TECHNOLOGY OF PETROCHEMICALS, LUBRICANTS, GREASES AND PETROLEUM REFINING

TECHNOLOGY OF PETROCHEMICALS, LUBRICANTS, GREASES AND PETROLEUM REFINING

Written By

EIRI BOARD OF CONSULTANTS & ENGINEERS

ENGINEERS INDIA RESEARCH INSTITUTE

4449, Nai Sarak, Main Road, Delhi - 110 006 (India)
Ph:. 91-11- 23918117, 23916431, 23840361, 31082370
Fax: 91-11- 2391 6431, 2391 8117
* E-Mail : eirisidi@bol.net.in
* Website: www.eiriindia.org

Sole Distributor :

INDIAN INSTITUTE OF CONSULTANTS, 4/27 ROOP NAGAR, DELHI - 07

PRINTED & PUBLISHED BY

ENGINEERS INDIA RESEARCH INSTITUTE

4449, Nai Sarak, Main Road, Delhi - 110 006 (India)
Ph:. 91-11- 23918117, 23916431, 23840361, 31082370
* Fax: 91-11- 23916431, 23918117
* E-Mail : eirisidi@bol.net.in
* Website: www.eiriindia.org

DISTRIBUTED BY

SMALL INDUSTRY RESEARCH INSTITUTE (SIRI)
INDIAN INSTITUTE OF CONSULTANTS

ISBN : 81- 86732-58-6
Printed in New Delhi (INDIA)

Rs. 900

Printed & Published by Sudhir Gupta for "Engineers India Research Institute" 4449 Nai Sarak, Main Road, New Delhi - 110 006

Preface

The book **Technology of Petrochemicals, Lubricants, Greases & Petroleum Refining** covers almost all the basic and advanced details to setup own Petrochemicals, Lubricants, Greases & Petroleum Refining Unit. The new edition of the book is covering latest technology including Petroleum Refinery and Petrochemicals, Hydrocarbons from Petroleum, Petrochemicals, Industrial Organic Synthesis, Lubricants, Manufacture of Oils and Greases, Distillation of Crude Petroleum, Petroleum Products, Purification of Petroleum Products, Refining of Petroleum, Testing of Petroleum, Application of Lubricating Agents, Formulating and Compounding of Lubricants, Reclamation of used Lubricating Oil, Re-Refining of Used Lube Oil, Formulating of Greases, Lubricants and their Manufacture, Various Formulations of Lubricants and Greases, Acetic Acid from Ethanol, Coolant (Engine), Cutting Oil, Ethanol (Biofuel) from Molasses, Formaldehyde, Food Grade Grease or Lubricant, Gas Filling of L.P.G. Cylinder, Grease (Lithium Based), Lube Oil from CNSL to Reduce Friction, Lube Oil and Grease, Microcrystalline Wax, Petroleum Jelly, Reclamation of used Engine Oil, Rust Prevention Lube Oil, Silicon Grease and Wire Drawing Lubricants. Apart from the above details and formulae, the book also deals with the project profiles on many industries, Suppliers of Plant & Equipments and Chemicals with Packaging materials have also been incorporated in this mega edition.

The book has been written for the benefit and to prove an asset and a handy reference guide in the hands of new entrepreneurs & well established industrialists.

Director

ENGINEERS INDIA RESEARCH INSTITUTE

Nai Sarak, New Delhi (INDIA)

E-Mail : eirisidi@bol.net.in

CONTENTS AND SUBJECT INDEX

CHAPTERS	PAGE NO.	CHAPTERS	PAGE NO.

Chapter 1

PETROLEUM REFINERY AND PETROCHEMICALS

NOMENCLATURE IN THE PETROLEUM INDUSTRY

Most petroleum types are complex mixtures that are difficult to characterise in detail, and therefore, many definitions used by the exploration, production, and refining sectors of the industry to describe petroleum and its products lack precision. Traditionally, the unit of crude-oil production has been the barrel, equal to 0.159 m^3, or 5.61 ft^3. Today, however, petroleum reserves are often given in metric tons. Density may be reported in metric units but is more often given in degrees API. The relationship between specific gravity and API also called API gravity, is defined by

$$\text{Sp gr (at } 16^{\circ}\text{C)} = \frac{141.5}{(\mathring{A}\text{PI} + 131.5)}$$

or

$$\mathring{A}\text{PI} = \frac{141.5}{\text{sp gr (at } 16^{\circ}\text{C)}} - 131.5$$

Other terms relating to physical properties are determined under defined conditions established by ASTM.

Gas production is generally given in cubic metres or cubic feet (28.3 m^3 = 1000 ft^3) and reserves are often quoted in trillions of cubic feet (10^{12} ft^3 = 28.3 x 10^9 m^3). Dry gas contains mostly methane; it is called wet gas if it contains more than 4 litres per 100 m^3 of natural gas.

Cycloalkanes (or cycloparaffins) are commonly called naphthenes. Naphtha, however, is a distillate boiling below 204-260°C. Gas oil boils slightly higher than kerosene (232-426°C). Cylinder oil is a viscous lubricating oil. The term distillate is sometimes used to denote distillate fuel oil as opposed to residual fuel oil.

ORIGIN OF PETROLEUM

Petroleum is a naturally occurring complex mixture consisting predominantly of hydrocarbons, frequently with other hydrogen and carbon compounds containing significant amounts of nitrogen, sulphur and oxygen as well as small amounts of nickel, vanadium, and other elements. It can occur in solid, liquid, or is gaseous form as asphalt, crude oil, or gas, respectively.

Organic matter is incorporated into sediments as they are deposited and some biogenic gas may be generated; with increasing depth of burial, temperature converts the organic matter to petroleum-like material; part of this material migrates from the source rock through carrier beds to the reservoir; here, compositional changes may be produced by increasing temperature, water washing, and bacterial degradation.

Organisms produce a wide range of organic compounds, and the types incorporated into source rocks influence the type of petroleum generated. Much of the algal-derived amorphous matter (kerogen) is rich in hydrogen and poor in oxygen and generates oil, whereas the woody type of kerogen is rich in oxygen and poor in hydrogen and generates mainly gas. The generation of petroleum is non-biological, induced by temperature and influenced by time. It follows essentially first-order kinetics and an increase of 10°C approximately doubles the rate. An important exception to thermal generation is the bacterial formation of methane. The bacteria are anaerobic, effective in sulphate-free anoxic conditions, and give shallow fields with gas that is isotopically light.

Movement of a separate crude-oil phase occurs when source rocks develop high internal pressures which squeeze oil droplets out and into adjacent permeable carrier beds. Here, buoyancy is the main driving force and migration distances can be in excess of 100 km. Oil may be remobilised after its initial accumulation in the reservoir which can lead to considerable compositional changes if both gas and oil are involved.

Petroleum composition can be changed by rising temperature or by contact with flowing water which may remove the more soluble components. If water brings bacteria and oxygen into contact with oil below 75°C, substantial degradation can result giving a higher-density, more sulphur-rich crude oil.

COMPOSITION OF PETROLEUM

The term petroleum, literally, rock oil, is applied to the deposits of oily material found in the upper strata of the earth's crust, where they were formed by a complex series of chemical reactions from organic materials, laid down in previous geological eras.

The elemental compositions of petroleum vary greatly from one deposit to another. Carbon and hydrogen make up the bulk, but other elements present include sulphur (trace to 8%), nitrogen (trace to 6%), oxygen (trace to 1.8%), and nickel and vanadium.

Modern techniques, such as gas chromatography (gc) and mass spectrometry (ms) and their combination (gc-ms), permit complete molecular characterisation of the lower boiling range (through C_7) without prior separation. However, isolation and identification of individual compounds is not practical for the higher distillate range. The crude is usually distilled, followed by liquid-liquid chromatography to separate saturated, aromatic, and polar compounds. The vacuum residuum includes the heaviest compound types that do not distill under commercial operating conditions. Special techniques are required for characterisation.

Saturated Hydrocarbons

n-Alkanes are found in all crudes and throughout the entire boiling range. *n*-Alkanes are present through *n*-$C_{44}H_{90}$ in the distillate range and have been identified as high as n-$C_{78}H_{158}$. Properties and concentrations vary greatly; carbon number and concentrations have a strong effect upon the pour point, i.e., the temperature at which crude or its products turn from a liquid to a solid. This is an important physical property often defining the necessary degree of processing.

All possible isoalkanes through C_8 have been identified in petroleum, together with many of the C_9 and some of the C_{10} compounds and a number of isoprenoids.

Cycloalkanes isolated from petroleum contain five-, six-, or seven membered rings. Alkyl derivatives of cyclopentane and cyclohexane are commonly found; dicycloalkanes have also been reported, e.g., *cis*- and *trans*-decahydronaphthalene and hexahydroindan. Cycloalkanes containing up to seven rings have been detected by mass spectrometry.

Analysis

All possible isomers with carbon number 7 or less and most of the C_8s can be separated by capillary gas chromatography. Hydrocarbon mixtures are analysed by mass spectrometry according to the number of rings present in the molecule. These methods have been standardised and published by ASTM. However, the saturated compounds need to be separated from the aromatic compounds before analysis, usually by liquid chromatography over silica gel. Alkenes interfere with this analysis.

Unsaturated Hydrocarbons

Both alkenes (olefins) and aromatic compounds occur in petroleum. Alkenes are rare, whereas aromatic compounds of almost every known type have been found, e.g., benzene and alkylbenzene derivatives (4.6-12.6%)

through the 22 isomeric C_{10} -alkyl isomers, indan and tetra-hydronaphthalenes and their methyl isomers, naphthalene and its I- and 2-alkyl derivatives, biphenyl and derivatives, and many multiring condensed aromatic compounds. Instrumental ASTM methods permits rapid compound-type analysis of aromatic compounds.

Sulphur, Nitrogen and Oxygen Compounds

Sulphur is found in all crudes in concentrations ranging from traces to 8.0%, mostly in the 0.5-1.5% range. It is present in aliphatic and aromatic compounds and also as elemental sulphur, hydrogen sulphide, and carbonyl sulphide (COS). Sulphur-specific flame photometric detectors in gas chromatography permit the rapid identification and measurement of sulphur compounds in the lower-boiling fractions. It is important to know the distribution of sulphur compounds within a crude. As the reserves of high quality, low sulphur crude diminish, crudes of poorer quality with high sulphur contents must be converted catalytically into low sulphur products.

Nitrogen concentrations are usually below 0.2%; but may be as high as 1.6%. Nitrogen compounds are concentrated in the high boiling fractions and in the residuum; very little is present in the fraction boiling below 300°C. Compounds containing oxygen as well as nitrogen are also found, e.g., hydroxypyridines and hydroxyquinolines. The nitrogen compounds affect processing, particularly of the higher-boiling fractions. Aromatic nitrogen-containing molecules are refractory and some are basic and may interact and adsorb onto acid catalysts and promote coke formation.

The oxygen content of most crudes is low. Oxygen is present mainly in the form of carboxylic acids, e.g., fatty acids through stearic, branched chain acids, alicyclic acids, and dicarboxylic acids.

Residuum

Specifications of a residuum fraction must always include the boiling range taken at the end of the distillate. Compound types are separated by chromatographic techniques. Unique to the residuum is solvent precipitation or deasphalting. The portion of the residuum insoluble in a large excess of *n*-heptane is known as asphaltenes (up to 25%), and the heptane-soluble fraction as maltenes. Saturated compounds may constitute 40 wt% of the residuum, usually much less.

Metals

In trace quantities, all metals through atomic number 42 (molybdenum) have been found, except rubidium and niobium; a few heavier elements have also been detected. Present in all crudes, nickel and vanadium are the most important. Analytical methods can detect metal concentrations in crudes at 10 ppb (10 ng/g).

A number of compounds, identified in petroleum, are referred to as biological markers or geochemical fossils. These are compounds whose basic carbon skeleton has survived chemical changes that occurred during petroleum genesis and whose structures are frequently found in terrestrial and marine life.

RESOURCES

Petroleum resources are distributed widely in the earth's crust as gases, liquids, and solids. The products derived from these naturally occurring resources are used mainly as energy sources, although substantial volumes serve as feedstocks in the plastics, chemical, and other industries.

Petroleum resources are classified as follows: The *resource base* is the total amount present in a specific volume of the earth's crust (also called in-place petroleum); *resources* represent the total amount of petroleum, including reserves, that is expected to be produced in the future; *reserves* constitute the petroleum that has been discovered and can be produced at the prices and technology that existed when the estimate was made; *proved reserves* are estimates of reserves contained primarily in the drilled portion of the fields; indicated reserves constitute known petroleum that is currently producible but cannot be estimated accurately enough to qualify as proved; *inferred reserves* are producible but the assumption of their presence is based upon limited physical evidence and considerable geological extrapolation; sub-economic resources constitute the petroleum in the ground that cannot be produced at present prices and technology but may become producible; *undiscovered resources* are estimated totally by geological speculation with no evidence by drilling available.

DRILLING FLUIDS

Drilling fluids and muds perform a variety of functions that influence the drilling rate, cost, efficiency, and safety of the drilling operation. They are pumped down a hollow drill string through nozzles in the bit at the bottom, and up the annulus formed by the hole or casing and the drill string to the surface. The bit is turned by rotating the entire string from the surface or by using a down-hole motor. After reaching the surface, the drilling fluid is passed through a series of screens, settling tanks or pits, hydroclones, and centrifuges to remove formation material brought to the surface. It is then treated with additives to obtain the desired properties. Once treated, the fluid is pumped back into the well and the cycle repeated.

Gas-based muds, ranging from compressed dry air or natural gas to mist to stable foams, are used mostly for the drilling of hard rock. About 90% of all drilling fluids is water-based systems, ranging from clear water without additives to high density muds containing clays and various organic additives. Offshore wells are frequently drilled with a seawater system, which needs more additives to achieve the desired flow and filtration properties.

Oil-based drilling fluids have diesel, a low-aromatic-content oil, or occasionally crude oil as a continuous phase with both internal-water and solid phases. Fluids with more than 5-10 vol% water are called invert oilbased muds or inverts. Oil muds are employed for high temperature wells where water-based systems may be unstable and where problems may arise from water-sensitive shale formations.

Properties

The density is adjusted with dissolved salts or powdered high density solids to provide a hydrostatic pressure against exposed formations in excess of the pressure of the formation fluids. In addition, the hydrostatic pressure of the mud column prevents collapse of weak formations into the borehole. Fluid densities may range from that of air to > 2500 kg/m^3 (20.8 lb/gal). Most drilling fluids have densities > 1000 kg/m^3 (8.33 lb/gal), the density of water. The hydrostatic pressure imposed by a column of drilling fluid is expressed as follows :

$$P = 0.098 L\rho_m \ (0.052\ L\rho_m)$$

where P = hydrostatic pressure in kPa (psi), ρ_m = drilling-fluid density in kg/m^3 (lb/gal), and L = column length or well depth in m (ft). Wells with bottom-hole pressure of 100 MPa (14,500 psi) at 5000 m are not unusual.

Viscosity and velocity must be high enough to remove drill cuttings and other formation material that may fall into the well bore. Low viscosity fluids are circulated at high rates and vice versa.

Density control

Mud density is controlled accurately by suitable weighting materials that do not adversely affect the other properties. Most important is the specific gravity of the weighting agent as well as its chemical inertness. Barite (barium sulphate, $BaSO_4$) meets these requirements; it is virtually insoluble in water and does not react with other mud constituents. The barite content in drilling mud can be as high as 2000 kg/m^3 (700 lb/ bbl). Other weighting materials include galena, haematite, magnetite, ilmenite, siderite, celesite, dolomite, and calcite.

The drilling rate is improved by solids-free fluids, which are designed for work-over and completion operations to avoid formation damage. Weighted fluids without solids are provided by solutions of various water-soluble salts (Table 1) for maximum densities. The incorporation of a limited amount of drilled solids is an economical way to increase mud density, but it also reduced penetration rates.

Table 1. Soluble salts that increase the density of drilling muds and work-over and completion fluids.

Salt	*Formula*	*Specific gravity*	*Saturated brine, 20-25°C* *Wt%*	*Density, g/cm³*
Potassium chloride	KCl	1.984	26.5	1.18
Sodium chloride	NaCl	2.165	28.5	1.20
Sodium carbonate	Na_2C03	2.532	22.5	1.24
Calcium chloride	$CaCl_2$	2.150	46.1	1.46
Potassium carbonate	K_2CO_3	2.428	52.9	1.56
Sodium bromide	NaBr	3.203	53.7	1.65
Calcium bromide	$CaBr_2$	3.353	58.7	1.70
Zinc chloride	$ZnCl_2$	2.910	81.2	2.14
Zinc bromide	$ZnBr_2$	4.201	81.7	2.65

Viscosity

The type of solids and the solids content of water-based muds control the viscosity. The reactive solids are composed of commercial clays, of which bentonite (montmorillonite), attapulgite, and sepiolite are the most important; organophilic clays, prepared from bentonite or attapulgite and aliphatic amine salts, are used for oil-based muds.

Organic polymers are used to increase viscosity and alsc to control filtration rates. Water-soluble polymers include starch, guar gum, sodium carboxymethyl cellulose, hydroxyethyl cellulose, xantham gum, polyacrylates, and polyacrylamides.

Viscosity is decreased by a reduction of solids, or deflocculation of claywater suspensions. Thinning is obtained by reducing plastic viscosity, yield point, or gel strength, or a combination of these properties. Typical mudthinning chemicals are polyanionic materials that are absorbed on the positive-edge sites of the clay particles, thereby reducing the attractive forces between the particles without affecting clay hydration.

Filtration control

Filtration control is particularly important in permeable formations where the mud hydrostatic pressure exceeds the formation pressure. It reduces drillstring sticking, torque, and drag due to filter-cake development; minimises damage to protective formations; and, in some areas, improves boreholes stability. Materials for this purpose include clays, organic polymers, and lignite derivatives. The bentonite present in freshwater systems acts as the primary filtration agent; concentration vary widely, but may range up to 100 kg/m^3 (35 lb/bbl).

Although a combination of bentonite clay and lignosulphonate provides filtration control in many water-based muds, organic polymers are generally needed as filtration aids, especially starches in concentrations of 6-29 kg/m^3 (2-10 lb/bbl). Fermentation by micro-organisms is prevented by saturating with salt or adding a preservative, e.g., paraformaldehyde or another biocide (ca 0.6-1.4 kg/m^3 or 0.2-0.5 bbl). Carboxymethyl cellulose is most commonly used in fresh- to seawater fluids (1.4-5.7 kg/m^3 or 0.5-2.0 lb/bbl).

Alkalinity control and removal of contaminants

Water-based drilling fluids are generally maintained at an alkaline pH by the addition of sodium hydroxide (3-14 kg/m^3 or 1-5 lb/bbl), lime (6-57 kg/m or 2-20 lb/bbl), or magnesium oxide.

Drilling-fluid contaminants are defined as any material or condition that adversely affects fluid performance. Drill solids are removed mechanically by various combinations of screens, hydroclones, and centrifuges. Electrolytes are removed by dilution and chemical treatment.

Shale stabilisation

Shales can be stabilised with an oil mud that prevents direct contact between the shale and the emulsified water. The most recent shaleprotective agents are the polymer/potassium muds. The reaction of potassium ions with clay results in potassium fixation and formation of a less water-sensitive clay. Potassium chloride is generally used in combination with a polymer. Ammonium chloride, ammonium sulphate, and diammonium phosphate have also been used, along with a number of anionic polymers.

Surfactants perform various functions in drilling fluids. Lignites and lignosulphonates act as emulsifiers, whereas aluminium stearate is used as a defoamer.

To function properly a drilling fluid must be circulated through the well and back to the surface. Loss of fluid, owing to openings in the formation, can result in a loss of hydrostatic pressure at the bottom of the hole, influx of formation fluids, and possibly loss of well control.

Lost-circulation zones are sealed off by the addition of flakes (shredded cellophane or paper, laminated plastic), fibrous materials (wood fibres, sawdust straw), or granules (ground walnut shells, rubber, plastics, limestones); concentrations of these materials range from 14 to 143 kg/m^3 (5-50 lb/bbl).

Lubricants and spotting fluids are added to overcome frictional resistance of the drilling string or sticking of the drill pipe. Blends of anionic and non-ionic surfactants and natural products are used as well as gilsonite and air-blown asphalts. String and casing corrosion is generally caused by oxygen dissolved or entrained in the mud, and can be prevented by excluding or scavenging corrosive gases and by maintaining a high pH.

ENHANCED OIL RECOVERY

Crude oil exists in contact with gases and water in sub-terranean rock formations called reservoirs. Wells serve as pressure sinks that allow the oil to be brought to the surface. Normal depletion, called primary recovery, results from the driving forces provided by dissolved gases of an associated aquifer. Following primary production, fluid may be injected into a portion of the wells to provide a secondary energy source. This is called secondary oil recovery, e.g., waterflooding or immiscible-gas flooding. Continued fluid injection, in time, results in ever-increasing production of injected fluid and eventually only injected fluid (i.e., water) is produced, leaving unrecovered oil behind as a residual oil saturation.

Enhanced oil recovery (EOR), often referred to as tertiary oil recovery, is recovery of oil over and above that which can be recovered by primary and secondary methods (Fig. 1). Estimates of the potential of EOR are highly speculative, but can be 5-10% of the oil discovered to date. Residual oil remains in a reservoir because of the high interfacial tension (IFT) between oil and water. Of importance is the interrelationship between capillary and viscous forces given by the capillary number:

capillary number = (velocity X viscosity)/IFT

where the velocity refers to the injected fluid and the IFT is measured between the oil and the injected fluid. High capillary numbers are required to get low residual oil saturations. For miscible fluids, the capillary number is infinite.

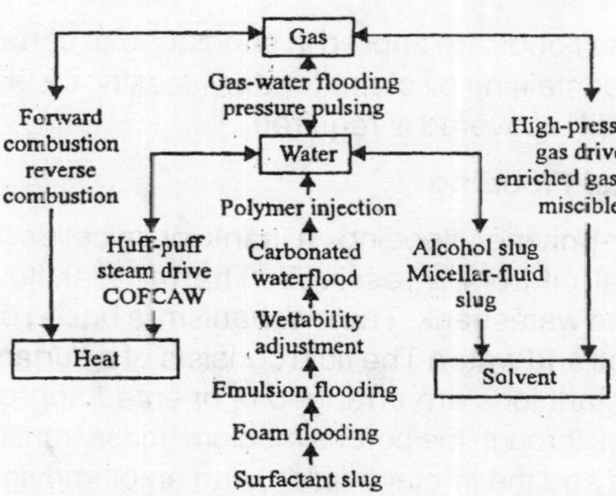

Figure 1. Improved methods for oil recovery (connecting lines indicate several combinations commonly in use), COFCAW is the combination of forward combustion and waterflooding.

Because of the density differences between gas, oil, water, and injected fluids, oil may be trapped high in the reservoir and not contacted by an injected water-base fluid. Gravitational forces are expressed in terms of densities. The economics of EOR methods are governed by the amount of oil that can be recovered and the cost of the injected fluids. A high initial investment is needed and oil production is delayed after initial injection of the fluid.

Miscible-Gas Drives

A gas can either miscibly or immiscibly displace oil, depending on the physical properties of the gas and the oil and the reservoir temperature and pressure. In a miscible-gas process, the residual oil is mobilised by an injected solvent (miscible gas) and the mobilised oil is displaced to a production well. A thorough understanding of the physical/chemical phenomena (displacement mechanisms) occurring within the oil-moving and solvent-moving zones is needed for a project design.

Miscible displacement may be controlled by either a first-contact or multiple-contact mechanism. In the former, the reservoir oil and injected solvent are mixed in all proportions at reservoir conditions and no phase separation occurs. In the latter, oil and solvent cannot be mixed in all proportions without phase separation upon equilibration. Miscibility is developed by either a condensation or a vapourisation (extraction) process.

First-contact miscible solvents include liquified petroleum gas fractions (LPGs) or enriched gas. Multiple-contact miscible agents include methane plus LPG components, carbon dioxide, methane, nitrogen, and flue gas. Enriched-gas flooding is an example of miscibility developed by the condensation process where the LPG components condense into the oil.

Application

Miscible gas floods are applied in sandstone or carbonate reservoirs of sufficient depth containing oil of moderate viscosity; ca 900--5400 m^3 of gas per cubic metre oil recovered is required.

Micellar-Polymer Flooding

In micellar-polymer flooding, a bank of micellar fluid is injected to displace residual oil from a reservoir. The micellar fluid is pushed by a polymerthickened water bank. The mechanism is based on reducing the IFT between crude oil and water. The fluid consists of a surfactant in a solvent in which the surfactant ions are arranged in oriented aggregates or micelles. As the fluid moves through the porous medium, mass transfer occurs between the injected fluid and the in-place fluids, and an oil-moving zone creates an ultra-low IFT condition which results in residual oil being displaced. The desired mobility of the various banks can be adjusted, and the proper mobility keeps the integrity of the bank and maximises sweep efficiency. This technique is still in the developmental stage.

Thermal Processes

Thermal processes utilise heat generated above ground or *in situ* to enhance oil recovery; they are applied primarily to heavy oils. The simplest process is steam injection. Steam is used as a driving fluid to displace oil from an injector to a producer, or in a cyclic-injection production sequence using the same well as both injector and producer with a soak period to heat the well, the so-called steam-soak or steam huff-and-puff process. Underground or *in situ* combustion processes utilise injected air or oxygen and hydrocarbons or coke within the reservoir as fuel.

REFINERY PROCESSES

Petroleum products derived from crude oil are a convenient source of energy. Since petroleum liquids are easy to handle and store, they are well suited for transportation fuels, e.g., for cars and airplanes. Other refinery products include lubricants, waxes, asphalt, solvents, and specialities such as liquefied petroleum gas (LPG), hydraulic fluids, and others. Petroleum is the principal raw material source for petrochemicals such as plastics, synthetic elastomers, certain alcohols, and other important products. The various fuel and chemical markets have their own product-quality requirements and it is the function of the refining operation to separate crude and other raw materials into fractions that are then processed to meet product specifications.

Crude petroleum contains a wide range of hydrocarbons from light gases to residuum that is too heavy to distill even under vacuum. Crude oil is primarily made up of paraffins, cycloparaffins (naphthenes), and aromatic compounds in varying proportions, some sulphur compounds, a small amount of nitrogen, but no appreciable amount of oxygen or olefins.

Refining processes can be grouped into three classes; separation, usually distillation to give the desired type of compounds; conversion, usually cracking, to change molecular weight and boiling point; and upgrading, e.g., hydrotreating, to meet product-quality specifications.

In general, refineries are located near a large body of water, partly to supply cooling water but also for transportation. Large refineries process about 80,000 m^3 (5 X 10^5 bbl) of crude per day, which corresponds to one supertanker load. Rail transportation would require 1600 tank cars per day to carry the same amount of crude.

Since the 1970s, the great increase in crude cost has been accompanied by greater emphasis on high value products at the expense of fuel products.

For example, fuel oil previously used in large power plants is displaced by coal or nuclear fuel. Increased attention to environmental aspects has led to demand for low sulphur products despite the trend toward higher sulphur crudes. Unleaded gasoline is another example of environmental concern.

Petroleum refining has shown a rapid growth and is now the largest manufacturing industry in India. Efforts to decrease the gasoline consumption (km/L) of vehicles by reducing their size and weight have been successful. More efficient engines are in wide use, particularly diesel engines, in which the fuel is injected directly into the combustion chamber. Diesel engines have efficiencies of about 35% versus ca 25% efficiency for gasoline engines.

Refineries range in size from 1600 m^3/d (10;000 bbl/d) to over 64,000 m^3/d (4 X 10^5 bbl/d). Small refineries make only gasoline, diesel, and domestic heating oils. Large refineries include the manufacture of lubricating oils and greases. Refining is also the main source of raw materials for petrochemical manufacture. A large steam-cracking unit for 500,000 t/yr of ethylene may consume ca 2 X 10^6 t/yr of oil feed (40,000 bbl/d), which may be 10% of the crude used in very large refinery. Clearly, chemical and fuel-refining operations must be carefully coordinated.

Processing Steps

Desalting

Salt and clay or other suspended solids are removed by washing with water at 65-90°C to reduce viscosity. Typical salt content of crude may be 280 g/100 m^3; desalting may remove over 90% without the loss of oil.

Distillation

The crude is separated in continuous-fractionation plate towers, as shown in Fig. 2. Primary distillation takes place at atmospheric pressure and the bottom temperature is limited to 370-400°C to prevents thermal cracking.

Naphtha, the fraction taken from the top, is mainly used for motor gasoline and processed further for octane improvement by catalytic reforming. The middle distillate includes diesel, and jet fuels, and heating oil. Kerosene and certain speciality solvents distill between these two fractions. The bottom fraction can be used as fuel oil but is usually vacuum distilled in order to increase the yield of high value distillate oil for catalytic cracking.

Vacuum distillation provides low sulphur oil by hydrosulphurising vacuum gas oil, which is then blended back into untreated vacuum bottoms. In addition, various speciality materials are obtained, such as wax and lube fractions.

Hydroprocessing

Hydroprocessing improves the quality of various products or cracks heavy carbonaceous materials to lower-boiling, more valuable products. Mild hydrotreating removes sulphur, nitrogen, oxygen, and metals, and

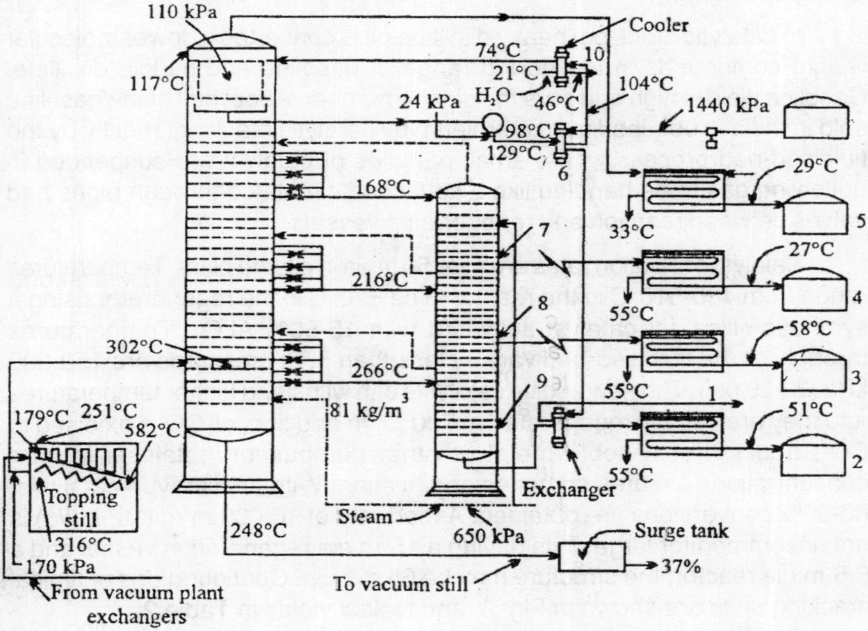

Figure. 2. Atmospheric distillation of crude. Multidraw crude oil topping plant. To convert kPa to psi, multiply by 0.145. 1. To vacuum-plant exchangers; 2. Gas oil 10.6%; 3. Kerosene 19.8%; 4. Naphtha 5.8%; 5. Light gasoline 26.8%; 6. Exchanger; 7. Steam; 8. 26 kg/m³; 9. 66 kg/m³; 10. 46°C.

hydrogenates olefins. A fixed-bed may be employed at 1.5-2.2 MPa (200-300 psig) and 350-400°C, without catalyst regeneration. Severe conditions are 7-21 MPa (1000-3000 psig) and 350-500°C with catalyst regeneration.

Hydrogen consumption increases with severity and depends on the amount of sulphur removed and the feed content of aromatic materials and olefins, which also consume hydrogen. Net consumption can range from 18 m^3/m^3 (100 ft^3/bbl) feed for hydrofinishing to well over 180 m^3/m^3 (1000 ft^3/bbl) feed in hydrocracking operations.

Hydrocracking

In hydrocracking, high molecular weight compounds are cracked to lower boiling materials. Severity is increased by operating at higher temperatures and longer contact time than in hydrotreating. Hydrocracking is used extensively on distillate stocks. It is of increasing importance in view of the trends to heavier crudes and the need for processing synthetic crudes.

Catalytic cracking

In catalytic cracking, heavy distillate oil is converted to lower molecular weight compounds in the boiling range of gasoline and middle distillate. Gasoline yield is high and so is the octane number. About half of the gasoline sold in India is obtained from petroleum by catalytic cracking, mostly by the fluidised-bed process where small particles of catalyst are suspended in upflowing gas to be handled like a liquid and circulated through pipes and valves between reaction and regeneration vessels.

Catalyst circulation rates are over 50 t/min in a large plant. Temperatures range from 480-510°C in the reactor to ca 620°C in the regenerator using a synthetic silica-gel catalyst activated with 15-60% Al_2O_3. Temperatures throughout the fluidised-bed vary by less than 5°C; pressures are 150-200 kPa (22-29 psi). The new zeolite catalysts can withstand higher temperatures and they are usually regenerated at 700°C. In addition, all CO is oxidised to CO_2; addition of a noble metal or other combustion catalysts in ppm concentrations assures complete combustion. With zeolite-type catalysts, 80-90% conversions are obtained. A feed rate of 16,000 m^3/d (10^5 bbl/d) is not uncommon for large units having a 15-m dia regeneration vessel and a 6.5-m dia reactor; the structure may be 65 m high. Configurations of typical cracking units are shown in Fig. 3, and typical yields in Table 2.

Coking

Both delayed and fluid coking are used on very heavy low value residuum feeds to obtain lower-boiling cracked products. Coking can be considered as high severity thermal cracking or destructive distillation. It is generally used on vacuum residuum (which is not a suitable feed for catalytic cracking) to generate lighter components. In delayed coking, a cyclic batch operation, the oil is held at 450°C and 35-70 kPa (5-10 psi) to deposit coke while cracked vapours are taken overhead. Fluid coking is a continuous process similar in design to fluid catalytic cracking.

Table 2. Catalytic-cracking operation.

	Operation	
	Maximum gasoline	*Maximum middle distillate*
Feed		
Boiling range, °C	260-566	343-566
Conversion, vol %	85	60
Yield[a]		
Methane and C_2 wt%	2.8	2.4

(Cont'd)

	Operation	
	Maximum gasoline	*Maximum middle distillate*
Propane, vol%	3.0	2.0
Propylene, vol%	7.0	6.0
Butane, vol%	8.8	5.2
Butene, vol%	7.6	7.9
C_5 naphtha up to 221°C, vol%	69.5	47.1
Heating oil, vol%	10.0	35.0
Slurry, vol%	5.0	5.0
Coke, wt%	5.3	5.4
RON[b] clear	92	92
Carbon on regenerated zeolite catalyst, wt%	< 0.20	0.35

[a] Because of expansion, vol% adds up to more than 100%.

[b] Research of octane number.

The products include gas, naphtha, gas oils, and coke. Hyderotreated coker gas oil augments supplies of residential heating oil; heavier fractions are cracked catalytically.

The sulphur content of the coke may be as much as 50% higher than that of the feedstock, but the coke can be used as fuel if SO, control is provided. Needle coke, a premium product especially suited for graphite production, is made by delayed coking of low sulphur, highly aromatic heavy oil obtained from catalytic or thermal cracking. It is the world's main source of graphite for carbon electrodes.

In flexicoking, high sulphur coke is gasified to clean fuel gas in a fluidised-solids circulating system. The coke is gasified with steam and either air or oxygen. The gas is scrubbed to remove sulphur compounds and impurities and thereby provides a cleaner fuel. Gasification is carried almost to completion while ash and metals build up to a high concentration in the purge solids. Yield pattern is given in Fig. 4.

Visbreaking

Viscosity breaking is one of the few thermal-cracking processes still used in refining other than coking. It reduces the viscosity of heavy fuel oil and permits handling at lower temperature. Vacuum residuum can usually be burned directly but would require perhaps 200°C for proper atomisation in burners. After visbreaking, a temperature of 100°C or less is adequate, which

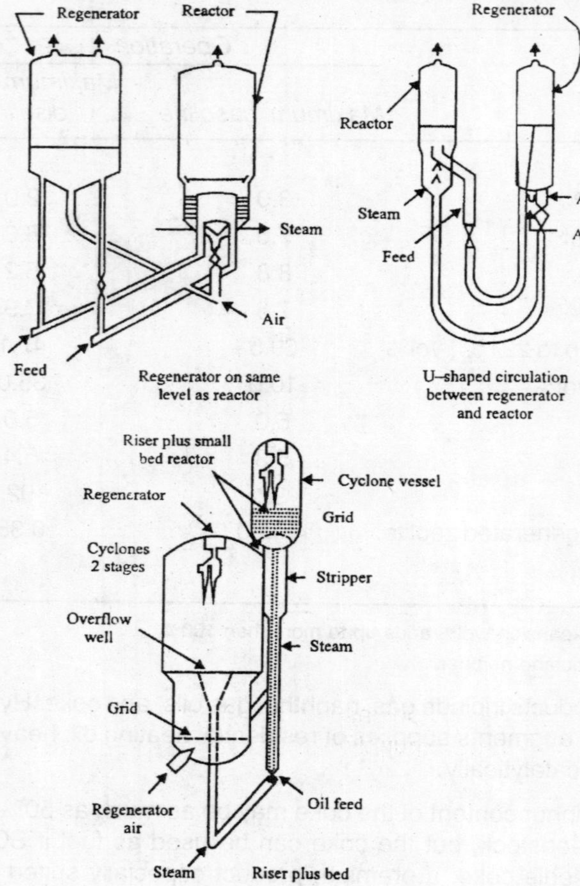

Fig. 3. Typical fluid-catalytic-cracking-unit configurations.

gives a fuel oil suitable for large commercial buildings, etc. In visbreaking, heavy oil is heated in a furnace to ca 480°C and held at this temperature in a soaking coil long enough to give the desired degree of cracking. The process yields 1-2% gas, 5-10% naphtha, and 20-30% distillate gas oil. In some case, the bottoms are distilled under vacuum to give a pitch that can be used in asphalt or roofing tar.

Steam-cracking

Steam-cracking is used primarily to produce olefinic raw materials for petrochemicals manufacture. It plays such an important role in refining, however, that the planning and operation of a large steam-cracking plant is usually closely integrated with a large refinery. Steam-cracking is carried out at ca 800-850°C and slightly above atmospheric pressure. Feedstocks range

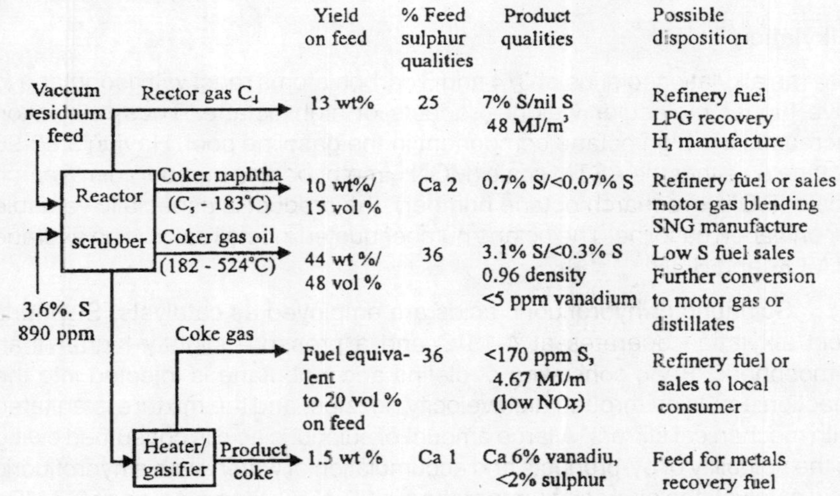

Fig. 4. Flexicoker yield pattern, product qualities, and possible dispositions. To convert MJ/m3 to Btu/SCF, multiply by 26.85.

from ethane to vacuum gas oil; heavier feeds give higher yields of by-products such as naphtha, etc. Steam is added with the feed to reduce the hydrocarbon partial pressure, thereby giving more olefins. The amount of steam may be equal in weight to the oil feed.

Catalytic reforming

Naphtha recovered directly from crude by distillation is called straight-run or virgin naphtha. It is too low in octane (30-50 clear octane) to meet quality requirements for motor gasoline and is upgraded by catalytic reforming. The feed is a naphtha fraction boiling in the 80-230°C range. Lighter fractions are not amenable to reforming, whereas heavier fractions would give products that remain outside of the gasoline boiling range since reforming gives only a small reduction in boiling point. Typical operating conditions are 430-520°C and 1-6 MPa (145-870 psi). By-product hydrogen amounts typically to 36-45 m^3/m^3 of feed (202-253 ft^3 /bbl) with a yield of C_5 and higher of 80-85 vol%.

For regeneration, the catalyst is burned in a low oxygen atmosphere; the on-stream run may last for one year or more before regeneration is needed. Currently, almost all catalysts are based on platinum or palladium. They lose their activity in the presence of sulphur or nitrogen compounds and are poisoned by metals such as arsenic or lead.

The following reactions occur in reforming (Fig. 5), dehydrogenation of cycloparaffins; isomerisation of paraffins; dehydrocyclisation of paraffins, hydrocracking of paraffins; and removal of sulphur, olefins, nitrogen, and oxygen.

Alkylation

In alkylation, olefins of 3, 4 and 5 carbon atoms react with isobutane to give higher molecular weight products of high octane. Thus, alkylation increases the high octane component in the gasoline pool. Having a 93-96 octane on either the ASTM scale (MON = motor octane number) or research scale (RON = research octane number), the product is especially valuable for unleaded gasoline. The octane number quoted in retail sales is an average of MON and RON.

Sulphuric or hydrofluoric acids are employed as catalysts. Sulphuric acid alkylation operates at 4-15°C and a pressure slightly higher than atmospheric. Feed consisting of olefins and isobutane is injected into the reaction emulsion through high velocity nozzles, and the mixture is agitated with mechanical stirrers. A large amount of sulphuric acid is consumed owing to the solubility of by-products and accumulation of water. With a hydrofluoric acid catalyst, the operating temperature is 25-45°C; the pressure of 0.7 MPa (101.5-145 psi) maintains the HF as a liquid phase.

Extraction

Extraction separates by chemical type rather than by boiling point and is much more expensive than distillation. It is used primarily for removal of aromatic material from naphtha fractions, upgrading middle distillates, and preparation of high quality lubricating oils.

Lubricants

Petroleum is the main source of lubricants for a wide range of uses. Lubricants are derived from distillates boiling above 370°C and they are separated by vacuum distillation and refined to meet specifications. Aromatic material is removed from the raw distillate by extraction with Nmethylpyrrolidine-2-one, phenol, or furfural. Wax is crystallised by chilling and filtered. Various additives play an important role in meeting quality requirements.

Gasoline Blending and Treatment

Separate components are blended to give various grades. Elaborate instrumentation controls in-line blending and offers large savings compared to blending in tanks. Leaded gasoline of reduced lead content is still being made, but may be phased out by about 1990. Naphtha-treatment processes, such as the Merox process, are used to extract sulphur compounds and to convert trace amounts of mercaptans to disulphides which are much less objectionable.

Today's unleaded gasoline usually contains additives for octane improvement, e.g., m ethyl tert-butyl ether and tert-butyl alcohol; gasohol contains ethyl alcohol.

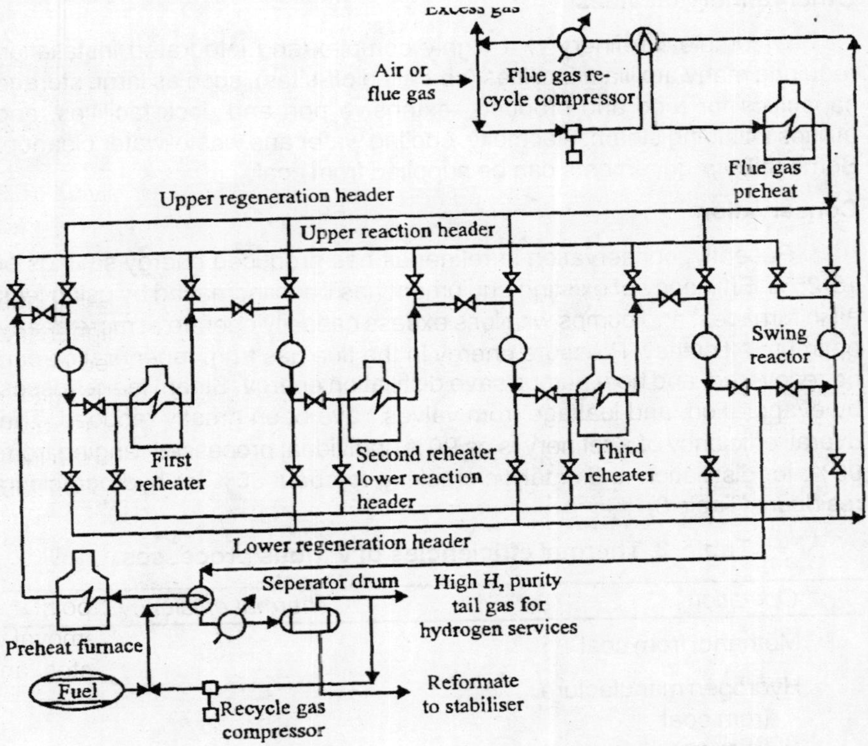

Fig. 5. Fixed-bed cyclic catalyic reforming

Hydrogen manufacture

The increase in hydrotreating has expanded the need for hydrogen beyond that available as a by-product from catalytic reforming. A common source is catalytic steam reforming of methane, refinery gas, or naphtha. Hydrocarbons treated with steam over a nickel-base catalyst at ca 2.8 MPa (400 psi) and 815°C give hydrogen and carbon oxides.

Sulphur recovery

Typical crude contains a large amount of sulphur. Thus, 10×10^6 t/yr of crude (200,000 bbl/d) with a sulphur content of 3% would yield 870 t/yr sulphur by-product. In refining, the sulphur compounds are converted to H_2S, which is removed by amine scrubbing. The H_2S is converted to pure sulphur in a Claus plant where one-third is allowed to react with the remaining H_2S in a series of catalyst beds. The reaction is exothermic and cooling is provided between beds together with separation of liquid sulphur. The final tail gas from a Claus plant is cleaned further before being released to the atmosphere.

Other refinery facilities

A complete refinery is a highly complex and integrated installation requiring many auxiliary facilities (so-called off-sites), such as large storage capacities for feed and products, extensive port and dock facilities, and utilities including steam, electricity, cooling water and waste-water cleanup. Some utility requirements can be supplied from coal.

Conservation

Recently, conservation in refineries has produced energy savings of 15-25%. Efficiency of existing equipment has been increased by using less air in furnaces, and pumps with less excess capacity operate at more nearly optimum efficiency. Pressure energy in the flue gas from regeneration can be recovered, and heat pumps save distillation energy. Steam leaks, losses by evaporation, and leakage from valves have been greatly reduced. The overall efficiency of a refinery is ca 90%, individual processes ranging from 95%; for distillation and catalytic cracking to about 80% for hydrocracking residuum (Table 3).

Table 3. Thermal efficiencies of various processes.

Operation	*Thermal efficiency,%*
Methanol from coal	50
Hydrogen manufacture	
from coal	55
from methane	60
SNG from coal	65
Coal liquefaction	70
Oil from shale	80
Fuel gas from coal	80-85

Environmental Aspects

Environmental aspects of refining concern air, water, and solid-waste problems (EPA classification). Petroleum refining was one of the first industries to be covered by Federal regulations mandating ambient airquality standards and allowable emissions (Table 4). State standards are at least as strict; Japan has very strict standards.

Table 4. National primary and secondary ambient air-quality standards.

Pollutant	*Type of standard*	*Averaging time*	*Concentration* $\mu g/m^3$	*ppm*
Carbon monoxide	Primary and secondary	1 h	40,000	35
		8 h	10,000	9
Hydrocarbons[a]	Primary and secondary	3 h	160[b]	0.24[b]
Nitrogen dioxide	Primary and secondary	1 yr	100	0.05
Photochemical oxidants[c]	Primary and secondary	1 h	160	0.08
Particulate matter	Primary	24 h	260	
		24 h	75	
	Secondary	24 h	150	
		24 h	60[d]	
Sulphur dioxide	Primary	24 h	365	0.14
		1 yr	80	0.03
	Secondary	3 h	1,300	0.5
Lead	Primary	90 d	1.5	
Ozone	Primary and secondary	1 h	235	0.12

a Non-methane.

b As a guide in devising implementation plans for achieving oxidant standards.

c Expressed as ozone by the federal reference method.

d As a guide to be used in assessing implementation plans for achieving the annual maximum 24-h standard.

Air-pollution control is directed toward the principal polutants; SO_x, NO_x particulates, CO, and hydrocarbons. Control measures on furnaces include the use of low sulphur fuels. The EPA standards regulate emission of flue gases from furnaces and catalyst regenerators as well as hydrocarbon vapours generated by leaks, evaporation, and handling.

Water pollutants include oil, H_2S or other sulphur compounds, and ammonia, phenols, chromium compounds, and chlorine used to control corrosion and biological fouling. The main sources of waste-water are cooling systems that may contain additives to inhibit corrosion or fouling; low toxicity inhibitors are now available. Process water containing H_2S, ammonia, and oil is termed sour water. It is stripped with steam, and treated in an API-type separator where the oil rises to the surface and is removed with the aid of air flotation.

Solid wastes consist mainly of spent catalysts, and ash if coal is the refinery fuel. Catalytic cracking units are subject to the following regulations: emission of particulates directly from regenerators should not exceed 1 kg/kg of coke burned; a stack opacity of 30 % maximum; and a maximum of 0.05 vol% of CO in gases discharged to the atmosphere.

Plant Economics

Utilities and general off-site expenditures include utilities production (equipment to generate steam and electricity), tie-in lines for power and water; roads and motor-vehicle access; port and dock facilities; tanks for feed and products; product loading and shipping; pipelines and railroads; repair shops, spare parts, and maintenance; technical service and engineering support; analytical and testing laboratories, an instrument and controls shop; business and accounting offices; and housing and facilities for construction crews. Investment for these facilities may amount to 40% of the costs of a new plant in a large existing refinery and often doubles the costs for a new installation.

Operating costs are strongly related to investment and include maintenance and repair; utilities; chemicals; catalysts and additives; and labour. Recently the costs have increased drastically both for the increased investment and the need for a higher return in order to make additional investment attractive. Capital charges include taxes and insurance.

Natural petroleum sources are still the lowest in cost of liquid fuels, but liquid from oil shale, fuel gas by coal gasification, and methanol plus substitute natural gas (SNG) from coal are now nearly competitive in some situations.

PETROLEUM PRODUCTS

The importance of petroleum products is reflected in the great consumption of crude oil, the starting material for these products.

Petroleum products include power fuels for passenger cars, trucks, aircraft engines, and gas turbines (gasoline, jet fuel, diesel fuel and LPG); heating oils; illuminating oils (kerosene); solvents (petroleum spirits, aromatic solvents); lubricants (engine oils, greases); building materials (asphalts); insulating and waterproofing materials; and other products, such as cutting oils, heat-treating oils, hydraulic oils, petroleum jelly, etc.

The amounts produced are influenced by several factors, especially feed costs, processing costs and market demands. Distillate fuels usually denote burner fuels, diesel fuels, and similar intermediate-volatility products taken as condensed vapours from a distillation process. Gasoline is also a distillate product but is identified separately. Residual fuels are the unvapourised products from distillation and include asphalt, petroleum coke, and heavy industrial and bunker fuels.

Because of Government regulations for the control of automobile emissions, new automobiles are equipped with catalytic mufflers for the reduction of unburned hydrocarbons emanating from engine exhausts. Since catalytic mufflers are rendered ineffective by leaded fuels, the production of unleaded gasoline has increased. High compression engines tend to develop knock, so that refiners developed processes to improve antiknock properties, even though they may reduce gasoline yields.

Aviation gasoline for commercial aircraft has been largely replaced by jet fuels, also called aviation turbine fuels.

Many petroleum products of commerce are blended, compounded, or otherwise modified from primary stock. Trade names are not necessarily those given by the refiner, and a product may have several trade names, depending on uses. Specifications for automotive gasoline are given in Table 5, and for diesel fuel in Table 6.

Table 5. Specifications for automotive gasoline.

	Volatility class				
Property	*A*	*B*	*C*	*D*	*E*
Octane number[a]	no limit specified				
Distillation temperature, °C					
10% evaporated, max	70	65	60	55	50
50% evaporated, min	77	77	77	77	77
50% evaporated, max	121	118	116	113	110
90% evaporated, max	190	190	185	185	185
end point, max	225	225	225	225	225
Temp. for vapour-liquid ratio of 20, min, °C	60	56	51	47	41
Vapour pressure, max, kPa[b]	62	69	79	93	103

(Cont'd)

Property	*Volatility class*				
	A	*B*	*C*	*D*	*E*
Lead content, max, g/L					
Unleaded grade	0.013	0.013	0.013	0.013	0.013
Conventional grade	1.1	1.1	1.1	1.1	1.1
Corrosion, copper strip, max, no.	1	1	1	1	1
Gum, existent, max, mg/ 100 mL	5	5	5	5	5
Sulphur, max, wt%					
Unleaded grade	0.10	0.10	0.10	0.10	0.10
Conventional grade	0.15	0.15	0.15	0.15	0.15
Oxidation stability, min	240	240	240	240	240

[a] Measure of anti-knock for spark ignition.

[b] To convert kPa to mm Hg, multiply by 7.5.

Table. 6. Specifications for diesel fuel oils (ASTM D 975-78).

Property	*Grade*		
	I-D	*2-D*	*4-D*
Distillation (90%) point, °C	288 max	282-338	
Flash point, min, °C	38	52	55
Water and sediment, max, vol%	0.05	0.05	0.05
Carbon residue on 10% bottom, max, %	0.15	0.35	
Ash, max , wt%	0.01	0.01	0.01
Viscosity at 40°C, kinematic, mm^2/s (= cSt)	1.3-2.4	1.9-4.1	5.5-24.0
Sulphur, max, wt%	0.50	0.50	2.0
Corrosion, copper strip, max, no.	3	3	
Cetane number[a], min	40	40	30

[a] Measure of ignition quality for autoignition.

PETROCHEMICALS

Petrochemicals are essentially the chemical compounds derived from petroleum sources. Thus cracking of petroleum produces ethylene which is converted to ethylene glycol, the latter being a typical petrochemical. The term is also applied to substances such as ammonia, because hydrogen used to form the ammonia is derived from natural gas. Thus synthetic fertilisers are considered to be petrochemicals. A number of chemical products are recovered from the abundantly available raw materials which include crude oil, natural gas, refined petroleum fractions and refinery gases. The bulk of petrochemicals obtained from common hydrocarbons are broadly grouped as under.

(1) *Paraffins (saturated):* Methane, ethane, propane, butanes (iso and normal), etc.

(2) *Olefins (unsaturated):* Ethylene, propylene, butylenes (butene 1 and 2 and isobutylene), etc.

(3) *Aromatics:* Benzene, toluenes, xylenes, etc.

The peculiarity of petrochemical industry is that most of the products can be made from more than one hydrocarbon raw material, depending on the availability of feedstock and economic feasibility of the processes.

The common techniques employed in petrochemical manufacture are the thermal and catalytic cracking, oxidation, hydrogenation, alkylation, chlorination, polymerisation, dehydrogenation, isomerisation, solvent extraction, crystallisation and other related processes. Apart from these, the manufacture of petrochemicals involves the application of a number of continuous physical operations, such as distillation, extraction, filteration, mixing, pumping, etc. To illustrate the scope of manufacture and possible lines of development, various petrochemical products obtained from paraffins, olefins, aromatics, etc. are given below.

Petrochemicals from Methane

Ammonia, nitric acid, ammonium nitrate, ammonium sulphate, urea, carbon dioxide, methyl alcohol, formaldehyde, isobutyl alcohol, acetylene, vinyl chloride, acrylonitrile, neoprene rubbers, acetaldehyde, acetic acid, perchloroethylene, trichloroethylene, carbon tetrachloride, chloroform, methyl chloride, methylene chloride, carbon black, carbon disulphide, etc. (Fig. 6).

Petrochemicals from Ethylene

Ethylene oxide, ethylene glycol, monoethanolamine, diethanolamine, triethanolamine, diethylene glycol, triethylene glycol, acrylonitrile, ethyl alcohol, acetaldehyde, acetic acid, acetic anhydride, polyethylene, ethyl benzene, styrene, polystryrene, ethyl chloride, ethylene dichloride, vinyl chloride, ethylene diamine, ethylene dibromide, etc. (Fig. 7).

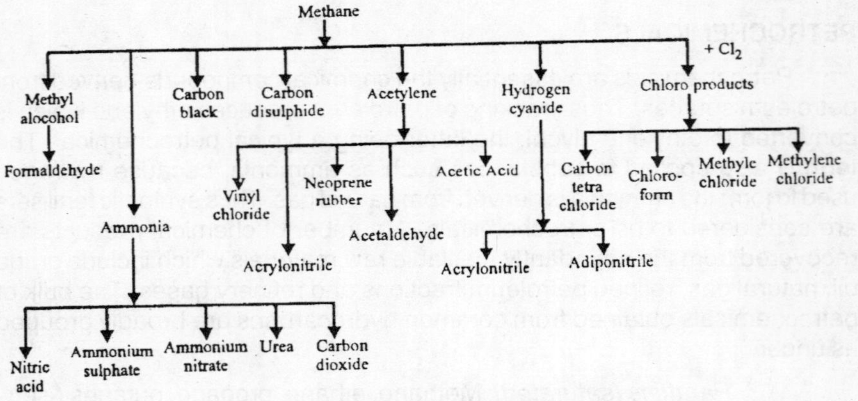

Fig. 6. Petrochemicals from methane.

Petrochemicals from Propane and Propylene

(1) *Propane:* Ethylene, methyl alcohol, formaldehyde, acetaldehyde, acetone (Fig.8).

(2) *Propylene:* Isopropyl alcohol, acetone, propylene trimer, nonyl phenol, propylene tetramer, dodecyl benzene, propylene oxide, propylene glycol, dipropylene glycol, allyl chloride, allyl alcohol, glycerine, epichlorohydrine, epoxy resins, propylene dichloride, acrolein, cumene, phenol, methyl styrene, polypropylene, etc.

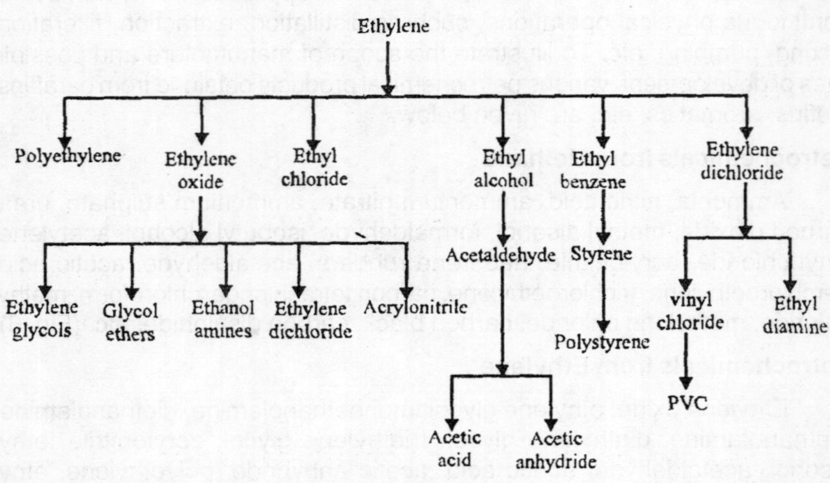

Fig. 7. Petrochemicals from ethylene.

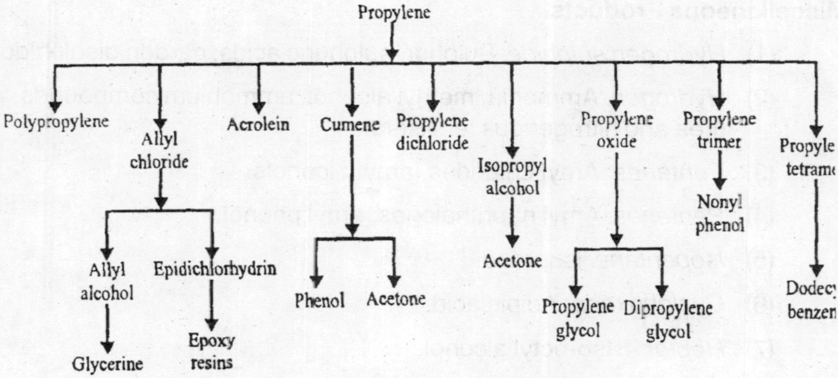

Fig. 8. Petrochemicals from propane and propylene.

Petrochemicals from Butanes and Butylenes

(1) *Butanes:* Acetic acid, acetaldehyde, acetic anhydride, methyl alcohol, formaldehyde, propionic acid, n-proply alcohol, butyric acid, n-butyl alcohol, isobutly alcohol (Fig. 9).

(2) *Butylenes:* N-butylenes, butadiene, synthetic rubber, sec-butyl alcohol, methyl ethyl ketone, isobutylene, butyl rubber.

Petrochemicals from Aromatics

(1) *Benzene:* Ethyl benzene, styrene, synthetic rubber, polystyrene, cumene, methyl styrene, dodecyl benzene, phenol, maleic anhydride, adipic acid, benzene hexachloride, etc.

(2) *Toluene:* Trinitrotoluene, etc.

(3) *Xylenes:* Para-xylene, terephthalic acid, meta-xylene, isophthalic acid, ortho-xylene, phthalic anhydride.

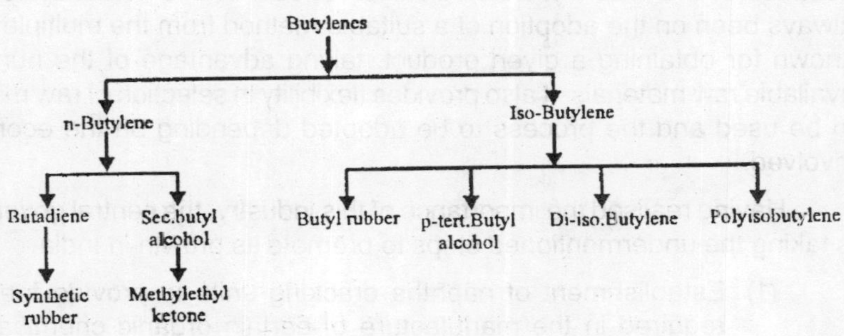

Fig. 9. Petrochemicals from butanes and butylenes.

Miscellaneous Products

(1) *Hydrogen sulphide:* Sulphur, sulphuric acids, carbon disulphide.

(2) *Hydrogen:* Ammonia, methyl alcohol, ammonium compounds, urea and nitrogenous fertilisers.

(3) *Pentanes:* Amyl chlorides, amyl alcohols.

(4) *Pentenes:* Amyl naphthalenes, amyl phenol.

(5) *Isopentane:* Isoprene.

(6) *Cyclohexane:* Adipic acid.

(7) *Heptane:* Iso-octyl alcohol.

(8) *Crude fractions:* Cresols, naphthenic acids, naphthalenes, sulphonates.

As a result of rapid development in the field of petrochemicals, a net work of industries, such as plastics, synthetic rubber, dyestuffs, intermediates, nitrogenous fertilisers, synthetic detergents, synthetic fibres, automotive chemicals, printing inks, etc. have come into existence and have experienced an enormous expansion in almost all industrial countries of the world.

The popularity of petrochemicals is attributed to the fact that it is possible to derive products of high purity from oil and natural gas. The range of products obtained from petroleum refining provide an easy and abundant supply of chemicals which are difficult to produce otherwise. In some cases the industries are entirely dependent on petroleum sources for supply of basic raw materials.

The promotion and rapid growth of petrochemical industry is ascribed to the cheap substitutes if provides in place of products hitherto obtained from conventional sources. The industry has made considerable progress because of the recent technological advances. In this field the focus has always been on the adoption of a suitable method from the multiple routes known for obtaining a given product, taking advantage of the numerous available raw materials. It also provides flexibility in selection of raw materials to be used and the process to be adopted depending on the economics involved.

Having realised the importance of this industry, the central government is taking the undermentioned steps to promote its growth in India.

(1) Establishment of naphtha cracking units to provide feedstock required in the manufacture of certain organic chemicals and intermediates;

(2) Utilisation of hydrocarbons and gases for the production of polymers and plastics, synthetic rubber, detergents, insecticides and pesticides, synthetic fibres, carbon black and other products; and

(3) Manufacture of nitrogenous fertilisers from naphtha and associated gases.

LUBRICATION AND LUBRICANTS

The process of reducing friction between two surfaces moving tangentially with respect to one another by interposing a substance of low shear strength between them is called lubrication and the interposed substance is known as a lubricant. Thus primary purpose of lubrication is suspension of moving surfaces to minimise friction and wear. The loss of energy due to friction is considerably reduced in this manner. The lubricant, in fact, acts in a number of manners. For example, it acts as a coolant or heat transfer medium by removing the heat of friction generated as a result of rubbing of surfaces. In lubrication, a thin film of lubricants is formed, between two rubbing surfaces, which does not allow a direct contact between the bubbling surfaces. In internal combustion engines, it acts as a seal by sealing the piston and cylinder wall at the compression rings. Thus there is no leakage of gases at high pressure in the combustion chamber.

Functions of Lubricants

The main functions of the lubricants are as follows :

(1) It reduces wear, and tear by avoiding direct contact between the rubbing surfaces.

(2) It reduces loss of energy in the form of heat by acting as coolant.

(3) It increases the efficiency of the machine.

(4) It minimises the liberation of heat.

(5) It reduces the maintenance as well as running cost of machine.

(6) It also acts as a seal to internal combustion engines.

Lubrication Principles

Several distinct regimes are commonly described to systematise the fundamental principles of lubricants. These range from complete separation of moving surfaces by a fluid lubricant, through partial separation in boundary lubrication to dry sliding where solid material properties and surface chemistry dominate. Presently, a change from sliding motion to rolling contact with elasto hydrodynamic lubrication also possible.

Tests of Lubricants

The most important tests of lubricants which are of prime importance in lubrication are copper strip corrosion, oxidation stability, inorganic sulphates and chlorides, steam emission number, viscosity, viscosity-temperature relation, viscosity index, volatility etc. In order to get efficient lubrication, there should be no change in these properties during lubrication. Moreover, there should be no effect of any chemical change such as decomposition, oxidation, reduction at higher temperature and emulsification during lubrication.

Viscosity. The behaviour of a lubricating oil or lubricant is determined by its viscosity. Viscosity is defined as the force in dynes necessary for the movement of 1 sq. cm. layer of a fluid with a velocity of 1 cm. per sec., past another parallel layer 1 cm away. The unit usually employed is centipoise. The measurement of viscosity is usually done in C.G.S. units and the unit is stoke. In case of thin oil which have very low viscosity, it is measured in centi-stokes. The viscosity measured by this method is called kinematic viscosity. In case of lubricants, viscosity depends upon the temperature. The viscosity has been found to decrease with increase in temperature.

Specific gravity. The specific gravity of an oil is defined as the ratio of the weight of a given volume of oil to the weight of the same volume of water. The test can be conducted either by using a hydrometer or a density bottle if greater accuracy is desired. The temperature of the test is important and always specified by the standard specification. It has been calculated that for insulating oils specific gravity varies by 0.0005 per every degree centigrade, the value decreasing with increasing temperature. The specific gravity of the oil is considered to have no important bearing on the utility of the oil. However, an upper limit of 0.89 to 0.90 is specified so that any water present in the oil may remain at the bottom only and not tend to float on the oil. A value lower than 0.85 adversely affects other properties, particularly viscosity so that normal insulating oils have specific gravity ranging from 0.85 to 0.90. The specific gravity is used extensively to facilitate volume to weight conversions.

Copper strip corrosion. Crude petroleum usually contains sulphur compounds, most of which are removed during the refining processes (sweetening). This test is designed to detect any traces of free or combined sulphur that may be present in an oil. A clean polished strip of pure copper metal of the specified dimensions is heated in a fixed quantity of the oil at a fixed temperature for the specified period of time. A black, brown, or grey tarnish indicates the presence of corrosive sulphur. The presence of sulphur promotes oxidation of oil in service and causes excessive formation of sludge. The sulphur also corrodes the copper and silver metal parts of the equipment.

Oxidation stability. The oxidation test is perhaps the most important test an oil must pass before it is accepted for service. An oxidation test submits the oil sample to accelerated oxidising conditions in a relatively short time than it is likely to meet in practice. The aim is to assess the behaviour of the oil during its long service from the results of the severe laboratory oxidation.

Though the conditions laid down in various oxidation tests of the standards are different, the accelerated conditions are brought by one or more of the following methods :

(1) Increase in temperature to the order of 100°-170°C.

(2) Inclusion of metals or soluble catalysts.

(3) Bubbling of air or oxygen in the oil during oxidation.

The oxidation stability test as laid down by the Indian Standard consists in ageing 100 grams of the oil at 150°C for a period of 45 hours during which purified air at the rate of two litres per hour is bubbled into the oil. A copper foil 51 x 32 x 0.1 mm after being cleaned and rolled into a cylinder is placed in the oil to act as a catalyst. The oxidation is carried out in a round bottomed flask of fixed dimensions fitted with a condenser through which cold water is circulated. This ensures that the volatile products of oxidation do not escape. At the end of the oxidation period the oil is diluted to four times its volume with normal-heptane and the amount of sludge and acids formed determined by analysis. The maximum limits fixed for new oils are acidity - 2.5 mg/ KOH/g and sludges 1.2% by weight. Formation of deterioration products above this level has been correlated by experience, to a faster rate of deterioration in service. Following are some of the other variation of the oxidation test :

(1) The oil is heated in a metal bomb for a fixed period under specified conditions of temperature and pressure, in an atmosphere of oxygen. The sludge and acids formed are subsequently determined (American method).

(2) The oil is aged in the presence of an electrical field and oxygen and the deterioration products determined after a fixed period of time (Swedish method).

(3) The tensile strength of cotton fibres immersed in the oil, which is being aged continuously, is tested periodically. The sludge formed is also determined (Swiss method).

The repeatability of the oxidation tests is poor and standards often fix the limits of difference between duplicate tests. The rate at which an oil will deteriorate during service can be assessed by the oxidation absorption tests.

Such tests though not specified by any standard are widely used to assess the quality of oils.

Inorganic sulphates and chlorides. The inorganic salts such as sulphates and chlorides may be present in the oil as left-overs from the refining processes. These salts ad to corrosivity of the oil. Their presence is determined by making an extract of the oil with hot water. The aqueous extract is treated with Barium chloride solution for sulphates or silver nitrate solution for chlorides. Any presence of a white haziness or precipitate indicates sulphates or chlorides respectively. A new oil must not contain any quantity of these salts.

Steam emulsion number. Water normally cannot remain in suspension in the oil. However the presence of soaps, polar contaminants etc., tends to increase its water retention capacity. The steam emulsion number is a measure of this capacity. In this test a known amount of steam is passed into a fixed quantity of the oil under prescribed conditions. The mixture is allowed to stand and the time taken for the condensed steam to separate out is noted. This lime in seconds is the steam emulsion number.

This test confirms the absence of soluble impurities if the oil has a low steam emulsion number.

Viscosity index. It may also be regarded as the average decrease in viscosity per degree rise of temperature between 100°F and 210°F. In the case of most lubricants, the viscosity index (V.I.) ranges from -50 to + 110. Lubricants having below or above viscosity index ranges than this are also known.

Pour point. It is an important property of a sample of lubricating oil and is defined as the temperature at which the oil ceases to flow when cooled under standard conditions. This property indicates the dissolved wax concentration in a given sample of lubricating oil.

Cloud point. It is another index of dissolved wax concentration, which may be defined as the temperature at which the cloudiness appears in a sample of oil, under standard conditions, because of wax separation. Lubricants also undergo oxidation, hydrolysis and pyrolysis. The property of lubricants to undergo oxidation is different for different lubricants and mainly depends upon the composition and purity of the lubricant. As a result of oxidation, the lubricant undergoes decomposition and its lubricating property is also affected. Hence certain anti-oxidants are employed in the lubricants to avoid oxidation.

Flash point. It is very important to test the *flash point* of the oil to be used as lubricant. It is not advisable to use an oil as lubricant, which flashes or reaches combustion temperature under the conditions of the lubrication. This is due to the fact that spontaneous combustion of oil vapours occurs if the oxidation is so rapid that heat of oxidation is not dissipated so quickly as to avoid the reaching of flash point or cbmbustion temperature. When lubricants such as esters are exposed to moisture at high temperatures and in the presence of acids and alkalies, they undergo decomposition as a result of hydrolysis. Polyethers and halides are hydrolysed only under drastic conditions of hydrolysis and poly siloxanes are hydrolysed easily by alkaline solutions. It is, therefore, necessary to use those lubricants, which are not capable of hydrolysing under lubricating conditions.

Interfacial tension

The interfacial tension between the oil and water is measure of the molecular attractive force between their unlike, molecules at the interface, *it* is expressed in dynes-centimetre. When an oil sample is poured in water the hydrocarbons comprising the oil arrange themselves at the interface and form a bond with the water molecules. This interface possesses a high tension. When the oil contains dissolved impurities which are polar in nature these tend to diffuse into the water through the interface consequently lowering the interfacial tension.

The interfacial tension is determined by means of suitable tensiometers (Torsion balance) in which the force required to lift a planar ring of platinum or a thin glass plate from the oil/water interface into the oil is measured. This value varies with temperature and ageing of the interface, and consequently the prescribed test conditions must be rigidly adhered to. A minimum interfacial tension value of 40 dynes/cm specified in some standards ensures freedom from all types of dissolved impurities.

Neutralisation number

Neutralisation number or the acid content of an oil is defined as the number of milligrams of potassium hydroxide required to neutralise completely the acids present in one gram of the oil. Neutralisation number is the sum of the organic and inorganic acids in the oil. To determine this a weighed quantity of the oil sample is boiled with a previously neutralised mixture of Alcohol and water (60:40). The resulting mixture is titrated while hot against a standard solution of potassium hydroxide using a suitable indicator. Organic acidity is the difference between the total and inorganic acidity. The maximum prescribed limit for total acidity in new oils is 0.05 mg/KOH/g.

Saponification value

The saponification number is defined as the number of milligrams of potassium hydroxide required to saponify completely the combined and free acids present in one gram of the oil.

It is determined by refluxing a weighed quantity of the oil dissolved in ethyl methyl ketone with an alcoholic solution of potassium hydroxide. The unconsumed alkali is measured by titration with standard hydrochloric acid. The amount of potassium hydroxide thus consumed is calculated. Under these conditions many of the soaps, metals, sulphur and its compounds, halogens and nitrogen compounds consume the alkali, in addition to the substances indicated in the acidity test. Also these are potential contaminates and if present in large quantities lead to a faster rate of oil deterioration.

Mechanism of Lubricants

Depending on the operating conditions three mechanisms may occur :

(1) Complete fluid or hydrodynamic lubrication.

(2) Boundary lubrication.

(3) Extreme pressure lubrication.

Complete fluid or hydrodynamic lubrication

In such type of lubrication, one of the rubbing surfaces is slightly displaced in relation to the other and a wedge shaped film of the lubricant is formed between the two surfaces rubbing against each other. The pressure developed in the wedge shaped film supports the load and prevents the direct contact between the rubbing surfaces. Since a solid-solid interface has been replaced by two solid-liquid interfaces (Fig 10), viscosity of the lubricant becomes a crucial factor. An example of this type of lubrication is the rotation of a shaft with respect to a stationary bearing. In Fig 10, the lubricant occupies the annular space between the shaft and the bearing and forms a hydrodynamic wedge. So long the shaft rotates, the wedge will remain and prevent contact between two solids. When the load becomes very high, the lubricant is squeezed out of the wedge and friction occurs.

Complete fluid lubrication is provided to delicate instruments such as watches, clocks, guns, sewing machines, scientific instruments etc. The most satisfactory and widely used lubricants for this type of lubrication are hydrocarbon oils, which are blended with selected long chain polymers in order to maintain suitable viscosity of the oil. Some anti-oxidants such as aminophenols are also added to hydrocarbon petroleum fraction because these usually contain minute amounts of unsaturated hydrocarbon petroleum fraction because these usually contain minute amounts of unsaturated hydrocarbons which are susceptible to oxidation under operating conditions.

Boundary lubrication

Boundary lubrication takes place under any of the following conditions :

(1) When the relative speed of the lubricated surface is insufficient to produce pressure in the lubricant film to carry the load. Such

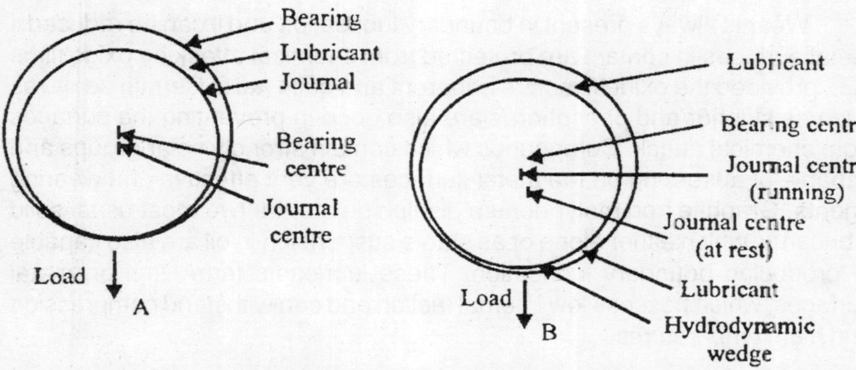

Fig. 10 Fluid film formation in bearing "A" at rest. "B" rubbing.

conditions are reached when a heavily loaded bearing is stopped or started.

(2) When the load on bearing exceeds the pressure generated in the lubricant film.

(3) When the surfaces are not perfect and the load is carried on high spots.

Boundary lubrication is therefore suitable when a continuous film of lubricant cannot persist and direct metal to metal contact is possible because of various reasons, for example, when a shaft starts moving from rest of speed is very low or load is very high or the viscosity of the oil is extremely low. Under all these circumstances friction between the lubricated surfaces lies on absorbed or boundary layer of lubricant. The load is carried by the layer of the absorbed lubricant or both the metal surfaces. The coefficient of friction in such a case is generally 0.05 to 0.15. This friction is generally dependent upon the nature of the material of the surfaces and also on some characteristics that can be determined by the chemical properties of the lubricant.

The effectiveness of boundary lubrication primarily depends upon the structure and chemical properties of the oil to be used. The lubricant used in such type of lubrication should have long chain and active atoms or groups capable of forming linkages with the metals or other surfaces. The other properties of boundary lubricants are good oiliness, low pour point, high resistance to oxidation and heat and high viscosity index. It should be noted that in fluid lubrication there is no friction between the surfaces and the wear is almost negligible. So in fluid lubrication wear decreases as the friction decreases. In boundary lubrication, decrease in friction does not decrease the wear to the same extent as the decrease in friction and so minimum friction is not achieved by minimum wear.

Wear is always present in boundary lubrication and it can be reduced if metal surfaces in contact are protected from chemical attack by oxide films etc., provided the oxide films are adherent and quite hard. Certain additives such as sulphur and phosphorus are also good in preventing the surfaces from chemical attack. Compounds which contain strongly polar groups and capable of absorbing on the metal surfaces are very effective and wearing agents. Graphite and molybdenum disulphide are the two most usual solid lubricants, which either alone or as stable suspension in oil are also capable of producing boundary lubrication. These lubricants form films on metal surfaces, which possess low internal friction and can withstand compression and high temperatures.

Extreme pressure lubrication

This mechanism is prevalent under conditions of high load and high speed and occurs at high temperatures. Under these conditions, the lubricant film may decompose and vapourise. This necessitates the addition of some chemicals to lubricant with a view to increase the chemical stability of the film. The additives contains chlorinated esters, sulphated oils and aryl(tricresyl) phosphates. These react with metal surfaces to form high melting chlorides, sulphides and phosphides. Their action is chemical, they do not reduce friction but prevent formation of welded joints.

Substances Used as Lubricants

Vegetable oils and fatty acids are most important substances which are used as lubricants. Tallow, lard, whale oils, neat foot oil, rosin oil, castor oil, olive oil, coconut oil, palm oil, oleic acid etc. are the various substances used as lubricants. Mineral oils compounded with fatty acids are known as compounded oils and these are also suitable as lubricants.

Lubricating oil not only reduce wear and friction between two moving or sliding metallic surfaces by providing a continuous fluid film in between them, but they also serve as coolant, sealing agent, corrosion preventors etc.

Characteristics of good lubricating oil

The characteristics of good lubricating oil are :

(1) High boiling point or low vapour pressure.

(2) Suitable viscosity for particular service condition.

(3) Low freezing point.

(4) High thermal stability.

(5) High oxidation resistance.

(6) Non-corrosive nature.

(7) Resistance to decomposition at higher or elevated temperatures.

Additives for Lubricating Oils

Although the bulk of additives is used in automotive lubricants, they also are used in oils for turbines, diesel and aircraft engines, two-cycle engines, hydraulic equipment, gears, and metal working. The common types of additives in the approximate order of their frequency of application are oxidation inhibitors, rust inhibitors, anti-wear agents, detergents-dispersants, pour-point depressants, viscosity index (V1) improvers and foam inhibitors.

Additives containing polar groupings such as fatty acids and their derivatives (e.g. multivalent metal soaps, known as metallic soaps), long chain alcohols and organic phosphides are used to ease boundary lubrication.

Certain additives such as long chain alkylated ring compounds, alkyl naphthalenes, polymers of long chin alkyl acrylate, metallic soaps of fatty acids etc. are used to reduce the temperature at which a liquid lubricant may become solid. This type of additives are known as pour depressants. Their function is colloidal and they prevent the wax crystals to grow.

Phenol and certain condensation products of chlorinated wax with naphthalene are also used as pour point depressing additives. They also prevent the separation of wax from the oil.

Additives such as phenols, their derivatives, amines, organic phosphides etc. are added to the lubricants to prevent the oxidation of lubricant and known as anti-oxidants.

The anti-oxidants or inhibitors retard the oxidation of oil by getting themselves preferentially oxidised. They are generally added to lubricant used in internal combustion engines, turbines etc., where oxidation causes a serious problem.

Additives containing strongly polar groups are added to increase the oiliness and film strength of the lubricants. Examples of such additives are amyl phenyl phosphate, methyl di chloro stearate, dibenzyl disulphide, tricresyl phosphate, sulphurised sperm oil etc.

Oiliness of a lubricant can also be increased by adding oiliness carriers such as vegetable oils (coconut oil, castor oil etc.) and fatty acids (palmitic acid, oleic acid, stearic acid etc.)

Additives such as high molecular weight compounds like hexanol are added as viscosity index improvers. Additives are also added as detergents of deflocculents to the lubricants. Examples of such additives are salts of phenol, carboxylic acids, sulphonic acids and alkyl phosphoric acids etc. Additives added as wear inhibitors prevent wearing of the lubricating surface. Alkaline earth phenolates are generally used as anti-corrosive wear agent and tricresyl phosphate is generally used as anti-abrasive wear agent.

Corrosion preventatives are organic compounds of phosphorus or antimony. Their function is to protect the metal from corrosion by preventing contact between the metal surfaces and the corrosive substances.

The gummy and acidic constituents of lubricants can be removed by a suitable refining processes. The tendency of emulsification of the lubrication oil is checked by certain additives to the lubricant. The additives are also added or used for number of other purposes. For example, polymeric thickners are used as additives for improving the viscosity index of the lubricant.

Extreme pressure additives such as compounds containing phosphorus, lead sulphur and chlorine (e.g. fatty acids, esters ketones, chlorinated wax, sulphurised wax etc.) are added to make lubricating oil to bear extreme pressure. Under extreme pressure a thick film of oil is not capable of maintaining the film and it needs to have high oiliness. High pressure additives are absorbed on the metal surface or chemically react with metal producing a surface layer of low shear strength on the metal surface. Hence tearing up of metal is prevented. High pressure additives also react on metal surface at high temperatures forming surface alloys and prevent welding to gather of the rubbing parts under severe operating conditions.

Additives such as fatty acids, oil soluble alkaline earth salts of fatty acids etc. are added to the lubricant as rust preventives. Additives such as alkali metal salts of carboxylic and sulphonic acids, non-ionic emulsifiers such as mono-esters of polyhydric alcohols, ether alcohols etc. are added to the lubricant which help the formation of emulsion with water. These additives are known as emulsifiers. It should be noted that additives are added to the lubricant taking all the factors including properties, application and effects of individual additives into consideration.

No single oil serves as the most satisfactory lubricant for various modern machineries. The properties of petroleum oils are greatly improved by adding various additives given above but the exact adjustment of the additives to a lubricating oil is one of the most complex problem. The socalled blended oils, are capable of giving desired lubricating properties, required for a particular machinery.

LUBRICANTS OF MINERAL ORIGIN

Lubricants are either of mineral origin or vegetable origin but lubricants of mineral origin are generally used as lubricants. Lubricants of vegetable origin such as vegetable oils and fatty acids are rarely used as lubricants, but they are generally used as additives to the mineral lubricants to improve their properties and qualities.

Large number of lubricants or lubricating oils are obtained from crude petroleum distillation as residue. These residues are either paraffins or asphaltic. Paraffinic residues are steam distilled to get an oil distillate and steam refined cylinder oil as the main fractions. Asphaltic residues are distilled to get various fractions with different viscosities. The lubricating oils obtained from mineral residues have a large number of impurities such as paraffin waxes, resins, asphalts etc. For a good lubricant these properties are undesirable, so it is necessary to remove them. For example, waxes increase the pour point and render the lubricant unfit for use at low temperatures. Asphaltic compounds undergo decomposition at higher temperature, causing carbon deposition and sludge formation. Resinous and asphaltic compounds are easily oxidisable and form sludge when the lubricant is used on the surfaces.

METHODS FOR REMOVING IMPURITIES

Sharpley's method

Sharpley's method is generally used for removing wax from lubricating oil. This method is based on the difference of density between precipitated wax and the solvent lubricating oil solution from which wax is separated by cooling or chilling. In this method, the lubricating oil containing wax and the solvent for dilution are mixed together and then heated to get a complete solution. The clear solution so formed is chilled down slowly to -20°F and then charged into a centrifugal rotating machine. The wax is separated from the solution of the solvent and lubricating oil. It should be noted the lubricating oil should be completely soluble in the solvent at moderately high temperature and wax should be so precipitated that it can be easily removed.

Acetone Benzene Solvent or Propane Dewaxing Method

Wax can also be removed by using acetone-benzene solvent method or propane dewaxing method. In acetone-benzene solvent method acetone and benzene (1:20) are mixed and then added to the oil at 120°F. The oil solvent mixture is then chilled to -30°F. The precipitated wax is removed by using continuous filtration drum type filter. In propane dewaxing method, lubricating oil is mixed with liquid propane solvent (propane remains liquid) at a pressure of about 200 lbs. per square inch in the ratio of I :2. Asphalt is thus precipitated which is removed by cooling is brought about by releasing the pressure and obtaining autogenous refrigeration. As a result, wax is thrown out.

Solvent Extraction Method

Aromatic compounds are removed by solvent extraction using different methods such as sulphur dioxide benzene process, nitrobenzene process, furfural process, phenol extraction process, chlorex process etc. In sulphur dioxide benzene process, aromatic compounds are removed by using a mixture of benzene (30:70) and sulphur dioxide.

In nitrobenzene method, the solvent and lubricating oil are mixed and extraction temperature is brought to 40°F. Two layers are separated when the mixture is allowed to stand. The lower layer contains naphthenic hydrocarbons in naphthalene and upper layer contains paraffin compounds with some dissolved nitrogen. The two layers are continuously separated and the solvent is removed by evaporation in a vacuum evaporator.

In furfural method, furfural is used as a solvent for the extraction of lubricating oil. It removes olefinic and aromatic compounds but does not remove paraffinic compounds. The lubricating oil is then treated with 200% by volume of furfural for extraction.

In phenol extraction method, phenol is used as an intermediate solvent between selective solvents like nitrobenzene and furfural and the high potency solvents. Phenol is cheap, stable and can be removed easily from the oil. It also reduces the viscosity sulphur content, oxidation number and carbon content as residue.

Chlorex process

In chlorex process, chlorex (β-β[1] dichloroethyl ether) is used for the extraction in the chlorex; oil ratio of 0.7:1.15. In this process viscosity and carbon residue of the lubricating oil are reduced and pour point is improved. Moreover, extraction also causes improvement in colour and oxidation stability.

Advantages

(1) It is less expensive.

(2) It provides satisfactory removal of asphaltic impurities and hence minimises the chances of carbon deposit formation during the use of refined lubricating oil.

(3) It gives high yield of refined oil and provides a very refined product which does not show much variation in viscosity due to increase in temperature.

Disadvantages

(1) It yields oil which is less resistant to oxidation.

(2) The refined oil also posses lower oiliness and hence its oiliness is improved by adding suitable additives.

Acid Treatment

Unsaturated hydrocarbons from the oil are removed by acid treatment. The lubricating oil is treated with 10% by volume of the oil of concentrated sulphuric acid. The principle of counter-current is used in the treatment. In order to avoid side reactions, generally the temperature is kept low. The oil is then separated from sulphuric acid sludge and is treated with dilute alkali and then with clay.

The acid refining can be followed after dewaxing process. If the oil still contains undesirable constituents like naphthenic and asphaltic impurities. These are eliminated by treating the oil with concentrated sulphuric acid and then agitated. Some of the impurities dissolved in the acid while others are converted into sludge. The later is removed by filtration and the filtrate is neutralised with requisite amount of NaOH so as to remove excess acid. The oil is finally decolourised by passing through fullers' earth at 100°-140°C. It should be noted that during above treatment of lubricating oils, not only the objectionable material and oxidisable impurities are removed, but polar bodies in lubricants are also removed. These polar bodies attach themselves to lubricated surfaces and provide better lubricant because of their chemical affinity. Hence the additives are now-a-days added to ultra purified and non-reactive oily substances and these additives are capable of giving polar properties to lubricating oils.

Classification of Lubricants

Lubricants are classified on the basis of their states of aggregation or consistency. They are :

(1) Liquid lubricants

(2) Semi-solid lubricants

(3) Solid lubricants.

Liquid lubricants (lubricating oils)

Most of the lubricating oils are of petroleum origin. When petroleum is distilled, a residual fraction collects at the bottom of the fractionating column. This oil on refractionation under reduce pressure gives three fractions-light, medium and heavy oils. These have to be purified before use as lubricants. The oil contains wax, asphalt (tar), coloured substances and oxidisable impurities. Wax prevents fluidity of the lubricant at low temperatures; asphalt deposits on the engine parts during use of the lubricant; and oxidisable impurities cause sludge formation.

Semi-solid lubricants or greases

A grease is a semi-solid lubricant obtained by thickening a lubricating oil through the addition of a metallic soap. The thickener also called a gelling agent, is usually a sodium, calcium or lithium soap. The long chain fatty acids forming the soap may be stearic acid, oleic acid or palmitic acid. If sodium soap is added to the lubricating oil, the grease is known as soda base grease; if calcium soap is added, lime base grease or cup grease results. The functions of the soaps are optimising the operating temperature, improving the resistance to oxidation and hydrolysis as well as adjusting the consistency. The different types of greases, their properties and uses are listed in Table. 7.

Though soaps are the usual thickening agents in the greases, graphite, asphalt (tar) or bentonite (clay) may also be used. Among synthetic greases, the silicones are the foremost.

Table 7. Properties and uses of various types of greases.

Greases	Properties	Uses
Soda base grease	Low water resistance; hence can be used only in dry conditions	Used in high temperature lubrication upto 175°C in ball bearings
Lime base or cup grease	General purpose greases. Can be used only upto 70°C. More resistant to water than soda base grease	Lubrication of pumps and tractors
Lithium-soap grease	Resistant to both heat and water.	For aircraft lubrication; from -55 to 150°C

Conditions in which Greases can be Used

(1) Oil is squeezed out due to heavier load or low speed, or the oil does not remain in place due to vertical flow or jerks.

(2) The design of the machine does not allow the lubricant to be retained.

(3) Lubricant should not contaminate the manufactured product, such as food, paper, textile etc.

(4) Lubricant has to act as a screen to prevent entry of dirt or moisture.

(5) Electrical motor bearings are to be fabricated.

(6) Frequent application of lubricant is inconvenient, as in automobile wheel bearings.

The important properties of greases are consistency, penetration index and drop point, of which, dropping point determination helps in finding the maximum temperature of use for grease. The dropping point of grease is the lowest temperature at which the grease, when heated under specified conditions, becomes sufficiently fluid to drop from a cup through a hole of standard dimensions.

Solid Lubricants

The reasons for which greases are preferred over lubricating oils hold preference of solid lubricant as well. Only those solids which have iaminar micro structure can be used as lubricants. Graphite and molybdenum disulphide are ideal lubricants on this basis.

Graphite may be used as powder or as colloidal dispersion in water or in oil. Colloidal dispersion of graphite is denoted by the dag (deflocculated Acheason's Graphite). Dispersions in water is known as aquadag and oily dispersion is called oildag. Graphite is not effective as a lubricatnt in vacuum and gets oxidised above 370°C. Graphite is used as a lubricant in I.C. engines, air compressors, lathes etc.

SYNTHETIC LUBRICANTS

Many lubricants even with additives can be used under various abnormal conditions, for example when the temperature is extremely high or the atmosphere is chemically reactive. Under such conditions synthetic lubricants having appropriate properties to be used under abnormal conditions are generally employed. Such synthetic lubricants are prepared by hydrocarbons, polyglycols, esters, polycarbonates, amines, silicones and fluorine derivatives etc.

In fact synthetic lubricants are developed to meet the most severe and drastic operations such as those existing in aircraft engines in which oil may have to be pumped at -50°C. During take off or landing the same oil may get heated to as high a temperature as 250°C. Hence it is necessary for the oil to maintain satisfactory properties. The oil to be used at high temperatures and high operating pressures is expected to have high resistance to oxidation and high viscosity, and at the same time it must also possess sufficiently low freezing point and it should also be noninflammable.

Modern Synthetic Lubricants

Modern synthetic lubricants are prepared by taking all these factors into consideration and have number of distinguishing characteristic features. They are inflammable and have high flash points, high viscosity index and high thermal stability at higher temperatures. For most common purposes blended petroleum oils are good and synthetic lubricants are needed only in special circumstances, e.g. in certain specialised military and industrial uses.

Polymerised Hydrocarbons

Polymerised hydrocarbons such as polymerised ethylene, propylene, butylene etc. having molecular weight ranging from 250 to 50,000 are used as synthetic lubricants. Although these hydrocarbons have chemical and physical properties similar to the lubricants obtained from petroleum fractions, but they have so distinct disadvantages over equivalent petroleum products.

For example they can be used at high temperatures as residue free high temperature lubricants, they are light in colour and free from nonhydrocarbons, having better electrical properties.

Polyglycols and Related Compounds

Polyglycols and related compounds such as polyethylene glycol, polypropylene glycol, their ethers and esters, higher polyalkylene oxides, polythioglycols and polyglycidyl ethers can be used as water soluble and water insoluble lubricants.

Water Diluted Lubricants

Water diluted lubricants can be prepared by polyethylene glycol or polypropylene glycol to be used in rubber bearings and joints. After applying to metal surfaces they can be easily removed by water flushing. Higher polyalkylene oxides and polyglycidyl ether absorb a considerable amount of water, although they are not soluble in water. Temperature has no effect on their viscosity. Polyalkylene oxides undergo decomposition into the .volatile parts under high temperature and these volatile parts undergo oxidation. Hence these lubricants are very useful at high temperatures and used in roller bearings of sheet glass machinery.

Natural Fats and Oils as Esters of Glycerides

They have high freezing point and can be easily oxidised. On account of this reason they cannot be used as lubricants. Diesters of glycol and aliphatic dibasic acid as well as that of aromatic dibasic acids and triesters of phosphoric acid etc. have been found to be good synthetic lubricants because their viscosity is not much affected by increase in temperature. Their volatility is very low, they can be easily oxidised by this property, this can be reduced by adding additives. They also act as good lubricant even at low temperatures. Esters as lubricants can however be decomposed by steam, acids and alkalies.

Organic Amines and Amides

Organic amines and amides are good synthetic lubricants having high viscosity index and low pour point. Silicones and the products obtained by hydrolysis and decomposition of organic chloro silicones are also employed as synthetic lubricants, because they have low viscosity temperature coefficients and are not readily oxidised upto about 200°C. They however oxidise quickly above 225°C. Silicones are very useful for low temperature lubrication of small parts.

Fluorocarbon and Other Compounds

Fluorocarbon and other compounds, e.g. tertiary amines, ethers, esters which can be completely fluorinated are also used as synthetic lubricants.

They are chemically inert and resist to all chemicals except sodium. They are not decomposed easily be heat. They are also not easily oxidisable.

PREPARATION OF GREASES

By saponification of fats

Greases are generally prepared by saponification of fat such as tallow or fatty acid with alkali such as lime caustic soda, followed by adding hot lubricating oil with constant agitation soaps are also added which act as gelling agents and give an interconnected structure. At high temperature, the interconnected structure which is held by intermolecular forces ceases to exist, because soap (gelling agent) dissolves in the oil and hence the grease undergoes liquefaction.

From fatty acids and lubricating oil

Greases can also be prepared by dissolving fatty acid in part of lubricating oil. Metal hydroxide is then added to it in form of dry oil slurry or as aqueous solution. The mixture of soap and oil is dehydrated by stirring and the balance of lubricating oil is added and homogenised. Since the gelling agents in soap based grease are crystallities of fibrous shape. Their gelling property is due to their ability to form a tangle in the interstices as a result of which the oil is held, the soap dissolved in oil. As a result, the fibrous structure no longer exists and liquefaction of grease takes place.

Greases can be made stable to oxidation and to provide lubrication under extreme conditions of load and sliding speed by adding additives to lubrication oils. The consistency of the greases considerably changes when the temperature is suddenly decrease, because the intersection of gelling agent and viscosity of oil changes with increase in temperature. The temperature at which the consistency of greases changes, determines the upper temperature limit of the applicability of the greases. Under certain conditions it is not possible to use liquid lubricant, so in such cases solid lubricants such as talcum, graphite, boron nitride, molybdenum disulphide are used.

Chapter 2

HYDROCARBONS FROM PETROLEUM

INTRODUCTION

Petroleum industry supplies a large number of saturated, unsaturated and aromatic hydrocarbons. Some of them include methane, ethane, ethylene, propane, propylene, butane, butylene, benzene and toluene. These hydrocarbons are used as basic **chemicals** for the manufacture of a large number of **petrochemicals** which are then used as **basic raw materials** for the manufacture of a large number of essential and useful commodities, such as fertilizers, fibres, rubbers, plastics and paints etc.

RAW MATERIALS

The **basic raw materials** supplied by the petroleum refineries or the **natural gas** companies are liquid petroleum gas (LPG), natural gas, gas from cracking processes, liquid distillate C_4 -C_9, distillates from special cracking processes and cyclic fractions for aromatics.

The preparation of some hydrocarbons from these raw materials are given below :

SATURATED HYDROCARBONS FROM NATURAL GAS

Natural gas leaving the wells consists of a large number of saturated hydrocarbons, such as methane, propane, butane, and other higher hydrocarbons. The natural gas is first dried and then passed into an absorption tower containing hexane fraction as absorbing medium. The tower operates at ordinary pressure and -35 to -45°C. Hydrogen and an excess of methane are not absorbed in the tower and they leave the absorber from the top. Other hydrocarbons and some methane are absorbed in the oil and the mixture is withdrawn from the bottom of the absorption tower and led into a **demethaniser**. A mixture of methane, ethane and propane leaves the demethaniser from the top. The components of this mixture are then separated in another absorber.

The hydrocarbon absorbed or dissolved in the oil from two absorbers are mixed and then separated from the oil by passing through a light oil still. A mixture of light hydrocarbon is obtained from the still as overhead. This mixture is then led through a number of fractionating columns to separate ethane, propane, pentane, butane and isobutane one by one. These hydrocarbons, alongwith ethylene, propylene and butylenes can also be obtained from **cracked refinery gases.**

USES OF SATURATED HYDROCARBONS

Methane - Methane is used in the manufacture of methanol, methanal, acetylene, formic acid, methyl ether, dimethyl sulphate, ethylene glycol, methylamines, hexamethylene tetramine, hydrogen cyanide, methyl chloride, methylene chloride, chloroform, carbon tetra chloride, carbondioxide, carbon monoxide, hydrogen etc.

Ethane - It is used in the manufacture of ethyl chloride, acetic acid, nitro ethane, ethylene, acetaldehyde, acetic anhydride, ethyl acetate, diethyl ether etc.

Propane - It is used in the preparation of propanol, propionic acid, nitromethane nitroethane, nitropropane, ethylene, isopropylamines, acetone, acetone cyanohydrin, tetra chloro ethane etc.

Pentanes - These are used in the preparation of amyl alcohols, acetaldehyde, butylenes, butadiene, thiophene etc.

IMPORTANT POINTS

- Halogenation of paraffins is an exothermic reaction, except iodination,which is endothermic.
- Carbon tetrachloride, an industrial solvent, is manufactured by chlorinating methane at 250 - 400°C.
- Pentanes from petroleum are chlorinated to a mixture of chloropentanes, which on hydrolysis,yield the corresponding alcohols. These are useful solvents.
- Chlorinated paraffin wax makes fabrics water proof and flame resistant.
- The oxidative reaction of paraffins is highly exothermic, so natural gas is widely used for heating, and gasoline as a motor fuel.
- In certain proportions, an alkane and air (or oxygen) explode violently if ignited, Because of this reason, explosions occur in coal mines due to methane.
- Carbon black can be manufactured by burning cheap natural gas (mainly CH_4) in limited supply of air for the rubber industry, painter's ink etc.

- Copper naphthenate or stearate is a catalyst in liquid phase oxidation of paraffins. The relative rates of oxidation are : Tertiary carbon > Secondary carbon > Primary carbon.
- Liquid phase of oxidation of paraffins may be carried out between 150°C and 200°C, and the gas phase oxidation at about 500°C.
- A straight chain paraffin is more readily oxidised than a branched chain paraffin.
- Industrially, alcohols, aldehydes, fatty acids etc are prepared by controlled high temperature oxidation of paraffins from petroleum.
- On heating with dilute nitric acid at about 200°C for several hours, paraffins form nitro-paraffins. Reactivity follows the order : Tertiary hydrogen > Secondary hydrogen > Primary hydrogen. Simultaneously, oxidation of paraffins also occurs and some polynitro derivatives are formed.
- When methane reacts with nitric acid at 475°C only 13% nitromethane is formed and oxidative products. predominate. But if nitration is carried out in vapour phase with nitric acid, mononitroalkanes are generally the main products. These can be separated by fractional distillation. At the high temperature, some fission of the carbon chain takes place and lower nitroalkanes are formed.
- Vapour phase nitration of propane from natural gas at ordinary pressure yields nitromethane (9 parts), nitromethane (26 parts), 1-nitropropane (32 parts) and 2-nitropropane (33 parts).
- The vapour phase nitration of ethane gives nitromethane (9 parts), nitroethane (I part). These nitroparaffins are used as industrial solvents for pyroxylene laquers, fuels etc.
- If n-butane is treated with $AlCl_3$ and a trace of anhydrous HCl (or $AlBr_3$ and a little HBr) at about 25°C, an equilibrium mixture of about 80% isobutane and n-butane is obtained. n-pentane can similarly be converted into mixtures of isopentane and n-pentane. This reaction is reversible and known as **isomerisation**. Normal straight chain paraffins knock badly in internal combustion engines under high compression but branched chain isomers are generally not. Modern petroleum refineries carry out the low temperature catalytic isomerisation of n-butane inorder to improve antiknock properties of gasoline or to increase the octane number of gasoline.
- Lower alkanes are remarkably stable at moderately high temperatures. For example, CH_4 decomposes into carbon and hydrogen slightly at a

about 800°C. Ethane decomposes into ethylene, methane and hydrogen partially at about 700°C. Propane forms propylene, ethylene, methane and hydrogen on partial decomposition at 600°C. In general, resistance to decomposition on heating decreases as the molecular mass of paraffin increases. Branched chain paraffins are less resistant to heat than n-chain paraffins (isomer). High boiling fractions of petroleum can be broken into smaller molecules(saturated and unsaturated) by pyrolysis or thermal cracking mainly to produce better high octane motor fuels. Cracking is usually done catalytically now a days.

➢ Because of low polarity of C - H bonds, paraffins generally resist attack by polar reagents.

➢ Methane from natural gas can be converted into carbon and hydrogen by cracking. Methane is the chief constituent of natural gas from oil or gas wells. Coal gas contains 20 - 30% of methane by volume.

➢ Methane is a common fuel in countries where natural gas is abundant or cheaply available. It can be converted into synthesis gas ($CO + H_2$) by partial oxidation with O_2 at about 1300°C. Acetylene can be obtained by heating methane in a limited supply of O_2 at 1500°C. A mixture of methane and steam, when passed over nickel catalyst at 850°C form CO and H_2.

$$CH_4 + H_20 \rightarrow CO + 3H_2$$

This mixture is used for the manufacture of HCHO. The latter is raw material for plastics. CO and steam at about 500°C and in the presence of ferric oxide as catalyst, yield $C0_2$ and H_2. The latter is used in the manufacture of ammonia and fertilizers.

➢ Ethane (CH_3 - CH_3) is present to the extent of 5 - 10% by volume in the natural gas. In minor amount it is also present in crude petroleum and coal gas. Some ethane is also formed when heavy petroleum fractions are cracked. Ethane is more reactive than methane. Ethane is converted into ethylene by pyrolysis, because ethylene is more important commercially.

➢ Propane ($CH_3CH_2CH_3$) is a minor constituent (upto 5% by volume) of natural gas. It occurs in crude petroleum and the gases formed during cracking of petroleum fractions.

➢ Propane is more reactive than methane and ethane. It can be readily liquefied at ordinary temperature. It is used as a domestic fuel. Propane is used for making nitroparaffins by vapour phase nitration. Liquid propane is used for dewaxing of lubricating oils. Controlled oxidation of propane under suitable conditions yields formaldehyde and acetaldehyde. On pyrolysis, propane yields ethylene and methane at about 800°C.

- n-butane and isobutane are present upto 1% by volume in natural gas, crude petroleum and in gases from cracking of oil fractions. n-butane and isobutane can be separated by selective adsorption or by fractional distillation under reduced pressure.
- A mixture of butane (n- and isobutanes), containing some propane, liquefied by compression is used for domestic heating and cooking as LPG.
- On pyrolysis, n-butane forms mainly propylene and methane with some ethane, ethylene, butene-1, butene-2 and hydrogen. Pure n-butane, mixed with dry air, is a standard fuel for heat treatment of special steels.
- On pyrolysis, isobutane mainly yields isobutylene and hydrogen.
- n-pentane, isobutane and neo-pentane occur to a very small extent (upto 1 % by volume) in natural gas in which n- and isopentances predominate. Crude petroleum also contains pentanes. **Petroleum ether** is mainly a mixture of pentanes and hexanes. A mixture of n-pentane and isopentane is industrially chlorinated at about 300°C mostly to monochloropentanes, which are hydrolysed to a mixture of alcohols.
- Natural gas, gasolines and fuel oils consist mainly of paraffin hydrocarbons.
- Natural gas is mainly a mixture of light hydrocarbons coming out from oil or gas wells. The gas from oil wells is **wet**. It is mixed with condensable hydrocarbons. The gas from gas wells is **dry**. The composition of natural gas varies widely with the locality, but its main component is methane (47-97%).
- Other constituents of natural gas are ethane, propane, butanes, pentanes and higher paraffins, CO_2, H_2S, N_2, and rarely helium.
- Water vapour is a common impurity in natural gas. It causes corrosion of pipelines and fittings and clogging of the passage of the gas by forming crystalline hydrates with some paraffins at low temperature. This can be removed by adsorption on silica gel, activated alumina etc or passing through towers containing hydrating agents such as di- and tri- ethylene glycol, by making use of counter current principle. The acidic gases CO_2 and H_2S are removed or separated by alkaline mono ethanolamines or a mixture of aqueous sodium carbonate,

arsenite and arsenate. The higher hydrocarbons are either liquefied under pressure and separated by fractional distillation at low temperature, or scrubbed in oil absorption towers containing suitable high boiling liquids. Methane from natural gas has widely been used as domestic and industrial fuel. Butadiene, made from n-butane of natural gas, is the chief component of synthetic rubber, which is cheaper and better than natural rubber. Common plastics such as polyethylene and polypropylene, are manufactured from the polymerisation of ethylene and propylene respectively. Ethylene is derived from ethane, propane or naphtha and propylene is obtained by propane by steam cracking. Synthesis gas ($CO+2H_2$), made from dry natural gas, is converted into several important chemicals such as CH_3OH and NH_3. A large number of other products such as CS_2, CH_3Cl, CH_2Cl_2, $CHCl_3$, CCl_4, HCN, C_2H_2 etc are made from natural gas. **Carbon black** is an important product obtained from CH_4 present in natural gas.

The composition of petroleum varies from place to place. The Pennsylvanian oil largely consists of straight chain n-paraffins. The Russian oil mainly contains naphthenes or cycloparaffins such as cyclopentane, cyclohexane and some of their derivatives. Some crude oils, e.g. from Texas or Mexico are mixed type. In general, straight chain paraffins (n-paraffin upto C_{78} has been found) very largely predominate in crude petroleums and branched chain paraffins occur to a limited extent only. Aromatic hydrocarbons such as benzene, tolune, naphthalene etc, are also present appreciably in some petroleum oils. Crude oil contains upto 4% sulphur, generally as alkylsulphides, hydrosulphides, hydrogen sulphide, thiophene, and less frequently as elemental sulphur. It has about 1% nitrogen as pyridine, quinoline derivatives, carbazole, pyrrole etc. Combined oxygen in the crude oil is present as carboxylic acids (naphthenic acids), ketones and phenols.

UNSATURATED HYDROCARBONS

ACETYLENE, C_2H_2

Acetylene is prepared from natural gas or from paraffin hydrocarbons.

(a) From Natural Gas- Methane obtained from natural gas is partially oxidised by oxygen into carbon dioxide and water. The excess of methane is then converted into acetylene in presence of heat evolved in the former reaction.

$$CH_4 + 2O_2 \rightarrow CO_2 + 2H_2O$$

$$2CH_4 \rightarrow C_2H_2 + 3H_2$$

Natural gas and almost pure oxygen are first preheated in preheaters to a temperature of about 550-650°C and the hot gases are then fed to a reactor which consists of three zones, viz, mixing, flame chamber and quinching. The gases are rapidly mixed in the first mixing zone and the mixture passes to the flame chamber containing specially designed burners.

Methane burns in oxygen in the flame chamber and heat of combustion increases the temperature of the gases to about 1500°C. For a contact period of 0.001-0.01 second, methane is cracked to acetylene under these conditions. The temperature is raised rapidly (since cracking of methane to acetylene is an endothermic reaction) and the reaction products quenched quickly with water jets in the quenching zone to avoid further reaction.

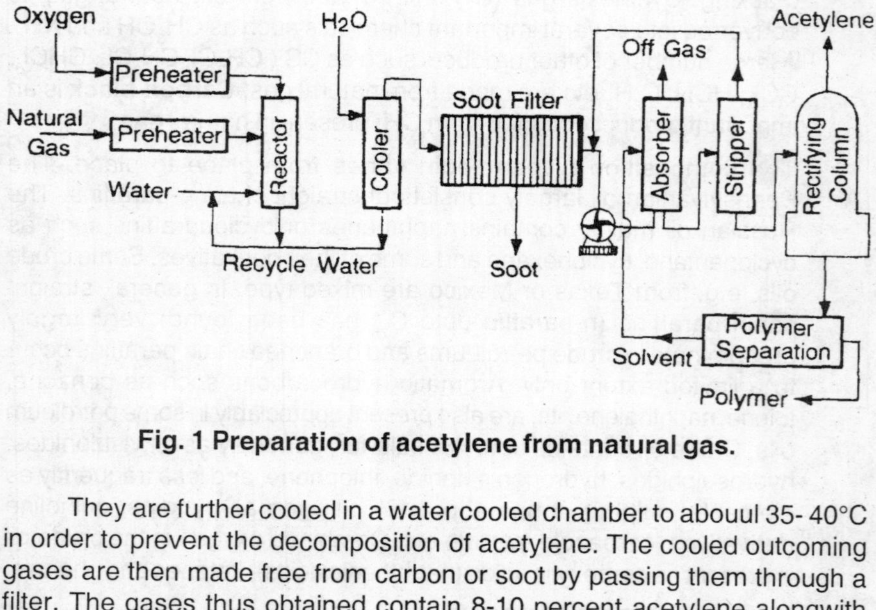

Fig. 1 Preparation of acetylene from natural gas.

They are further cooled in a water cooled chamber to abouul 35- 40°C in order to prevent the decomposition of acetylene. The cooled outcoming gases are then made free from carbon or soot by passing them through a filter. The gases thus obtained contain 8-10 percent acetylene alongwith hydrogen, carbon monoxide, methane, carbon dioxide and some polymerised acetylene. 99.5% pure acetylene is obtained from the mixture by extraction with a suitable solvent, such as dimethyl formaide. The mixture of gases is first compressed to about 8-10 atmospheric pressure and then passed into an absorber containing dimethyl formamide. Acetylene, polymers of acetylene, some ethylene and CO_2 are absorbed by the solvent and unabsorbed gases leave the absorber as overhead. These gases are used as fuel for steam boiler, combustion chamber etc. The solvant containing absorbed acetylene is first passed to a stripping column in order to remove less soluble components and then sent to a rectifying column in order to get pure (99.5%) acetylene as overhead.

(b) From Paraffin Hydrocarbons- Acetylene is also manufactured by the thermal decomposition or pyrolysis of natural gas rich in butane. The natural gas rich in butane is diluted with steam and then pyrolysed in a furnace at about 1300°C under atmospheric pressure for a contact period of 0.03 second.

$$\underset{\text{Butane}}{C_4H_{10}} \xrightarrow{\text{Steam}} \underset{\text{Acetylene}}{CH \equiv CH} + \underset{\text{Ethylene}}{CH_2 = CH_2} + CO + H_2$$

$$\underset{\text{Ethylene}}{CH_2 = CH_2} \rightarrow CH \equiv CH + H_2 \qquad \underset{\text{Methane}}{2CH_4} \rightarrow \underset{\text{Acetylene}}{CH \equiv CH} + 3H_2$$

Synthesis gas ($CO + H_2$) is obtained as a byproduct. The thermal decomposition is carried out in a furnace which essentially consists of a rectangular steel box filled with refractory brick check work. The furnace

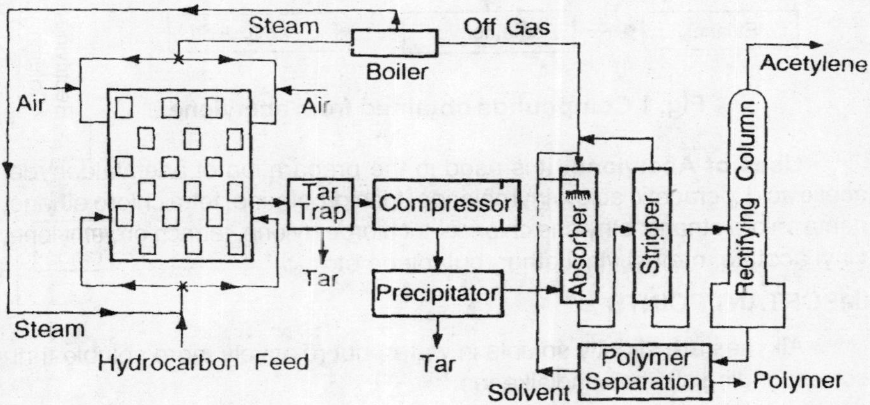

Fig. 1 Preparation of acetylene from paraffin hydrocarbons.

works on **regenerative principle of heat economy** and operates on a four minute cycle. The checkwork in the furnace is initially heated for one minute by burning gaseous fuels in it and then natural gas diluted with steam is pyrolysed for one minute. This operation is then repeated in the opposite direction.

The natural gas rich in butane is first diluted with steam (1 : 8) and then pumped in the furnace by making use of large vacuum pump. They are then subjected to thermal decomposition at about 1300°C under atmospheric pressure for a contact period of 0.03 seconds. The pyrolysed gaseous mixture which leaves the furnace at about 300-325°C is quickly quenched in a tar trap, where steam and various tars are removed. The resulting gases are compressed and then passed through an electrical precipitator to make them free from adhering tar. The purified compressed gaseous mixture is then passed into an absorber containing dimethyl formamide solvent. Acetylene is absorbed by the solvent and then recovered by the method similar to that described earlier. The yield varies from 30-50 percent, depending upon the hydrocarbon feed or amount of butane in the natural gas.

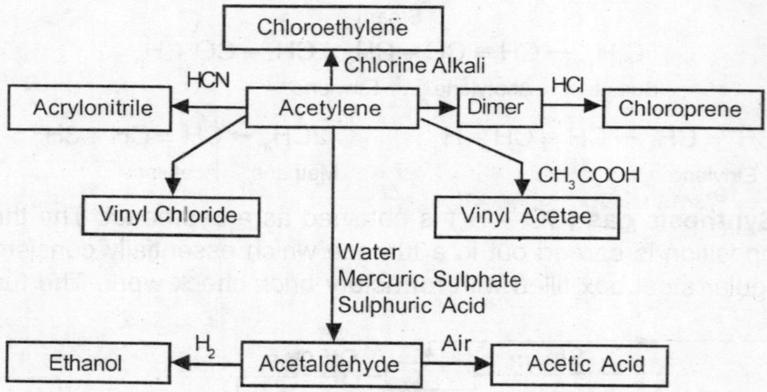

Fig. 1 Compounds obtained from acetylene.

Uses of Acetylene- It is used in the preparation of acetalaldehyde, acetic acid, peracetic acid, vinyl chloride, trichloroethane, tetra chloro ethane, penta chloro ethane, ethylene chloride, trichloroethylene, tetrachloro ethylene, vinyl acetate, methyl vinyl ether, butadiene etc.

IMPORTANT POINTS

Alkynes are slightly soluble in water, but relatively more soluble than corresponding alkanes and alkenes.

Alkynes burn with a luminous flame and form an explosive mixture with air or oxygen.

Alkynes are readily reduced to alkenes on catalytic hydrogenation, preferably with a poisoned catalyst or with sodium in liquid ammonia. Further reduction gives paraffins or alkanes.

Alkynes are generally less reactive than alkenes. Thus a halogen adds up to the double bond in preference to a triple bond.

The addition of halogen halides to acetylene is generally carried out in gas phase or in a solvent with mercuric chloride or cuprous chloride as a catalyst. Vinyl chloride which is polymerised to polyvinyl chloride (PVC) is manufactured from dry acetylene and hydrogen chloride at 160-250°C in the presence of mercuric chloride as catalyst.

$$HC \equiv CH + HCl \rightarrow \underset{\text{Vinyl chloride}}{CH_2 = CHCl}$$

Chloroprene for the synthetic rubber neoprene is commercially prepared from vinylacetylene, $CH_2 = CH.C \equiv CH$, and hydrochloric acid.

$$2CH \equiv CH \xrightarrow{CuCl} \underset{\text{Vinylacetylene}}{CH_2 = CH.C \equiv CH} \xrightarrow[CuCl]{HCl} \underset{\text{Chloroprene}}{CH_2 = C.C1.CH = CH_2}$$

Pure acetylene under ordinary pressure is passed into 20% H_2SO_4 containing 1 % $HgSO_4$ at 70-100°C to obtain acetaldehyde, which can be reduced to ethyl alcohol or oxidised to acetic acid, the two very important industrial chemicals.

$$CH \equiv CH + H_2O \rightarrow \underset{\text{Vinyl alcohol}}{CH_2 = CHOH} \rightarrow CH_3CHO$$

$$\underset{\text{Propylene}}{CH_3C \equiv CH} + H^+ \rightarrow CH_3C^+ = CH_2 \xrightarrow{OH^-} \underset{\text{Unstable}}{CH_3 - \underset{\substack{|\\ OH}}{C} = CH_2} \rightarrow \underset{\text{Acetone}}{CH_3 - CO - CH_3}$$

Acetone can also be prepared by passing steam and acetylene over zinc oxide-ferric oxide catalyst at 470°C.

$$2CH \equiv CH + 3H_2O \rightarrow CH_3COCH_3 + CO_2 + 2H_2$$

Vinyl acetate is manufactured from acetylene and acetic acid in vapour phase at (175-200°C) in presence of zinc acetate, and polymerised to polyvinyl acetate (PVA), a plastic resistant to chemicals.

$$CH \equiv CH + H^+ \xrightarrow{+} CH = CH_2 \xrightarrow{CH3COO^-} \underset{\text{Vinyl acetate}}{CH_3COOCH = CH_2}$$

Propyne yields an acetate with acetic acid and an ether with ethyl alcohol.

$$CH_3C \equiv CH + CH_3COOH \rightarrow \underset{\text{Isopropenyl acetate}}{CH_3 - \underset{\substack{|\\ OOCCH_3}}{C} = CH_2}$$

$$CH_3C \equiv CH + C_2H_5OH \rightarrow \underset{\text{2-Ethoxy propane}}{CH_3 - \underset{\substack{|\\ OC_2H_5}}{C} = CH_2}$$

Vinyl ethers can be manufactured by reacting acetylene (diluted with N_2) with an alcohol under 15 atmospheres at 160-175°C in presence of caustic potash. They are then polyrnerised into plastics, used in the textile and lacquer industries.

$$HC \equiv CH + CH_3OH \xrightarrow{KOH} CH_2 = CH - OCH_3$$

Vinyl methyl ether

Alkynes combine with CO and water in the presence of nickel carbonyl at moderate temperatures and unsaturated acids are formed. If water is replaced by an alcohol, an ester is formed. Various acrylic acids and their esters are thus prepared commercially for acrylic plastics.

$$HC \equiv CH + CO + H_2O \xrightarrow{Ni(CO)_4} CH_2 = CH.COOH$$

Acrylic acid

$$CH_3C \equiv CH + CO + H_2O \rightarrow CH_3 - \underset{\displaystyle COOH}{\underset{|}{C}} = CH_2$$

Methacrylic acid

$$HC \equiv CH + CO + CH_3OH \rightarrow CH_2 = CH - COOCH_3$$

Methyl acrylate

$$CH_3C \equiv CH + CO + CH_3OH \rightarrow CH_3 - \underset{\displaystyle COOCH3}{\underset{|}{C}} = CH_2$$

Methyl methacrylate

When acetylene is passed into a concentrated solution of cuprous chloride and ammonium chloride, containing a little dilute HCl, at 50-75°C, a dimer vinyl acetylene is formed. It reacts with HCl at 160°C in the presence of cuprous chloride to yield chloroprene, which polymerises to neoprene, a synthetic rubber.

Benzene is formed if acetylene is passed through a red hot glass tube at about 500°C. Acetylene in benzene solution under 15 atmospheres and in the presence of triphenyl phosphene-nickel carbonyl catalyst, forms benzene in 88% yield.

$$3CH \equiv CH \xrightarrow{500°C} C_6H_6$$

Methyl acetylene forms symmetrical trimethyl benzene or mesitylene in presence of sulphuric acid.

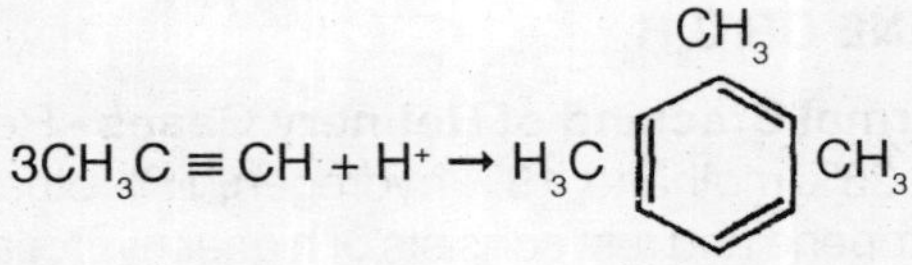

Propyne Mesitylene

Commercially, acetylene can be obtained by the pyrolysis of natural gas (rich in butane), which is diluted with steam at about 1300°C under atmospheric pressure for a contact period of 0.03 seconds. Synthesis gas ($CO + 2H_2$) is a byproduct. The pyrolysis of coke oven gas also yields acetylene.

$$C_4H_{10} \xrightarrow{\text{Stream}} HC \equiv CH + CH_2 = CH_2 + CO + H_2$$

$$CH_2 = CH_2 \rightarrow HC = CH + H_2$$

$$2CH_4 \rightarrow HC = CH + 3H_2$$

Partial oxidation of natural gas or propane with pure oxygen at about 1500°C for a contact period of 0.001 to 0.01 second gives acetylene. The temperature is gradually increased and the reaction products are quickly quenched with water jets. Synthesis gas is the major product. The outcoming gas contains 8-10% acetylene. 99.5% pure acetylene is obtained by extraction with a suitable solvent.

$$2\ CH_4 \rightarrow HC \equiv CH + 3H_2$$

Acetylene and hydrocyanic acid gas (10 : 1) are passed into cuprous chloride solution in dilute HCl at 70°C under atmospheric pressure to obtain acrylonitrile, which is used in the manufacture of acrylic fibres (orlon), nitrile rubber etc.

$$CH \equiv CH + HCN \rightarrow CH_2 = CHCN \text{ (Acrylonitrile, 80\% yield)}$$

Acetylene reacts with formaldehyde (or other aldehydes and ketones) in presence of copper acetylide catalyst to form an alkyne diol, which can then be converted to butane -1, 4-diol by catalytic hydrogenation and then into 1,3-butadiene by dehydration.

$$HC \equiv CH + 2HCHO \rightarrow HO.CH_2 - C \equiv C - CH_2OH \xrightarrow[\text{200°C, 280 atm}]{H_2}$$

$$\underset{\text{1,4 Butanediol}}{HO.CH_2 - CH_2 - CH_2 - CH_2OH} \xrightarrow[-H_2O]{H_3PO_4} \underset{\text{1,3,-butadiene (divinyl)}}{CH_2 = CH - CH = CH_2}$$

ETHYLENE, ETHENE OR C_2H_4

(a) **From Thermal Cracking of Refinery Gases -** Refinery (cracked) gases contain about 25% methane, 19% hydrogen, 15% ethane, 7% ethylene, 12% propane, 6% propene and rest consists of higher hydrocarbons, hydrogen sulphide, carbon dioxide, carbon monoxide, nitrogen etc.

The refinery gas is first passed into the bottom of an absorption tower from the top of which ethanolamine sloution trickles down. This solution absorbs whole of the H_2S and a part of CO_2 gas present in the refinery gases. The amine solution containing absorbed H_2S and CO_2 is removed from the bottom of the absorption tower and heated to remove H_2S and CO_2 and used again in the process. The remaining CO_2 is removed from the refinery gases by passing them through caustic soda solution in a scrubber.

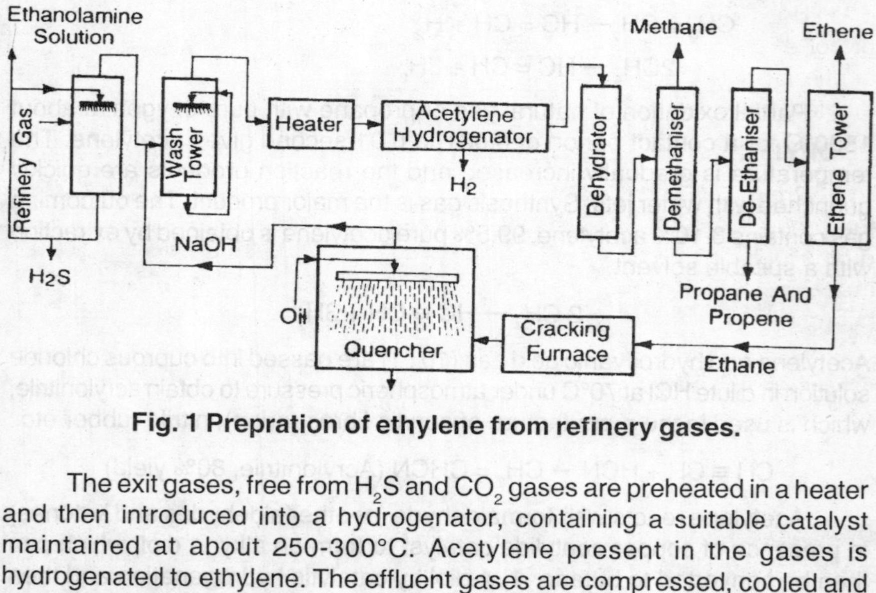

Fig. 1 Prepration of ethylene from refinery gases.

The exit gases, free from H_2S and CO_2 gases are preheated in a heater and then introduced into a hydrogenator, containing a suitable catalyst maintained at about 250-300°C. Acetylene present in the gases is hydrogenated to ethylene. The effluent gases are compressed, cooled and then led through a dehydrator containing alumina. The mixture is further cooled in a refrigerator and the partially liquefied mixture thus obtained is first conveyed to a demethaniser inorder to separate methane from the mixture. The mixture then passes to another fractionating column, called de-ethaniser. The latter sets free propane, propene, and other higher hydrocarbons from the mixture. The remaining gases then pass to a third fractionating column, called ethylene column in which ethylene is separated as overhead from ethane (bottoms). Ethane from the bottom of the ethylene column is conveyed to a cracking furnace, where it is heated with steam at atmospheric pressure and at about 800°C for one second in absence of air.

$$CH_3.CH_3 \rightarrow CH_2 = CH_2 + H_2$$

The resulting cracked gases are recycled to the caustic soda scrubber.

(b) **From Natural Gasoline, Heavy Naphtha and Gas Oil -** All these petroleum fractions are first mixed with super heated steam and the mixture is introduced into a cracking furnace. The resulting cracked gases are led through a heat exchanger, as a result of which steam is produced. This steam is sufficient to be used with the petroleum fractions. From heat exchanger the gases are allowed to pass through a fractionating column, where gases are separated from the oils. The overhead gases are sent to a depropansing column. The gases leaving this column as overhead contain ethane and ethylene as the main products. These gases are passed through ethylene column, which separates ethylene as overhead from ethane. The latter is converted into ethylene by a method similar to that described earlier.

Uses of Ethylene - It is used in the manufacture of ethanol, ethylene glycol, ethylene oxide, ethylene chloride, ethylene chlorohydrin, acetaldehyde, acetic acid, ethyl acetate, diethyl ether, ethyt chloride, tetra ethyl lead, ethylene bromide, acrylonitrile etc.

PROPYLENE, PROPENE OR C_3H_6

Propylene is obtained as a byproduct during the catalytic cracking for the production of ethylene. Propylene is also produced in large quantities during petroleum cracking. Refinery off gas, separated during catalytic cracking of gas oil to produce gasoline, contains large amounts of C_3 hydrocarbons. They are separated to get propane and propylene. Propylene can also be prepared from cracking of propane.

Uses of Propylene- It is used in the production of glycerol, allyl alcohol, allyl chloride, isopropyl alcohol, isopropyl ether, isopropyl amine, acetone, acetyl acetone, cumene, propylene oxide, propylene glycol, propionic acid, n-propyl alcohol and acrolein etc.

BUTYLENES OR BUTENES

Butene-1, butene-2 and isobutene occur in the gases from petroleum cracking. C_4 olefins can be produced either by catalytic dehydrogenation of butane followed by selective solvent purification or by the cracking of naphtha. C_5 olefins can be prepared by the dehydrogenation of pentanes. C_6 and C_8 olefins are produced by the dimerisation of propylene and butylene respectively. Other higher olefins such as C_9 and C_{12} can be obtained by trimerisation and tetramerisation of propylene respectively.

Uses of Butylenes- These are used in the preparation of butanol, butadiene, methyl ethyl ketone, ethyl butyl ketone, tertiary butyl alcohol, poly butylenes, butyl rubber, iso-octane etc.

IMPORTANT POINTS

Ethylene, $CH_2 = CH_2$ occurs in gases from petroleum cracking and in coal gas, making its flame luminous.

Dehydration of ethyl alcohol with excess sulphuric acid gives ethylene.

Industrially, ethane and propane of natural gas are heated with steam at about 800°C for 1 second in the absence of air to make ethylene.

$CH_3 - CH_3 \rightarrow CH_2 = CH_2 + H_2$ $\qquad$ $CH_3 - CH - CH_3 \rightarrow CH_2 = CH_2 + CH_4$

Ethylene is one of the most important chemical and used industrially in the manufacture of polyethylene, power alcohol, ethylene oxide, ethylene glycol, mustard gas etc. Ethylene is produced in fruits till the cells are disintegrated, and accelerates ripening. Hence it is used in artificial ripening of green fruits. Ethylene produces anaesthesia on inhalation but it is not used as an anaesthetic.

Propene, $CH_3 - CH = CH_2$, is produced in large quantities during petroleum cracking. Propylene has widely been used in making isopropyl alcohol, acetone, glycerine etc. Propylene glycol, an antifreeze for automobile radiators, is manufactured from propylene.

Propylene and ethylene are copolymerised and the product made into a special type of synthetic rubber.

Butene-1 and butene-2 occur in the gases from petroleum cracking. Butene-I is manufactured by passing n-butane of natural gas over alumina and chromium oxide at about 600°C. n-butyl alcohol and conc. H_2SO_4 yield mostly butene-1 and some of butene-2. Isobutyl alcohol likewise yields isobutylene. Synthetic rubber is manufactured from butadiene, $CH_2 = CH-CH= CH_2$, derived from butene-1.

Butenes polymerise more readily than ethylene and propylene. Isobutene forms a dimer iso-octane, with 65% H_2SO_4. Butenes are converted into corresponding alcohols, which are valuable industrial solvents.

1,3-butadiene occurs in varying amounts in gases from petroleum cracking. It is mostly prepared by catalytic dehydrogenation of n-butane of natural gas and of butene-I (from cracked petroleum gases).

AROMATIC HYDROCARBONS

(1) Benzene-A suitable fraction of petroleum containing cyclohexane, methyl cyclohexane, methyl cyclopantane and hexanes is catalytically reformed to get aromatic hydrocarbons. Hydrogenation, isomerisation and cyclisation take place simultaneously in the process. Cyclohexane and methyl cyclohexane are thus converted into benzene as a result of dehydrogenation and dehydrogenation as well a dealkylation respectively. Hexane is converted into benzene by cyclisation and dehydrogenation.

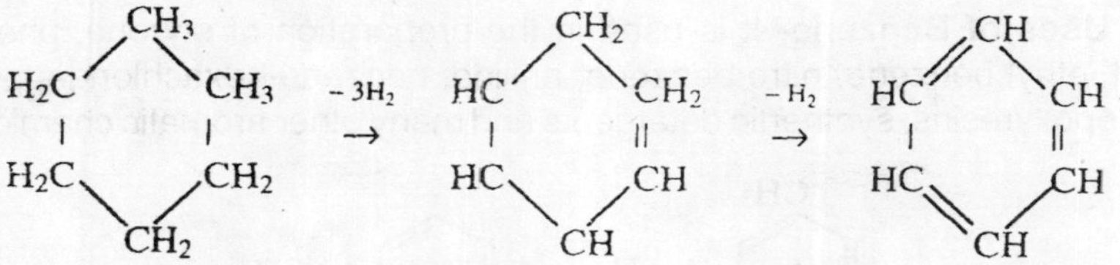

n-Hexane Benzene

The recycle hydrogen under a pressure of 100-300 p.s.i. and at 480-550°C is added to the hydrocarbons and then passed into a reactor containing molybdenum trioxide and chromium trioxide at catalysts. Platinum may also be used as a catalyst. Usually a series of four reactors with a preheater between any two reactors are used, because of the exothermic nature of the hydrogenation reaction. Conversion of C6 paraffins into benzene is about 80% per pass. The benzene originally present in the petroleum passes through the process unaffected and is extracted with the synthetic product. The gases from the reactor are led to a separator, where hydrogen formed during the reaction is separated and recycled to be used again. The liquid from the separator is sent to a stabilizer, where a mixture of light hydrocarbons leaves the stabilizer as overhead. The latter is conveyed to a debutaniser. The liquid at the bottom of the stabilizer is sent to the fractionating column. The overhead from this column contains mainly the benzene and bottom contains a mixture of high boiling hydrocarbons. The overhead is intorduced into a solvent extraction tower in which aqueous diethylene glycol comes down from the top. The bottoms, from the fractionating column are recycled. Aromatic hydrocarbons are absorbed by the solvent in the extractor. The solvent containing aromatics is taken out from the extractor and taken in a stripper, where water is removed as overhead. Aromatic hydrocarbons are removed from the solvent (from the bottom) and then subjected to fractional distillation in a benzene tower to ger pure benzene. Solvent from the bottom of the stipper is reused in the process. Other aromatics, such as toluene, xylenes etc. leaving the tower from the bottom are separated and collected by fractional distillation. In this manner about 10% benzene, 50% xylenes and 40% toluene are obtained. Toluene and xylenes (dimethyl benzenes) obtained in this manner may also be demethylated in presence of hydrogen with or without chromium oxide or platinum catalyst into benzene and methane at about 500-650°C under 500-1200 p.s.i.

Benzene of very high purity *is obtained and requires no solvent extraction.*

The above conversion is economical as benzene is more costly than toluene and xylenes. Moreover, toluene and xylenes are in much less demand than benzene.

Uses of Benzene- It is used in the preparation of styrene, phenol, nylon, ethyl benzene, nitro benzene, aniline, benzene hexachloride, picric acid, epoxyresins, synthertic detergents and many other aromatic chemicals.

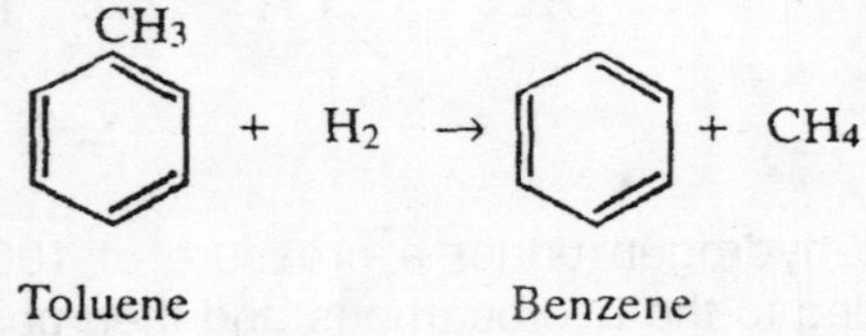

TOLUENE OR METHYL BENZENE, $C_6H_5CH_3$

During the catalytic reforming of a selected fraction of petroleum, called naphtha, toluenes and xylenes are produced in large amounts. This fraction mainly contains methyl cyclohexane, ethyl cyclopentane and diethyl pentane. Methyl cyclohexane, for example, forms toluene (80-90%) and hydrogen by dehydrogenation process.

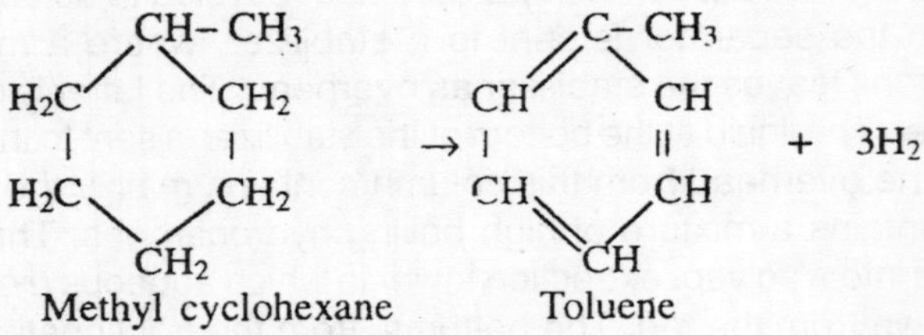

The naphtha fraction is first preheated by passing through a heat exchanger and then converted into vapour in a furnace at about 560-565°C. The vapour is then mixed in the furnace with recycle gas containing excess of hydrogen and again heated to 575°C. The hot gaseous mixture under a pressure of 10-20 atmospheres and a temperature of 560-575°C is passed through a reactor containing a catalyst of 10% molybdenum dioxide on alumina. The time of contact between gases and catalyst is about 15 sec. per pass. The conversion is about 80-90%. The gases from the reactor are allowed to pass through heat exchangers and then to a liquid condenser and separator. The separated gas containing excess of hydrogen is compressed to 5-15 atmospheres, heated in a furnace and recycled to the reactor. The remaining gas and liquid are passed to the fractionating columns, where these are separated into the following three fractions :

(i) Aliphatic hydrocarbons upto four carbon atoms. These are used as fuel.

(ii) Gasoline fraction containing C_5 - C_8 hydrocarbons.

(iii) Hydroformates containing 20-21 percent toluene. It may be recycled through the reactor or may be subjected to fractional cistillation. The fractions are collected. The first fraction is called benzene fraction, the second or middle fraction is called toluene fraction, as it contains about 65% toluene and third or last fraction is called xylene fraction.

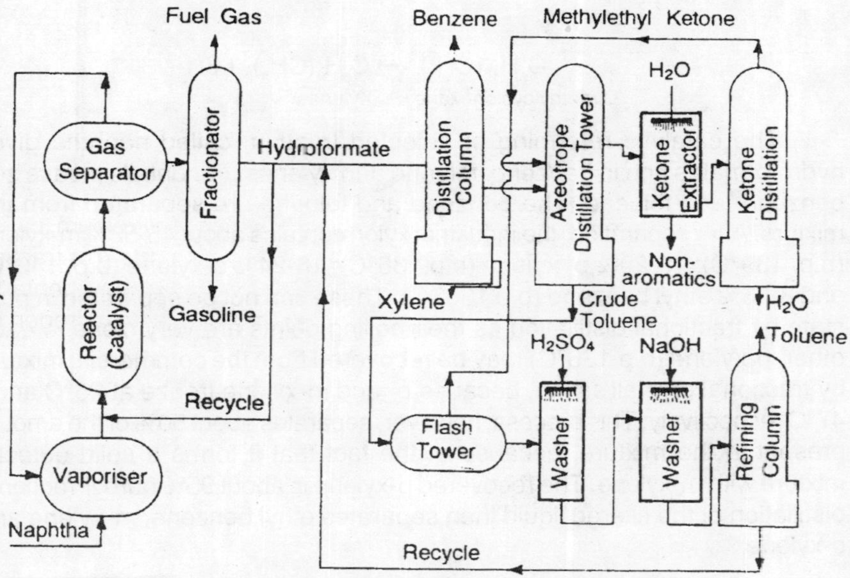

Fig. 1 Prepration of toluene from naphtha.

The middle fraction is introduced into an azeotropic distillation tower containing a mixture of 90% methyl ethyl ketone and 10% water. The non aromatics, such as paraffins and naphthenes get associated with the solvent which carries them out of cistillation tower. Toluene moves down the tower and collected from the bottom as crude toluene. Crude toluene thus obtained is passed through a flash tower where some toluene and remaining ketone are obtained as overhead. The overhead is recycled to the azeotropic distillation tower. The ketone free toluene from the bottom of the flash tower is washed with conc. H_2SO_4 to remove adhering olefins, then with water and finally with caustic soda solution. The resulting toluene is then distilled to get about 90% pure toluene.

It should be noted that nitromethane, methanol etc. may also be used as solvents in place of methyl ethyl ketone. Moreover, distillation may also be carried out instead of aze otropic distillation solvent extraction method.

Uses of Toluene-It is used in the preparation of benzyl chloride, benzal chloride, benzyl alcohol, benzaldehyde, benzoic acid, T.N.T. phthalic anhydride etc.

XYLENES OR ORTHO, META AND PARA DIMETHYL BENZENES, $C_6H_4(CH_3)_2$

Petroleum fractions, containing dimethyl cyclohexane are industrially converted into xylenes by catalytic reforming, Benzene and toluene are also formed during the reaction.

$$\underset{\text{Dimethylcyclohexane}}{C_6H_{10}(CH_3)_2} \xrightarrow{H_2} \underset{\text{Xylenes}}{C_6H_4(CH_3)_2} + 3H_2$$

The catalytic reforming of selected fraction, called naphtha gives hydroformates rich in benzene, toluene and xylenes. For details please see benzene, and toluene. The benzene and toluene are separated from the mixture. After separation, the industrial xylon contains about 45-52% m-xylene (b.p. 139°C); 18-20% p- xylene (b.p.136°C); 18-24% o-xylene (b.p. 142°C) and 8-13% ethyl benzene (b.p 136° C). These can not be separated in pure state by fractional distillation as their boiling points are very close to each other. p-xylene (b.p.136°C) may be recovered from the commercial mixture by fractional crystallisation, because o- and m-xylene freeze at 25°C and -47°C respectively. This process, however, separates about 50% of the amount present in the mixture, because of the fact that it forms a solid eutectic mixture with m-xylene. The recovered p-xylene is about 95% pure. Fractional distillation of the filtered liquid then separates ethyl benzene, m-xylene and o-xylene.

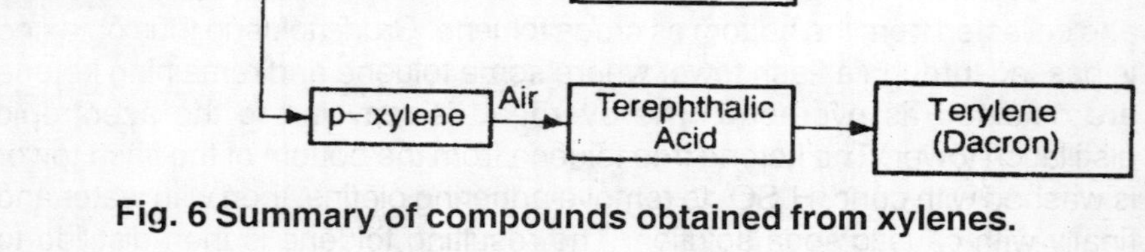

Fig. 6 Summary of compounds obtained from xylenes.

They can also be separated from the industrial mixture by selective sulphonation as follows.

The mixture of xylenes and ethyl benzene is dried by passing over activated alumina and then cooled. The Cooled mixture is treated with cold 80% H_2S0_4. Under these conditions, sulphuric acid sulphonates only the more reactive m-xylene to from m-xylene-4 sulphonic acid. The o- and p-xylene remains unaffected. These are separated by distillation. The mixture of o- and p- xylene is then sulphonated with 98% H_2SO_4 at 20°C. The resulting o- xylene sulphonic acid and p- xylene 2-sulphonic acid are separated by fractional crystallisation from the diluted sulphonated mixed solution. The p-isomer crystallises first being less soluble than o- derivative. o-, m- and p-xylenes are then obtained almost in pure form by hydrolysing their sulphonic acid derivatives with 25% hydrochloric acid under pressure.

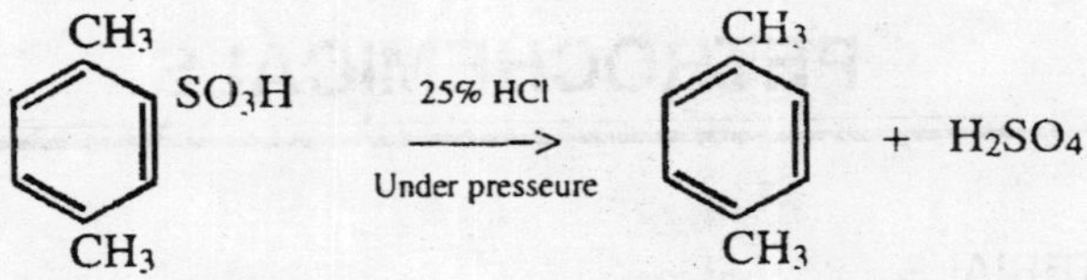

Ethyl benzene present in the xylene fraction also becomes separated during operation.

Uses of Xylenes-They are used in the manufacture of phthalic anhydride, isophthalic acid, terephthalic acid, terylene of dacron etc.

Chapter 3

PETROCHEMICALS

RAW MATERIALS

The basic raw materials supplied by the petroleum refineries or the natural gas companies are liquid petroleum gas (LPG), natural gas, gas from cracking processes, liquid distillate C_4 - C_9, and distillates from special cracking processes, as well as cyclic fractions from aromatics. These mixtures are usually separated into individual constituents in the petroleum refineries and then chemically converted into their reactive **precursors,** before being subjected to the chemical conversions necessary for the manufacture of petrochemicals used by manifold industries.

TABLE 1 : PRIMARY PRECURSORS: PETROLEUM-PETROCHEMICAL COMPLEX

Raw materials by distillations	Precursors (basic chemicals) by conversion	Intermediates by conversion	Finished products by conversions
Paraffins and cyclics	Olefins, diolefins, acetylene, aromatics	Various inorganics and organics	Inorganics and organics
Natural gas			Carbon black
Sulphides	H_2S	S	H_2SO_4
Hydrogen		Synthesis as	NH_3
Methane			Methanol
			Formaldehyde
Refinery gases	Acetylene	Acetic acid	Acetates
	Isobutene	Acetic anhydride	Fibres
Ethane*	Ethylene	Isoprene	Rubber
Propane*	Propylene	Ethylene oxide, etc.,	Rubber and fibre
n-Butane*	n-Butane	Butadiene	Rubber
Hexane			
Heptanes			
Refinery nephthas			
Naphthenes	Cyclopentadiene	Adipic acid	Fibres

(Cont'd)

Raw materials by distillations	Precursors (basic chemicals) by conversion	Intermediates by conversion	Finished products by conversions
		Ethylbenzene	Styrene
		Styrene	Rubber
		Cumene	Phenol
			Acetone
		Alkylbenzene	
		Cyclohexane	
Toluene	Toluene	Phenol	Plastics
		Benzoic acid	
Xylenes	o- m-, p-xylene	Phthalic anhydride	Plastics
Methyl naphthanes	Naphthalene	Phthalic anhydride	Plastics

*From LPG and refinery cracked gas. (demethylaiton etc.)

Note : Aromatics are also obtained by chemical conversions

The birth of petrochemicals is one of the fabulous stories connected with modern chemical and chemical engineering works. The petroleum companies in their own plants, in wholly owned subsidiaries or in association with strictly chemical manufacturing companies, have entered into the manufacture of petrochemicals, or chemicals derived from petroleum raw materials, including natural gas. Almost all the petrochemicals actually entering into industrial use arise by the chemical reactions of the various chemical conversions as do many of the strictly petroleum products, such as high octance gasoline and upgraded lubricanting oils. The petrochemicals are fundamentally the basic chemical raw materials, which are further converted into fertilizers, plastics, rubbers, fibres and paints etc. Petrochemicals are significant in making lubricant oil additives, pesticides, and solvents and as another and large source of aromatic compounds.

The lower members of the parraffin and of the olefin series of organic raw materials are of great importance in the manufacture of petrochemicals.

TABLE 2. THE PRINCIPAL CHEMICAL CONVERSIONS

Acylation	Fermentation
Alcoholysis	Fridel Crafts (Reactions)
Alkylation	Halogenation
Amination by reduction	Hydroformylation (Oxo)
Ammonolysis	Hydrogenation, dehydrogenation, and hydrogenolysis
Aromatisation	Hydrolysis and hydration
Calcination	Ion-exchange
Carboxylation	Isomerisation

(Cont'd)

Causticization	Neutralisation
Combustion	Nitration
Condensation	Oxidation
Dehydration	Polymerisation
Diazotisation and coupling	Pyrolysis or cracking
Double decomposition	Reduction
Electrolysis	Silicate formation
Esterification	Sulphonation

These are the precursors and chief raw materials for petrochemicals. Various physical separation methods such as distillation, azeotropic and extractive distillation, superfractionation, crystallisation, molecular sieve adsorption, and solvent extraction have been used for the separation of petrochemical raw materials and products. Solvents such as liquid SO_2, NH_3 and many organic ones, either pure or in more suitable mixtures, are used for the purpose. Other examples are Modex for separating straight chain paraffins from branched chain paraffins, and Unisorb for separating aromatic hydrocarbons from non-aromatics in treating kerosenes, and light catalytic-cycle oils.

The petrochemicals have largely been manufactured by chamical conversions. Most of these are characterised by **continuous processing** in large volume and under the control of modern instrumentation. Many are also system-controlled through computers.

MANUFACTURE OF PETROCHEMICALS

The production of commercially produced petrochemicals is based largely on efficient, and in may cases noval chemical processing. The basis for these chemical processes is the chemical reaction or the chemical conversion.

Chemical processing may be defined as the industrial processing of chemical raw materials leading to the products of enhanced industrial value. Generally this involves a chemical conversion or reaction, as in the manufacture of sulphuric acid from sulphur by oxidation ($S + O_2 \rightarrow SO_2$ and $SO_2 + O \rightarrow SO_3$) and hydration ($SO_3 + H_2O \rightarrow H_2SO_4$). The production of fibres, such as nylon from hexamethylene diamine and adipic acid is also included in chemical processing by more complicated chemical reactions. In all these chemical changes, physical operations such as heat transfer and temperature control are also invluded. These are necessary to ascertain good yields required by the industry as, for example, in the oxidation of SO_2 to SO_3 in the contact process of manufacturing H_2SO_4. There are some cases, where no chemical reaction is involved, but only physical changes occur. For example, distillations to separate and purify petroleum fractions and to obtain pure alcohol after fermentation. Another example is mass transfer of liquids or solids in suspension from place to place or to a chemical reactor.

TABLE 3. PETROCHEMICALS FROM METHANE

Basic derivatives and sources, %	Uses, %
Ammonia	Agricultural chemicals (as ammonia, salts, urea)
Petroleum sources :	
Methane hydrogen, Fibres, plastics	
Refinery hydrogan	Industrial explosives
Electrolytic, H_2, coal	Other
Carbon black	Rubber compounding
Natural, gas	Pigments, metallurgy
Liquid petroleum	
Methanol	Formaldehyde (mainly for resins)
Petroleum sources :	
Methane	Methanol antifreze
Propane-butane	Ethylene glycol
Coal	Other
Chloromethanes	Solvents ; cleaners
Methane chlorination	Chlorofluorcarbons for refrigerants, aerosols
Other sources	
Acetylene	Vinyl chloride, vinyl acetate
Petroleum (mainly methane)	Chloroprene (neoprene)
Calcium carbide, balance	Chloroethylene
	Acrylonitrile
	Other
Hydrogen cyanide	Acrylonitrile (with ethylene oxide or acetylene)
	Adiponitrile
	Other

ALKYLATION, DEALKYLATION, AND HYDRODEALKYLATION

Benzene can be **alkylated** in the presence of phosphoric acid as catalyst, with propylene in vapour phase at 250°C and 100 psia, to from cumene or isopropyl benzene, using refinery propylene - propane fraction. Polyalkylation can be avoided or minimised by using an excess of benzene. The benzene and cumene are recovered and purified, after flashing off the propane and unreacted propylene. $AlCl_3$ and H_2SO_4 can also be used as catalysts for alkylation.

Dealkylation is carried out in producing aromatic hydrocarbons such as benzene, toluene, xylenes and naphthalene from petroleum. **Tetra ethyl lead (TEL)** is the alkylated product and is the most important antiknock compound for gasoline. TEL can be commercially prepared by the action of ethyl chloride on a lead sodium alloy.

$$4PbNa + 4C_2H_5Cl \rightarrow Pb(C_2H_5)_4 + 3Pb + 4NaCl$$

The plant for the reaction consists of a heating jacket, a heavy duty stirrer to stir the Na - Pb alloy, and a reflux condenser. The alloy should be finely divided and temperature of the reaction must be less than 70°C. The reactants are first heated and then cooled to keep the temperature 40 - 60°C. After 2 to 6 hours, the excess of ethyl chloride is distilled off and TEL is steam distilled from the mixture. Now Tetra methyl lead (TML) is partially replacing TEL, due to its high antiknock qualities in high compression engines with highly aromatic, high octane gasolines. Moreover, TML is more stable than TEL at higher temperatures. TEL has also been prepared by electrolytic alkylation process.

$$2RMC1 + 2RC1 + Pb \xrightarrow{DC} R_4Pb + 2MgCl_2$$

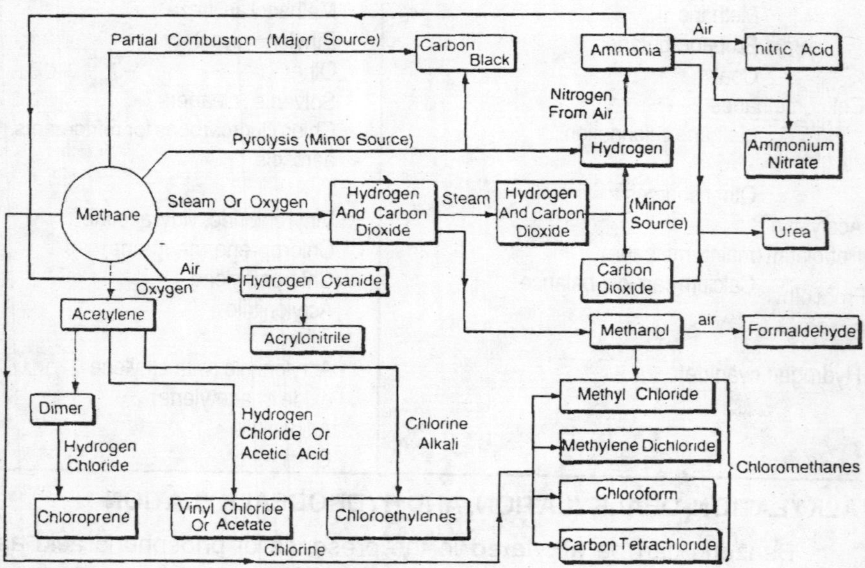

Fig. 1. Petrochemicals from methane.

AMINATION BY AMMONOLYSIS AND REDUCTION

Amination by ammonolysis is the reaction in which an amino compound is formed by using NH_3 or substituted ammonia as the reagent. Other amines are prepared by the reduction of a nitro compound. A mixture of mono - , di - and triethanolamines can be obtained when ethylene oxide is passed through 28% aqueous ammonia solution at 30 - 40°C.

$$\underset{\diagdown O \diagup}{CH_2 - CH_2} + NH_3 \text{ (Excess)} \rightarrow HOCH_2CH_2NH_2 + (HOCH_2CH_2)_2NH + (HOCH_2CH_2)_3N$$

The rate of reaction of ethylene oxide with ammonia is approximately the same as with mono ethyloamine or diethyloamine. Hence the ratio of ethylene oxide to ammonia is the primary variable in changing the relative amounts of the ethanolamines. The process involves the exothermic, rapid, liquid phase reaction of ethylene oxide with aqueous ammonia. The well stirred vertical steel reactor has its contents pumped through the external cooler in order to maintain the reaction temperature. The reactor contents are removed for product recovery and purification. The unreacted ammonia is removed by stripping. The products are obtained by fractionation under vacuum.

Methylamines have various uses as intermediates in further synthesis. They can be manufactured by the ammonolysis of methanol.

TABLE 4. PETROCHEMICALS FROM ETHYLENE

Basic derivatives and sources, %	Uses, %
Ethylene oxide	Ethylene glycol
Via direct oxidation (newer plants)	Di- and triethylene glycols,
Via chlorohydrin	Ethanolamines,
	Nonionic detergents
	Other
Ethyl alcohol (industrial)	Aldehydes
From ethylene	Other chemicals
By fermentation	Solvent
	Other
Polyethylene	Film, sheet, moulding and extrusion
Styrene	Polystyrene
From ethylene and benzene (or reformate)	Styrene-butadiene rubber and latex
	Miscellaneous resins
	Other
Ethyl chloride*	Tetraethyl lead (TEL)
Ethylene + HCl	Minor amounts for other ethylations
Chlorination of ethane	(such as ethyl cellulose)
Ethylene dichloride	Vinyl chloride
By direct chlorination	Scavenger in antiknock fluid
By-product of ethylene chlorohydrin production	Other
Ethylene dibromide	Scavenger in antiknock fluid

* In one process, hydrogen chloride from ethane chlorination is used as reagent for production of ethyl chloride from ethylene.

PYROLYSIS OR THERMAL AND CATALYTIC CRACKING

The process of pyrolysis is extremely important for making petrochemical precursors such as olefins. The most important petrochemical and product obtained by pyrolysis is **carbon black.** Isoprene can be manufactured by cracking or synthesis.

Dehydration is mainly used for the production of ethers by the dehydration of alcohols. Methyl, ethyl and isopropyl ethers are very important from commercial point of view. The ethers can be produced by liquid phase dehydration of the corresponding alcohol , in presence of H_2SO_4 as a catalyst. The ethers can also be prepared by vapour phase dehydration over acidic catalysts such as alumina. However, the most important source of ethers is byproducts of the production of the corresponding alcohol by hydration of the olefin over an acidic catalyst. Excess of ether can be recycled over an appropriate catalyst to produce alcohol.

ESTERIFICATION

Esters are used for solvents, plasticisers, monomers, medicines, and perfumes etc. Certain nitrate esters, such as nitroglycerine and nitrocellulose, are used as powerful explosives.

Ethyl acetate is an important solvent, particularly in lacquers. It can be manufactured by the following reaction.

$$CH_3CH_2OH + CH_3COOH \xrightarrow{H_2SO_4} CH_3COOC_2H_5 + H_2O$$

This reaction is forced to completion by removing the products as soon as they are formed and using an excess of either CH_3CH_2OH or CH_3COOH. The raw materials are acetic acid, ethyl alcohol in excess, and H_2S0_4 as a catalyst. They are mixed, conducted through heat exchangers, and passed through an esterifcation column, the overhead of which is ternary azeotrope (b.p = 70.2°C) having the composition 82.16% ethyl acetate, 8.4% ethyl alcohol, and 9% water. Some water is added to the condensate frequently in order to remove most of the alcohol. The latter is returned to the system. The ester carrying about 4% of watet is rectified through a column, the water going overhead as a constant boiling mixture. All the acetic acid reacts by virtue of the mass action of excess alcohol combined with removal of the products. The process is conducted in a continuous manner. The equipment is mostly constructed from copper.

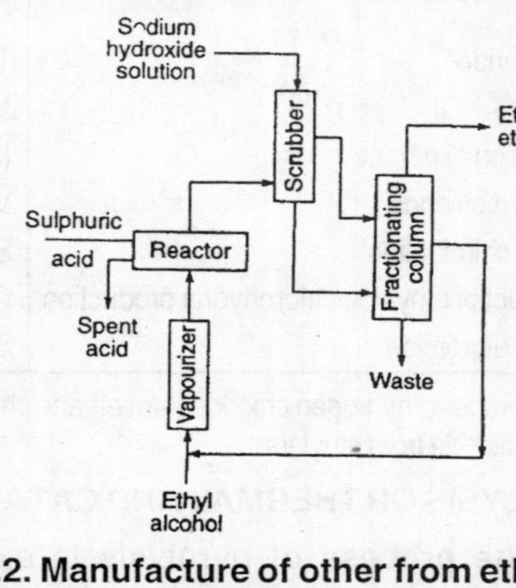

Fig.2. Manufacture of other from ethanol by dehydration

TABLE 5. PETROCHEMICALS FROM PROPYLENE AND BUTYLENES

Basic derivatives and sources, %	Uses, %
Isopropyl alcohol	Acetone (by dehydrogenation or oxidation)
From propylene	Other chemicals
Propane-butane oxidation, small	Solvent and miscellaneous
Dodecene (tetramer)	Detergents: dodecylbenzene sulfonate,
Nonene (trimer)	nonlyphenyl polyglycol ethers
Cumene	Phenol and acetone
Allyl chloride	Glycerol, epichlorohydrin, allyl chemicals
Propylene oxide	Mainly propylene glycol, other chemicals
Polypropylene	Film sheet moulding and extrucsion, rubber
Butadiene	Styrene-butadiene rubbers
From butylenes (refinery cracked gas)	Acrylonitrile-butadiene rubber
From butane ad hoc	Styrene-buradiene paint latex
Miscellaneous hydrocarbon cracking	Adiponitrile and hexamethylenediamine for nylon Other
Secondary butyl alcohol	Mainly methyl ethyl ketone
Oxo alcohols (via C_8 aldehydes), "isooctyl alcohol	Detergents, plasticizers
Butyl rubber (copolymer of isobutylene and isoprene)	Inner tubes, mechanical rubber goods
Diisobutylene	Mainly detergents, plasticizers
Triisobutylene	
Polyisobutylene	Adhesives, sealants, electric insulation, Tube-oil additives
Tertiary butyl alcohol	Solvent

Amyl, butyl, and isopropyl acetates can be prepared from the respective alcohol and acetic acid. All are important lacquer solvents. **Butyl acetate** is the most important nitrocellulose lacquer solvent. Methyl salicylate, methyl anthranilate, diethyl phthalate, and dibutyl phthalate can also be made by similar methods.

Esterification of acetylene by addition of various lower organic or inorganic acids is an excellent method of producing unsaturated vinyl esters which are used in polymerisation reactions. The most important esters are vinyl esters such as vinyl acetate, vinyl chloride, acrylonitrile and vinyl fluoride. The addition reaction can be carried out in the liquid or in the vapour phase, depending on the properties of the acid. In either case polymerisation of the vinyl ester product is prevented.

Vinyl acetate can be manufactured by the following reaction.

$$CH \equiv CH + CH_3COOH \rightarrow CH_3COOCH = CH_2$$

Commercially, **vinyl acetate** can be prepared by vapour phase process. Glacial acetic acid and the recycle acid are mixed and heated in a stainless steel vessel. Fresh and recycle acetelene are mixed and bubbled through the acetic acid. The desired ratio of acid to acetylene can be achieved by controlling the temperature. The vapour mixture is preheated and passed through the vertical reactor tubes, which are filled with zinc acetate or activated carbon catalyst. Since the reaction is exothermic, heat liberated in the reaction is removed through the catalyst tube walls. The effluent gases are cooled and condensed except the unconverted acetylene. Acetic acid can be recovered by distillation and recycled, along with acetylene. Liquid phase method has also been used. Vinyl acetate (The yield is 80 - 95%) is purified by distillation and then stabilised by adding inhibitor such as diphenylamine or hydroquinone.

TABLE 6. CYCLIC PETROCHEMICALS

Basic products and sources, %	Uses, %
Banzene	Styrene
From petroleum	Phenol via cumene (definitely petrochemical)
From coal	Phenol via sulfonation or chlorination
	Synthetic detergents
	Miscellaneous chemicals and other uses
j	
Toluene	Motor and aviation gasoline
From petroleum	Explosives
From coal	Toluene diisocyanate, vinyltoluene, other chemicals
	Solvent for coatings
	Other
Xylene	Coatings and solvents
From petroleum	Aviation gasoline
From coal	Isomer separaton (for phthalic acids
	Other
Ethylbenzene	Styrene
From benzene predominant	
Direct from reformate, small	
Cyclohexane	Polyamides* (nylons)
From petroleum naphthas, > 65	
From benzene by hydrogenation	

* The hexamethylenediamine required comes mostly from petroleum via adipic acid or butadiene.

The basic processing scheme given above is widely used in the manufacture of other vinyl esters. A different acid such as HCl, HCN or HF is used, and a liquid or vapour phase may be chosen depending on the volatility of the raw material. Acetylene can be polymerised to vinyl acetylene in a horizontal copper vessel using a weak NH_4Cl solution of Cu_2Cl_2 and KCl as a catalyst. The reactor gas is passed through a condenser to remove water, and fractionated. The vinylacetylene is treated with cold aqueous HCl at 35 - 45°C to form **chloroprene** in presence of aqueous Cu_2Cl_2, as catalyst.

$$2CH \equiv CH \xrightarrow{55\text{-}65^{\circ}C} CH_2 = CH - C \equiv CH \xrightarrow[CU_2Cl_2,\ 40^{\circ}C]{+HCl} CH_2 = C.Cl - CH = CH_2$$

Acetylene Vinyl acetylene Chloroprene

The esters of allyl alcohol, such as diallyl phthalate , can be prepared by direct esterification of phthalic anhydride and allyl alcohol. The esters of allyl alcohol are useful bifunctional polymerisation monomers.

Various acrylic esters, such as ethyl acrylic, are widely used in polymerisation, and can be manufactured by direct esterification of the acrylic acid with the appropriate alcohol.

TABLE 7. END PRODUCTS OF THE PETROCHEMICAL INDUSTRY

Product	Product
Industrial gases	Flavours and perfumes
Industrial carbon	Detergents
Ammonia	Plastics, polymers, plasticizers synthetic fibers
Nitrogen industries	Rubber, rubber chemicals
Sulphur and sulphuric acid	Synthetic motor fuels
Aerosols	Lubricant and gasoline additives and synthetic lubricants
Explosives	Floatation and antiknock compounds
Surface coatings	Alcohols
Adhesives	Solvents
Paints, varnishes, lacquers	Dyes, lakes, tonners
Agrochemicals	Medical products
Food additives	
Fertilizers and pesticides	

HALOGENATION AND HYDROHALOGENATION

Chlorination of aliphatic hydrocarbons - The direct chlorimation of lower aliphatic hydrocarbons can be carried out through both liquid and vapour phase reactions, using various temperatures and pressures in presence or absence of a catalyst and various products are obtained, which are separated by rectification. These chloroaliphatics are commercially used, e.g, for the production of amyl alcohols from chloropentanes and as solvents, particularly is dry cleaning under flammable conditions. The chloromethanes such as methyl chloride, dichloro methane (or methylene chloride), and chloroform are all obtained by the chlorination of methane. Methyl chloride can also be made from CH_3OH and hydrogen chloride, and chloroform from the decarboxylation of trichloroacetic acid with lime.

Methyl chloride is used as an alkylating agent and refrigerant. Methylene chloride is used as a dewaxing solvent for oils, and chloroform is used as a solvent, intermediate, and medicinal substance. Chloroform is, however, mostly used in producing fluorocarbons . Carbon tetrachloride is also made from chlorination of methane. In chlorinating, the Cl_2 and CH_4 (including recycle) are charged (in the ratio 0.6 : 1.0) to the reactor and the temperature in the primary reactor is maintained at 650 - 700 F. using the products to preheat the reactants. The conversion of Cl_2 and CH_4 are 100% and about 65% respectively. The effluent gases contain methyl chloride 6 parts, methylene chloride 3 parts, chloroform I part and carbon tetrachloride 0.25 part. In addition, they also contain unreacted CH_4 and the HCl, and traces of chlorine and heavy chlorinated products. The secondary chlorination takes place in liquid phase at ambient temperature in presence of light (mercury arc catalysed) in a reactor converting CH_2Cl_2 to $CHCl_3$ and $CHCl_3$ to CCl_4 in another reactor.

Ethane can also be chlorinated under very similar conditions as methane and chlorinated ethanes, such as ethyl chloride , are formed. Ethyl chloride has widely been used in the manufacture of tetraethyl lead (TEL). Since polychlorinated ethanes are not desirable, a large excess of ethane is used.

$$CH_3 - CH_3 + Cl_2 \rightarrow CH_3CH_2Cl + HCl$$

In order to utilize the byproduct, HCl, a mixture of ethane and ethylene is used and the following reaction takes place over Friedel Crafts catalysts.

$$CH_2 = CH_2 + HCl \xrightarrow{AlCl_3} CH_3CH_2Cl$$

Ethylene dichloride can be prepared by addition of halogen to unsaturated hydrocarbon (ethylene) because it serves to give various derivatives, such as **ethylene dichloride, ethylene dibromide, dichloro ethylene, trichloro ethylene and tetrachloro ethane.**

$$CH_2 = CH_2 + Cl_2 \xrightarrow{C_2H_4Br_2} Cl - CH_2 - CH_2 - Cl_2 \text{ (Ethylene dichloride)}$$

The chlorine gas is passed through a tank containing ethylene dibromide, $C_2H_4Br_2$, and the mixed vapours are led to a chlorinating tower, where they are allowed to react with a stream of ethylene. The reaction takes place at 40 - 50°C. The products from the tower pass through a partial condenser, followed by a separator, the crude ethylene dichloride passing off as a gas and the liquid ethylene dibromide being returned to the process. The product is used in the preparation of ethylene diamine and **Thiokol rubber.** Ethylene dichloride is also used as a solvent, and as an additive to TEL to vapourise any lead.

Ethylene dibromide or ethylene bromide is manufactured by direct addition of bromine to ethylene. **Ethyl bromide** is now prepared using the following reaction initiated by gamma radiation from Co - 60.

$$C_2H_4 + HBr \rightarrow C_2H_5Br$$

The reaction is exothermic and gamma radiation only acts as initiator of the reaction. The process is a two phase gas - liquid reaction and makes use of the recirculation system. C_2H_5Br is used in large quantities as an additive to

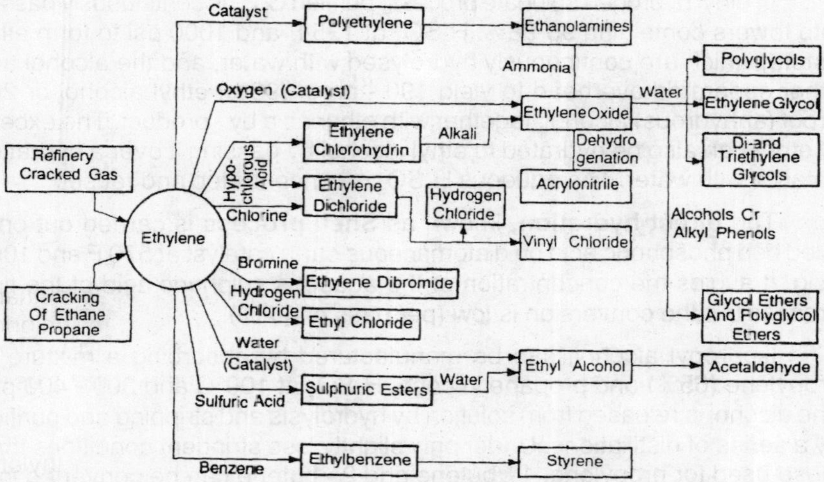

Fig. 3. Petrochemicals from ethylene.

TEL in gasoline in order to prevent the deposition of lead oxide on the valves of the gasoline engine.

Perchloro ethylene has widely been used in dry cleaning and vapour degreasing. It is now manufactured as a means of disposal of junk chlorinated hydrocarbons of one to three chlorine atoms. These are allowed to react with excess chlorine and conducted through a reactor at 700°C, causing chlorinolysis to occur and yielding CCl_4 and perchloro ethylene, $CCl_2 = CCl_2$. Either of these can be recycled to extinction so that the supply can be controlled.

$$2CCl_4 \rightleftharpoons C.Cl_2 = C.Cl_2 + 2Cl_2$$

Pentanes can be chlorinated to amyl chloride, which are then hydrolysed to amyl alcohols.

HYDRATION AND HYDROLYSIS

The principal examples of this chemical conversion for petrochemicals are in **ethyl and other alcohols.** There are two main synthetic processes for the manufacture of ethyl alcohol, the ethyl hydrogen sulphate one and the vapour phase direct hydration. In both, the raw material is ethylene.

(1) $$3C_2H_4 + 2H_2SO_4 \rightarrow C_2H_5HSO_4 + (C_2H_5)2SO_4$$

$$C_2H_5HSO_4 + (C_2H_5)_2SO_4 + (H_2O) \rightarrow 3C_2H_5OH + 2H_2SO_4 + (H_2O)$$

$$2C_2H_5OH + H_2SO_4 \dashrightarrow C_2H_5OC_2H_5 + H_2SO_4.H_2O \text{ (Byproduct)}$$

(2) $$C_2H_4 + H_2O \xrightarrow{H_3PO_4} C_2H_5OH$$

In ethyl hydrogen sulphate process, purified C_2H_4 is continuously passed into towers containing 95-98%. H_2SO_4 at 135 F and 1000 psi to form ethyl esters, which are continuously hydrolysed with water, and the alcohol and ether separated overhead to yield 190 - proof (95%) ethyl alcohol or 200 proof (anhydrous) alcohol, together with ether as a by - product. The excess of ether can also be hydrated to ethyl alcohol by passing it over a hydration catalyst with water. The aqueous H_2SO_4 is concentrated and reused.

The **direct hydration,** known as **Shell process** is carried out on a fixed bed phosphoric acid on diatomaceous earth catalyst at 570 F and 1000 psig. It avoids the concentration of the aqueous sulphuric acid of the first process but the conversion is low (per pass of 4.2%).

Isopropyl alcohol, can be manufactured by absorbing a mixture of propylene (65%) and propane in conc. H_2SO_4 at 100°C and 300 - 400 psi. The alcohol is released from solution by hydrolysis and stripping and purified by a series of distillations. Under only slightly less stringent conditions than those used for propylene, 1 - butene and 2 - butene can be converted into isobutyl alcohol and isobutylene can be converted into **tertiary butyl alcohol.**

Ethylene glycol, an important antifreeze, is made by several processes, involving hydrolysis. For example, ethylene chlorohydrin (produced by the reaction of ethylene and chlorine water) is treated with sodium bicarbonate solution.

$$CH_2 = CH_2 + Cl_2 + H_2O \rightarrow CH_2 - OH - CH_2 - Cl + HCl$$

$$CH_2OH - CH_2Cl + NaHCO_3 \rightarrow CH_2OH - CH_2OH + NaCl + CO_2$$

The ethylene chlorohydrin is produced by passing ethylene and chlorine in water at 50 - 120F. Ethylene oxide can also be prepared from ethylene chlorohydrin by adding caustic and rectifying the vapours. The chlorohydrin solution is concentrated to 35 - 40% and allowed to react with $NaHCO_3$ solution in a closed, stirred, steam jacketed Kettle. Hydrolysis takes place smoothly at 70 - 80°C with the evolution of CO_2. Glycol solution is concentrated by distillation. As the high boiling ethylene glycol can only be separated with difficulty from the salt, it is better to make ethylene oxide from ethylene chlorohydrin by heating with caustic soda or hydrated lime. Ethylene oxide can be hydrated to glycol by treating with weakly acidic water under low pressure.

Diethylene glycol is prepared as a byproduct from the manufacture of ethylene glycol. It is used as a humectant for tobaccos and as an emulsifying agent. In recent years, ethylene glycol is prepared by the reaction of ethylene with oxygen and water.

$$CH_2 = CH_2 + \tfrac{1}{2}O_2 \rightarrow \underbrace{CH_2 - CH_2}_{\diagdown O \diagup} \text{ or } C_2H_4O$$

$$C_2H_4O + H_2O \rightarrow CH_2 - OH - CH_2 - OH$$

Ethylene, oxygen and recycle gas are charged to a tubulor reactor, which is filled with sulphuric acid or silver as a catalyst. The reactor is operated at 200 - 300°C. Ethylene oxide is recovered from the gaseous reactor effluent by absorption in water. The wet ethylene oxide is reacted with water in presence of acid at 50 - 100°C to form ethylene glycol. The crude glycol is dehydrated and fractionated from di - and tri - glycol byproducts.

Amyl alcohols are prepared from pentane via a two step process, which involves chlorination and hydration. Anhydrous pentane and chlorine vapours are mixed and charged to a furnace, where the pyrolysis of the chloropentanes is minimised by cooling the reactor effluent. The **monochloro pentane or amyle chloride** is recovered from unreacted pentane, hydrogen chloride, and polychlorinated pentanes. The amyl chlorides are hydrolysed with aqueous caustic soda in the presence of sodium oleate as a catalyst to form amyl alcohol. After the hydrolysis the brine phase is decanted, and the organic phase is run to steam stripping columns, where pentanes and amyl chlorides are removed. The amyl alcohols are recovered by distillation.

HYDROGENATION AND DEHYDROGENATION

Hydrogenation yields many useful products for the chemical industries. In addition to hydrogenating the double bonds, this reaction it also capable of in eliminating other elements from a molecule, such as oxygen, nitrogen, sulphur, carbon, and halogens. Hydrogenation is carried out under pressure and usually at elevated temperatures in the presence of a suitable catalyst.

Temperature usually lies upto 500°C, but in many cases it is less than 400°C. The catalyst used depends on the temperature and noble metals such as Pt or Pd are used upto 150°C, nickel and copper from 150 - 250°C and various combinations of metals and metal oxides at higher temperatures. Pressure increases the rate of reaction of hydrogenation. Many of the foregoing remarks on hydrogenation are also applicable for dehydrogenation, but the main differences are in the pressure and its effect on the equilibrium and the catalyst. **In dehydrogenation,** lower pressures are used, or a vacuum, and noble metal (Pt), copper and iron oxides are used as catalyst.

Methanol, which is one of the most important of the high pressure organic synthesis used today, is prepared by the hydrogenation of carbon monoxide.

$$CO + 2H_2 \rightleftharpoons CH_3OH \quad \Delta H = -24.6 \text{ kcal}$$

The catalyst commonly used is silver or copper promoted with oxides of zinc, chromium, manganese, or aluminium. Contact of the gases with hot iron must be avoided and so copper lined reactors are used. The appropriate amounts of gases are mixed and compressed to 4500 psi. The high pressure results in more favourable chemical or equilibrium. After oil purification, the gases go to the reactors, where the equilibrium yield is about 60% at 300°C. The gaseous products then pass through the heat exchangers to high pressure condensers, where CH_3OH is condensed at 3500 - 4000 psi, the gases being recirculated. The conversion to alcohol is low, since the catalyst only operates at high temperatures where the equilibrium constant is poor. The yield of methanol, is however, very high. Methanol finds a wide variety of uses, such as denaturant, antifreeze, fuel and solvent. It is also the starting material in the preparation of methylamines, formaldehyde and dimethyl aniline.

Styrene is prepared from ethyl benzene by dehydrogenation. Many of the lower molecular **aliphatic ketones** are prepared by the dehydrogenation of the corresponding alcohols. For example, acetone, methyl ethyl ketone, and cyclohexanone are produced in this manner. The most important ketone produced is acetone which is mainly used for cellulose acetate and manufacture of other chemicals, such as phorone, mesityl oxide, methyl isobutyl ketone, and methyl methacrylate. It is also used as a solvent. Its main supply is by :

(a) *Catalytic dehydrogenation of isopropyl alcohol.*

(b) A *byproduct of cumene phenol process, and*

(c) Fermentation and Oxidation (Butane).

The dehydrogenation of isopropyl alcohol to acetone can be represented as,

$$CH_3CHOHCH_3\,(g) \rightarrow CH_3COCH_3\,(g) + H_2\,(g)\ \Delta H = 15\ \text{k.cals}$$

The reaction results in an 85 - 90% conversion at 350°C and above, and over metallic copper or zinc acetate catalyst, and is often carried out at 30 psi. Acetone is recovered by condensation from the hydrogen and is purified by distillation.

NITRATION

Nitration is one of the most important means of introducing nitrogen into hydrocarbons. Nitric acid is a powerful oxidising and nitrating agent. A basic development in the field of nitration has been the vapour phase low pressure nitration of aliphatic hydrocarbons, particularly propane.

Since 1940, alkanes are being industrially nitrated in vapour phase in stainless steel reactor under about 10 atmospheres with moderately concentrated nitric acid (35 - 70%) between 400 - 450°C for a short contact period. As a result, only mononitro paraffins are formed. The nitro group may enter any position in the carbon chain. Since paraffin molecule undergoes cracking partially during nitration, usually a mixture of nitro paraffins is formed. From propane, e.g, 1 - nitropropane (25%), 2 - nitropropane (40%), nitroethane (10%) and nitromethane (25%) are formed. Methane is most difficult to nitrate directly. Higher alkanes are more easily converted into nitroalkanes. Oxidative reactions also take place. The usual byproducts are alcohols, aldehydes, fatty acids, carbon monoxide, carbon dioxide etc.

$$\text{Propane} + HNO_3 \rightarrow CH_3CH_2CH_2NO_2\,(25\,\%) + CO_2$$
$$CH_3CHNO_2H_3\,(40\,\%) + H_2O$$

$$CH_3CH_2NO_2\ (10\ \%) + NO$$

$$CH_3NO_2\ (25\ \%)$$

The material of construction of the apparatus is essentially stainless steel, in a continuous series of heaters, reactors, condensers, distillation columns, pumps and control instruments.

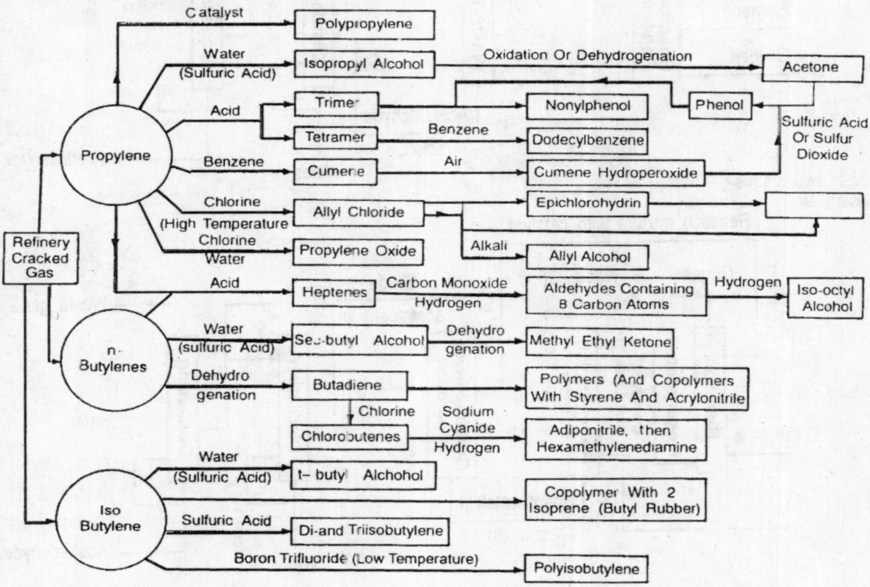

Fig. 4. Petrochemicals from propylene, n-butylene and isobutylenes.

A small amount of air or oxygen may be added to improve the yield. The liquid phase nitration of alkanes is very slow, oxidative products predominate. C_1 - C_3 nitroparaffins are the most important commercially. Propane and butane are nitrated on an industrial scale. The unreacted hydrocarbons are recycled. Nitroparaffins are separated by fractional distillation. Nitroparaffins are used as solvents and propellants and to make derivatives, e.g, hydroxylamine. Nitroalkanes are used as military propellants. Nitromethane, nitroethane, 1 - and 2 - nitropropanes are good solvents for nitrocellulose lacquers, alkyd resins, polyvinyl plastics etc. They also dissolve oils, fats and waxes. Many of them are intermediates in the manufacture of synthetic detergents, insecticides, drugs and explosives.

OXIDATION

Oxidation is one of the most valuable conversion for petrochemicals. Generally oxidation involves fission of C - C and C - H bonds with the formation of C - O bonds. The cheapest reagent for oxidation is air or oxygen. Oxygen is often more economical than air, largely because of enhanced yields,

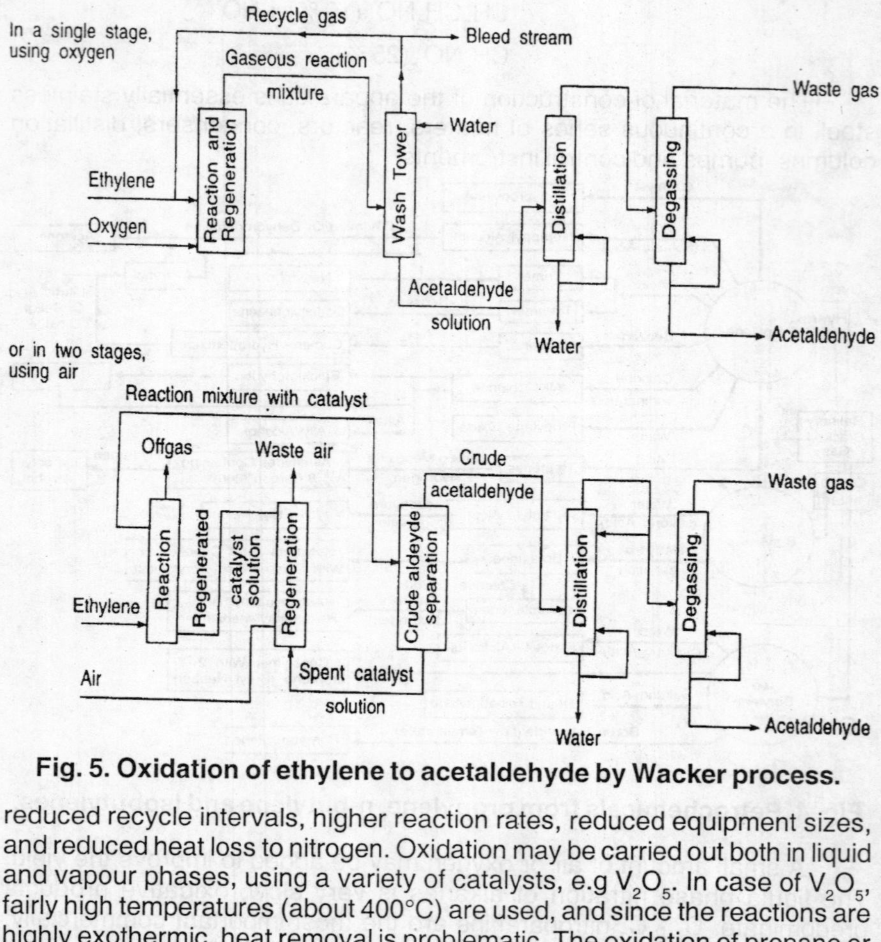

Fig. 5. Oxidation of ethylene to acetaldehyde by Wacker process.

reduced recycle intervals, higher reaction rates, reduced equipment sizes, and reduced heat loss to nitrogen. Oxidation may be carried out both in liquid and vapour phases, using a variety of catalysts, e.g V_2O_5. In case of V_2O_5, fairly high temperatures (about 400°C) are used, and since the reactions are highly exothermic, heat removal is problematic. The oxidation of propane or butane as such or as LPG gives a large number of oxygen containing compounds. Some of them are acetic acid, acetic anhydride, formaldehyde, acetaldehyde, acetone, butyraldehyde, ethyl acetate, butanol, vinyl acetate etc. **Partial oxidation** is used to increase the temperature and to oxidise partially a hydrocarbon, e.g, natural gas to make acetylene.

LPG oxidation takes place with air or preferably O_2, because of greater production from a given plant. Products without catalyst are acetaldehyde, formaldehyde, methanol, and many other oxygenated petrochemicals. The longer the normal paraffin chain length and the higher the pressure, the easier is the oxidation. Catalysts are important and selective. For example, liquid phase oxidation of butane in presence of cobalt as catalyst yields 76% acetic acid and 6% formic acid, but in presence of manganese catalyst the yield is 62% acetic acid and 23% formic acid.

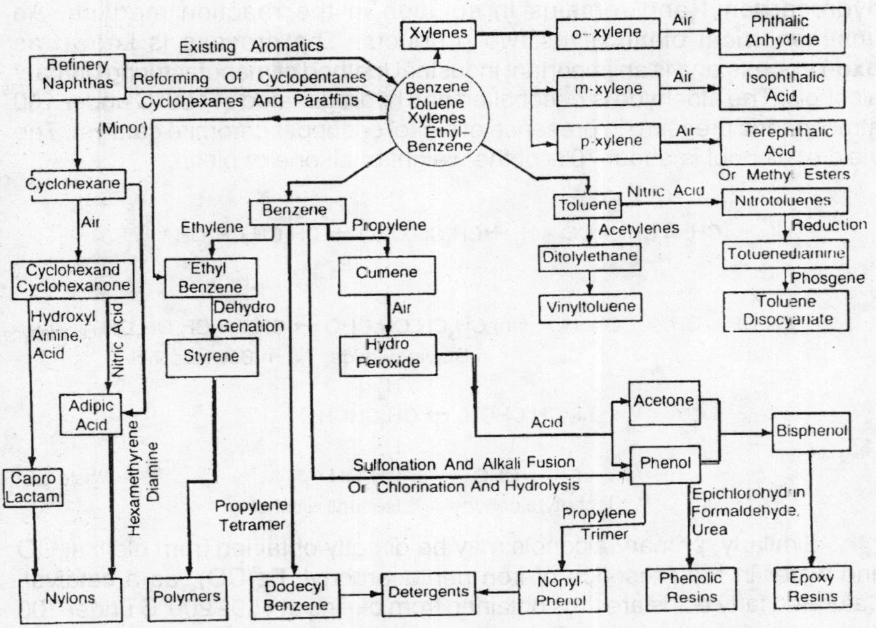

Fig. 6. Petrochemicals from benzene, toluene and xylenes.

OXO OR HYDROFORMATION

The oxo method is a process of converting α-olefins to aldehydes and/or alcohols containing one additional carbon atom. The olefin in liquid state is reacted with a mixture of H_2 and CO in the presence of a soluble cobalt catalyst to produce the aldehyde (and some alcohol). All or a part of aldehyde is then hydrogenated over a nickel catalyst to form alcohol. The reaction is exothermic. The usual raw materials are synthesis gas ($CO + H_2$) and olefins. The principal olefins used are propylene and C_7 - C_{12} copolymers of propylene and isobutylene.

$$CH_3CH_2CH_2 + CO + H_2 \xrightarrow[150^\circ C,\ 250\ arm]{CO} CH_3CH_2CH_2CHO + \underset{\substack{|\\ CH3}}{CH_3CHCHO} + CH_3CH_2CH_2CH_2OH + \underset{\substack{|\\ CH3}}{CH_3CH_2CH_2OH}$$

The products are n - butyraldehyde, isobutyraldehyde, n - butanol and isobutyl alcohol.

CARBONYLATION

Olefins combine with CO and H_2 in molar ratio at 160-175°C under about 200 atmospheric pressure in the presence of cobalt hydrocarbonyl, $HCo(CO)_4$, as a catalyst to form the corresponding aldehydes. In practice, cobalt naphthenate is added to the reactor, which is converted there into hydrocarbonyl and remains in solution in the reaction medium. An unsymmetrical olefin gives two products. The process is known as **oxo-process** and is an important industrial method of manufacturing primary alcohols. The aldehyde is decobalted and hydrogenated at 150°C under 100 atmospheric pressure in presence of nickel or copper chromite catalyst. The yield of alcohol is about 70% of the weight of alkene or olefin.

$$CH_2 = CH_2 + CO + H_2 \rightarrow CH_3CH_2CHO \xrightarrow{H_2} CH_3CH_2CH_2OH$$

$$CH_3CH = CH_2 + CO + H_2 \rightarrow \text{(i) } \underset{\text{n-Butyraldehyde}}{CH_3CH_2CH_2CHO} \xrightarrow{H_2} \underset{\text{n-Butyl alcohol}}{CH_3CH_2CH_2CH_2OH}$$

$$\text{(ii) } \underset{\text{Isobutyraldehyde}}{CH_3\underset{|}{\overset{}{C}}HCH_3 \; (CHO)} \xrightarrow{H_2} \underset{\text{Isobutyl alcohol}}{CH_3CHCH_3 \; (CH_2OH)}$$

Similarly, primary alcohols may be directly obtained from olefins, CO and water in the presence of iron pentacarbonyl, $Fe(CO)_5$ as a catalyst. Saturated fatty acids are thus obtained from olefins at 150 - 200°C under 100 atmospheres in presence of nickel carbonyl catalyst.

$$RCH = CHR' + 3CO + 2H_2O \rightarrow \underset{\text{Primary alcohol}}{RCH_2CHR'CH_2OH} + 2CO_2$$

$$CH_2 = CH_2 + CO + H_2O \xrightarrow{Ni(CO)_4} \underset{\text{Propionic acid}}{CH_3CH_2COOH}$$

OXIDISING CHLORINATION

Hydrogen chloride is obtained as a byproduct in the chlorination of paraffins and aromatic hydrocarbons of petroleum refining that is widely used in industrial organic synthesis. Utilization of the byproduct is -an urgent problem associated with :

(a) *Decreasing the cost of chlorination products.*

(b) *Improving sanitary conditions, and*

(c) *Combatting the corrosion of metals.*

Part of the hydrogen chloride is used in the manufacture of hydrochloric acid by the counter current absorption of HCl by water. The local demand for hydrochloric acid, however, is usually much smaller than the possibility of producing it from hydrogen chloride. The transportation of hydrochloric acid over long distances involves much difficulties because of its high corroding ability.

One of the best ways of utilising HCl is the method of oxidising chlorination. This method is used today for the manufacture of vinyl chloride from ethylene. The ethylene is converted into 1,2 - dichloroethane in a reactor for oxidising chlorination and catalytic decomposition of dichloroethane so formed yields vinyl chloride. The formed HCl is recycled into the reactor.

$$2\begin{array}{c}CH_2\\ \|\\ CH_2\end{array} + 4HCl + O_2 \rightarrow \begin{array}{c}CH_2Cl\\ |\\ CH_2Cl\end{array} + 2H_2O$$

$$\begin{array}{c}CH_2Cl\\ |\\ CH_2Cl\end{array} \rightarrow \begin{array}{c}CH_2\\ \|\\ CH_2Cl\end{array} + HCl$$

The oxidising chlorination proceeds at 260 - 300°C in the presence of copper chloride catalyst on an inert carrier. The catalytic decomposition of dichloroethane is carried out at 500°C on a porous pumice catalyst.

The combined processing of ethylene and acetylene from gases of petroleum refining also gives vinyl chloride. The hydrogen chloride formed in the production of vinyl chloride from ethylene is used for the hydrochlorination of acetylene.

$$\begin{array}{c}CH_2\\ \|\\ CH_2\end{array} \xrightarrow{Cl_2} \begin{array}{c}CH_2Cl\\ |\\ CH_2Cl\end{array} \xrightarrow{Pyrolysis} \begin{array}{c}CH_2\\ \|\\ CHCl\end{array} + HCl$$

$$\begin{array}{c}CH\\ |||\\ CH\end{array} \xrightarrow{HCl} \begin{array}{c}CH_2\\ \|\\ CHCl\end{array}$$

Another economical way of utilising hydrogen chloride is the combination of methane chlorination with oxidising chlorination to produce chlorine derivatives of methane.

$$CH_4 + 4Cl_2 \rightarrow CCl_4 + 4HCl \qquad CH_4 + 4HCl + O_2 \rightarrow CCl_4 + 2H_2O$$

In addition to CCl_4, this process also yields CH_2Cl_2 and $CHCl_3$. The CCl_4 is used as a solvent, as fumigant in agriculture and as a fire extinguisher. Chloroform ($CHCl_3$) is valuable intermediate in the synthesis of freons, fluoro plastics etc.

Oxidising chlorination is also used in the manufacture of chlorobenzene from a vapour and gas mixture of benzene, hydrogen chloride, air or oxygen at 225°C on a mixed catalyst (Al_2O_3 - $CuCl_2$ - $FeCl_3$).

$$C_6H_6 + HCl + 0.5O_2 \rightarrow C_6H_5Cl + H_2O$$

A chromium-cesium catalyst has been proposed for oxidising hydrogen chloride to chlorine, that is, for regenerating chlorine from the flue gases of organic compound chlorination.

POLYMERISATION

Polymerisation is the name of a process in which a number of molecules of a monomer unite to form a large, polymer molecule with an elemental composition identical to that of the initial monomer.

Because of the reactive double bond, an olefin reacts with itself inter-molecularly many times in the presence of a suitable catalyst and form a big or macromolecule. This process, known as **polymerisation** is now defined as inter-molecular combination which is functionally capable-of proceeding indefinitely. Ethylene polymerises to polyethylene or polythene in presence of traces of oxygen (0.01-0.1%) or peroxide under 1000-2000 atmospheres at 100-250°C, following free radical mechanism.

$$nCH_2 = CH_2 \rightarrow [CH_2 - CH_2]_n \text{ or } [- CH_2 - CH_2 -)_n$$

Monomer Polymer

The polymer so formed consists of 1000 or more ethylene molecules and has the same percentage composition as ethylene, the monomer. Here the monomer simply adds on, head to tail, until the chain reaction terminates. Because nothing is lost during the process, it is known as **addition polymerisation.** The polymerisation of butadiene into polybutadiene is also addition polymerisation.

$$CH_2 = CH- CH= CH_2 \rightarrow [-CH_2 - CH= CH- CH_2 -]_n$$

Another typical example of addition polymerisation is **natural rubber,** a high polymer of isoprene, $CH_2 = C(CH_2).CH = CH_2$.

There is another type of polymerisation, known as **condensation polymerisation,** in which monomer molecules react to form a bond between the molecules and some of the atoms present are lost in the form of a product. **Thiokol,** a polysulphide polymer is formed by condensation polymerisation.

Reaction between chlorine atoms or ethylene dichloride and sodium atoms of sodium tetrasulphide takes place. A bond is formed between sulphur and carbon atoms and long chain polymer known as thiokol. NaCl is formed as a byproduct.

$$Cl - CH_2 - CH_2 - Cl + Na - \underset{\underset{S}{\|}}{S} - \underset{\underset{S}{\|}}{S} - Na \rightarrow \left[- CH_2 - CH_2 - \underset{\underset{S}{\|}}{S} - \underset{\underset{S}{\|}}{S} - \right] + NaCl$$

Ethylene dichloride Sodium tetra sulphide Polyethylene tetrasulphide

Because of the introduction of **emulsion polymerisation and co-polymerisation process,** several high quality rubbers have been developed in recent years. The most important synthetic rubber is a copolymer of butadiene and styrene. This rubber is called GRS or SBR rubber. Neoprene is another modern synthetic rubber.

Butadiene is mostly prepared by catalytic dehydrogenation of n- butane (of natural gas) and of butene-1 (from cracked petroleum gases). Dry and almost pure n-butane, preheated to 600°C is passed over a catalyst bed of activated alumina impregnated with 20% chromic oxide under 0.15 atmosphere for 4-10 minutes at 600°C. The process is **endothermic.** Both butene-1 and butadiene are formed. Unreacted butane and butene-1 are separated and recycled. Butene-1 from petroleum refineries is likewise dehydrogenated to butadiene.

$$\underset{\text{n-Butane}}{CH_3CH_2CH_2CH_3} \xrightarrow{-H_2} \underset{\text{Butene-1}}{CH_2 = CH - CH_2 - CH_3} \xrightarrow{-H_2} \underset{\text{1,3-Butadiene}}{CH_2 = CH - CH = CH_2}$$

Acetylene may also be converted into butadiene by heating to 100°C with 30% aqueous formaldehyde under 5 atmospheres in presence of copper acetylide. 2-butyne-1, 4-diol so formed is hydrogenated to butene-1, 4, diol at 200°C under 280 atmospheres. This with hot phosphoric acid, forms **tetrahydrofuran (THF)** which is finally dehydrated to butadiene at 270°C in presence of sodium phosphate.

$$2HCHO + HC \equiv CH \rightarrow \underset{\text{2-Butyne-1, 4, diol}}{CH_2OH.C - C.CH_2OH} \xrightarrow{H_2} \underset{\text{Butane-1, 4 diol}}{CH_2OH - CH_2 - CH_2 - CH_2OH}$$

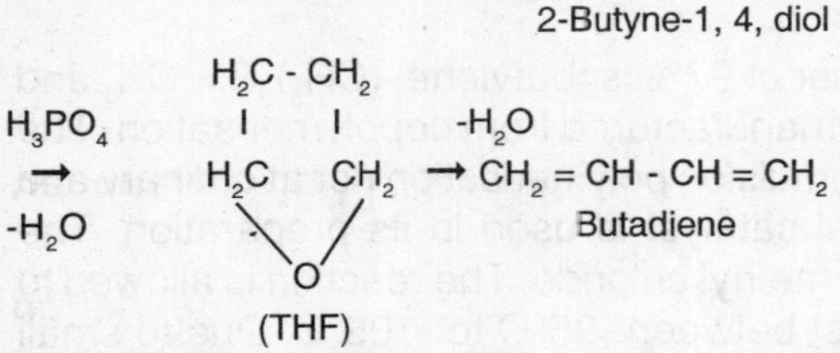

Butadiene can also be prepared by passing ethyl alcohol vapour over alumina/zinc oxide catalyst at 400°C. As a result, dehydration and dehydrogenation take place simultaneously, and butadiene is formed in about 60% yield.

$$2C_2H_5OH \rightarrow CH_2 = CH - CH = CH_2 + 2H_2O + H_2$$

Butadiene is copolymerised with styrene, $C_6H_5 - CH = CH_2$ into **GRS or Buna S rubber.**

$$\underset{\text{Butadiene}}{CH_2=CH-CH=CH_2} + \underset{\text{Styrene}}{C_6H_5-CH=CH_2} \rightarrow \underset{\text{GRS or SBR unit}}{-CH_2-CH=CH-CH_2-CH_2-\underset{\substack{|\\ C_6H_5}}{CH}-}$$

Buna N is a copolymer of 75% butadiene and 25% acrylonitrile, $CH_2 = CHCN$, and is prepared by emulsion polymerisation. Buna N is used in making fuel tanks, gasoline hoses, conveyor belts, higher altitude aircraft components etc. It is also used in tank linings, gaskets, printing rollers, adhesives, oil resistant foams, and automobile parts etc.

Neoprene is the first synthetic rubber made commercially in 1932. Acetylene is dimerised in the presence of cuprous chloride to vinyl acetylene which, with cone. HCl, cuprous chloride and ammonium chloride, yields 2-chlorobutadiene or **chloroprene.** The emulsion polymerisation of chloroprene at ordinary temperature gives neoprene. Polymerisation, which is very rapid, follows free radical mechanism.

$$2CH \equiv CH \xrightarrow{CuCl} CH_2 = CH.C \equiv CH \xrightarrow[CuCl]{HCl} CH2 = C.Cl - CH = CH_2$$

Vinyl acetylene Chloroprene

$$- CH_2C.Cl = CH - CH_2 -$$

Neoprene unit

Neoprene can be valcanised by heating alone (non-sulphur). Zinc oxide and magnesium oxide have also been used as vulcanising agents. Antimony sulphide has been found to be more effective. Neoprene is resistant to weathering, many common chemicals, oils and flame. Neoprene is used as standard engineering material in oil refining plants, for making gaskets etc. Neoprene is also used in conveyor belts, for printing rollers and rubber cements.

Butyl rubber is a co-polymer of 97% isobutylene, $(CH_3)_2C = CH_2$ and 3% butadiene or isoprene and is manufactured from copolymerisation. The butyl rubber is neither formed by emulsion polymerisation nor at ordinary and elevated temperatures. No usual catalyst is used in its preparation. The monomers are dissolved in liquid methyl chloride. The reaction is allowed to take place in presence of catalyst between -95°C to -105°C. Due to small proportion of isoprene the percentage of double bonds is very little in butyl rubber. Butyl rubber is used in making tubes and tyres, hoses, conveyor belts, tank linings etc.

Chapter 4

INDUSTRIAL ORGANIC SYNTHESIS

INTRODUCTION

The products of organic synthesis have been used in all the branches of chemical industry either as finished products or chiefly as raw materials for other manufacturing processes (semi-products). The amount and variety of organic synthesis products made by chemical industry continue to grow from day by day. These products include organic alcohols and acids, synthetic motor fuel (synthin), various monomers and the synthetic resins, rubber, plastics, adhesives, solvents, heat carrying agents, coolants, floatation agents, synthetic detergents and other surfactants, insecticides, a large number of different paints and varnishes, antifreeze and antiknock compounds, hundreds of kinds of dyes, pesticides, photochemicals, perfumes and plant growth stimulators.

THE RAW MATERIALS AND BASIC PROCESSES

The raw materials used in ,the organic synthesis industry should solve important problems of chemical industry such as,—

(a) *Combining manufacturing, processes for the complete, utilization of the raw materials, and*

(b) *The replacement of food and ,t egetable products with non- edible and mineral materials.*

The main kind of raw materials are natural and accompanying hydrocarbon gases, gaseous and liquid products of petroleum refining and also synthesis gas ($CO + H_2$), coke oven gas and the industrial tars produced in the thermal processing of wood, coal, shale, and peat.

The substances involved in the manufacture of complex organic compounds are divided into the following groups.

(a) The initial materials or the raw materials.

(b) The intermediate products.

(c) The end products.

The initial materials or the raw materials - Methane, ethylene, propylene, butylene, acetylene, benzene, toluene and other individual hydrocarbons are the most important of the substances used in organic synthesis. They can be obtained by chemical processing of gaseous, liquid and solid fuels. At one time the principal source of the raw materials for organic synthesis was the coal tar obtained in coking and low temperature carbonisation, and raw materials of plant and animal origin were also used extensively. But in **recent years**,liquid hydrocarbons contained in petroleum, natural gas and casing, head gases, and also the gases formed in processing petroleum have become more important and major source. At present many of these initial or raw materials are produced in amounts of tens and hundreds of thousands of tonnes per year.

The intermediate products - Ethylene oxide, acetaldehyde, phenol, nitrobenzene, and many others are obtained by processing the initial materials and they are themselves materials used in making more complex organic compounds such as plastics, fibres, dyes, pharmaceuticals, physiologically active agents etc. The ties between the initial raw material and the end product can be represented as,

Initial material → Intermediate product I → Intermediate product II → Intermediate product III →End product.

For example, benzene, a product of petrochemical and coke-benzene industries, is an excellent solvent for fats, rubbers, resins, sulphur and other compounds. Benzene is also a raw material (initial material) used in the manufacture of nitrobenzene, aniline, chlorobenzene, phenol, ethyl benzene, isopropyl benzene, styrene, DDT, maleic anhydride, phenyl ethyl alcohol, monosulphonic acid and other chemical products and also the intermediate products used in manufacturing dyes, synthetic rubber, plastics, varnishes, insecticides, pharmaceuticals and disinfectants, explosives etc.

The product prepared by the oxidation of ethylene, that is, ethylene oxide is used for the manufacture of ethanolamine, ethylene glycol, di- and polyethylene glycol, acetaldehyde, dioxane, ethylene chlorohydrin, styrene etc. and from them synthetic resins, synthetic rubbers, plastics, varnishes, fibres, detergents, antifreeze and other industrial products.

In **recent years**, the organic synthesis industry makes use of the following principal kinds of raw materials.

(a) *Natural gas and casing-head gas.*

(b) *Gaseous and liquid hydrocarbons obtained by distillation of petroleum.*

(c) *Cracking and pyrolysis of petroleum products.*

(d) *Solid paraffinic hydrocarbons and heavy petroleum residues.*

(e) *Coke oven and shale gases.*

(f) *Coaltar and tars obtained from shale, wood and peat.*

In addition, a large number of inorganic compounds have also been used. They include acids, alkalies, soda ash, chlorine etc. Without these chemicals many of the processes cannot be carried out.

In general, a purified raw material must first be obtained, which can then be processed into semiproducts as well as pure products. All raw materials are subjected to purification to remove water vapour, mechanical admixtures, sulphurous compounds and other impurities and then separated to get individual hydrocarbons. The gaseous hydrocarbons are generally separated by making use of the following methods :

(a) Compression under cooling. (b) Absorption - desorption. (c) **Adsorption - desorption.**

Liquids are usually separated by distillation and rectification. For separation, a combination of two or more methods can also be used in industrial processing.

These methods of separating raw materials and modern processing methods have been used to obtain the most important of the intermediate products, which serve as the direct starting materials for organic synthesis. Such substances include synthesis gas (a mixture of CO and H_2), saturated aliphatic hydrocarbons from methane to pentanes, individual monolefins (C_2 and higher) and their mixtures, diolefins (butadiene, isoprene etc.), acetylene and aromatic hydrocarbons (such as benzene, toluene, xylene etc.).

CHEMICAL PROCESSES USED IN INDUSTRIAL ORGANIC SYNTHESIS

The methods employed for processing any raw material depend mainly on.

(a) *The nature of the product to be obtained from it, and*

(b) *The composition and properties of the initial hydrocarbons.*

The manufacture of organic synthesis products is based on standard reactions of organic chemistry such as **halogenation, sulphonation, oxidation, reduction, hydrogenation, dehydrogenation, hydration, dehydration, hydrochlorination, dehydrochlorination, nitration, alkylation, cyclization, isomerisation, condensation, polymerisation, esterification etc.** The organic chemical industry is mainly based on synthesis reactions, that is, on obtaining complex compounds from simple ones. However, decomposition reactions have also been used. The direction of a chemical reaction and its rate depend on chemical and physical parameters of the process, that is, temperature, pressure, duration, state of aggregation and the ratio of the reactants, the use of catalysts, solvents, the ways of supplying and removing heat etc. Organic synthesis processes occur in a kinetically controlled manner and hence their overall rate is determined by the rate of chemical reaction.

Several parallel and consecutive reactions generally occur in organic synthesis instead of one chemical reaction. As a result, **byproducts or waste products** are also obtained in addition to the desired product. The rate constant of the overall process may therefore be a complex function cf the rate constants of the separate reactions [$k = f(k_1, k_2, k_3, k_4 \text{ - - -})$].

The functional relationship may vary greatly with the increase in temperature, and pressure, the concentration, of the reactants, and other regime parameters. The **selectivity** of a process with respect to the desired product is given by the ratio of the rate constant of the principal

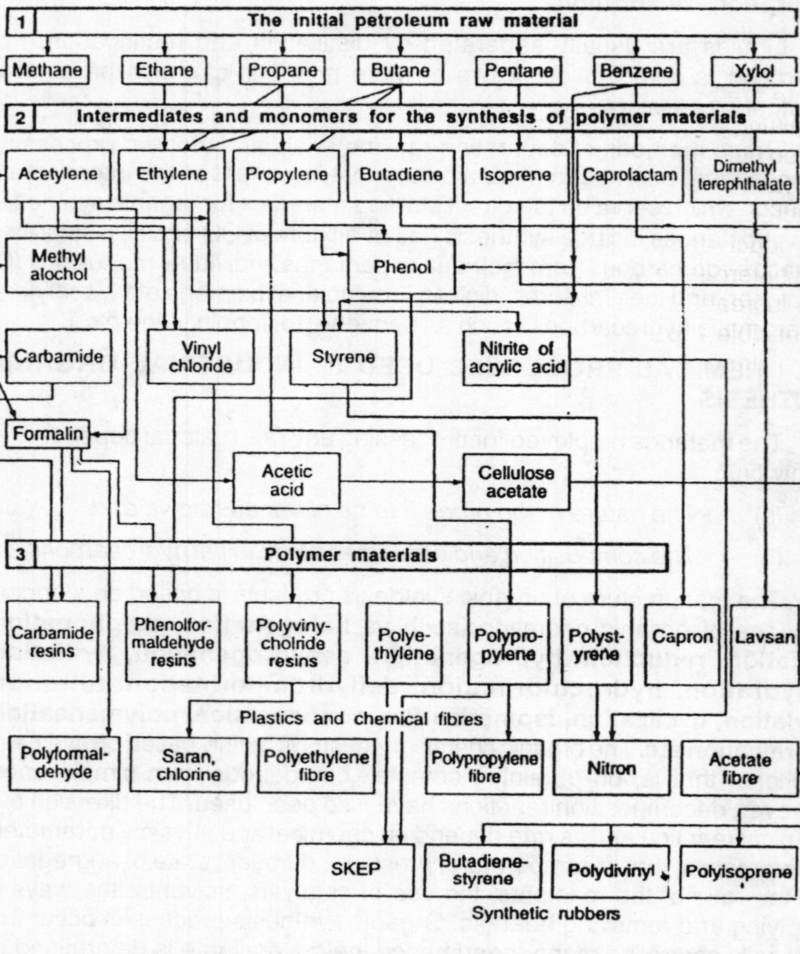

Fig. 1 Petroleum products used as raw materials in industrial synthesis.

reaction to that of the side reactions. In accordance with this, a commonly used means for accelerating the processes of organic synthesis is to use selective catalysts which are capable of accelerating the rate of main reaction only. Here not only the functional relation changes, but also the reaction order. Different ways of accelerating a process are used in the technology of organic synthesis. Among them are :

(a) *An increase in the driving force of the process*

(b) *An increase in the rate constant of the reaction.*

(c) *An increase in the phase contact surface area in heterogeneous processes.*

In gas reactions such as **chlorination, oxidation and hydrogenation,** widely used in organic synthesis, the driving force of the-process and its rate are increased by changing the temperature and pressure and thereby shifting the equilibrium towards maximum formation of end products and also by using catalysts that accelerate the process by decreasing the energy of activation. In **sorption process,** the driving force of the process is increased by increasing the concentration of the reactants or removing the product (desorption) from the reaction zone. The phase contact surface area in heterogeneous processes taking place in the diffusion, controlled region is increased by intensive mixing of the reacting masses. Mixing makes it possible to increase the rate constant due to lowering of the diffusion resistances preventing the reaction of the components (replacement of molecular diffusion by convection).

Polymerisation, hydrogenation and other processes resulting in a decrease in volume are often carried out at medium or high pressures. to accelerate the process and to increase the equilibrium yield. **Gas-absorption, processes,** which are frequently encountered in organic synthesis, can be carried out with advantage at high pressures. The inverse processes of **desorption, dehydrogenation, splitting of molecules** to produce gaseous products should-be carried- out under vacuum.

Not only catalysts, but initiators, and photosynthesis and irradiation techniques have also been used to increase the rate constant in making organic intermediates. For example, oxidation of paraffinic hydrocarbons, chlorination of benzene, polymerisation of ethylene, the manufacture of graft polymers, vulcanisation of rubber etc. can be carried out using ionising radiation, and in many cases the products formed are much better than those obtained in an ordinary manner. Thus sulphochlorinated polyethylene, following irradiation, possesses higher heat resistance and also resistance to acids and strong oxidising agents, including ozone, One of the most important advantage of radiation-chemical reactions is considerable reduction of the induction period.

The intensification of organic synthesis processes is also associated with the use of continuous apparatuses. Preference has been given to continuous apparatuses such as column type reactors, tubular reactors, and contact apparatuses, made from corrosion resistant and heat resistant materials. Whether or not a given method should be used for intensifying a process depends on economic factors particularly on the need to use complex equipment. Development of'new production schemes and new processes has been accompanied by continuous improvements in the design of equipment. New and improved apparatus provides a continuous process throughout the complete chain of manufacturing operations and integral utilization of raw materials. Modern organic synthesis plants are made up of a combination of various production sections, where, in addition to the basic end products, various coproducts, formerly the waste products, are recovered and processed.

Organic synthesis processes can be classified according to various features, but generally they are divided according to the raw materials used.

It should be noted that utilization of various means for intensifying production processes is often limited by the low stability of the organic compounds at higher temperatures (due to decomposition of the molecules of the starting materials and the products).

Processes of organic synthesis have had a great effect on the technology of petroleum processing plants. Since the organic synthesis manufacturing processes are almost limitless, only some of the most typical and economically important are discussed in this chapter.

PETROCHEMICALS

***Petrochemicals** are those chemicals. which are derived from petroleum, including natural gas.* The first petrochemical, except carbon black, manufactured on an industrial scale was **isopropyl alcohol in 1920.** Their number has now increased to more than 4000. The petrochemical industry has grown up so rapidly that even the monopoly of coal to supply aromatic chemicals has disappeared. This is partly due to the large production of aromatic compounds by physical separation from petroleum, but principally because of the conversion of petroleum raw materials into aromatics. The petrochemicals now form the basic raw materials in the manufacture of a large number of other materials, such as fertilizers (ammonia), plastics, fibres, rubbers (nylon, polyester, acetate etc.) and paints. They have also been used in the manufacture of pesticides, lubricants, adhesives and solvents. Many important processes, such as production of ammonia, acetone,- ethyl alcohol, acetic acid, acetic anhydride, glycerine and others are now based wholly or significantly upon petrochemicals. It will not *be amiss to say that more than 80% of the organic chemicals used in chemical industry are based on petrochemicals.*

The production of petrochemicals is based on chemical conversions which are usually continuous and give rise to large volumes of the petrochemicals. The manufacturing procedures of some of the petrochemicals are given below :

METHYL ALCOHOL, CH_3OH

(I) From Synthesis Gas- Methanol is synthesised from carbon monoxide and hydrogen (synthesis gas) under high pressure in the presence of a catalyst.

$$CO + 2H_2 \ CH_30H \ ; \Delta H \rightarrow 24.6 \text{ k. cals.}$$

Hydrogen and carbon monoxide are obtained from the natural gas. The latter is desulphurised by passing over activated carbon, preheated and mixed with steam and carbon dioxide under 2 atmospheric pressure. CO_2 required for the reaction is obtained by burning natural gas in excess of air.

$$CH_4 + 2O_2(\text{air}) \rightarrow CO_2 + 2H_2O$$

The mixture of natural gas, carbon dioxide and steam is then passed through alloy steel tubes, packed with promoted nickel catalyst and then heated to about 800°C in a furnace. As a result, synthesis gas ($CO + 2H_2$) is obtained.

$$3CH_4 + CO_2 + 2H_2O - 4CO + 8H_2$$

Synthesis gas ($CO + 2H_2$) or a mixture of carbonmonoxide and hydrogen (1 : 2) is compressed to 3000-5000 p.s.i, and then preheated at 300°C by passing through a **heat exchanger.** The pre-heated mixture is passed into a copper lined **steel converter** containing a bed of mixed catalysts, e.g., zinc oxide with 10% chromium oxide, Cr_2O_3. The reaction is highly exothermic and takes place with a decrease in volume. The enhanced pressure would, therefore; result in more favourable equilibrium (Le Chatelier Principle). Since the reaction is exothermic. The temperature of the reaction is maintained at about 300°C by cooling once the reaction has started. The temperature is also kept constant by controlling the space velocity of the incoming gases and proper heat exchange. The issuing gases are cooled to 0°-20°C and then condensed in high pressure **condensers,** where methanol is condensed at 3000- 4000 p.s.i. The liquid methanol is drawn off and the residual gases are recycled. The crude methanol, on distillation gives 99% pure methanol. The yield is about 60% without recycling. Dimethyl ether (1-2%) and higher alcohols, such as -n-propanol and isopropanol (0.3-0.5%) are obtained as byproducts.

IMPORTANT POINTS

Methyl alcohol is an important raw material for the manufacture of formaldehyde, dimethyl sulphate, dimethyl terephthalate, methyl acetate, dimethyl formamide, tetra ethyl lead, inhibitors, antifreeze; methylamine, the methyl ester of acrylic acid, varnishes, dyes and a large number of other products. Pure methyl alcohol is used as a solvent and as a high octane admixture to motor fuels.

In the manufacture of methyl alcohol, a synthesis gas mixture with a $CO : H_2$ ratio of 1 : 4 to 1 : 8 is used. The process is carried out at 350 - 400°C and 200-300 atm. pressure in the presence of a mixed zinc-chromium ($ZnO + Cr_2O_3$) catalyst. The basic reaction is

$$CO + 2H_2 \rightleftharpoons CH_3OH + 111\ kJ \quad (1)$$

If the pressure is below 200-300 atm. and temperature is above 350-400°C, then the following side reactions may also occur simultaneously.

$$CO + 3H_2 \rightleftharpoons CH_4 + H_2O + 209\ kJ \quad (2)$$

$$2CO + 2H_2 \rightleftharpoons CH_4 + CO_2 + 252\ kJ \quad (3)$$

$$2CO \rightleftharpoons C0_2 + C \quad (4)$$

$$CO + H_2 \rightleftharpoons HCHO + 8.4\ kJ \quad (5)$$

$$2CH_3OH \rightleftharpoons CH_3 - O - CH_3 + H_2O \quad (6)$$

$$CH_3OH + nCO + 2nH_2 \rightarrow CH_3(CH_2)nOH + nH_2O \quad (7)$$

$$CH_3OH + H_2 \rightarrow CH_4 + H_2O \quad (8)$$

The amount of a given side product depends on temperature, pressure, composition of initial gas mixture, the selectivity and the physical conditions of the catalyst. Methane as a rule is the most significant admixture. The formation of methyl alcohol results in maximum decrease in volume as compared to the side reactions 2-8, and hence increase in pressure would shift the equilibrium towards the right (formation of CH_3OH). Since the reaction (1) is exothermic, the increase in temperature will shift the equilibrium to the left and degree of conversion of synthesis gas into CH_3OH decreases. However, if the temperature is not high enough, the rate of reaction will be slow and hence the process is carried out within a narrow temperature range with fluctuations not exceeding 20-30°C.

Because of insufficient activity and selectivity of the catalyst used, the actual yield is always less than the equilibrium value.

The zinc-chromium catalyst, employed in industry is made by precipitating oxides of zinc and chromium in the ratio $ZnO : Cr_2O_3 \approx 2 : 1$. The catalyst is reduced in a stream of the synthesis gas. The period during which the catalyst operates continuously without needing regeneration is from 4 to 6 months.

Studies of synthesis of CH_3OH over a $ZnO + Cr_2O3$ catalyst in a fluidised bed in a wide range of temperatures (300-400°C) and pressures (50-250 atm) at a very high space velocities of 358000 to 800000 per hour, $H_2 : CO = 2.6 : 8$, mean diameter of the catalyst pellets 0.38-2.5mm, showed that the overall rate of the synthesis reaction depends on hydrogen adsorption.

Industrially, synthesis of methanol is carried out according to the flow diagram of Fig. 3. The initial gas mixture, after preliminary removal of

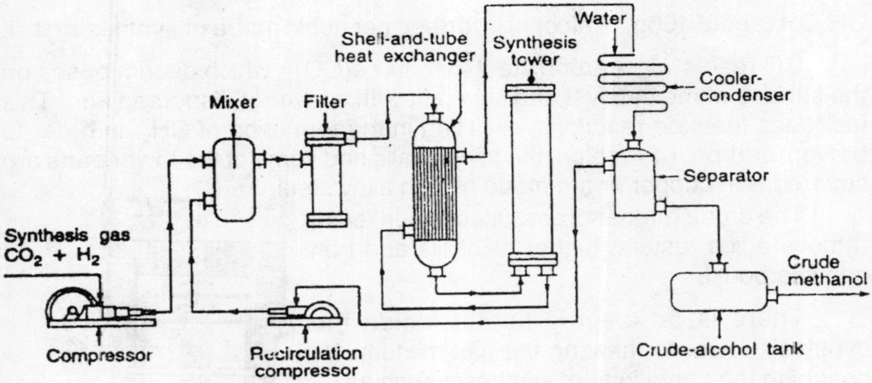

Fig. 3. Industrial methanol synthesis from CO and H_2.

Fig.3. Industrial methanol synthesis from CO and H_2.

impurities, is compressed in a five stage compressor to 250 atms. A cooler removes the heat of compression after each stage. Fresh gas is then mixed with recycled gas in a mixter and after passing through a filter for removing oil, it enters into the tubes of a heat exchanger, where it is heated to about 220°C by the gases leaving the reactor and then it is introduced into the synthesis tower. The temperature in the tower is maintained by the heat of reaction, part of which is taken up by the gas mixture flowing through the heat exchanger tubes on its way to catalyst zone. For controlling the temperature, cold gas mixture can also be introduced into the synthesis tower. Synthesis towers differ in the type of packing used. In **shelf type towers** the catalyst is placed in several beds and gas is consecutively allowed to pass through each bed. Fig. 4 shows a methanol synthesis tower in which the catalyst basket, electric heater and heat exchanger are all contained in a single body.

The synthesis gas ($CO + H_2$) enters at the top and passes down through the annular space between the tower body and the catalyst basket. The gas then flows through the intertube space of the heat exchanger, where its temperature is in creased by removing heat from the synthesis gases flowing inside the heat exchanger tubes. The contact gases leave the tower at the bottom and after giving up heat to initial gas mixture in the heat exchanger, they flow through a water cooler condenser to a separator. Here the crude CH_3OH (96%) is separated from the unreacted gases, which are compressed by a recycle compressor to the pressure of the initial gas and are transferred to the mixer and methyl alcohol is transferred to a crude alcohol tank. Since the impurities and products of various side reactions such as methane, nitrogen, carbon dioxide etc, accumulate in the circulating gas mixture, it is periodically brought up to standard by burning part of the recycle gas. About 700 m^3 of CO and 1400-2000 m^3 of H_2 are consumed to produce 1 ton of

CH_3OH (about 400g. of alcohol is formed per cubic metre of synthesis gas).

CO reacts with carbon steel to form $Fe(CO)_5$, which decom poses on the surface of the catalyst and covers it with a layer of dispersed iron. This facilitates the side reactions, resulting in the formation of CH_4. In order to prevent carbonyl corrosion, the tower walls and some of the tower parts are covered with copper or are made of high alloy steel.

The crude methanol produced is purified to remove acids, esters, higher alcohols and iron pentacarbonyl.

There is an electric heater inside the synthesis tower for heating the gas mixture. By changing the conditions of synthesis such as,

(a) The temperature.

(b) The pressure.

(c) The CO-to-H_2 ratio of the initial gas mixture, and

(d) The composition of the catalyst,

not only methyl alcohol, but also higher alcohols, aldehydes, ketones, esters, organic acids, saturated and unsaturated hydrocarbons with any desired chain length upto that of solid paraffins,but primarily with unbranched structures can be obtained. The initial gas mixture must be carefully purified to remove sulphurous compounds, tars, dust and other harmful impurities.

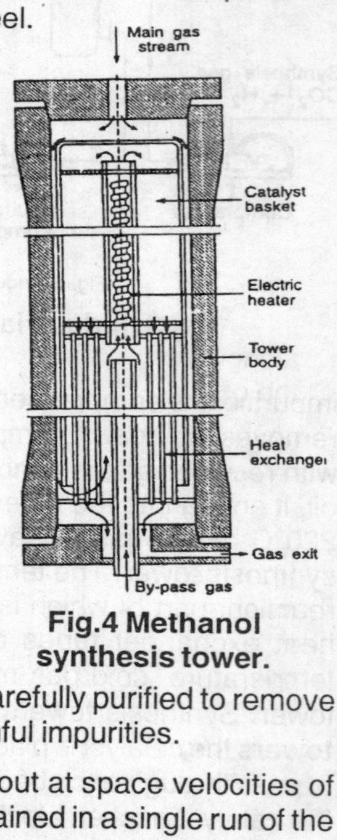

Fig.4 Methanol synthesis tower.

In industrial conditions, synthesis is carried out at space velocities of 20,000 - 40,000 hour-1 and the yield of CH_3OH obtained in a single run of the mixture through the catalyst is about 4%. If space velocity is increased to 100,000 hour-1, conversion of the initial mixture for one pass is reduced but if recycle schemes are used, the amount of methyl alcohol produced increases because the degree of conversion is lower than increase in the space velocity.

(2) From Carbon dioxide and Hydrogen-Carbon dioxide obtained from the burning of natural gas in air can also be used instead of carbon monoxide.

$$CH_4 + 2O_2(air) \rightarrow CO_2 + 2H_2O \qquad CO_2 + 3H_2 \rightarrow CH_3OH + H_2O$$

The crude methanol thus obtained contains about 25 percent water. The mixture of methanol and water is conveyed to a continuous refining column and the overhead from this column is dimethyl ether and some methanol. The bottoms are allowed to pass through a second column, where methanol is collected as overhead, while water comes out from the bottom. If a fraction is collected from the portion near to the bottom of the column, it is found to contain about 30% methanol, 50% higher alcohols and ethanol and 20% water.

(3) By Partial Oxidation of Natural Gas - Methanol can also be obtained by the- partial oxidation of natural gas and other lighter hydrocarbons by air in presence of a catalyst at temperatures between 430-480°C and pressures from 7-20 atmospheres. A suitable catalyst is aluminium phosphate mixed with metal oxide. The product contains about 35% methanol and varying amounts of formaldehyde, higher aldehydes, ketones, alcohols, water etc. The mixture is fractionally distilled to get pure compounds.

$$CH_4 + O_2(air) \xrightarrow[\text{Catalyst 7-20atm.}]{410\text{-}480^{\circ}C} CH_3OH + HCHO + \text{Higher aldehydes} + \text{ketones} + \text{alcohols} + \text{water}$$

(4) By Vapour Phase Oxidation of Propane or Butane - Methanol alongwith a complex mixture of organic compounds can also be produced by the oxidation of propane or butane with oxygen of air.

$$C_3H_8 \text{ or } C_4H_{10} + O_2 \text{ (air)} \rightarrow CH_3OH + HCHO + CH_3CHO + \text{Other aldehydes} + \text{Ketones},$$
$$+ \text{Acids} + \text{Alcohols} +. CO + CO_2 + N_2 \text{ etc.}$$

Propane or butane is first mixed with compressed air and recycle gases from the **absorber** in the ratio of 1 : 2 : 7 parts by volume respectively. The mixture is then compressed to about 6-7 atmospheric pressure and introduced into a **tube furnace** where it is heated to about 380°C. The hot gaseous mixture is then fed to a reactor which is a steel tube with a section near the outlet packed with ceramic shapes. The temperature in the reactor increases to about 450°C, because of the exothermic nature of the reaction. The oxidation of hydrocarbon takes place in the reactor tube and any peroxide formed is decomposed by the ceramic shapes. The hot reaction gases are then passed through a **quencher scrubber** which operates under controlled temperature and pressure conditions in such a manner that organic compounds other than formaldehyde are not absorbed and they leave the scrubeer as ovehead. In the quencher, the hot gases meet a .spray of cold dilute (10-14%) aqueous formaldehyde solution. Formaldehyde vapours are **absorbed** in aqueous formaldehyde solution and a concentrated aqueous solution of formaldehyde is collected from the bottom of the **quencher** and sent for recovery of formaldehyde. The gaseous mixture then passes through a **scrubber**, where it meets a spray of water. As a result, unreacted hydrocarbons and fixed gases like N_2, CO and $C0_2$ etc. separate out and most of organic compounds go into the solution. A major part (about 70%) of this hydrocarbon mixture is recycled and mixed with compressed air and propane or butane as described above, while 25 percent is passed for hydrocarbon recovery.

The aqueous solution containing most of the organic compounds is collected at the bottom of the water scrubber. It is, withdraw from the water scrubber and fed to a **flash tower**, where low boiling organic compounds are vapourised and the vapours leave the tower as overhead. The latter is conveyed to a **purification unit** where it is subjected to distillation with combination of straight extraction. Here about forty components, including methanol are separated.

The dilute acidic solution collected at the bottom of the **flash tower** is withdrawn from the bottom, cooled, neutralised with sodium hydroxide solution and recycled to the **quencher scrubber.**

It has been observed that 10 kg of butane gives 2.0 kg of methanol, 3.3 kg of formaldehyde, 3.1 kg. of acetaldehyde, 0.4 kg of acetone and about 1.2 kg of mixed solvents.

Methanol is a colourless, mobile, inflammable liquid (b.p. 64.5°C) with a characteristic smell and burning taste. It is highly poisonous, causing blindness and-death. It is. soluble in water, ether and alcohol.

Methanol finds a wide variety of direct industrial uses, such as antifreeze for automobile radiators, fuel and solvent for shellac, paints, lacquers, ethyl cellulose etc. It is a starting material in such reactions as the preparation of formaldehyde, methyl amine and dimethyl aniline. About half of the methanol produced is converted into formaldehyde, which is required in huge quantity for plastics.

ETHANOL OR C_2H_5OH OR INDUSTRIAL ALCOHOL

(1) From Ethylene and Sulphuric Acid - Ethanol may be synthesised by first absorbing ethylene (obtained by cracking a mixture of ethane and propane followed by purification) in 94-95% sulphuric acid to give a mixture of ethyl hydrogen sulphate and diethyl sulphate.The mixture is then hydrolysed to get ethanol and sulphuric acid. The alcohol is purified by distillation and the sulphuric acid is concentrated and reused in the process.

Absorption : $CH_2 = CH_2 + H_2SO_4 \rightarrow \underset{\text{Ethylhydrogen sulphate}}{CH_3CH_2OSO_3H}$

$$2CH_2 = CH_2 + H_2SO_4 \rightarrow \underset{\text{Diethyl sulphate}}{(CH_3CH_2)_2SO_4}$$

Hydrolysis : $CH_3CH_2OSO_3H + H_20 \rightarrow CH_3CH_2OH + H_2SO_4$

$$(CH_3CH_2)_2S0_4 + 2H_20 \rightarrow 2CH_3CH_20H + H_2SO_4$$

$$CH_3CH_2OSO_3H + (CH_3CH_2)_2SO_4 + 3H_2O \rightarrow CH_3CH_2OH + 2H_2SO_4$$

Side Reaction : $2C_2H_5\,OH \xrightarrow{H_2SO_4} \underset{\text{diethyl ether}}{C_2H_5OC_2H_5} + H_2O$

Ethylene (35-95%) under 150-200 p.s.i. pressure is passed into the bottom of an **absorption tower,** from the top of which 90-95% sulphuric acid

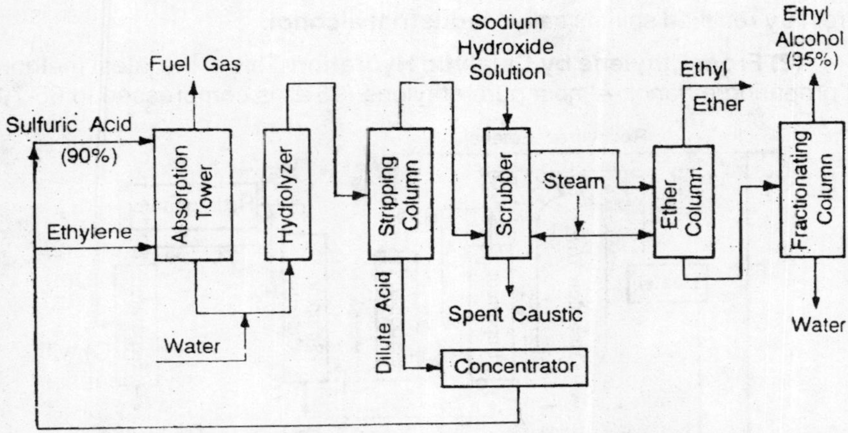

Fig. 5. Manufacture of C_2H_5OH by esterification and hydrolysis.

is sprayed, so that ethylene is absorbed in sulphuric acid. The reactions are exothermic and the temperature is maintained at 50-80°C by controlling the rate of feed of ethylene and sulphuric acid. Catalysts such as oxides of iron or copper may be added for better absorption. Ethyl hydrogen sulphate and diethyl sulphate are thus formed. The unabsorbed gas escapes from the top of the absorption tower and is used as a fuel. The mixture of esters is dicharged from the bottom of the tower and pumped into the bottom of a hydrolyser after diluting it with 1-2 volumes of water. The mixture is kept at 70°C for about 4 hours in the hydrolyser. The esters are hydrolysed by water to form ethanol. Diethyl ether (5-10%) is also formed. The mixture of crude ethanol, dilute sulphuric acid, diethyl ether etc. passes through a **stripping column** from the bottom of which steam is led in. Alcohol, ether and traces of acid are carried over by the stream as overhead. Dilute sulphuric acid is withdrawn from the bottom of stripping column and concentrated in **vacuum evaporators** and reused in the process.

The overhead containing ethanol, diethyl ether and traces of acid is then passed into the bottom of a **scrubber** from the top of which NaOH solution is sprayed. The alkali neutralises the acid and the spent alkali is withdrawn from the bottom. The mixture of alcohol, ether and water vapours leaves from the top, which is then condensed to get the liquid mixture. The liquid mixture is passed into an **ether column** from the bottom of which steam is allowed to pass. The overhead is diethyl ether which is dehydrated and used as such or subjected to catalytic hydration to get ethyl alcohol. The alcohol collected at the bottom of the ether column is conveyed to a **fractionating column,** where it is purified by fractional distillation. The vapours of 25% alcohol escape from the top of the fractionating column and they are condensed to give 95% pure ethanol. The ethanol thus formed is called **rectified spirit.** One gallon of 95% ethanol is obtained from 4 lb of ethylene.

Ordinary rectified spirit is called **industrial alcohol.**

(2) From Ethylene by Catalytic Hydration-This is the latest method of preparing ethanol. Almost pure ethylene (95%) is compressed to 65-70

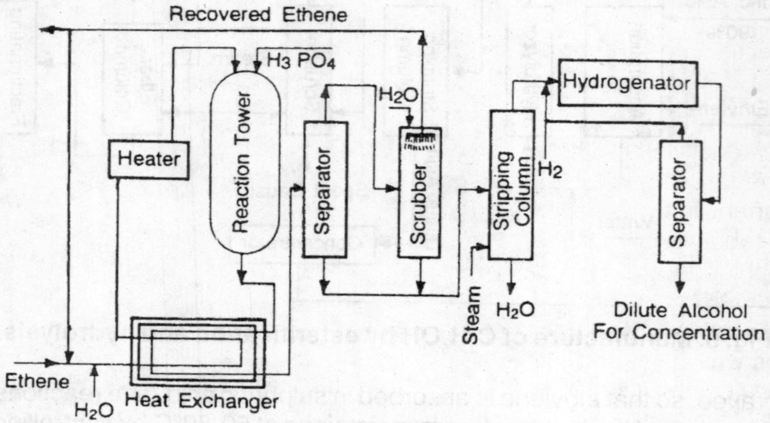

Fig. 6. Preparation of ethyl alcohol by catalytic hydration.

atmospheric pressure and mixed with unreacted recycle ethylene. The combined compressed ethylene mixture is then mixed with water (0.6 mole per mole of ethylene). The ethylene water mixture is **vapourised** by passing through a **heat exchanger** and the vapours are again heated to 300°C in a **gas fired furnace.** The hot vapours are then led to a reactor, where they pass over the catalyst (inert diatomaceous earth soaked with 85-90% phosphoric acid). The ethylene is hydrated with water to form ethanol. Conversion per pass is, however, low, i.e., about 4% only. The gases from the reactor are passed through a **dilute caustic soda solution** to remove the adhering acid that may have been vapourised. The reaction is exothermic. The mixture is then passed into **high pressure separator,** where ethylene (unreacted) separates out as a gas from alcohol water mixture. The gas is **scrubbed** with water in a **scrubber** to remove traces of alcohol and then recycled. Some acetaldehyde also results due to the hydration of acetylene (present as impurity in 95% ethylene). Alcohol water mixture containing some acetaldehyde is passed into a **stripping column,** where steam is led in from the bottom. As a result, concentrated alcohol solution **together** with acetaldehyde passes as overhead and water is withdrawn from the bottom. The overhead is vapourised and then **hydrogenated** with hydrogen gas in presence of nickel as a catalyst. As a result of catalytic hydro-genation, acetaldehyde is converted into ethyl alcohol. The excess of hydrogen is separated by **condensation** of the products and again used. The liquid from the bottom of the hydrogenator is purifed by **fractional distillation** to get 95% alcohol, called **rectified spirit or industrial alcohol.**

$$H_2O + CH_2 = CH_2 \xrightarrow{H_3PO_4} CH_3CH_2OH$$

$$CH \equiv CH + H_2O \rightarrow CH_3CHO \qquad CH_3CHO + H_2O \xrightarrow{Ni} CH_3CH_2OH$$

The yield of ethanol is 95-97%.

IMPORTANT POINTS

Ethylene, propylene, butylene and butadiene (divinyl), all of which are highly reactive compounds, are very important in industrial organic synthesis. Of the large number of reactions into which olefins take part, the most important industrially are **polymerisation** (polyethylene, polypropylene, polyisobutylene etc.), **hydration** (alcohols), **chlorination** (dichloroethanes, allyl chloride etc.), **oxidation** (ethylene oxide), **oxo-synthesis** and many others. Processes in which olefin hydrocarbons are hydrated are extensively used now, because ethyl, isopropyl and other alcohols can be manufactured in this way.

From year to year the production of alcohol from food grains or food product raw materials is being replaced by its production through synthesis, hydrolysis and sulphite process. One ton of ethylene is equivalent to 4 tons of food grain. Synthetic alcohol made from ethylene costs several times less than that made from food products and less labour is involved in its production.

Synthetic alcohol is widely used in industry for making synthetic rubber, celluloid, acetaldehyde, acetic acid, artificial silk, pharmaceuticals, perfumes, cordite, as a solvent etc.

Hydration of ethylene can be carried out by two methods (a) Using sulphuric acid **(Sulphuric acid hydration),** and (b) By the forward reaction of ethylene with steam over a solid catalyst **(vapour phase-catalytic hydration).** The sulphuric acid industrial method consists of four operations.

(a) *Absorption of ethylene with sulphuric acid to produce ethyl sulphate*

(b) *Hydrolysis of the esters.*

(c) Separation of the alcohol and its rectification.

(d) *Concentration of sulphuric acid.*

The reaction between ethylene and sulphuric acid occurs in two stages :

(a) *Physical dissolution of ethylene into the acid, and*

(b) *Homogeneous reaction of both components to form alkyl sulphates.*

$$C_2H_4 + H_2SO_4 \rightleftharpoons C_2H_5HSO_4$$

$$C_2H_5HSO_4 + C_2H_4 \rightleftharpoons (C_2H_5O)_2SO_2$$

Under the conditions in which the process is carried out, diethyl sulphate can react with H_2SO_4 to form ethyl sulphate.

$$(C_2H_5O)_2SO_2 + H_2SO_4 \rightleftharpoons 2C_2H_5HSO_4$$

Sulphuric acid absorbs ethylene at a slower rate than other gaseous olefins (e.g. hundreds of times slower than isobutylene). The rate of absorption of ethylene increases, as the ethylsulphuric acid (ethyl sulphate), in which

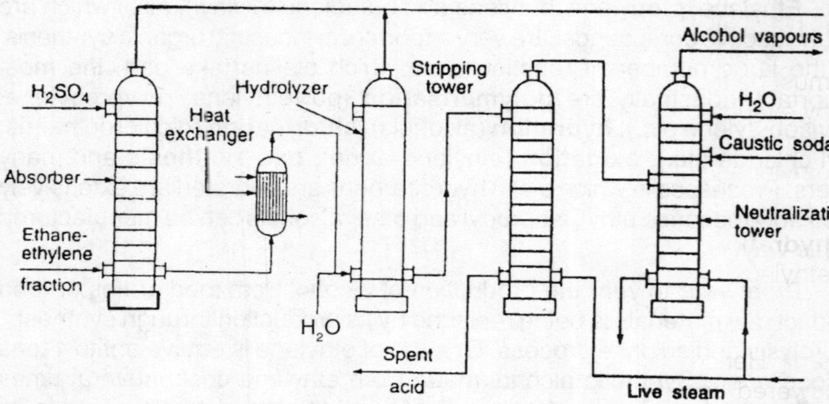

Fig.7. Flow diagram of the process for manufacturing ethyl alcohol by sulphuric acid-ethylene hydration.

ethylene is dissolved better, is formed. But the rate of overall reaction decreases because of simultaneous decrease in the concentration of H_2SO_4. The required concentration of 0.6 mole C_2H_4 per mole of H_2SO_4 in the upper part of the absorber is achieved with 97.5% H_2SO_4 in 75 minutes (That is, twice as rapid as with 95% H_2SO_4 (135 minutes). Hence it is best to use 97-98% H_2SO_4.

The optimum temperature for the reaction is 65-75°C. If it is increased the amount of ethyl sulphuric acid formed decreases. When the pressure is increased, the rate of absorption and the degree of saturation of H_2SO_4 with ethylene increase.

Intensive agitation is very important for the process. For this bubble type towers are used, because they provide better agitation than that obtained by packed towers. In the second stage, ethyl and di-ethyl sulphates undergo, hydrolysis.

$$C_2H_5HSO_4 + H_2O \rightleftharpoons C_2H_5OH + H_2SO_4$$

$$(C_2H_5O)SO_2 + 2H_2O \rightleftharpoons 2C_2H_5OH + H_2SO_4$$

Along with above reactions, diethyl ether,is also formed.

$$(C_2H_5O)_2SO_2 + C_2H_5OH \rightleftharpoons C_2H_5OC_2H_5 + C_2H_5HSO_4$$

$$(C_2H_5O)_2SO_2 + H_2O \rightleftharpoons C_2H_5OC_2H_5 + H_2SO_4$$

In addition, acetaldehyde is formed and polymerisation of ethylene may also occur. Inorder to reduce the amount of diethyl ether, hydrolysis is generally carried out at the maximum possible rate and the alcohol formed is immediately .stripped from the solution, ,so as to keep its concentration very low.

The weak sulphuric acid formed after the formation of alcohol is subjected to purification for removing tarry impurities, and after concentration is again,fed to the absorber. For producing one ton of alcohol two tons of conc. H_2SO_4 must be fed to the absorber, i.e. 4 tons of weak acid must be concentrated by evaporation. The sulphuric acid method yields 1.2 tons of cruce alcohol and about 100 kg of ethyl ether per ton of ethylene used. About 90% of ethylene feed is converted into alcohol.

In recent years an improved method, known as **vapour phasecatalytic hydration** with a recycle flow scheme has widely been used. Hydration of ethylene is an exothermic reversible reaction.

$$C_2H_4 + H_2O \rightarrow C_2H_5OH + 45.6 \text{ kJ}$$

Hence according to LeChatelier's principle, the temperature must be lowered and pressure be increased to shift the equilibrium towards the hydration of ethylene.But below 280°C, the rate of hydration is slow and use of pressures above 80 atm is not economical. Phosphoric acid deposited on car rier Kieselguhr, silica gel or alu minosilicate is used as the catalyst. The use of a carrier with large pores causes an increase in the rate of diffusion.

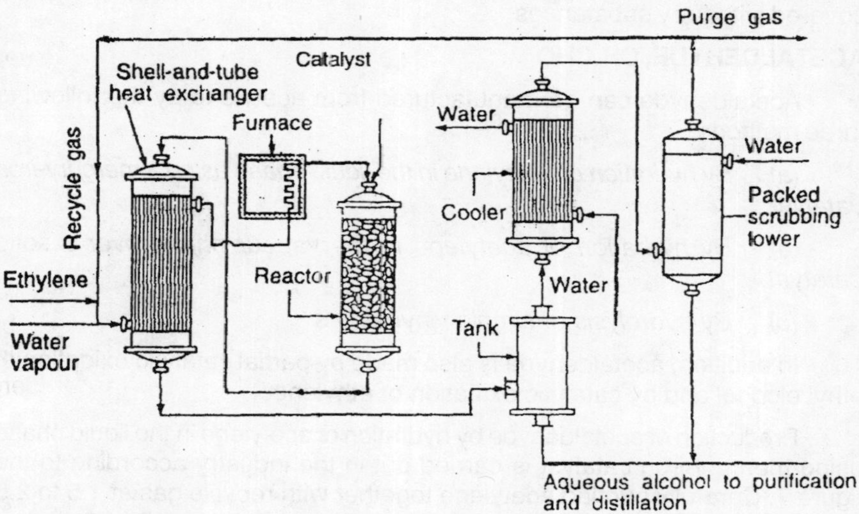

Fig. 8. Flow diagram of process for manufacturing ethyl alcohol by catalytic hydration of ethylene in vapour phase.

From experiments it has been shown that process variables of the reaction between gaseous ethylene and water vapour for a good yield should be : (a) Temperature of 280-290°C (b) Pressure, of 70-80 atm. (c) Ethylene concentration in the recycle gas of 80- 85% by volume (d) Molar ratio of water to :ethylene of 0.6 : 1.0075 : 1 (e) Phosphoric acid concentration on the surface of catalyst atleast 83%, and (f) Space velocity of 1800-2500 hour. These conditions yield a water alcohol solution containing 15-16% alcohol with 4-5% C_2H_4 conversion in one pass. Overall useful consumption of ethylene is about 95%. The remaining 5% ethylene is converted into 2% diethyl ether, 1% acetaldehyde and 2% dimers and polymers.

The direct hydration of ethylene involves the following continuous operations.

(a) *Preparation of initial vapour-gas mixture.*
(b) *Hydration of ethylene.*
(c) *Neutralisation of the vapours of reaction products.*
(d) *Recuperation of the heat of recycle streams, and*
(e) *Purification of the recycle gas.*

The hydration of ethylene is carried out in catalytic reactor lined with copper to protect it against corrosion.

About 0.685 tons of ethylene, 5.6 kg of phosphoric acid, 2 kg of carrier and 16 kg of caustic soda are consumed per ton of ethyl alcohol produced. The service time of catalyst is upto 600 hours. This time can be increased by spraying pulverized phosphoric acid into the reaction during the course of the reaction. After which it has to be replaced because its surface gets covered with tarry substances.

ACETALDEHYDE, CH_3CHO

Acetaldehyde can be manufactured from acetylene by the following three methods.

(a) *By hydration of acetylene in the liquid phase using a mercury-iron catalyst.*

(b) *By hydration of acetylene in the vapour phase over a* solid *catatyst.*

(c) *By hydrolysis of simple vinyl ethers.*

In addition, acetaldehyde is also made by partial catalytic oxidation of ethyl elcohol and by catalytic oxidation of ethylene.

Production of acetaldehyde by hydration of acetylene in the liquid phase using mercury-iron catalyst is carried out in the industry according to the figure 7. Carefully purified acetylene together with recycle gas at 1.5 to 2.5 atm pressure is continuously passed in a hydrator through a liquid catalyst containing a solution of Hg(II) sulphate in H_2SO_4. The Hg (II) is reduced to Hg(I) and then to Hg because acetaldehyde is a reducing agent.

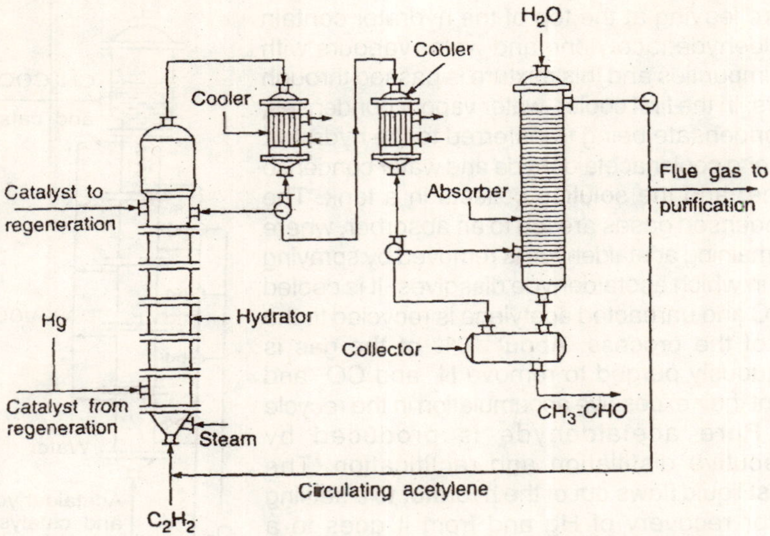

Fig. 9. Flow diagram of manufacture of acetaldehyde by liquid phase hydration of acetylene

$$2Hg_2SO_4 + H_2O + CH_3CHO \rightarrow Hg_2SO_4 + H_2SO_4 + CH_3COOH$$

$$Hg_2SO_4 + H_20 + CH_3CHO \rightarrow 2Hg + H_2SO_4 + CH_3COOH$$

Inorder to maintain the necessary composition of the catalyst liquid, Hg metal and an oxidising agent are added which in the presence of H_2SO_4 transform the mercury metal to Hg(II) sulphate required for the hydration of acetylene.

$$2Hg + Fe_2(SO_4)_3 \xrightarrow{H_2SO_4} Hg_2SO_4 + 2FeSO_4$$

$$Hg_2SO_4 + Fe_2(SO_4)_3 \rightarrow 2HgSO_4 + 2FeSO_4$$

Hg metal is periodically introduced. It is sprayed into the reactor through a funnel at the top (about 0.1 kg of Hg is lost per ton of CH_3CHO produced). Under these conditions 50-60% of C_2H_2 is hydrated.

$$CH \equiv CH + H_2O \rightarrow CH_3CHO + 151\ Kg$$

The hydrator is a column with a conical bottom and a widened top. It is made of ferrosilicon or of stainless steel. Each of the bubbler trays of the hydrator operates in accordance with a model which is closer to complete mixing then to plug flow both w.r.t. the gas and the liquid. The gas and liquid move through the tray in cross flow. Since there is a large number of trays in the tower process calculations can be carried out for counter current plug flow through the tower. The temperature in the hydrator is maintained at

80-100°C by introducing live steam. The steam gas mixture leaving at the top of the hydrator contain acetaldehyde, acetylene and water vapours with other impurities and this mixture is passed through coolers. In the first cooler, water vapour condenses, the condensate being transferred to the hydrator. In second cooler acetaldehyde and water condense together and the solution collects in a tank. The uncondensed gases are fed to an absorber, where the remaining acetaldehyde is removed by spraying water in which acetaldehyde dissolves. It is cooled to 10°C and unreacted acetylene is recycled to the head of the process. About 10% of the gas is continuously purged to remove N_2 and CO_2 and prevent their excessive accumulation in the recycle gas. Pure acetaldehyde is produced by consecutive distillation and rectification. The catalyst liquid flows out of the hydrator to a settling tank for recovery of Hg and from it goes to a regeneration tank. The catalyst liquid contains approx. 200g/L of H_2SO_4, 0.5- 0.6g/L mercuric oxide and 40g/L iron oxides. The yield of acetaldehyde w.r.t. acetylene reacted is about 90-95%. One ton of acetaldehyde can be produced from 680 kg of acetylene, 0.1 kg of Hg, 3 tonnes of steam and some amount of H_2SO_4, HNO_3 and iron sulphate.

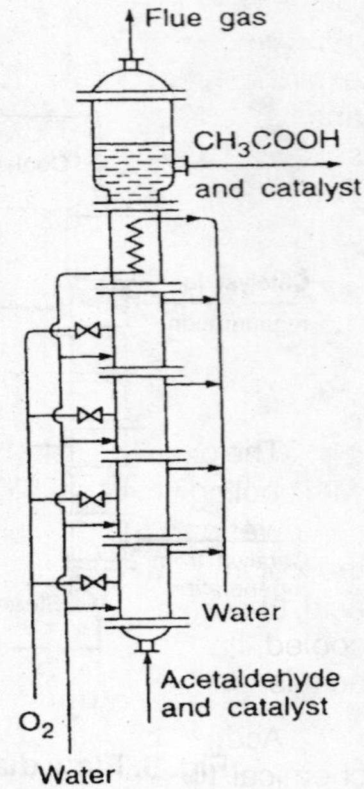

Fig10. Flow diagram of manufacture of acetic acid by odidation of acetaldehyde.

Since mercury is toxic, oxides of Zn, Mg, Ni; Fe, Co, Cr and other metals have also been suggested as catalysts. Heterogeneous catalytic processes of this type can be carried out by using a fluidised bed of the catalyst. The yield of acetaldehyde is 88- 90% of the converted C_2H_2. The degree of conversion per pass is 50%.

ACETIC ACID, CH_3COOH

Acetic acid has been manufactured for a very long time by dry distillation of wood and fermentation of ethyl alcohol. Now acetaldehyde is processed into acetic acid by its liquid phase oxidation by the oxygen of the air at 60-70°C in presence of a catalyst, a solution of manganese acetate, $Mn(CH_3COO)_2$, in acetic acid. The unstable peracetic acid is formed as an intermediate product of oxidation.

$$CH_3CHO + O_2 \rightarrow CH_3COOOH$$

The peracetic acid reacts with a second molecule of acetaldehyde to form a peroxide compound that decomposes into two molecules of acetic acid.

$$CH_3COOOH + CH_3CH0 \rightarrow CH_3CO.O.O.CHOH.CH_3 \rightarrow 2CH_3COOH$$

Accumulation of peracetic acid in the apparatus may cause an explosion. To prevent this, the gas vapour mixture is diluted with nitrogen and the temperature is maintained between 60-75°C. The use of manganese salts as catalyst promotes the reduction of peracetic acid to acetic acid. The process is carried out in tray type oxidising tower similar to that used in making acetaldehyde. The industrial process consists of three stages:

(a) *Oxidation of acetaldehyde.*

(b) *Absorption of acetaldehyde from the discharged gases.*

(c) Separation of acetaldehyde from acetic acid.

The oxidising reactor is column assembled from aluminium sheet drums with cooling coils. A solution of acetaldehyde and catalyst is introduced into the lower part of the column. The oxygen is fed in along the entire height of the column. The vapour gas mixture leaving the reactor contains acetic acid, unreacted acetaldehyde and byproducts of the reaction. The mixture is cooled, the acetaldehyde is recycled to the reactor, while the crude acetic acid is distilled. The yield of acetic acid is 90%.

Acetic acid is semi product of organic synthesis for the production of chemical fibres and plastics, solvents, lacquers and varnishes, fragrant substances, and many other products. Its salts are used as mordants and medicines.

ISOPROPANOL $CH_3CHOHCH_3$

Isopropanol is commercially made from propylene, present in petroleum cracking gases. The mixture of cracked gases rich in propylene is first desulphurised and then passed into the bottom of an **absorption tower** at about 27°C, from the top of which 85% sulphuric acid trickles down. Sulphuric acid meets the propylene gas in a counter current manner and the reaction is exothermic in nature. The tower is, therefore, cooled by circulating brine to prevent the rise in temperature. Nearly half of the propylene is absorbed in the sulphuric acid and isopropyl hydrogen sulphate is the chief product with a little di-isopropyl sulphate. Ethylene (present in the cracked gaseous mixture) is not absorbed under these conditions. The unabsorbed gases are recycled. The higher olefins, such as butenes and pentenes, it present in the cracked gases, are also absorbed alongwith propylene.

The reaction mixture containing isopropyl hydrogen sulphate and di-isopropyl sulphate from the bottom of the **absorption tower** is charged into a closed **lead lined tank**, where the products are.diluted to 20% strength with water. The heat of dilution hydrolyses the isopropyl sulphate into isopropanol and sulphuric acid.

The isopropyl alcohol is removed by passing steam through the reaction mixture and then purified by **distillation.** An **azeotrope** with 91 % isopropanol and 9% water- distils from the top of the **rectifying or distillation column.** It also contains some higher alcohols-which are removed; the azeotrope

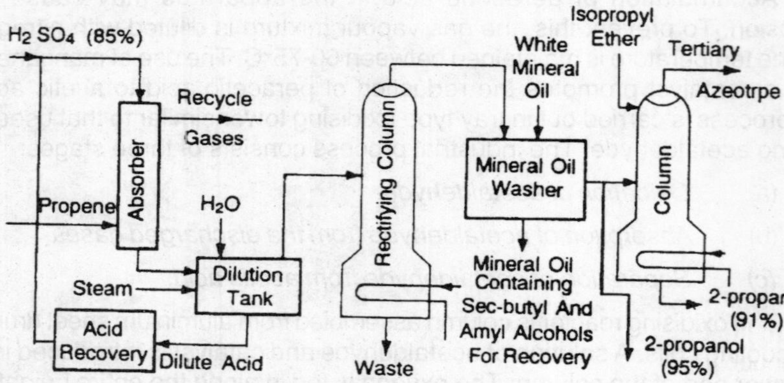

Fig. 11. Preparation of isopropyl alcohol from propene.

mixture is passed through a **mineral oil washer** which selectively absorbs the higher alcohols..

Absolute isopropanol (about 99%) is obtained by the redistillation of 91% alcohol with a little di-isopropyl ether. At about 61.4°C, a ternary azcotrope containing 91.1% isopropyl ether, 5.8% isopropanol and 3.1% water is removed from the top and the anhydrous isopropanol is drawn off from the bottom of the distillating column. The azeotrope is washed with water and various components of it are recovered by fractional distillation. The yield of alcohol is about 70%. The dilute sulphuric acid formed in the reaction is first concentrated and then recycled to be used again. The acid is, however, run to waste after certain cycles, because of the accumulation of tarry material in it.

$$\underset{\text{Propylene}}{CH_3CH = CH_2} + H_2SO_4 \rightarrow \underset{\text{Isopropyl hydrogen sulphate}}{CH_3CH(OSO_3H)CH_3} \xrightarrow{H_2O} CH_3CHOHCH_3 + H_2SO_4$$

Isopropanol is a coiourless'mobile liquid (b.p.82^{0}C). If is soluble in water, ether and ethanol.

It is used as a solvent, as an antifreeze and a component of shaving lotions, nail polishes etc. It is also used in the preparation of acetone.

ETHYLENE GLYCOL, $CH_2OH.CH_2OH$

Ethylene glycol is manufactured from ethylene obtained from cracked petroleum by the following two processes.

(a) Ethylene is passed under a pressure of 200 atmospheres at 200°C into a **tower** of hydrated lime so that it contains about 28 gms. of ethylene per litre of alkali solution. From there, the solution is pumped into a **chlorination chamber** under the same pressure. The chlorine reacts with hydrated lime to form calcium oxychloride ($CaOCl_2$), which immediately decomposes to form bypochlorous acid and calcium chloride.

$$CaO + Cl_2 \rightarrow CaOCl_2 \xrightarrow{Cl_2 + H_2O} 2HOCl + CaCl_2$$

The hypochlorous acid then reacts with ethylene to form ethylene chlorohydrin.

$$CH_2 = CH_2 + HOCl \rightarrow \underset{\text{Ethylene chiorohydrin}}{CH_2(OH).CH_2Cl}$$

The ethylene chlorohydrin solution is withdrawn from the **chlorination chamber** and treated with the requisite quantity of sodium bicarbonate in a **steam jacketed vessel** fitted with stirrer at about 70-80°C. The treatment is continued for about 5-6 hours to ensure complete hydrolysis. Ethylene glycol is recovered by distillation under reduced pressure. The yield is about 65-70%.

$$CH_2(OH).CH_2Cl + NaHCO_3 + H_2O \rightarrow CH_2OH.CH_2OH + CO_2 + NaCl + H_2O$$

(b) Ethylene cholrohydrin can also be converted into ethylene glycol by an indirect method in which chlorohydrin solution is heated with lime or calcium hydroxide to get ethylene oxide. The latter is readily separated from the salts by distillation.

$$CH_2(OH).CH2Cl + Ca(OH)_2 \rightarrow 2\underset{\text{Ethylene oxide}}{\underbrace{CH_2 - CH_2}_{\diagdown O \diagup}} + CaCl_2 + 2H_2O$$

Ethylene oxide can also be prepared by passing a mixture of pure ethylene and air (1 : 10) under atmospheric pressure over silver oxide catalyst at about 300°C for a contact period of about one second. As a result, 60-70% ethylene is converted into ethylene oxide which is absorbed in a liquid and unoxidised ethylene gas and air are recycled. Ethylene oxide is then hydrated with water at 195°C for one hour in a tower or it maybe hydrated with 1% H_2SO_4 at 60°C for about half an hour to get ethylene glycol. The crude glycol thus formed is distilled under reduced pressure to get pure glycol and to separate di- and triethylene glycols which are also foumed during the reaction.

$$CH_2 = CH_2 + \tfrac{1}{2}O_2 \text{ (air)} \xrightarrow{Ag_2O} \underbrace{H_2C - CH_2}_{\diagdown O \diagup} \xrightarrow{H_2O} \underset{\text{Ethylene glycol}}{CH_2OH.CH_2OH}$$

Ethylene glycol is a colourless, syrupy liquid (b.p.197°C) and it is hygroscopic with sweet taste. It is heavier than water (Sp. gr. 1.116) with which it is soluble. It is used as an antifreeze for automobile radiators.

GLYCERINE, $CH_2OH.CHOH.CH_2OH$

Synthetic glycerol can be prepared from propylene obtained from cracked petroleum gases by two different routes.

(1) Via Allyl Chloride. Dry propylene gas (4 moles) is first preheated to about 400°C and then mixed with chlorine gas (1 mole) coming under a pressure of 4 atm. and at 20°C. The mixed gases are then heated in a **steel tube reactor** at 400°C-500°C for 2-3 seconds. The reaction is exothermic and so the temperature is maintained constant by means of insulation provided with the reactor.

The product is then cooled by passing through a **cooler** and then introduced into a **fractionating column,** where allyl chloride is collected at the bottom and excess of propylene, alongwith hydrogen chloride leaves the column at the top. These are separated and propylene is recycled.

Allyl chloride is then introduced in a **tank fitted** with a stirrer and treated with chlorine and water i.e. hypochlorous acid) at about 35°C. As a result, dichlorohydrin is formed. The product is sent to a **separator**, where it is separated into two layers, the aqueous layer of hypochlorous acid and non aqueous layer of dichlorohydrin as the main product. The aqueous layer of hypochlrous acid is separated from the non aqueous layer and recy cled. The non aqueous layer is introduced into a **reactor**, where it is allowed to react with milk of lime at about 60°C, and the product is **steam distilled.** As a result, epichlorohydrin distils over with steam. Epichlorohydrin is purified by distillation and then **hydrolysed** with 10% caustic soda solution at about 150°C for half an hour. Dilute glycerine (5%) and sodium chloride are thus formed. The product is first steam distilled under vacuum to get 8% refined glycerol. The latter is further purified as usual by vacuum distillation. The yield is about 80%

$$\underset{\text{Propylene}}{CH_3CH = CH_2} + Cl_2 \rightarrow \underset{\text{Allyl chloride}}{CH_2ClCH = CH_2} + HCl$$

$$\underset{\text{Allyl chloride}}{CH_2ClCH = CH_2 + HOCl} \rightarrow \underset{\text{Dichlorohydrin}}{CH_2ClCHCl.CH_2OH}$$

$$\underset{\text{Dichlorohydrin}}{2CH_2ClCHC1.CH_20H} + Ca(OH)_2 \rightarrow \underset{\text{Epichlorohydrin}}{2CH_2C1\text{-}\underbrace{CH\text{-}CH_2}_{O}} + CaCl_2 + 2H_2O$$

$$CH_2Cl\text{-}\underbrace{CH\text{-}CH_2}_{O} + NaOH + H_2O \dashrightarrow \underset{\text{Glycerine}}{CH_2OH.CHOHCH_20H} + NaCl$$

(2) Via Acrolein- Propylene may also be converted into glycerol via acrolein. Propylene, steam and oxygen (4 : 4 : 1) is led into a reactor containing copper oxide catalyst maintained at a temperature of 350°C and 2 atmospheric pressure for a contact period of 0.8 seconds. Propylene is thus oxidised to acrolein. The reaction mixture is cooled and distilled to separate acrolein from unreacted propylene and other products. The purifled acrolein vapour is then reacted with isopropanol vapour (molar ratio 1 : 3) at 400°C in presence of magnesia and zinc oxide catalysts. Allyl alcohol and acetone are thus formed.

They are separated by distillation. Finally, allyl alcohol is oxidised with an aqueous solution of H_2O_2 (molar ratio 1 : 2) in presence of tungustic oxide at 60-70°C for about 2 hours. As a result, very pure glycerine mixed with water is obtained. The glycerine water mixture is then concentrated in vacuum to give very pure glycerine. Isopropanol, used in the process, is also prepared from propylene.

$$CH_2 = CH - CH_3 + O_2 \rightarrow CH_2 = CHCHO + H_2O$$

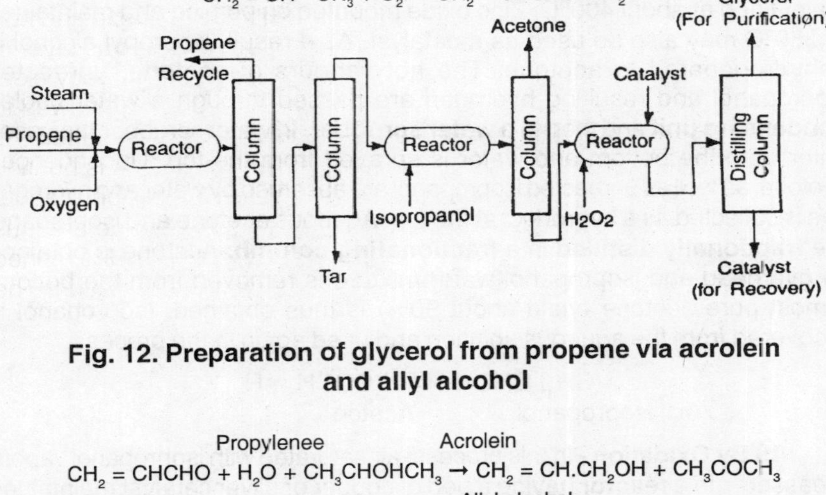

Fig. 12. Preparation of glycerol from propene via acrolein and allyl alcohol

$$\underset{\text{Acrolein}}{CH_2 = CHCHO} + H_2O + \overset{\text{Propylenee}}{CH_3CHOHCH_3} \rightarrow \underset{\text{Allyl alcohol}}{\overset{\text{Acrolein}}{CH_2 = CH.CH_2OH}} + CH_3COCH_3$$

$$\underset{\text{Allyl alcohol}}{CH_2 = CH.CH_2OH} + H_2O_2 \rightarrow \underset{\text{Glycerine}}{CH_2OH.CHOH.CH_2OH} + H_2O$$

Glycerol or glycerine is a clear, colourless, odourless, syrupy, hygroscopic liquid (b.p. 290°C) with a sweet taste. It is heavier than water (Sp. gr. 1.265) and soluble in water or alcohol in all proportions.

It is used in the manufacture of alkyd resins, drugs, toilet soaps, tooth pastes, food and beverages, explosives, printing inks, transparent soaps etc.

ACETONE, PROPANONE, CH_3COCH_3

Acetone is usually manufactued either by catalytic dehydrogenation of isopropyl alcohol or by its oxidation.

(a) Catalytic Dehydrogenation-The vapour of isopropanol is preheated

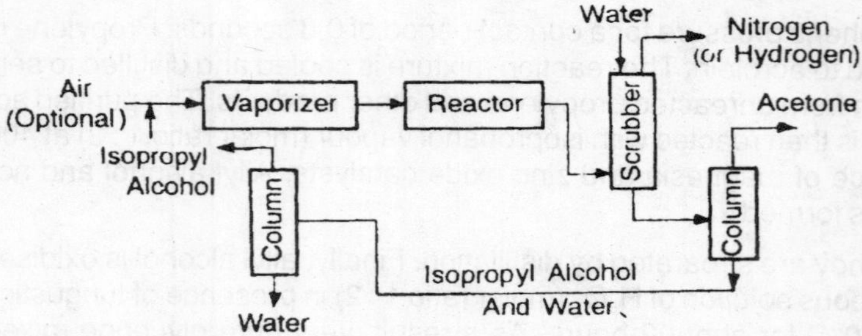

Fig. 13. Preparation of acetone by oxidation of isopropanol.

in a **heat exchanger** by outgoing gases and then passed under a pressure of 3-4 atmospheres into a **reactor** containing finely divided copper catalyst maintained at about 400°C. Zinc oxide mounted on pumice and maintained at 380°C may also be used as a catalyst. As a result, isopropyl alcohol is dehydrogenated to acetone. The hot vapours of acetone, unreacted isopropanol and resulting hydrogen are passed through a water cooled **condensing unit** and then to a **water scrubber.** In water scrubber the gases enter from the bottom and water is sprayed from the top. Uncondenced acetone, as well as unreacted isopropanol are absorbed by water and hydrogen gas is collected as a byproduct at the top. Aqueous acetone and isopropanol are **fractionally distilled** in a **fractionating column.** Acetone is obtained as overhead and isopropanol water mixture is removed from the bottom. Almost pure acetone (yield about 90%) is thus obtained. Isopropanol is recovered from the aqueous solution and used again in the process.

$$\underset{\text{Isopropanol}}{(CH_3)_2CHOH} \rightarrow \underset{\text{Acetone}}{CH_3COCH_3} + H_2$$

(b) By Oxidation - In this process, air saturated with isopropanol vapour is passed into a **reactor** having a bed of copper or silver catalyst maintained at 400-500°C. The hot exit gases are **cooled** partially and **absorbed** in water. Nitrogen escapes to the atmosphere. Because of the presence of copper catalyst, some dehydrogenation also takes place simultaneously with oxidation. Acetone is purified as described above. The yield is about 85-90%.

$$(CH_3)_2CHOH + \tfrac{1}{2}O_2 \rightarrow CH_3COCH_3 + H_2O$$

(2) By Oxidation of Propylene - A mixture of very pure propylene and oxygen is passed under 6-7 atmospheres into the bottom of a **reactor** containing a catalyst solution of cupric chloride and a small amount of palladium chloride. As a result, propylene is oxidised to acetone.

The exit gases are then passed through a **water scrubber,** where acetone dissolved in water and unabsorbed gases leaving from the top are recycled. The acetone solution is distilled to get pure acetone.

$$CH_3CH = CH_2 + PdCl_2 + H_20 \xrightarrow{CuCl_2} CH_3COCH_3 + 2HCl + 2Pd$$

Palladium formed according to the above reaction is oxidised back into palladium chloride by cupric chloride.

$$2CuCl_2 + Pd \rightarrow 2CuCl + PdCl_2$$

Cupric chloride Cuprous chloride

The cuprous chloride formed according to the above reaction is oxidised back into cupric chloride by oxygen.

$$2CuCl + 2HCl + ½ O_2 \rightarrow 2CuCl_2 + H_2O$$

Acetone is a colourless inflammable, pleasent smelling, volatile liquid (b.p 56°C). It is soluble in water, ethanol and ether. It is used as a solvent for acetylene, nitrocellulose and cellulose acetate. It is also used in the preparation of sulphonal (a soporific), irone (an artificial scent), cordite (smokeless powder), plaxiglass (a plastic), chlorofrom, iodoform etc. '

PHENOL, C_6H_5OH

Phenol is manufactured by a number of processes

(1) Cumene Process - Benzene and purified propylene obtained from petroleum industry are mixed in liquid or vapour phase in presence of

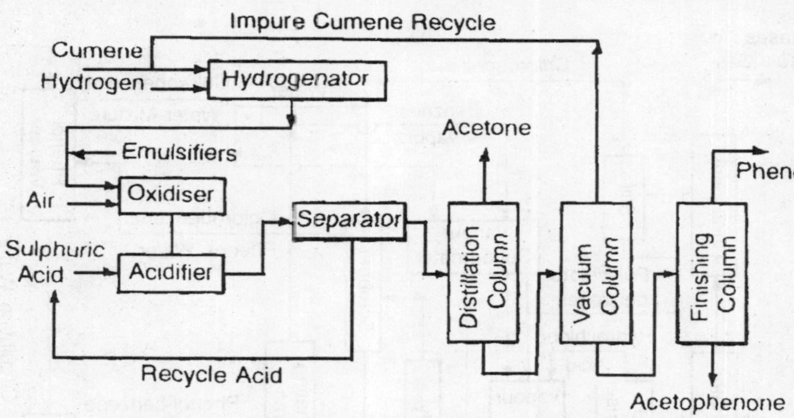

Fig. 14. Manufacture of phenol (Cumene Process).

phosphoric acid on kieselguhr. As a result, cumene or isopropyl benzene is formed. The cumene thus formed is made into the form of an emulsion with dilute aqueous sodium carbonate solution, using sodium stearate as an emulsifier. The emulsion is then oxidised in an oxidiser with air under atmospheric pressure for 3-4 hours in presence of a catalyst, such as copper, cobalt or manganese salt. The temperature and pH of the reaction are maintained between 160-260°C and 8.5-10.5 respectively. As a result of oxidation, cumene hydroperoxide is formed. The peroxide thus formed is then decomposed by 5-50% sulphuric acid in an **acidifier** at 45-65°C under pressure. As a result of decomposition, phenol (15%), acetone (9%), cumene (73%) are formed along with some a- methylstyrene and acetophenone. These. are separated in a **separator.** The cumene is recycled to be used again and phenol is either extracted or recovered by fractional distillation. The yield is about 70-80%. Acetone is also formed as a byproduct (0.6 lb. per lb. of phenol).

$$\underset{\text{Propylene}}{CH_3CH=CH_2} + \underset{\text{Benzene}}{C_6H_6} \rightarrow \underset{\text{Cumene}}{C_6H_5CH(CH_3)_2} \xrightarrow{O_2} \underset{\text{Cumene hydroperoxide}}{C_6H_5C(CH_3)_2\text{-}O.OH} \xrightarrow{\text{dil.}H_2SO_4} \underset{\text{Phenol}}{C_6H_5OH} + \underset{\text{Acetone}}{CH_3COCH_3}$$

(2) **Raschig Process -**This process was developed in **Germany in 1940.** Benzene is first converted into chlorobenzene by passing a mixture of benzene vapour, hydrochloric acid vapour and airunder normal pressure at about 23°C in presence of a copper iron catalyst, supported on alumina. The reaction is exothermic in nature and so the temperature is maintained constant by external cooling. The conversion per pass is about 10%.

$$C_6H_6 + HCl + ½O_2 \rightarrow C_6H_5Cl + H_2O$$

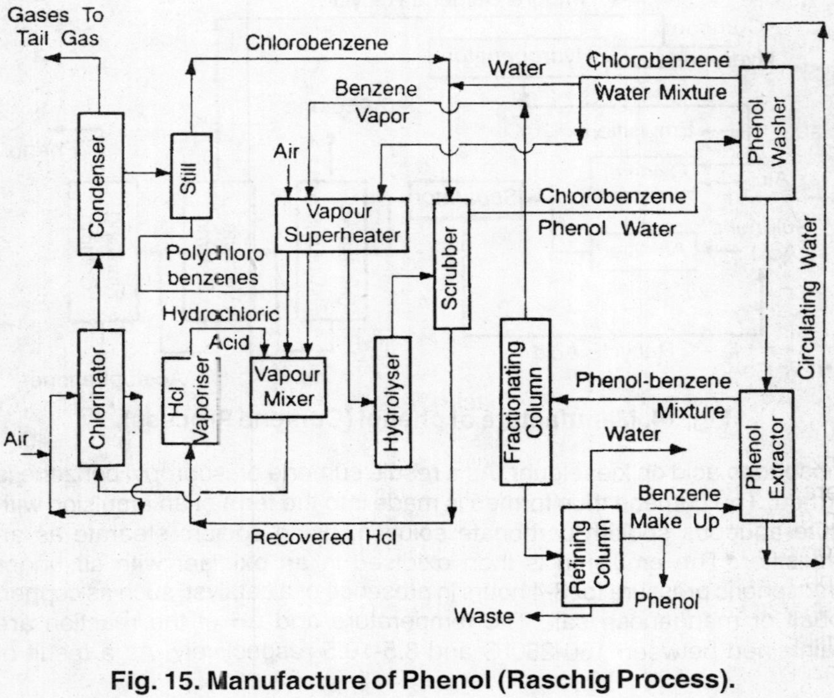

Fig. 15. Manufacture of Phenol (Raschig Process).

The chlorobenzene after separation from unchanged reactants is hydrolysed into phenol by heating with steam at about 400-500°C in presence of silica catalyst. The conversion is again about 10% per pass in this second step.

$$C_6H_5Cl + H_2O \rightarrow C_6H_6OH + HCl$$

Hydrogen chloride set free in the reaction is recovered and recycled. Crude phenol (97%) obtained according to the above reaction is purified by distillation under vacuum. The yield is about 75-85% on benzene. A small amount of HCl is sufficient to convert large amounts of benzene into phenol.

(3) Dow Toluene Air Oxidation Process - Toluene in liquid phase is oxidised with air in a reactor under 40-70 p.s.i. in presence of a soluble cobalt catalyst (cobalt naphthenate) maintained at 150°C. Benzoic acid and water are thus formed. The reaction is exothermic and temperature is maintained by external cooling. The crude molten benzoic acid at about 150-200°C is conducted from the reactor to a distillating column, where it is rectified to pure benzoic acid, toluene (unreacted) and water. Th toluene is separated and recycled to the first **oxidising reactor.** The pure benzoic acid is fed to a second reactor, where it is oxidised to phenol by air and steam under 20-25 p.s.i. at 230°C in presence of cupric benzoate catalyst promoted with manganese. The reaction mass is periodically withdrawn from the second reactor into an extractor, where it is washed with water to remove unwanted tars and benzoic acid and steam are returned to second reactor. The phenol, water and unreacted benzoic acid are conducted ovehead to two distillation columns in series. In the first column, crude phenol is separated from overhead and unreacted benzoic acid is recycled to the second oxidising reactor. In the second column pure phenol is obtained as overhead and leaves aromatics and benzoic acid to the feed of preceeding crude phenol column. The yield of phenol on benzoic acid is about 75-80%.

$$C_6H_5CH_3 + 1\tfrac{1}{2}O_2 \rightarrow C_6H_5COOH + H_2O \leftrightarrow C_6H_5COOH + \tfrac{1}{2}O_2 \rightarrow C_6H_5OH + CO_2$$

(4) Sulphonation Process - It is one of the oldest method of manufacture of phenol. Benzene sulphonic acid is first prepared by passing vapour of benzene into concentrated sulphuric acid at about 150-170°C. The water formed during sulphonation is distilled off inorder to prevent dilution of sulphuric acid and to avoid the backward reaction. Benzene sulphonic acid is then neutralised with aqueous sodium sulphite to form sodium salt of benzene sulphonic acid. The sodium salt (Sodium benzene sulphonatc) is filtered off and then fused with caustic soda in a cast iron vessel at about 340-380°C in the ratio (I : 3) for about 5-6 hours. As a result, sodium phenate is formed. The melt is cooled, extracted with water and then acidified with sulphur dioxide. The latter is obtained as a result of neutralisation of benzene sulphonic acid with sodium sulphite. The upper oily layer of crude phenol is distilled under vacuum to get pure phenol. The yield is about 80-90% on benzene.

$$C_6H_6 + H_2SO_4 \rightleftharpoons \underset{\text{Benzene sulphonic acid}}{C_6H_5SO_3H} + H_2O \xrightarrow{Na_2SO_3} \underset{\text{Sod. benzene sulphonate}}{C_6H_5SO_3Na} \xrightarrow[NaOH]{\text{Fusing}} Na_2SO_3 + \underset{\text{Sodium phenoxide}}{C_6H_5ONa}$$

$$\underset{\text{Sodium phenoxide}}{2C_6H_5ONa} + SO_2 + H_2O \rightarrow \underset{\text{Phenol}}{2C_6H_5OH} + Na_2SO_3$$

The lower layer contains sodium sulphite which is separated and used for the neutralisation of benzene sulphonie acid. Phenol is a colourless, crystalline solid (m.p,42°C). It has a characteristic phenolic or carbolic smell. It is deliquescent in nature and becomes pink or red on exposure to light and air on account of oxidation. Phenol is readily soluble in organic solvents, such as benzene, ether, ethanol, acetic acid etc. Phenol is used in the manufacture of bakelite, synthetic tannins, dye intermediates, salicylic acid, picric acid etc. Hydrogenated phenol, called cyclohexanol is used as an industrial solvent for rubber, lacquers, nitrocellulose etc.

FORMALDEHYDE, HCHO

Formaldehyde i's mainly prepared from methanol, either by its catalytic vapour phase oxidation or by combined oxidation hydrogenation process.

(a) **Oxidation Dehydrogenation Process -** Fresh and recycle methanol are first vapourised, super heated by steam and then passed to a methanol air mixer. Purified air is compressed and then mixed with preheated vapours of methanol (vapours are preheated in a heat exchanger so that the mixture contains about 30-50 percent methanol by volume). The mixture is then preheated to about 300°C by passing through a preheater and then rapidly through a water jacketed reactor containing several layers of silver gauze catalyst. The catalyst is maintained at about 400-500°C. The time of contact of gaseous mixture with the catalyst is about 0.01 sec. About 65% of the CH_3OH is converted into HCHO per pass. The hot gases enter a cooling column for partial separation of unreacted methanol from formaldehyde, and then a **scrubber** fed with cold water. They are finally vented to atmosphere. The exit gases contain 20-22 percent H_2, 74-75 percent N_2 and traces of CO_2, CO, CH_4 and O_2. The reactor effluent contains about 25% formaldehyde water and about 15% unreacted methanol. The mixture is sent to a **methanol fractionating column,** where 37% formaldehyde solution (Formalin) together with a few percent of required amount of methanol is removed from the bottom. The water intake adjusts the formaldehyde to 37% strength. The excess of methanol is collected as overhead and recycled in the process. The yield is 85-90%, the formaldehyde being marketed as a 37% aqueous solution, **called formalin.**

$$CH_3OH + \tfrac{1}{2}O_2 \rightarrow HCHO + H_2O$$

$$CH_3OH \rightarrow HCHO + H_2$$

(b) Oxidation Process-In this process methanol vapours are mixed with 5-10 times excess of air and the mixture is passed through a reactor containing a catalyst which consists of a mixture of molybdenum, iron or vanadium maintained at 350-450°C.

$$CH_3OH + \frac{1}{2}O_2 \text{ (air)} \rightarrow HCHO + H_2O$$

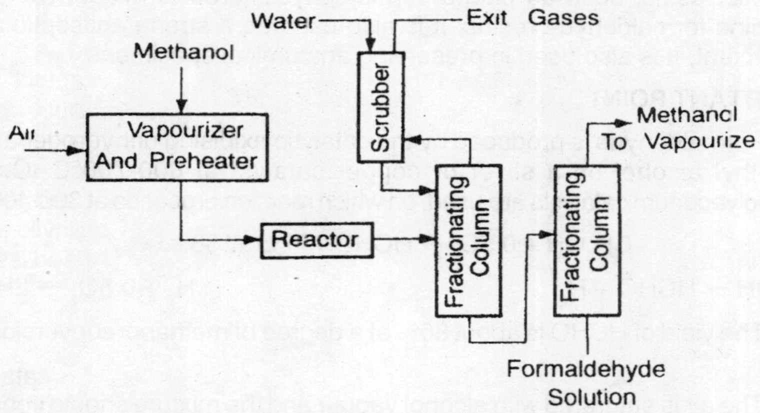

Fig. 16. Manufacture of Formaldehyde.

Under these conditions only oxidation takes place and a very high conversion (about 90%) is effected.

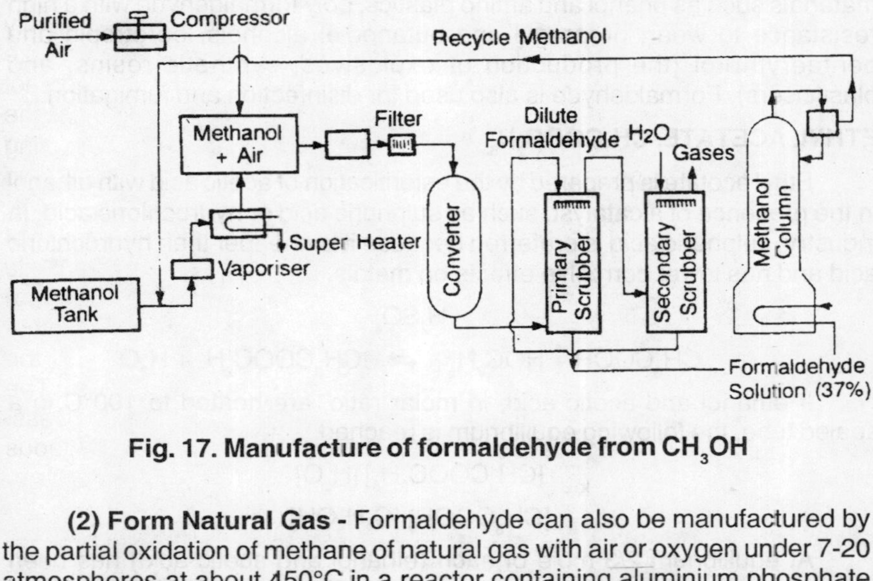

Fig. 17. Manufacture of formaldehyde from CH_3OH

(2) Form Natural Gas - Formaldehyde can also be manufactured by the partial oxidation of methane of natural gas with air or oxygen under 7-20 atmospheres at about 450°C in a reactor containing aluminium phosphate and a metal oxide as catalyst. The gaseous products containing formaldehyde (25%), methanol (35%), acetaldehyde (6%) etc. are cooled rapidly.

Formaldehyde is separated from other products by fractional distillation and then made free from traces of formic acid by passing through a bed of basic synthetic resin. Formaldehyde is a colourless, pungent smelling gas, highly soluble in water. The major use of formaldehyde is in the preparation of synthetic resins, such as phenol formaldehyde, urea formaldehyde and melamine-formaldehyde resins. It is also used as a strong antiseptic and disinfectant, It is also used in preserving anatomical specimens.

IMPORTANT POINT

Formaldehyde is produced by the catalytic oxidising dehydrogenation of methyl alcohol on a silver or copper catalyst at 600-700°C. Oxide iron-molybdenum catalysts are used, on which reaction proceeds at 300-400°C

$$CH_3OH + 0.5O_2 \rightarrow HCHO + H_2O - 158\ kJ$$

$$CH_3OH \rightarrow HCHO - H_2 \qquad\qquad H_2 + 0.5O_2 \rightarrow 2H_2O$$

The yield of HCHO is about 80% at a degree of methanol conversion of 85%

The air is saturated with alcohol vapour and the mixture should contain about 5g/L of CH_3OH to ensure safety and the required direction of the process.

Rapid lowering of temperature prevents the oxidation of formaldehyde to CO, CO_2 and H_2O.

Formaldehyde is a valuable raw material in the production of variety of materials such as phenol and amino plastics, poly formaldehyde with a high resistance to wear, propargyl and butanediol alcohols, eurotropin and pentaerythritol (the production of explosives, synthetic resins, and plasticisers). Formaldehyde is also used for disinfection and fumigation.

ETHYL ACETATE, $CH_3COOC_2H_5$

Ethyl acetate is prepared by the esterification of acetic acid with ethanol in the presence of a catalyst, such as sulphuric acid or hydrochloric acid. In industry, sulphuric acid is preferred because it is cheaper than hydrochloric acid and has lower corrosive effects on metals.

$$CH_3COOH + HOC_2H_5 \overset{H_2SO_4}{\rightleftharpoons} CH_3COOC_2H_5 + H_2O$$

If ethanol and acetic acid, in molar ratio, are heated to 100°C in a sealed tube, the following equilibrium is reached.

$$k = \frac{[CH_3COOC_2H_5]\,[H_2O]}{[CH_3COOH]\,[C_2H_5OH]}$$

At equilibrium 2/3 mole of each (ethanol and acetic acid) has been converted into ethy acetate and water and 1/3 mole each of ethanol and acetic acid remaining free. In other words. yield of ethyl acetate is 66.7%

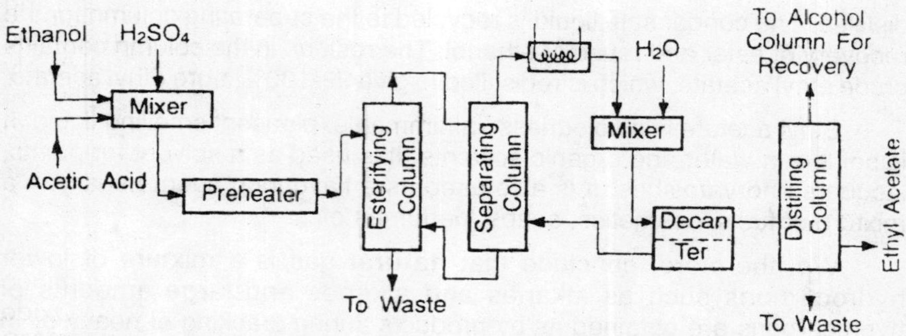

Fig. 18. Manufacture of ethyl acetate.

only. The equilibrium constant can be calculated by applying law of mass action,

$$k = \frac{C_{ester} \times C_{wacer}}{C_{acid} \times C_{alcohol}} = \frac{2/3 \times 2/3}{1/3 \times 1/3} = 4$$

If the equilibrium constant and other conditions are unaltered, *the yield of ester may be increased by taking one of the reactants in excess and removing the water formed during the reaction.* Thus with 4 moles of ethanol and 1 mole of acetic acid, the yield of ethyl acetate increases to about 93%. It is more economic, however, to remove water as soon as it is formed inorder to force the reaction to completion. It has been observed that in presence of a catalyst, such as sulphuric acid (which forms H_3O+ ion with the water), the reaction goes practically to completion at elevated temperatures.

Dilute acetic acid produced by fermentation is mixed with excess of 25% ethanol and about 1 °/r of sulphuric acid (69 Be) and the mixture is **preheated** by passing through a **preheater** and then introduced into an esterification column made of copper. The mixture is refluxed for some time and a suitable amount of distillate, containing about 70% alcohol, 10% ethyl acetate and 10% water, is removed from the top of the column at about 80°C and again refluxed. A ternary azeotrope mixture (83% ethyl acetate, 9% ethanol and 8%o water) is removed from the top of the column and maintained at about 70-80°C. The whole mixture is intorduced into a decanter, where it is diluted with water and allowed to settle into two layers. The upper layer contains 93% ethyl acetate, 5% water and 2% ethanol, while lower aqueous layer contaius, small amount of alcohol and ester. This aqueous layer is recycled into the bottom of the separating column, where ester is removed as a constant boiling ternary mixture. The ethanol is recycled to the lower part of the esterification unit, where it is vapouroised. Some sulphuric acid present at the bottom of the separating column is withdrawn and run to waste. The upper layer is allowed to overflow to a drying column, where it is distilled. The condensate liquid is recycled to the separating column for the recovery of ester and reuse of ethanol. The residue in the column contains crude ethyl acetate, which is redistilled to give 99-100%, pure ethyl acetate.

Ethyl acetate is a colourless, inflammable, pleasent smelling liquid. It is soluble in water and organic solvents. It is used as a solvent for paints, lacquers and varnishes. It is also used as a flavouring agent usually in a mixture of fuels, cosmetics, soaps, perfumes etc.

We, therefore, conclude that **natural** gas is a mixture of lower hydrocarbons such as alkanes and alkenes and large amounts of hydrocarbons are obtained as by-products during cracking of heavy oil in petroleum refineries. These hydrocarbons are excellent raw materials for the manufacture of a large number of chemical compounds, called petrochemicals. These petrochemicals are then used in industry for the preparation of other numerous compounds such as **explosives solvents, fertilizers, paints, dyes and drugs etc.** Some of the petrochemicals obtained from saturated and unsaturated hydrocarbons (obtained from petroleum) are given in Table 1.

TABLE 1 : PETROCHEMICALS

Hydrocarbon	Petrochemical
Metane (CH_4)	Formaldehyde, formic acid, acetylene, ethylene-glycol, dimethyl ether, methyl amine, hexamethyl-tetramine, dichloro monofluoro methane, dichloro difluoro methane, mono, di-, tri- and tetra chloro methane etc.
Ethylene (C_2H_4)	Ethanol, ethylene oxide, ethylene glycol, ethylene chlorohydrin, vinyl chloride, acetic acid, acetaldehyde diethyl ether, ethyl acetate, ethyl chloride, tetra-ethyl lead, butyric acid, PVC and of ethene plastic etc.
Ethane (C_2H_6)	Ethyl chloride, ethylene, acetic acid, acetic anhydride, diethyl ether, ethyl acetate, acetaldehyde etc.
Propane (C_3H_8)	Propyne, ethylene, nitroethane, nitromethane, nitropropane, propionic acid, isopropy lether, acetone, acetone cyanohydrin etc.
Propene (C_3H_6)	Allyl chloride, glycerol, allyl alcohol, isopropyl alcohol, acetone, propylene glycol, diacetone alcohol, propionic acid, acrolein, cumene, n-propyl alcohol, isopropyl ether etc.
Butanes (C_4H_{10})	Butylene, thiophene, butadiene etc.
Butenes (C_4H_8)	Butanol, tert, butyl alcohol, butyl rubber, iso-octane, ethyl butyl ketone, methyl ethyl ketone etc.
Pentane (C_5H_{12})	Amyl chloride, amyl alcohol, amyl phenols etc.
n-Hexane	DDT, benzene, phenol, gammaxene, styrene, polystyrene, plastics etc.
n-Heptane	Toluene, benzaaldehyde, benzoic acid, TNT, benzyl chloride benzal chloride, benzo trichloride, terephthalic acid etc.
Acetylene (C_2H_2)	Vinyl acetylene, acetaldehyde, acetic acid, vinyl chloride, trichloro ethane, ethylene chloride, vinyl acetate, butadiene, acrylic fibres etc.
Cyclo alkanes	Toluene, xylene, benzene, adipic acid, hexamethylene diamine etc.

1, 3-BUTADIENE OR DIVINYL

Compounds with conjugated double bonds such as divinyl (1,3-Butadiene), isoprene, chloroprene and those with a single double bond such as isobutylene, styrene, a-methylstyrene, acrylonitrile, etc are used in the manufacture of synthetic rubbers. Most of these compounds are obtained by dehydration of the corresponding hydrocarbons, which are present in industrial petroleum gases, casing-head gases, natural gasoline and some fractions of petroleum processing gases, and also by synthesis (e.g. ethyl benzene and isopropyl benzene). Divinyl or 1,3-butadiene is obtained by catalytic decomposition of ethyl alcohol and also by dehydration of butane and butylene in one or in two stages.

(1) From Ethyl Alcohol - A portion of ethyl alcohol is first converted into acetaldehyde by passing the vapours of alcohol over red hot copper at about 250°C. The byproducts, ethyl acetate and acetic acid (formed as a result of dehydrogenation of alcohol), are separated form the unreacted alcohol by distillation. Acetaldehyde and ethyl alcohol are then passed in a proportion 1:3 (mols) in a reactor at about 325°C in presence of a catalyst, which is silica gel impregnated with 2% of tantalum oxide (Ta_2O_5). The catalyst is regenerated periodically by burning off the deposited carbonaceous matter. The products from the reaction are then condensed under pressure. The propylene and ethylene gases leave the reactor as overhead, while the bottom liquid contains butadiene, along with some unreacted ethyl alcohol, and acetaldehyde and some other products. The bottom liquid is then subjected to fractional distillation under pressure and the butadiene fraction (96%), thus obtained is refined by treating it with chlorex ((β -β-dichloro ethyl ether) and finally distilled to get 98.5% butadiene. The chlorex dissolves all undesirable non paraffin constituents. In order to prevent polymerisation of the butadiene formed, it is necessary to add some inhibitor before fractional distillation under reduced pressure. The condensate containing butadiene and inhibitor is then washed to remove inhibitor and excess of ethyl alcohol (recovered) is reused.

$$CH_3CH_2OH \xrightarrow[250^oC]{Cu} CH_3CHO + H_2$$

$$\underset{\text{3 moles}}{CH_3CH_2OH} + \underset{\text{1 mole}}{CH_3CHO} \xrightarrow[325^oC,\ \text{I at. Pr.}]{\text{Silica gel. } Ta_2O_5} \underset{\text{1 : 3 butadiene}}{CH_2 = CH - CH = CH_2} + 2H_2O$$

In **India,** ethyl alcohol is cheaply available as it is obtained by the fermentation of molasses, a byproduct of sugar industry. In **Russia and America,** butadiene is obtained from butane, recovered form **petroleum or natural gas.**

IMPORTANT POINTS

The overall process can be described by the following reactions.

$$2C_2H_5OH \xrightarrow[370'C]{ZnU + Al_2O_3} CH_2 = CH - CH = CH_2 + 2H_2O + H_2 - 80\ kJ$$

This reaction passes through a number of stages.

(a) $CH_3CH_2OH \rightarrow CH_3CHO + H_2$

(b) $CH_3CHO + CH_3CHO \rightarrow CH_3CHOHCH_2CHO \rightarrow CH_3 - CH = CH - CHO + H_2O$
Crotonaldehyde

(c) $CH_3 - CH = CH - CHO + 2H \rightarrow CH_3 - CH = CH - CH_2OH$ (Crotyl alcohol)

(d) $CH_3 - CH = CH - CH_2OH \rightarrow H_2O + CH_2 = CH - CH = CH_2$

Simultaneously, side reactions also take place. In fact, the catalytic de composition of ethyl alcohol is a complex chemical process, because, in addition to the main products, up to 60 other different compounds such as acetaldehyde, water, hydrocarbons, higher alcohols etc are also formed.

The yield of 1,3-Butadiene depends on the following factors :

(a) *The activity of the catalyst.*

(b) *The temperature of the catalytic reaction.*

(c) *The ratio of the basic components in the initial mixture.*

(d) *The presence of impurities, etc.*

In industry, complex catalysts are used which contain both dehydrating and dehydrogenising components.

Since the process takes place at a high temperature, heat must be added to increase the temperature of the gas mixture and to compensate for the endothermic effect. The use of improved catalysts with higher selectivity has resulted in increased yield of divinyl. Because the process is accompanied by an increase in the gas volume, a decrease in pressure favours the yield of divinyl. The process involves the following basic operations.

(a) *Evaporation of eyhyl alcohol.*

(b) *Catalytic decomposition of the alcohol vapours.*

(c) *Recovery and purification of 1,3- butadiene (divinyl).*

(d) *Regeneration or replacement of the catalyst.*

The alcohol is evaporated, the vapour is superheated and at a high temperature of 180 - 200°C, it enters into the super heater of the reactor furnace (which is lined with fire brick and has double walls which form a narrow annular space, serving as combustion chamber in which a liquid or gaseous fuel is burned), where it is heated to 370 - 410°C.

The combustion products pass through channels into the alcohol super heater and then to the inner department of the furnace, which has retorts filled with the catalyst located around the perimeter. The catalyst is periodically unloaded through the branch pipe at the bottom of the retort. The gases from the furnace retorts enter a collector and at 360°C are directed to the unit for condensing and distilling the alcohol. On their way they pass through

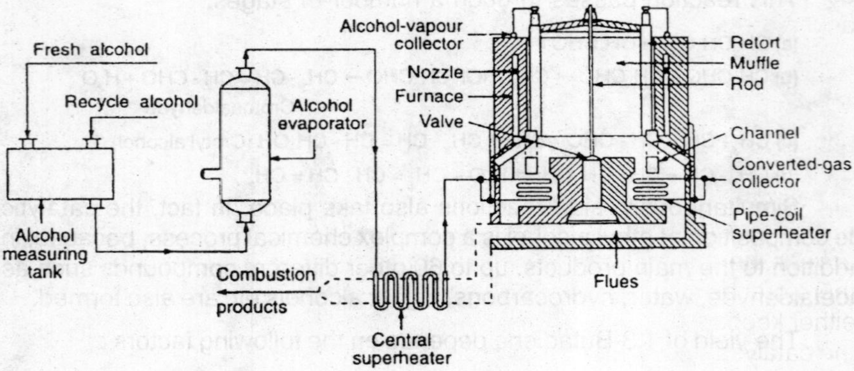

Fig. 19. Unit for manufacture of 1,3-Butadiene from ethyl alcohol.

waste-heat boilers, where they are cooled to 180°C. The gases are subjected to condensation by cooling them with water and cold brine under vacuum in a group of consecutive condensers. The condensed unreacted alcohol is recycled. 1,3-butadiene (b.p. = -4.5°C), is absorbed in ethyl alcohol. It is stripped from the alcohol solution and after careful purification enters the polymerisation unit.

(2) From Petroleum - Of the light hydrocarbons, on which the petroleum chemical industry is mostly based, the C4 hydrocarbons are most important. The petroleum, as found in nature contains 1-2 percent of C_4 hydrocarbons (0.9% butane + 0.3% isobutane). It is during refinery operation, usually cracking that large quantities of C4 hydrocarbons are obtained. N-butane, isobutane, 1-butene, 2- butene and isobutene are obtained on thermal and also on catalytic cracking. Butadiene is obtained by low pressure steam cracking and is about 37.7% by weight in C4 fractions. Dehydrogenation is an important process for the production of butenes form n-butene and of butadiene from n-butane and butenes. The reaction can he carried out thermally or catalytically. The production of butadiene increases with temperature and low pressure. Whatever be the source of butane, it is converted into butadienc by the dehydrogenation process.

Butadiene is separated by extractive distillation form the C4 hydrocarbons. It is carried out by adding furfural in which butadiene is largely soluble. Butene-2 is removed by straight distillations as bottoms. The overhead consists of butadiene and butene 1. In presence of furfural, the overhead is butene-1, whereas the bottoms are rich in butadiene. The hydrocarbons are separated form the solvent and on distillation 98.5% butadiene is obtained. The separation of butadiene by azeotropic distillation with ammonia has been effected successfully in fractionating columns. This process is not in use these days. Cuprous ammonical acetate solution absorbs butadiene, which is regenerated in a concentrated form. Catalytic dehydrogenation is performed first by removing iso-butylene through sulphuric acid extraction.

$$(CH_3)_2C = CH_2 + H_2SO_4 \rightarrow (CH_3)_3COSO_3H$$

Butene, which is free from isobutylene is passed over calcium nickel phosphate catalyst stabilized with 2% chromium oxide at temperature, which is more than 620°C, and a low butene pressure. Steam, which is preheated to 700°C, is used as a diluent to obtain low-n-butene partial pressure, which has several advantages. Butadiene polymerises at high temperatures and covers the catalyst with carbonaceous matter. These reactions should, therefore, be minimised or avoided by adding suitable inhibitors. Water gas, either keeps the catalyst free from carbonaceous matter or removes it from the catalyst. The overall conversion into butadiene is 40-50% per pass.

$$\underset{\text{Butylene}}{C_4H_8} \xrightarrow[\text{625-700°C}]{Ca_8Ni(PO_4)_6} \underset{\text{1 : 3 butadiene}}{CH_2 = CH - CH = CH_2}$$

Another catalyst, iron oxide promoted with potash and chromic oxide dehydrogenates butenes mixed with steam (1:4) at 620-680°C. The conversion is 25-30 percent per pass. n-butane is catalytically dehydrogenated over alumina-chromia catalyst at 570-600°C to give butadiene and butene mixture. The presence of water spoils the catalyst and , therefore, the fuel must be absolutely dry.

$$\underset{\text{n-Butane}}{C_4H_{10}} \xrightarrow[\text{500-600°C}]{CrO_3 + Al_2O_3} \underset{\text{Butene}}{C_4H_8} + \underset{\text{1 : 3 butadiene}}{CH_2 = CH - CH = CH_2}$$

IMPORTANT POINTS

- Dehydrogenation of n-butane into 1,4-butadiene initially forms n-butylenes after which divinyl or 1,3-butadiene is produced by further dehydrogenation.

$$CH_3 - CH_2 - CH_2 - CH_3 \overset{\text{536-600°C}}{\rightleftharpoons} CH_3 - CH = CH - CH_3 + H_2 - 126 \text{ kJ}$$

$$CH_3 - CH = CH - CH_3 \rightleftharpoons CH_2 = CH - CH = CH_2 - 116 \text{ kJ}$$

- The heat of reaction depends on the structure of' initial compounds. The course of dehydrogenation reactions depends on
  - (a) *The composition and activity of the catalyst.*
  - (b) *The temperatute and pressure.*
  - (c) *The duration of the process.*
  - (d) *The presence of impurities in the starting material.*
- The yield of divinyl is limited not only by the thermodynamic equilibrium

but also by hydrocarbon cracking reactions which also occur simultaneously.

- The optimum time of contact for converting n-butane to n-butylenes decreases with an increase in temperature. At 550-575°C and over industrial alumino-chromium catalysts it amouts to about 2 sec. conversion of n-butane in a single pass through the catalyst is 40-60% an the yield of n-butylenes is 35-40% w.r.t. initial material.
- Dehydrogenation of' butane in a moving or fluidised catalyst bed provides continuous action and increases the capacity of the reactor. Dehydrogenation of n-butylenes is usually carried out in an adiabatic catalytic reactor (The catalysts are mixtures of' metal oxides) at 600-650°C together with superheated water vapour which is introduced to reduce the partial pressures of reactant gases.
- The divinyl yield is 80-85% w.r.t. the gaseous reaction products.
- The apparent activation energy of the reaction over mixed oxide catalysts (oxides of Fe, Cu, Mg, Cr, 7.n and K) is 75-80 kJ/mole.

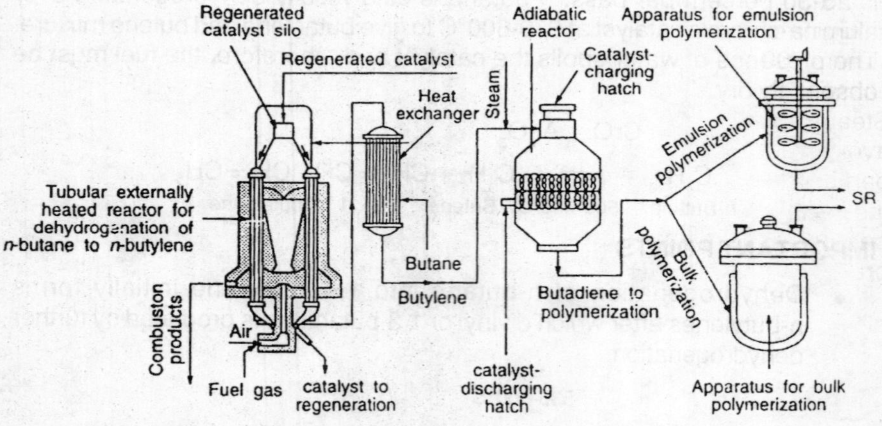

Fig. 20. Manufacture of divinyl (1.3-Butadiene) and then rubber from butanes.

STYRENE

Styrene is manufactured by **Dow Process.** In this process benzene, mostly free from sulphur (thiophene) is dried azeotropically, as water increases the consumption of aluminium chloride used as a catalyst in this process. Moreover, it also causes corrosion due to HCl formation. The dried benzene is fed to a reactor, called **alkylator** and ethylene gas is passed through it at 85-90°C and 5 psig pressure in presence of $AlCl_3$ acting as a catalyst. The temperature in the alkylator is maintained by water cooling. Small amount of ethyl chloride is also continuously fed in the alkylator for supplying HCl which acts as a promoter. Ethylene is passed until the reaction is complete. Excess of ethylene is recycled. The alkylated mixture contains 35-40% ethyl benzene, 40-50% benzene and 2-10% polyethylbenzene and other higher boiling fractions. The catalyst forms a complex containing $AlCl_3$, 26-28%, benzene and ethyl benzene 50% and rest high molecular weight hydrocarbons. The catalyst complex forms a separate layer and is worked to separate hydrocarbons and the catalyst in solution.

$$C_2H_4 + C_6H_6 \rightarrow C_6H_5C_2H_5$$

The alkylated mixture containing benzene, monoethylbenzene, polyethyl benzene and high boiling fraction hydrocarbons is fractionated into columns, which work at different pressures (column 1- one atm., column 2 at 200 mm. Hg column 3 at 400 mm Hg) to separate benzene (column 1), ethyl benzene (column 2) and polyethylbenzene (column 3) and tar. The vapours of ethyl benzene thus obtained are then passed over a catalyst heated to 600-660°C. The catalytic dehydrogenation of ethyl benzene is an endothermic reaction and is favoured by low pressures. the catalysts employed are oxides of metals like zinc, chromium, iron, magnesium or aluminium either separately or mixtures. The best catalyst consists of Fe_2O_3 on MgO base with small amounts of $CuO + K_2O$. This catalyst is usually known as **1707.** Superheated steam (700-720°C), and ethyl benzene at 400°C are fed into a reactor which contains the catalyst. The temperature of the reactor is kept at 600-660°C. Steam provides necessaryheat for the reaction, controls high temperature to avoid cracking, reduces partial pressure to favour styrene production (as partial pressure of the product gasses styrene and hydrogen are reduced, the backward reaction is avoided) and keeps the catalyst free from deposited carbon. The super steam also minimise undesirable side reactions by preventing decomposition.

$$\underset{\text{Ethyl benzene}}{C_6H_5C_2H_5} \rightleftharpoons \underset{\text{Styrene}}{C_6H_5CH = CH_2} + H_2$$

The products are condensed to 100-110°C. The condensate contains styrene 35-37%, ethyl benzene 59-60%, toluene 1-2%, benzene 0.5-2% and tar 0.2-0.5%. The uncondensed gases contain CO, CO_2, water and some hydrocarbons. Pure styrene is recovered from the condensate by vacuum distillation in fractionating columns operated at 20-40 m.m. of Hg 99.9% pure styrene is thus obtained. The byproducts of the industry consist of 20% aluminium chloride solution, benzene which is reused, toluene, tars and polymers.

Chapter 5

LUBRICANTS

LUBRICANTS

A substance which is capable of reducing the friction between two surfaces which are sliding over each other is called lubricant. Lubricant reduces the coefficient of friction between two rubbing surfaces of the machinery. The loss of energy due to friction is considerably reduced in this manner. The lubricant, in fact, acts in a number of manners. For example,

(a) *It acts as a coolant or heat transfer medium by removing the heat of friction generated as a result of rubbing of surfaces.*

(b) *In lubricaion, it does not allow a direct contact between the rubbing surfaces. A thin film of lubricant lies between these rubbing surfaces under proper conditions of lubrication.*

(c) *In internal combustion engines, it acts as a seal by sealing the piston and cylinder wall at the compression rings. Hence there is no leakage of gases at high pressure in the combustion chamber. Lubrication also avoids power loss in the internal combustion engines.*

Hence the main functions of a lubricant are:

(a) *It reduces wear and tear and surface deformation, by avoiding direct contact between the rubbing surfaces.*

(b) *It reduces loss of energy in the form of heat by acting as a coolant.*

(c) *In increases the efficiency of the machine by reducing the waste of energy.*

(d) *It redcues expansion of metal by local frictional heat.*

(e) *It minimises the liberation of frictional heat and hence avoids seizure of moving surfaces.*

(f) *It prevents or minimises unsmooth relative motion of the moving or sliding parts.*

(g) *It reduces the maintenance as well as running cost of the machine to a large extent.*

(h) As *seen above it also acts as a seal in internal combustion engines.*

Petroleum is the main source of lubricants or lubricating oils, but synthetic lubricants have also been prepared in recent years for specific purposes.

PROPERTIES OF LUBRICANTS

The most important properties of lubricants which are of prime importance in lubrication are viscosity, viscosity temperature relation, viscosity index, volatilily etc. In order to get efficient lubrication, there should be no change in these properties during lubrication. Moreover, there should be no effect of any chemical change such as decomposition, oxidation, reduction at higher temperature and emulsification during lubrication. The behaviour of a lubricating oil or lubricant is determined by its viscosity. Viscosity is defined as the force in dynes necessary for the movement of 1 sq. cm. layer of a fluid with a velocity of 1 cm per sec, past another parallel layer lcm away. The unit usually employed is centipoise. The measurement of viscosity is usually done in C.G.S. units and the unit is stoke. In case of thin oils which have very low viscosity, it is measured in centi-stokes. The viscosity measured by this method is called kinematic viscosity. In United States another unit of viscosity, known as Saybolt Universal viscosity (SUV) is frequently employed in petroleum industry. It is expressed as the number of seconds required for 60 cc of the oil to run through a standard orifice from a cylinder filled to a definite level at a standard temperature. In case of lubricants, viscosity depends upon the temperature. The viscosity has been found to decrease with increase in temperature. For example, the viscosity of petroleum products such as spindle oil, neutral oil, red and pale oils, bright stocks and steam cylinder oils (all used as lubricants) at 20°C are 8-100, 30-300, 50-2000, 2000-5000 and 2000-10000 centistokes respectively. The values of viscosity of the same lubricants at 100°C become 1 to 5, 3 to 5, 5 to 25, 20 to 60, and 20 to 80, respectively.

The variation of viscosity of an oil with temperature is given by Viscosity Index (V I), defined by the expression,

Viscosity Index (V.I.) $X = V_L - V_X \times 100$

Where V_L = S.U.V. of a standard low viscosity oil at 100°F

V_H = S.U.V. of a standard high viscosity oil at 100°F

Viscosity Index may also be regarded as the average decrease in viscosity per degree rise of temperature between 100°F and 210°F. In the case of most lubricants, the viscosity index (VI) ranges from -50 to +110. lubricants having below or above viscosity index ranges than this are also known. Solvent refining usually improves viscosity index of oils. Lubricants having lowest possible viscosity index are in great demand for aircrafts where bearings are exposed to temperature between - 80°C and +200°C. Liquids which have low viscosity and low viscosity temperature coefficient are composed of easily movable or flexible molecules, while those having high viscosity and high viscosity temperature coefficient are composed of rigid molecules. This is due to the fact that decrease in viscosity with increase in temperature is due to increase in the free volume that is available for the molecules to move in. In the case of lubricants having larger molecules, heat also provides energy required to deform the large molecules to make them able to slip past each other and thus decreasing the viscosity.

Viscosity of a lubricating oil also increases by mixing polymers with the lubricants. In practical work, viscosity is measuerd as S.U.V as in U.S.A by Saybolt viscometer, and not in centi-stockes or poises. When a lubricant is used in the form of a very thin film as in rolling contact bearings or in general boundary lubrication, the volatility of the lubricant is necessary to be taken into consideration. When lubricants containing volatile impurities are used, these volatile impurities may escape during the function of the machinery. As a result, the pure lubricant (without volatile impurities) may reduce in quality and may cause, lubricant starvation. If *we use* a *multicomponent* lubricant *and one or* more of the *components* undergo volatilization. then the residue may change very undesirably with respect to its property of viscosity which may increase to a considerable extent.

Pour point is an important property of a sample of lubricating oil and is defined as the temperature at which the oil ceases to flow when cooled under standard conditions. This property indicates the dissolved wax concentration in a given sample of lubricating oil.

Cloud point is another index of dissolved wax concentration, which may be defined as the temperature at which the cloudiness appears in a sample of oil, under standard conditions, because of wax separation. Lubricants also undergo oxidation, hydrolysis and pyrolysis. The property of lubricants to undergo oxidation is different for different lubricants and mainly depends upon the composition and purity of the lubricant. As a result of oxidation, the lubricant undergoes decomposition and its lubricating property is also affected. Hence certain anti-oxidants are employed in the lubricants to avoid oxidation.

It is very important to test the flash point of the oil to be used as lubricant. It is not advisable to use an oil as lubricant, which flashes or reaches combustion temperature under the conditions of the lubrication. This is due to the fact that spontaneous combustion of oil vapours occurs if the oxidation is so rapid that heat of oxidation is not dissipated so quickly as to avoid the reaching of flash point or combustion temperature. When lubricants such as esters are exposed to moisture at high temperatures and in the presence of acids and alkalies, they undergo decomposition as a result of hydrolysis. Polyethers and halides are hydrolysed only under drastic conditions of hydrolysis and poly siloxanes are hydrolysed easily by alkaline solutions. It is, therefore, necessary to use those lubricants, which are not capable of hydrolysing under lubricating conditions.

Different lubricating oils employed in the moving parts of an **internal combustion** engine undergo thermal decomposition or pyrolysis, producing free carbon, in varying amounts. This property is usually expressed by the coke number, which gives the amount of carbon deposited by a weighed sample of lubricant oil in a standard apparatus and under a standard set of experimental conditions. Samples having lower coke numbers are recommended as better lubricants. When organic lubricating oils are exposed to temperatures greater than 300°C, they generally undergo cracking, which is a free radical mechanism. The rate of cracking is different for differnet iubricants and is generally enhanced by oxidation. Hence lubricants used should not crack under lubricating conditions.

There are some lubricating oils which are capable of mixing with water to from an emulsion (emulsification) and this emulsion has the tendency to deposit dirt, grit particles and other foreign matter. When lubricant containing these solid particles is used in the lubricating system,it may cause abrasion and may even damage the sensitive parts of the machinery. there are certain additives which are mixed with the lubricants to check the emulsification tendency of the lubricant. A good lubricant is that which does not form emulsion under lubricating conditions, and if it forms an emulsion, the emulsion should break off immediately or very quickly. For example, in the case of steam turbines it is essential that the emulsion formed by the lubricant with water should separate very quickly, otherwise the lubricant is useless for the purpose. Oiliness is another important property of lubricants. When a lubricating oil is subjected to pressure under lubricating conditions it has the tendency to be squeezed out. The capacity of a lubricant to stick on to the surface under pressure or load is called oiliness. Lubricants having high oiliness stick on in between the lubricating surfaces and do not come out when they are subjected to high pressure or load. *Vegetable oils have oiliness, but mineral oils have much less or no oiliness. Additives such as vegetable oils and fatty acids such as oleic acid, steric acid etc are added to mineral oil to improve their oiliness.*

CLASSIFICATION OF LUBRICATION

Lubrication can be classified into the following types:

(a) Complete Fluid Lubrication. (b) Boundary Lubrication.

(c) Extreme Pressure Lubrication.

(a) ***Complete Fluid Lubrication -*** In such type of lubrication, one of the rubbing surfaces is slightly displaced in relation to the other and a wedge-shaped film of the lubricant is formed between the two surfaces rubbing against each other. The pressure developed in the wedge-shaped film supports the load and prevents the direct contact between the rubbing surfaces. The lubricant film covers or fills the irregularities of the sliding or moving surfaces and the lubricant forms a thick layer in between them. As a result, there is no direct contact between the material surfaces and wear is considerably reduced. The resistance to movement of moving or sliding parts is only because of the internal resistance between the particles of the lubricant moving over each other. The friction between two lubricated surfaces depends upon the dimensions of the film and viscosity of the lubricant.

In **fluid film lubrication**, e.g., the lubricant must have minimum viscosity under working conditions and at the same time it is expected to remain in place and separate the surfaces. In such a system, friction does not depend upon the load, but depends upon the viscosity, thickness of the lubricant and relative velocity as well as area of the moving or sliding surfaces. The coeffieient of friction in such cases is extremely low, being of the order of 0.001 to 0.03. In the case of a shaft running at a fair speed, hydrodynamic friction occurs and a film of lubricating oil covers the irregularities of shaft and that of bearing surfaces. Moreover, there is no direct contact of metal surfaces with each other. As a result, the resistance to movement is caused due to the internal resistance of the lubricant.

Complete fluid lubrication or hydrodynamic lubrication is provided in delicate instruments such as watches, clocks, guns and light machines such as sewing machines, scientific instruments etc. The most satisfactory and widely used ubricants for this type of lubrication are hydrocarbon oils, which are blended with selected long chain polymers inorder to maintain suitable viscosity of the oil in summer, winter and other seasons of the year. Some antioxidants such as aminophenols are also added to hydrocarbon petroleum fractions because these (latter) usually contain minute amounts of unsaturated hydrocarbons which are susceptible to oxidation under operating conditions.

(b) ***Boundary Lubrication*** - This type of lubrication may take place under any of the following conditions.

(a) When the relative speed of the lubricated surfaces is insufficient to develop pressure in the lubricating film to carry the load. Such condition may develop when a heavily loaded bearing is suddenly stopped or started.

(b) When the load on bearing becomes greater than the pressure developed in the lubricating film.

(c) When the surfaces are not perfect and the load is carried on high spots.

Boundary lubrication or thin film lubrication is, therefore, suitable when a continuous film of lubricant can not persist and direct metal to metal contact is possible because of various reasons, e.g. when a shaft starts moving from rest or speed is very low or load is very high or viscosity of the oil is extremely low. Under all these circumstances friction between the lubricated surfaces lies on absorbed or boundary layers of lubricant. The load is carried by the layers of the adsorbed lubricant on both the metal surfaces. The coefficient of friction in such a case is generally 0.05 to 0.15. This friction is dependent mainly upon the nature of the material of the surfaces and also on some characteristics that can be determined by the chemical properties of the lubricant.

The effectiveness of boundary lubrication primarily depends upon the structure and chemical properties of the oil to be used fot boundary lubrication. The lubricant used in such type of lubrication should have long hydrocarbon chains, polar groups (to enhance spreading and orientation over the metallic surfaces at high pressure), lateral attraction between the chains and active atoms or groups capable of forming linkages with the metals or other surfaces. *Other important properties of boundary lubricants are good oiliness, low pour point, high resistance to oxidation and heat and high viscosity index.* In lubrication, the layer of lubricant, which is just in immediate contact with surface is held there by physical adsorption type of forces or chemical type of forces which result because of chemical reaction between the lubricant and the metal surface or by the combination of both physical and chemical type of forces. The tenacity with which this layer of the lubricant adheres to the surface depends directly on the oiliness of the lubricant. Next layer is several molecules thick and remains stationary. This is called boundary layer. After this there is a fluid film of the lubricant, which carries the load and is continuously sheared. In case the fluid layer is squeezed out due to some reason, then boundary layer remains in contact with the lubricated part. As a result, **boundary or thin film lubrication is developed. Localized excessive wear or seizing, welding or galling** may also be produced and there is complete squeezing out of all the layers, which may take place at high point on the rubbing surfaces.

Lubrication by **boundary lubrication** does not depend upon the viscosity and resistance to shearing of the lubricant because lubricant layer in this type of lubrication is in immediate contact with the metal surface. However, these properties have been found to affect lubrication, because true boundary lubrication conditions are difficult to achieve. These properties of lubricant determine the formation of a wedge of the lubricant between the surfaces in case of fluid **lubrication. In boundary lubrication** metals are not effectively separated by a lubrication film. The thin film of the lubricant is penetrated by irregularities of the metal surfaces which are never absolutely plane. A layer of lubricant which is many molecules thick may, no doubt, reduce the number of metal contacts, but can not remove all the contacts, even under mild conditions of movement. The lubricant should therefore be capable of repairing the disruptive film of the lubricant, so that **best boundary**

lubrication may result. When the boundary lubrication has to work under vacuum, the lubricaing film goes out. Hence friction increases because of the direct contact of the metals being taking place. **The presence of air increases the efficiency of boundary lubrication** because of the formation of protective iron oxide film on the surfaces. *When lubricants are fatty acids, the presence of moisture has been found to increase the effectiveness of boundary lubrication.*

It should be noted that in fluid lubrication there is no friction between the surfaces and the 'wear is almost negligible. So in fluid lubrication wear decreases as the friction decreases. In boundary lubrication, decrease in friction does not decrease the wear to the same extent as the decrease in friction and so minimum friction is not achieved by minimum wear.

Films which are chemically attached are generaly produced by organic acids which react with metals. The contacts between the surfaces can be reduced effectively by these films, if these acids can undergo **condensation and polymerisation**. *This indicates why oleic acid (which can polymerise) is a better lubricant than stearic acid (which can not polymerise). The lubricating property of oleic acid is also reduced if unsaturated impurities are removed from it.*

Vegetable as well as animal oils (glycerides of higher fatty acids) and their soaps possess the property of adsorption or surface attachment. They are either physically adsorbed to metal surfaces or react chemically at the metal surfaces, forming a thin film of metallic soap which act as lubricant. The load is carried by the two layers of adsorbed lubricant.

The fatty acids form solid metal soap films on the surface of the metals. In many cases, this soap formation with fatty acids takes place through the oxide of the metal which reacts to form soaps. *Hence lubricating property of fatty acids decreases if this oxide layer on the surface is removed or cleaned by freshly cutting the surface. The fatty acids are also useless as lubricants, if the oxide film is formed in the absence of moisture or water. In other words, best lubricating properties of fatty acids can be obtained by the action of air and water on metal surfaces.*

No doubt, the fatty oils possess a great property of adhesion, called **oiliness,** but they tend to break down at higher temperatures. **Hence vegetable oils are not suitable for use in cylinders of an internal combustion engine. Mineral oils** are thermally more stable than vegetable oils, but they have a lesser property of adhesion **(called oiliness)** than vegetable oils. **The oiliness of mineral oils** can, however, be improved by adding small amounts of fatty oils or fatty acids.

The removal of metal when intimate contact between the surfaces takes place is called wear, which causes a damage to the surfaces in the form of seizure, flow or displacement of the metal.

Wear is always present in boundary lubrication and so it can be reduced if metal surfaces in contact are protected from chemical attack by oxide films etc, provided the oxide films are adherent and quite hard. Certain **additives** such as sulphur and phosphorus, are also good in preventing the surfaces from chemical attack. **Compounds which contain strongly polar groups and capable of absorbing on the metal surfaces are very effective anti wearing agents. A lubricant may contain both anti-wear and anti-friction agents.** In such cases, the material having greater concentration as will as activity well predomitate. For example, the effect of 5% oleic acid **(antifriction agent)** will be offset by 1 % tricresyl phosphate (anti-wear agent) if both of them are present in the lubricant. Lacquers and some **nitrogen compounds** which form layer of nitrides on surfaces have also been found to be good **anti-wear agents.**

Graphite and molybdenum disulphide are the two most usual solid lubricants, which either alone or as stable suspension in oil are also capable of producing **boundry lubrication.** These lubricants form films on the metal surfaces, which possess low internal friction and can withstand compression and high temperatures.

(c) **Extreme Pressure Lubrication -** We know that in boundary lubrication, there is always some contact between the surfaces through the thin film of oil. As a result, friction is developed which generates heat as well as high temperature Hence welded junctions as well as metal tearing takes place. If the load or pressure is too high, the contacts between the metal surfaces increases and if temperature is also too high, deformation, seizures, welding etc take place to a large extent. The temperatures are dependent upon the sliding velocity between the surface and the pressure. Hence, when there is high load and high temperature generation between the sliding surfaces, **extreme pressure lubricants** are used. This type of lubricants contain organic compounds containing sulphur, phosphorus, lead, chlorine etc. as **extreme pressure additives.** Sulphur and chlorine present in these additives react with metal to form sulphides and chlorides (when both sulphur and chloride are present). These metallic chlorides, sulphides or phosphides have high melting points and act as good lubricants under extereme pressure and extreme temperatures. The organic compounds decompose and form high melting lubricating films on the metal surfaces. These additives form a more durable film on the metal surfaces and thus film is capable of withstanding high loads and high temperatures. As seen above, these additives are the organic compounds having active radicals or groups such as chlorine (as in chlorinated esters), sulphur (in sulphurized oils) or phosphorus (as in tricresyl phosphate). Some examples of **extreme pressure additives** are compounds containing oxygen (fatty acids, ketones, esters etc), containing sulphur or sulphur and oxygen, chlorinated wax, sulphurized fats, sulphurized olefins, organic compounds containing lead and both chlorine and sulphur etc.

These additives form layers of films having low shear strength (which does not allow the metal to tear away) and they also act as **fluxing agents,** which contaminate the metal surface and hence prevents welding.

SUBSTANCES USED AS LUBRICANTS

Vegetable oils and fatty acids are the most important substances which are used as lubricants. Tallo, lard, whale oils, neat foot oil, rosin oil, sperm oil, castor oil, olive oil, coconut oil, palm oil; oleic acid etc are the various substances used as lubricants. **Mineral oils** compounded with fatty acids are known as **compounded oils** and these are also suitable as lubricants.

Fatty oils such as castor oil, coconut oil, etc posses oiliness, and they undergo **emulsification** in presence of water and steam. However, they are gummy, acidic, corrosive and expensive. It has been observed that fatty acids are absorbed in preference to mineral oils on the metal surface when both of them are present in the lubricant. Layer of fatty acid thus formed is very thin and with such a film conditions of **boundary lubrication** are reached.

Lubricating oils not only reduce wear and friction between two moving or sliding metallic surfaces by providing a continuous fluid film in between them, but they also serve as coolant, sealing agents, corrosion preventores etc. **The most important characteristics of** a good lubricating oil are

(a) *A high boiling point or low vapour pressure.*

b) *Suitable viscosity for particular service condition.*

(c) *Low freezing point.*

(d) *High thermal stability.*

(e) *High oxidation resistance.*

(f) *Non-corrosive nature.*

(g) Resistance to decomposition at higher or elevated temperatures.

Animal and vegetable oils have good oiliness and thus stick to the surface of machine parts even under high pressure (or load) and higher temperatures, but they are costly, undergo oxidation readily, form gummy and acidic products and get thickened in contact with air and undergo hydrolys is in contact with aqueous medium or moist air.

Hence in recent years they are not widely used. If used, then they are not used as such, but used as blending agents, with other lubricating oils like mineral oils. After the advent of petroleum industry use of vegetable oils as lubricants is almost restricted.

Olive oil is a colourless to golden yellow oily liquid that is extracted from the olive trees. The lower grade olive oil is used as lubricant for bearing and machine parts subjected to low pressure and high speeds. High grade olive oil is used for edible purposes. **Castor oil** is colourless to pale green oil having a sp. gravity of 0.96. It can be obtained by compression of castor seeds and it possesses an excellent **oiliness.** It is used as a lubricant for bearings and machine parts which are subjected to high speeds but low pressure. **Castor oil** is immiscible with petroleum. **Palm oil** is a pale yellow, pleasent smelling oil liquid having sp. gravity of 0.91 and is obtained by compression of kernels of palm fruits. It is widely used as a lubricant for delicate articles such as watches, clocks, sewing machines and scientific in struments **Rape seed oil (collza)** is a pale yellow liquid extracted from colza plant and used as a lubricant for steam cylinders and delicate apparatus. Hazel nut oil can be obtained form the hazel nuts and used for lubrication of watches, clocks etc. **Olive oil, palm oil, castor oil, rape seed oil and hazel nut oil are the examples of vegetable oils. Whale oil** is a very thin pale yellow oily liquid having sp. gravity of 0.88 and is obtained by the distillation of different parts of sperm whale flesh. It is used for the lubrication of light machineries. **Tallow oil** is a transparent oil that can be obtained by the compression of cattle fat under high pressure. It is generally used for high pressure and low speed machines. **Lard oil** is colourless oil and is obtained from fats, kidneys and intestines of pigs. Ordinary machines are lubricated by lard oil. **Neat foot oil** is a pale yellow oil of sp. gravity 0.915 and has a characteristic smell. It can be obtained by boiling foot of neat with water. It has been used as lubricant for sewing machines, watches, clocks and other delicate articles. **Lard oil, tallow oil, whale oil and neat foot oil are the examples of animal oils.**

ADDITIVES FOR LUBRICATING OILS

The gumy and acidic constituents of a lubricant can be removed by a suitable **refining process.** The tendency of emulsification of the lubricating oil is checked by certain additives to the lubricant. The additives are also used for a numner of other purposes. For example. **polymeric thickeners are used as additives for improving the viscosity index of the lubircant.** These are long chain polymers having very high molecular weight (3000-30,000). Examples of such polymers are polystyrene or alkyl styrene polymers, alkyl acrylate and polyester polymers, polyisobutylene type polymers etc.

Additives containing polar groupings such as fatty acids and their derivatives (e.g multivalent **metal soaps,** known as metallic soaps), long chain alcohols and organic phosphites are used to ease boundary lubrication. Certain additives such as long chain alkylated ring compounds, alkyl naphthalenes, polymers of long chain alkyl acrylates, multivalent metal soaps of fatty acids etc are used **to reduce the temperature at which a liquid lubricant may become solid.** This type of additives are known **as pour depressants. Their function is colloidal and they prevent the wax crystals to grow.**

Phenol and certain condensation products of chlorinated wax with naphthalene arc also used as **pour point depressing additives.** Thay also prevent the separation of wax from the oil.

Additives such as phenols, their derivatives, amines, organic phosphides etc are added to the lubricants **to prevent the oxidation of lubricant and known as anti-oxidants.**

The **antioxidants or inhibitors** retard the oxidation of oil by getting themselves preferentially oxidised. They are particularly added to lubricant used in internal combustion engines, turbines etc., where oxidation causes a serious problem.

Additives containing strongly polar groups are added to increase the oiliness and film strength of the lubricants. Examples of such additives are amyl phenyl phosphate, methyl di-chloro stearate, dibenzyl disulphide, tricresyl phosphate, sulphurised sperm oil etc.

Oiliness of a lubricant can also be increased by adding **oiliness carriers** such as **vegetable oils** (coconut oil, castor oil etc) and **fatty acids** (palmitic acid, oleic acid, stearic acid etc).

Additives such as high molecular weight compounds like hexanol are added as viscosity index improvers. Additives are also added as **detergents or deflocculents** to the lubricants. Examples of such additives are salts of phenol, carboxylic acids, sulphonic acids and alkyl phosphoric acids etc. Additives added as **wear inhibitors prevent wearing of the lubricating surface.** Alkaline earth phenolates are generally used as **anti-corrosive wear agent** and tricresyl phosphate is generally used as **anti-abrasive wear agent.** Corrosion preventatives are organic compounds of phosphorus or antimony. Their function is to protect the metal from corrosion by preventing contact between the metal surfaces and the corrosive substances.

Extreme pressure additives such as compounds containing phosphorus, lead, sulphur and chlorine (fatty acids, esters, ketones, chlorinated wax, sulphurised olefins, sulphurised wax, organic compounds containing sulphur, sulphur and oxygen, and containing trivalent and pentavalent phosphorus etc) are added **to make lubricating oil to bear extreme pressure.** Under extreme pressure, a thick film of oil is not capable of maintaining the film and it needs to have high oiliness. High pressure additives are absorbed on the metal surface or chemically react with metal, producing a surface layer of low shear-strength on the metal surface. Hence tearing up of metal is prevented. High pressure additives also react on metal surfaces at high temperatures forming surface alleys and prevent welding together of the rubbing parts under severe operating conditions.

Additives such as fatty acids, oil soluble alkaline earth salts of fatty acids etc are added to the lubricant as **rust preventives**. Additives such as alkali metal salts of carboxylic and sulphonic acids, non-ionic emulsifiers such as mono-esters of polyhydric alcohols, ether alcohols etc are added to the lubricant **which help the formation of emulsions with water. These additives are known as emulsifiers.** Additives such as siloxane derivatives are used as foam **depressants**. Oil insoluble glycols and glycerols are also used for the same purpose.

It should be noted that additives are added to the lubricant taking all the factors including properties, application and effects of individual additives into consideration.

No single oil serves as the most satisfactory lubricant for various modern machineries. The properties of petroleun oils are greatly improved by adding various additives given above but the exact adjustment of the additives to a lubricating oil is one of the most complex problem. The so called, **blended oils,** are capable of giving desired lubricating properties, required for a particular machinery.

LUBRICANTS OF MINERAL ORIGIN

Lubricants are either of mineral origin or vegetable orign. Lubricants of mineral origin are generally used as lubricant. Lubricants of vegetable origin such as vegetable oils and fatty acids are rarely used as lubricants, **but they are largely used as additives to the mineral lubricants to improve their properties** and qualities. A large number of lubricants or lubricating oils are obtained from crude petroleum distillation as residues. These residues are either paraffinic or asphaltic. Paraffinic residues are steam distilled to get an oil distillate and steam refined cylinder oil as the main fractions. Asphaltic residues are distilled to get various fractions with different viscosities.

The lubricating oils obtained form mineral residues have a large number of impurities such as paraffin waxes, resins, asphalts, oxy and thio derivatives etc. These impurities are undesirable for a good lubricating oil and so these are nessarary to be removed. For example, waxes increase the setting point. Wax in the lubricant also increases the pour point and renders the lubricant unfit for use at low temperatures. **Asphaltic compounds** undergo decomposition at higher temperature, causing carbon deposition and sludge formation. **Resinous and asphalic compounds** are easily oxidisable and form sludge when the lubricant is used on surfaces. **Oxy- and thio derivatives** are also easily oxidisable and should be removed from the lubricating oils.

Wax from the lubricating oil is generally removed by **Sharples method,** which is based on the difference of density between the precipitated wax and the solvent lubricating oil solution from which wax is separated by cooling or chilling. In this method, the lubricating oil containing wax and the solvent for dilution are mixed together and then heated to get a complete solution. The clear solution so formed is chilled slowly to -20°F and then charged into a centrifugal rotating machine rotating at about 15000 rounds per minute. Wax is separated from the solution of the solvent and lubricating oil. It should be noted that lubricating oil must be completely soluble in the solvent at moderately high temperature and wax should be so precipitated that it could be easily removed. **Wax can also be removed by using acetone-benzene solvent method or propane dewaxing method.** In **acetone benzene method,** acetone and benzene (1 : 20) are mixed and then added to the oil at 120°F The oil solvent mixture is then chilled to -30°R The precipitated wax is removed by using continuous filtration drum type filter. In **propanedewaxing method,** lubricating oil is mixed with liquid propane solvent (propane remains liquid at a pressure of about 200 lbs. per sq. inch)in the ratio 1 : 2. Asphalt is thus precipitated which is removed by cooling which is brought about by releasing the pressure and obtaining autogenous refrigeration. As a result, wax is also thrown out.

In **dewaxing,** solvents other than propane, such as trichloro ethylene, mixture of benzene and ethylene dichloride are also mixed with the oil and then refrigerated. The precipitated wax is then removed by passing the oil wax suspension through a centrifuge or continuous filter. The solvent present in the oil can also be recovered by distillation. **Aromatic compounds** are removed by **solvent extraction** using different methods such as **sulphur dioxide-benzene process, nitrobenzene process, furfural process, phenol extraction process, Chlorex process etc. In sulphur dioxide-benzene process,** aromatic compounds are removed by using a mixture of benzene and sulphur dioxide (30:70). **In nitrobenzene method,** the solvent and the lubricating oil are mixed and extraction temperature is brought to 40°F. Two layers are separated when the mixture is allowed to stand.The lower layer contains naphthenic hydrocarbons in naphthalene and upper layer contains paraffn components with some dissolved N_2. The two layers are continuously separated and the solvent is removed by evaporation in a **vacuum evaporator. In furfural method,** furfural is used as a solvent for the extraction of lubricating oil. It removes olefinic and aromatic hydrocarbons but does not remove paraffinic compounds. The lubricating oil is treated with 200% by volume of furfural for extraction. **In phenol extraction method,** phenol is used as an intermediate solvent between selective solvents like nitrobenzene and'furfurol and the high potency solvents. Phenol is cheap, stable and can be removed easily from the oil. It also reduces the viscosity, sulphur content, oxidation number and carbon content as residue. In Chlorex process, chlorex (β - β' dichloroethylether, $ClCH_2$, CH_2OCH_2 CH_2O) is used for the extraction in the chlorex : oil ratio of 0.7:1.5. In this process viscosity and carbon residue of the lubricating oil are reduced and **pour point** is improved. Moreover, extraction also causes improvement in colour and oxidation stability.

Solvent extraction method has a number of advantages

(a) It *is much less expensive.*

(b) *It provides satisfactory removal of asphaltic impurities and hence minimises the chances of carbon deposit formation during the use of refined lubricating oil.*

(c) *Gives a high yield of refined oil and provides a very refined product, which does not show much variation is viscosity due to increase in temperature.*

One of the most important **disadvantages** of solvent extraction method is that it yields oil which is less resistant to oxidation. As a result of solvent extraction, natural oxidation lubricators present in the oil are removed. The refined oil also possessess lower oiliness and hence its oiliness is improved by adding suitable additives.

Unsaturated hydrocarbons from the oils are removed by **acid treatment.** The lubricating oil is treated with 10% by volume of the oil of conc. H_2SO_4. The principle of counter-current is used in the treatment. In order to avoid side reactions, generally the temperature is kept low. Oil is separated from H_2SO_4 sludge. The oil so obtained is treated with dilute alkali and then with clay.

The **acid refining** can also be followed after dewaxing process, if the oil still contains undesirable constituents like **naphthenic and asphalic impurities.** These are eliminated by treating the oil with conc. H_2SO_4 and then agitated. Some of the impurities dissolve in the acid, while others are converted into tarry sludge. The latter is removed by filtration and the filtrate is neutralised with requesite amount of NaOH so as to remove excess of acid. The oil is finaly decolourised by passing through fuller's earth at 100-140°C temperature. It should be noted that during above treatments of lubricating oils, not only the objectionable bodies and oxidisable impurities are removed, but polar bodies in lubricants are also removed. These polar bodies attach themselves to lubricated surfaces and provide better lubrication because of their chemical affinity. Hence additives are now a days added to ultra purified and non- reactive oily substances, and these additives are capable of giving polar properties to the lubricating oils.

SYNTHETIC LUBRICANTS

Mineral lubricants, even with additives can not be used under various abnormal conditions, e.g. when the temperature is extremely high or the atmosphere is chemically reactive. Under such conditions synthetic lubricants having appropriate properties to be used under abnormal conditions are generally employed. Such synthetic lubricants are prepared by **hydrocarbons, polyglycols, esters, polycarbonates, amines, silicons and fluorine derivatives etc.**

In fact, synthetic lubricants are developed to meet the most sever and drastic operation conditions, such as those existing in aircraft engines in which oil may have to be pumped at -50°C . During take off or landing, the same oil may get heated to as high a temperature as 250°C. Hence it is necessary for the oil to maintain satisfactory properties. The oil to be used at high temperatures and high operating pressures is expected to have high resistance to oxidation and high viscosity, and at the same time it must also possess sufficiently low freezing point and it should also be non-inflammable.

Modern synthetic lubricants have been prepared by taking all these factors into consideration and have a number of distinguishing characteristic features. They are inflammable and have high flash points, high viscosity index and high thermal stability at higher temperatures. They are, however, very costly and so they are used only when they are badly needed. For most common purposes, blended petroleum oils are good and synthetic lubricants are needed only in special circumstances, e.g, in certain specialized military and industrial uses.

Polymerised hydrocarbons such as polymerised ethylene, propylene, butylene etc having molecular weights ranging from 250 to 50,000 are used as **synthetic lubricants.** Although, these hydrocarbons have chemical and physical properties similar to the lubricants obtained from petroleum fractions, but they have some distinct advantages over equivalent petroleum products. For example, they can be used at high temperatures as residue free high temperature lubricants, they are light in colour and free from non-hydrocarbons and they have better electrical properties.

Polyglycols and related compounds such as polyethylene glycol, polypropylene glycol, their ethers and esters, higher polyalkylene oxides, polythioglycols and polyglycidyl ethers can be used as water soluble and water insoluble lubricants.

Water diluted lubricants, e.g. can be prepared by polyethylene glycol or polypropylene glycol to be used in rubber bearings and joints. After applying to metal surfaces they can be easily removed by water flushing. Higher polyalkylene oxides and polyglycidyl ethers absorb a considerable amount of water, although they are not soluble in water. Temperature has no effect on their viscosity.

Polyalkylene oxides undergo decomposition into the volatile parts under high temperature and these volatile parts undergo oxidation. Hence these lubricants are very useful at high temperatures and used in rolling bearings of sheet glass machinery.

Natural fats and oils are esters of glycerides. They have high freezing points and can be easily oxidised. That is why they can not be used as lubricants. Diesters of glycol and aliphatic dibasic acids as well as that of aromatic dibasic acids and triesters of phosphoric acid etc have been found to be good synthetic lubricants, because their viscosity is not much affected by increase in temperature, their volatility is very low, they can be readily oxidised, but this property can be reduced by adding additives. Moreover, they also act as good lubricants even at low temperatures. Esters as lubricants can, however, be decomposed by steam and acids as well as alkalies.

Organic amines, imines and even anodes are good synthetic lubricants having high viscosity index and low pour point. Silicones and the products obtained by hydrolysis and decomposition of organo chlorosilicones are also employed as synthetic lubricants, because they have low viscosity temperature coefficients and are not readily oxidised upto about 200°C. They are, however, oxidised quickly above 200°C and undergo cracking at about 225°C. Silicones are very useful for low temperature lubrication of small parts.

Fluorocarbons and other compounds, e.g, tertiary amines, ethers, esters, which can be completely fluorinated are also used as synthetic lubricants. They are chemically inert and resistant to all chemicals except molten sodium. They are not decomposed easily by heat. They are also not easily oxidisable.

GREASES

Greases are the products composed of a dispersion medium (liquid) which is retained in the cells of a structural frame formed by solid particles of a dispersed phase (thickening) with particles of colloidal size.

Greases behave like solids at low loads. They undergo deforming plastically and become fluid like liquids at a critical load and regain the properties of a solid as the load is removed. This ensures the proper lubrication of engines and mechanisms when ordinary lubricating oils are ineffective. The best greases retain their properties in friction pairs at temperatures from -100°C to + 300°C, rotation speed upto 100,000 rmp, contact stresses above 5000 MPa, in high vacuum, in outer space, under water etc.

Mineral and synthetic oils are used as the liquid base in the manufacture of greases. According to the type of thickener, greases are classified as,

(a) **Soap greases**, which are thickened by soaps such as organic salts of Na, Ca, Ba, Li, and Pb.

(b) **Hydrocarbon greases** are those which are thickened by paraffins, petroleum and ceresins.

(c) **Inorganic greases** are those which are thickened by bentonite clays, graphite and molybdenum disulphide.

(d) **Polymeric greases** are those thickened by high molecular compounds.

The principal operation characteristics of a grease are determined mainly by the thickener. For example, a grease thickened by seresin, whose m.p is 75°C, can operate at temperatures upto 60 - 65°C irrespective of the type of oil used in it (petroleum oil or synthetic).

On the bases of application, greases are classified as :

(a) *Antifriction greases, which decrease friction and wear in friction pairs,*

(b) *Friction greases, which increase friction and prevent slippage.*

(c) *Protective greases, which prevent corrosion.*

(d) *Dispersing greases which improve the alignment of mating parts.*

The major portion of greases relates to the antifriction class. Many of them also possess high protective properties and are called all purpose greases.

Some grades of greases possess unique properties. For example, greases thickened by perfluorinated alkyl polyesters or polytetrafluoroethylene (teflon) do not react with hydrocarbon jet fuels, hydrazine, hydrogen peroxide, fuming nitric acid and liquid oxygen.

The process of manufacture of greases includes the following operations.

(1) *Preparation of components (fusion, dehydrogenation and preheating to the specified temperature).*

(2) *Batching components in a reactor.*

(3) *Compounding.*

(4) *Cooling, and*

(5) *Discharging (pouring).*

The quality of a grease and the strength of its colloidal structure depends on :

(a) *Composition.*

(b) *Process conditions.*

(c) *Conditions of cooling.*

LUBRICATING GREASES

When liquid lubricants are applied to metal surfaces, the bearings or other parts are to be sealed to avoid the loss of lubricant due to deforming effect of gravity. Sealing may, however, be, avoided by using lubricants which are capable of resisting deforming effect of gravity. This type of lubricants are used generally in the solid form and known as greases or semi-solid lubricants. Greases are composed of lubricating oil with an added gelling agent which gives stiffness to the mixture. Fatty acids, and soaps of metals like Al, Ca, Na, Li etc are usually used as gelling agents, but sometimes soaps of K, Pb, Ba and Mg etc have also been used. Fatty acids that have been used as gelling agents are oleic acid, palmitic acid, and stearic acid. Carboxylic acids obtained from castor oil and hydrogenated fish oils are also used as gelling agents. Non-soap gelling agents such as carbon black, organobentonite, asphaltenes etc are also used in the preparation of greases.

Generally petroleum fractions are used as lubricating oils in the preparation of greases but synthetic oils such as polymerised ethylene oxides, fluorocarbons and siloxanes havd also been used.

Greases are generally prepared by saponification of fat such as tallow or fatty acid with alkali such as lime, caustic soda etc, followed by adding hot lubricating oil with constant agitation. Soaps, which are added as gelling agents, give an interconnected structure. At high temperature, the interconnected structure which is held by inter molecular forces, ceases to exist, because soap (gelling agent) dissolves in·the oil and hence the grease undergoes liquifaction.

Grease can be **manufactured** by dissolving fatty acid in a part of lubricating oil. Metal hydroxide is then added to it in the form of dry oil slurry or as aqueous solution. The mixture of soap and oil is dehydrated by stirring and the balance of lubricating oil is added. Finally, using some shear device, it is homogenised. As we know, gelling agents in soap based greases are crystallities of fibrous shape. Their gelling property is due to their ability to form a tangle in the intersticies as a result of which the oil is held by capillary forces. When the temperature is high, the soap dissolve in oil. As a result, the fibrous structure no longer exists and liquefaction of grease takes place.

It is also possible to make greases stable to oxidation and to provide lubrication under extreme conditions of load and sliding speed, by adding additives to lubricating oils. But these additives are required in much greater amounts than the quantity required for the lubricating oils because of interfering action of the gelling agent. The consistency or yield value of greases, which depends on the structure and interaction of the gelling elements and also on the viscosity of the oil, is an important property of greases and can be expressed in terms of depth of penetration in the grease of a cone of specified dimensions under specified conditions. Consistency of greases varies from a heavy viscous liquid to that of a stiff solid mass. The heat resistance of greases can be improved by adding inorganic and thickening agents such as carbon black, finely divided clay. Colloidal silica, bentonite etc are also added.

The consistency of the greases cosiderably changes when the temperature is suddenly decreased, because the interaction of gelling agents and the viscosity of the oil changes with increase in temperature. The temperature at which the consistency of the greases changes, determines the upper temperature limit **of the applicability of the grease.** Under certain conditions it is not possible to use liquid lubricants. In such cases **solid lubricants** such as talcum, graphite, boron nitride, molybdenum disulphide etc are used. Greases can support much heavier loads at lower speeds because they have higher shear or frictional resistance. Greases also have a tendency to separate into oils and soaps. The main function of the soap is to act as **thickening agent** so that grease sticks firmly to the metal surfaces.

The consistency, water resistance, oxidation resistant and the temperature upto which the grease can be used are all decided by the nature of soap. Hence, greases are sometimes classified as cup greases (calcium based greases), soda base greases, lithium base greases, axle greases etc, depending upon the soap used in the manufacture of greases.

Cup greases or calcium base greases are the emulsions of petroleum oils with calcium soap and can be prepared by adding calculated amount of $Ca(OH)_2$ to a hot petroleum oil such as tallow, with constant agitation. These greases are water resistant because they are insoluble in water. They are cheap and has widely been used at low temperatures upto 60-65°C. Above 80°C, soap begins to separate from these greases. Soda base greases are petroleum oils thickened by mixing sodium soap. They are soluble in water and so they are not water resistant. They can be used upto 175°F in ball bearing, where the lubricant gets heated as a result of friction.

Lithium based greases are petroleum oils thickened by adding lithium soaps. These are resistant to water and used at low temperatures only. Axle greases are cheap resin greases which are prepared by adding lime or heavy metal hydroxide to resin and then allowed to stand, as a result of which, grease floats on the surface as a stiff mass. It is separated and mixed with filters such as tale and mica. These greases are insoluble in water and so they are water resistant and can be suitably used for delicate equipments working under low speeds but high loads.

Greases can also be prepared by dispersing graphite, soap stone etc in mineral oils.

CHEMICAL PROPERTIES OF GREASES

(a) *Oxidation :* Due to oxidation catalysing effect of soap oil interface, greases are less stable to oxidation than the component lubricating oil present in the oil. In order to prevent oxidation of grease, antioxidants or inhibitors are added to the grease.

(b) *Water Resistance :* In presence of hydrophilic gelling agents, the presence of moisture in the grease becomes deterimental. **Most of the gelling agents are hydrophilic in nature,** Sodium and potassium soap greases are soluble in water and so they are less resistant to water. Lithium and multivalent metal soaps are much less soluble in water and so greases produced by them are resistant to water and resist emulsification by water quite satisfactority.

SOLID LUBRICANTS

The most important solid lubricants that have widely been used are graphite and molybdenum disulphide. Graphite consists of multitude of flat plates, one atom thick and these plates are held by weak bonds so that the force required to shear the crystals in a direction parallel to the layer is small. This causes the parallel layers to ,slide over one another. Solid lubricants are sometimes mixed with some organic compounds, so that they can stick firmly to the metal surfaces.

Graphite is the most widely used of all solid lubricants. It is very soapy to touch, non-inflammable, resistant to oxidation by air below 375°C, and can be used upto very high temperatures in the absence of air. Suspension of graphite in oil or water is prepared in presence of tannin, which acts as an emulsifying agent. Graphite dispersed in oil is called oil dog, and graphite dispersed in water is called aquadog. Oildog is generally used in internal combustion engine, because it provides a tight fit contact by forming a film between the piston and rings and hence increases the compression. Aquadog is used where a lubricant free from oil is needed, e.g, in food stiff industry. Graphite greases(graphite mixed with greases) are used at very high temperatures.

Molybdenum disulphide has a sandwitch like structure in which a layer of a molybdenum atom lies between two layers of sulphur atoms. It provides low shear strength in a direction parallel to the layers because of poor interlaminar attraction. Molybdenum disulphide has very low coefficient of friction and is thermally stable in air up to 400°C. Its fine powder may be sprinkled on surfaces sliding at high velocities. As a result, it fills low spots in metal surfaces forming the film. It has also been used mixed with solvents and greases. **Solid lubricants** are generally used either in the form of dry powder or mixed with water or oil. The coefficient of friction of solid lubricants lies between 0.005 and 0.01. Soap stone, talc, mica, etc have also been used as solid lubricants, inaddition to graphite and molybdenum disulphide.

Solid lubricants are generally used :

(a) *Where operating conditions are such that a lubricating film is difficult to be secured by use of lubricating oils or greases.*

(b) *Where* contamination of *lubricating oil or greases by dust or grit particles is not acceptable, e.g. in commutator bushes of electric generators and motors.*

(c) *Where the operating temperature or load is extremely high, even for a semisolid lubricant (grease) to stick in position.*

(d) *Where combustible lubricants have to be avoided.*

LUBRICANT EMULSIONS

A dispersion system consisting of two immiscible liquids is called an emulsion and it is stabilized by adding a third component, called **emulsifying agent.** *Emulcifiers or emulsifying agents are the substances which exhibit polar as well as non- polar character, because they contain hydro-phobic as well as hydrophilic end.* The hydrophobic end of the emulsifier molecule is preferable wetted by oil (water hating) and hydrophilic end (water loving) will be wetted by water. Hence emulsifier molecule is adsorbed at the interface of the two immiscible phases or liquids (oil and water), resulting in the formation of a protective film around the dispersed droplets. A well known example of emulsifying agent is sodium soap, which is the sodium salt of long chain fatty acid (e.g, $C_{15}H^{31}COONa$). It possesses hydrophilic or water loving group -COONa and hydrophobic or water hating end $C^{15}H^{31}$.

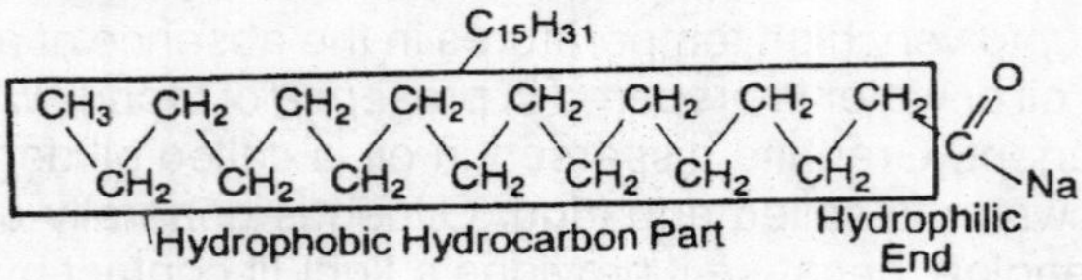

Fig. 1. Structure of sodium palmitate as emulsifier.

There are two types of emulsions. These are **oil in water emulsion and water in oil emulsion.** Oil in water emulsions are obtained by adding an oil to a suitable quantity of water in presence of 3-20% water soluble emulsifying agent, such as sodium soap or sodium and potassium salts of sulphonic acids. These emulsions are generally used as cooling and lubricating liquids for cutting tools. These emulsions are also used as rust preventers and used as lubricant for certain heavy sliding components such as pistons in marine diesel engines.

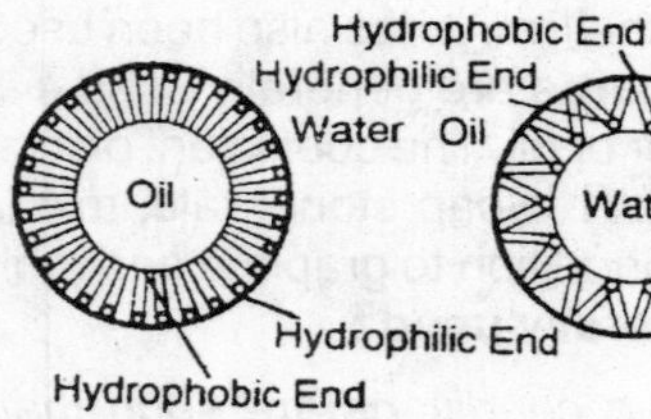

Fig. 2. Function of emulsifier molecules around the droplets in o/w and w/o emulsions.

Water in oil emulsions (W/O) are prepared by mixing water containing 1-10% water soluble emulsifier such as alkaline earth soap (calcium stearate) to the oil. This type of emulsions are widely used to lubricate compressors and provide cooling effect because of evaporation of water, in addition to lubrication. These emulsions possess higher viscosity, than that of the oil from which they are prepared.

SOME TESTS SCARRIED OUT ON LUBRICANTS

(1) Pour Point : This important property of a sample of lubricating oil is the temperature at which the oil ceases to flow when cooled under standard conditions. **Pour point** is the temperature, being multiples of 5°F, which is 5°F above the temperature at which the oil just fails to flow when cooled under prescribed condititons. It indicates the dissolved wax concentration in a given sample of lubricating oil and also determine the temperature below which oil can not be used as lubricant in the engine.

Pour point apparatus consists of a jar, closed from above by a cork through which a thermometer is inserted. Another jacket cylinder surrounds the jar. A disc of cork is inserted and fixed at the bottom, the jacket cylinder and jar containing the lubricant sample under test stands over the disc of cork. The whole apparatus is surrounded by a cooling bath.

The sample is cooled in the cooling bath till it does not flow on tilting the jar. The jar is then held in a horizontal position for exactly 5 seconds. If the sample shows any movement or the flow, the jar is again placed into the jacket and again cooled for another 5°F, when oil does not flow or shows no movement during these five seconds, the temperature of the thermometer is recorded. 5°F is then added to the thermometer reading and the result is **pour point** of the lubricant.

(2) **Viscosity and Viscosity Index** : When the conditions are such that perfect fluid lubrication takes place, then viscosity is a measure of bearing friction, heat generation and rate of flow under specified conditions of load, speed and design. The variation of viscosity with temperature is known as **Viscosity Index.** Viscosity index may also be regarded as the rate of change of viscosity with temperature and is a measure of paraffinic nature of a lubricating oil, because the rate of change of viscosity of paraffins is low. The **Viscosity Index** can be determined by determining the viscosity of the oil at different temperatures. The co-relation of specific gravity and viscosity, generally known as viscosity gravity constant, is also a measure of paraffinic nature of lubricating oils because paraffins are less dense than the naphthenic hydrocarbons.

In **United States , Saybolt Universal Viscosity (S.U.V),** which can be expressed as the number of seconds required for 60 cc of the oil to run through a standard orifice from a cylinder filled to a defnite level at a standard temperature, is frequently used. S.U.V can be determined by Saybolt Viscometer. The **Viscosity Index** is expressed as

$$\textbf{Viscosity Index (V.I) X} = \frac{V_L - V_X}{V_L - V_H} \times 100$$

Where V_L = S.U.V of a standard low viscosity oil at 100°F

V_H = S.UX of a standard high viscosity oil at 100°F

In **Great Britain** for measuring the viscosity in seconds, Redwood Viscometer is used. Thus time in seconds is proportional to the true viscosities.

Viscosity is the most important property of any lubricating oil, because it determines the main operating characteristics of the lubricant. For example, it is not possible to maintain a liquid oil film between two moving or sliding surfaces if the viscosity of the lubricant is too low and hence excessive wear will occur. Excessive friction will take place, if the viscosity of the lubricant is too high.

Viscosity of liquids decreases with increasing temperature and so lubricating oil becomes thinner as the operating temperature is raised. It is, therefore, necessary that viscosity of the lubricating oil should not change

underfuctuating temperatures. As seen above, the rate of change of viscosity of an oil with temperature is measured in terms of viscosity Index. An oil has a low viscosity index (V.I.) if its viscosity decreases rapidly with increase in temperature, and an oil has a high viscosity index (V.I.), if its viscosity is only slightly affected on increasing the temperature.

To determine the viscosity index, the viscosities of the lubricating oil are first determined at 100°F and 210°F. In case of a good oil the difference between the two values should be minimum. The difference will be large, if the oil is of poor quality. This difference is generally compared with two standared oils one with viscosity index (V.I.) of 100 and another with viscosity index 0. These reference oils are series of paraffinic base Pennsylvnian.oils (VI =100) and naphthanic base Gulf oils (V.I. = 0) respectively. Their viscosties at 100°F and 210°F are marked. The oils having V.I. = 100 are known as **H-Oils (High Viscosity Index Standard)** and those having V.I. = 0 are called as **L- Oils (Low Viscosity Index Standards).**

The viscosity as well as the viscosity index of a lubricating oil depend mainly upon the molecular structure of the oil. **A high viscosity Index (V.I.)** is exhibited by molecules of a linear or rod like structure which possesses flexibility through free rotation about the chemical bonds. A low freezing point or high viscosity of an oil can be achieved if short side chains are attached to the main chain of the linear molecule, because side chains prevent alignment of the neighbouring molecules. **In general, a lubricating oil having high molecular weight possesses high viscosity as well as high boiling point.**

It is also possible to increase the **viscosity index** of lubricating oils by adding certain polymers which are partially miscible with the oil. At low temperatures, the added polymer dissolves in the oil only slightly and so there is a slight change in the viscosity of the oil, but at high temperature, the solubility of the polymer in oil is more and hence its effect will be to increase the viscosity of the oil to a considerable extent. In general, polymer blends of lubricating oils having very slight temperature coefficients of viscosity or even none at all can be produced by adding requisite quantities of organic polymers.

The viscosity of a lubricating oil can be determined by making use of a **viscometer** in which a known volume of the lubricating oil is allowed to flow from a given height, through a standard capillary tube under its own weight and the time of flow-in. seconds is noted. This time is proportional to the true viscosity of the oil.

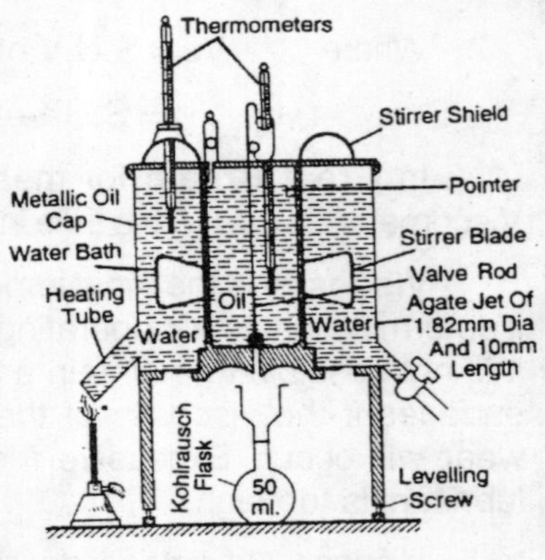

Fig.4. Redwood viscometer No.1

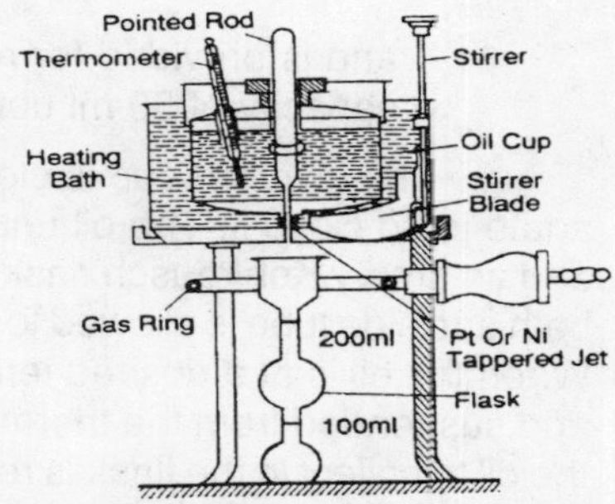

Fig. 5. Engler's viscometer.

As seen above Saybolt viscometer and Redwood viscometers are generally used in U.S.A. and Great Britain respectively for measuring the ciscosities of the lubricating oils and results are expressed in terms of time taken by the oil to flow through a particular instrument. For example, if time of flow of an oil through Red wood viscometer at 20°C is 60 seconds, it indicates that its viscosity is 60 Redwood seconds at 20°C.

In India, Redwood viscometer is generally used for determining the viscosity of a lubricating oil. These are generally of two types. Redwood viscometer No.I. is commonly used for determining the viscosities of thin lubricating oils. It has a jet or bore diameter of 1.62 m.m. and length 10 m.m. Redwood viscometer No. 2 is generally employed for the measurement of viscosities of highly viscous oils and has a jet diameter of 3.8 m.m. and length 15 m.m. The Redwood viscometer No. 1 consists of the following parts.

(a) **Oil Cup -** It is a silver plated brass cylindrical vessel 90 mm in height and 46.5 mm in diameter. The upper end of the cup is open and the lower end is concave internally to ensure complete drainage of oil. The bottom of the cylinder is provided with a tapering central hole in which an agate jet with bore of diameter 1.62 mm and length 10 mm is fitted. The jet is opened or closed by a value rod which is a small silver plated brass ball fixed to a stout wire. The level to which the cup is to be filled with oil is indicated by a pointer, which is a stout wire fixed in the side of the oil cup. The wire is turned upwards and is tapered to a sharp point to indicate the level properly. The lid of the cup is fitted with a thermometer for indicating the oil temperature.

(b) **Heating Bath -** Oil cup is surrounded by a cylindrical bath made of copper. It contains water and also provided with a tap for emptying water from it. It has also got a side tube projecting outwards and attached to it. It is used for heating the bath water by making use of a gas burner or spirit lamp.

(c) **Stirrer -** The heating bath containing water contains a stirrer having four blades or vanes for stirring -the water in the bath for keeping the temperature of the water bath uniform throughout.

(d) **Spirit Level -** The lid of the cup is provided with a spirit level for vertical levelling of the jet and the entire apparatus is kept on three legs, provided at the bottom with levelling screws.

(e) A flask, known as **Kohlrausch flask,** is specially shaped flask, and is provided for receiving oil from the outlet The flask has a capacity of 50 ml upto the mark in its neck.

The levelling cup is cleaned and ball of value rod is placed on the agate jet to close it. The oil under test is filled in the cup upto pointer level and an empty Kohlrausch flask is placed below the jet. Water is filled in the bath and side tube is allowed to heat slowly with constant stirring of the bath. When the oil is at a desired temperature, say 100°F, the ball value is lifted and suspended from the thermometer bracket. The time taken for 50 ml of the oil to collect in the flask is recorded and the valve is immediately closed, inorder to prevent the flow of oil. viscosity of the oil is expressed in Redwood No. 1 seconds at the particular temperature. Viscosity can also be determined by Engler's viscometer is which water-bath is heated by a gas ring. The water temperature is maintained uniform by making use of a stirrer. The oil cylinder is fitted with three gauge points for indicating the amount of oil to be filled in it. Gauge points also help in levelling of the instrument. The oil cover of oil cylinder carries a thermometer which is also used for stirring the oil by rotating it gently. The oil cylinder is also provided with a jet made of platinum or nickel and it is slightly tappered. A valve pin, which seats on the jet, is lifted when the test is started and stop watch is immediately started when the time for flow of 200 ml of the oil is to be determined. The time of out flow of 200 ml of water at 20°C has been taken as 52 seconds and viscosity is measured in degrees of Engler's degrees. The viscosity in degrees E, can be calculated by dividing the time in seconds for outflow of 200 ml of the oil by the time of outflow of 200 ml of water at 20°C.

It should be noted that:

(a) The diesel engine lubricating oils have time of flow not exceeding 700 seconds at 20°C and time of flow not exceeding 50 seconds at 90°C, using Redwood No 1. viscometer.

(b) The ***kinematic viscosity in centistoke*** *can 6e calculated by using the relation.* y = Ct - B/t

Where, C and B are constants of the viscometer. t is the time of flow in seconds. In case of Redwood viscometer NoI, it is the time of flow of 50ml of oil and values of B and C are given below.

TABLE 1.

Value of t	Value of B	Value of C
34-100 sec.	1.78	0.00260
above 100 sec.	0.50	0.00247

(c) Relation between E (= Degrees Engler), R.I (=Seconds Redwood) and S.V (= Seconds, Say bolt Universal) for higher viscosities are given below: Vk in the following relations indicates kinematic viscosity.

TABLE 2.

E= 0.132 Vk	Vk = 7.58 E	Vk = 0.216 S.U.	Vk = 0.247 R.I.
R.I. = 4.05 Vk	R.I. = 30.7 E	E = 0.0285 S.U.	E = 0.326 R.I.
S.U. = 4.62 Vk	S.U. = 35.11 E	R.I. = 0.87 S.U.	S.U. = 1.14 R.I.

Example 1 : A *lubricating oil has Saybolt universal viscosity of 58 seconds at 210°F and 564 seconds at 100°F. The low VI standard Gulf oil has Saybolt universal viscosity of 58 seconds at 210°F and 758 seconds at 100°F. The high VI standard Pennyslyvanian oil gave the Saybolt universal viscosity value of 58 seconds at 210°F and 420 seconds at 100°F. Calculate the VI of the lubricating oil.*

Solution : We know **V.I., X =** $\frac{V_L - V_X}{V_L - V_H} \times 100$

In the present problem V_L=758 seconds, V_H = 420 seconds, Vx = 564 seconds. Thus,

$$\textbf{V.I.} = \frac{758 - 564}{758 - 420} \times 100 = \frac{194}{338} \times 100 = 57.396$$

Example 2 : An *oil of unknown VI. has a Saybolt universal viscosity of 58 seconds at 210°F and 560 seconds at 100°F. The high viscosity index standard (ie pennysylvanian) oil has Saybolt viscosity of 58 seconds at 210°F and 420 seconds at 100°F The low viscosity index standard (ie Gulf oil) has a Saybolt universal viscosity of 560 seconds at 210°F and 770 seconds at 100°F Calculate the viscosity index of unknown oil.*

Solution : V .I. = $\frac{V_L - V_X}{V_L - V_H} \times 100$

In the present problem, V_L= 770 secnonds, VH = 420 seconds and Vx = 560 seconds. Thus.

$$\textbf{V.I.} = \frac{770 - 560}{770 - 420} \times 100 = \frac{210}{350} \times 100 = \mathbf{60}$$

Example 3 : The *following observations were made with a sample of diesel oil using Redwood viscometer No. 1. Volume of sample = 50 ml, temp. of the oil = 20°C and time of flow = 500 seconds. Calculate the absolute kinemetic viscosity of the oil.*

Sulotion : We know ϒ -Ct - B/t

In the present problem t= 500 seconds and so the values of B and C are respectively 0.50 and 0.00247. Thus,

ϒ= [(0.00247 x 500) - (0.50 x 500)] _ [1.235 - 0.001] = **1.234 Centistokes.**

(3) Emulsification - Emulsification is the property of oils to get intimately mixed with water, forming an emulsion. A number of lubricating oils are capable of forming emulsions with water very easily. Emulsions also have a tendency to attract dirt, grit, foreign matter etc, as a result of which abrasion and wearing out of the lubricated parts of the machinery may take place. **A good lubricating oil forms an emulsion with water which undergoes de-emulsification very quickly.** The tendency of a lubricant to form an emulsion can be quantitatively determined by the **emulsion test,** in which an emulsion of the lubricating oil and water is prepared under specified standard conditions. The emulsion is then allowed to stand so that it undergoes **de-emulsification.** The time in seconds in which the emulsion separates out (de-emulsifies) into its constituents is noted as the steam emulsion number, (S.E.N.). A good lubricant possesses a low **steam emulsion number.** In an actual procedure, 20 ml of oil is taken in a test tube and steam is bubbled through it at 100°C, till the temperature is raised to 90°C. The tube is then kept in a thermostat maintained at 90°C so that oil and water separate out as distinct layers. The time in seconds in which oil and water separate in distinct layers is called steam emulsion number.

(4) Precipitation Number- Precipitaion number of a lubricant indicates the amount of precipitated asphalt when diluted with petroleum ether and then centrifuged, and is a property of lubricant which can differentiate between different classes of lubricaing oils. The precipitated asphalt is filtered, washed, dried and weighed. Precipitation number is expressed as the percentage of weight of oil taken.

(5) Cloud Point- This is an index of dissolved wax in a lubricating oil and defined as the temperature at which cloudiness appears in a sample of oil under standard conditions of wax separation.

(6) Neutralisation Number- The acidity and alkalinity of an oil is determined by this test and it may be defined as the weight in milligrams of KOH required to neutralise the acid content of one gm of oil. Lubricating oils containing detergents are alkaline in nature and then neutralisation is called **alkaline neutralisation.** A *lubricating oil should possess acid number or acid value (determination of acidic constituents present in oil is called acid number of acid value) less than oil. Values greater than 0.1 shows that oil has been oxidised. Hence lubricating oil in such a case causes gum and sludge formation as well as corrosion.*

Take 10-20 gm. of oil in a conical fkask and add 50cc water, 50cc alcohol and few drops of phenolphthalein as indicator. Titrate the solution with N/10 KOH solution till pink colour is obtained at the end point.

$$\textbf{Neutralisation Number} = \frac{\text{No. of cc of N/ 10 KOH x 5.6}}{\text{Weight of oil}}$$

In presence of additives, the neutralisation number of the lubricating oil is greater than 0.10, while in the absence of an additive, the neutralisation number or acid number is riot more than 0.10.

(7) Copper Strip Test - The presence of corrosive or tarnished materials or chemically active substances in the oil can be determined by placing a polished copper strip in the lubricating oil for a specified time. If the copper strip becomes tarnished then the lubricant is supposed to contain the above materials. This is also known as corrosive stability test. A **good lubricant should not tarnish the** copper strip. The corrosion effects of oil are prevented by adding some **inhibitors** such as organic compounds of arsenic, antimony, chromium, bismuth, lead and phosphorus.

(8) Specific Gravity- The specific gravity of an oil in American Petroleum Institute (A.PI.) degrees is given by the expression

$$\textbf{Degrees of A.P.I} = \frac{141.5}{\text{Sp. Gravity/60°F}} - 131.5$$

141.5 is termed the modulus of A.PI scale. A.P.1 hydrometer is adapted to the simplified numerical system and starts at 10, which is equivalent to 1 for the unit specific gravity of water at 60°F *Liquids lighter than water are thus asigned values higher than 10 and liquids heaver than water are assigned values lesser than 10. Heavier naphthalenic base-mineral oils have lower A.R1. gravity than those of lighter paraffin-base oils.*

(9) Saponification Number - The number of milligrams of KOH required to saponify 1 gm of lubricating oil is known as **saponification number.** 2.5 g. of accurately weighed sample is saponified by adding 25cc of N/2 alcoholic KOH and heating on a water bath atlest for an hour. 25cc of N/2 alcoholic KOH are also heated in a separate flask to be used for blank titration. After about an hour, both solutions are titrated with N/2 HCl using phenolphthalein as an indicator . The difference in the titration value of blank and the sample is equivalent to N/2 alcoholic KOH equivalent to N/2 HCl solution used for the saponification of the sample. Suppose the difference be *a* cc of N/2 HCl. Thus

$$\textbf{Saponification Value} = \frac{a \times 28.05}{\text{Weight of oil}}$$

Vegetable and animal oils undergo saponification but mineral oils do not undergo saponification. The small saponification number in case of mineral oils may be due to the presence of minute amounts of fatty matter. Thus. Saponification value indicates whether the **oil is animal, vegetable or mineral oil or a compounded oil which contains both mineral oil and vegerable oil.** In the case of compounded oil, the fat added to determine the percentage of compounding in an oil can be calculated by using the formula,

$$\textbf{\% Fatty Oil} = \frac{C}{F} \times 100$$

where C and F are the **saponification numbers** of the compounded oil and fatty oil respectively.

(10) Ash Test : This test is performed by heating or burning a known amount of the lubricating oil in a crucible to burn out all the combustible products and weighing the residue. The percentage of ash in a lubricating oil, particularly in used oil, determines the materials that may cause wear and abrasion.

(11) Coke Number : Different lubricating oils used in moving parts of an internal combustion engine undergo thermal decomposition, producing free carbon in varying amounts. This property is expresed as the **coke number** and gives the amount of carbon deposited by a known amount of lubricating oil in standard apparatus and under a standard set of experimental conditions. **Better lubricating oils have low coke numbers.**

TABLE 3 : SAPONIFICATION NUMBERS OF OILS

Oil	Saponification Number	Oil	Saponification Number
Lard oil	192-198	Rapeseed oil	170-179
Tallow	193-198	Soyabean oil	189-197
Fish oil	140-193	Peanut oil	186-197
Sperm oil	120-140	Cotton seed oil	191-197
Castor oil	176-187		

(12) Aniline Point : It is defined as the minimum equilibrium solution temperature for equal volumes of aniline and the lubricating oil sample. **Aniline point** is helpful in indicating the possible deterioration of the oil in contact with packings, rubber sealings etc. Low aromatic content in the lubricant is desirable because aromatic hydrocarbons have a tendency to dissolve natural rubber as well as a number of synthetic rubbers and protect the lubricating oils from deterioration. A *high aniline point of lubricant indicates that it contains higher percentage of paraffinic hydrocarbons and lower percentage of aromatic hydrocarbons.*

For the detrmination of aniline point, equal volumes of aniline and sample are mixed in a tube and the mixture is heated till a homogeneous solution results. The tube is then cooled slowly at a controlled rate. The temperature at which the oil and aniline phases separate out, is noted as the **aniline point.**

(13) ***Drop Point*** *: It is the temperature at which a semisolid grease passes into the liquid state and hence determines the maximum temperature of the applicability of the grease. Drop* **point** is determined by making use of the apparatus shown in fig. 6, which consists of a metal cup, heaving an

opening of standard size at the bottom. The cup is enclosed in a glass case having tight lid. the cup is provided with a thermometer, which is inserted in such a manner that bulb of the thermometer lies just above the sample of grease. The apparatus is placed in an outer glass beaker containing water. It is also provided with a stirrer for uniform heating of water and the beaker is slowly heated at the rate of 1°C per minute. As the temperature increases, the semisolid grease passes into the fluid state. The temperature at which first drop falls from the opening is noted as the **drop point.**

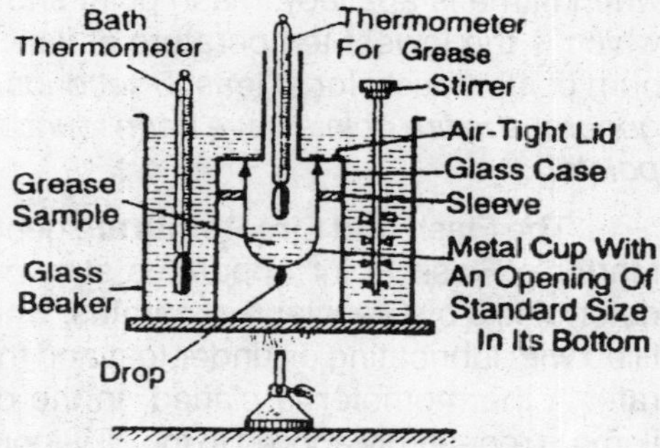

Fig.6. Determination of drop point.

(14) **Consistency or Yield Value :** It is expressed in terms of penetration and defined as the distance in tenth of millimetre that a standard cone penetrates vertically into the smaple of grease or semisolid lubricant, under the standard conditions of **load (150g), temperature (25°C) and time (5 seconds).** The consistency of grease is influenced by structure and interaction of gelling agents and also by visocity of the oil used. The interaction of gelling agents and the viscosity of the oil change with increasing temperature. Hence consistency of the grease changes when temperature decreases abruptly. This ***temperature*** *determines the upper temperature limit of the applicability of the grease and is known as* ***drop point.***

(15) **Flash Point :** During use, lubricants are also be subjected to high temperatures and at such high temperatures they have a tendency to volatilise and cause loss of lubricant. A good lubricant is that which does not volatilise under the conditions of lubrication. If, however, they volatilise, the vapours formed by them should not catch fire under the conditions of the lubrication. *Hence a good lubricant should form inflamrnable vapours only at a temperature which is greater than the working temperature of the lubricant. Flash* point is the lowest temperature at which the lubricant oil gives off enough vapours that ignite for a moment when a small flame is brought in contact with it (i.e. vapours form inflammable mixture with air and catch fire

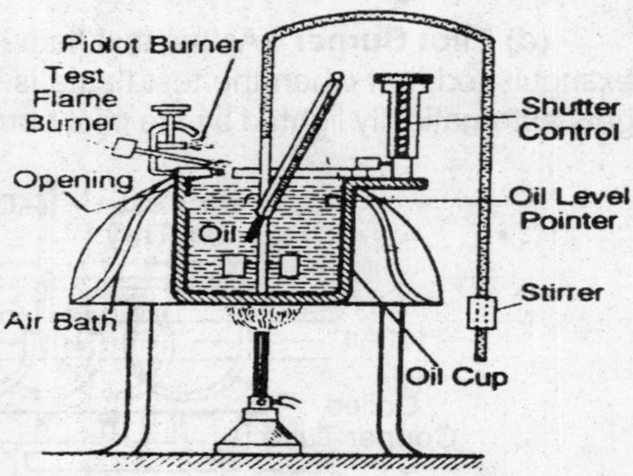

Fig.7. Penskey - Marten's Flash Point Apparatus

when flame is applied). Flash point should not be confused with fire point, which is the lowest temperature at which the vapours of the lubricating oil burn continuously for at least 5 seconds, when a flame is brought near it. *In general, the fire points have been found to be 5 to 40°C higher than the flash points.*

The Flash **and Fire Points** are generally determined by using Penskey Marten's Flash Point Apparatus shown in Fig. 7. Flash point can also he determine d by Cleveland apparatus, which consists of an *open cup of* brass filled with lubricating oil under test and the oil is heated at a certain constant rate. A thermometer is placed in the oil to note the temperature. Naked flame is repeatedly applied to the oil vapour at regular intervals of temperature. The temperature is noted as the **flash point** at which vapours of oil catch fire. Penskey Marten's Flash Point Apparatus consists of the following parts:

(a) Oil Cup : The oil cup is about 5 cm in diameter and 5.5 cm deep. In it there is a groove or level to which the oil is to be filled. The cup lid is provided with four openings of standard sizes and one of them is fitted with the thermometer. Second opening is used for introducing test flame, through the third opening passes a stirrer carrying two brass blades and fourth opening is used for introducing the air.

(b) **Shutter** : It is level mechanism provided at the top of the cup. By moving the shutter, opening in the lid is exposed to flame carried by a flame exposure device. Flame exposure device is a small flame which is connected with the shutter in such a manner that when the opening in the lid is exposed by the shutter, the flame of this device is dipped into the opening.

(c) Air Bath : Oil cup is supported by its flange over an air bath, which is heated by a gas burner.

(d) Pilot Burner : As the test flame is introduced in the opening, it is extinguished, but when the test flame is returned to its original position, it gets automatically lighted by the pilot burner.

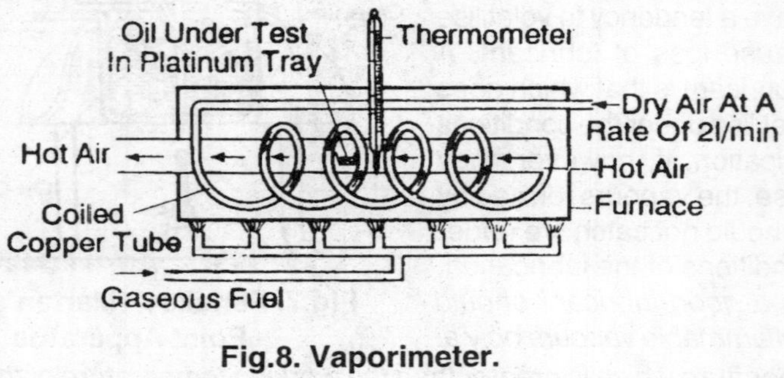

Fig.8. Vaporimeter.

The oil is filled up to the mark in the oil cup and it is heated by a burner through an air-bath. Shutter is moved and the oil is exposed to flame at every 2°F rise in temperature of the oil. Heat is applied so as to raise the oil temperature by about 5°C per minute. During heating of the oil, stirring of the oil is carried out by the stirrer continuously. The temperature at which a distinct flash (a combination of weak sound and light) appears inside the cup by applying the test flame through the opening provided for the purpose, is noted as the flash point. The heating is continued thereafter and the test flame is applied as before. When the oil ignites and continues to burn at least for 5 seconds, the temperature is recorded as the fire point of the oil.

(16) **Volatility** : We have seen that certain lubricating oils, when used in heavy machinery working at very high temperatures, undergo volatilisation leaving behind a residual oil, which has different lubricating properties than that which was used originally. For example, its viscosity is increased after volatilisation at high temperature. A good lubricant should therefore possess low volatility. **The volatility** of a lubricating oil can be determined by using vaporimeter shown in Fig. 8. It consists of a furnace heated by some fuel gas. A coiled form of copper tube is siturated in the centre of the furnace and air can be passed through the tube. A known weight of the lubricating oil is taken in a platinum tray and it is introduced into the copper tube. Now dry air is passed through the copper tube at the rate of about 2 litres per minute. After one hour of heating, the tray is taken out of the copper tube, cooled and weighed. The loss in weight is calculated as percentage volatilisation.

(17) Carbon Residue : Lubricating oils contain a good percentage of carbon in combined state. Carbon residue percentage in an oil is proportional to the amount of carbon deposited in the combustion chamber. In addition to carbon residue, however, other conditions in the engine also influence the carbon deposits. The lubricating oils decompose on heating, depositing a certain amount of carbon, which is not tolerable, especially in internal combustion engines and air compressors. A good lubricant is that which deposits least amount of carbon when in use. The determination of carbon residue is carried out either by Conradson method or by Ramsbottom method. In Conradson methed, a known amount of the lubricating oil is taken in a silica crucible and the crucible is placed in a skidmore iron crucible of 75-80 ml capacity, which is also provided with a lid having a small tube opening for the escape of volatile matter. The whole combination is kept in a wrought iron crucible which is covered with chimney shaped iron hood. This wrought iron crucible is now heated slowly for 10 minutes till flame appears. Now heating is slowed down and continued for 5 minutes more, Finally heating is done strongly for about 15 minutes, till vapours of all volatile matter are

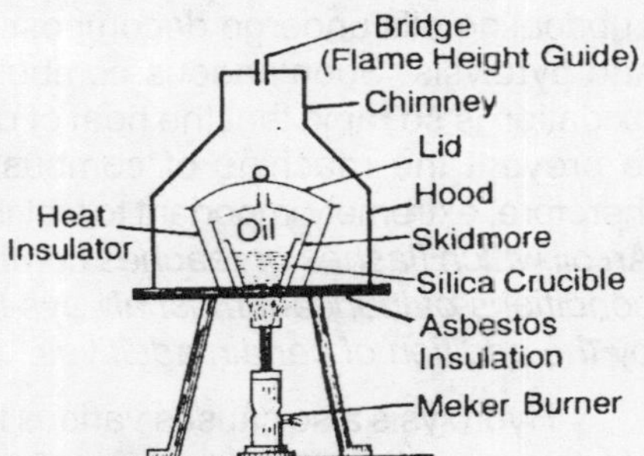

Fig.9. Conradson's apparatus for the estimation of carbon residue

completely burned. The crucible is allowed to cool and weight of residue left is calculated. The result is expressed in percentage of the original weight of oil taken. The Ramsbottom apparatus consists of an electrically heated small furnace which is provided with a number of holes at the top to contain glass bulbs in which the samples of oil are placed. The weighted amount of the oil sample is taken in the special type of bulb of thick glass (known as coking bulb). The inlet of the bulb consists of a small capillary and the oil is injected into the bulb through the capillary inlet by means of a hypodemic syringe. The temperature of the furnace is raised to 500-500°C and the bulb containing the oil is placed in one of the holes in the furnace. It is electrically heated for about 30 minutes in the furnace at 500-500°C. The bulb is then taken out and cooled in a desiccator and then weighed. The result is then expressed as percentage of the original weight of oil taken.

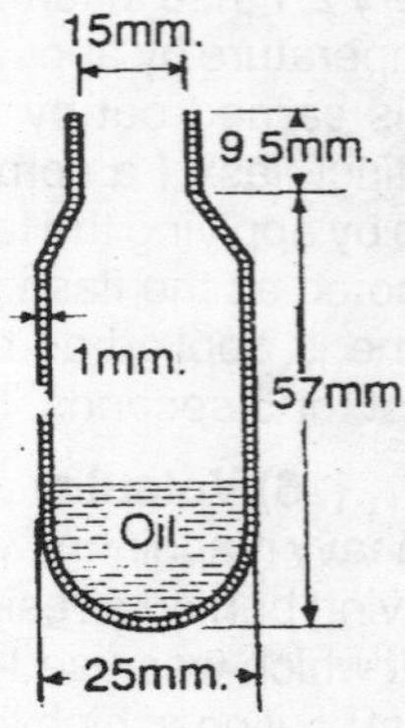

Fig.10. Coking bulb.

(18) **Decomposition Stability :** Lubricating oils are expected to be stable to decomposition at the working temperatures, but it is not so. Lubricating oils undergo decomposition as a result of oxidation, hydrolysis and pyrolysis. Spontaneous combustion of oil vapours takes place when oxidation is so rapid that the heat of oxidation is not dissipated so quickly as to prevent the reaching of combustion temperature or flash point. It is, therefore, extremely important to test the flash point of the oil used as lubricant. *An oil which flashes or reaches combustion temperature under the working conditions of lubricant must always be avoided. Oxidation can be inhibited by the addition of certain additives.*

Hydrolysis also causes various lubricants to decompose. The presence of moisture in the oil causes hydrolysis of such components as esters in the lubricant and releases alcohols and destructive fatty acids. Esters when exposed to moisture at high temperature or in the presence of acids and alkalies are decomposed. Poly ethers and halides get hydrolysed under drastic conditions. Poly *siloxanes get hydrolysed in alkaline solutions. Hence a good lubricant is that which is not hydrolysed under the working lubricating conditions.*

Pyrolysis is the cracking of petroleum chains, which takes place at high temperatures found with in the engine bearings. Pyrolysis is the main cause of the deposition of gummy and carbon sediments within the lubricant. When lubricating oils are exposed to temperatures greater then 300°C, they undergo cracking, which is generally a free radial chain reaction and generally accelerated by oxidation. The rate of **cracking is different for different** oils. A good lubricant should not crack under lubricating conditions. A common test for determining the oxidation stability of the lubricating oil is Slight Oxidation Test. log. of the lubricating oil sample is taken in a special flask and air in the flask is displaced with 02. The flask is placed on an oil-bath at 200'C and heated for about 2.5 hours. The flask is then taken out, cooled and the contents are diluted with petroleum naphtha. It is allowed to stand for one hour and precipitate, if any, is filtered, washed, dried and weighed. The result is expressed as the percentage of original weight of the oil taken. A good lubricant must possess a low slight oxidation number.

CUTTING FLUIDS

Cutting fluids are those liquids which are used to cool as well as lubricate. Emulsions of oil in water have widely been used as cutting fluids for tools used in machine shop for cutting, threading, sawing, turning, drilling etc. The function of cutting fluids is to cool the tools or to lubricate the fools or to cool as well as lubricate the tools. The cutting fluids provide cooling as well as lubrication in those machines where the friction is very high, because of contact between the work piece and the tool. As a result, large heat is generated as local heat and the tool becomes heated and may even lose its hardness and temper. The most important characteristies of a good cutting fluid are :

(a) Good *lubricating property.*

(b) Low Viscosity.

(c) Chemical and thermal stability.

(d) *Non-corrosive nature towards the tool as well as metals of the work piece.*

(e) *High thermal conductivity.*

In fine work, a stream of oil such as lard oil, rapeseed oil or sperum oil is directed over the work piece. In such a case, the oil acts as a cutting fluid and functions more as a lubricant and less as cooling agent or heat carrying agent. When the speed is low and the pressure is too high e.g. in broaching , the oils are widely used as cutting fluids. **Compounded oils** obtained by mixing petroleum oils with vegetable oils and animal oils are also used as cutting fluids. In **rough or routine work** such as grinding and truning, no lubrication is required and cooled action is sufficient. In such cases, water, being a good cooling agent, is widely used as cutting fluid.

In most cases, use of either oil or water alone is not sufficient, because in such cases cooling and lubrication both are required simultaneously. In such cases oil in-water emulsions are most satisfactory as cutting fluids. These emulsions are obtained by mixing small amounts of petroleum oil in water in presence of an emulsifying agent such as soap, lard oil, sperum oil, tallow oil, sulphonated oils (such as sulphuric acid treated castor oil, chloro-sulphonated organic compounds etc). In addition, some glycols or alcohols are added to prevent gelling or thickening. Certain germicides like sodium nitrite, triethanol amine etc are also added. **Emulsions as cutting fluids act as** : (a) *Lubricant to reduce frictional heat. (b) Medium for transfer of heat produced.*

As a result, these emulsions reduce power consumption and wear of the tool. **It should be noted that cutting emulsion should not cause rusting of the metals involved.**

SELECTION OF LUBRICANTS

In selecting a lubricant for a particular job, a careful study of various properties and their correct interpretation is extremely important, because properties of a properly selected lubricant should remain same and do not change under service conditions, otherwise there may be a lot of problems. For example,

Cutting fluids are used as lubricants in cutting, grinding, turning, and machining of the metals. 'In such operations, the friction is very high because of close contact between the work piece and the tool and this generates a large amount of local heat. Heat so liberated may overheat the tool and may lower its temper and hardness. Hence **lubricants used as cutting fluids act**

(a) To cool *the tools so as to reduce wear and prevent metal losing its hardness.*

(b) To cool *the metal work piece and to prevent distortion and dimensional inaccuracies.*

(c) *To reduce power consumption by providing lubrication.*

(d) To *improve the finish of the surface.*

In **light cuttings,** oil emulsions have been found to be most effective. These emulsions have smaller lubricating effects than cutting oils, but they are more efficient as cooling media, because of high heat capacity of water that is present in the emulsion. In heavy cuttings, the most efffertive lubricants are, however, cutting oils, which are generally the mineral oils of low viscosities having additives such as fatty oils, chlorinated compounds and sulphurized fatty oil. These additives attach themselves to the surface of continuously exposed fresh metals due to the polar groups present in them. A considerable reduction in friction is obtained because shear strength of cutting oil films is much smaller than that of the metal. Hence there is a considerable decrease in the power consumption as well as in heat generation. For spindles moving at very high speeds in **textile industry,** thin oils, containing oxidation and rust inhibitors are widely used. In **internal combustion engines,** the lubricant has to be exposed to high temperatures. It indicates that lubricant used in internal combustion engines should have **high viscosity index** (low variation of viscosity with temperature and **high**

thermal stability (It should not undergo easy evaporation and decomposition at high temperatures). Petroleum oils containing additives (which impart high viscosity index and oxidation resistance to the oils) are widely used as lubricating oils for **internal combustion engines. Lubricants for delicate materials** such as watches, clocks, sewing machines, scientific instruments etc are not subjected to high temperatures or to water or to extreme load. For such prupose, **vegetable oils and animal oils** such as palm oil, neat foot oil, castor oil etc are most appropriate.

For **high pressure and low speed** tractor rollers, lathes, railway track joints, concrete mixtures etc, it is not possible to maintain oil grease films. So in such a case **solid lubricants** such *as graphite, soapstone,* mica are-used either in the dry powder form or as emulsion in oil or water.

In gears, the lubricants are subjected to very high pressure or loads. Hence lubricants for use in gears must have good oiliness, good load carrying capacity, good resistance to oxidation and should not be removed by centrifugal force from the point or place of application. Thick mineral lubricating oils with extreme pressure additives such as metallic soaps and compounds containing chlorine; sulphur or phosphorus are most suitable for use in gears. **Greases and blended thick oils** are most suitable to be used as lubricants for **high pressure and low speeds** such as rail axle boxes, tractor roller, wire ropes etc.

Oil with low pour point, low viscosity and low cloud point are used as lubricants for **refrigeration system.** Naphthalene base oils, which possess all these properties are thus widely employed for refrigeration systems. The **pour point** for the lightest grade and highest grade oils are -40°F and -13°F respectively. The viscosity of these oils varies from 85 to 325 Saybolt Universal Seconds at 100°F.

The function of a lubricating oil in an electrical transformer is to insulate the windings and to remove the heat generated, when the transformer is subjected to on-load. The lubricant used for these transformers should, therefore, possess **low viscosity and good dielectric properties.** Moreover, transformer oil is also exposed to air to a very small extent and so, when the transformer is on-load, such exposure to air, high temperature, electrical stress and catalytic influence of copper etc cause various chemical changes in the oil leading to the formation of acids as well as sludge. The acids so formed may attack the copper conductors, the transformer tank, the cotton insulation etc. The sludge formed may coat the windings and interferes with cooling in the refrigeration system and may even increase the temperature. The chemical changes resulting in the formation of acids and sludge may be accelerated at high temperature. To avoid or minimise the formation of acids and sludge, **highly refined minerals oils** having high insulating properties, optimum oxidation resistance, and high chemical stability are used for refrigeration system.

LUBRICATING OIL CLASSIFICATION AND THEIR USES FOR DIFFERENT TYPES OF MACHINERY

According to their viscosity (Redwood No. 1 in Seconds), lubricating oils have been **classified** into 5 groups (British Specification No. 210). The terms such as **light, medium and heavy** have been used for these different viscosity classifications of lubricating oils (Table 4).

TABLE (4) VISCOSITY CLASSIFICATION OF LUBRICATING OILS FOR GROUPS 1, 2, 3, 4, AND 5

Group	Extra Light	Light	Medium	Medium Heavy	Heavy	Extra Heavy	Super Heavy
Grou 1 at 140 °F	-	60 - 75	75 - 90	-	90 - 112	> 112	-
Grou 2 at 140 °F	-	50 - 60	60 - 80	80 - 125	125 - 175	> 175	-
Grou 3 at 140 °F	< 50	50 - 60	60 - 80	80 - 125	125 - 175	> 175	-
Grou 4 at 140 °F	70 - 90	90 - 130	130 - 175	175 - 250	250 - 375	375 - 500	> 500
Grou 5 at 200 °F	-	100 -160	160 - 190	190 - 210	> 210	-	-

Chapter 6

MANUFACTURE OF OILS AND GREASES

SELECTIVE SOLVENTS

Lubricating oils and other lubricating materials are used to reduce friction and to prevent the associated heating and seizure in engines, machines and mechanisms. They are also capable of protecting the metal surfaces from the harmful effect of substances formed on combustion of fuels. High quality lubricating oils, particularly those having a high viscosity index, are essential for effective and smooth operation of modern machines and mechanisms. They not only ensure a longer service life of machines but also decrease the consumption of lubricating oils. High grade lubricating materials can be prepared by making use of a better oils base (base component) by properly selecting petroleum grades and process conditions and by using appropriate additives. In the process of oils manufacture, selective solvents are of vital importance.

The use of selective solvents for purification of oils is based on different solubility of hydrocarbons in particular solvents. There are some solvents, such as ethyl ether, trichloromethane ($CHCl_3$), carbon tetrachloride (CCl_4) etc. which form homogeneous solutions with liquid hydrocarbons at normal temperature. There are other solvents, which form two phase mixtures, one of the phases containing hydrocarbons (petroleum products) and a small amount of solvent and the other phase being formed by the solvent with a small portion of dissolved hydrocarbons of the original fraction. A homogeneous solution can only be obtained with a very high quantity of the solvent.

A solvent to be used for selective purification of oils should meet the following important requirements.

(a) It should extract only undesirable components.

(b) It should not have any effect on the useful components.

(c) It should form two separate phases upon purification.

The phase containing useful components of oil, such as paraffinic and naphthenic hydrocarbons, is called the raffinate phase and the phase containing the undesirable or unwanted impurities is known as extract phase. The raffinate phase gives the purified end product, known as raffinate, on distillation of the solvent. The extract phase gives the residue, known as extract, when distilled to remove the solvent.

The results of the purification mainly depend on :

(a) Selectivity of the solvent, that is, the ability of the solvent to extract impurities from the product that has to be purified, and

(b) On the dissolving power of the solvent.

The higher the dissolving power of the solvent, better is the quality of the raffinate. A solvent of high dissolving power has, therefore, a lower selectivity. The solubility of oils in solvent mainly depends on their hydrocarbon composition and to some extent on the fractional composition. High boiling oils are less soluble in a solvent than low boiling oils. The solvent-to- product ratio, which depends on the conditions of the process, starting material and solvent used, is also of great importance.

For a given solvent-to-product ratio, the solubility of hydrocarbons of petroleum fraction increases as the temperature increases to a definite temperature, known as critical solution temperature (CST). Above CST, hydrocarbons from a perfect mixture with the solvent (homogeneous single phase system). It is interesting to note that :

(a) The CST of hydrocarbons decreases sharply with increase in the number of rings in their molecules.

(b) Hydrocarbons with longer alkyl chains have a higher value of CST.

(c) Pentacyclic naphthenic hydrocarbons intensively lower the CST than the hexacyclic hydrocarbons.

(d) Naphthenic benzene hydrocarbons have a lower CST than naphthenic hydrocarbons having corresponding structure.

(e) Normal paraffinic hydrocarbons have highest value of CST.

The solubility of oils depends on :

(a) Their composition.

(b) The nature of the solvent, and

(c) Additives (water and organic substances).

In the presence of water, the dissolving power of certain solvents such alcohols and water, decreases, which is characterised by increasing CST of oil in these solvents. Similarly, the dissolving power of certain solvents such a phenol, furfural and ketones increases on addition of benzene or toluene, but CST as well as selectivity decrease. The CST of raffinate is higher than that of the starting materials and so the difference in temperature between these two, known as temperature gradient of extraction, is of great importance.

For example, the temperature gradient of extraction for furfural extraction columns is 35-40°C. In many cases, recirculation of an intermediate product is carried out. The extract solution passing from the extraction apparatus is cooled by 25-30°C, which decreases the solubility of the dissolved oil and precipitates partially from the solution which still carries a large amount of useful compounds. So precipitated product is recycled for purification.

Furfural, which gives a high yield of oils, has widely been used for the purification of medium-viscosity distillates. Phenol is preferred when purification of residual products is required. Residual materials and materials with a high concentration of tars are deasphaltized in a propane solution before the selective purification. In some cases, a mixture of phenol and cresol or furfural in a propane solution is used for this purpose. Double solvents are more useful because they replace two processes-deasphaltizing of residual materials and selective purification. In all these cases, the raffinate obtained is dewaxed by solvents, as a result of which dewaxed oil and gatch (from oil distillates) or petroleum (from residues) are obtained. Dewaxed oils are then subjected to hydrofining.

Figure 1 shows the flow diagrams of manufacture of oils with the use of selective solvents.

(a) In flow diagram I, deasphaltization of goudron and purification of deasphaltizate are carried out separately.

(b) In flow diagram II, these two processes are combined and carried out by making use of double solvents.

In both cases, dewaxed oils are subjected to hydrofining. The flow diagram of oil manufacture by using selective solvents has two main flows.

(a) **Distillate flow** (starting material, oil distillates), that is, selective purification by phenol or furfural, as a result of which raffinate (purified distillate) and extract are obtained. Then dewaxing in a solution or acetone (methyl ethyl ketone), benzene and toluene, which gives dewaxed distillate oil and gatch (high in paraffins), and finally hydrofining of dewaxed distillate oil, which makes distillate components of the oil of low and medium viscosity.

(b) **Residue flow** (starting material, goudron or concentrated long residuum). It involves deasphaltization by propane to form deasphaltizate and asphalt ; selective purification of deasphaltizate by furfural or phenol, which gives raffinate and extract ; dewaxing in a solution of acetone, benzene and toluene (acetone may be replaced by methyl ethyl ketone, dichloroethane etc.), which produces a dewaxed component of residual oil and petroleum ; hydrofining of the dewaxed oil which gives a residual component of a high viscosity. The process of purification or residual oils by furfural and propane, that is, double solvent process, has a higher selectivity and a lower solvent-to-material ratio than the ordinary industrial solvents such as phenol, phenol-cresol-propane etc.

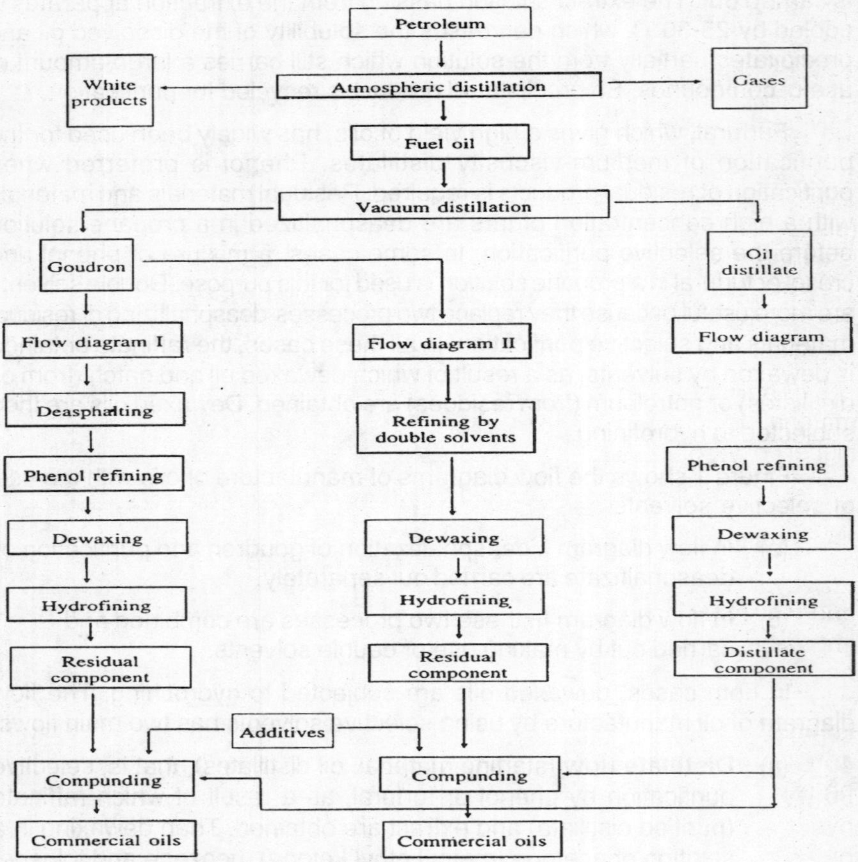

Fig.1. Flow diagram of oil manufacture

In some cases, the components obtained are commercial oils such as transformer oil (from distillates) or aviation oil (from residual products). In most cases, however, the commercial oils are prepared by mixing distillate and residual components and various additives. Gatch is used as the starting material for preparing solid paraffins. Petroleum is purified to prepare medical petroleum or processed into ceresins.

DEASPHALTIZATION OF GOUDRON BY PROPANE

Deasphaltization is the principal process in the manufacture of high viscosity oils from residual products of petroleum distillation (goudron, long residuum) which contain asphaltenes. The process is based on the ability of liquefied hydrocarbons to dissolve hydrocarbons under appropriate conditions and they have no effect on tar-asphaltene substances. When liquid propane is added to the starting material at elevated pressures, tar asphaltene substances having a high density separate in the form of precipitate from the solution. During settling, they absorb a certain amount of oil. The degree of separation of tar asphaltenes can be increased to a definite limit, by increasing the use of propane per unit mass of the material or by increasing the temperature.

As a result of deasphaltization, two layers are formed. The solution of deasphaltizate in propane forms the upper layer and solution of asphalt (bitumen) in propane forms the lower layer. The deasphaltization of goudron is carried out by commercial propane having atleast 95% purity. It should contain not more than 2% of C_2H_6 and 3% of C_4H_{10}. It should also be free from sulphur compounds because they may cause corrosion of the equipment and pipelines.

The **propane-material** ratio is determined by the nature of the starting material and the temperature of deasphaltization. This ratio is lower at a higher concentration of tar-asphaltene products in the material and vice-versa. Goudron from a low sulphurous petroleum can be deasphaltized at a ratio of 4.5-5 : 1, whereas goudron from a sulphurous petroleum grade can be deasphaltized at a ratio of 2.5 : 3 : 1.

At a higher **temperature** and with the same propane-material ratio, tars and polycyclic hydrocarbons pass more easily into the lower layer, which improves the colour of deasphaltizate and decreases it viscosity, density and coking ability, but at the same time also decreases the yield of deasphaltizate. At an appropriate pressure and propane-material ratio, the separation of tar- asphaltene substances, can be carried out at 40-90°C. At 40°C, part of tars remain in the solution, while at 90°C (which is very close to 96.8°C, the critical solution temperature of propane), many valuable hydrocarbons are not dissolved in propane and precipitate with tars. Thus process should be carried out between 50 to 85°C. For maximum extraction of valuable hydrocarbons from the material, the temperature in the deasphalting column is kept at 50-65°C at the bottom and at 75-80°C at the top (for better separation of hydrocarbons from tars). This temperature gradient of deasphaltization can be obtained by internal or external heating of the flow of oil propane solution at the column top and by heating of propane and material in external heaters.

The pressure in the deasphalting column is generally maintained at 3.5-4 MPa, depending on the temperature in the column.

The deasphaltizate layer is distilled to run off propane in the regeneration unit of the plant and to obtain the deasphaltizate, an end product. On removal of propane, the asphalt layer gives the residue (asphalt or bitumen). The yield and quality of asphaltizate depends on process conditions and the composition of the starting material. The yield of deasphaltizate is lower at a lower content of coke. A high content of coke, however, may cause complications in subsequent selective purification of deasphaltizate.

The effectiveness of deasphaltization depends on the depth of distillation of the petroleum residue. The materials of a wider fractional composition are deasphalted less easily than those from which low molecular fractions have been run off. Tarry goudrons from sulphurous petroleum grades may, however, contain 15-20% of heavy fractions upto 500°C, which promote the dissolution of useful high molecular hydrocarbons in propane.

Deasphaltization can be carried out in one or two stages. The deasphaltizate from the first stage is used for making motor oils and then from the second stage, for obtaining viscous oils for rolling mills.

In **single stage deasphaltization** of goudrons by propane, the starting material is pumped through a steam heat exchanger, where it is heated to the specified temperature and then fed to a deasphalting column. Liquefied propane from a tank is pumped through a heat exchanger and enters the bottom portion of the deasphalting column. Propane moves upwards and comes in contact with descending heavy oil. The solution of deasphaltized oil is removed from the top of the deasphalting column, passes successively through a pressure regulator and horizontal propane evaporators heated respectively by low pressure and high pressure steam and enters a steaming column, where the rests of propane are stripped off by direct steam. The prepared deasphaltized oil is pumped off into a tank.

The asphalt solution from the bottom of deasphalting column is led into a furnace and then to an evaporating column where the main portion of the propane is evaporated and the rests of propane are stripped off by direct steam in atmospheric steaming column. The asphalt is pumped from the column bottom to a tank. High pressure vapours of propane from the evaporators as well as evaporating column are fed to condensers and then to liquefied propane tank. The low pressure vapours of propane from the steaming columns are freed from steam in a mixture condenser and then fed into the intake line of compressor. After that they are supplied into the main pipeline of the regenerated propane. The plant is automatically controlled. The temperature of the material at the exit from the furnace is 200-250°C and that at the inlet to the deasphalting column is 100-150°C. The pressure of propane is 1.8 : 2.0 MPa at the compressor discharge, 3.5-4.0 MPa in the deasphalting column, and 0.15 MPa in the steaming columns.

The deasphalting column, the principal unit of the plant is a vertical cylindrical vessel separated into two portions by a partition. In the lower portion, which operates at pressures upto 4 MPa, there are upto 8 shutter trays or sections. Distributors for the supply of the material and reflux liquid are arranged above the trays and a distributor for propane, below them.

The most important disadvantage of singlestage deasphaltization is a great loss of valuable hydrocarbons in asphalt. For deeper extraction of these hydrocarbons, two stage deasphaltization is used. The plant contains additionally a deasphalting column of the second stage, two evaporators for stripping of propane from a deasphaltizate solution at the second stage, heat exchanger for the heating of goudron, pumps for supplying propane to the second stage and pumping off the deasphaltizate, and a steaming column for the second stage deasphaltizate.

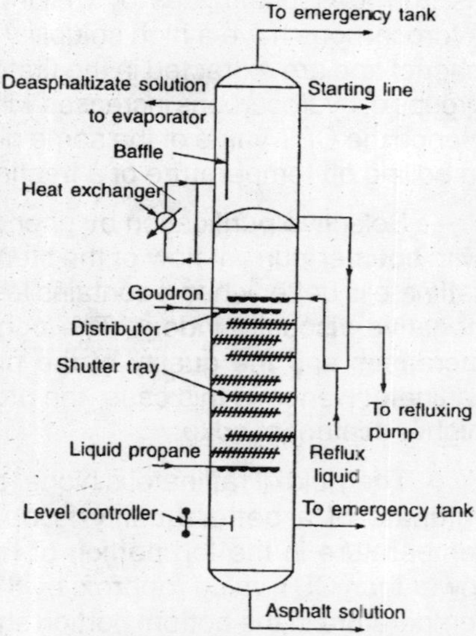

Fig.2. Diagram of a deasphalting column.

In two stage deasphaltization of goudron by propane, the asphalt solution from the first deasphalting stage is fed to the second stage of deasphaltization, and an addition flow of propane is supplied. The pressure and temperature in the second stage column are maintained at lower levels. The yield of a deasphaltizate from the second stage may vary in a wide range depending on the starting material. The yield of asphalt decreases with an increase in the yield of deasphaltizate. Two stage deasphaltization is especially advantageous for the processing of materials low in tars and high in oil fractions. Oils obtained from the deasphaltization of the second stage have higher viscosity or low viscosity index and contain more benzene hydrocarbons than those obtained from the first stage deasphaltizates.

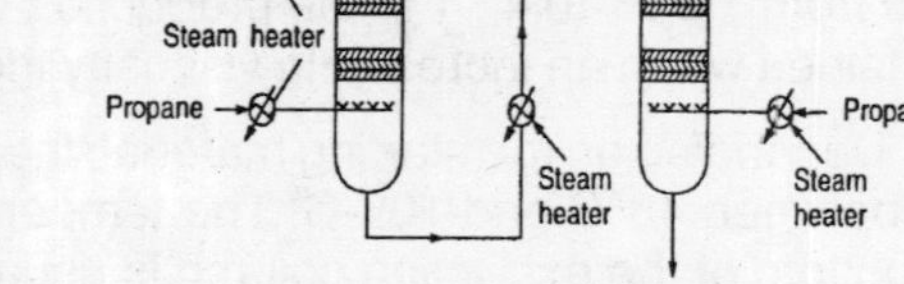

Fig.3. Diagram of the extraction unit of a plant for two stage deasphaltization of goudron by propane.

SELECTIVE PURIFICATION OF OIL DISTILLATES AND DEASPHALTIZATES

An important characteristic of the quality of oils is the ability of coking which is mainly due to the presence of tars, asphaltenes and benzene hydrocarbons (especially polycyclic hydrocarbons). Benzene hydrocarbons remain partially in deasphaltizates and in small amounts in oil distillates. Polycyclic benzene hydrocarbons can be removed from oil distillates as well as from deasphaltizates by making use of selective **purification**. These hydrocarbons have a high solubility in selective solvents such as furfural or phenol and are extracted in the first place from oils. The solubility of various groups of hydrocarbons increases with an increase in their boiling temperature. Hence the CST value of the same petroleum grade increases with increase in boiling off temperature of a fraction.

Selective purification by phenol is carried out in an extraction column with counter-current flow of the starting material and phenol. The quality of raffinate is better when it contains less heavy benzene hydrocarbons (with a negative viscosity index). The content of heavy benzene hydrocarbons increases and the quality of the product decreases, with a high yield of raffinate. Hence in this case, the product has a lower viscosity index and a higher content of coke.

The yield of raffinate.is higher at a lower temperature of extraction, but raffinate of a better quality is obtained at a higher temperature. The temperature in the top portion of the extraction column is usually slightly lower than CST value (approx. by 8 - 10°C in purification-of distillates). The temperature in the bottom portion should be greater than the setting point of the material and above the m.p of the solvent employed.

The yield of raffinate is lower at a higher **phenol-material ratio**. The quality of the product improves with increasing ratio to a definite limit at which-the state of over **purification** is reached. An over purified oil has high quality indices but it is extremely unstable. Hence, when oils of higher viscosity index are required, they are over purified and stabilized by adding additives. Taking this fact into consideration, the degree of purification is usually determined by the coking ability of raffinate. An abnormally low coking ability means over purification of an oil. The phenol-material ratio is usually maintained in the range from 0.9 : 1 to 2 : 1 in making distillate oils and in the range from 1.5 : 1 to 4 : 1 in the production of residual oils. A higher ratio is maintained when an increase in viscosity index is required.

Depending on the starting material, the temperature of purification may vary between 48°C and 105-C. The temperature gradient between the top and bottom of the extraction column is usually 10 - 30°C. The selectivity of phenol can be improved by adding 4 - 8% by mass of water. The content of water may be increased upto 12% for the lightest distillate oils. In phenol purification of sulphurous materials, the equipment is subjected to a strong corrosion attack of phenol and H_2S in the presence of water. In order to lower the temperature of regeneration and thus to reduce the corrosion, the regeneration of solvent is carried out in vacuum. Residual materials should be purified by dry phenol (containing not more than 0.8% water) as for as possible.

The conditions of selective purification determine the quality of the base oil obtained to a large extent. Deep seiective purification gives base oils of an elevated viscosity index almost from all grades of petroleum. Much better results can be obtained by hydrogen improvement of oil distillates and deasphaltizates with subsequent shallow selective purification. A zeolite containing catalyst has been recommended for hydrofining. The optimum conditions of hydrofining are : Temperature = 360°C (± 10°C), the volume flow rate of starting material = 1.5-2.0 hour $^{-1}$, and the circulation of hydrogen containing gas = 500 - 700 m^3/m^3.

Extraction is carried out in one or more stages in a counter current flow. Counter current extraction is often used in the manufacture of oils. The use of solvent in the counter current process is only 1/2 or 1/3 of that used in the parallel flow process. The process can be carried out with recirculation or with varying temperature conditions.

A plant for selective purification by phenol or another solvent consists mainly of two units.

(a) **An extraction unit** for the removal, of undesirable components from oil, and

(b) **A regeneration unit,** for the regeneration of the solvent from the solutions of raffinate and extract.

For selective purification of oil distillates and deasphaltizates by phenol, the starting material is pumped through shell-and-tube heat exchanger and then fed to the top of an absorber. The vapour of an azeotropic mixture of water and phenol are supplied from drying column under the lowermost tray of the absorber, where the starting material absorbs phenol from the azeotropic mixture and water vapours discharged to the atmosphere are condensed and the condensate is used for steam generation. The starting material from bottom of the absorber is pumped through a heat exchanger and introduced into the middle portion of an extraction column. Phenol from intermediate tank is pumped through a heater and then to the top of the extraction column. In addition, phenol water is fed into the bottom portion of extraction column. The temperature at the bottom of the extraction column is controlled by circulating a part of the extract solution through a cooler.

The raffinate solution from the top of extraction column is collected in a tank. The regeneration of phenol from the raffinate solution is carried out in two stages in evaporating columns. The raffinate solution from the tank is pumped through a heat exchanger and then through the coils of a furnace and enters evaporating or raffinate column. The phenol vapours from the top of that column are condensed and cooled in heat exchanger and cooler and the condensate so obtained is fed to a dry phenol tank. The raffinate solution, containing about 5-6% of phenol flows from one evaporating column to another, where direct steam is introduced through the bottom.

The vapours of phenol and water from the top of the evaporating column are condensed in condenser, and the condensate is collected in a tank.

After removal of phenol, the raffinate is pumped through heat exchanger into a cooler and then to a tank.

The regeneration of solvent from the extract solution is carried out in there stages. The extract from the bottom of the extraction column is pumped through a heat exchanger into the middle portion of drying column. The vapours of azeotrophic mixture of phenol and water from the top of that column are introduced into an adsorber or condensed in condenser, and the phenol water is pumped into a tank and then to the bottom of extraction column by a pump. The extract solution passes through a heater, heated by condensing phenol vapours. The dehydrated extract solution from the bottom of drying column is pumped through the coil of pipe furnace and fed to column, which is heated by the extract solution circulating through another coil of furnace. Phenol vapours are taken from the top of the. column and condensed in heater and heat exchanger at 0.3 MPa pressure, and the condensate is passed through cooler and collected in dry phenol tank. The final steam- stripping of phenol is carried out in steaming column. The vapours of water and phenol are removed from the top of that column, and the extract solution from the bottom is pumped through a cooler into a storage tank. Liquid phenol is supplied as reflux liquid. The plant has automatic means for controlling flow rates, temperature and pressures.

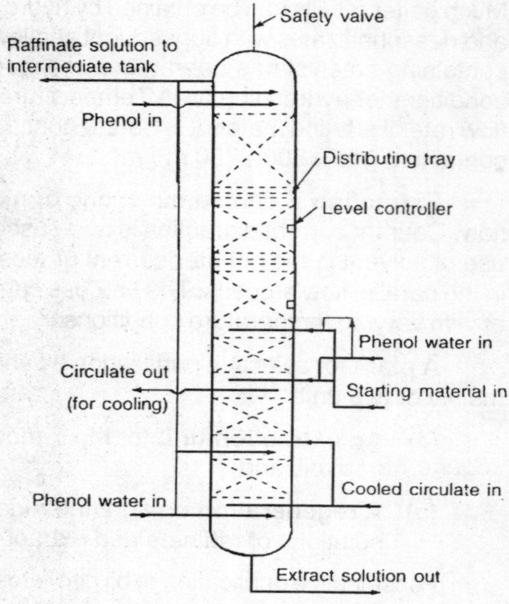

Fig.4. Diagram of an extraction column.

The process can also be carried out in a **rotary** disc contactor, in which centrifugal forces are utilized for better contact and phase separation. The rotary disc contactor is a vertical cylindrical vessel with a vertical shaft rotated by an electric motor mounted on the top of the apparatus. The shaft is provided with discs which rotate in the space between fixed stator discs attached to the contactor walls. The liquids being mixed are whirled and agitated vigorously by the discs, which ensure good contact between them. The upper and lower sections of the contractor serve for settling the raffinate and extract solutions. In these sections, the shaft in enclosed is a tube and the settling chambers are separated from the zones by supply of the solvent and material by fixed large-mesh grids.

COMBINED PROCESS OF DEASPHALTIZATION AND SELECTIVE PURIFICATION

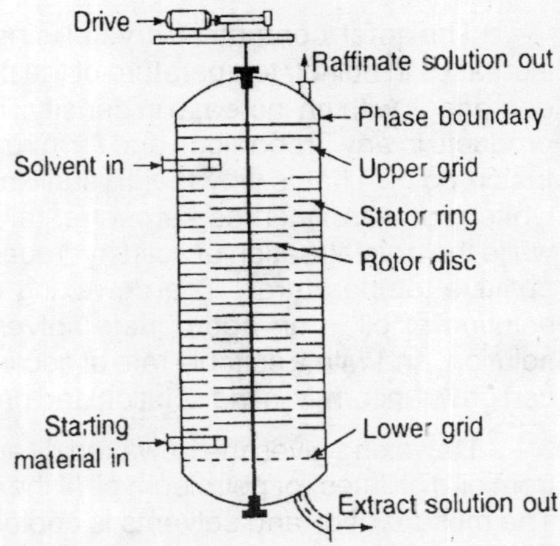

Fig.5. Diagram of a rotary disc contactor.

The combined process of deasphaltization and selective purification of oils makes use of propane for dissolution of valuable components of oils and a mixture of phenol and cresols for the dissolution of undesirable components. Double solvents such as propane and furfural have also been used, because they give better results, particularly when selective purification of oil distillates is carried out by furfural as furfural is regenerated in a common system of the plant. The yield of raffinate increases with an increase in the concentration of propane in the mixture, but the raffinate has poor characteristics. The quality of the raffinate decreases with an increase in the content of phenol in a phenol-cresol mixture. Inorder to avoid this, the flow rate of solvents is increased, which decreases the plant productivity. With an excessively low concentration of phenol, the yield of raffinate decreases. Depending on the starting material, the solvent mixture may contain 35-60% of phenol and 40-65% of cresol.

Plants operating by the combined process have better technico-economical characteristics and produce more raffinate of better quality than separate plants for deasphaltization and selective purification. The purification by double solvents is especially effective in the manufacture of residual oils from petroleum grades having a high content of tars. The process can also be recommended for making high viscosity oils. The average losses of valuable hydrocarbons with asphalt and extract are 32-35%o in single stage deasphaltization, 22-25% in two stage deasphaltization, and only 12% in the combined process with double solvents.

DEWAXING OF RAFFINATES

Raffinates obtained from oil distillates and residual products of petroleum processing have generally a high setting point. Hence they can not be used directly as commercial oils, because of the presence of solid hydrocarbons in them. These solid hydrocarbons are necessary to be separated from them. In the process of dewaxing, solid hydrocarbons precipitate from raffinates or petroleum fractions and crystailise from the solution, when temperature is lowered. High molecular paraffinic, naphthenic, naphthene-benzene and benzene hydrocarbons with long alkyl chains of n- and weakly branched structure can be separated from petroleum fraction in this way.

The total content of crystallising hydrocarbons increases with an increases in boil-off temperature of the petroleum fractions, but their solubility decreases with an increase in density. They can be mixed with all petroleum products in any proportions and form real solutions at temperatures near the fusion point. That is why the crystallisation of paraffins hydrocarbons from white products, such as kerosene, takes place at negative temperatures, while the crystallisation of solid hydrocarbons from oil fraction takes place at positive temperatures. The dewaxing of oils is carried out by cooling the solution of oil in an appropriate solvent. Because of low viscosity of the solution, and with a suitable rate of cooling, the crystals of solid hydrocarbons can grow uniformly in the solution and precipitate easily from the liquid phase.

Dewaxing gives the dewaxed oil and gatch (in the dewaxing of raffinate from oil distillates) or petroleum oil (if the raffinate is from petroleum residues). The mixture of oil and solvents is cooled to a definite temperature, which is determined by the desired setting temperature of the oil and by the solvent or solvent mixture used. The difference between the temperature of dewaxing and the temperature of setting of the final dewaxedoil is called temperature effect of dewaxing (TED) or temperature gradient of dewaxing. The temperature effects of dewaxing the oil from various solutions are as follows :

(1)	Liquid propane	13 to 21°C
(2)	Mixture of acetone, benzene, and toluene (30 : 35 : 35)	11°C
(3)	Mixture of methyl ethyl ketone, benzene and toluene (50 : 25 :25)	-3 to -6°C
(4)	Mixture of dichloroethane and benzene (70 : 30)	-6 to -11°C
(5)	Methyl isobutyl ketone	0°C

For example, if it is required to produce oil with the setting temperature at -15°C, the solution of raffinate in a mixture of acetone, benzene, and toluene should be cooled to -26°C.

The solvent used for dewaxing must dissolve the oil and precipitate solid paraffins. It must also have a low TED value and good filtering ability. A mixture of solvents is used in those cases when the capability for precipitating solid hydrocarbons is combined with the capability for dissolving the oil. The most important solvent mixtures used in industry for the dewaxing are :

(a) Methyl ethyl ketone-benzene-toluene

(b) Acetone-benzene-toluene

(c) Methyl isobutyl ketone-benzene-toluene.

In these mixtures, methyl ethyl ketone and acetone act as precipitators of solid hydrocarbons and benzene and toluene are as oil solvents. The combination of a mixture can be changed according to the nature of the starting material and the desired degree of separation of solid hydrocarbons. A high concentration of ketone (acetone, methyl ethyl ketone etc) in a mixture increases the degree of separation of solid hydrocarbons and the rate of filtering.

At higher viscosity of raffinate, a greater amount of solvent is required for decreasing the viscosity of the solution and to ensure the free growth of crystals. The amount of dissolved solid hydrocarbons increases with an increase in the use of solvent. It also increases the setting temperature of the dewaxed oil. In general, the solvent-to-material ratio is usually greater (4 : 1 to 6 : 1) for residual oils.

In dewaxing process, the mixture is cooled in two stages. At the first stage, the mixture is cooled quickly by water to a temperature slightly above the cloud point. At the second stage (from the appearance of the cloudiness to the temperature at which crystallisation takes place intensively), cooling is carried out slowly, at a rate of 80°C/hour. The final cooling to the temperature of filtering can be done more quickly.

Oils with a low temperature of setting are prepared by deep dewaxing plants for deep dewaxing of distillate oils by methyl ethyl ketone which shows better results than those making use of acetone.

The dewaxing plant has the following principal units :

(a) Crystallisation and filtering unit.

(b) Solvent regeneration unit.

(c) Cooling unit.

(d) Inert gas system.

The main apparatuses used in the dewaxing plant are crystallisers and filters for separation of solid hydrocarbons from oil solutions. Crystallisers serve for cooling of the oil solution and precipitation of paraffin crystals from it. A crystalliser is essentially a horizontal tube-in -tube heat exchanger, inner tube of which has spring- biased scrapers for the removal of the paraffin layer from its walls. The inner tubes of the sections are connected by bent tubes and the outer tubes, by flanged pipe connections. The solution of the oil to be dewaxed is pumped through the inner tubes, and the cooled dewaxed solution or ammonia moves in counter current manner in the annular space. In order to minimise the heating from outside, crystallizers are heat insulated properly.

Crystallizers in which cooling is carried out by a cold dewaxed oil solution are called regenerative crystallizers. In ammonia crystallizers, the material solution is cooled because of the evaporation of liquid ammonia, which is pumped into an accumulator provided above the cooling unit. Liquid ammonia from the bottom portion of the accumulator is introduced into the bottom portion of the outer tube of the crys talliser. Evaporation of NH3 takes place here and its vapours pass from the top portion of the tube into the top portion of the accumulator from where they are sucked off by the compressor of the refrigerating unit.

The liquid is discharged from the bottom portion of a crystalliser and gases, from the top portion.

Solid hydrocarbons are usually separated from an oil solution in vacuum filters or in centrifuges. A vacuum filter has a steal drum rotating on bearings in an air tight housing. The filter drum is divided into 30 sections by longitudinal partitions. In each section, 18 pipes pass into the drum. They are connected with collectors (9 pipes in each). Both collectors communicate with the distribution head of the vacuum filter. A filtering cloth on metallic mesh is stretched onto the drum surface.

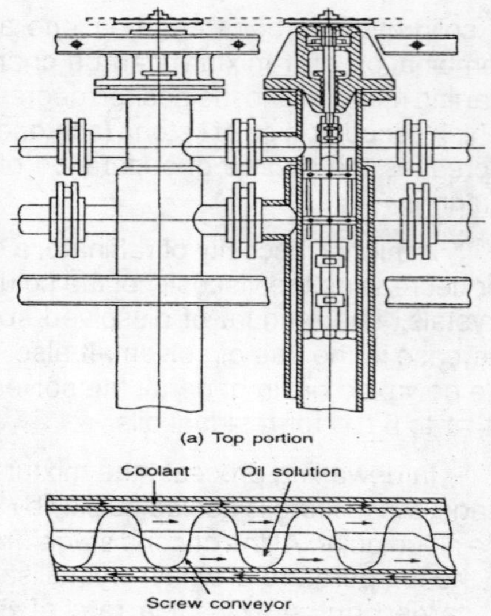

(b) Longitudinal section of crystallizer tube

The temperature required for dewaxing is usual ly formed by a refrigeration plant with ammonia content. The lowest temperature attainable on ammonia evaporation (- 57°C) is obtained in the plant at pressure of 0.03 MPa in the intake line of compressors.

The cooling temperature that can be attained at an in crease of pressure upto 0.09 MPa is - 36 or - 37°C.

In plants for deep dewaxing and preparation of oils with the setting temperature below - 60°C, refrigeration is carried out in two stages, the first stage operating on ammonia and the second, on ethane (liquid ethane can form a temperature of - 72°C on evaporation).

The dewaxed oil has different properties from the raffinate from which it is formed. It has higher density and coking ability and slightly smaller viscosity index and setting temperature, because of removal of solid hydrocarbons. The density, viscosity index, coking ability and setting temperature of raffinate and dewaxed oil are given below :

	Raffinate	Dewaxed oil
Density $d^{20}_{4.4}$	0.886	0.900
Viscosity index	110	82
Coking ability, %	0.12	0.18
Setting temperature, °C	+ 38	-18

PREPARATION OF BASE COMPONENTS AND PREPARATION OF COMMERCIAL OILS

Dewaxed oil contains a certain amount of tar asphaltenes, selective solvents and other substances, as a result of which they can not be used immediately as commercial oils. It should be purified by clays or by hydrofining.

Most grades of commercial oils (except transformer, aviation and some special oil grades) are prepared by mixing or compounding distillate and residual components of base oil and various additives.

At some plants, oils are prepared by pumping the required oil components successively into the mixing vessel in proportions determined in the laboratory, after, which circulation is effected by the scheme - vessel bottom-pump-vessel bottom. By another more effective method, oil components and additives are added in pipelines by using automatic mixing stations. This method has widely been used in industry.

OIL ADDITIVES

In modern mechanisms and engines, the lubricants must resist oxidation ever at higher temperatures of the order of 320°C and above. These requirements are not even satisfied by oils prepared from selective petroleum grades by deep refining. Because of this reason, their properties are improved by adding various complex synthesised substances, known as additives.

Viscosity additives are used for making oils with a high viscosity index upto 160 and low setting temperature. Polyisobutylene, polymethacrylates and vinypols are the examples of viscosity additives. The purified distillate of a viscosity 4-6 is used as the oil base. Such oils are called multigrade oils.

Depressor additives or depressors decrease the setting temperature of oils. For example, a depressor based on naphthene dialkyl derivatives, when added to oil in an amount of 0.2-1 %, decreases the setting temperature by 10-12°C.

Anti-acid and anti-corrosion additives are added to prevent the corrosion of metallic surfaces by acid products which are formed during the operation. Such additives are made from amine-and phenol base derivatives, compounds of sulphur, phosphorus etc, and their combinations. Ionol and n-oxidiphenyl amine are most effective additives of this type.

Anti-scuffing and anti-wear additives improve the characteristics of industrial and transmission oils. 'They are most effective if prepared on refined oil base with an addition of sulphur and phosphorus compounds.

Dispersing and neutralising additives dissolve and neutralise the acid substances which form in oils at high temperatures. These compounds are washed off, as it were, from the surface of valves and other members, which ensures a longer service life of an engine or mechanism. These additives are synthesised on the bases of barium, magnesium and calcium alkyl phenolate. Even more effective are some noval ashless dispersing additives such as those of alkyl salicylates and succinimide additives. They are prepared by the reaction of butylene or isobutylene polymers of a molecular mass of 600-1000 with maleic anhydride, after which the substance formed is combined with polyalkyl amines.

GREASES

Greases are the products composed of a dispersion medium (liquid) which is retained in the cells of :a structural frame formed by solid particles of a dispersed phase (thickening) with particles of colloidal size.

Greases behave like solids at low loads. They undergo deforming plastically and become fluid like liquids at a critical load and regain the properties of a solid as the load is removed. This ensures the proper lubrication of engines and mechanisms when ordinary lubricating oils are ineffective. The best greases retain their properties in friction pairs at temperatures from -100°C to + 300°C, rotation speed upto 100,000 rmp, contact stresses above 5000 MPa, in high vacuum, in outer space, under water etc.

Mineral and synthetic oils are used as the liquid base in the manufacture of greases. According to the type of thickener, greases are classified as,

(a) **Soap greases,** which are thickened by soaps such as organic salts of Na, Ca, Ba, Li, and Ph.

(b) **Hydrocarbon greases** are those which are thickened by paraffins, petroleum and ceresins.

(c) **Inorganic greases** are those which are thickened by bentonite clays, graphite and molybdenum disulphide.

(d) **Polymeric greases** are those thickened by high molecular compounds.

The principal operation characteristics of a grease are determined mainly by the thickener. For example, a grease thickened by seresin, whose m.p is 75°C, can operate at temperatures upto 60 - 65°C irrespective of the type of oil used in it (petroleum oil or synthetic).

On the bases of application, greases are classified as :

(a) Antifriction greases, which decrease friction and wear in friction pairs,

(b) Friction greases, which increase friction and prevent slippage.

(c) Protective greases, which prevent corrosion.

(d) Dispersing greases which improve the alignment of mating parts.

The major portion of greases relates to the antifriction class. Many of them also possess high protec tive properties and are called **all purpose greases.**

Some grades of greases possess unique properties. For example, greases thickened by perfluorinated alkyl polyesters or polytetrafluoroethylene (teflon) do not react with hydrocarbon jet fuels, hydrazine, hydrogen peroxide, fuming nitric acid and liquid oxygen.

The process of manufacture of greases includes the following operations.

(1) Preparation of components (fusion, dehydrogenation and preheating to the specified temperature).

(2) Batching components in a reactor.

(3) Compounding.

(4) Cooling, and

(5) Discharging (pouring).

The quality of a grease and the strength of its colloidal structure depends on :

(a) Composition.

(b) Process conditions.

(c) Conditions of cooling.

Chapter 7

DISTILLATION OF CRUDE PETROLEUM

PREPARATION OF PETROLEUM FOR PROCESSING

Crude petroleum obtained from the oil wells contains gases, salt, water and mechanical impurities. During the exploitation of petroleum deposit, the content of petroleum in crude product gradually decreases and that of water increases even upto 95 to 98%. Settled petroleum has even been found to contain great amount of salts, upto 6 g/L. The dissolved gases evolve from the petroleum at the wells because of reduction in pressure. The gas liberated is known as casing-head gas which is fed to the gasoline plants for further processing. The crude petroleum obtained from the oil wells is usually a weak, unstable emulsion of petroleum and water. In further processing, especially on pumping, it is converted into a stable emulsion which is difficult to be separated. The crude petroleum is, however, required with least content of water and salt. Hence deep purification is necessary at the well or at the nearest petroleum storage station.

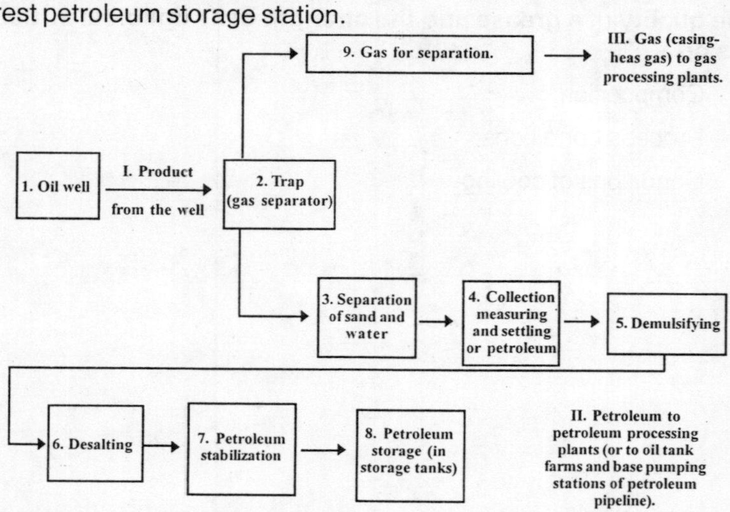

Fig.1. Principal diagram of petroleum and gas collection at oil wells.

Depending on the quality characteristics of crude petroleum and gas, the process of purification may be different. At most of the wells the crude petroleum is subjected to dehydration down to 1-2% of water and then partially desalted. The crude petroleum after processing should not contain 0.1-0.3% of water and 100 mg/L of salt. Hence all grades of petroleum should be demulsified in order to facilitate their processing in petroleum processing plants. For effective operation of petroleum processing plants, the crude petroleum to be processed must contain not more than 2 mg/L of salts and 0.2% of water. Hence crude petroleum obtained from oil wells is purified at petroleum processing plants, because presence of water in crude petroleum can sharply impair the productivity of plants and cause an excessive loss of power for evaporation and condensation of water. Salts and mechanical impurities present in it may cause erosion and clogging of pipes of furnaces and heat exchangers, lower the heat transfer coefficient, and increase the ash content in fuel oils and goudrons produced. In addition, dissolved salts in crude petroleum cause the corrosion of the equipment by HCl, formed as a result of hydrolysis of some chlorides such as $MgCl_2$.

$$MgCl_2 + H_2O \rightarrow MgOHCl + HCl$$

Sulphurous grades of petroleum may increase the corrosion of gasoline condensers and coolers, especially if water is present in the form of vapour. In the presence of moisture, first a protective film of FeS is formed, which is converted into $FeCl_2$ in the presence of HCl.

$$Fe + H_2S \rightarrow FeS + H_2 \qquad FeS + 2HC1 \rightarrow FeCl_2 + H_20$$

It is dissolved in water, so that iron is exposed to react with H_2S etc.

DESTRUCTION OF PETROLEUM EMULSION

Petroleum emulsions are hydrophilic (petroleum-in-water) and hydrophobic (water-in-petroleum). The colour of emulsion varies from yellow to dark brown. The viscosity of petroleum emulsions increases with increase in water content upto 60-80%, and then decreases. The stability of emulsions depends on the presence of emulsifying agent (substances soluble in one of the liquids which form films on droplets and thus prevent these from coalescing). Emulsifying agents may also be hydrophilic or hydrophobic. Hydrophilic emulsifiers are readily soluble in water and insoluble in petroleum. Examples of hydrophilic emulsifiers are sodium salts of naphthenic acids, sulpho acids etc. Hydrophobic emulsifying agents are soluble in petroleum but insoluble in water and include naphthenate, finely divided clay, metal oxides such as that of Ca, Mg, Fe, and Al, and tar asphaltene compounds etc. An emulsifying agent promotes the formation of an emulsion which corresponds to the type of that agent. Emulsions may be stable because water droplets and solid particles can store charges of static electricity. These charges cause mutual repulsion of water droplets. A hydrophilic emulsion (petroleum-in-water emulsion) is dissolved in water and settles to the bottom in gasoline, while an opposite effect has been observed in case of hydrophobic emulsion (water-in-petroleum type). Hydrophilic emulsions conduct electric current, while hydrophilic emulsions are non-conductive.

Crude petroleum containing emulsions can not be processed directly and it is subjected to demulsification, that is, emulsion is destroyed to separate petroleum from water and other impurities. Fresh emulsions are destructed more easily and hence demulsification should be performed as soon as possible. The removal of water from, and destruction of emulsions, in crude petroleum can carried out by :

(a) Mechanical Methods.

(b) Thermal Methods.

(c) Thermochemical Methods.

(d) Electrical Methods.

The mechanical method of demulsification is based on settling, centrifuging and filtering. In most cases, settling is the first stage of demulsification. Centrifuging and filtering are effected in laboratories for the determination of water content in petroleum and trapped product.

The thermal method of demulsification of petroleum is based on heating. During heating of an emulsion, the films of emulsifying agents expand and break, and so water droplets can coalese. Thus water accumulates at the bottom and petroleum forms the upper layer. Petroleum is usually settled in settling tanks and heated at a temperature upto 70°C. Some emulsions are difficult to be destroyed even at 120°C. In such cases, heating is carried out at a higher temperature with more careful tightening in order to minimise the loss of light fractions or other methods of demulsification are used.

The chemical method of demulsification has widely been used in recent years. The emulsifying agent destroys the emulsion by substituting or dissolving the active emulgator. In recent years, demulsifying agents of the type of non-ionogenic surfactants (based on ethylene and propylene oxides) have widely been used for this purpose. They promote the formation of emulsions of an opposite type to that already present in petroleum. When two emulsions come in contact, their emulsifying capacity is destroyed and the original emulsion is separated into layers.

In thermochemical method, a demulsifying agent is added to the petroleum during heating. The method is very efficient if high quality demulsifying agents are used. A more advanced thermochemical method consists in dehydration of petroleum in an air tight apparatus at 0.9 MPa pressure in the presence of an active demulsifying agent. Petroleum, preliminarily heated in heat exchangers or furnaces at about 150-155°C is allowed to settle. Water is settled at the bottom. This method has actually been used for the destruction of stable emulsions in heavy grades of petroleum.

The electric method of demulsification has widely been used at oil walls and at petroleum processing plants. In this method, an electric field formed by a high voltage AC is applied to the emulsion. The electric field destroys the emulsion films.

ELECTRIC DESALTING PLANTS

The technique of electric desalting of petroleum has changed radically in recent years and now new and more efficient plants have been employed. In addition, the electric and thermochemical methods of dehydration and demulsification are applied in combination.

Plants in which the process of dehydration and desalting of petroleum is effected are known as electric dehydrators (Fig 2).

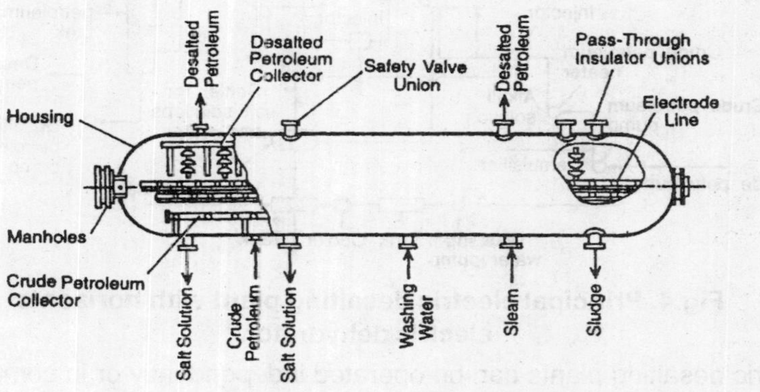

Fig.2. Horizontal electric dehydrator.

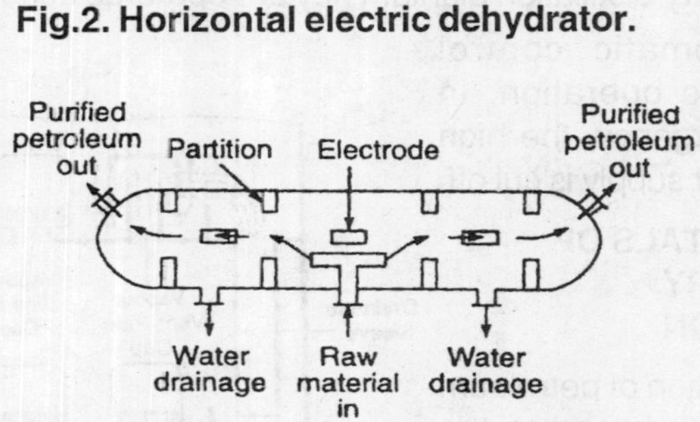

Fig.3. Electric sectional dehydrator.

Two rectangular frame electrodes are suspended at a height slightly below the cylinder axis, in the cylindrical housing of the plant. The distance between the electrodes is 25-40 cm. Crude petroleum is first fed into a layer of clarified water, then to the zone under the electrodes and finally passes through the lower electrode space. The material is then displaced into the zone above the electrodes and higher in the direction of outlet collectors. with processed petroleum, which are arranged above the cylinder uniformly along its whole length. An electric desalting plant may have one or more electric dehydrators connected in one or two stages.

Another type of electric dehydrator (Fig. 3) is provided with a number of separate sections formed by partition walls. The section have individual electrodes and communicate with one another through opening provided in the partition walls at the level of interelectrode spaces.

The principal diagram of an electric desalting plant is shown in Fig. 4.

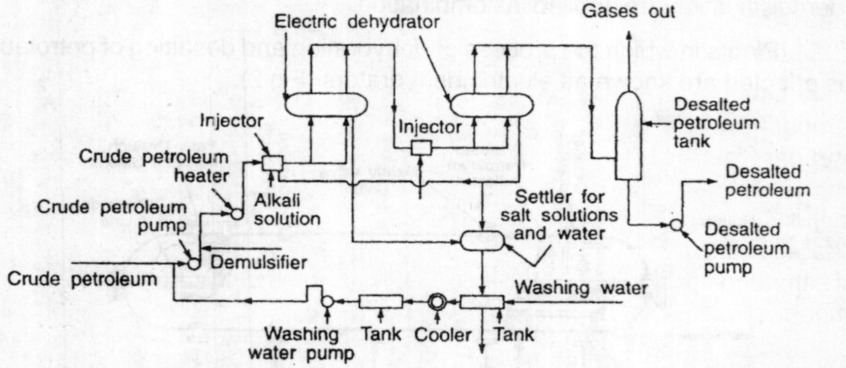

Fig.4. Principal electric desalting plant with horizontal electric dehydrator.

Electric desalting plants can be operated independently or in combination with preliminary distillation plants. They are operated according to a process chart. Automatic control ensures safe operation. In case of emergency, the high voltage power supply is cut off.

FUNDAMENTALS OF PRELIMINARY DISTILLATION

Separation of petroleum into fractions is based on the difference in the boiling points of the components. For example, if a mixture contains two components than the component having lower

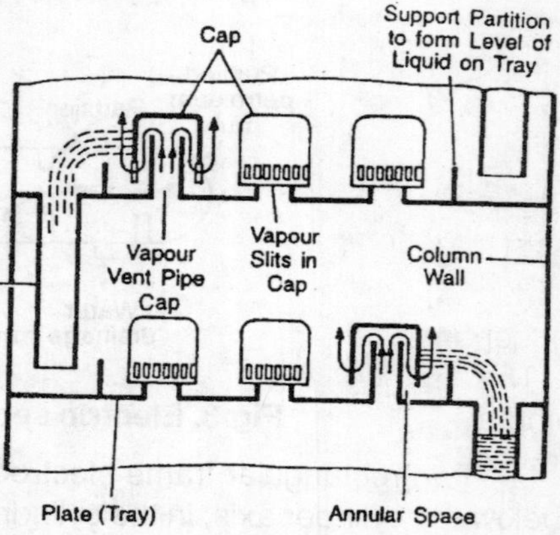

Fig.5. Bubble cap type tray.

boiling point (low boiling component) will be evaporated, and the component having higher boiling point (high boiling component) will remain in the form of liquid. The vapours are condensed to get what is known as distillate, and the remaining liquid is called residue. In other words, low boiling component passes to the distillate and high boiling component, to the residue. This process is called simple distillation. For more perfect separation of components, fractional distillation has been used. Fractional distillation means distillation combined with rectification. The rectification means counter-flow contact of the vapours formed in distillation with the liquid obtained by the condensation of vapours. For carrying out rectification in a distillation column, it is essential to form an ascending flow of vapours and descending flow of liquid. The vapour flow is due to the heat supplied to the bottom section of the column and the liquid flow is because of cold spraying in the top section. A bubble cap type tray of a rectification column is shown in Fig. 5.

Two phases meet on a column tray; a vapour phase at a higher temperature and a liquid phase at a lower temperature. Vapours are cooled and part of the high boiling component is condensed to liquid. The liquid phase is heated and part of the low boiling component evaporates and passes to the vapour phase. The process occurs repeatedly on each plate. During distillation and rectification of petroleum and petroleum products, the pressure of saturated vapours and the equilibrium between vapours and liquid play an important role.

A bubble cap fractionating column is shown in Fig. 6, and the construction of the bubble plate is shown in fig. 7 a and b. There is a layer of liquid at each plate and the liquid flows from one plate to another by a series of overflow pipes. The vapour rises through bubble caps in the plate. The upward movement of the vapour through the caps prevents the liquid descending through them.

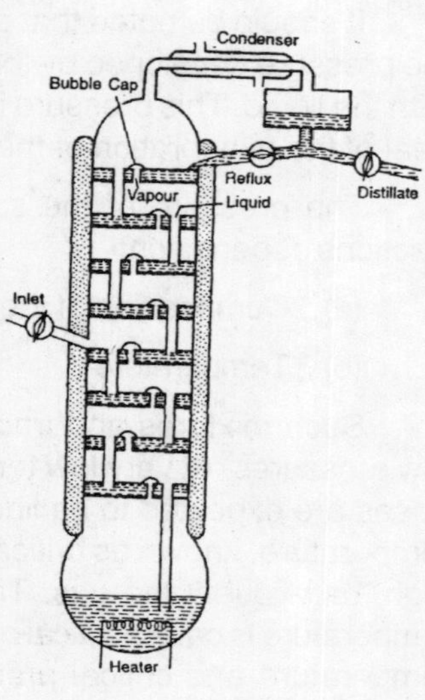

Fig.6. Bubble cap fractionating column.

A column (Fig. 7c) is heated by a coil at the bottom. There is a condenser B at the top of the column. The condensed liquid is collected in vessel C. The liquid thus collected may be withdrawn through D or returned back through E. The ratio of material returned to material withdrawn is called the reflux ratio. Material can also be withdrawn from the bottom of the column or fractions can be collected at various heights.

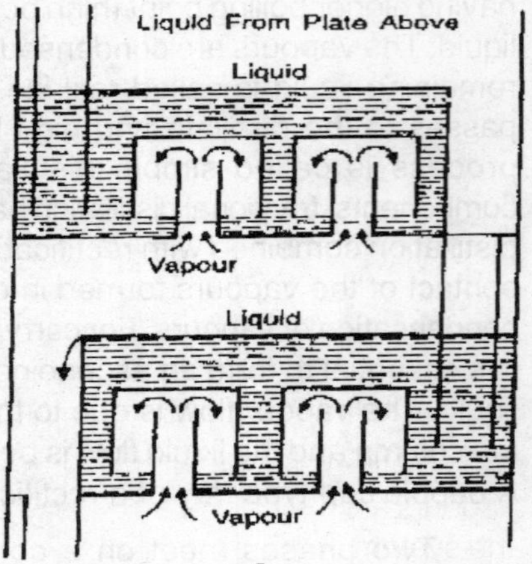

Suppose a mixture of liquids A and B is heated. The vapours consisting more of the more volatile component B than A rise up. The vapours of A undergo condensation on coming in contact with a large cooling surface of the fractionating column, while vapours of B pass over and can be collected in the receiver. The condensed liquid containing the excess of less volatile component A descends down the fractionating column and meets the fresh hot rising vapours. As a result of this contact, the ascending vapours are robbed off the less volatile component A which undergoes condensation and comes down with the descending liquid, while the condensed liquid loses its more volatile component B which rises up with the ascending vapours enriched much with B. The process is repeated until the vapours reaching the top of the column consist mainly of the component B, while the liquid coming down the column contains mainly the component A. In this way an almost complete separation is effected.

It should be noted that pressure of the saturated vapours of a liquid is the pressure developed by the vapour at a given temperature in equilibrium with the liquid. This pressure increases as the temperature is increased and heat of the evaporation of the liquid is decreased.

The pressure of the saturated vapours of mixtures and petroleum fractions depends on

(a) Composition of the liquid and vapour phases.

(b) Temperature.

Such mixtures and fractions obey the Raoult's and Dalton's laws at low pressures. At very low temperatures and sufficiently high pressures, all gases are expected to be liquefied. For each gas, however, there exists a temperature, known as critical temperature, above which no pressure, how high, can liquefy the gas. The vapour pressure corresponding to critical temperature is called critical pressure. The specific volume of a gas at critical temperature and critical pressure is called critical volume. At the critical point, continuity existing between the gaseous and liquid states disappears. The pressure of saturated petroleum vapour does not obey Raoult's law and Dalton's law in the region of high pressures.

METHODS OF PETROLEUM DISTILLATION

There are two main methods of petroleum distillation.

(a) With gradual, or multiple, evaporation in boilers, and

(b) With single or fresh evaporation in pipe furnaces.

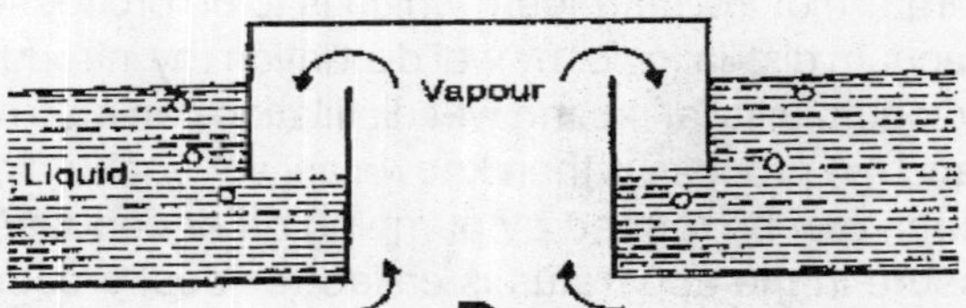

B

With gradual evaporation, the vapours are immediately removed from the system as soon as they are formed in the boilers, where multiple evaporation takes place. As the liquid passes from one boiler to the next boiler in the set of boilers, individual components are evaporated and removed in order of increasing boiling points. In modern plants of petroleum processing, gradual evaporation is almost completely out of use.

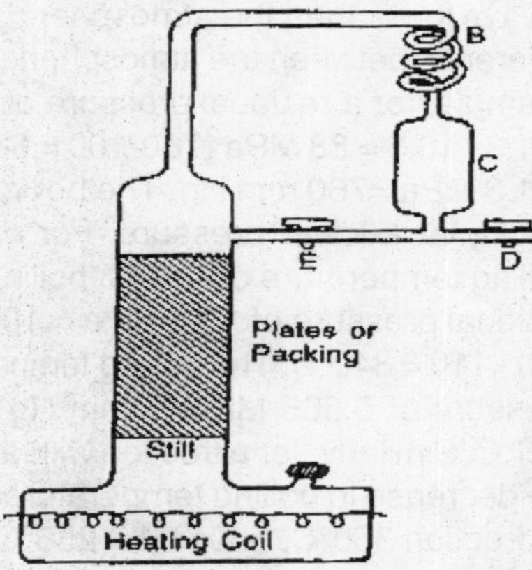

C

Fig. 7.

With flash evaporation, the product is heated in a pipe furnace upto a specified temperature and required distillate is obtained. The vapours are not separated from the liquid during the whole time of heating (composition of the system remains same). As the desired temperature is attained, the vapour phase formed in the system is separated from the liquid phase. The separation is effected in a column or evaporator where the heated product is supplied from the pipe furnace. Before separation the vapour and liquid phase remain in equilibrium and so the process is known as equilibrium flash evaporation. Hence, in flash evaporation of petroleum, the whole mixture of vapours formed at a given temperature is separated atonce frcm the liquid residue and then fractionated into fractions.

Unlike gradual evaporation in boilers (which takes few hours), the petroleum distillation with flash evaporation takes place in a few minutes and can be performed at a lower temperature, because low boiling fractions promote the evaporation of high boiling fractions at lower temperatures.

If the temperature and time of heating of petroleum are increased, the decomposition of the high molecular hydrocarbons may take place. This is called cracking, which takes place at 320-360°C, depending on the composition of petroleum. In some cases, e.g, when high boiling fractions are required for manufacturing the distillate oils and starting materials for catalytic cracking, petroleum must be heated above 360°C. For preventing the decomposition of high molecular hydrocarbons, it is necessary to decrease the boiling temperature of the petroleum which is to be processed. This can be achieved by vacuum distillation or by wet distillation (by introducing steam). In some cases, vacuum distillation and wet distillation can also be employed simultaneously and the process is then known as wet-vacuum distillation. A vacuum in a column can be formed by pumping off or condensation of the gases. The pressure in the apparatus is called residual pressure which is always lower than the atmospheric pressure. Vacuum is determined as the difference between the atmospheric pressure and the residual pressure. For example, for a residual pressure of 13.3 MPa (100 mm Hg), the vacuum is 101.3 - 13.3 = 88 MPa (760-100 = 600 mm Hg). The atmospheric pressure = 101.3 MPa =760 mm Hg. The boiling temperature of a fraction lowers more quickly at a lower pressure. For example,for a fraction with the average boiling temperature of 450°C, boiling temperature decreases by 110°C at a residual pressure of 13.3 MPa = 100 mm Hg, that is, the fraction will boil at 450 - 110 = 340°C. The boiling temperature decreases by 214°C at a residual pressure of 0.665 MPa (5 mm Hg). Thus fraction will boil at 450 - 214 = 236°C. Similarly, for a fraction with an average boiling temperature of 500°C, the decrease in boiling temperature at 13.3 MPa (100 mm Hg) is 117°C and for fraction 350°C, 350 - 94 = 256°C.

The method of wet distillation is widely used in petroleum processing, especially in fuel oil distillation. The effect of steam in petroleum distillation is as follows. Numerous steam bubbles have a very large free surface area in petroleum and the latter evaporates into them. The pressure of petroleum vapours is smaller than the atmospheric pressure and can not overcome the latter, but it is summed up with the pressure of steam, so that the total pressure is slightly greater than the atmospheric pressure and is sufficient for boiling and distillation of petroleum.

The steam is blown through a nozzle provided above the bottom of the apparatus and its pressure is maintained at a level sufficient to overcome the head of the liquid column, the pressure in the apparatus, and the hydraulic resistance of the pipelines. The pressure in direct steam.is maintained at not less than 0.2 MPa. The steam used should be dry. It is achieved by steam superheating in furnace coils.

In vacuum distillation, the boiling temperature can only be lowered by forming a sufficiently low residual pressure, but this makes the distillation apparatus not only expensive but also difficult to operate. Wet distillation without vacuum consumes much steam and also involves large expenditures on steam generation. Hence, the most efficient method of distillation of high molecular petroleum products is wet vacuum distillation, that is, a combination of vacuum with the supply of direct steam into the product that is to be distilled. This method is used in distillation of fuel oil with the formation of oil distillates and starting materials for catalytic cracking and hydrocracking.

Industrial flash distillation of petroleum is carried out in pipe furnaces where petroleum is heated to the direct temperature and fed to a rectification column in which it is separated into two phases. The first, vapour phase moves upwards and the second, liquid phase flows into the bottom portion of the column. The process gives fractions with particular temperature ranges of boiling off. This process of separation of petroleum into fractions by multiple evaporation and condensation of hydrocarbons is known as rectification. In the rectification of binary mixtures, the low boiling component is removed as vapours through the top of a column and the high boiling component remains in the liquid state and is drained off through the column bottom.

Figure 8. shows schematically the process of rectification of a binary mixture such as benzene and toluene. Upon heating in a furnace, the mixture is fed through pipeline I into rectification column 1. Low boiling compound benzene vapours are removed by pipeline II to condenser 2, from where part of condensed benzene is fed by pipeline III for refluxing and the remaining part is pumped off through cooler 3 by pipeline IV into a storage tank. A heater, fed by steam through pipeline VI, is arranged at the bottom of the column. Toluene (high boiling component) is removed from the column by pipeline V, via a cooler, to a storage tank. In the separation of benzene-toluene mixtures into fractions, the temperature at the top of column must be 80.4°C, i.e., corresponds to the boiling point of pure benzene. The temperature at the bottom must atleast be 110°C.

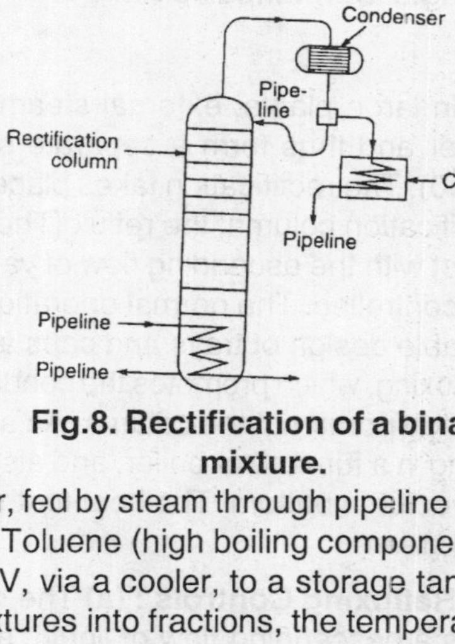

Fig.8. Rectification of a binary mixture.

Rectification of ternary mixtures (e.g. benzene, toluene and xylene) needs two columns. Xylene is taken off from the bottom portion of the first column, and mixture of benzene and toluene is withdrawn from the top of the first column and toluene is taken off from the top of the first column and separated into benzene and toluene in the second column as shown above.

For the rectification of complex mixtures of the type of petroleum, (n-1) simple columns are required for n compnents or fractions to be separated. But this scheme is very complicated. More often, a combined column is used, which consists of a number of simple columns with internal or external sections (Fig. 9).

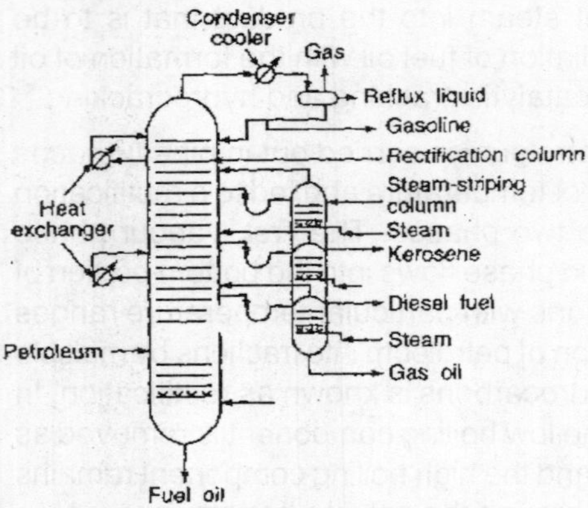

Fig.9. Combined column.

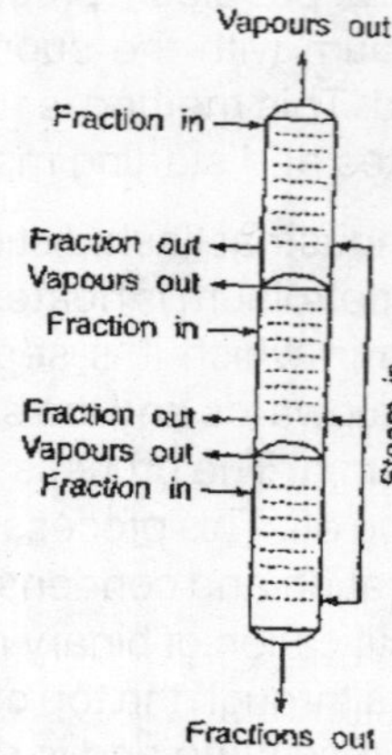

Fig.10. Multisection steam stripping column

In large plants, external steaming sections are mounted one above another and thus form a separate steaming or steam stripping, columns (Fig. 10). The rectification takes place on each tray. For normal operation of a rectification column, the reflux (The liquid on trays) must be in the closest contact with the ascending flow of vapours. Temperature is also necessary to be controlled. The normal operation of rectification column is ensured by a suitable design of trays and caps and the temperature control is ensured by refluxing, which promotes the condensation of the high boiling components in the top portion of the column. An ascending flow of vapours is formed by heating in a furnace or boiler, and also by partial evaporation of liquid phase in the column bottom. The heat for this purpose is obtained by boilers or by direct steam.

Refluxing Controls : (a) The temperature at the top of a column. (b) Forms a descending flow of liquid, and (c) ensures a gradual decrease in temperature of vapours as they pass from bottom upwards in the column. There are three main types of refluxing

(a) Cold Refluxing.
(b) Hot Refluxing.
(c) Circulating Refluxing.

The flow rate of the cold reflux liquid is lower at lower temperature of the liquid at the entry to the column and a higher latent heat of evaporation. The temperature of the product supplied as the reflux liquid to the column top is usually 30-50°C. The ratio of the flow rate of the reflux to the yield of the light component (rectified product) is known as reflux-to-product ratio.

A disadvantage of hot refluxing is a strong corrosion of the elements of partial condensers, which may cause leakage and passage of starting material to the distillate and a condenser is also difficult to be cleaned.

In circulating refluxin!gl the reflux liquid from some trays is drained off to the outside, passes through a heat exchanger, where it gives up its heat to the starting material and is thus cooled. It is returned into the column onto the next upper tray. Circulating refluxing is carried out in an upper or middle section of a column and is generally combined with cold retluxing. Circulating refluxing removes vapours from the top portion of rectification column. In addition, it makes it possible to preheat the starting material more intensively. The flow rate of the reflux liquid in the column top should not vary appreciably.

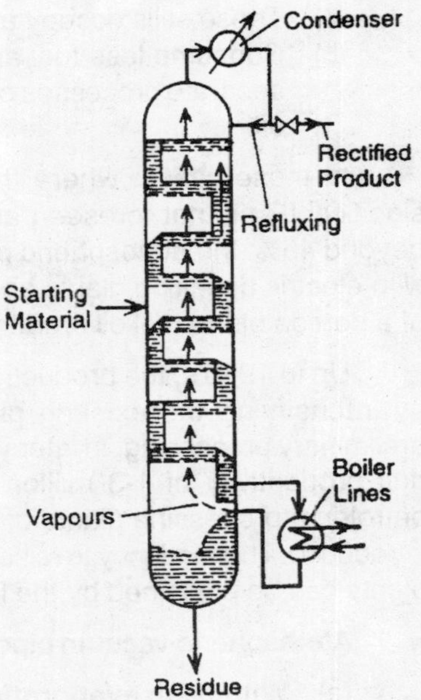

Fig.11. Material flow in a column

Depending on the starting material and pressure and flow rate of steam, the temperature in rectification columns and their portions can vary within wide limits. For example, from 80 to 120°C for gasoline vapours, from 190-220°C for Diesel fuel distillate in atmospheric columns, from 220-360°C for oil (vacuum) distillates at a residual pressure of 5.32-10.64 kPa (40-80 mm Hg) in a vacuum column.

Distillation of **white products (gasoline, kerosene, Diesel fuel etc.)** is carried our in tubular apparatuses operating at **atmospheric pressure-atmospheric pipe stills.** The process in an atmospheric pipe still gives fuel oil as residue. The fuel oil can be distilled in vacuum stills to obtain oil distillates or starting materials for catalytic and hydrogen cracking. In most cases, atmospheric and vacuum distillation of petroleum is carried out in a single plant, known as **atmospheric vacuum pipe still.**

In atmospheric-vacuum distillation of petroleum, the residue is goudron, which is used further in manufacturing boiler fuels or as starting material for making thick residual oils, bitumens and coke.

Modern processing plants characterised by a high yield of white products or a large volume of manufacture of oils and bitumens are f mainly equipped with atmospheric-vacuum pipe stills, usually together with an electric desalting unit, because

(a) These stills occupy a smaller area than atmospheric stills, and

(b) Consume less fuel and electric power than would be needed in separate processes of atmospheric and vacuum distillation of fuel oil.

In those cases, where the production of oils and bitumens is not significant or is not foreseen and yield of white products does not go up beyond 45%, the atmospheric pipe stills are generally used in combination with electric desalting plants and an additional plant for vacuum distillation of a portion of the fuel oil produced.

Up to 1950's, the productivity of petroleum processing was increased by intensifying the existing plants and construction of new plants for preliminary processing. In later years, plants for preliminary processing for a unit productivity of 1-3 million tons/year were put into operation. Then petroleum processing plants of annual productivity of 12 million tons were introduced. The tendency to raise the unit productivity of petroleum processing plants can be explained by the fact that larger plants are more efficient.

Atmospheric-vacuum pipe stills may be of various types, such as :

(a) With flash evaporation.

(b) With double flash evaporation in two columns.

(c) With preliminary evaporation of light gasoline fractions.

In flash evaporation plant, petroleum is pumped by a pump through heat exchangers into electric dehydrator and then fed to pipe furnace,(under the pressure formed by that pump) and rectification column. Plants of this type are most efficient for processing of petroleum grades with not more than 15% of gasoline fractions. With a higher content of gasolines, an exceptionally high pressure is to be formed at the pump discharge, in furnace coils, and in the column. Thus plants of other types are preferred for the processing of such grades of petroleum.

In double flash evaporation plants, petroleum is pumped by a pump through heat exchanger and electric dehydrator into topping still. The petroleum residue from the bottom of still is pumped by hot pump through a furnace and fed to atmospheric rectification column. Such plants are used for distillation of petroleum grades with not more than 15% of gasoline fractions. They are more complicated than flash evaporation plants because an extra column and the hot pump are required. Moreover, a high temperature of heating is required for the product in the still, since the light fractions distilled in the first column can not promote evaporation of heavier hydrocarbons.

In Preliminary Evaporation Plants, light gasoline fractions are run off in a separate evaporator and the topped petroleum is fed to a rectification column for distillation of white products. Petroleum is heated in heat exchanger fed through electric dehydrator into a preliminary evaporator and the topped petroleum is pumped by hot pump into a pipe furnace and further into rectification column. Vapours from the evaporator are also supplied to the column. In other words, the plant operates by the method of double flash evaporation with rectification being carried out in a single column and hence it combines the advantages of the two schemes described above, the main being that there are not elevated pressures in the pump-heat exchanger-electric dehydrators - furnace system. The combined rectification of light and heavy vapours in the column makes it possible to run the process at lower final temperatures of heating. These plants have widely been used for the distillation of non-stabilized and dehydrated grades of petroleum. However, the main column in such plants is quite complicated in design.

In atmospheric - vacuum plants, the petroleum is pumped by a pump through heat exchangers and electric dehydrator into the pipe furnace, where from it is fed to rectification column. Here, white fractions are separated at atmospheric pressure and 350°C, and the residue (fuel oil) at the bottom of the column is pumped by hot pump through pipe furnace into rectification column to separate fuel oil into fractions. Furnace and rectification column operate under vacuum.

The broad oil fraction obtained in atmospheric - vacuum plants (with or without electric dehydrators) can be used as the starting material for the manufacture of distillate oils and the catalytic and hydrogen cracking. By making use of one or two vacuum columns, these plants have also been employed in obtaining narrower distillate fractions for making oils: 300-400°C, 350-420°C, 420-460°C or 420-490°C. They can also be produced in separate vacuum plants by distillation of fuel oil. In all the cases, fuel oil distillation is carried out in vacuum inorder to decrease the boiling temperature of hydrocarbons, which makes it possible to run off the fractions that boil at atmospheric pressure and 500°C temperature at 420°C. In producing oil distillates, their decomposition is minimised by increasing the rate of flow of steam and lowering the pressure gradient in vacuum column.

In vacuum columns for making narrow oil fractions, the number of trays is increased and a steaming column is provided for each run-off fraction. With a large number of trays, it is, however, more difficult to maintain vacuum in the evaporation zone, where the starting material is fed. In such cases, double flash evaporation is used and it can be effected by two methods.

(a) Light fractions are run off in the first column and the residue from that column is heated in a second column where the remaining fractions are run off.

(b) A broad oil fraction is run off in the first column as in flash evaporation and is separated into narrower fractions in the second column.

Vacuum in a column can be formed by vapour condensation in barometric mixture condensers.

In Noval Plants, the effectiveness is increased by using surface condensers of the shell-and-tube type instead of mixture condensers. As a result, direct contact between the cooling water and vapour gas mixture is eliminated.

The use of surface condensers makes it possible to lower substantially the flow rate of wastes and the losses, and also the capital expenditures on the construction of sewage and purification units.

The best technico-economical results are obtained in plants where preliminary distillation is combined with thermal and catalytic processes.

DISTILLATION OF CRUDE PETROLEUM

Crude petroleum is a greenish red to black fluorescent emulsion with sandy oil and water as pumped out from wells. It also contains dissolved gases, liquids, with low, medium and high boiling points and widely varying viscosities and solids as well as semisolids. The crude oil is pumped under pressure to cylindrical tanks through underground pipes. In these tanks the emulsion is allowed to settle, as a result of which the emulsion is broken into two separate layers by heating which also releases the dissolved gases with the crude oil. These gases are disposed off as wet natural gas. The oil separates as a top layer. While wet sand (sand + water) forms the lower layer. Both layers are separately withdrawn. Some gas is also separated during distillation. Electrostatic separation of oil and water has also been carried out by passing crude oil between electrically charged insulated plates. Excessive salt content of the crude oil is reduced by washing with water.

In most modern refineries the batch stills have been replaced by pipe stills. Petroleum is refined by continuous distillation in these pipe stills which are also fitted with tubular furnace and tall fractionating column (a multiplate bubble cap tower). These save time, labour and fuel and as a result of fractional distillation, a number of fractions viz., gas, gasoline (or petrol), kerosene oil, gas oil and high boiling residue are obtained in a continuous process. The high boiling residue is generally further fractionated under low pressure into lubricating oils, paraffin wax etc. More gasoline may also be recovered by subjecting the residue to catalytic cracking. The fractions obtained vary with the nature of crude petroleum.

TABLE 1

Fraction	Composition	Boiling Range	Uses
Gas - Cymogene and Rhgolene		0-30°C	Liquid cymogene is used in the manufacture of ice. Rhigolene is used in medicine as local anaesthetia.
Crude Naphtha - on refractionation it further gives:	C_5H_{12}-C_8H_{14}	30°- 150°C	
(a) Petroleum ether		30°-70°C	As solvent in exraction of oils and fats and rubber industries, for dry cleaning.
(b) Gasoline or Petrol	C_6H_{14}-C_8H_{18}	70°-90°C	Motor fuel, dry cleaning etc.
(c) Ligroin or light Petroleum	C_6H_{14}-C_8H_{18}	90°-120°	In dry cleaning, as a solvent.
(d) Benzene Petrol	C_8H_{18}-$C_{10}H_{22}$	120°-160°C	In dry cleaning. In oil and paints industry as solvent).
Kerosene oil	$C_{10}H_{22}$-$C_{18}H_{38}$	150°-300°C	As a fuel, as an illuminant and for makin oil as.
Gas oil or Heavy oil	$C_{18}H_{38}$-$C_{42}H_{88}$	Above 300°C	
Residue		Above 400°C	As fuel in Diesel engines, cracked to get more gasoline. further fractionated under reduced pressure to yield
(a) Paraffin Wax	C_{20}-C_{30}	On coolin	
(b) Lubricating oils	C_{16}-C_{22}		For manufacture of candles and boot polishes. For lubrications.
(c) Vaseline			
(d) Pitch			In toilet goods and ointments.
(e) Petroleum coke (on redistillation of tar)			In paints and varnish. As fuel.

The uncondensed gases are mainly used as a fuel for heating the still containing crude petroleum, but a portion is liquefied and used as domestic fuel after filling in special type of cylinders under pressure. The upper layer of crude oil is used as cooling agent in the condensers, where it gets heated

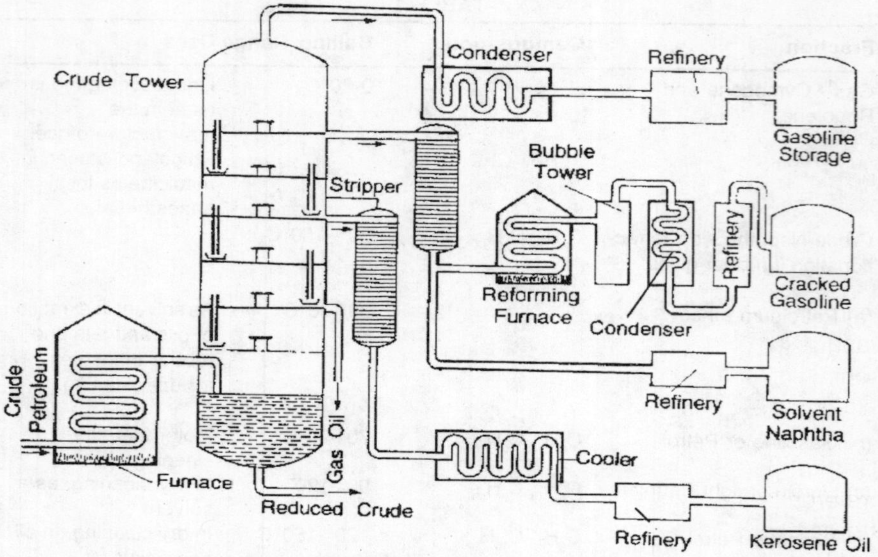

Fig.12. Distillation of petroleum.

to about 150°C. The hot oil at about 150°C is then allowed to pass through long coil of pipes, heated in a fire box. Here it gets heated to about 400°C, when cracking takes place and gases are formed. The heated crude oil then passes to a large insulated vessel, called evaproator, where all components volatising upto 400°C, vapourise and escape at the top from where they are conveyed to a fractionating column, where fractional condensation takes place. A residue of fuel oil is left in the evaporator and periodically removed from the bottom of the evaporator.

In fractionating column, high boiling fraction condense first and low boiling fractions last. The various products, with their boiling ranges and uses are listed in Table 1.

The **main fractions** of petroleum distillation are purified to improve the odour, colour etc. The disagreeable odour of the various fractions of crude naphtha and kerosene oil etc. is due to the presence of sulphur compounds, such as hydrogen sulphide and thioalcohols. The gasoline is therefore passed to the refining tank to remove sulphur compounds and diolefins and finally to storage. The gasoline is made free from bad odour by NaOH washing followed by sweetening (The process of converting thio alcohols into disulphides by adding sweetening agents, such as sodium hyposulphides (thio alcohols) to alkyl disulphide R2S2 which has less objectionable odour). Sulphur may be more or less completely removed with alcoholic caustic soda, and sodium butyrate. Bauxite at about 450°C or liquid sulphur dioxide removes much of the colouring matter. The diolefins are polymerised when the gasoline is treated with 94% H_2SO_4 at ordinary temperatures. The sulphuric acid also absorbs most of the sulphur compounds as well. The sulphuric acic treatment is no longer used now. This is due to the fact that acid also removes aromatic hydrocarbons which have high anti-knock properties.

The cracked gasoline is usually refined by vapour phase treatment. The vapour is allowed to pass through a tower containing hydrated aluminium silicate as well as nickel and cobalt oxides acting as catalyst at about 310-340°C. The compounds of sulphur are preferentially adsorbed on the surface of the catalyst. These are then removed from the surface as H_2S or SO_2 during regeneration of the catalyst.

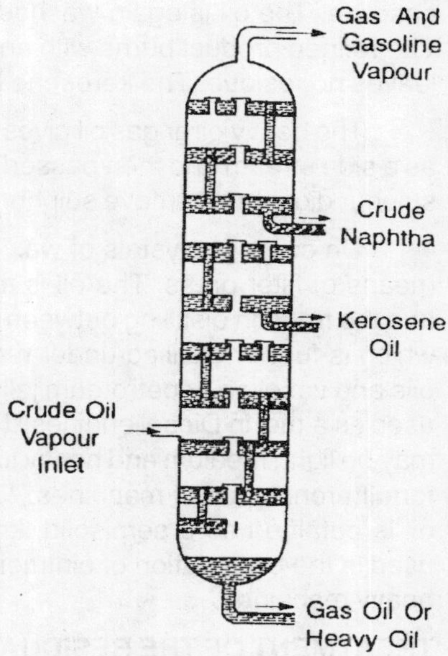

Fig.13. Distillation Column.

Kerosene oil obtained from distillation usually contains impurities of tarry matter, unsaturated hydrocarbons and sulphur compounds, which should be removed before it is put to use. The unsaturated hydrocarbons in kerosene are removed by washing with liquid sulphur dioxide or treatment with conc. sulphuric acid. This treatment decomposes unsaturated hydrocarbons and when allowed to settle, the acid and tarry products form a lower layer and are easily removed.

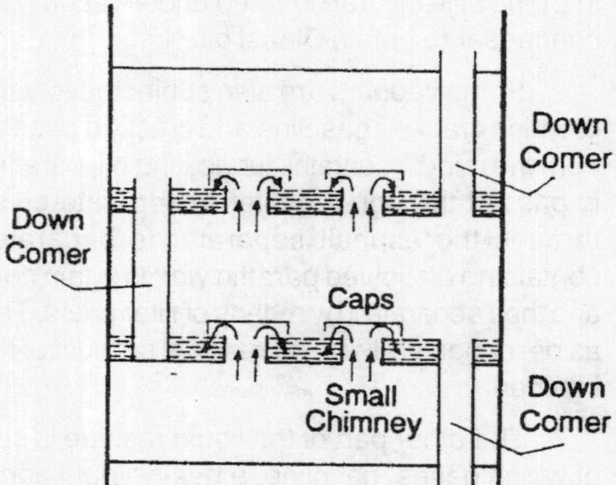

Fig.14. Bubble tower.

The oil is then mixed with caustic soda solution and compressed air is passed through to neutralise the acid. The caustic soda layer is then removed by washing the oil with water several times. The oil is finally redistilled and made free from sulphur compounds, (if present) as described in case of gasoline. The oil is again washed with water several times and redistilled. The refined product burns with an almost non sooty flame from a wick, and leaves no residue. The kerosene is decolourised like gasoline.

The heavy oil or gas oil gives a variety of valuble products. It is removed as a side stream and then passed through a cooler and extracted with liquid sulphur dioxide to remove sulphur compounds and then sent to the storage.

On cooling, crystals of wax separate out which are then removed by means of filter press. The oil is then distilled under atmospheric pressure and the fraction distilling between 280- 400°C is collected. It is called fuel oil which is further distilled under reduced pressure to get fuel oil, lubricating oils and vaseline or petroteum jelly. Fuel oil is the first fraction and is mainly used as a fuel in Diesel engines. The second fraction is lubricating oil, which may be light, medium and heavy lubricating oil. These are used as lubricants for different types of machines. The last fraction of the distillation of heavy oil is obtained as a semisolid, known as vaseline or petroleum jelly. It is used in the preparation of ointments, in toilet industry and as a lubricant for heavy machines.

TREATMENT OF THE RESIDUAL LIQUID

A dark coloured thick liquid comes.out through the bottom of the distillation still and is known as Tar. A part of the residual liquid is vapourised in a pipe still and fractionated under vacum. The overhead is condensed in a condenser to obtain Diesel oil.

Some vapours are also subjected to vapour phase cracking as a result of which cracked gasoline and cracked gases are obtained. The side stream from the middle contains lubricating oil, paraffin wax and asphalt. This stream is passed through a cooler to separate crystals of paraffin wax and then through the asphalt separator to separate asphalt. The lubricating oil containing dissolved paraffin wax is again cooled to separate wax as a solid and then separated by means of filter press. The lubricating oil is then obtained as described earlier. The residual product of the vaccum distillation is asphalt bitumen.

The other part of the liquid residue is subjected to cracking as a result of which gases, gasoline, a heavy liquid and petroleum coke are obtained. Gases leave the cracking tower at the top and the liquid is subjected to fractional distillation in pipe stills.

Gasoline obtained as overhead is condensed in a condenser and sent to cracked gasoline stroge before making it free from sulphur compounds and diolefins. The residual liquid from the last still is subjected to destructive distillation. The volatile products are condensed to get heavy fuel oil. The residue left in the still is called petroleum coke. Natural gasoline is obtained from wet natural gas and the gas obtained from crude petroleum.

PROCESSING OF LIQUID FUELS SUCH AS PETROLEUM AND PETROLEUM PRODUCTS

Petroleum and the products obtained by processing it are the most important liquid fuels. In order to develop deep petroleum processing methods, it is necessary to study the composition and various kinds of petroleum, the behavior of hydrocarbons during the processing operations, catalytic processes of hydrocarbon conversion and a number of other problems.

The products of the petroleum refining process are fuels such as gaseous and liquid fuels, lighting kerosene, solvents, lubricants, greases. solid and semisolid mixtures of hydrocarbons, paraffin, ceresin, vaseline etc; petroleum bitumens, and pitches, petroleum acids and their derivatives such as alkaline naphthenates, sulphoacids, fatty acids etc., individual hydrocarbons such as ethylene, propylene, methane, benzene, toluene, xylene and others, which are extremely useful raw materials for chemical industry. The most important among these are liquid and gaseous fuels, lubricants and individual hydrocarbons. Liquid petroleum fuels, depending on their use, can be classified as carburator motor (aviation automobile and tractor petrol), jet (Jet and turbojet engines), diesel, gas turbine and furnace fuels.

Petrols must possess definite properties such as definite fractional composition, vapour pressure and detonating properties. They must be non-corrosive and chemically stable. The vapour pressure should not exceed a definite limiting value. The detonating properties of a petrol are very important. In the cylinder of an internal combustion engine, a mixture of petrol and air is first compressed and then ignited by a spark created by a spark plug. The gases formed as a result of combustion of the fuel drive the piston. The higher the degree of compression of the gas mixture in the cylinder, the higher will be the efficiency of the engine. The degree of compression is, however, limited by the process of combustion of the mixture in the cylinder. The rate at which the flame spreads through the gas in the cylinder, varies, when the mixture is ignited by a spark. Under normal conditions, the rate of propagation is 10 to 15 m/sec, but at a certain level of compression, the mixture detonates and the flame propagation rate rises to 1500-2500 m/sec. Detonation results in knocking and over heating of the cylinder, dark exhaust gases are produced, consumption of fuel increases, wear increases and motor power decreases.

The detonating properties of a petrol are described by its octane number. The petrol octane number is determined by comparing its detonation during compression in a cylinder of an internal combustion engine with that of a standard mixture, consisting of iso-octane (2,2,4 trimethyl pentane) and n-heptane, under similar conditions. Iso-octane, which does not detonate easily, has an octane number of 100, and n-heptane, with an extremely high tendency to detonate, has an octane number of 0. The octane number of a petrol will then be equal to the content of iso-octane in a standard mixture which detonates at the same compression as the petrol being tested.

Automobile petrols have octane numbers of 76 to 95. Petrols more stable than iso-octane have octane numbers above 100. Aviation petrols, for planes with piston engines, are manufactured with octane numbers above 100. Chemical stability is characteristic of the tendency of a petrol to form tar and to change chemically during storage or in the internal combustion engine. It depends on the composition of the fuel and is lower if olefins and diolefins are present. The corrosive effect increases with an increase in sulphur content and acidity of a petrol.

Tractor fuel mainly kerosene, is described by the same characteristics as motor petrol. The octane number of kerosene should at least be 40.

Diesel fuels such as kerosene, gas oil and solar distillate are used in internal combustion piston engines in which ignition results from the compression of the gas. Economic operation of diesel motors depends on the fractional composition and cetane number of the diesel fuel. A diesel fuel should mainly contain a narrow fraction which boils, usually from 200-350°C. The cetane number characterises the capability of a fuel to ignite in the motor cylinder. The greater the cetane number, the better is the fuel. The cetane number is determined by comparing the behavior of a diesel fuel in motor with the behavior of a standard mixture of cetane ($C_{16}H_{34}$), whose cetane number is 100 and α-methyl naphthalene ($C_{10}H_7CH_3$) whose cetane number is 0.

Furnace fuel oils are mazout and other distillate residues. If mazout is not used for making lubricants, petrol or other motor fuels, it is burned in furnaces of locomotives, steam boats, power plants etc. **Jet engine fuel** is a kerosene fraction and is used for powering jet engines.

Gaseous petroleum fuels include casing head gas and the gases produced by processing petroleum and petroleum products. According to their applications, lubricating oils can be classified as industrial oils (spindle oil, machine lubricating oils etc), oils for internal combustion engines (motor and tractor engine oil, aviation lubricating oils etc.), transmission oils, turbine oils, compressor oils for steam engines (cylinder oils) and special purpose oils.

The quality of an oil is determined by its lubricating property, viscosity, solidification temperature and flash point, density, moisture content, acidity, tendency to coke, ash content and stability. Preliminary processing of petroleum consists in removing dissolved gases, mineral salts, moisture and mechanical impurities such as clay and sand, from the crude petroleum. Impurities are partly removed at the well and partly at the petroleum refining plants.

Gases are removed in traps, in which both the pressure and the velocity of the petroleum stream are reduced, so that the dissolved gas can be liberated. In many cases, natural gasoline, the lightest hydrocarbon mixture is also separated with the dissolved gas. The natural gasoline is removed from the gas by absorbing it with solar oil or adsorbing it on activated charcoal.

Mineral salts are removed in a desalting process in which petroleum is repeatedly scrubbed with warm water to dissolve the salts. The emulsion so formed is separated from the petroleum during dehydration. Dehydration can be carried out by setting and physical impurities are then partly removed together with water. Since petroleum forms highly stable emulsions with water, complete dehydration is only possible if the emulsion is destroyed by deemulsifying agents such as sodium salts of naphthenic acids. Electrical dehydration is very effective method and consists in passing a film of petroleum at a high temperature between electrodes to which alternating current is fed at a voltage of 30,000-40,000 volts. As a result, emulsion is destroyed, water drops undergo coagulation and then water is separated from petroleum by settling.

Stabilization of petroleum is carried out by desalting and dehydration. This process decreases losses of light hydrocarbons during transportation and storage and provides a constant level of vapour pressure. Stabilization is achieved by stripping the propane-butane, and in some cases also part of the pentane fraction of the hydrocarbons. The stabilization unit is provided with furnaces for heating the petroleum and distillation tower for separating the propane-butane fraction, which is a valuable raw material for the chemical industry. Depending on the kinds of products to be obtained from the petroleum, three modes of petroleum processing are employed. These are : (1) Fuel processing, which yields motor and furnace fuels. (2) Fuel-lubricant processing, in which both fuels and lubricants are the products, and (3) Patrochemical processing, by which not only fuels and lubricants are produced, but raw materials such as olefins, aromatic and paraffinic hydrocarbons etc are also produced. These methods can be divided into two classes (a) Physical processing methods, which produce individual hydrocarbons or more often, their mixtures from the petroleum or petroleum products, utilizing differences in their physical properties such as boiling point, crystallisation temperature, solubility etc. The widely used method is straight run distillation method of petroleum and petroleum products, that is, separation of petroleum into fractions with different boiling points (b) Chemical methods, which are based on deep, chemical, destructive transformations, of hydrocarbons contained in the petroleum or petroleum products, effected by temperature, pressure or catalysts. Most extensively used are various forms of cracking. Petroleum processing using catalytic conversion techniques have also been employed.

The apparatus for treating petroleum and petroleum products serve first of all for heating them to a high temperature, then for dividing the products obtained, and when needed, for carrying out catalytic reactions. Pipe furnaces are used for heating petroleum and petroleum products. Heat is transferred from gaseous combustion products to the pipes (through which the liquid materials flow) by radiation and by convection. The furnace uses a gas fuel which is fed to prism shaped ceramic burners in the furnace walls. By flameless combustion of the gas fuel in the burners of the ceramic plates are heated to incandescence and heat is intensely radiated to the surface of radiant tubes. The gaseous combustion products flow through the convection chamber and transfer heat by convection to the tubes carrying the material on its way to processing. Flameless combustion furnaces with vertical radiant tubes are also available.

At present flameless combustion pipe furnaces are used for heating petroleum and petroleum products. The furnace is made of prefabricated ribbed pannels. There is a layer of heat insulating bricks between the ribs of the pannels which keeps the outside wall temperature at about 45°C. The liquid materials flow through tubes joined in series. The first pass through convective heating chamber tubes in the convection heating chamber and then enter the radiant heating tubes. These tubes are located along the partition walls, the hearth and the roof of the furnace. The gas fuel used in the furnace is fed to prism shaped ceramic burners in the furnace walls. The ceramic plates are heated to incandescence by flameless combustion of the gas fuel in the burners and heat is intensely radiated to the surface of radiant tubes. The gaseous combustion products flow through the convection chamber and transfer heat by convection to the tubes carrying the material on its way to

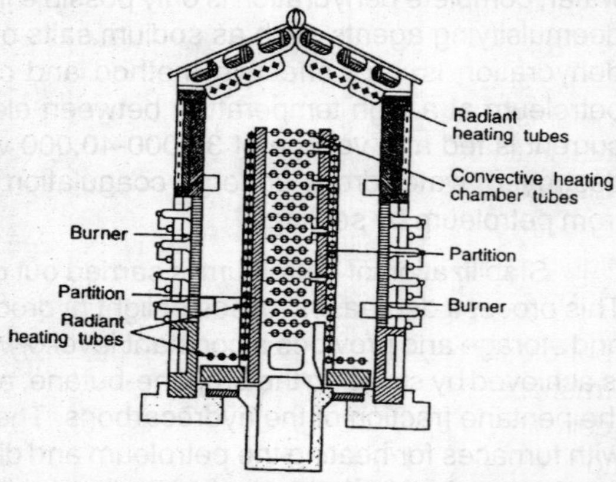

Fig.15. Flameless combustion pipe still.

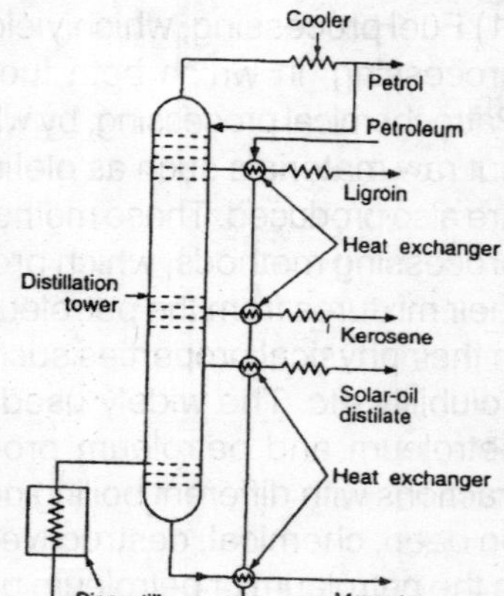

Fig.16. Schematic diagram of a petroleum distillation unit.

processing. A feature of modern pipe furnaces is a high degree of utilization of the excess heat of the off gas combustion products and the heated liquid, which are employed to produce steam. Flameless combustion furnaces with vertical radiant tubes are also available.

A flow diagram of a single stage unit is given in Fig. 16. A pump forces the petroleum consecutively through shell-and-tube heat exchanger, where it absorbs heat from the distillates and is heated to about 170-175°C and then through the tubes of the first pipe still. The petroleum in the tube is under a small excess pressure created by the pump. From the pipe still the petroleum (at about 300-350°C and in a liquid vapour state) is fed to the lower part of the distillation tower, where the pressure is decreased, and the volatile fractions evaporate and separate from the liquid remainder, known as mazout. The vapours of these fractions rise up through the column and are distilled. The distillates are removed in a condensed state of various heights. They are then subjected to distillation in stripping towers and cooled first in shell and tube heat exchanger by the petroleum entering the unit and then in water coolers. Petrol vapours are removed at the top of the column and are cooled in condenser, where they are converted into liquid. Part of the liquid petrol is returned to the column as reflex.

A two stage unit consists of two similar blocks, a block of straight run petroleum refining (Fig 16), and a second block for separating mazout into fractions. The mazout, which is removed at the bottom of the tower, is delivered to a pipe still, where it is heated to 400-420°C, and is then transferred to a tower which operates under vacuum. Residual asphalt is removed from the lower part of the tower and lubricant distillates are removed at several heights. The petrol yield of straight run distillation depends on the composition of the petroleum and lies between 3 and 15%.

Straight run petrol mainly contains paraffinic and naphthenic hydrocarbons, but petrols obtained from petroleum with a high aromatic hydrocarbon content are the exceptions. Depending on composition, the octane number of petrols varies from 50 to 78. Petrols with octane numbers upto 87 - 95 are obtained by adding ethyl fluid.

The products of petroleum processing are mainly separated by distilling them in towers of various types, but bubble cap towers are most commonly employed. A distinct feature of petroleum refining towers is that they consist of a number of primary, independent columns placed one above the other with liquid products removed at various heights. The liquid enters into stripping sections, located outside the tower, where steam is passed through it. As a result, vapours of low boiling fractions are formed, which are returned to the tower. Distillation towers are generally operated under pressure, at atmospheric pressure or under vacuum. The catalytic processes of petroleum refining units are carried out in reactors of different designs. The catalytic converter units include both reactors and regenerators, because catalyst in these processes quickly loses its activity. The reactors and regenerators may be with the catalyst in a filtering bed, a fluidised bed or with a moving catalyst.

Straight run distillation of petroleum (Physical petroleum refining), is based on the differences in the boiling points of the various petroleum products. As a result of this distillation, petrol (upto 170°C), ligroine (160-200°C), kerosene (200-300°C), gas oil (300-350°C) and remainder, called mazout are formed as fractions or distillates. Each of these fractions can be redistilled and separated into fractions with a narrow range of boiling points, producing different kinds of distillates. Petroleum distillation is carried out under atmospheric pressure. The mazout or fuel oil can also be subjected to fractionation. Distillation of mazout is generally carried out under vacuum inorder to avoid decomposition of hydrocarbons present in it at high temperatures. The mazout fractions or distillates are Spindle oil (230-250°C), Machine oil (260-305°C), Light cylinder oil (375-325°C), Heavy cylinder oil (350-370°C) and residual asphalt (350-370°C). These distillates which are obtained by distillation of mazout, are raw materials for making lubricants.

Now-a-days petroleum and mazout are distilled in pipe still units where following operations take place (a) Preheating of raw material by interchange with the distillation products in heat exchangers (recuperation). This is main stage of heating raw material in the pipe still. (b) Separation of vapours formed from the liquid remainder, and (c) Their distillation in distillation towers, condensation and cooling of the distillation products in coolers, which also serve as raw material heaters.

The petroleum distillation unit may be single stage and two stage units. In single stage unit, fractions, ranging from petrol upto high boiling fractions are produced from the petroleum at atmospheric pressure. In two stage unit, petroleum is first distilled at atmospheric pressure to obtain petrol, ligroine, kerosene, gas oil and mazout, and then lubricating oil distillates are separated from the mazout under vacuum. Two stage units for petroleum distillation are called atmospheric-vacuum units.

High temperature chemical processing of petroleum and petroleum products is a method of destructive treatment of petroleum, which leads to intensive changes in the molecular structure of initial materials. One such process is cracking of petroleum distillation fractions.

Cracking is the splitting of molecules of the initial material into smaller ones. Cracking not only causes decomposition, but also accompanied by secondary processes of synthesis of larger molecules.

Reforming is the cracking of low octane petrol or ligroine to raise the octane number of a carburetor fuel or to obtain hydrocarbons for organic synthesis. Cracking and reforming at higher temperatures in the absence of a catalyst are called thermal cracking and thermal reforming. In presence of' a catalyst, these processes are known as catalytic cracking or catalytic reforming. Therncal cracking is carried out at 470-540°C and at pressures upto 60 atm. In spite of complex nature of hydrocarbon conversions during cracking, some of the rules governing the behavior of various hydrocarbon groups have been formed :

(a) At high temperatures, rupture of the molecular chains and dehydrogenation of methane hydrocarbons may occur.

(b) The olefins formed undergo further transformations.

(c) When naphthene hydrocarbons are dehydrogenated, aromatic hydrocarbons are formed. Thus dehydrogenation of cyclohexane gives benzene.

(d) Aromatic hydrocarbons may rupture at C_{aryl} - C_{alkyl} bond and split off a side chain. As a result, simple aromatic and unsaturated hydrocarbons are formed. For example, ethyl benzene yields benzene and ethylene.

(e) Condensation of the aromatic hydrocarbons, which results in coke formation is also possible.

(f) The unsaturated hydrocarbons formed in cracking enter into condensation, alkylation and cyclisation reactions with each other and with the initial substances to form aromatic and other complex hydrocarbons.

(g) Hydrocarbon reactions often take a chain mechanism. In order to determine the nature of the products obtained by cracking, one must know which of the reactions of hydrocarbon conversion are more probable according to the reaction thermodynamics.

(h) At higher temperatures the strength of hydrocarbon bonds is lower. The thermal stability of paraffin hydrocarbons of a homologous series decreases as the size of the molecule increases. Thus on heating the hydrocarbons with longer chain split first. The split position shifts towards the end of the chain with an increase in the temperature and this leads to the formation of more stable, short chain hydrocarbons, upto CH_4. However, above 820K, methane also starts decomposing into carbon and hydrogen.

(i) Below 500K, the methane and naphthene hydrocarbons are more stable, but at higher temperatures, the aromatic hydrocarbons and olefins are the most stable. Therefore, at high temperatures they still accumulate in the cracking product. For a dehydration reaction the change in free energy is ΔG = 130 - 0.14 TkJ/g.mole and for a reaction resulting in rupture of the carbon chain, $\Delta G = 80 - 0.14\ T$ kJ/g.mole. **This indicates that chain rupture is more probable than dehydration.** A thermodynamic analysis of the process shows that a given change in the cracking temperature promotes one certain reaction of the number of them which are possible thermodynamically. Since cracking is kinetics limited, the temperature also has a significant effect on the rate of the process. The dependence of the reaction rate on the temperature is expressed by the **Arrhenius equation** and the temperature coefficient of the reaction is about **2. The activation energy for paraffinic and naphthenic hydrocarbons amounts to about 200-300 kJ/mole, and for aromatic hydrocarbons about 300-400 kJ/mole. Thus according to their rate of conversion, hydrocarbons are arranged in the order : Paraffinic, naphthenic, aromatic.**

The most important of the products manufactured at most plants is petrol. At some temperature, decomposition of the less stable heavy hydrocarbons begins and lighter hydrocarbons, which are a part of the composition of petrol, are formed. As the temperature increases, the process rate also increases and the petrol yield (for constant residence time in the reactor and constant pressure) grows. However, increase in temperature causes further decomposition of the lighter hydrocarbons to form gases. Hence there should be a certain optimum temperature at which maximum yield of petrol is obtained.

The rate of decomposition of hydrocarbons is not affected by the pressure on the one hand, an increase in pressure slows down the reversible cracking reactions which result in the formation of gaseous products and thus increases the petrol yield. On the other hand, it favours secondary reactions which give rise to heavy products, and hence petrol yield is decreased. Consequently, if it is desired to increase the yield of liquid products the process should be carried out at high pressures, and if, it is necessary to obtain large amounts of gases, cracking should be carried out at low pressure.

The course of cracking reactions is affected by the residence time of the hydrocarbons in the high temperature zone. When the residence time of the products in the high temperature zone is increased, the degree of decomposition of heavy hydrocarbons increases and yield of petrol also increases with it. A further increase in the residence time causes fission of the lighter hydrocarbons and formation of gases and hence petrol yield decreases.

Because of this the degree of conversion during one passage through the cracking apparatus is limited to 50-70%. Then, after the cracking products, e.g, petrol and a heavy remainder, are removed and the so called intermediate fraction is again subjected to cracking, either separately, or in a mixture with fresh raw material. This latter process is called cracking with recirculation, or recycle.

PETROLEUM PROCESSING EQUIPMENT

STORAGE TANKS

Petroleum and petroleum products, including liquefied hydrocarbon gases, are stored in specially designed tanks which are usually made of killed open hearth steel and may either be cylindrical or domed shaped (globe-roof). All storage tanks are provided with :

(a) Level guages.
(b) Safety valves.
(c) Sampling devices.
(d) Non-freezing drainage means.
(e) Unions for ventilation and removal of gas rests.
(f) Manholes, and
(g) Inner ladders.

In order to ensure the desired head of the pump, storage tanks for liquefied gases are built on concrete foundations of a sufficient height. Storage tanks for petroleum and petroleum products can be built either on the ground level (such storage tanks are known as land tanks) or beneath the ground (such storage tanks are known as submerged tanks). Land tanks are commonly made of steal and submerged tanks are made of plain or reinforced concrete. In some cases, storage tanks are also made of bricks, stone or other materials and faced inside with steel sheets to protect the walls against the aggressive action of petroleum products. In very cold countries, storage tanks are made of steels retaining their strength at low temperatures.

For safe operation, horizontal cylindrical storage tanks are designed to withstand a gauge pressure upto 0.5 MPa (capacity of tank upto 100 m^3) and vertical steel tanks of a capacity of 50,000 m^3 or more, are designed to withstand a gauge pressure of 0.25 kPa.

Storage tanks breathe during operation. Intense breathing has been observed when the product is pumped in and displaces the gas from a tank, or is pumped off and then the tank is filled again with the surrounding air or gas. Light breathing is because of variation in temperature. At an increase in temperature, the pressure of the gas inside increases and the gas is partially displaced from the tank, and *vice versa*. Storage tanks are equipped with various devices in order to compensate for breathing, allow proper maintenance, measure the liquid level, take samples of the product, remove the settled water, and sometimes to heat the product. Storage tanks for white products are provided with an essential element known as hydraulic safety valve, which functions in combination with breathing valve and a fire-safety

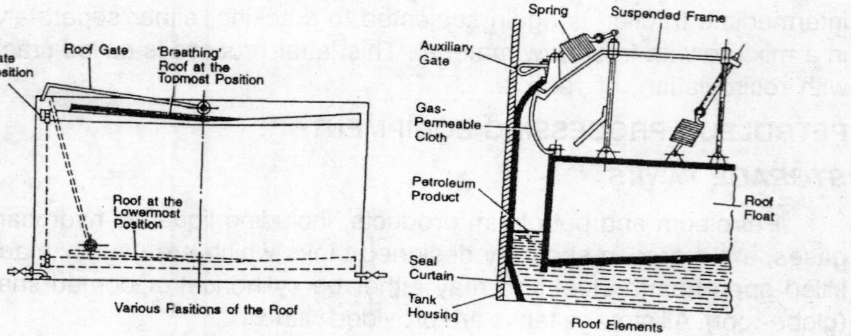

Fig.17. Breathing storage tanks. (a) Various portions of the roof. (b) Roof elements.

valve. It is designed for a higher pressure (upto 2.1 kPa) and higher vacuum (0.3 kPa), than the breathing valve and opens in cases when the breathing valve fails to operate for some or other reasons.

In recent years, storage tanks of the float-roof type (breathing tanks) have found wide applications for storage of light grades of petroleum and of gasoline fractions. The roof of such a tank can move up and down freely, which minimises the breathing effect and hence reduces the loss of light petroleum products sharply.

RECTIFICATION COLUMNS

Rectification columns of various designs, such as packed columns and rotating-cone columns are used.

Packed Columns - A column may be packed with ceramic rings (Fig. 19) lumps of coke, polyhedral prisms, etc. In order to increase the surface area, some type of rings are made with internal partitions. The packing is laid on trays with holes of two types :

(a) Smaller holes for the passage of refux, and
(b) Larger holes for the passage of vapours.

Such type of rectification columns, however, fail to ensure a close contact between vapours and reflux. Such type of columns are mostly used for periodic rectification when a high productivity is not required.

CAP TRAY OR BUBBLE TRAY COLUMNS

This type of columns have widely been used for distillation of crude petroleum and petroleum products. A column has a cylindrical housing with top and bottom end portions and trays arranged on angle pieces around the column periphery. The trays are mounted horizontally and each of them is provided with openings with pipe unions covered by caps and a draining arrangement for slipping the fluid on to the next lower tray. The pipe unions

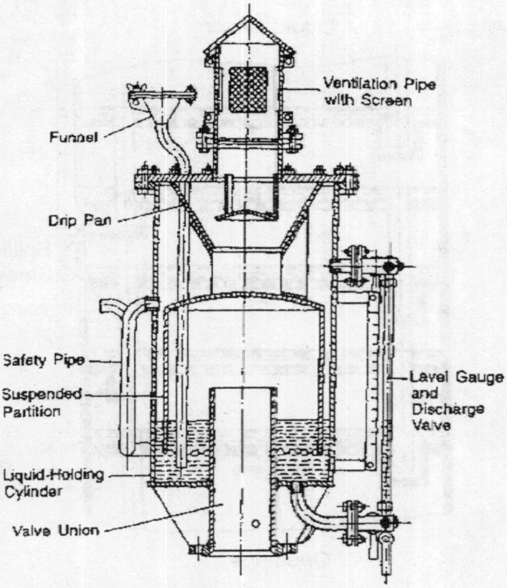

Fig.18. Hydraulic safety valve.

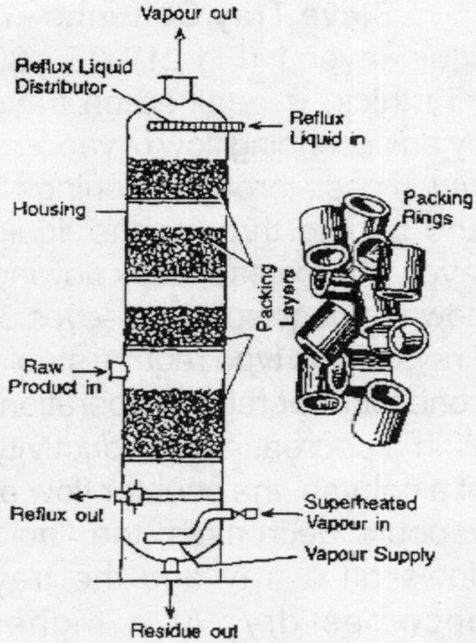

Fig.19. Packed columns.

and the slits between the caps act for the passage of vapours which bubble through the liquid. The evaporation of low boiling components from reflux and the condensation of high boiling components take place on every tray. Bubble cap tray columns differ mainly in the design of caps and spilling means. Various types of caps are shown in Fig. 20. In recent years, columns with valve type trays are more common.

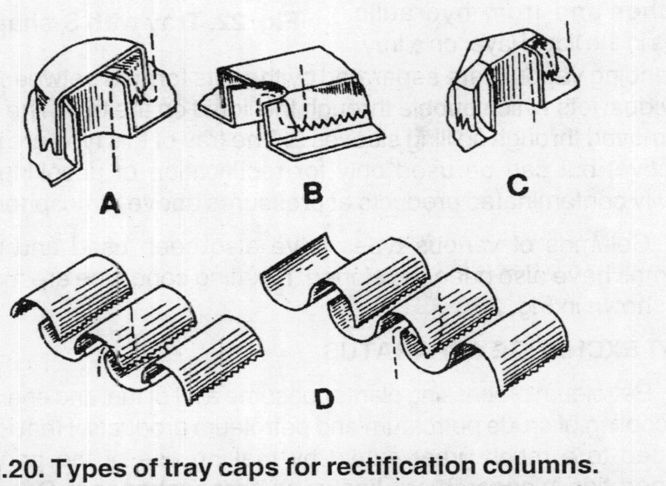

Fig.20. Types of tray caps for rectification columns. (a) Cylindrical (b) Rectangular (c) Hexagonal (d) Tunnel-type.

Sieve Tray Columns - A liquid layer 1 (Fig 21), 25 - 30 mm thick, is retained on trays by an ascending flow of vapours which pass through openings 2 and bubble through the liquid layer, the excess reflux flowing down through spilling sleeves 3. Trays of this type require stable conditions for reliable operation. With a decrease in productivity of a column, the counter flow of vapours decreases, the liquid flows off a tray and the tray becomes dry. At a higher productivity, the counter flow of vapours increases and removes from the liquid layer a greater amount of heavier hydrocarbons which disturbs the equilibrium and impairs the rectifying effect of the column.

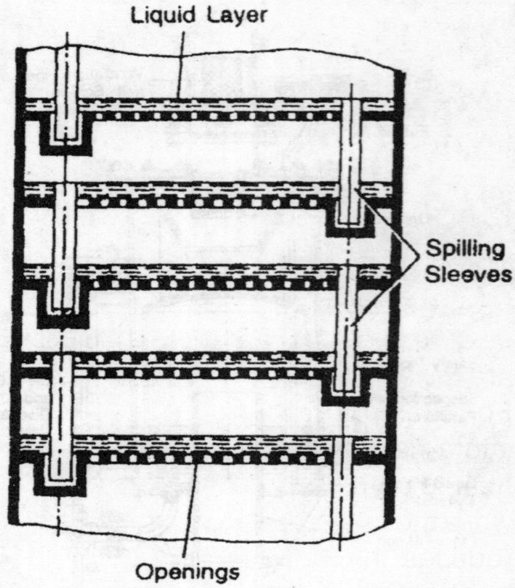

Fig. 21. Sieve tray.

Columns with S-Shaped Caps - Caps I (Fig 22) are stamped from steel sheets. The edges of caps engage one another and from hydraulic gates in the liquid layer on a tray. Ascending vapours are separated by the slits formed between the caps into individual jets which bubble through the liquid on the tray. The excess reflux is removed through spilling sleeves 2. The tray of this type are no doubt very effective, but can be used only for rectification of uncoking and not too heavily contaminated products at pressures above atmospheric.

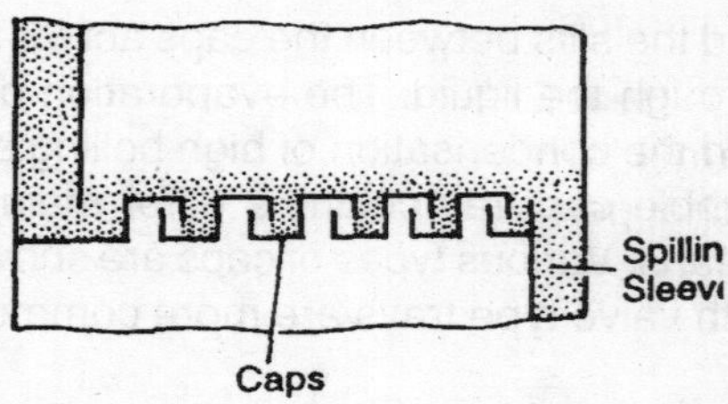

Fig. 22. Tray with S-shaped caps.

Columns of various types have also been used and new types of columns have also been developed. Rotating cone type are most promising and shown in Fig. 23.

HEAT EXCHANGE APPARATUS

Petroleum processing plants consume a lot of fuel and energy for heating and cooling of crude petroleum and petroleum products. Heat losses may be reduced to a much great extent by making use of the principle of heat regeneration in apparatuses known as heat exchangers. Depending on the purpose, all heat exchange apparatus can be divided into three main parts.

(1) Heat Exchangers.
(2) Steam Space Heaters or Boilers.
(3) Condensers.

The principle of operation of these apparatuses is that the two products are contacted through the walls of an apparatus or tubes so that the heat of the hotter product is given to a colder product (an exception is mixture condensate where the two products are mixed with each other in the apparatus). For example, fuel oil from a distiller is led into a heat exchanger where it supplies its heat to crude petroleum and is thus cooled, while the crude petroleum is heated up. This reduces the fuel consumption needed for heating up the crude petroleum to the specified temperature. It also reduces the consumption of cooling water required for cooling fuel oil to the given temperature.

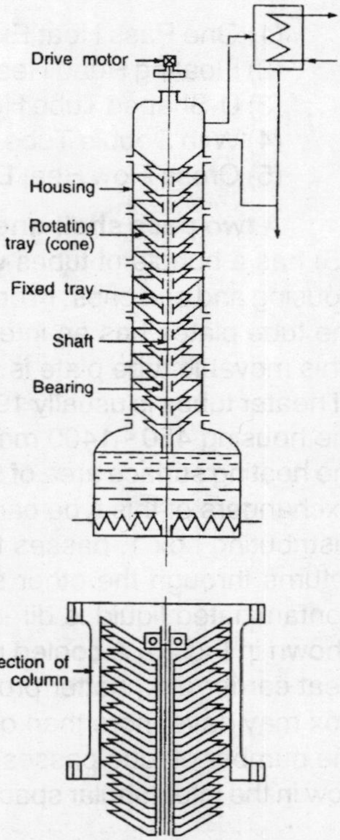

Fig.23. Rotating cone column.

Heat Exchangers - Heat generation is mainly effected in two types of head exchangers. These are:

(a) Shell and Tube Heat Exchangers.
(b) Double Pipe Type Heat Exchangers.

Shell-and-tube heat exchangers have widely been used, especially in large and combined plants. This type of heat exchanger consists of a bundle of tubes fastened at the ends in tube plates and the whole assembly is enclosed in' a shell housing. One of the heat carriers circulates through the tubes and the other, in spaces between the tubes. Heat exchange takes place through the tube walls. Shell-and-tube heat exchangers can be divided into the following main types.

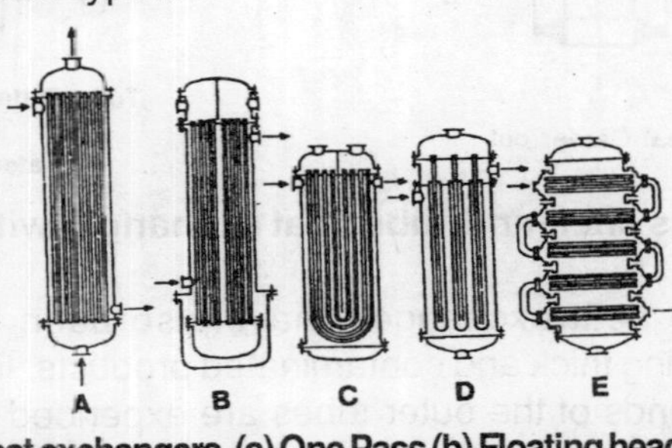

Fig.24. Rigid type heat exchangers. (a) One Pass (b) Floating head (c) With U shaped tubes (d) With double tubes. and (e) Cross-flow heat exchanger.

(1) One Pass Heat Exchangers.
(2) Floating Head Heat Exchangers.
(3) U-Shaped Tube Heat Exchangers.
(4) With Double Tube Heat Exchangers.
(5) Cross Flow Heat Exchangers.

A two pass shell-and-tube heat exchanger with a floating head (Fig. 25) has a bundle of tubes with their ends expanded in tube plates 2 of the housing and end caps. In order to compensate for thermal expansion, one of the tube plates has an internal cap which can move freely in the housing. This movable tube plate is known as floating head 3. The outside diameter of heater tubes is usually 19-25 mm, their length 6 - 9 m, and the diameter of the housing 450 - 1400 mm. Modern shell-andtube heat exchangers have the heating surface area of 50 - 2000 m^3. The heat exchange process in heat exchangers of this type can be explained as follows. A liquid is supplied to distributing box 1, passes through the tube bundle to floating head 3, and returns through the other set of tube bundle. Usually a thicker and more contaminated liquid is directed through the tube bundle. In the apparatus shown in Fig 25, A cooled product moves through the tube bundle and the heat carrier (i.e., hotter product) in the intertubular space. The distributing box may have more than one longitudinal partition to increase accordingly the number of tube passes. Transverse partitions may increase the rate of flow in the inter tubular space and this increases the heat transfer coefficient.

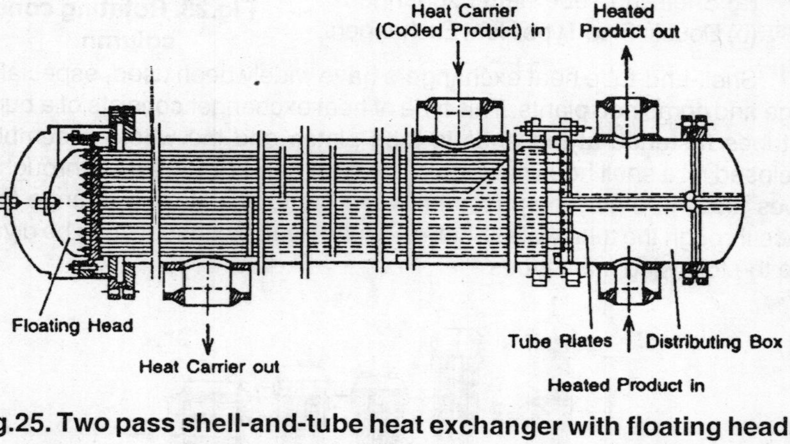

Fig.25. Two pass shell-and-tube heat exchanger with floating head.

Double pipe heat exchangers have also been used extensively, especially for heating thick and contaminated products. In such type of heat exchanger, both ends of the outer tubes are expended in the tube plates. Inner tubes are expanded at one tube plates and connected by U-shaped tubes at the other end. The diameter of the tube may even be as large as

150mm. Steel finned tubes (Fig. 26) are generally used for increasing the area of heating surface and intensifying the heat exchange, which can even be raised by 50-80%.

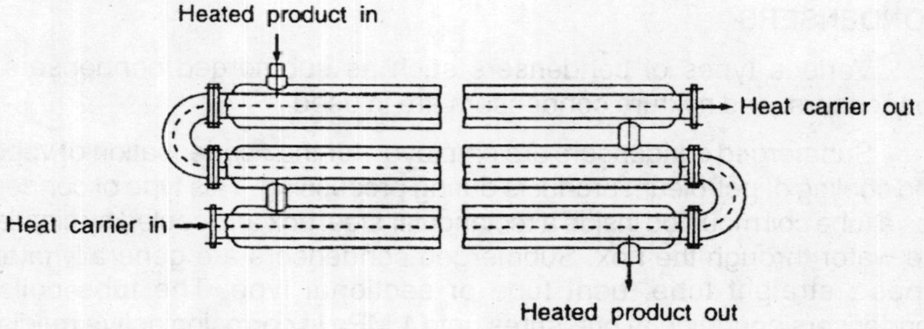

Fig.26. Double pipe heat exchanger.

In recent years, plate heat exchangers have been used because of their advantages over shell-and-tube heat exchangers. Some of their advantages are :

(a) A lower mass of metal.
(b) Smaller dimensions.
(c) More extensive heat exchange.

Knock down heat exchangers with corrugated plates (Fig. 27) have been manufactured industrially for the chemical and petroleum processing industries.

Fig.27. Finned tube.

STEAM SPACE HEATERS OR BOILERS

Heaters of this type are used instead of fire heating devices in various plants, including gas-fractionate plants, where heating is not required at high temperatures. The heat carrier, usually steam is supplied to a tube bundle and the product to be heated is fed to the bottom portion of the apparatus. During heating, lighter products are evapo-rated and their steam is recycled to the rectification column. Heavy residue is drained off continuously from the heater. In order to obtain a sufficient area of the evaporating surface, the distance from the liquid surface to the top of the apparatus housing must not be less than 0.35 of the inner diameter of the housing and the level of the liquid should atleaste be 100 mm above the tube bundle, which is mounted in the lower half of the apparatus. Steam space heaters are made with the total surface area of the tubes from 50 - 540 m^2.

CONDENSERS

Various types of condensers such as submerged condensers, air condensers, and mixture condensers are in used.

Submerged condensers are employed for the condensation of vapours and cooling of petroleum products during processing. This type of condenser has a tube coil mounted inside a rectangular steel box and cooled by circulating the water through the box. Submerged condensers are generally of three types : straight tube, bent tube or sectional type. The tube coils for condensers operating at pressures upto 1 MPa in corrosion active media are constructed of cast iron. Steel tubes are used for pressures upto 4 MPa and temperatures in coil upto 425°C. Brass tubes and brass plated tube plates are employed for sulphurous grades of petroleum.

Drip condensers are provided with a number of straight tubes arranged horizontally above one another and connected into a single coil by means of headers or U-tube sections. Cooling water circulates into perforated tubes mounted above the coil. Water flows down over the surface of cooling tubes in the form of thin layer and hence absorbs heat very effectively. Partial evaporation of water also improves the heat exchange conditions and decreases the rate of flow of water for cooling.

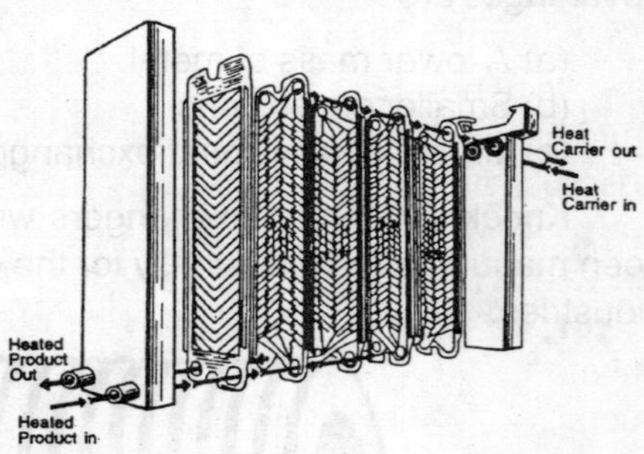

Fig.28 Plate type heat exchanger

Air condensers are capable of cooling petroleum products down to 35°C in summer time. This is achieved by contact of a powerful air flow with the surface of finned or smooth tubes made of nonferrous metal (or bimetallic tubes with a non-ferrous metal at the air side), in which vapour or liquid products to be cooled circulate.

Air condensers are more advantageous than submerged condensers. Some of their advantages are :

(a) A smaller mass of metal.
(b) Low consumption of electricity.
(c) They can be used in water- deficient regions.
(d) Lower water consumption, which makes it easier to purify sewage waters.

(e) Capital investment is lower.

Mixture condensers are mainly used for condensation of light petroleum products which can easily be separated from water. Barometric mixture condensers are sometimes used to form vacuum columns. The height of barometric tube should be slightly greater than the height of water column that counterbalances the atmospheric pressure (that is, slightly above 0.1 MPa).

PIPE FURNACES

Pipe furnaces have been used for high temperature heating of petroleum and petroleum products in their processing. In thermal processes, pipe furnaces also act as reactors. In pipe furnaces, fuel oil or gas is burned in burners arranged in a radiant chamber from which the combustion products pass to a convection chamber and than to a gas collector (provided with a gate valve to control the drought) and are ejected through a stack to the atmosphere. A gaseous or liquid product to be heated is allowed to pass in a single or more flows through the upper tubes of a convection coil and through the tubes of wall screens of the radiation chamber, where it is heated to the needed temperature and passed out of the furnace.

In general, a pipe furnace is made of two chambers. (a) The combustion chamber or radiation chamber, where radiation tubes are installed which absorb mainly the radiant heat, and (b) The convection chamber, where convective tubes utilise the heat of the combustion gases which leave the radiation chamber at a relatively high temperature, upto 950°C. The number of convective tubes for heating the petroleum products can be reduced substantially, if it is possible to utilized heat of these gases for other purposes such as air heating or steam superheating.

According to the method of heat transfer, pipe furnaces may be classified as convective, radiant convective, and radiant pipe furnaces. According to shape they are classified as cylindrical, vertical, box type, with an inclined roof etc. According to number of chambers, and the thermal power, they are classified as small upto 12.75 mln kJ, medium size, upto 62.85 mln kJ, and large, above 62.85 mln kJ.

In modern plants, radiant type furnaces have widely been used. They are usually of vertical type with more than one radiant chamber and one of them have a common convection chamber.

According to the method of radiant heat transfer, pipe furnaces are classified into the following groups.

(a) Those furnaces in which the radiant heat of the flame plays the prevailing part and radiation of the furnace lining and gases is not so necessary.

(b) Those furnaces in which the combustion process occurs beyond the radiation chamber, and

(c) Those furnaces, in which radiant heat of solids is utilized, usually using radiation pieces, flat flame or multi flame surface combustion.

The most perfect and efficient type of pipe furnace has radiation walls assembled of surface combustion burners Fig. 30. Radiant (surface combination) furnace a tube coil heated by radiant heat from two sides (Fig 29).

This type of furnaces are fired by gaseous fuel in surface combustion panel burners, which are made in the form of ceramic prisms that are mounted side by side to form the furnace wall. In operation, the temperature of a ceramic panel burner block (from the side of the combustion chamber) may be as high as 1200°C. The outer surface of the burner remains at about 45°C because of continuous cooling by the air-gas mixture-supplied by an injector. The heat transfer in the furnace is effected mainly from the incandescent radiant walls arranged at a distance of 600-1000 mm from a tube screen.

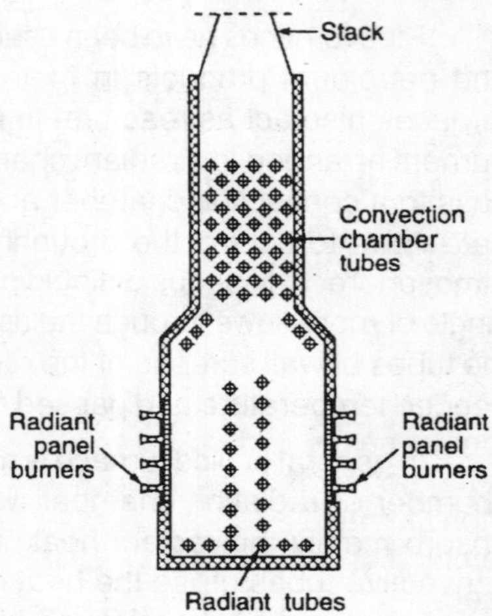

Fig. 29

Fuel combustion required for heating of petroleum products is a chemical reaction in which there is a combination of organic substances present in the fuel with oxygen or air. Complete combustion of the elements of fuel gives CO_2, SO_2 and H_2O vapours. As a result of incomplete combustion, CO and free carbon, known as carbon black may be formed. For complete combustion, air should be in excess of the theoretically required amount. 10-10.5 m^{-3} of air is required per kg of liquid fuel.

The ratio of the amount of air actually given to a furnace to that theoretically required is known as excess air coefficient, a. A high value of a indicates improper operation of a furnace and results in much heat loss with exhaust gases. With normal operation, the value of cc is 1.2-1.5 for gas fired furnaces and 1.02-1.05 for surface combustion furnaces.

The efficiency of operation of pipe furnaces can be determined in term of the following main characteristics :

(a) The heat density of the furnace space which is the quantity of heat consumed per hour per square metre of the furnace space. In modern pipe furnaces it may be 146700-293300 kJ/(m^2h)

(b) The heat density of the surface of radiant pipes which is the amount of heat transferred by a squire metre of the surface of pipe per hour. For most furnaces, it is between 62400 to 209500 kJ/(m^{2}h). For surface combustion furnaces it is 209 to 398 mJ/(m^{2}h).

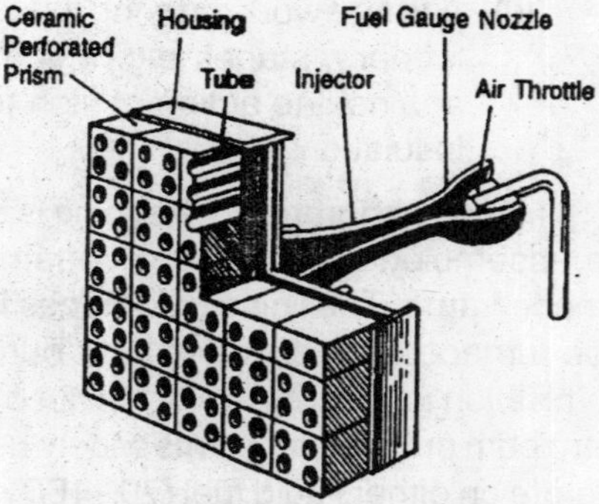

Fig.30. Radiant (surface combustion) panel burner.

(c) The heat density of the surface of convective pipe, which is the quantity of heat transferred by a squire metre of the surface of pipes per hour. For smooth pipes, the heat density is 33520 to 50280 kJ/(m^{2}h).

The temperature of flue gases at the entry to the convection chamber is usually 700 - 900°C. At a higher temperature coking may take place. In some types of furnace, the temperature of flue gases is lowered at the entry to the convection chamber by recirculation. The heat of the flue gases is often utilized by means of recuperators (heat exchangers in which the air for combustion is preheated by the heat of flue gases). If air preheating is not used, the temperature of gases should be as low as possible. How ever, at too low temperature, the surface area of convective pipes must be substantially increased, which increases the dimensions and cost of the furnace. Hence the temperature of flue gases should be 100 - 150°C greater than the temperature of the product to be heated in the furnace.

The efficiency of a furnace is the ratio of the amount of heat utilized in the furnace to the total amount of heat introduced. For most furnaces, it is equal to 0.6 - 0.8. Surface combustion furnaces have the highest efficiency of 0.8 - 0.82. The efficiency can be increased by decreasing the excess air coefficient and temperature of the flue gases.

A pipe furnace consists of the following main elements :

(a) A coil made of seamless tubes upto 24 m. in diameter and with wall thickness of 6 - 15 mm, connected by means of welded U-tubes.

(b) Tube plates, made of refractory cast iron or steel sheets, for supporting the pipes of the radiant and convective sections.

(c) Pipe suspensions for holding the radiant pipes between tube plates and thus preventing them from sagging. Pipe suspensions are subjected to high temperatures and so they are made of refractory steel.

(d) A frame work carrying the load of the pipes, roof, suspended roof, ladders, stages etc. It is made from steel beams for protection against the action of high temperatures by refractory linings and insulation.

In modern furnaces, the lining is made of shaped refractory brick. Bricks are assembled into blocks on beams or rods, which are fastened to the furnace frame. The lining of furnaces is usually encasted into metal housing. Pipe furnaces are provided with burners for liquid or gaseous fuels. Fuel atomisation in burners is carried out by means of steam, air or mechanically. Petroleum processing plants widely use combined gas oil burners which can operate on either liquid fuel (70 - 160 kg/h) or on gaseous fuels (upto 100 M^3/h). This type of burner is shown in Fig 31.

Liquid fuel is supplied at a pressure of 0.8 - 1 MPa through internal

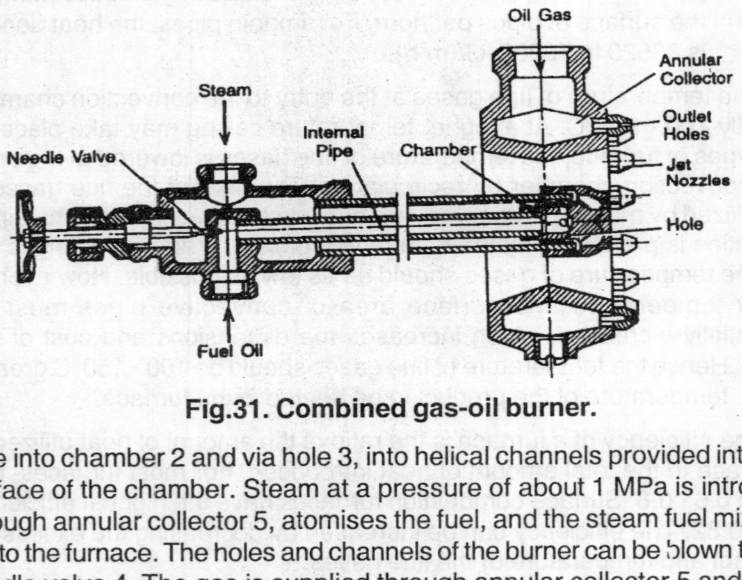

Fig.31. Combined gas-oil burner.

pipe into chamber 2 and via hole 3, into helical channels provided into outer surface of the chamber. Steam at a pressure of about 1 MPa is introduced through annular collector 5, atomises the fuel, and the steam fuel mixture is fed to the furnace. The holes and channels of the burner can be blown through needle valve 4. The gas is supplied through annular collector 5 and further via jet nozzles 7 into the furnace. A central channel and one or more outlet holes 6 are bored in the jet nozzles.

PIPELINES

Enormous amount of crude petroleum, gas and petroleum products are transported via main pipelines. At petroleum processing plants, process pipelines are used for the transportation of many products, from crude petroleum to diverse end products. Interplant pipelines connect various processing plants with one another and also with storage tanks. The operating conditions of pipelines of petroleum processing plants depend on a number of factors, depending on the type of product to be pumped, the pressure and the temperature of transported media.

Depending on their operating conditions, pipelines may be made of metallic or non-metallic tubes. In most cases they are made of carbon steel, but in special cases, e.g. catalytic cracking reforming, hydrogen refining, isomerisation, manufacture of synthetic alcohols, acids etc, alloy steels (containing Cr, Ni, and Mo) , copper and copper alloys, nickel and nickel alloys, aluminium and plastics have also been used for the construction of pipelines. High alloy steels are high in Cr (up to 18%), Ni (upto 20%), W (2-3%) and also contain minor amounts of niobium, titanium and boron. Tubes made of such austenitic alloys can withstand temperatures upto 1100°C and possess high resistance to corrosion at working temperatures. They also have good weldability.

The diameter of the tubes and their applications depending on pressure, temperature and quality of the metal are specified by state standards. Seamless tubes made of carbon steel grades CT.2, CT.3, CT4, CT.5 are widely used for making process pipelines in weakly corrosive media upto 450°C. In some cases, welded tubes are used, e.g. for pumping of petroleum products and vapours at wall temperatures less than 300°C. Stainless steel tubes. of diameter 25-64 mm and 3-8 m long are sometimes replaced by tubes made of steel grades CT.2 or CT.3 lined inside with polyethylene (1.5-2 mm layer), glass (1-2 m layer) or rigid PVC (2 mm or thicker layer). Such tubes can be used for the transportation of aggressive media at gauge pressures upto 1.5 MPa and 60-100°C. Bimetallic tubes made of carbon steel/stainless steel or carbon steel/copper etc. are also used in recent plants.

FITTINGS

Fittings are sued for controlling the flow of liquids, gases, gas liquid mixtures, suspensions, powers etc, transported through the pipelines. According to their purpose all fittings can be classified into the following classes.

(1) Closing valves, which are meant for controlling the characteristics of the flow.

(2) Safety valves, which let out or bypass a portion of the. working medium when the pressure in the system rises to a value which is dangerous for the strength of the system. These valves also prevent back flow of the medium.

(3) Control valves, which are meant for controlling the characteristics of the flow, that is, pressure, flow rate, temperature etc, by varying the flow area.

(4) Measuring valves, which determine the level of the medium, and

(5) Miscellaneous valves, which are intended, e.g, for admitting air into or removing air from the pipeline.

All fittings should be tight as well as reliable in operation. They should be corrosion resistant and explosion safe. The required strength is mainly determined by the working pressure and temperature. According to normal bore diameter, all valves are classified into small (Normal Bore diameter, Dn, i.e. inside diameter of the pipe line in which the valve is to be fitted is ≤ 40 mm), medium (Dn = 50 - 250 mm), and large (Dn > 250 mm). The nominal pressure corresponds to the admissible working pressure of a valve at the normal temperature. Depending on the nominal pressure, all valves can be classified as low pressure valves (Dn upto 1 MPa), medium pressure valves (l .6 - 6.4 MPa), and high pressure valves (10 - 100 MPa). Special fittings have also been manufactured for operation in vacuum and at super high pressures above 100 MPa. The mechanical properties of most materials become worse with increasing temperature. Hence, the admissible working pressure for valves operating at high temperatures is lower than the nominal pressure. The working temperature is the highest temperature at which the working medium can be pumped through a pipeline for a long time. With an increase in the working temperature above 120°C the working pressure should be decreased relative to the normal pressure by 30 - 40%.

COMPRESSORS AND PUMPS

Compressors are used for compression and transpuitatiun of gases while pumps are used for transportation of liquids. Both compressors and pumps may be piston type, centrifugal, axial, rotary and jet type.

Compressors have widely been employed in petroleum processing and petrochemical industry. The pressure of gases in compressors is increased because of an increase in gas energy which is effected by the mechanical energy of a motor. On the basis of principle of operation, compressors may be turbocompressors (axial and centrifugal), which are also known as radial compressors, and positive displacement compressors (reciprocating piston compressors, free piston compressors and membrane type compressors). In membrane compressors, a membrane plays the part of the piston. Rotary compressors are also included in positive displacement compressors.

In turbo compressors, the transformation of energy occurs in two stages.

(a) The KE of the gas is increased by the supply of mechanical energy from outside.

(b) The KE of the gas is partially transformed into the energy of pressure of the gas.

These two stages may also take place simultaneously. In positive displacement compressors, the gas is compressed by the piston in the cylinder to a specified pressure and then displaced from the cylinder. There are many advantages of turbo compressors over other types of compressors. For example,

(a) They have relatively small mass and diamentions (due to the fuel that the gas flows continuously and at a high rate).

(b) There is no reciprocating movement of compressor elements.

(c) The gas is supplied uniformly.

(d) It is possible to connect a compressor to a high speed steam or gas turbine or electric motor.

(e) They can develop high flow rates in a single unit,so that a small number of compressors can serve the need of a process.

According to the principle of operation, turbo compressors may be related to power turbo machines such as blade-type machines. In addition to turbo compressors, this class of machines includes steam and gas turbines, certifugal and axial pumps, and hydraulic turbines. A common feature of such mechanes is blading provision, that is, provision of stationary and moving blades which interact with the flow of working medium. Turbo compressors are most closely related with centrifugal pumps as far as nature of energy transformation is concerned.

Centrifugal compressors can be characterised by a radial direction of the flow. They have a number of rotating bladed wheels which entrain and accelerate the flow of air or other gases introduced through an inlet opening. Piston type compressors are similar in design. Multistage compressors are manufactured either with the cylinders connected in series along the axis (Tandem type or with the cylinders arranged in parallel (compound type). Two stage horizontal compressors are often made with a single cylinder and a stepped, or differential piston. The gas is first compressed in a cylinder by the wider portion of a piston, cooled in intermediate cooler, and led to the cylinder at the other side of the piston and compressed to the final pressure. Compressors with cylinders arranged at an angle to one another, known as V-shaped compressors, have also been made for greater compactness. Compressed gas from piston compressor is fed to consumers via gas collectors or receivers which serve as a buffer. Petroleum processing plants usually make use of centrifugal and piston pumps, because

(a) They are less expensive.

(b) They have smaller diamensions.

(c) They are simple in design and operation.

(d) They can pump liquids more uniformly.

High viscosity petroleum products and crude petroleums are pumped only by piston pumps,, because centifugal pumps fail to pump these liquids effectively and efficiently. In order to facilitate suction, the pumping stations are located as close to the storage tank as possible. A single stage centrifugal

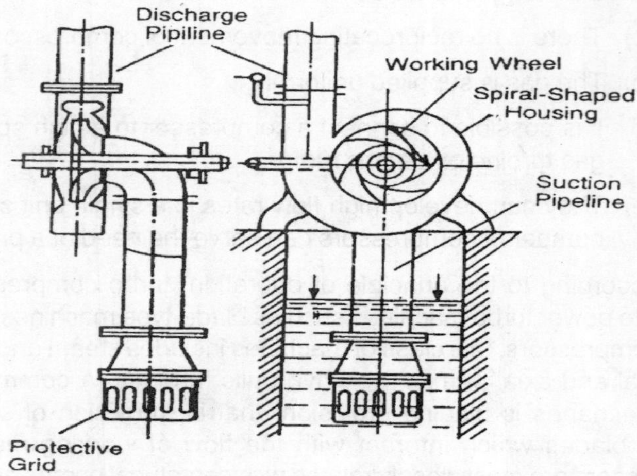

Fig.32. Single stage centrifugal pump.

pump (Fig. 32) has working wheel, with blades bent backwards. The wheet rotates at high speed inside spiral shaped housing. The liquid from suction pipelines (which has an intake valves having protective grid) is fed along the wheel axis and whirled by the blades. The pressure of the liquid increases under the influence of centrifugal force and the liquid is discharged into stationary housing and discharge pipeline. In this process, a negative pressure is developed, at the inlet to the wheel and the pressure difference ensures continuous supply of the liquid from the reservoir. Electrically driven multistage pumps provided with a number of working wheels are used, when a high pressure is required. The wheels are arranged in a common housing. In many pumps the speed of the flow is transformed into the energy of pressure due to a special spiralshaped discharge channel in the housing. Piston pumps may differ in the principle of action (single or double action pumps), the type of drive, and the design of the piston (piston type or plunger type pumps). In plunger pumps, the piston contacts directly the liquid or is separated from the liquid by an elastic impermeable membrane. Such type of pumps are also known as membrane pumps.

Single action pumps perform one suction pass and one discharge pass during the double stroke of the piston, that is, pump the liquid non-uniformly. A horizontal double action plunger pump (Fig. 33) has two valves at each side of the plunger, that is, four valves in all. The liquid is sucked in into the left hand portion of the cylinder with the piston moving in the right direction, and discharged from the right hand portion. With the reverse stroke of the piston, the liquid is sucked in into the right hand portion and discharged from the left hand portion. Such type of pumps work more uniformly than single action pumps.

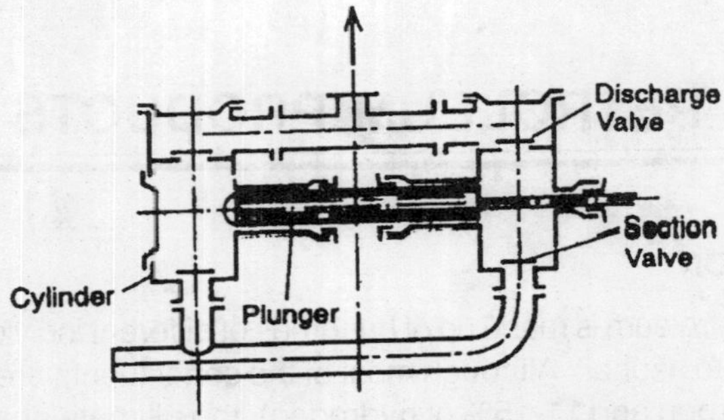

Fig.33. Horizontal double-action plunger pump.

Chapter 8

PETROLEUM PRODUCTS

INTRODUCTION

Crude petroleum is made up of hundreds of different individual chemicals, from methane to asphalt. Although most of the constituents are hydrocarbons (83-87% of carbon and 11-15% of hydrogen), the ultimate analysis indicates the presence of nitrogen (0-0.5%, sulphur (0 to 6%), and oxygen (0 -3.5%) also. The hydrocarbons may be divided into two chemical classes

(a) Open chain, or aliphatic compounds containing n-paraffin series, CnH_{2n+2} isoparaffin series, CnH_{2n+2} and olefin series, CnH_{2n}. The n- paraffinic series of hydrocarbons comprises a large fraction of most petroleums and n-paraffins predominate in most straight run gasolines. The branched chain isoparaffin series compounds are very desirable and are frequently manufactured by catalytic reforming, alkylation, and isomerisation. The olefin series is either not present or exists in very small quantities. Cracking processes produce large amounts of olefins, which are very useful because of their excellent antiknock properties and chemical reactivity. Many higher members of olefin series are present in cracked gasolines and in residual products.

(b) Ring compounds, containing naphthene series, CnH_2n and aromatic or benzene series, C_nH_{2n-6}. The members of naphthene series are completely saturated. It is the second most abundantly occurring series of compounds in most crude petroleums. Some members of this series are methyl cyclopentane, cyclohexane, dimethyl cyclopentanes, and methyl cyclohexane. These naphthenes predominate in most gas oils and lubricating oils from all types of crude petroleums. They have also been found to be present in residual products. Small amounts of aromatic compound are present in most petroleums. These compounds are produced by chemical processing and have high antiknock properties. Some members of aromatic series present in petroleum are benzene, toluene, ethylbenzene and xylenes.

Petroleum products have long been divided into salable cuts by fractionation in refining operations. This is a separation by boiling ranges. The natural separation into natural gas and ordinary crude, that takes place when petroleum leaves its underground reservoirs, is based on the same principle. Such refinery fractions are roughly classified as follows,

(a) Natural (or casing head) gasoline and natural gas, LPG, light distillates such as motor gasolines, solvent naphtha, jet fuel, kerosene and light heating oils.

(b) Intermediate distillates, such as heavy fuel oils, Diesel oils, gas oils and heavy distillates such as heavy mineral oils (medicinal), heavy floatation oils, waxes and lubricating oils (large range).

(c) Residues such as lubricating oils, fuel oils, petroleum, road oils, asphalts, and coke.

Natural gas occurs as accumulations in underground, porous reservoirs, with or without petroleum oil. Natural gas is mainly composed of paraffin series of hydrocarbons from methane to pentane, carbon dioxide, nitrogen and sometimes helium. The most important products obtained from natural gas are fuel, natural gasoline, LPG, carbon black, helium, hydrogen, and petrochemicals.

Gasoline extracted from natural gas is called straight run or refinery gasoline (which is distilled from crude oil). Natural gasoline is called casing head gasoline. The recovery of natural gasoline from natural gas gives a high volatile gasoline for blending into a motor fuel. Natural gasoline can be isomerised into pure isobutane and isopentane for alkylation with light olefins as butylene to get alkylated gasoline. When crude oil is forced from a well by the pressure of natural gas, some of its lighter components are vapourised into the gas. Hence the composition and characteristics of the recovered gasoline are determined by the composition of the oil.

A great demand for light hydrocarbon liquids for petrochemicals and fuels, is met by a deeper extraction of these products from natural gas. Two of the major processes used to achieve these are

(a) Refrigerated absorption, and

(b) Low temperature distillation.

A third method using adsorption on solids is not efficient for high recovery of ethane and propane.

Natural gas is particularly devoid of unsaturated hydrocarbons and hydrogen, but these compounds are present in the cracked gases of refineries. The oil industry is now developing along the line of synthesis, due to large quantities of unsaturated and hence chemically reactive hydrocarbons produced by cracking processes. The unsaturated (olefinic) hydrocarbons of these cracked gases are used in the manufacture of polymerised and alkylated gasoline, antifreezes, petrochemicals, explosives, solvents, medicinals, fumigants, resins, synthetic rubber, and many other products. Olefins are also manufactured by dehydrogenation of paraffins. Light hydrocarbons such as propane and butane, which are produced as byproducts from natural gasoline, are now used as liquefied petroleum gas (LPG) for domestic gas and heating and for city gas, as well as for direct motor fuel in tractors, trucks and buses. It is also used for the manufacture of petrochemicals. Since the heating value of the pure gas is very high, it is mixed with an inertx gas before using. Bottled gas or liquefied gas is used by many rural dwellers who are too far from and gas mains, for cooking, lighting, heating water, and gas refrigeration.

Precursors for petrochemicals are converted from gas, natural or cracked, LPG, and cyclic cuts. To emphasise the increasing importance of acetylene, olefines and aromatic hydrocarbons for petrochemicals, these are called as precursors to intermediates. These precursors are either chemically converted from the natural petroleum raw materials or isolated from cracked stocks. The principal precursors are acetylene, propylene, benzene, xylenes, ethylene, butane, toluene and naphthalene.

Light distillates embrace naphthas and refined oils,aviation gasoline, motor gasoline, petroleum solvents, and jet fuel kerosene. Gasoline is the most important petroleum product and heads the list of light distillates. Aviation gasoline, with an octane number of 100 or even higher, is composed of about 1/3 alkylate, derived from isobutane and gaseous olefins, blended with catalytically cracked gasoline and suitable crude distillate, to which TEL is added to reduce the knocking property. Sulphur present in it markedly reduces the effect of TEL in increasing the octane number. The colour of the gasoline indicates about its quality. Oil soluble dyes are added to leaded gasoline. Dyes also mask the off white colours of cracked gasoline. The term naphtha indicates any light product having properties intermediate between gasoline and kerosene. Naphthas are widely used as solvents in paints and dry cleaning. Kerosene is used in jet aeroplanes than aviation gasoline. Kerosene is also used as a fuel and as an illuminant. Light heating oils are used as a fuel in home furnaces.

The use of additives to petroleum products is of great importance in improving the performance of petroleum products in general, when added to gasolines, distillates, fuel, lube oils, and brake fluids. Tetra ethyl lead (TEL) is the best known additive used as antiknock compound. Organophosphorus additives such as phosphorodithionates or tricresyl phosphate effectively reduce surface ignition and hence combustion deposits. Antioxidants such as phenol derivatives (2,6-di-tert-butyl-4- methyl phenol) stabilize the diolefins in gasoline and reduce the gum formation. Antistall additives (carburettor de-icing) increase in volume with cold weather, and consist of freezing point depressants, such as isopropyl alcohol.

Rust inhibitors are amino alkyl phosphates. Alkyl nitrates are used as additives for increasing cetane number of Diesel oils. Additives for lubricating oils consist of zinc dithiophosphates, prepared from reaction of phosphorus pentasulphide with alcohol or phenols, followed by neutralisation with zinc oxide. They inhibit corrosion and oxidation and prevent the formation of varnish or sludge in internal combustion engines. Alkaline earth aromatic sulphonates, metal phosphates etc are used for detergent action and retardation of ring sticking. Ethylene glycol is still used as antifreeze.

Intermediate distillates include gas oil, heavy furnace oil, cracking stock, Diesel fuel oil, absorber oil, and distillates cracked and reformed to produce gasoline of required quality. Generally distillates are blended with heavy tar to reduce the viscosity of tar so that it can be marketed as a fuel oil. Special heavy naphthas are used to reduce the viscosity of asphalt so that it can be used as road oil. This material is also called cut back asphalt. Gas oil is now used as a fuel or cracked into gasoline. Diesel fuel is a special grade of gas oil which has now become most important. The proper viscosity of. Diesel fuel is essential. Distillates may also be used as vehicles for insecticides. Heavy distillates furnish lubricating oils, heavy oils for various purposes and waxes. Heavy distillates are also hydrocracked to lighter distillate fuels and to gasoline. Paraffin wax is first obtained as crude scale wax.

Residues include asphalt, residual fuel oil, greases, coke and petroleum. Petroleum coke is commercially used for electrodes, in paints, in ceramic industry and in the manufacture of C_aC_2. Asphalt is used as a paving or roofing material or for water proofing structures. The properties of asphalt can be markedly altered by heating it to a high temperature and partially oxidising it by blowing air through it. Such material is known as oxidised asphalt and is used in the manufacture of roofing and for grouting.

CLASSIFICATION OF PETROLEUM PRODUCTS

The products obtained from petroleum can conveniently be divided into four groups :

Group I - Fuels - This group includes liquefied hydrocarbon gases, fuels for carburettor engines (gasolines), fuels for jet (kerosene) and for turbojet engines, Diesel fuels; boiler fuels etc.

Group II - Lubricating oils - This group includes various lubricating oils, paraffins, ceresins and petroleum.

Group III - Miscellaneous petroleum products - This group includes plastic greases, bitumens, coke etc.

Group IV - Chemical and petrochemical products - This group includes hydrocarbons of various classes which serve as starting products for organic and petrochemical synthesis.

LIQUEFIED HYDROCARBON GASES AND FUELS

Liquefied hydrocarbon gases mainly consist of propane and butane along with small quantities of propylene and butylene. They have widely been used as domestic fuel which may be commercial propane (atleast 93% of propane), commercial butane (atleast 93% of butane) or their mixture (in winter, with a greater proportion of propane). Liquefied gases or their constituents of higher purity have been used as starting materials for the manufacture of various chemical products and olefins (by pyrolysis).

(a) Fuels for carburettor engines - This group of fuels includes aviation gasoline, and tractor kerosene. The pressure of saturated vapours (kPa) for aviation gasoline and motor gasoline should be 29.3 to 47.9 and 66.5 to 93.1 respectively. For summer grades, the pressure of saturated vapours for motor gasoline should not exceed 66.5. The fractional composition of fuels is of great importance. For example, the 10% boiling point of gasoline (the point at which 10% of the fuels boils off) can characterise the starting properties and reliability of an engine starting under various conditions, particularly, at low temperature of the ambient air. 50% boiling point of gasoline characterises the speed of engine heating during starting, the smoothness of switching from one' operating mode to another, and the stability of engine operation. The 90% and 97.5% boiling points of aviation gasoline and the temperature of the end of boiling of motor gasoline determine the homogeneity of the fuel mixture, that is, the completeness of fuel combustion in the engine. In the case of incomplete combustion of the fuel, liquid substances may penetrate into the crankcase and dilute the lubricating oil. Hence a quick wear of the engine is caused. Incomplete combustion also causes a serious air pollution.

Antiknock rating is another most important characteristic of fuels which determines their proper combustion in carburettor engines. With detonation combustion, the rate of flame front propagation increases very quickly and causes explosion or knock, in an engine. As a result, the engine may quickly be out of operation. The antiknock rating of fuels is evaiuated in terms of octane number (ON).

Aviation gasolines are used as fuel for carburettor engine planes and helicopters. Aviation gasolines are prepared by compounding of a base gasoline (obtained by catalytic cracking or catalytic reforming), high octane components (such as iso- octane, alkyl gasoline, isopentane, benzene hydrocarbons etc), tetraethyl lead (TEL), and other additives raising the octane number, and of inhibitors (that is, substances which prevent fuel oxidation). With aviation gasolines, oxy-diphenyalamine is used as inhibitor. These components are taken in proportions required to get gasoline having desired grade and quality.

The boiling-off points of 90 percent, 50 percent and 10 percent gasolines should not be greater than 145°C, 105°C and 75°C to 88°C respectively.

Motor gasolines are used in automobile carburettor engines. Their antiknock rating is also expressed in terms of octane number. the octane numbers are determined by using mixtures of iso-octane (O.N = 100) and n-heptane (O.N = 0). The current control of fuels is done by using secondary reference fuels haying various values of octane number. The octane number of gasoline increases (a) By adding benzene hydrocarbons (b) By adding isomeric paraffin hydrocarbons, and (c) By decreasing the point of fuel boiling off. If these measures are not capable of giving gasolines of desired octane number, an antiknock agent is used. Various metalorganic and organic substances can be used as antiknock agents, but most important is tetra-ethyl lead, in the form of ethyl liquid or ethyl fluid. The hydrocarbons, in order of increasing effect of TEL on octane number can be written as :

Paraffins - Naphthenes - Benzenes - Olefins

The effectiveness of gasoline decreases with in increase in the content of TEL. The sensitivity of gasolines to TEL also decreases sharply with an increasing concentration of sulphur, which reacts with lead and petrifies the effect of TEL. Thus starting materials and some grades of gasolines should be purified from sulphur compounds before adding TEL.

For easier operation of engines, motor gasolines are manufactured as **summer and winter kinds**. The winter gasolines have a higher pressure of saturated vapours. More over, they have different temperatures of boiling off of intermediate fractions and of the end of boiling.

New, more efficient automobile engines have a high compression ratio and can be run on high octane gasoline. Motor gasolines are prepared by compounding various components such as high octane gasolines of catalytic cracking and catalytic reforming, alkylates and isomerisates of light fractions of preliminary distillation. In the preparation of low octane gasolines, use is made of gasolines of thermal cracking and coking, gasolines obtained by straight - run distillation of petroleum, which have a higher temperature of boiling off, and dearomatised products (refined petroleum) obtained in the manufacture of benzene hydrocarbons by catalytic reforming of gasoline fractions.

Since tar, if present in gasoline, can disturb the operation of engines, their content in gasolines should not exceed 5 mg-7 mg/ 100 mL.

In Diesel engines air is compressed and its temperature rises and the Diesel fuel injected into the engine is ignited by the hot air. The capability of Diesel fuels for self ignition is measured in terms of cetane number (It is the index of ignitability of Diesel fuel). Cetane number is numerically equal (in percentage) to the content of cetane (n-hexadecane, $C_{16}H_{34}$) in a mixture of cetane (cetane number = 100) and a-methyl naphthalene (cetane number = 0). The cetane number depends on the composition of fuel, The highest cetane number is shown by paraffin hydrocarbons, a lower cetane number by naphthenes, and the lowest cetane number by aromatic or benzene hydrocarbons (because of which they are undesirable in Diesel fuels). The cetane number can be increased by mixing Diesel fuel with certain components containing paraffin hydrocarbons of normal structure or by giving special additives.

Diesel engines are of three main kinds :

(a) **High speed engines** (above 1000 rounds per minute) for agricultural machines, Diesel locomotives, cross country vehicles etc.

(b) **Medium speed engines** (about 500-1000 rmp) for locomotives and as auxiliary motors or ships.

(c) **Low speed engines** (less than 500 rpm) used as main marine engines and Diesel generators.

Diesel fuels have been made for summer, winter, winter northern and arctic operation. They must have cetane numbers of atleast 45 and are recommended for use at air temperatures respectively above 0°C. -20'C, -30°C and -50°C.

Depending on the content of sulphur in the original petroleum, Diesel fuel fractions may be **low sulphurous** (upto 0.25 S) and **sulphurous** (0.7 - 0.8% S) The content of sulphur can be reduced by hydrogen refining. **Low sulphur fuels** are less corrosive and less liable to carbonisation. Inaddition, they form exhaust gases low in sulphurous and sulphuric anhydrides. The viscosity of the Diesel fuel has been standardised in order to ensure atomisation and reliable operation of fuel supply system. Heavy fraction in the fuel can cause incomplete combustion and smokes in exhaust gases and carbonisation of engine.

Medium speed Diesel engines can be run on heavy distillate fuels and low speed engines, on fuel obtained by dilution of fuel oils by distillates, including Diesel fractions, to obtain the desired viscosity (36-67 mm^2/s at 50°C). The setting point of the mixture may be -5 to 5°C.

FUEL OILS OR BOILER OILS

Fuel oils have been used in many branches of chemical technology and particularly in thermal power plants. Fuel oils are generally graded as marine grades, furnace fuel oil grades 40 (medium) and furnace fuel oil grade 100 (heavy oil). The relative viscosity of fuel oils should not be more than 5 and 12mm^2/s for medium and light grades and 8 and 16mm^2/s at 80°C for furnace grades 40 and 100 respectively. Fuel oils of a higher viscosity have a higher flash point, which is specified at 90°C and 110°C (in an open vessel) for furnace grades 40 and 100. The setting point of fuel oils is limited at -5° to 25°C or upto 42°C for fuels obtained by high paraffin petroleum.

According to the sulphur content fuel oils are divided into low sulphurous (upto 0.5% S), medium sulphurous (0.51 to 1.0% S), and high sulphurous (1.01 - 3.5% S).

The quality of fuel oils is decided by the following characterist cs.

(a) Viscosity, which determines the ease of transportation of the fuel and the probable degree of heating for effective atomisation.

(b) Setting point, which determines the conditions of storage and application of the fuel at various temperatures of the air.

(c) Sulphur content, which determines the degree of corrosion of the engine and the exhaust of sulphurous compounds to the atmosphere.

The heat of combustion (calorific value) of the fuel oils depends on their composition. The low calorific value of low sulphurous and medium sulphurous fuel oils must not be less than 41454 kj/Kg for marine grades, 40740 kj/Kg for furnace grade 40 and 4053 kj/Kg for furnace grade 100 (recalculated to dry fuel). Fuel oil grades are selected according to the condition of operation of engine. Thicker and cheaper grades are usually emp oyed at stationary plants where the fuel can be heated up and filtered. Marine grades of fuel oils (used in marine power plants) have lower content of ash, water, sulphur and tars in comparison with furnace grades. Fuel oils are prepared by mixing residual products of preliminary distillation such as residual fuel oil, semigoudron and goudron with residual products of thermal and some catalytic processes (cracking residue, gas oil, reflux, polymers) and residual products of oil manufacture.

FUELS FOR JET AND GAS TURBINE ENGINE

Fuels for aviation jet engines may be sub-sonic and supersonic speed fuels. The supersonic fuels must have an elevated density and a sufficiently high calorific value inorder to ensure the required power of the engine and the desired flight range. At higher speeds of flight, fuel is heated much more. For example, in flights at speeds three times the sonic speed, the temperature of the fuel may increase upto 325°C. Jet engine fuels, known as aviation kerosene are kerosene fraction of preliminary distillation of petroleum having the temperature of the beginning of boiling from 150°-195°C and the boiling off point from 250°C to 315°C. Fuels for jet engines must easily be vapourisable, have a high calorific value (lowest calorific value should not be less than 42950 - 44160 kj/Kg), high thermal stability, a low temperature of the beginning of crystallisation (not more than -60°C). and cause no corrosion of engine parts or elements. Jet engine fuels having highest thermal stability can be obtained by catalytic refining in hydrogen atmosphere under pressure. Gas turbine fuels for terrestrial machines differ from aviation kerosene by a wide fractional composition and a higher content of sulphur (upto 3%). Their relative viscosity at 50°C must not be more than 2.

LUBRICANTS, PRODUCTS OF OIL PARAFFIN PROCESSING AND OTHER PETROLEUM PRODUCTS

In addition to high quality fuels, lubricating materials are also essential for normal operation of various machines and engines. **All lubricants can be divided into four groups : These are gaseous, solid, liquid and semisolid (thickened), or greases.**

Some gases are capable of reacting with metals to from a lubricating film which decreases friction and wear. Solid lubricants, such as graphite or molybdenum disulphide can be used at very high temperatures and under heavy load where ordinary lubricants, including oils and greases, are not effective.

A new branch of science, known as chemmotology deals with the properties, quality and applications of fuels, lubricants, and special liquids in engineering. Chemmotology deals with the complex interrelationship between the fuel, lubricants, engines and operating conditions. By determining an optimum relationship between the elements, it is possible to increase the life time of engines, machines and mechanisms, lower the consumption of fuels and lubricants, and greatly improve the quality and effectiveness of operation in many branches of engineering.

LUBRICATING AND OTHER OILS

Petroleum processing industry manufactures mineral oils of various kinds such as motor oils (aviation, Diesel and automobile grades), industrial oils, turbine oils, electro insulating oils, compressor oils, etc. Viscosity plays a vital role in all kinds of oil. It should be sufficiently low to ensure lubrication and easy start of engines at low temperatures, while it should be sufficiently high to properly lubricate even the hottest part of an engine. This requirement is met by oils having a high viscosity index. Other important characteristics of oils include

(a) Their oxidation stability at the elevated temperature.

(b) A low setting point, especially for winter grades.

(c) Good anticorrosive properties, etc.

All grades of lubricating oils for modern mechanisms and engines especially for Diesel engines, contain additives for improving the performance of lubricating oils. Diesel and automobile oils are manufactured by mixing purified residual and distillate oils.

Aviation Oils - These oils have been utilised for the lubrication of aviation piston engines. They can be prepared by goudron residue after distillation of specially selected petroleum grades by deep refining with selective solvents and sometimes by mixing with distillate oils.

Aviation engines operate under heavy loads and at high temperatures, so that the oils for them will have a high chemical stability and great lubricating power.

Industrial Oils - These oils are used for the lubrication of machines and mechanisms of industrial equipment which are operated at relatively low atmospheres and for friction pairs of machines and engines not subjected to the effect of steam, hot air or gases. Industrial oils are generally classified according to their viscosity and the conditions and field of application. Taking into consideration the viscosity, the industrial oils may be classified as light (3.5-10 mm 2/s at 50°C), medium (10-58 mm^2/s at 50°C), and heavy (11-96 mm^2/s at 100°C). Depending on the conditions of applications, they are classified into oils for light and moderate speeds and loads and heavy duty oils.

On the bases of field of application, they are classified as oils for gear transmission, slip guides, spindles, instrument oils, break-in oils, and special oils.

Industrial oils should be pressure and corrosive resistance, and must be capable of retaining their fluidity at the working temperatures. They should also be stable against foaming and oxidation.

Turbine Oils - These oils are used for lubrication of bearings and auxiliary mechanisms of turbo machines (steam and gas turbines), turbo compressors, hydraulic turbines, marine turbines etc. They have also been utilized as pressure fluids. Turbine oils without additives can be prepared by contact acid refining, while those with additives can be manufactured by selective refining from low sulphurous and sulphurous grades of petroleum. In turbine oils, additives are added to improve their antioxidising, deemulsifying, anticorrosive and antifoaming properties. Turbine oils must have a high chemical stability and separate easily from water which enters occasionally in the lubricating system.

Insulating Oils - Oils are liquid dielectrics and therefore can be used for insulation of current conducting elements such as transformers, capacitors, cables etc. Insulating oils are also capable of removing heat and favour quick arc extinction between electric contacts. Transformer oils, capacitors oils and cables oils belong to the group of insulating oils.

Transformer oils are used for long operation at 70-80°C in the atmosphere of air and that is why they should have a very high chemical stability and should not form low molecular acids on oxidation. Moreover, transformer oil are also expected to have dielectric characteristics. Most grades of transformer oils have a viscosity which is less than 9 mm2/s at 50°C.

Transformer oils can be replaced by other oils.

Compressor Oils - These oils are used for lubrication of cylinders, valves and piston rods of compressors operating at 200-225°C and 20 - 20.5 MPa pressures. The pressure oils must have an appropriate oxidation stability. Compressor oil grade 12 M, having a kinematic viscosity of 11-14 mm, 2/s at 100°C, has been used for single stage horizental and vertical compressors for a pressure of 0.7 - 0.8 MPa and for two stage compressors for an average pressure upto 5 MPa. Compressor oil grade 19T, having a kinematic viscosity of 17-21mm2/s at 100°C has been utilized in multi stage high pressure compressors upto 20 - 30 MPa. The oxidation stability of these oils is ensured by deep refining.

Oils for Steam Engines - These oils are classified into two groups. For saturated steam and for super saturated steam machines. These oils have low evaporability and a high viscosity. The kinematic viscosity at 100°C is 9-13 mm^2/s for cylinder oil grade -2 and 44-64 mm^2/s for grade - 52, known as vapour oil. Cylinder grade oils of grade -2 are manufactured from distillates and vapour oil (grade-52) is prepared from residues by deasphalting with propane or by the distillation of gourdron in high vacuum.

Synthetic Oils - These oils are essentially organic or elemento organic compounds containing silicon, iron etc. They are intended for heavy duty applications.

PARAFFINS, CERESINS AND PETROLEUM

Paraffins - These are soft (liquid) or solid petroleum products having crystalline structure and can be obtained from distillates of paraffinic and high- paraffinic grades of petroleum.

Solid petroleum paraffins are crystalline products of white to bright brown in colour, depending on the amount of oil. Paraffins are classified in many grades such as high purified grades (fusion point 50-52°C), grade C (fusion point 42-52°C), unpurified grade HC (fusion point 42-50°C), and unpurified high fusion grade HB (fusion point 57-64°C). High purified grades are generally used for electrical engineering industry and perfumery, grade C is generally used for the manufacture of synthetic fatty acids, unpurified grade HC is used for the manufacture of matches and unpurified high fusion grade HB is used for various applications. The oil content in paraffins varies from 0.8 to 0.5% for high purified grades and upto 2.2 to 2.3 and even 5.0% for other grades.Special grades of paraffin, to be used in food industry are also manufactured by deep refining of raw paraffins and mainly employed for impregnation of packing materials either contacting loose dry foodstuffs or non- contacting foodstuffs. The oil content by mass in contacting loose dry foodstuff and non- contacting foodstuffs are upto 0.9% and 2.3% respectively. Some paraffin grades are also used in the manufacture of candles.

Ceresins - It is mixture of solid hydrocarbons which are obtained in the processing and refining of ozokerite, unpurified petroleum ceresin or their mixtures. Ceresins have been used in the manufacture of greases, wax alloys, insulating materials etc. The most important characteristic of ceresins is the dropping point, °C. The dropping points such as 80, 75, 67 and 57°C are the basis of gracing ceresins and the volume resistivity at 100°C is only specified for grade 80 ceresin .for which it should not be less than 1 x 10^{12} ohm.cm. Synthetic high fusion ceresin has the highest dropping point. It is a mixture of solid hydrocarbons of the methane family, majority of which have normal chains. It is obtained by synthesis of CO_2 and H_2 (Fischer-Tropsch process). The dropping point of this grade of ceresin must not be less than 100°C and the volume resistivity at 100°C should not be less than 10^{14} ohm.cm.

Medical or Liquefied Petroleum - It is obtained by fusion of ceresin, paraffin, purified petroleum or their mixture with petroleum oil. The dropping point of medical petroleum is 37-50°C.

Capacitor Petroleum - This product is used for filling in and impregnating of capacitors. Its kinematic viscosity at 60°C must atleast be 28 m m^2/s. The volume resistivity of this product must atleast be 1 x 10^{12} ohm. cm at 100°C.

MISCELLANEOUS PETROLEUM PRODUCTS

Greases - Grease is a thick product consisting of oil and a thickener. Various soaps such as calciumsodium, aluminium, lithium, barium etc have commonly been used as thickeners. Greases thickened by hydrocarbon components such as ceresin, paraffin or petroleum have widely been used for protective coatings. They are stable physically as well as chemically, but their operation range is limited to 50-60°C. Special greases have also been produced, in which various compounds are used instead of oil as a liquid phase.

Greases are preferred in those cases where mineral oils do not act as proper lubricants for machines and mechanisms, and also for tightening gaps. Sometimes, greases are also used as a slushing compound. They protect mechanisms against corrosion during storage and then may act as lubricant in operation.

Petroleum Bitumens - Bitumens are generally produced by oxidation of goudrons from heavy tarry grades of petroleum. They can also be obtained by mixing with asphalt, extracts of oil manufacture and asphaltite. The most important characteristics of bitumens are : (a) Needle penetration (b) Ductility, and (c) Softening temperature, which is responsible for the thermal stability of bitumen. The penetration and ductility at low temperatures (in combination) determine the capacity of bitumen to retain its elasticity.

Petroleum bitumens are mainly used in road construction. Dirt and gravel roads are .sometimes impregnated by liquid bitumen obtained by dilution of bitumen with a less viscous petroleum product, such as fuel oil. Special grades of bitumen to be applied in civil engineering and for manufacture of paints, and varnishes have also been manufactured.

Petroleum Acids and their Salts - Naphthenic petroleum acids are mainly present in some grades of petroleum. They are separated during alkali refining of fuel and oil distillates as sodium salts (soaps) and used for the manufacture of naphthenate soap, acidol and acidol-naphthenate soap. Naphthenate soap, which contains about 43% of petroleum acids, is a mixture of sodium soaps and petroleum acids, mineral oil and water. Acidol, which contains 42 - 50% of petroleum acids, consists of petroleum acids with an admixture of mineral oil. Acidol-naphthenate soap, which contains 67 - 70% of petroleum acids, is a mixture of free naphthenic acids and their sodium soaps. All these products are used as substitutes of fats in the manufacture of industrial soaps, because they have high emulsifying and foaming properties. They have also been employed for dyeing in textile industry and as drying agents in paints and also for wood impregnation. The content of mineral oil in these products should not be above a specified limit.

Solvents - Gasoline (fraction 45-170°C), white spirit (fraction 165-200°C) and solvent naphtha (mixture of xylenes) have widely been used as solvents in paints and varnish industry. Gasolines (Galosha) and gasoline with 98% boiling off point at 110°C are used in the rubber industry. The common solvent used in food industry is extraction gasoline (fraction 70-95°C) and also the petroleum ether (fraction 40-70°C and 70-100°C). These and some other solvents such as benzene have also been used in some other industries as well. All solvents are specified for the content of benzene and unsaturated hydrocarbons and sulphur compounds.

Solvents are usually obtained from accompanying petroleum gases and low sulphurous petroleum grades in gas fractionation, preliminary distillation of petroleum and in catalytic reforming (from refined products). The required fraction is sometimes separated in deep distillation plants. The fractions so obtained are then purified specially for minimising the content of benzene hydrocarbons and sulphur compounds.

Domestic Kerosene - It is obtained by straight run distillation of petroleum. Inorder to ensure normal burning it should have a specified composition of paraffin hydrocarbons. It should also burn without forming fly ash (The height of non- smoky flame should not be less than 20 rnm). It should also have an appropriate brightness of flame.

Coke - Coke is a product of petroleum coking. It is used in making electrodes, abrasives and some other materials and as a solid fuel. Electrode coke has a highest industrial significance for electrolytic manufacture of aluminium and in making artificial graphites which are used as antifriction materials in mechanical engineering.

Carbon Black - Carbon black or commercial carbon is an amorphous substance usually in the form of powder with black spherical particles 30-40 pm in diameter. Depending on the method of manufacture, the commercial carbon is called channel black or furnace black. In rubber and paint industries, it is used as a filler and as a dyer in the manufacture of printing ink, ebonite, electrodes etc. The principal standardised characteristics of carbon black are :

(a) *Adsorption (b) Dispersion (c) Colouring power (d) Absence of foreign inclusions (e) Uniform distribution in rubber mixers, and (f) Fractional composition.*

At petroleum processing plants, carbon black can be prepared from gases, green oil (obtained in pyrolysis of kerosene-solar oil fractions), coke residue (from coking plants), gas oil of catalytic cracking, and extraction of oil processing after thermal treatment in cracking plants, coal tar pitch, and atomised extracts from gas oil of secondary processes.

Softeners - Residual products of straight run distillation of petroleum (softener fuel oil), shale oil and some products of oil processing can be used as softeners. They have widely been employed in the rubber industry and as softeners of rubber mixtures in rubber regeneration.

PRODUCT OF PETROCHEMICAL AND BASIC ORGANIC SYNTHESIS

The basic organic and petrochemical synthesis industry is a link between petroleum processing and chemical recovery coke industries and all other branches of organic synthesis. It provides the required starting materials-organic products, and also supplies national economy with valuable final products. A large number of products of basic organic and petrochemical synthesis are not the end products, but infact they are intermediates,which include many organic compounds of chlorine in which chlorine atoms can be substituted by other atoms or groups of atoms.

Starting Substances for Polymer Materials - The manufacture of starting materials plays an important role in basic organic synthesis and petrochemical synthesis. It provides starting materials for the manufacture of plastics, synthetic rubber, synthetic lacquers, glues, film materials, fibres etc. Polymer materials, having various properties and diverse applications are now manufactured in hundreds of kinds the most important among them are polyethylene, polystyrene, polyvinyl chloride, polypropylene, and synthetic rubbers. Many of them have been used as starting materials for the manufacture of commercial goods. For example, various rubber articles, including tyres, are made from synthetic rubbers. Many articles made from polyehtylene and polypropylene can successfully replace non-ferrous metals. etc.

Plasticisers and other Auxiliary Substances for Polymer Materials - In addition to the basic materials for manufacture of synthetic polymers, plasticisers and various auxiliary materials have also been prepared which either facilitate the process of synthesis or improve the properties of final products. For example, even 30- 40% of plasticisers are added to certain polymers, especially to synthetic rubber and polyvinyl chloride, in order to improve the elastic and plastic properties of these materials.

High boiling esters such as dibutyl phthalate, dioctyl phthalate, tricresyl phosphate etc and some esters of higher alcohols and dicarboxylic acids and of higher carboxylic acids and diatomic alcohols are the most important plasticisers among various types of plasticisers.

Softeners obtained at petroleum processing plants are used in the manufacture of synthetic rubber. Other auxiliary substances used in polymer technology and in other processes include initiators, catalysts, inhibitors, regulators etc. The plastic industry has grown very rapidly in recent years. The basic and intermediate raw materials mostly come from natural gas and petroleum. Other sources of raw materials are coal mines. forests, farms, paper and textile mills etc. The phenyl, formaldehyde, solvents, dyes, maleic and phthalic anhydrides, olefins and various other organic chemicals are supplied by coal mines and petroleum. Cellulose paper products and fabrics for laminated plastic are supplied by paper and textile mills. Lactic acid (from milk or corn sugar) is supplied by farms. Glycerine is obtained by the synthesis of petrochemicals or from fatty oils. The petroleum contains mainly the open chain or aliphatic hydrocarbons and ring compounds.

The open chain or aliphatic compounds comprise : (a) N-paraffin Series,(C_nH_{2n}+2) which comprises a large fraction of most petroleum. Important members of this series are n-hexane (> 2%) and n-heptane (2.5-1.7%). The n-paraffins predominate in most straight run gasolines. (b) Isoparaftin Series (C_nH_{2n}+2) which are frequently manufactured by catalytic reforming, alkylation and isomerisation. Naturally occurring members are 2- and 3- methyl pentanes (0.8-1.5%), 2,3- dimethyl pentane and 2-methyl hexane (1.2-1.3%). (c) Olefin Series (C_nH_{2n}), which is either not present or exists in very small quantities. Cracking process produces large amounts of olefins. Examples of pure lower members are ethylene, propylene and butylene. Cracked gasoline and residual products contain higher members of the series.

The ring compounds comprise : (a) Naphthene Series (C_nH_{2n}) is the second most abundantly occurring series of completely saturated compounds in crude petroleum. Members are methyl cyclopentane (0.5-1.3%), cyclohexane (0.64- 0.78%), dimethyl cyclopentanes (1.0-1.75% and methyl cyclohexane (1.82.4%). These naphthenes predominate in most gas oils and lubricating oils from all types of petroleum. (b)Aromatic or Benzene Series (C_nH_{2n}-6), compounds are produced by chemical processing and like olefins have high anti knock qualities. Members are benzene (0.06-1.5%), toluene (0.5-0.6%), ethyl benzene (0.2-0.9%) and xylenes (0.9-1.1%).

Inter-relationship of precursors from natural gas, petroleum cuts and coal

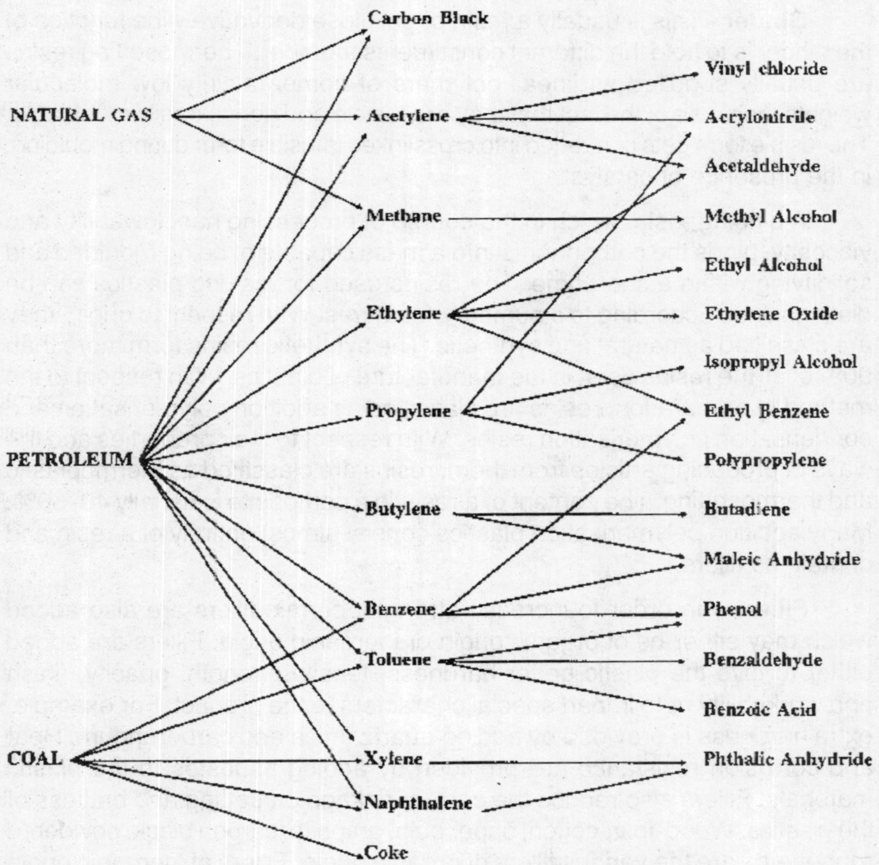

Petroleum products have long been divided into salable cuts by fractional distillation in refning operations. Such refinery fractions are generally classified into three groups.

(a) **Natural or Casing**- head Gasoline and Natural Gas, LPG. light distillates, motor gasolines, solvent naphtha, jet oil, kerosene and light heating oils.

(b) **Intermediate Distillates**- heavy fuel oil, Diesel oils, gas oils, heavy distillates, heavy mineral oils, heavy floatation oils, waxes (candles, sealing, paper, treating, insulating) and lubricating oils.

(c) **Residues**- Lubricating oils, fuel oils, petroleum, road oils, asphalts, coke etc.

Plastics are made from moulding compositions, which are prepared from two or more of the following material groups.

Binder - This is usually a resin or cellulose derivative. The function of the binder is to hold the different constituents together. Thermosetting resins are usually supplied as linear polymers of comparatively low molecular weights, because of the fact that they are fusible and hence easily mouldable. The fusible form gets converted into crosslinked infusible form during moulding, in the presence of catalyst.

A binding resin, which in the course of processing has flowability and viscosity, binds the components into a mass capable of being moulded and solidifying within a short time. The resins used for making plastics can be distinguished according to a number of features. With respect to origin, they are classified as natural and synthetic. The synthetic resins form more than 90% of all the resins used in the manufacture of plastics. With respect to the method of preparation, resins are classified as addition polymerisation and condensation polymerisation resins. With respect to their properties and the ways of producing articles from them, resins are classified as thermoplastic and thermosetting. The content of a resin in a composite is usually 40- 50%. Many addition polymerisation plastics consist almost entirely of a resin and contain no fillers.

Fillers - In order to increase strength, certain fillers are also added which may either be of organic origin or inorganic origin. Fillers are added either to give the plastic better hardness, tensile strength, opacity, finish and workability or to impart special characters to the product. For example, extra hardness is provided by adding quartz, mica and carborundum. Heat and corrosion resistance are provided by adding asbestos to the plastic materials. Fillers also reduce the cost, shrinkage on setting and brittless of the plastics. Wood flour, cotton, paper pulp, graphite, carbon black, powdered rubber etc., are the various fillers of organic origin. Fillers of inorganic origin include asbestos, powdered mica, silicate clays, talc, kieselguhr, zinc and lead oxides, cadmium and barium sulphides, and metals of iron, lead, copper and aluminium in powdered form. The percentage of filler varies with the nature of the plastic formed and properties required and can be as high as 50% of the total moulding mixture. Those fillers which are added to increase the mechanical strength, are called reinforcing fillers. For example, addition of carbon black increases the tensile strength of natural rubber to about 40%

and also the abrasion resistance.

TABLE 1 : CLASSIFICATION OF FILLERS

Organic Origin	Inorganic Origin
(1) Cellulosic - Wood floor, cotton, a-cellulose, paper pulp, shredded textiles, bagasse, corn husks, seed hulls etc.	**(1) Mineral Fillers** - Asbestos, powdered mica, silicate clays, talc, kieselguhr, barites, pumice, emery, zinc oxide, lead oxides, cadmium sulphide and barrium sulphide.
(2) Carbonaceous - Graphite, carbon black	**(2) Powdered Metals** - Fe, Pb, Cu and Al.
(3) Miscellaneous - Powdered rubber, plasticizers.	

Fillers are very important components of a composite. They are added to impart valuable service properties such as high strength, heat resistance, low shrinkage during solidification and lower the cost of the article formed. The filler also reduces combustibility of wares made from the plastic and often increases water resistance and improves the appearance or dielectric properties. Fillers are usually cheap and available organic and inorganic compounds in the powder, fibre, sheet and flaky forms. For example, they can be in powder form (wood, mica, quartz meal, carbon black, graphite, barium sulphate, kieselguhr, kaolin, talcum etc.), fibrous form (cotton, asbestos, textile combings, glass fibre etc) and sheet form (paper, cotton, mica, wood veneer, glass cloth etc.). Fibrous fillers ensure high strength properties. Graphite improves the antifriction properties. Asbestos and mica provide an increased heat resistance. Fillers form upto 60% of the mass of the plastics.

According to their composition plastics can be classified into filler plastics and non-filler plastics. Non-filler plastics contain pure polymer or very small amounts of admixtures. Filler plastics contain mixtures containing fillers, plasticizers, stabilizing agents, solidifying agents etc., uniformly distributed throughout the binder (resin).

(a) Polyethylene, polypropylene, polystyrene, fluoroplastic, polyamides, polyfornaaldehyde, polycarbonate, polyvinyl butyral plastics are classified as non-filler plastics.

(b) Foam, porous and honeycomb plastics, expended polystyrene, foam phenoplast, polyurethane foam (porolon) etc are classified as plastics containing gas-air filler.

(c) Phenoplasts, phenoliths, aminoplasts etc contain fillers such as wood meal, talcum, ground quartz, graphite, barite, aluminium oxide etc in the powder form.

(d) Fibre filled phenol resin, press materials, asbestoresols, fibre glass materials and faolites contain wood pulp, asbestos and glass fibre, textile combings, wood, glass etc in the fibrous form.

(e) Hardened paper, cloth laminate, glass fibre laminates, asbestos cloth laminates and wood laminates contain sheets of paper, cloth, asbestos cloth, glass fibre cloth etc. in the sheet form.

Chemical Intermediates - Phenol, formaldehyde, hexamethylene diamine, phthalic anhydride, vinyl chloride, vinyl acetate, olefins, styrene, ethylene, propylene, acetylene, butadiene, adipic acid etc. are the important chemical intermediates for resins used in plastics.

Catalyst - Monomers combine together to form polymers. In this polymerisation process, there are certain chemicals which may increase the rate of polymerisation and these chemicals are known as catalysts or accelerators. Catalysts or accelerators are used only in case of thermosetting resins. The function of these catalysts or accelerators is to accelerate the polymerisation of fusible resin into cross linked infusible form during moulding operation. Thermosetting resins may use either an acid or basic catalyst, depending upon the properties required. For resins of vinyl group, peroxides are used to initiate the polymerisation of the monomers such as vinyl acetate and methyl methacrylate to form polyvinyl acetate and polymethyl methacrylate resins. In general, catalyst used for compounding are H_2O_2, benzoyl peroxide, acetyl sulphuric acid, metals such as Ag, Cu and Pb, metallic oxide such as ZnO, ammonia and its salts etc.

Alkaline substances such as ammonia, caustic soda and slaked lime catalyse the hardening or curing of phenol formaldehyde resins. Acid catalysts are used to catalyse the curing of urea formaldehyde resins.

Accelerators give the necessary solidification rate at lower temperatures.

Plasticisers - Plasticisers are the substances compatible with the resin. Compatibility is the ability of a resin to dissolve in the plasticizer. Plasticisers are mainly low volatility liquid substances, which increase the plasticity of the composition at elevated temperatures and make the fabricated ware more cold resistant, more elastic and resilient. Plasticisers also affect the mechanical properties of the materials and increase the service life of the plastics. An increase in the amount of plasticiser lowers the tensile and compressive strength of the polymer, but at the same time sharply increases the impact strength and the ability of stretching. The most commonly used plasticisers are high boiling liquids such as castor oil, dibutylphthalate, tricresylphosphate and solids such as phthalates, alkyl and aryl phosphates etc. Plasticisers are usually cyclic or acyclic organic chemicals that are added to synthetic plastics and resins : (I) In order to increase workability during fabrication. (2) In order to improve the natural properties of resin. (3) In order to develop some new properties not present in the original resin. (4) In order to reduce the viscosity of the resins so that they can be easily shaped at high temperatures and pressures. (5) In order to impart flexibilitv and other desirable properties in the finished product.

A plasticiser is generally a high boiling liquid and is relatively nonvolatile at room temperature. It should be a good solvent for the material that has to be plasticised. For example, cellulose acetate should be soluble in the plasticiser dimethyl phthalate. In general, the material and the plasticiser should be compatible. Thermoplastic materials such as nitrocellulose, cellulose acetate and polyvinyl chloride, when hot pressed without making use of any plasticiser, are hard and somewhat brittle materials having softening temperature too high for easy hot shaping. When these thermoplastic substances are compounded with a suitable plasticiser or a mixture of plasticisers, the properties of the compounded materials are greatly improved and become quite different from those of the original materials. The impact strength of the compounded material gets increased and it becomes soft. So its softening temperature is lowered at the expense of surface hardness, which is also lowered. By properly selecting a plasticiser and the amount to be added, it is possible to obtain a tough, pliable material of easy flow.

To the thermosetting materials, a plasticiser is added to serve as a flux and hence it helps the material to flow more easily under hot pressing conditions. For example, furfural is added as a flux in a phenolic moulding material. After acting as a flux, furfual is absorbed by the plastic by chemically combining with the plastic. The action of plasticisers is considered to be due to neutralisation of part of the intermolecular forces of attraction between macromolecules of resins. As a result, they impart greater freedom of movement between the polymeric macromolecules of resins and increase the flexibility as well as plasticity of the compounded material, but decrease the tensile strength and chemical resistance.

Cresyl diphenyl phosphate, tricresyl phosphate, triphenyl phosphate, butyl phthalate, diethyl phthalate, diisodecyl phthalate, octyl decyl phthalates etc. are various cyclic plasticisers used in the manufacture of synthetic plastics and resins. Acyclic plasticisers include adipic acid esters, epoxidised esters, oleic acid esters, phosphoric acid esters, stearic acid esters, azelaic acid esters etc. Most common plasticisers are non-drying vegetable oils, camphor, phosphates and esters of stearic, phthalic or oleic acid.

Lubricants - In order to facilitate the moulding operations, particularly in cold moulding compounds, some lubricants, such as stearates, oleates, waxes and other metallic soaps are also added. Lubricants also

impart a flawless, glossy finish to the products and prevent the plastic material from sticking to the fabrication equipment.

Stabilizers - The object of adding stabilizers is to improve thermal stability during processing. For example, stabilizers are added to vinyl chloride and vinylidene chloride polymers because they have a tendency to undergo decomposition and discolouration at moulding temperatures. Stabilizers are either opaque moulding compounds (such as white lead, litharge, red lead, lead silicate, lead naphthenate etc) or transparent moulding compounds (such as lead, cadmium and barium stearates). Stabilizers make the plastic capable of retaining its original properties for a long time.

Colouring Matter - Organic dystuffs and inorganic pigments are used as colouring materials.

Synthetic Surfactants and Detergents - Surfactants and detergents are extensively used domestically as powders and liquids for washing and cleaning. The substances are characterised by a combination of hydrophobic and hydrophilic groups in the molecule. During washing, this combination facilitates wetting of the fabric and passage of dirt to the washing water. Detergents may be ionogenic and non-ionogenic, depending on the presence or absence of groups capable of dissociating in aqueous solutions ionogenic substances may be classified as anionic or cationic, with their surface active properties being determined by the activity of anions or cations respectively.

Most of the anion active surfactants are sodium salts of sulphonic acids and acid esters of sulphuric acid, particularly (a) Alkylaryl sulphonates with C_{10} - C_{15} alkyl group, (b) Alkyl sulphonates with 12-18 carbon atoms, and, (c) Alkyl sulphates with an alkyl group roughly of the same length.

R -  - S020Na (a) $RS0_3Na$ (b) $ROSO_2ONa$ (c)

In recent years, non-ionogenic substances have also been used widely. They have been synthesised from ethylene oxide and various organic compounds such as carboxylic acids, alcohols, amines etc, having active hydrogen atoms. Their hydrophilic properties are because of a $(CH_2CH_2O)_n$ chain which is obtained by successive attachment of ethylene oxide molecules : RO - $(CH_2$ - $CH_2O)_n$ - H. Inorder to improve their capacity of washing and decrease the consumption, detergents are mixed with various additives and these compositions are known as washing. Such compositions, e.g., washing powders contain sodium phosphate, pyrophosphate, and hexa methaphosphate, sodium silicate, sulphate, carbonate etc.

Synthetic Fuels, Lubricants and Additives - This group includes synthetic motor and jet fuels, lubricating oils, additives, antifreezing agents, braking and pressure fluids.

Solvents and Extractive Agents - Synthetic solvents and extractive agents may belong to various groups of organic compounds such as chlorine derivatives, alcohols, cellosolves, ethers, ketones, esters etc.

Miscellaneous Products - They include insecticides, medicaments and explosives.

DYE INTERMEDIATES

The raw materials used for the manufacture of dyes are mainly aromatic compounds, such as benzene, toluene, naphthalene, anthracene, phenol, pyridine, carbazole, pyrene etc. These raw materials are known as primaries and exclusively obtained in the past from the distillation of coal tar. In recent years, petroleum and natural gas have become important sources of primaries such as benzene, toluene, naphthalene, xylene etc. Aromatic hydrocarbons in recent years have also been obtained from other sources such as water gas, methane, and olefines by catalytic processes.

A large number of inorganic compounds have also been used in dye industry to serve various purposes. These materials include sulphuric acid, oleum, nitric acid, acetic acid, caustic soda, hydrochloric acid, chlorine, bromine, sodium chloride, sodium nitrite, sodium carbonate, sodium sulphate, sodium hydro sulphite, sodium sulphide, sodium dicromate, manganese dioxide, aluminium chloride etc. The primaries of dyes are never directly used in the synthesis of dyes. They are first converted into a large number of derivatives, which are in turn made into dyes. The derivatives or derivates are generally known as dye intermediates, because they act as intermediate between the primaries and the final dye.

A large number of important reactions such as nitration, oxidation, halogenation, sulphonation, reduction, condensation etc have been used in the production of intermediates. These reactions give rise to the formation of substituted hydrocarbons which are functional in nature (They contain functional groups which undergo further chemical reactions to produce dye).

Sulphonation, nitration, amination by reduction, halogenation, dehydration, Friedel-Craft's reaction etc are the most important and common unit processes which are involved in the synthesis of dyes.

Aliphatic compounds, aromatic compounds and heterocyclic compounds are the three main types of intermediates needed for the manufacture of dyes.

The most common aliphatic compounds used as dye intermediates are alcohols, carboxylic acids, esters, chloro derivatives, aldehydes, ketones, amines etc. They are mainly used as solvents or as reagents or reactants. The common alcohols used are methyl alcohol, ethyl alcohol, butyl alcohols, amyl alcohols, ethylene glycol, glycerol etc. The common carboxylic acids used are formic acid, acetic acid, malonic acid, maleic acid, succinic acid etc. Many of the carboxylic acids and their esters such as formic, acid, acetic acid, ethyl acetate etc are generally used as solvents.

Methyl chloride, dichloromethane, ethylene dichloride, trichloro ethane, carbon tetra chloride chloroform etc are the halogen compounds of aliphatic series which are used as solvents. Many aliphatic chloro compounds such as vinyl chloride, chloro acetic acid, phosgene, thiophosgene ($CSCl_2$), and epichlorohydrin are used in various condensation reactions to get aromatic as well as heterocyclic intermediates and dyes. Chloral (CCl_3CHO) is used in the production of isatin. Acetyl chloride and other acid chlorides are used in many organic reactions such as Friedel Crafts reaction for the production of intermediates.

Aldehydes and ketones are generally used in the manufacture of ranges of intermediates. Paraformaldehyde, acetaldehyde, benzaldehyde, methyl isopropyl ketone etc are used for this purpose.

Aliphatic amines undergo condensation reactions with many organic aromatic compounds having active phenolic or chloro groups. For example, o^- and p^- nitro chloro benzenes react with secondary amines, such as diethylamine to yield corresponding o^- and p^- substituted amino nitrobenzenes. Methyl amine reacts with sodium salt of chloro acetic acid to form sarcosine. Monoethanolamine reacts with quinizain to produce a dispense dye. In addition, some other aliphatic compounds such as urea, ethylene oxide, acetonitrile, thio urea, acrylic acid, dimethyl sulphate, acrylonitrile etc have also been used in the manufacture of intermediates and dyes.

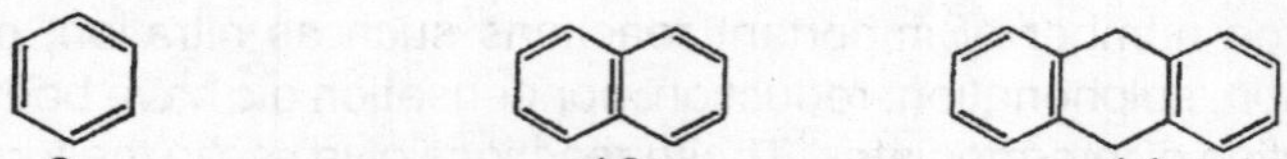

6π 10π 14π

The aromatic dye intermediates are commonly prepared from benzene, naphthalene and anthraquinone. Biphenyl, acenaphthene, benzanthrone, pyrene, perylene etc have also been used in making aromatic dye intermediates, but less frequently.

The reactivity of aromatic compounds depends mainly upon the availability of in electron cloud on the system. The increase in the π electron cloud follows the order : **Benzene (6π) < Naphthalene (l0π) < Anthracene (14π).**

The reactivity increases in the same order towards electrophiles, but decreases in the same order towards nucleophiles. Electron donating groups in the aromatic hydrocarbons facilitate the attack of an electrophile and resist the attack of a nucleophile as compared to the unsubstituted hydrocarbon, because of removal of π electron cloud away from the benzene ring system. $-NH_2$, -OH, -SH, $-CH_3$ etc are the examples of electron withdrawing groups.

Electron withdrawing groups in the benzene or atomatic hydrocarbons resist the attack of electrophile but facilitate the attack of a nucleophile as compared to the unsubstituted hydrocarbon, because of removal of n electron cloud away from the benzene ring. $-NO_2$, -CHO, $-SO_3H$,- COOH, -CN etc are the examples of electron withdrawing groups. The electron donating groups in the benzene ring facilitate further substitution in ortho and para positions and electron withdrawing groups favour meta position, because of the conjugative effect. Chlorine in chlorobenzene becomes electron withdrawing, because of the fact that it is more electronegative than the carbon atom to which it is attached. Due to inductive effect, $-CH_3$ group in toluene is electron donating. In general, electron rich and electron deficient positions in benzene as well as in other aromatic compounds are attached by electrophiles and nucleophiles respectively.

The introduction of an amino group into an aromatic nucleus by replacement of another functional group is known as amination, which generally takes place in presence of a catalyst. In amination primary amines and ammonia act as nucleophilic reagents.

Ammonolysis is carried out under pressure using gaseous ammonia or aqueous ammonia in presence of a metallic catalyst such as copper oxide, cuprous oxide or cupric chloride. The choice of catalyst, depends upon the compound to be subjected to ammonolysis. For example, in case of aniline, which is easily oxidised, a reducing catalyst such as cuprous chloride is preferred. In case of amino anthraquinone, which is likely to be reduced easily, an oxidising catalyst such as cupric chloride is preferred. Alumina and sulphites have also been used as catalysts in gaseous and liquid phase ammonolysis respectively.

The conversion of a nitro compound into the corresponding amine is the most common and important reduction method in the manufacture of dye intermediates. Nascent hydrogen, sodium sulphide (Na_2S), sodium hydrosulphide (HS), sodium poly sulphide (Na_2Sx), zinc in alkaline aqueous or alcoholic medium, catalytic reduction (such as Ni, Cu Pt, W, Mo etc) have generally been used as reducing agents.

Oxidation reaction may be carried out by air in the presence of a catalyst (e.g V_2O_5) or by using oxidising agents such as $KMnO_4$, MnO_2 etc.

The introduction of -CHO group into the benzene ring is known as formylation, which is carried out by the hydrolysis of dichloromethyl group. The latter is introduced in the benzene ring by chlorination of side chain -CH3 in the absence of a halogen carrier. For example, chlorination of toluene in absence of halogen carrier gives benzal chloride which yields benzaldehyde when hydrolysed with milk of lime. Formylation of tertiary amines is carried out by nitrosation followed by reaction with formaldehyde.

Chlorine is widely used for halogenation. Chlorination is generally carried out with dry chlorine gas in absence or presence of a catalyst. Thionyl chloride, PCl_3, PCl_5 sulphuryl chloride etc have also been used as chlorinating reagents in some cases.

The replacement of one or more hydrogen atom of the benzene ring by $-NO_2$ group is known as nitration. Nitric acid in water or organic solvent is used as a nitrating agent in case of highly reactive compounds and mixed acid (Conc. HNO_3 + Conc. H_2SO_4) is used for the nitration of less reactive compounds. If benzene ring contains one of the $-CH_3$, -Cl, -Br, -OH, -I, $-NH_2$ etc groups, the nitro group enters to the otho and para positions. If benzene nucleus contains any of the $-NO_2$, -COOH, -CN, $-SO_3H$, -CHO groups, the nitro group enters to the meta position. NH? group in compounds to be nitrated is necessary to be protected against oxidative destruction by **acetylation**. When nitration is complete, the acetyl group is removed by hydrolysis. .

Nitrosation reaction is commonly used for getting nitrosation intermediates. For example, nitrosation of dimethyl aniline and phenol is done by $NaNO_2$ and dilute HCl or dilute H_2SO_4 in cold. The N=O acts as an electrophile or attacking species.

Friedel Crafts reaction is a reaction between hydrocarbon such as benzene with alkyl chloride (alkylation) or acyl chloride (acylation) or aroyl chloride (aroylation) or acid anhydride (acylation or aroylation) in presence of a catalyst such as $AlCl_3$,$AlBr_3$ or BF_3 (Lewis acid). Acetylation with acetyl chloride or acetic anhydride is known as acetylation and aroylation with benzoyl chloride is known as benzoylation.

Many heterocyclic intermediates have also been used in dye industry. Some of the important ones are ethylene oxide, pyrrole, thiophene, oxazole, thiazole, imidazole, pyrazole, triazole, pyran, pyridine, pyrimidine, triazine, azine, oxazine, thiazine etc. Ethylene oxide and epichlorohydrin are important among three membered heterocyclic ring systems. Pyrrole, thiophene, oxazole, thiazole, imidazole and triazole are important among five membered heterocyclic systems. Phthalocyanines, phthalogens and some natural colouring matters (e.g chlorophyll) possess pyrrole rings in the form of tetrazaporphin and porphin ring structures. Indoles are used in the indigoid vat dyes.

Coumarin and xanthene are important among pyran heterocyclic intermediates. Coumarin structure is found in fluorescent brighteners, while xanthene structure is found in many basic dyes such as rhodamines. Pyridine skeleton has been found in pyridine derivatives, quinoline derivatives, naphthalimides and acridines etc. Pyridine derivatives find use as diazonium components for disperse and cationic dyes. A number of pyridine derivatives have been used as coupling components. Quinoline derivatives such as

8-hydroxy quinoline consist of a number of coupling components. Tetrahydroquinoline derivatives such as 8-hydroxy quinoline consist of a number of coupling components. Tetrahydroquinoline and tetrahydrobenzoquinoline derivatives find use as coupling components. Naphthalimide dyes such as 5aminonaphthalimide derivatives are important fluorescent dyes. Pyrimidine skeleton has been found in some anthraquinonoid dyes and a number of coupling components (amino pyrimidines and barbituric acid). Azine, oxazine and thiazine systems have been found in azine, oxazine and thiazine classes of dyes. For example, methylene blue is a thiazine dye.

LACQUERS

The dispersion of cellulose derivatives such as cellulose nitrate, resins and plasticizers in solvents and diluents is generally known as lacquer. Such a dispersion dries upon by evaporation of its volatile constituents and provides protective as well as decorative coating. Lacquer may be regarded as a modified form of spirit varnish that gives a transparent film. A clear lacquer is called pigmented lacquer or lacquer enamel if it also contains a pigment.

Film forming materials in a lacquer are either cellulose derivatives (such so nitrocellulose, ethyl cellulose, cellulose acetate etc) or synthetic resins (such as damar, copal, estergum (natural resins) and phenol formaldehyde, alkyd etc (synthetic resins).

The function of cellulose derivatives is to provide durability, hardness and water proofness, while that of natural and synthetic resins is to improve adhesion, water resistance capacity and the quality of retention of original gloss., Hence resins'are mainly used to improve the properties of the film.

Nitrocellulose is prepared by treating cotton linters (cellulose) with nitrating mixture consisting of conc. HNO_3 and conc. H_2SO_4, while cellulose acetate in prepared by treating cotton linters or cellulose with acetic anhydride. The cellulose acetate provides a non - inflammable film and so has been used with advantage over cellulose nitrate. Moreover, nitro cellulose without any treatment is highly viscous and a large amount of solvent is needed to dissolve desired amount of nitro cellulose, because of its less solubility in solvents. As a result, the resulting solution is too thin to give a fine of desired properties.

The solubility of nitrocellulose in solvents can be increased and hence viscosity can be decreased by heating nitro cellulose with water at 130°C. The aqueous suspension is passed through a steel pipe against the pressure of a stand pipe at the exit. The suspension is allowed to remain inside the pipe for about half an hour and rate of flow is controlled. The mixture overflows the tube and is then centrifuged. The viscosity is decreased because long chain molecules of nitro cellulose ester are degraded as a result of hydrolysis.

The solvents used are esters (such as ethyl, butyl, amyl acetates), ketones (such as methyl ethyl ketone, cyclohexanone), ethers (such as cellosolve) and alcohols (such as ethyl, butyl and amyl alcohols).

The function of the solvent is to dissolve the film forming substances as well as to suspend the pigments. Rate of evaporation as well as solvency of the film forming material depend upon the type of solvent used. The choice of solvent depends upon the film forming material and the rate of evaporation, because drying of lacquer is an evaporation process and properties of the film obtained from lacquer depends upon the conditions of evaporation (not on the nature of film). The choice of solvent is governed by a number of factors such as rate of evaporation, solvency of film forming material, viscosity of the solution, stability, odour, purity, availability, blushing behaviour, compatibility with resins and other in gradients etc.

A defect known as blushing is developed, if a film is formed by very rapid evaporation of solvents and diluents, as a result of which cooling of film to 30 - 40°F below .the atmospheric temperature takes place. This causes the condensation of moisture upon lacquer film. Blushing can be avoided by using a solvent of high boiling point and hence slower rate of evaporation.

Solvents are generally classified according to their rate of evaporation and vapour pressure at room temperature.

Diluent is a non-solvent miscible with the solvent used. Diluents used are generally coal tar products (such as toluol, benzol, solvent naphtha etc) or petroleum products (such as petroleum naphtha). The purpose of diluent is to reduce the viscosity of the lacquer as well as its cost. It should be noted that dilutent is added in quantities insufficient to cause precipitation of the nitro cellulose.

Plasticizers such as dibutyl phthalate, butyl stearate, tributyl phosphate etc are added to reduce brittleness and improve adherence. Castor oil is used as a plasticizer if pigments are used in the lacquer.

Chlorinated diphenyls, aroclors etc are also added to the lacquers to decrease the inflammability of the nitrocellulose film. The lacquers are manufactured by dissolving first the resin in the diluent and cellulose ester in the solvent. Now both the solutions are mixed and more solvent and diluent are added. Finally a suspension of pigment in nitrocellulose solution or in the plasticizer is introduced to get the lacquer.

Lacquers are generally used in the preparation of artificial leather and for giving finish to automobile parts (it resists abrasion, cracking and chalking). Lacquers are also used in interior decoration such as painting of wood work and furniture etc.

SOLVENTS AND THINNERS

The most common and the cheapest solvent is water. In addition to water, a large number of other substances have also been employed as solvents. These include esters, ketones, alcohols, ethers, halogenated hydrocarbons, petroleum hydrocarbons, coal - tar hydrocarbons and turpentine etc. Solvents belonging to more than one class have also been used as solvents. For example, methyl ether of ethylene glycol is an ether as well as an alcohol. It is, however, difficult to distinguish between solvent and thinner. In general, a solvent is used to dissolve substances and a thinner is employed to make the solution less expensive, otherwise the process of thinning would be one of adding more solvent. These classes merge with plasticizers, which may be regarded as solvents with boiling points sufficiently high so that they will not evaporate at ordinary temperatures.

A solvent with a flash point below 100°F is usually called inflammable. If it flashes above that temperature, it is called combustible.

Esters are the compounds which result from the reaction of an alcohol and an organic acid with the loss of water.

$$CH_3COOH + C_2H_5OH \rightarrow \underset{\text{ester}}{CH_3COOC_2H_5} + H_2O$$

Acetates, propionates, butyrates and lactates are commonly used as solvents, while ethyl, methyl, propyl, and butyl alcohols are commonly used for their preparation. Esters have fruity smell, e.g., ethyl acetate smells like apple and amyl acetate resembles the bannana smell. They can be easily saponified on warming with aqueous alkali to give the alcohol and a salt of the acid. They burn with blue to yellow flames. The presence of one type of ester can be easily identified and confirmed by density and boiling point determination. If the ester is blended with unsaponifiable material not readily separable by distillation, then the amount of ester is determined by saponification.

Ketones frequently used as industrial solvents are acetone, methyl ethyl ketone and methyl acetone, (a mixture of 48% acetone, 28% methyl acetate and 24% methyl alcohol). All ketones are soluble in water. alcohol and esters. Ketones are unsaponifiable and can be readily identified by their odours. Ketones containing methyl group are identified by iodoform test. This test is also positive in case of ethyl alcohol. Ketones give the test at room temperature, while ethanol must be heated to 60°C.

$$3I_2 + 6NaOH \rightarrow 3NaOI + 3NaI + 3H_2O$$

$$CH_3COCH_3 + 3NaOI \rightarrow CH_3COONa + CHI_3 + 2NaOH$$

Or

$$CH_3COCH_3 + 3I_2 + 4NaOH \rightarrow CH_3COONa + 3NaI + CHI_3 + 3H_2O$$

Ketones can also be tetsed with sodium nitroprusside reagent. A deep red colour is produced with ketones.

Monohydric alcohols can be distinguished by their odours. They burn with a clear colourless blue flame. Ethanol and isopropanol can be identified by iodoform test.

Among the dihydric alcohols, ethylene glycol and propylene glycol are commonly used as solvents. These are soluble in water and many of them can easily be identified with their densities and boiling points. Quantitatively, they can be identified by acetylation with acetic anhydride.

Chlorinated hydrocarbons have high specific gravity, always greater than one. Thus they sink when poured in water. The density increases with higher degree of chlorination. All are toxic and introduction of chlorine decreases inflammability. In fact those containing three or more chlorine atoms are expected to be non - inflammable. Chlorinated hydrocarbons are identified by their densities and positive green flame test.

Petroleum solvents usually contain paraffinic or naphthenic hydrocarbons and the quality varies with the source of the crude oil. The grades range from light naphthenic hydrocarbons and the quality varies with the source of the crude oil. The grades range from light naphthas or petroleum ethers with specific gravities of 0.627 - 0.72 to petroleum solvents of sp. gravities upto 0.82. The common trade names are petroleum naphtha, V .M. and P naphtha, safety solvent (stoddard solvent) and kerosene of which first two are inflammable and last two are combustible. All petroleum solvents when heated burn with a more or less yellow flame, sometimes giving a little smoke. Petroleum solvents are usually miscible with absolute alcohol. They are also miscible with aromatic hydrocarbons and with ethyl ether and are not saponifiable.

Aromatic hydrocarbons are coal tar distillates. The most common are benzene, toluene, xylenes and high flash naphtha. Aromatic hydrocarbons burn with a smoky flame. These solvents are soluble in alcohol and in ether and are not saponifiable. The solvents are quantitatively identified by nitration with conc. HNO_3 and conc. H_2SO_4 or by sulphonation.

Wood turpentine and gum turpentine are the common turpentine solvents. These solvents are easily identified by specific gravity and odour.

The above solvents can, therefore, be identified by making use of properties such as sp. gravity, boiling point or boiling range and other properties. They are, however, difficult to evaluate if they are present in mixtures. They are first separated and then identified by the properties already given. Boiling range may be useful but many pairs of solvents form isotropic mixtures which have a boiling point below that of ether. Separation of two or more solvents may be made by solubilities or by fractional distillation.

Many solvents have characteristic odours that may at least identify the presence of that solvent in the mixture. Sp. gravity determination is also helpful. A sp. gravity less than 0.780 would normally indicate the presence of ethyl ether or a petroleum solvent, while a sp. gravity of more than I will show the presence of chlorinated hydrocarbons. Solubility in water is also helpful in identification. To a 5 ml of sample in a graduated culinder add 20 ml of water. Shake well and separate the layers. Any lost in volume of the sample indicates the presence of alcohols, ketones, glycols and various other solvents, some of which are partly soluble in water. If there is no appreciable loss in the volume of solvent, it means that only hydrocarbons and/or higher alcohols are present.

Chapter 9

PURIFICATION OF PETROLEUM PRODUCTS

INTRODUCTION

Since the products obtained by distillation and cracking contain olefins, diolefins and sulphur, oxygen and nitrogen containing compounds, petroleum products are subjected to purification, because these compounds cause instability and formation of carbon deposits on the cylinder walls of internal combustion engine and give a dark colour and unpleasant odor to the products. Purification is the final stage in the manufacture of motor fuels and lubricating oils.

Both chemical as well as physico-chemical purification methods have been used. The chemical methods include purification with sulphuric acid and hydrofining and physico-chemical methods include adsorption and absorption.

The existing methods for purification of petroleum products can be divided into absorptive,adsorptive, hydrogenising, chemical and electric-field purification etc.

In absorptive and adsorptive purification and in purification by selective solvents, the purifying agent can be used repeatedly, which is more economical than using sulphuric acid or alkalies in other processes. In sulphuric acid and alkali purification and water washing, a product is allowed to come in contact with a reagent (or water) and the phases so formed are separated by precipitation. The precipitation requires much time and large storage tanks for petroleum products. Moreover, these processes form a large amount of waste products, e.g, acid goudrons in sulphuric acid purification and alkaline wastes in alkali purification, which result in large expenditure and losses of petroleum products. Oil purification by selective solvents is carried.out in few stages, and a certain group of harmful impurities are removed in every stage. For example, tar-asphaltene compounds are separated by deasphalting and tars and part of polycycle benzene hydrocarbons by selective purification.

Paraffins or ceresins are separated by dewaxing. The colour is improved by hydrofining.

White products can be purified by simple methods, because they contain less impurities. High octane gasolines should have a reiatively high content of benzene hydrocarbons, which can be achieved by catalytic reforming. On the other hand, presence of benzene hydrocarbons is not desirable in other types of petroleum products. For example, their presence in kerosenes give smoky flame. Since benzene hydrocarbons are toxic, their content in solvents such as white spirit, extraction gasoline etc. must be limited. Hence for preparation of these products benzene hydrocarbons should be removed from the distillates to a certain limit. A high voltage d.c field method has widely been used for the purification of petroleum products in recent years. The quality of purified products such as fuels, oils and lubricants can also be improved by adding additives. For example, inhibitors are added to some products to increase their stability. Tetraethyl lead (TEL) is added to gasolines for increasing their octane number.

ABSORPTIVE AND ADSORPTIVE PURIFICATION

The absorptive purification of gaseous liquid petroleum products are carried out in separate plants or in purification units of combination plants.

Absorptive purification is used to purify dry gases containing a high concentration of H_2S and vapours of light fractions and liquid hydrocarbons (C_3, C_4 and C_5) with a relatively low content of sulphurous compounds. The common industrial absorbents are ethanolamines, sodium phenolate, potassium triphosphate, alcacide etc. Ethanolamines have widely been used in modern plants. They can be obtained by reacting ethylene oxide and ammonia. Gases are purified by 15 - 30% aqueous solution of amines. The purifying capacity of solution increases with,

(a) Decrease in temperature.

(b) Decrease in H_2S concentration in a gas.

(c) Increase in pressure, and.

(d) Increase in circulation ratio.

The absorption of H_2S at 25 - 40°C is accompanied by liberation of heat. With an increase in temperature upto 105 - 130°C, the sulphides formed as a result of absorption are decomposed and H_2S gas is evolved. H_2S is separated and processed into sulphur and sulphuric acid. The absorption of H_2S and CO_2 by aqueous solution of mono- and diethylamines (MEA and DEA) is an example of chemisorption. Other conditions being equal, the absorptivity of H_2S is 3 - 5 times that of CO_2. When temperature is increased from 25°C, the absorption of H_2S decreases and that of CO_2 increases. The absorptivity of H_2S by an absorbent is lower at a higher concentration of CO_2

in the gas that has to be purified. MEA can dissolve unsaturated, hydrocarbons C_4 and higher, if they are present in the gas being purified. As a result, the solution is foamed and tarred. Foaming of MEA can disturb the proper functioning of trays in the absorber. The DEA has a higher boiling point and dissolves heavier hydrocarbons less readily and thus decreases the probability of foaming of the solution. Thus DEA makes it possible to perform the process in tray absorbers at a higher flow rate of the gas. Hence DEA is more widely used than MEA. Triethanol amine is suitable in those cases when only H_2S is to be separated without removing CO_2.

The adsorptive purification of gases and liquid petroleum products is carried out by making use of various adsorbents such as silica gel, discolouring clays, amorphous or crystalline aluminosilicates (zeolites), activated carbons etc. Adsorptive purification is mainly used for gases employed in chemical synthesis. Various microimpurities of H_2S, CO_2, H_2O etc. can be retained by the pores of an adsorbent. In some cases, adsorbents are used for removal of water microimpurities of various products in which presence of moisture is harmful. Adsorptive purification is based on the ability of adsorbents to promote the polymerisation and condensation of unsaturated hydrocarbons, if present in the product which is to be purified, and also on their ability to adsorb certain hydrocarbons and other compounds. Tar-asphaltene substances can be adsorbed most readily, followed by benzene, naphthenic and paraffinic hydrocarbons. Unsaturated hydrocarbons, especially diolefins, are adsorbed on amorphous aluminosilicates more readily than other hydrocarbons and even more intensively than tars. They are polymerised in the process. Paraffinic hydrocarbons are easily adsorbed on crystalline aluminosilicates (zeolites). This property of zeolites is used in increasing the octane number of gasolines, for preparation of n-paraffinins in dewaxing of distillates etc. In some cases, oils are purified finally by discolouring clays. Most clays possess no discolouring properties in the natural form, some of them, such as gumbrine can be activated by treating with H_2SO_4 or HCl at 95°C followed by washing and drying. As a result, its adsorptivity increases 2 - 4 times. In contact purification by discolouring clays, the yield of end products is 97 - 98% for distillates and 95 - 96% for residual oils.

Circulation purification, in which the product is passed through a layer of adsorbent upon acid treatment, is sometimes used for the purification of special oils, petroleum, waxes and ceresins. Continuous purification of petroleum products on adsorbents is, however, more effective and can be used instead of selective purification for preliminary and final purification of high quality raffinates. The plants for effecting the process have four units in which the following processes are carried out.

(a) Adsorption and desorption.

(b) Stream stripping of a solvent from the solution of a tarred adsorbent.

(c) Oxidising regeneration and cooling of an adsorbent, and

(d) Regeneration of the solvent.

SULPHURIC ACID PURIFICATION

In sulphuric acid purification, the product is mixed with a small amount of sulphuric acid (93% H_2SO_4) at room temperature. As a result, purified product is obtained with the undesirable impurities being converted into a sludge. The sludge is a waste product which can be used to make H_2SO_4. The H_2SO_4 purification is troublesome, large amounts of reagents are used and produces waste products which are difficult to utilize.

Sulphuric acid purification can remove a considerable amount of unsaturated hydrocarbons, asphaltenes, tars, nitrogen and sulphur compounds from the petroleum products. Sulphuric acid of 93 - 98% has practically no effect on paraffinic and naphthenic hydrocarbons at room temperature. Fuming sulphuric acid can, however, react with paraffinic hydrocarbons at elevated temperature to form sulpho acid, which can also be formed by the reaction between benzene hydrocarbons and sulphuric acid. The degree of extraction of benzene hydrocarbons by H_2SO_4 from oil fractions decreases with increase in boil off temperature of fractions. For deeper extraction, the use of fuming acid is to be increased, which causes great loss of distillates in purification.

Unsaturated hydrocarbons may react with sulphuric acid at low temperatures to form acid esters, known as alkyl sulphuric acids, and at higher temperatures (above 40°C) to form natural esters. The latter can also form acid esters on heating.

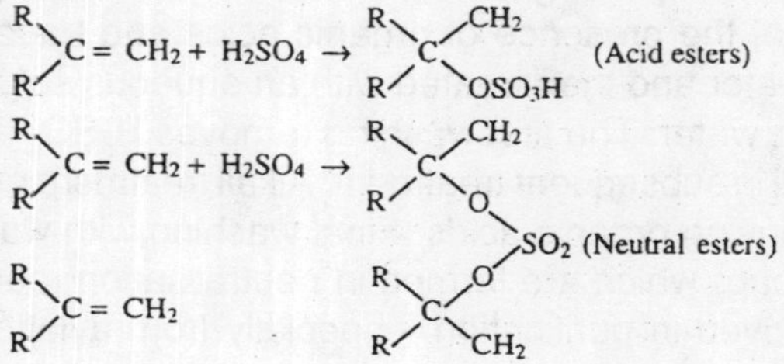

Acid esters are concentrated in acid goudron and natural esters, which are colourless oily liquids readily soluble in organic solvents, in the refined product. The acid and neutral esters can be hydrolysed with an aqueous solution of alkali at 60 - 70°C to form corresponding alcohols.

With a high content of unsaturated hydrocarbons in a petroleum product, H2S04 purification should be done at reduced temperatures for reducing the amount of neutral acids formed.

Tar asphaltene substances readily react with H2S04 to form heavy products such as asphaltenes, sulphoacids etc, which settle on the bottom of the reactor as the main constituent of goudron. Some of these substances and reaction products are also soluble in H2S04.

Among sulphur compounds, mercaptans and thiophenes may react with H_2SO_4. H_2S from the petroleum product should be removed before purification by H_2SO_4, because H_2S can react with H_2SO_4 to form elemental sulphur which gets dissolved in the petroleum product and will react with hydrocarbons during subsequent distillation and form H_2SO_4 again. The reaction of mercaptan (RSH) with H_2S takes place in several stages and forms disulphides.

$$2RSH + H_2SO_4 \rightarrow RS - SR + SO_2 + 2H_2O$$

Disulphides are dissolved in the purification product. Here an active sulphur compound (mercaptan) causing corrosion is converted into an inactive disulphide.

Thiophenes and their homologues react with H_2SO_4 to form thiophene sulphonic acids.

Nitrous bases react with H_2SO_4 to form sulphates which pass to goudron.

Naphthenic acids are partially soluble in the sulphuric acid and partially be sulphurised. Naphthenic acids of higher molecular mass are more easily sulphurised.

The products obtained by H_2SO_4 purification include a refined product (distillate), gaseous SO_2, and acid goudron which settles on the bottom of the reactor. The yield of the goudron is greater at a higher molecular mass of the product and a deeper degree of purification. The refined product is always acid because of the presence of organic acids and traces of H_2SO_4. It is washed with water and then treated with an aqueous solution of alkali and then again with water. The first washing removes H_2SO_4 and thus reduces the use of alkali in subsequent treatment. Alkali treatment makes the product neutral by removing organic acids. Final washing with water removes ash component (soap) which are formed in neutralisation reactions. They can hardly be removed in purification, especially from aviation kerosene and oils.

Acid goudrons are further processed to obtain demulsifiers, fuels and regenerated acid. Alkali wastes are used to prepare acid oil, emulsion oil and naphtha-soap. Because of great use of H_2SO_4 and high loss of oils, H_2SO_4 purification is mainly employed in producing white oils. Other grades of oils are generally obtained by using selective solvents.

ALKALINE PURIFICATION

Alkaline purification of distillates is carried out more frequently by making use of caustic soda (NaOH) and less frequently by using soda ash (Na_2CO_3). Alkaline treatment removes acid oxygen containing compounds such as phenols, naphthenic acids etc, and some sulphur compounds such as H_2S and mercaptans, from the petroleum products. Alkaline purification is usually carried out in addition to prior H_2SO_4 purification in order to neutralise the unreacted acid and the acid products of the reaction with hydrocarbons (sulphoacids and sulphonic esters). The reaction between the alkali and acid compounds gives sodium salts forming alkaline wastes. Part of the salt remaining in the product are removed by washing with water.

There are many disadvantages of alkaline purification of gasoline distillates. For example,

(a) Alkali is difficult to be regenerated and so large amount is consumed in the process.

(b) The sulphur-alkali wastes of the process are contaminated with phenols and are strong pollutants for the environment. Special sewage systenas are therefore required for the removal and purification of wastes.

These disadvantages can be removed by making use of regenerative regents such as potassium triphosphate, ethanolamines etc, in which upto 97% of H_2S can be removed from the product. Alkalisation is, however, used for the processing of white petroleum products, especially those with a high content of naphthenic acids. The process is also used for the separation of naphthenic acids which are useful products. With gasolines of petroleum distillation or obtained from secondary processes, hydrotining is generally used instead of alkali purification.

HYDROFINING

In recent years, the hydrofining process has widely been used. It consists in treating the products being purified with H_2 in presence of aluminocobaltmolybdenum catalysts at 380-420°C and pressure from 35 to 40 atm. In the hydrorefining process hydrogen reacts with sulphur-, nitrogen- and oxygen containing compounds to form NH_3 and H_2O, which can easily be separated from the substance to be purified.

$$RSH + H_2 \rightarrow RH + H_2S \qquad RNH_2 + H_2 \rightarrow RH + NHa$$

The dienes are also hydrogenated and in this way stability of the product increases.

$$> C = C < + H_2 \rightarrow > CH\text{-} CH <$$

Hydrofining can also be utilized for producing petroleum products from high sulphur petroleums.

PURIFICATION IN A D.C. ELECTRIC FIELD

The main apparatus used in this method of purification is an electric precipitator which is based on the combination of petroleum purification by chemical reagents (or washing with water) and subsequent coalescence of particles of the reagent in an electric field. The electric field or forces destroy easily the emulsion and eliminate the difficulties associated with phase separation. Electric purification is now used increasingly in petroleum processing and other branches of industry and electric purification units are now included in almost all schemes of new petroleum processing processes.

Electric purification is not only applicable in refining of petroleum products, but in all cases where it is required to separate two phases, one of which is non-conductive (dispersion medium) and the other is conductive. The process of electric purification takes place in two stages. (a) Coalescence of dispersed phase particles in an electric field, and (b) Precipitation of coarsened particles under the influence of gravity. The efficiency of electric purification depend mainly on

(a) Temperature

(b) Pressure

(c) Hydraulic conditions of mixing and precipitation

(d) Properties of reagents, and

(e) Electric field strength.

The products of higher molecular mass and higher setting or fusion point need a higher temperature of the process. This is necessary for decreasing the viscosity of the dispersion medium and the easier precipitation of dispersed phase particles. In desiccation of white petroleum products, the solubility of water in them increases with increase in temperature. Electric purification can remove freely dispersed water but does not remove the dissolved water. Hence jet fuels, in which the moisture content is very limited, must be desiccated at 20 - 35°C and Diesel fuels and gasolines, at 35 - 40°C.

Depending on the product to be purified, the pressure is controlled in electric purification. It is usually between 0.2 to 2.0 MPa. The lower value corresponds to heavy products, and the higher value, to lighter ones including liquefied gases.

With more intensive mixing, the greater portion of particles decreases in size and more time is required for purification (either by natural precipitation or in the electric field). The size of the dispersed particles should be such as to ensure the closest contact between the two phases and to prevent the formation of an emulsion, which is difficult to be destroyed even in an electric field.

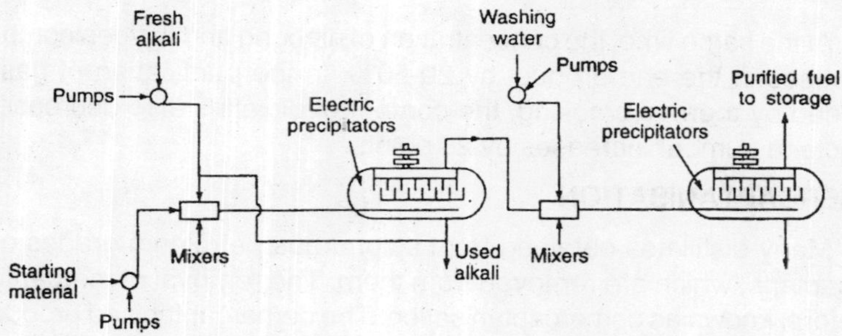

Fig. 1. Unit for alkali purification of jet and Diesel fuels.

The unit for alkali purification of jet and Diesel fuels (Fig. 1) performs alkali purification, water washing and filtering of the product. In the purification of jet fuel the unit operates as follows. The fuel at 30 - 35°C, along with 4 - 6% alkali solution, is fed by a pump into a mixer, from where the mixture is allowed to pass to an electric precipitator. Alkali solution from the bottom of the precipitator is recycled and the jet fuel -from the top is supplied into a water mixture where naphthenic acids and traces of alkali are washed off by water. The mixture so obtained is then fed to another precipitator for removing water. Water is drained into the sewage system and the desiccated fuel passes through a filter (in order to separate scale and mechanical impurities) to a storage tank.

NEW METHODS OF PURIFICATION

In the processing of fuel oil by water superheated to 300°C (water fuel oil ratio 10 : 1) upto 50 % of sulphur can be removed from fuel oil. Membranes have been used particularly in the separation of hydrogen from synthesis gas. The films of polyethylene, polypropylene, vinyl fluoride, polybenzyl glutamate etc have been tested as membranes.

A continuous industrial process has also been developed for the removal of sulphur compounds from petroleum distillates with transition metals in low voltage state. Such compounds as iron carbonyls and dodecacarbonyl, $Fe_3(CO)_{12}$ are capable of combining with mercaptans, sulphides disulphides, and elemental sulphur to form stable complexes containing mercaptides. The substances so formed can be separated by filtration or adsorption and used for the preparation of concentrated mixtures of sulphurous compounds or sulphonic acids. The filtrate or purified product contains much less of sulphurous compounds and other harmful impurities. Diolefins, nitrogen and oxygen compounds, which are present in the purified product are not harmful because they are combined in other complexes and their concentration decreases.

At the same time, the concentration of nitrogen and oxygen compounds decreases in the end product by 20-50%. In the purification of gasolines obtained by thermal cracking, the content of diolefins also decreases and the octane number increases by 20 points.

DEMERCAPTANISATION

Many distillates obtained from sulphurous petroleum grades contain mercaptans, which are removed from them. The removal of mercaptans is, therefore, known as demercaptanisation. The demercaptanised products are non- corrosive and have a pleasant odour. The process is generally used for the purification of gasolines and aviation kerosenes. The process of demercaptinisation can be carried out by oxidising and extractive methods.

In oxidising mercaptanisation, mercaptans are converted into disulphides which remain dissolved in the gasoline. This type of process includes plumbite and hypochlorite purification, and also purification by cupric chloride, sulphurous dyes etc. The mechanism of plumbite purification is given below.

(1) $2RSH + Na_2PbO_2 \rightarrow RS-Pb-SR + 2NaOH$

(2) $RS-Pb-SR + S \rightarrow RS-SR + PbS$

At the second stage, lead mercaptides $(RS)_2Pb$ are converted into disulphides by a reaction with sulphur. The solution becomes clear because lead mercaptides and disulphides are soluble in the product, while lead sulphides separates as a precipitate.

The solution is renewed after a few days of the operation, and the used solution is regenerated by air blowing.

$$4NaOH + PbS + 2O_2 \rightarrow Na_2PbO_2 + Na_2SO_4 + 2H_2O$$

In extractive processes, mercaptans are extracted from the product and can be used for various purposes. Extractive methods include. (a) Alkali-methanol process (b) Purification by a mixture of sulphuric acid and sulphurous anhydride etc.

STABILIZATION

In many cases even after purification, the petroleum products remain unstable. Stabilisation of petroleum products consists in adding very small amounts of antioxidants or inhibitors which sharply decrease the rate of oxidation of tarry substances, diolefins etc. and in this manner the pctroleum products are made stable for storage. Inhibitors or antioxidants used are phenols, aromatic amines, aminophenols etc.

Chapter 10

REFINING OF PETROLEUM

Approval of refinery.

(1) No person shall refine, crack, reform or blend petroleum unless the project report with specifications and plans showing the general arrangements of tanks, stills, furnaces, electrical installations, pump houses, arrangement for drainage treatment and disposal of effluents, arrangement for fighting fire, fencing gates and all plants and buildings at the place where it is proposed to refine, crack, reform or blend petroleum (hereinafter in this Chapter referred to as the refinery) has been approved by the Chief Controller.

(2) The design and layout of the various block/facilities/process units in new crude oil refineries shall be as per design philosophy given in OISD Standard-118. This will apply to new crude oil refineries/gas processing installations approved by the Chief Controller after publication of this rule.

(3) Any person desiring to refine, crack, reform or blend petroleum shall submit to the Chief Controller an application along with-

(i) a copy of the project report and specifications and plans referred to in sub-rule (1) in triplicate, and

(ii) a scrutiny fee of rupees five thousand paid in the manner specified in rule 13.

(4) The Chief Controller on receiving the project report with specifications and plans may require submission of such further particulars as he may specify after satisfying himself that petroleum can be so refined, cracked, reformed or blended, shall return to the applicant one set of the specifications and plans signed by him and conveying his sanction subject to such conditions as he may specify.

Retention of plans and specifications.

A copy each of the approved plans and specifications and containing any alterations sanctioned under rule 164 from time to time shall be kept at the refinery.

Alteratio:

(1) No alterations in refinery involving the general arrangements or the design of tai stills, furnaces, plants, pump-houses, electric installation or firefighting facilities shall be carried out without the previous sanction in writing of the Chief Controller.

(2) The occupier of a refinery wishing to carry out any of the alterations referred to in sub-rule (1) shall submit to the Chief Controller an application along with-

(i) specifications and plans, in triplicate, showing proposed alterations together with reason therefor, and

(ii) a scrutiny fee of rupees one thousand paid in the manner prescribed in rule 13.

(3) The Chief Controller on receiving the specifications and plans for the alterations and reasons therefor, may require submission of such further particulars as he may specify and after satisfying himself that the proposed alterations can be carried out, return to the applicant one copy of the specifications and plans signed by him and conveying his approval subject to such conditions as he may prescribe.

Use of fire-proof materials.

All buildings and facilities in which petroleum is handled shall be built of fire-proof materials.

Situations of storage tanks.

No storage tanks for petroleum shall be situated nearer than 90 metres to any still, boiler or furnace:

Provided that this rule shall not apply to a storage tank containing petroleum Class C for use as a fuel for a boiler and such a storage tank shall not be larger than is necessary to conserve 24 hours fuel for the fire which it services.

Situation of storage tanks and facilities for liquefied petroleum gases.

No storage tank or filling facility for liquefied petroleum gases shall be nearer than 90 metres to any still, boiler or furnace or nearer than 30 metres to any storage tank, pump-house or any facility for the blending or filling of petroleum or to any protected work.

Situation of flare.

No flare shall be situated nearer than 90 metres to any tank, still, pump-house or any facility for the refining, cracking, reforming, blending, storage or handling of petroleum or liquefied petroleum gas, other than knockout drum and condensate recovery pump attached to such flare.

Drainage.

(1) Adequate arrangements shall be made to ensure that effluents and drainage passing from the refinery does not cause pollution of rivers, irrigation channels, water reservoirs or foreshore and does not harmfully affect animal or vegetable life in any way.

(2) Effluent drainage from pump-houses and all other points where oil may be entrained shall be passed through an efficient oil interceptor system of adequate size.

(3) All chemical waste shall be rendered harmless before they leave the refinery area.

(4) The whole of the sewerage shall be independent of other drainage systems.

(5) All drains shall have adequate capacity to prevent any flooding or backing-up and be of such construction as to prevent leakage from them to the surrounding grounds.

(6) Drains for carrying waste chemicals shall be of a type which is not affected by the chemicals in question.

(7) Trash racks shall be fitted to the drains where there is a possibility of rubbish being carried forward and forming a plug.

(8) Manholes shall be provided in closed drains where there is an abrupt change of directions and also at reasonable intervals in straight sections to permit rodding.

(9) When vents are provided to release gases separated from contaminated effluents in closed drains, they shall be sited where they are unlikely to cause danger or annoyance.

(10) All drains shall be fitted with fire traps/water seals at suitable points to prevent the passage of flame.

(11) Where gas traps are provided in the drains they shall be constructed on the upstream side of the oil interceptors and such gas traps shall be fitted with vents to liberate the gas at such a height that danger or annoyance is not caused.

Fire and Smoking.

(1) No fire furnace, source of heat or light capable of igniting inflammable vapours shall be allowed except in the firing space of stills and boilers.

(2) No smoking shall be allowed except in spaces or buildings specially approved for the purpose by the Chief Controller.

Permits to carry out maintenance and repair work.

(1) No maintenance or repair work and no entry into confined spaces including a closed drain or manhole shall be permitted except under and in accordance with the conditions of a written permit as per OISD Standard-105 issued by a competent person authorised by the occupier of the refinery.

(2) The competent person referred to in sub-rule (1) shall, before issuing the permit, satisfy himself by inspecting and testing, whenever necessary, that the conditions of the vessel, site or equipment are entirely safe for the work which is to be undertaken and shall specify on the permit the conditions under which the work can be carried out safely.

(3) Permits for carrying out maintenance or repair work shall be issued for limited and stated period during which known conditions will remain safe and such permits shall not be renewed without re-inspection and re-testing of the vessel, site or equipment.

(4) All gas tests for the purpose of issuing a permit shall be carried out by suitably trained persons by an instrument which is calibrated and checked at such intervals as are recommended in this behalf by the manufacturers of such instruments in the manual of instruction pertaining thereto.

(5) In the case of vessels which had contained products blended with leaded fluid, the regulations laid down by the suppliers of the fluid shall be fully observed.

Fire Control.

(1) Every crude oil refinery shall be fully protected against fire by a well organised and trained fire fighting service with necessary materials and fixed, mobile and portable equipments for fighting fires in line with the Oil Industry Safety Directorate's Standard-116. This will apply to new crude oil refineries/ gas processing installation approved by the Chief Controller after publication of this rule.

(2) An adequate supply of water shall be available at all strategic points in the refinery by means of an independent ring main or grid provided with isolating valves. The main shall be kept constantly pressurized by two or more boosting pumps of adequate capacity preferably working automatically as any significant loss of pressure in the main occurs. At least one of the boosting pumps shall be independent of the normal power supply.

(3) All mains shall be fitted with hydrants at convenient places not more than thirty metres apart in hazardous areas and not more than 45 metres apart in non-hazardous area. Such hydrants shall be of design suitable for operating conditions and for connecting mobile pumps.

(4) Static water supply of adequate capacity shall be provided where mains water supply may be subject to interference.

(5) All refinery personnel shall be practiced in the use of first-aid, fire-fighting appliances and selected refinery personnel shall be trained in all aspects of fire-fighting.

(6) The Chief Controller may relax any of the provisions of sub-rules (1) to (5) or require additional fire-fighting provisions to be made if he deems such relaxation or additional fire-fighting provisions necessary in respect of any class of refinery.

Removal of Petroleum.

All petroleum as it leaves the stills with the exception of such quantities as may be pumped direct to service tanks for fuel, shall at once be pumped out into the refinery storage tanks and shall not be stored in the immediate neighbourhood of stills and boilers:

Provided that the Chief Controller may permit petroleum to be disposed of otherwise.

Prevention of danger from static electricity.

Adequate provision shall be made to prevent accumulation of dangerous static charge of electricity.

Warning notices.

(1) Warning notices regarding prevention of unauthorised person, naked lights, smoking and other hazards shall be displayed prominently at strategic locations in the refinery.

(2) No fireworks of any kind shall be carried out within a radius of one kilometre from the refinery except with the prior permission of District Magistrate.

Marking of pipelines and cables.

(1) All above-ground pipelines and cables shall be identified by taping, stenciling, colouring distinctively or by any other suitable methods.

(2) All overhead pipelines and cables crossing roads shall be adequately protected against accidental damage.

(3) Pipelines and valves at loading and discharging berths shall be prominently marked to identify the product.

(4) The route of all underground cables shall be marked by prominent markers. At least two such markers shall be visible from any point on the route of the cable.

(5) The route of all underground pipelines shall be marked by prominent markers or by any other effective means to prevent accidental damage to the pipelines.

Inspections.

All plants, instruments and equipments including fire-fighting equipment shall be inspected and tested at intervals, the frequency depending on practical or other relevant factors, and records of all such inspections shall be maintained.

Safe operations.

(1) All operators employed in a refinery shall be adequately trained in the safe operation of plants and equipment.

(2) Written procedures shall be established for operators to start up, shut down and gas-free plants or sections of plants safely and to take safe action under emergency conditions.

(3) Checks shall be made at all stages of the operations by supervisors to ensure that vessels and equipments are properly isolated or connected up, as required, and to ensure that safety facilities are commissioned as the operation proceeds.

Report of fire.

The occurrence of any fire in refinery shall be reported immediately by the person in-charge of the refinery for the time being to the Chief Controller and to the nearest police station.

Closing of refinery.

If refinery is closed down, the area within the fence surrounding it shall be cleared of all petroleum having flash point below 93 degree C as soon as possible.

Chapter 11

TESTING OF PETROLEUM

Drawing of sample.

(1) In all cases, the sampling officer shall personally superintend the drawing of the sample and the sample shall be drawn in the presence of at least one witness. Where the sample is drawn from an original unopened receptacle containing petroleum otherwise than in bulk the opening shall be sufficient to admit of the sample being rapidly transferred from the receptacle.

(2) Two bottles, each of a capacity of 1 litre shall be filled to nine-tenths of their capacity with the sample and corked. The corks shall be driven home and cut-off level with the neck; and melted sealing wax shall be worked into the corks and the bottles shall be efficiently sealed.

(3) In the case of petroleum imported into India the bottles containing the samples shall, after being sealed, be labelled with the name of the consignee, particulars of the ship or vehicle by which it is imported and such other distinguishing marks as may be necessary.

Forwarding and retention of samples.

One of the bottles referred to in subrule (2) or rule 186 shall be preserved for reference in case of need and the other shall be forwarded to the testing officer.

Procedure of delivery of samples.

(1) When the master of, or the agent for, a ship or the agent of the importer has made the declaration required under rule 17 or rule 26, the sampling officer shall obtain samples of all the petroleum which is intended to land at the port or place of import. If the importer so desires, the sampling officer shall also take samples of all the petroleum which is intended to land at any other port or place of import in India:

Provided that no sample need be taken of petroleum if it is declared to be the petroleum Class A.

(2) The master of ship or the person for the time being in-charge of the vehicle by which petroleum is imported shall deliver to the sampling officer, without charge, samples of every variety of petroleum comprised in the

petroleum of which samples are to be taken under sub-rule (1). Such samples shall, if the sampling officer so requires, be taken from the particular receptacles indicated by him:

Provided that when the petroleum is in cases, samples shall be taken as the landing proceeds.

Selection of samples from imported cargo.

The minimum number of samples to be selected from each brand or quality contained in the cargo to the imported shall be as follows:

(i) in cases-one sample for every 10,000 cases or part thereof;

(ii) in casks or drums, declared to be uniform quality-one sample for every 600 kilolitres or part thereof;

(iii) in bulk or in tanks-one sample from each tank or tank compartment.

Standard test apparatus.

The standard test apparatus shall-

(a) agree in every respect with the Indian Standard Specification No. IS-1448 (Part I): (P 20) or (P 21) as applicable and for the unit being in force; and

(b) have been tested and certified by an officer appointed by the Central Government under sub-section (1) of section 15 of the Act.

Certification of apparatus.

(1) When any apparatus for determining the flash point of petroleum is submitted to the officer appointed under sub-section (1) of section 15 of the Act for comparison with the standard test apparatus, the officer shall examine the apparatus including the thermometers and the barometers or aneroid.

(2) No certificate shall be granted under section 16 of the Act if the apparatus, any thermometer or barometer is in any respect outside the tolerances laid down or variations permitted under the Indian Standard Specification No. IS-1448 (Part-1): (P 20) or (P 21), as applicable, and for the time being in force.

(3) A certificate in Form IV shall be granted in respect of any apparatus which has been found to agree with the standard test apparatus within the limits specified in IS-1448 (Part I) (P 20) (P 21) was applicable and for the time being in force.

(4) A certificate granted under this rule shall be valid for a period of three years.

Register of certificates.

A register of all certificates granted under rule 191 shall be maintained in Form V by the officer appointed under sub-section (1) of section 15 of Act.

Method of test.

(1) The testing officer shall test the samples in the manner laid down in the Indian Standard Specification No. IS-1448 (Part I); (P 20) or (P 21), as applicable, and for the time being in force.

(2) In all cases at least three samples shall be separately tested, the average of the three readings being corrected for the thermometer correction, if any, and for the barometric correction in case of dispute.

(3) If the average flash point is not lower than 23°C, the whole of the petroleum represented by the samples shall be deemed to be petroleum Class B or petroleum Class C according to the average flash point determined by the test.

(4) If the petroleum to be tested is viscous or solid or contains sediments or thickening ingredients, such petroleum shall be tested in accordance with the methods specified in the Fifth Schedule.

Procedure when tests show want of uniformity.

(1) If the testing officer after testing samples taken from an imported cargo, considers further testing necessary to satisfy himself that none of the petroleum is petroleum Class A, he shall report to the Commissioner of Customs accordingly.

(2) On receipt of a report under sub-rule (1)-

(a) when the consignment is imported in cases or casks or drums, the Commissioner of Customs shall cause the petroleum in question to be landed and stacked in lots of not more than 1,500 cases or casks or drums each, or to be discharged into boats each containing not more than 1,500 cases, casks or drums, and the sampling officer shall select and deliver to the testing officer one sample from each lot.

(b) when the consignment is imported in bulk, the sampling officer shall forward a second sample and Commissioner of Customs may, until the receipt of the testing officer's further report, prevent the landing of any portion of the contents of the tank in question or may permit it to be landed as provided under rule 21.

(c) if the petroleum has already been landed and stored under rule 21-

(i) if it is otherwise than in bulk it shall be divided into lots, and samples of each lot shall be selected as provided in clause (a); (ii) if it is in bulk, samples shall be drawn from each separate storage tank containing the petroleum.

Certificate of tests.

(1) The testing officer shall, as soon as practicable, and ordinarily within twenty-four hours after receipt of samples make out a certificate in Form VI and shall forward it in the case of samples, of petroleum taken on board a

ship or a vehicle by which petroleum is imported to the Commissioner of Customs and in the case of other samples to the officer submitting the sample.

(2) The testing officer shall, at the request of any person concerned furnish him with a certified copy of the certificate in Form VI on payment of a fee of rupees two hundred.

Fee for inspection and comparison.

(1) The fee for each inspection of the standard test apparatus shall be rupees one hundred.

(2) The fee for comparing a privately owned test apparatus with the standard test apparatus shall be as follows:-

	(in Rupees)
Test apparatus	800
Barometer	200
Thermometer	100

Fee for testing.

(1) The fee for testing each sample of petroleum shall be rupees five hundred:

Provided that the aggregate fees chargeable under this sub-rule shall not, in the case of any single consignment of petroleum in any one ship, other vessel, train or place, exceed rupees one thousand.

(2) The fee for re-testing each sample under section 20 of the Act shall be rupees one thousand. It shall be refunded if the original test is proved to be erroneous.

Power to enter, inspect, search and seize.

(1) Any, officer, specified in column (1) of the table below may within the jurisdiction specified in the corresponding entry in column 2 of the said table-

(a) enter, inspect and search any place where he has reason to believe that any petroleum is being imported, transported, stored, produced, refined or blended or is under transport and inspect all receptacles, plants and appliances used in connection therewith in order to ascertain if they are in accordance with provisions of the Act and of these rules;

(b) search for petroleum therein;

(c) take samples for testing of any petroleum found therein and make payments by cash for value of samples taken; and

(d) seize, detain and .remove any petroleum or any material suspected to be petroleum or any equipment or appliances used therein together with connected documents thereof in respect of which he has reasons to believe that any of the provisions of the act or of these rules have been contravened.

TABLE

Designation of the Officer	Unit or Jurisdiction
(1)	(2)
Chief Controller & Controller	Whole of India
All District Magistrates	Their respective Districts
All Magistrates subordinate to District Magistrate	Their respective Jurisdiction
Police Officer not below the rank of an Inspector	The area over which their authority extends

(2) Whenever any officer other than the Chief Controller, seizes, detains or removes any petroleum or any material connected therewith or any connected documents thereof under this rule, he shall forthwith report the fact by telegram to the Chief Controller and Controller having jurisdiction over the place where seizure, etc., has taken place and whenever any officer not being the district authority seizes, detains or removes any petroleum or any material connected therewith or any connected documents thereof under this rule, he shall intimate the facts of the case to the Chief Controller and the Controller having jurisdiction.

(3) Whenever any samples are taken in accordance with this rule, they shall be tested in accordance with the relevant provisions of Chapter X of these rules.

(4) Whenever any petroleum is seized under this rule, it shall be stored, under adequate guard until examination by Chief Controller or Controller and receipt of instructions from him as to its disposal.

(5) Whenever searches are made under this rule the same shall be carried out in accordance with the provisions of the Code of Criminal Procedure, 1973 (2 of 1974). All officers of the police and district authorities shall assist the Chief Controller in the execution of the Act and rules.

(6) Whenever any person by himself or any person in his employment voluntarily obstructs or offers any resistance to or otherwise interferes with or refuses or fails to give or wilfully gives false or misleading information to the officer duly appointed under this rule who is acting in accordance with his duty thereunder such person shall be deemed to have committed an offence under the Act.

Destruction of petroleum.

The Chief Controller or Controller may destroy any petroleum or any material or equipment connected in respect of which the Chief Controller or Controller has reason to believe that any of the provisions of the Act or of these rules have been contravened or which in his opinion is no longer fit for storage, transport or use. The petroleum shall be destroyed at the expenses of the licensee or the occupier of the premises, as the case may be.

Chapter 12

APPLICATIONS OF LUBRICATING AGENTS

Lubrication is an essential feature of all modern machinery and has been throughout the ages. The first authenticated use of lubricants is found in the relics of ancient Egypt. It is possible that the massive stones of the pyramids were flated into place on thin semi-fluid layers of mortar. The colossi of the same period were dragged over the yielding sand on logs of wood used as sliders, not rollers.

Solid Lubricants

A solid lubricants, as the name implied, is any solid material, which reduces the mechanical interaction between surfaces that are in relative motion against the action of a load.

Types of Solid Lubricant Systems

Lubricant Powders

The mechanism by which solids reduce friction and wear are still no completely resolved. Graphite and molybdenum disulphide are the most common substances in gereral use and both posses the lamellar structure, which is typical of many solid lubricants. Powders can be supplied to moving surfaces dispersed in a carrier gas stream.

Resin Bonded Dry Films

In this form, the lubricating solid is bonded to one or two of the substrates by a resin system. This serves to increase the adhesion of the solid to the surface, particularly during the early life of the solid to the surface, and also provides a reservior of lubricant to replenish meterial lost during operation. This is the most common form fo dry film lubrication. The lubricant/resin system is normally used in the form of dispersion in a volatile carrier and is applied by brush, drip or spray.

Dry Film with Inorgabic Binders

The maxiumum operating temperature of resin bonded systems is generally limited by the thermal instability of the binder. In order to extend the operating range, inorganic materials, such as silicates and cermics, have been introduced in place of the resin. These binders freqently allow periods of operation above the oxidations temperature of the lubricant by restricting the rate at which oxidation occurs.

Dispersions in Non Volatile Carrier

These generally consist of finely divided particles of solid lubricant in the form of a stable dispersion in oils, synthetic fludis or greases. Such systems are freqyently used to fortify conventional lubricants.

Wear Reducing Solids

These materials are not normally classed a lubricants since they do not reduce the coefficient of friction to low level. However, they do allow surfaces to side without severe seizure, as in the case of oxide films. For prolonged operation above the oxidation temperature of conventional solid lubricants, ceramic surface coating or components machined from solid ceramic will provide stable bearing with a useful life.

Soft Metal Films

A thin layer of a soft metal or alloy on a hard substrate will reduce the coefficent of friction and wear rate by virtue of alow shear strength coupled with a low area of contact.

Plastic Lubricants

Some thermoplastics are able to reduce the friction and wear between moving surfaces, provided the loads are not high. Polyterafluoroethylene is probably the best example. It can be applied to sufaces in the form of a dispersion to provide a dry lubricanting film. Alternatively the plastic can be incorporated into the bearing during manufacture.

Chemical Reaction Films

Lubricating surfaces may be formed or replenished by chemical reaction with the sliding surfaces using either gaseous or solution techniqes. Hydrogen suplhide will react with molybdenum disulphide film and some halogen substituted hydrocarbon vapours will produce lubricating layers on steel. Photosphating of steel is widley used to assist lubrication.

Synthetic Lubricants

The American Society for Testing Materials (ASTM) definition for synthetic lubricant is : A synthetic lubricant is a product, which consists of stocks manufactured by chemical synthesis and containing necessary performance additive. The base stocks are tailored through molecular restructuring to meet predetermined physical and chemical qualities.

The demand for lubricants of improved performance has been created principally by developments in aviation, initially by requirements of military aircraft in World War II and then, especially with the increasing use of gas turbine engines, in civil aircraft.

With continued development of both military and civil aircrafts of higher speeds and performance, the need for lubricants and hydraulic fluids capable of withstanding greater extremes of temperature and also giving less fire hazard is still increasing. In addition to aircraft uses, a considerable stimulus to the development of synthetic lubricants has from military requirements in missile and weapon development as well as in naval craft and military vehicles.

Industrial uses of synthetic lubricants have tended to follow military uses. Of particular importance are their uses as fire resistant hydraulic fluids, automotive brake fluids and lubricants for extreme environment applications.

Economic disparity with mineral oils has tended to inhibit commercial development of synthetic lubricants other than for military use, but gradually their value is being recognised in extending the design and application of lubricatred mechanisms generally.

Apart from the ability to lubricate rubbing surface, a good lubricant must has some or all of the following attributes. It must :

Be chemically inert and have good oxidation and thermal stability.

Be resistant to degradation by mechanical shearing force and preferably be highly incompressible.

Have good viscosity characteristics, i.e., it must have the correct room temperature viscosity and exhibit a small change of viscosity with temperature.

Have a low pour point for low temperature application and remain stable and non volatile for high temperature applications.

Be compatible with and have little effect on materials of construction including metal and non-metallic materials such as seal and flexible hose elastomers.

Be non-corrosive and non-toxic.

Preferably be non-inflammable and for some applications, resistant to nuclear radiation.

The classes of chemical compounds or polymers, which are selected as synthetic lubricants, usually give some sign of hav ing some of the desirable physical and chemical properties.Within a class of compounds or polymers, considerable variation within the individual members of the class is usually possible by using different substitute groups in the basic chemical structure formula and by changing the molecular weight.

By this way, it is possible to choose base lubricant stocks having primarily the required bulk properties of chemical inertness and stability to heat and oxidation, a high boiling point and low freezing point, and also essentially the best viscosity/temperature characteristics.

Variations of structure and molecular weight within the class will generally permit adjustments of viscosity and other properties, but more flexibility in adjustment of properties is obtained by the use of additives.

The finished synthetic lubricant will contain a base stock, additive to impart certain performance characteristics and may contain a carrier for the additives. Should the carrier be a mineral oil, the mineral oil content should be no higher than 10 to 15% of the lubrianct, if it is to be considered a true synthetic product.

Synthetic lubricating oils are relatively pure compounds made by chemical synthesis, most often from petroleum based hydrocarbons. While the use of synthetic lubricants as motor oils in the retail market is new, synthetics have been used for many years in special aviation and industrial applications, where the oils are subjected to extremely high temperatures or a flammable environment. Mineral oils would not be suitable for these applications.

Synthetic lubricants are generally much more costly than mineral lubricating oils. The base fluids can be classified as follows :

1. Synthesised hydrocarbon fluids (SHF)

   Aromatics
   Polybutene
   Cycloaliphatics

2. Esters
   Diabasic acid esters
   Phosphate esters
   Silicate esters

3. Ethers
   Polyethylene glycol ether
   Polyphenyl ether

4. Other silicones

5. Halogenated fluids

Application Areas

Generally, all lubricants are meant to reduce friction, temperature and wear, to control corrosion and to remove contaiminants. In addition, lubricants perform specialised functions such as to transmit power as in hydraulics and as seals like in case of grease. Synthetic lubricants can be justified when one or more of the above functions are no longer performed suitably by mineral oils. Major applications of synthetic fluids in the modern world are as follows :

Polyaphaolefins

Engine, gear, turbine and compressor oils, grease, hydraulic and power steering fluids.

Dialkylbenzes

Engine, gear, turbine and hydraulic oils and greases.

Organic esters

Engine, gear, turbine and compressor, hydraulic and jet engine oils and greases.

Polyglycols

Fire resistance fluids, brake fluids, gear oils, circulating oils, gas compressor oils and greases.

Phosphate esters

Fire resistant fluids.

Table 1: Principal Classes of Synthetic Lubricants

Class	Typical Structural Formula
Polybutene	$(-CH_2-CH_2-CH_2-CH_2-)n$
Diester	$C_8H_{17}-O-CO-C_5H_{16}-CO-O-C_8H_1$
Polyglycol	$HO\,(-CH_2-CH(CH_3)-O-)_nH$
Chlorinated hydrocarbon	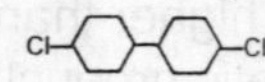
Chlorofluorocarbon	
Polyphenyl ether	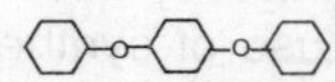
Neopentylpolyol ester	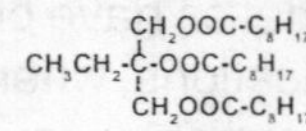
Silicon	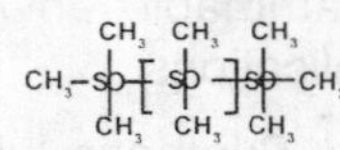

Automotive applications

Automotive engine oils are one of the largest potential uses for synthetic luids. Polyaphaolefins and organic esters are widely employed as base fluids for enginelubricants.

The superioer qualities of these synthetics form the basis for these diverse engine lubricants and provide the following benefits :

Fuel saving between 2.8 and 4.3%.

Outstanding engine wear protection and cleanliness in both petrol and diesel car engines.

Excellent results in turbocharger passenger air engines.

Easier cold starting and faster oil flow to critical parts during start up.

Good engine response and smooth running operation.

Provides outstanding engine protection for up to 25000 km or 1 year oil changer.

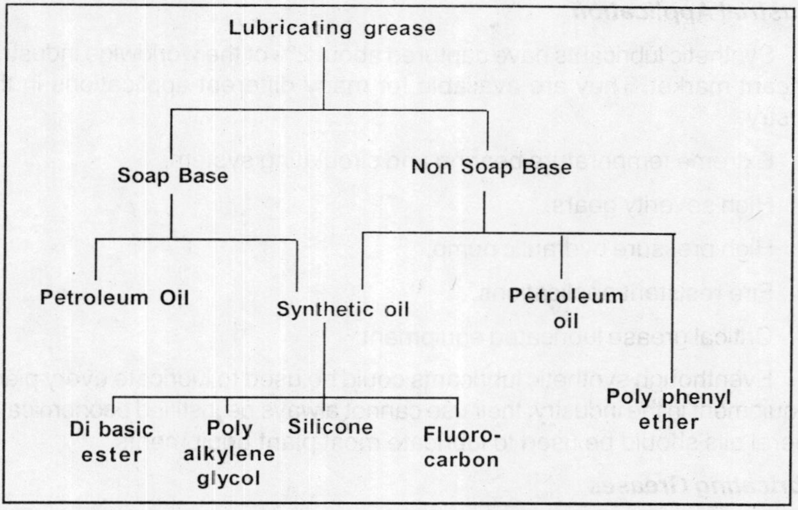

Fig. 1 : Classification of Lubricating Greases

The synthetic oil proeprties, which provide these benefits are :

Very high natural viscosity index (7/50).

Very low pour point (-54°C)

Excellent thermal and oxidation stability with additives.

Good rust and corrosion protection.

High load carrying capacity.

Fully compatible with conventional mineral oils.

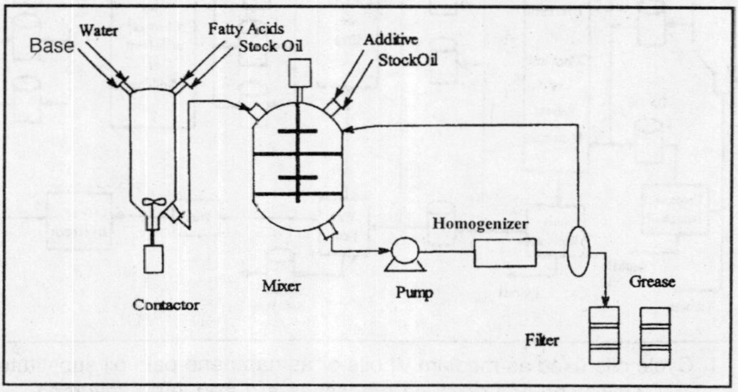

Fig. 2 : Traditional Method of Manufacturing Greases

Industrial Application

Synthetic lubricants have captured about 2% of the worldwide industrial lubricant market. They are available for many different applications in the industry.

Extreme temperature bearing and circulating system.

High severity gears.

High pressure hydraulic pump.

Fire resistant applications.

Critical grease lubricated equipment.

Eventhough synthetic lubricants could be used to lubricate every piece of equipment in the industry, their use cannot always be justified economically. Mineral oils should be used to lubricate most plant equipments.

Lubricating Greases

The amount of lubricating grease used in the industry is small, compared with the amount of lubricating oil used. The comparatively complex nature of grease, however, has promoted much reserach. The technology of grease manufecture is largely concerened with means of economically and homogeneously dispersing the thickner or gelling agent in the liquid phase.

Fundamental knowledge on the nature of the grease system has increased rapidly in the past decade and studies with the electron microscope, in particular, have contributed greatly to understanding,

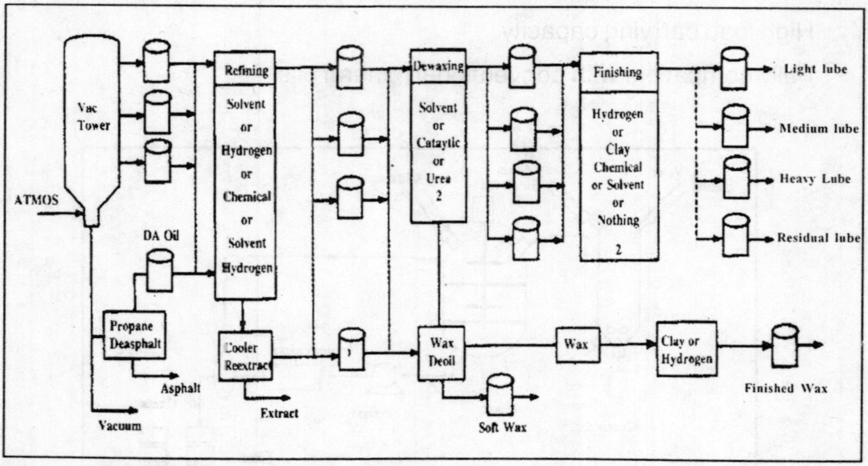

1. Cycle oils used as medium VI oils or as napthene pale oil substitutes
2. Dewaxing and finishing processes are frequently reversed

Fig . 3 : Process Flow for Manufacture of Paraffinic Lube Oils

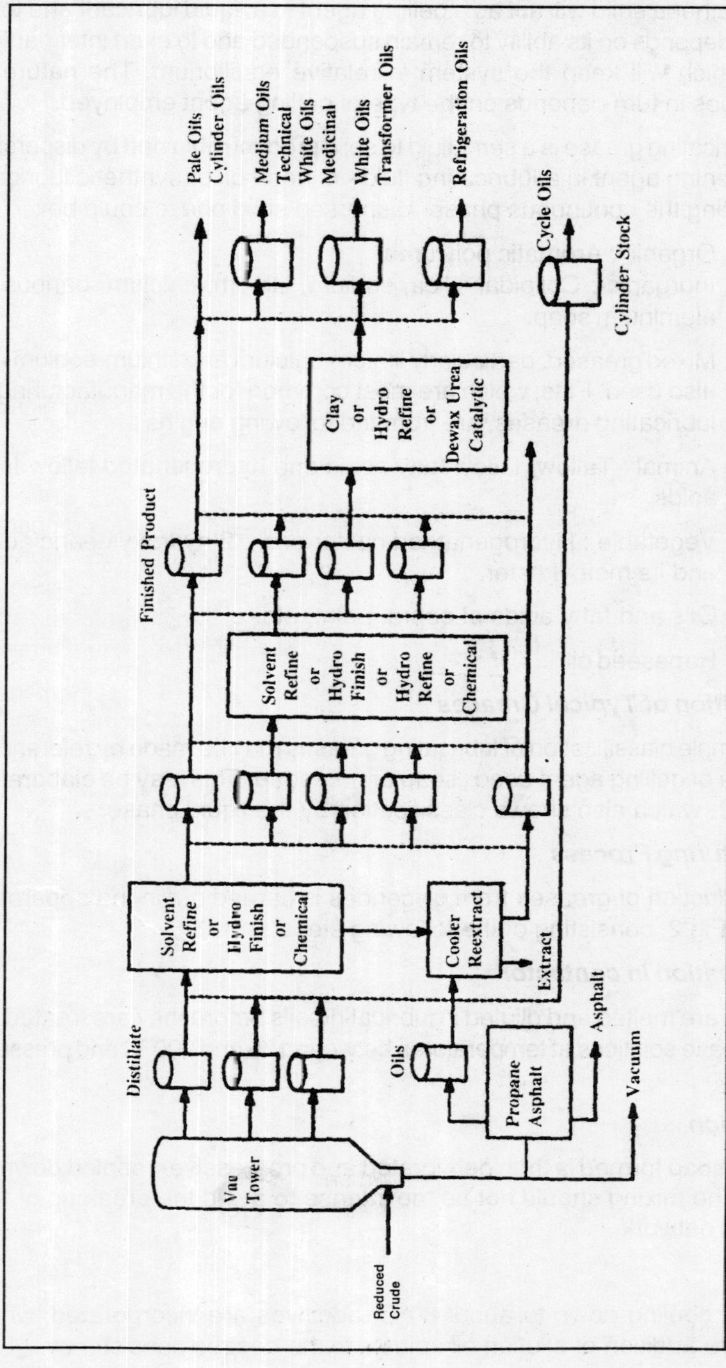

Fig. 4. Process flow for Manufacture of Naphthenic Lube Oils.

Whether a solid will act as a gelling agent in a liquid lubricant and form a grease depends on its ability to remain suspended and to exert inter particle forces, which will keep the system in relative equilibrium. The nature of these forces in turn depends on the type of gelling agent employed.

Lubricating grease is a semi-fluid to solid product, obtained by dispersion of a thickening agent in a lubricating fluid - mineral oil or synthetic lubricant - constituting the continuous phase. Dispersed solid phase could be :

- Organic : Aromatic poly urea.
- Inorganic : Colloidal silica, sodium, lithium, calcium, barious or aluminium soap.
- Mixed greased, particularly lithium-calcium and lithium-sodium are also used. Fats, which are most common for the manufacturing of lubricating greases, are from the following origins :
- Animal : Tallow, tallow fatty acids and hydrogenated tallow fatty acids.
- Vegetable : Hydrogenatged castor oils, 12 hydroxystearic acids and its methyl ester.
- Oils and fatty acids of copra, palm, etc.
- Rapeseed oil.

Composition of Typical Greases

A simple classification of lubricating greases may be made by references to the type of gelling agent used : soap or non-soap. This may be elaborated as in Fig.1. which also shows classification by the liquid phase.

Manufacturing Process

Production of greases from glycerides is carried out in the apparatus shown in Fig.2. consisting of the following steps :

Saponification in contactor

Fats are melted and diluted in lubricating oils before they are treated by aqueous base solutions at temperatures between 175 and 200°C and pressure of 10 bars.

Dehydration

The soap formed is then dehydrated and progressively cooled down in a mixer. The mixing should not be too intense to avoid the break up of the fibrous gel network.

Cooling

After cooling down to about 80°C, additives are incorporated, while progressive addition of dilution oil adjusts to the desired consistency.

Milling, filtering, deaeration

To homogenize perfectly the soap dispersion grease is "smoothed out" in mills with a grinding wheel set at a distance of 50 to 250 mm, or extruded by draw plates of smaller diameter. But the rolling of grease induces intorduction of air bubbles, which must be eliminated under vacuum.

Grease Formulations and Evaluation

Despite intensive research on grease in recent times, it its still barely possible to define requirements for specific applications, particularly rolling bearing lubricants. The method of processing also has such an important effect on the quality and behaviour of grease that development of a formulation is still to a large extent empirical. However, from experience, it is possible to eliminate some obviously unsuitable formulations and to restrict the area of investigation.

Temperature requirement may narrow the choice to small number of gelling agents and liquid lubricants. The need for additives to perform specific functions may also be self-evident. A limited number of promising types may then be slected for investigation. The first requirement is appropriate laboratory scale processes of manufacture, which, if the formulation shows promise, can be translated to plant scale.

Grease so prepared experimentally must be evaluated by appropriate test methods before a decision can be made to attempt manufacture on a plant scale with a view to field trials. In some cases, however, new methods are involved, which require manufacture of apparatus, development of skills in operation and possibly correlation programs to ensure adequate precision.

Promising formulations may be examined on a larger scale by processing in pilot units of about one tenth of main plant capacity. Such an intermediate stage can produce enough grease for field tests, with a fair probability of good reproduction on main plant scale.

Laboratory evaluation of experimental grease can be a lengthy and costly process. In addition to simple standard tests such as consistency, drop point and oil separation, performance tests, mechanical stability tests, corrosion tests, water resistance tests and others, which are time consuming for production control, may also be conducted.

Lubricating Oils

Manufacturing processes

The manufacture of mineral lubricating oil base stocks consists of five basic steps :

- Distillation

- Deasphalting to prepare the feed stocks.
- Solvent or hydrogen refining to improve viscosity index and quality.
- Solvent or catalytic dewaxing to remove wax and to improve the low temperature properties of paraffiic lubes.
- Clay or hydrogen finishing to improve colour, stability and quality of the lube base stock.

Fig. 3 and 4 are simplified processing diagrams showing some of the ways these processes are combined to manufacture paraffinic and naphthenic lube base stocks and byproducts, respectively. The finished lube base stocks are blended with each other and/or with additives using batch and continuous methods to prepare fully formulated lubricants.

The most common route is the mixed processing route, which consists of solvent refinishing, solvent dewaxing and hydrogen finishing, although a few refiners still use the solvent and clay processing route or the hydrogen refinishing and solvent dewaxing route. The all-hydrogen processing (lube hydro cracking, catalytic dewaxing and hydro refinishing) route is used by few refiners for the manufacture of limited number of paraffin base oils.

Mineral Lubricating Oils

The low cost and available large volume of mineral oils derived from petroleum crude oil makes them the most widely used of all lubricants. The lubricating oil base stocks contain a mixture of the many different hydrocarbons naturally present in crude oil. The base stocks can be placed into three general classes :

- Paraffin, having a high viscosity index (90-100) with a pour point of 0 to 20°F.
- Naphthenic, with a low viscosity index (0-40) and a low pour point of - 50-20°F.
- Lube base stocks having an intermediate viscosity index prepared from paraffinic and naphthenic mixed base crude oils with inherent qualities between the two extremes of paraffinic and naphthenic crudes.

Automotive Gear Oils

In automotive equipment, there are various types of gears to be lubricated in addition to automatic transmission. These include manual transmission, gearboxes, differentials and universal Joints.

Because of the difference in design and in service conditions, there are a number of gear lubricants, each formulated to satisfy a specific requirement. Some gears are operated under light loads, in which case an oxygenation inhibited mineral oil is adequate.

The viscosity of a gear lubricant has some effect on load carrying capacity, leakage and gear noise. At low temperature , viscosity determines the ease of gear shifting and has considerable influence on the flow of the lubricant to bearings and to gear tooth surfaces Higher viscosity grades, which are expected to operate at higher temperatures and do not require as good cold fluidity properties, are defined by viscosity ranges at 212°F.

In addition to providing the proper lubrication properties, the additives used in gear oils provide protection against deterioration in storage, oxidation, foaming, corrosion and rusting.

Chapter 13

FORMULATIONS AND COMPOUNDING OF LUBRICANTS

Introduction

Since oil is the primary ingredient in a lubricant formulation, the choice of such oil is the first step insetting up a formula. With a given specification or requirement, the factors to consider in selection of an oil are -

Availability, cost, viscosity, degree of refinement, temperature characteristics, or compatibility with other ingredients or with the materials with which it may come in contact.

Additives for Straight Mineral Oil Gear Lubricants

All gear oils should contain a foam inhibitor, probably in the range of 5 to 10 parts per million. In order to arrive at approximately the correct proportion of such an additive, it is best to use a concentrate. This may be a 10 per cent dispersion of a dimethyl silicone in either kerosene or carbon tetrachloride.

For special applications other types of additives may also be found necessary in what can be classed as straight mineral oils.

Formulation of Open or Exposed Lubricants

Open gear lubricants are most often composed of asphaltic materials which may not be blended with lubricating oils.

Ingredients	%
Lead naphthenate	7
Chloronaphtha xanthate	6
Butyl stearate	1
Mixture of 40% pale oil and 60% asphalt	86
Total	100

Formulation of mild type E.P. Lubricants

Formulation of mild type E.P. lubricants contain 5 per cent or more of lead and 2 to 3 percent of sulphurized lard oil. The fact should be confirmed that the lead soap will stay in solution or suspension in the oils chosen. In order to insure such solubility, various solubilizing agents are sometimes added to the blends. Oleic acid or an alkyl phenol in proportions of 1 to 2 percent have been suggested for this purpose. Likewise 2 per cent or more of the extract from solvent refining of lubricating oil has been used.

Aircraft Lubricants

The ideal jet-engine lubricant would be one which would serve both turbo-jets and turbo-props irrespective of the source of the engine.

In formulating aircraft turbine lubricants, the first requirement is a satisfactory base fluid. These include di-(2 ethylhexyl) sebacate, dicotyl sebacate, di-(3, 5, 5-trimethylhexyl) sebacate, or dinonyl sebacate.

A typical formulation for a jet turbine lubricant is as follows:

Ingredients	Purpose	Percent
Dodecylamine dodecyl acid Phosphate	E.P. agent	0.12
Dodecyl dihydrogen phosphae	E.P. agent	0.08
Tricresyl phosphate	Anti-wear agent	2.0
Phenyl alpha naphthylamine	Oxidation inhibitor	1.0
Quinzarin	Metal deactivator	0.02
Dimethyl silicone	Anti-foam agent	0.001
and poly 1,2, Oxypropylene glycol		96.78

Miscellaneous Formulations

Aluminium Based Lubricants

Ingredient	kgs.
Petroleum oil	95
Powdered aluminium	5
Total	100

Antimony Based Lubricants

Ingredient	*lbs.*
Petroleum oil	45
Tallow	67
Black antimony	1
Gum camphor	1

Copper Based Lubricants

	Ingredient	Parts by wt.
(i)	Oil of tar	10 kg.
	Powdered copper	10 kg.
	Petroleum oil	10 kg.
	Graphite	2 kg.
	Powdered mica or soap stone	20 kg.
	Tallow or stearin	50 kg.
(ii)	Copper powder	1 kg.
	Petrolatum	1 lit.
	Lubricating oil	1 lit.

Mercury Based Lubricants

Ingredient	*lbs.*
Mercury	16
Sulphur	40
Tallow	1
Lard	16

Mica Based Lubricants

	Parts by wt.	
Ingredients	For high temp.	For low temp
Mica	1	0.2
Chalk	1	1
Tallow	2	1

Sulphur Based Lubricants

Ingredient	lbs.
Sulphur	3 gal.
Sodium chloride	5 gal.
Lard oil	1 gal.

Zinc Based Lubricants

Ingredient	% by wt.
Zinc oxide	40

	Lead oxide	40
	Olive oil	10
	Gourd core oil	10

Glycerine Based Lubricants

	Ingredient	Parts by wt.
(i)	Ethylene glycol	63
	Water	30
	Polyglycol ether	7
	Total	100
(ii)	Ethylene glycol	52
	Polyethylene glycol ether	6
	Water	25
	Neutral sulphuric ester of vicinoleic acid	16

	Ingredient	*Parts by vol.*
(iii)	Ethylene glycol	28
	Butanol	12
	50% aqueous solution of a neutral sulphuric ester of ricinoleic acid	20

Asbestos Based Lubricants

	Ingredient	%
(i)	Natural asbestos	5-50
	Lubricating oil or grease	90-38.5
	Ground borax	1.5-2.5
	Granular soapstone	2.5-10

	Ingredient	*Qty.*
(ii)	Tar	1 oz.
	Rosin	6 ozs.
	Plumbago	6 ozs.
	Glauber's salt	1 oz.
	Tallow	3 ozs.
	Petroleum oil	1 gal.
(iii)	Powdered graphite	28 lbs.
	Turpentine	50 gallons
	Lubricating oil	50 gallons
	Creosote Oil	50 gallons
	Ether	5 lbs.
(iv)	Graphite	1 oz.
	Camphor	1 oz.
	Carbon disulfide	2 ozs.

	Engine oil	1 quart
	Light hydrocarbon oil	3 quart
	Ingredient	*Parts by wt.*
(v)	Graphite	8
	Oil of citronella	1
	Castor oil	16
	Turpentine	96

Graphite Based Lubricants

1. Stick Form

Ingredient	
Ozokerite	30
Beeswax	13
Rosin	10
Castor oil	5
Graphite	33
Carbon black	9
Total	100

The rosin and castor oil mixture is stirred over direct heat unt€ a clear liquid results, which is poured into the waxes that have been melted by hot water or steam heat. The pigments are stirred in, heating is continued, and when a smooth cream is obtained, the heating is stopped and cooling allowed to proceed until i! becomes viscous. Then it can be poured into cold moulds of the hinge type.

2. Paste Form

Ingredient	*Parts by Wt.*
Paraffin wax	10
Candelilla wax	10
Graphite	20
Naphtha	59
Lavender Oil	1
Total	100

The waxes are melted by hot water or steam and poured into the naphtha, which has been heated to the same temperature as the wax and in a similar manner.

The graphite and perfume oil are stirred into this and kept hot until a smooth slurry results, when heating can be stopped. When cooling has proceeded to the point where stirring is difficult, the mixture can be poured into tin cans to cool and set.

Liquid Graphite Lubricant

	Ingredient	*Parts by Wt.*
(i)	Asphalt (By product)	11
	Asphalt (Gilsonite)	6
	Paraffin wax	10
	Naphtha	25
	Graphite	20
	Carbon Tetrachloride	25
	Oil soluble nigrosine	3
	Total	100

The natural asphalt is first crushed and heated until it can be stirred, then the by product asphalt is poured in and heating continued until a homogeneous liquid results. The paraffin is then added and after it has melted, the container is removed from the flame and the naphtha stirred in. When it is homogenous, the black liquid is passed through a screen to remove coarse minerals always present in gilsonite. In the meantime, the graphite and nigrosine are soaking in the carbon tetrachloride, and when both containers are at room temperature, the contents are mixed and are ready for packaging. In view of the fact that graphite forms aggregates or lumps in mixtures, where water is absent, it might settle to the bottom on long standing and not be redispersed with vigorous shaking. However, the paraffins present in this mixture have a thickening effect and offset settling.

	Ingredient	*Parts by wt.*
(ii)	Rosin	7
	Crude montan wax	2
	Naphtha	2
	Caustic soda	1
	Water	70
	Nigrosine	3
	Graphite	12
	Lamp black	3
	Total	100

Grease for Pressure Lubricants

Ingredient	*Parts by wt.*
Refined montan wax	22
Oleic acid	5
Engine oil (6-7°E at 50°C)	67
Lime hydrate	3

Greaseless Lubricating Pencil, Type 1

Ingredient	*Parts by wt.*
Beeswax	100
Graphite powdered	50-100

Melt together and stir until a little above room temperature. Pour into moulds and allow to cool.

It is useful for lubricating hinges, automobile doors, etc., as it will not run off and stain.

Greaseless Lubricant Pencil, Type 2

Ingredient	*Parts by wt.*
Bees wax	80
Diglycol stearate	20
Graphite powder	100-200

Melt together and stir until just cold enough to pour. Pour into moulds and allow to set.

Greaseless Lubricating Pencil, Type 3

Ingredient	*Parts by wt.*
Petroleum	10
Paraffin wax	10

Melt together, mix well, and pour into cardboard moulds.

Grease for Parting the Punch from the die

Ingredient	*Parts by wt*
Beeswax	1
Rosin	1.5
Venice turpentine	1.5

Laboratory Stopcock Lubricant, Type 1

Ingredient	*Parts by wt.*
Standard viscous oil (No. 24 or 32)	80
Beeswax	20
Total	100

Heat the oil to 100-120°C, add the beeswax, and mix thoroughly, No. 24 gives a lubricant of medium body, No. 32 gives a very firm, viscous product.

Laboratory Stopcock Lubricant, Type 2

(i)	Petroleum	100
	Beeswax	10
	High grade red rubber tubing (Small pieces)	20

Heat together for several hours at 150°C, until the mixture is homogeneous. Our into a widemouthed jar.

(ii)	White petroleum	77.5
	Paraffin wax	15.0
	Pale rubber latex	7.5

Heat on an oil bath for 6 hours at 130°C.

Simple Lubricant

Technical caustic soda (38°Be)	3
Crude montan wax	15
Dark mineral oil	82

Lubricating Compound for Drawing Aluminium, Type 1

Ingredient	*Parts by wt.*
Diglycol stearate	6
Glycowax	2
Water	56

The entire mass is heated to about 180°F, and then stirred at moderate speed Until uniformly dispersed. Small parts, such as collapsible tube blanks, are dipped into the hot d spersion while in a wire basket and then centrifuged to remove excess lubricant. If a microscopic protective film is not required on the finished work, the glycowax may be replaced with additional diglycol stearate.

Lubricating Compound for Drawing Aluminium, Type 2

(A)	Diglycol stearate	10
(B)	Paraffin wax (145°F)	60
(C)	Boiling water	400

Melt (A) and (B) and then add (C) slowly, with vigorous mixing.

Lubricating Compound for Tin Stamping

Diglycol stearate	1
Water	100

The diglycol stearate is dispersed by heating while stirring in the water. This is applied prior to stamping and is considerably cheaper than the old wax lubrication method. It permits stamping of lacquered metal without fracturing the coating.

Light Coloured Lubricating Grease

Powdered lime hydrate	5
Oleic acid	10
Doubly bleached montan wax	25
Pale spindle oil	80

Dark Coloured Lubricating Grease

Rapeseed oil or Deodorised train oil	5
Technical caustic soda (10%)	10
Crude montan wax	25
Mineral oil (0.910)	260

Metal-Etching Stop Off 1

Wax	4
Rosin	2
Pitch	1

This coating is used as a general stop-off and is made by melting the ingredients in a kettle and then adding 4 ozs. of finely powdered asphalt.

The following stop off is also recommended particularly as being very hard and offering good resistance to strongly etching solutions.

Metal Etching Stop Off-2

Black Pitch	1
Japan wax	2
Rosin	1
Gum Dammar	1

Add to these, melted together in a kettle, 1 oz. of turpentine.

A series of etchants is available but usually dilute solutions of nitric acid are used on metals other than gold or platinum. Strong acids are not suitable because of the lifting of the stop off by evolution of gas resulting in non-uniform and dull etching.

Metal Stamping Lubricant

Ingredient	*Parts by wt*
Diglycol stearate	1
Water	100

The wax is dispersed by heat in the water and is stirred until cool. The dispersion can be sprayed on lacquered metal sheets or, in semi-automatic operations, brushing or spraying is satisfactory. This operation, carried out prior to stamping, is a considerable improvement over the old hot paraffin wax method by eliminating spotting and a greasy surface of the finished lacquered stampings, in addition to considerable reduction in operating and material costs.

Plastic-Mould Lubricant

Ingredient	*Parts by wt.*
Bright Drying Camauba Wax Emulsion	2 ozs.
Pine oil	5 drops

Spray this into the mould before use for easy ejection of moulded articles.

Porcelain-Mould Oil

Ingredient	*Parts by wt.*
Stearic Acid	24
Ozokerite	1
Paraffin wax	3
Heavy mineral oil	82

Rod Lubricant

Ingredient	*Parts by wt.*
Yellow ceresin	25
Sperm oil	25
Tallow	50
Melt together	
Yellow ceresin	1
Refined Spindle Oil	3-8
Melt at low temperature	

Soldering Paste, Type 1

Ingredient	*Parts by wt.*
Ceresin	10
Stearic acid	30
Rosin	22
Anhydrous zinc chloride	38
Total	100

The first three substances are melted in a steam heated kettle and when liquid, the zinc chloride is stirred in.

Soldering Paste, Type 2

Ingredient	*Parts by wt.*
Ammonium chloride	29
Sulphur powder	33
Rosin	2
Paraffin wax	9
Tallow	21

Salt	5
Balsam	1
Total	100

The paraffin and tallow are melted together in a steam heated kettle and while molten the other solids are stirred in; the balsam is added after the mixture has been removed from the heat.

Clay Base Lubricants

Ingredient	*Parts by wt.*
White clay	1 lb.
Paraffin wax	2 lbs.
Graphite	2 ozs.
Petroleum Residue	10 lbs.

Free Sulphur Lubricants

Ingredients	*Qty.*
Sulphur	10 ozs.
Sodium borate	2 ozs.
Ammonium carbonate	4 ozs.
Ammonium chloride	4 ozs.
Chalk	10 lbs.
Lime water	12 gallons

Salts Containing Lubricants

	Ingredient	*Qty.*
(i)	Lubricating oil	1 gal.
	Ammonium sulphate	16 ozs.
	Soda	16 ozs.
	Ammonium chloride	16 ozs.
	Ammonium phosphate	5 ozs.
	Sodium tungstate	6 ozs.
	Graphite	6 ozs.
(ii)	Calcium oxide	14 lbs.
	Pulverized chalk	20 ozs.
	Potassium carbonate	22 ozs.
	Calcined magnesia	16 ozs.
	Sodium carbonate	15 ozs.

	Ingredient	*Parts by wt.*
(iii)	Sodium chloride	25
	Borax	2
	Powdered coal	10
	Water	63
	Total	100

Sulphur Based Cutting Oil

Lard oil	85
Flowrs of sulphur	15
Total	100

Finished oil

Sulphur	4.43
Lard oil	15.94
Mineral oil, 100 to 200 vis. pale oil	80.00

Sulphur Base Cooling Oil

Finely ground sulphur	0.90
Asphalt base red oil, 250 vis. at 100°F	99.10
Total	100.00

Procedure: The mineral oil is first charged in a steam jacketed kettle and heated to 245°F.

The sulphur is then sifted in. Agitation may be accomplished, if so desired, by means of a small pump so arranged as to take suction at the bottom of the kettle and discharge back into the kettle just below the surface of the oil. Circulation should be carried on while heating the oil. For ten minutes the batch of oil is kept at a temperature of 250°F, when the steam in the jacket is turned of.

The batch is slowly cooled over a period of about three hours to a temperature of 110° F, when it may be drawn into barrels or other containers for shipment.

Sulphur Base Cutting Oils

Ingredient	*Parts by wt.*
Wool fat or distilled wool grease	30.00
Sulphur	13.00
Lard oil	26.00
28° Paraffin oil	30.00

Ordinary Cutting Oil

Ingredient	*Parts by wt.*
28° Be, paraffin oil (140 - 170 vis. at 100°F)	98.00
Lard oil	1.75
Cooling base	0.25
Sulphur, Degras, Lard oil	equal pts.

Thread Cutting Oil

Ingredient	*Parts by wt.*
Whale oil	20.00
Acidless tallow oil	5.0
Pale oil, 100 vis.	75.00
Total	100.00

Acid Base Cutting Oil

Ingredient	Parts by wt.
Lard oil	30.00
Paraffin oil, 28° Be	70.00
Total	100.00

Cutting Compound Paste

Ingredient	Qty.
Oleic acid	5 gals
Lard oil	10 gals
Paraffin oil	30 gals
Raw Degras	35 lbs.
Sal soda	135 lbs.
Water	210 lbs.
Oil of mirbane	2 ozs.

Procedure: Charge in a steam jacketed mixer all of the oils and the degras and bring to 80° F.

Mix the sal soda (crystallized sodium carbonate) and water together and bring to 100°F, when all of the soda should be dissolved.

Add the soda solution to the ingredients in the mixer and heatto 130°F.

Heating should be continued until a temperature of 210°F, is reached, which completes the batch.

Soap-based Acetylenic Glycols

A typical lubricant that can be used in water solution for the wet drawing of steel, copper coated steel, liquorfinished steel, galvanized steel, and other types of metal wire drawing is as follows:

Ingredient	*Percent*
Tall oil fatty acid	17.8
45% KOH	7.2
Polyoxy propylene derivative of prolpylene glycol, mw 2,000 (Pluracol P-2010)	6.7
Water	68.3
Total	100.0

Polybutene-based Lubricant

A lubricant for metal working, such as forging, which contains a major portion of polybutene .and minor portions of tin or lead soaps, a solid lubricant, such as graphite, and a dispersing agent. For hot forging, it is preferred to dilute the lubricant with kerosene. The following formulations are given to illustrate the lubricant of the process:

Example 1	*Percent*
Lead naphthenate	4.7
Dispersing agent (polyamino alkenyl succinimide)	4.7
Lubricity agent (synthetic sperm oil)	4.7
Graphite	4.7
Antioxidant (hindered phenol)	0.5
Polybutene (viscosity 3,400 55 at 100°F)	80.7
Total	100

Example 2	*Percent*
Stannous oleate	7.5
Dispersing agent (polyamino alkenyl succinimide)	4.7
Lubricity agent (epoxidized soybean oil)	1.4
Lubricity agent (lanolin)	3.9
Antioxidant (hindered phenol)	0.5
Graphite	4.7
Polybutene (viscosity 3,400 55U at 100°F)	77.7

The above lubricants can be diluted 1 : 1 (by weight) with kerosene and employed in the hot forging of aluminium automotive wheel hubs. Idle temperature is about 650°F and work-piece lay on temperature is about 800°F. The lubricant is sprayed onto the die surfaces for both blocking and finishing operations. Little or no build-up of residue is noticeable on the dies and no problem is found with the workpiece sticking to the dies.

The lubricant flashes quickly and burns cleanly, resulting in little or no smoke and essentially no hydrocarbon emission. In the finishing operations, which require two forging strokes, it is found that only one application of lubricants needed. As a comparison when using conventional lubricants in the forging operation, the application of lubricant is necessary for each finishing stroke.

This type of lubricant is suitable for metal washing, such as forging, etc.

Textile lubricants

A finished lubricant suitable for the lubrication of a circular knitting machine is prepared by blending together the following composition in the weight percentages indicated below:

Ingredient	Weight Percent
Base oil”	95
Zinc dialkyl dithiophosphate	0.5
Oleic acid	0.5
Sufurized sperm oil	3.0
Zinc oxide concentrate	1.0
Total	100.0

‘Mixture of about 55 weight percent of a solvent neutral lubricant oil of 100 SUS viscosity and 45 weight percent of solvent neutral mineral lubricating oil of 150 SUS viscosity both viscosities at 100°F.

Machinery Lubricants

I. Lubricants-sewing machine oils

	Ingredient	Qty.
(1)	Olive oil	3 pts.
	Almond oil	2 pts.
	Rapeseed oil	1 pts.

Procedure: Prepare a homogeneous consistent solution with alcohol.

	Ingredient	*Qty.*
(2)	Pale oil of almonds	9 ozs.
	Rectified benzoline	3 ozs.

	Oil of lavender	1 oz.

Procedure: Mix and filter.

	Ingredient	*Qty.*
(3)	Petroleum	3 ozs.
	Pale groundnut oil	7 ozs.
	Almond oil	40-50 drops

Procedure: Mix and filter.

	Ingredient	*Qty.*
(4)	Oil of almonds (Pale)	9 ozs.
	Rectified benzoline	3 ozs.
	Oil of lavender	1 oz.

Procedure: Mix and filter.

2. Lubricating oil for motor cylinders

Ingredient		Qty.
Castor oil		30 gals.
Engine oil (Sp, Gr. 0.902)		30 gals.
Benzene		30 gals.
Camphorated oil		10 gals.
	Total	100 gals.

Procedure: Mix all the constituents and use 2-3 volumes in 1000 volumes gasoline.

3. Machinery lubricant (in summer)

Ingredient	*Qty.*
Tallow	15 pts.
Rosin oil	2 pts.
Rapeseed oil	13 pts.

4. Machinery lubricant (for winter)

Ingredient	Qty.
Tallow	7 pts.
Rosin oil	2 pts.
Rapeseed oil	13 pts.

5. High pressure machinery lubricant

	Ingredient	Qty.
(1)	Kerosene oil	10 pts.
	Rapeseed oil	4 pts.
	Coconut oil	1 pt.
	Lime	1 pt.

Procedure: Prepare a saturate d solution of lime in water and boil together with the oils till a homogeneous paste-like product is obtained.

Ingredients	*Qty.*
(2) Kerosene oil	10 pts.
Linseed oil	5.7 pts.
Lime	2.5 pts.

Procedure: Prepare as above.

6. Oil for cleaning Rifle Barrels

ingredients	*Qty.*
White oil	2 fl. oz.
Sperm oil	1 fl. oz.
Oil of turpentine	1 fl. oz.
Acetone	1 fl. oz.

7. Oil for clocks, watches and similar delicate machines

(1) Take refined rapeseed oil or fine olive oil. Mix caustic soda to it in the ratio of 1 : 100 by weight. Keep it aside for 2 or 3 days, shaking the mixture occasionally. Add a large amount of water, let it settle and decant or syphon the floating oil. To remove the colouring water, shake 10 pts. of oil so obtained with 2 pts. of 90% alcohol. Cork well the bottles, shake up, and kept it in the sun for about a fortnight. Shake occasionally, when the water white oil should be syphoned off and at once filled up in phials. The residual spirit can be purified by means of distillation.

(2) Put a clean strip of lead in olive oil in a white phial. Place it in the sun till no more sediment is deposited. Syphon out carefully the clear white oil.

(3) Put some oil in a beaker. To this add double as much in double the amount 96% alcohol. Shake well. Cover and keep in a dark place for 24 hours or more. Take olive oil in a clear bottle and to this add ten times the volume of oil, distilled water and for 5 minutes, let agitate, allow to stand for half an hour and then freeze like ice-cream In a freezing mixture of ice and salt, when clear, liquid oil at the top should be syphoned.

8. Oil for cycles

	Ingredients	*qty.*
(1)	Sperm or whale oil	20 pts.
	Vaseline	5 pts.
	Mineral oil	traces
(2)	Refine rapeseed oil	20 pts.
	Water-white petroleum	5 pts.

Chapter 14

RECLAMATION OF USED LUBRICATING OIL

Introduction

Lubricating oil deteriorates, and becomes contaminated with foreign materials, in service. In circulating systems, where a quantity of oil is involved, it is desirable to maintain the oil as clean as possible to provide maximum lubrication efficiency, and to keep wear and damage of lubricated parts to a minimum.

When the lubricating oil reaches the end of its life in the engine, what most probably happens is additive depletion. Because of the engine operation, these chemicals, slowly lose their effectiveness. This is the time to change the oil. This used oil can be re-refined for use. Technically speaking, re-refined oil can be used to replace some of the original base stocks. For some applications, in fact, they are better. But the usages depends heavily on the process used to manufacture the re-refined oil and so many other things like the chemical compatibility etc.

Reconditioning of a used oil may be accomplished by full flow, by-pass, of batch methods - or combination of these. In the full-flow system, the entire flow of oil from the nain pressure line is continuously filtered. In the by-pass system, a fraction of the total of flow is continuously filtered and returned to the oil reservoir. In the batch system, as the name implies, all the oil is removed from the lubrication system and is reconditioned as a batch.

Nature of Contaminants in Used Lubricating Oil

Contaminants in a used oil may be divided into two classes:

(1) Products resulting from chemical action within the system, including effects due to fuels; and

(2) Foreign material which enter the system.

Products resulting from chemical action within the system are as follows:

(a) Carbon, and other products of partial decomposition of oil or of incomplete combustion of fuel;

(b) Oxidation products (which may be either soluble or insoluble in the oil), due to chemical action at high temperatures;

(c) Gummy product, both soluble and insoluble, resulting from polymerization (combining) of unsaturated components in the oil; and

(d) Sulphur compounds, formed by sulpur in the oil or fuel.

Foreign materials may include some of the following:

(I) Dirt and dust from the air;

(II) Metal particles resulting from wear of operating parts of the machine, or left over from machining operation during an overhaul;

(III) Foundry core-sand from castings;

(IV) Water condensed from air moisture or products of fuel combustion; and

(V) Fuel dilution.

Purification of Oils

Three basic methods of treating contaminated oils are used, both singly and in combinations:

(1) Gravity purification,

(2) Filteration, and

(3) Reclamation

1. Gravity Methods of Purification

Gravity methods which are based on the relative weights of clean oil and the contaminants to be separated out, include the use of settling tanks and of centrifuges.

Settling Tank

In a settling tank method, a batch of dirty oil is allowed to stand for ten or more days in a tank, and insoluble matter (including water), which is heavier than oil, settles to the bottom under the influence of gravity. The tank should be free from vibration and the oil is undisturbed. Small particles and dispersed insoluble oxidation products are not removed in this process.

Best results are obtained when the oil is heated to the range of 1 20°F to 160°F to reduce the oil viscosity, thus facilitating settling.

Drawbacks to the settling tank method of purification are : the time element, the space requirements for tanks, extra oil charge for the engine during settling process, and the fact that impurities are only removed periodically.

This method is adaptable to straight mineral oils, but is generally unsatisfactory with heavy duty additive-type oils.

Centrifuge

A centrifuge works on the principle of separation by centrifugal force. This force, supplied by the high-speed rotation of the bowl containing the contaminated oil, is several thousand times the force of gravity. As a result, the centrifuge is much faster and more efficient than the settling tank. Substances having a higher density than the oil, such as water and heavy particles, are thrown out against the walls of the centrifuge with greater force than the oil. As a result, a stable oil water boundary is established, under proper operating conditions. Oil and water leave by separate outlets, the oil discharge tube being nearer the center. The sediment is removed from the walls by cleaning at regular intervals. For some types of centrifuge; special arrangements are provided to prevent mixture of purified oil with incoming contaminated oil, in the vicinity of the oil-water boundary.

"Through-put" capacity is the maximum number of gallons of contaminated oil which can be sent through the centrifuge each hour, with no regard for the degree of purification. The effective capacity of the centrifuge, which is much more meaningful, is the rate at which contaminated oil may be processed to give the desired degree of purification. This rate depends upon prevailing conditions and what is deemed to be a desirable degree of purification in each case.

In so-called wet centrifuging, water is intentionally added to the entering stream of contaminated oil. This added water may have a washing effect on the oil and a tendency to carry away more of the lighter solid, as well as some acids which are more soluble in water than in oil.

A centrifuge is especially well adapted to a by-pass system, in which part of the oil being circulated is by-passed through the centrifuge each cycle. Centrifuge are also suitable for the batch system of purification.

Filteration

Filters may be applied on full-flow, by-pass or batch systems where there is sufficient pressure to overcome the internal resistance of the filter. There are three principal types of filters:

(1) Mechanical,

(2) Absorption, and

(3) Adsorption.

Where a filter is installed in the lubrication system of machinery, such as an engine, a relief valve is provided to cut off flow to the filter at a predetermined pressure. This is for the protection of the engine against loss of oil supply. Filters may be integral units composed of a filter element in a sealed container, in which case the entire unit must be replaced. When blocked with filtered material, or they may be replaceable element type, wherein the container can be opened for the replacement of the used element.

Regenerating Process of Used Lubricating Oils

Lubricating oils are discarded after a specific period of use, to give engines longer life and better performance. These are either drained into rivers or burnt in air, causing pollution of air and water. Thus the re-refining of used lubircating oil is another way of tackling the disposal problem through reutilisation. 80-90% of used lubricating oils remain unchanged, these can be economically regenerated.

India depends mostly on the foreign market to meet her requirements of lubricants and greases. The deficit in indigenous availability of lube stock is fulfilled through import. As such, the import of base stock and lubircant technology is making the important product "Lubricant" costilier, with the passing of each day. The economic factor alone is the most critical factor forindustry to recognise the conservation of lubricant as an important area.

Regeneration of lubricating oil, a practice in many oil rich countries, should be popularized as this will stop drainage of foreign exchange and conserve our existing stock.

Contaminants Present in Used Lubricating Oils

Contaminants present in used lubricating oils can be classified as:

1. Volatile, (2) Oils soluble compounds, (3) Oil insoluble compounds.

Unburnt fuel and water constitute volatile component while in use in the engines, lubricating oils from primary oxidation products which polymerise and are finally converted to asphalts by pyrolysis. These constitute oil soluble compounds. The third category of compounds includes dust, metallic particles, soot, degraded additives; metal soaps etc.

Principles of Used Lubricating Oils Regeneration

Re-refining and reclamation are the two procedures used in regeneration. Re-refining may involve the following steps:

(1) Settling and Dehydration.

(2) Acid treatment.

(3) Clay treatment of acid treated oil.

(4) Removal of clay by filteration.

(5) Distillation or fractionation.

(6) Blending with bright stock and incorporation of additives.

Re-refined oil compares well with the virgin oil. Reclamation, on the other hand, involves steps like settling, dehydration, removal of asphalts and other solid bodies. It does not remove diluents and certain oil degraded products.

Existing Process for Regeneration of Used Lubricating Oils

Processes employed in United States:-

1. In the process followed at Mohawk Refinery Co. Newark N.J. a 10,000 gall. dish bottomed tank is charged with feed stock which is heated to 82°C (dispersant filled oils require higher temp.) with 98% sulphuric acid and settled, leaving mainly saturated naphthenic and paraffinic molecules. After acid and settling treatment 82-84% of the feed remains. This is followed by heating to 316°C in the clay contact step. In a flash chamber, clay and residue drop down while overheads are pulled down to reflux with a product stream joining the second tower. Here the lighter ends are gathered for process fueling, and the bottoms are recycled. Two lubricants products result a 350-SSU at 37.8°C stream and 110/120 SSN at 37.8°C light distillate.

2. S and R Oil Co. Houston Tex. re-refiner processes (i) 360,000 gal./mo. of crank case drainings. First the waste oil runs through a pipe still for dehydration. Next, acid treatment in air blown agitator is followed by clay containing at 204°C. Then filteration takes place using sweetland filters, rotary vacuum filters or even plate and frame presses. The final step is blotter pressing to remove any remaining clay.

3. Diamond Head Oil Refining Co. Keramey, N.J. does not use acid in its re-refining processes but employs more severe clay treatment, coupled with higher temperatures.

4. Anew re-refining method for lubricating oils is said to offer favourable economies and eliminate refiner's own water pollutants acid sludge and filter cake. The process has been developed at Villanova University.

The new process has five basic steps:

1. After the moisture content is reduced to less than 0.1 percent by heating to 138°C the acidic contaminants are neutralized by sodium hydroxide or other undisclosed agents.
2. Dilution with light naphtha as a coagulant followed by solids removal.
3. Atmospheric distillation to recover the light naphtha for recycle.
4. Vacuum fractionation to recover product and split out No. 1 heating oil.
5. Clay treatment. The oil is heated with clay to 338°C for about an hour under a nitrogen blanket and with mechanical agitation. The mix is then cooled to 149°C and the clay is removed via a rotary vacuum filter.

By products of the process are a carbonaceous material similar to carbon black and a potential rubber extender oil. Out of total lubricating market in U.S. reclaimed oil accounts for about 6%.

In the field of re-refining of used lubricating oils, acid treatment is being replaced by light hydrocarbon treatment (propane and naphtha) resulting in better yields and obviating the problem of the disposal of acid sludge.

Research is being carried out in different countries of the world to evolve further cheaper methods of used oil regeneration.

Characteristics of a Used and Regenerated Heavy Duty Motor Oil.

Properties	*Used Oil*	*Regenerated Oil*
Appearance	Dark	Clear and Bright
Density D420	0.892	0.890
Flash point, opn cupOC	260	236
kinematic viscosity, cs		
at 37.8OC	165.4	162.4
98.9OC	17.66	17.3
Viscosity Index	...	H6.5
Acidity, mg KOH/gm.	3.0	...
Conradson carbon	0.805	0.26
Residue % wt.		
Ash sulphated, % wt.	0.36	...

A flow diagram for a process on regeneration of used lubricating oil is given in Fig. 1 which gives complete idea.

Plants are said to be running on this process.

Process developed at the Regional Research Laboratories, Jorhat Assam (Indian Patent No.127751) consists of the following steps :

1. Clay Treatment

Used lubricating oil together with activated fuller's earth and water is heated to suitable temperature in a closed vessel with constant stirring.

2. Filteration

Oil from (step 1) is cooled and then passed through a filter press.

3. Distillation

Filtered oil (step 2) is then subjected to vacuum distillation. Some portion of the distillate collected is discarded as heating oil. Distillation is continued upto a still temperature ensuring more or less complete recovery

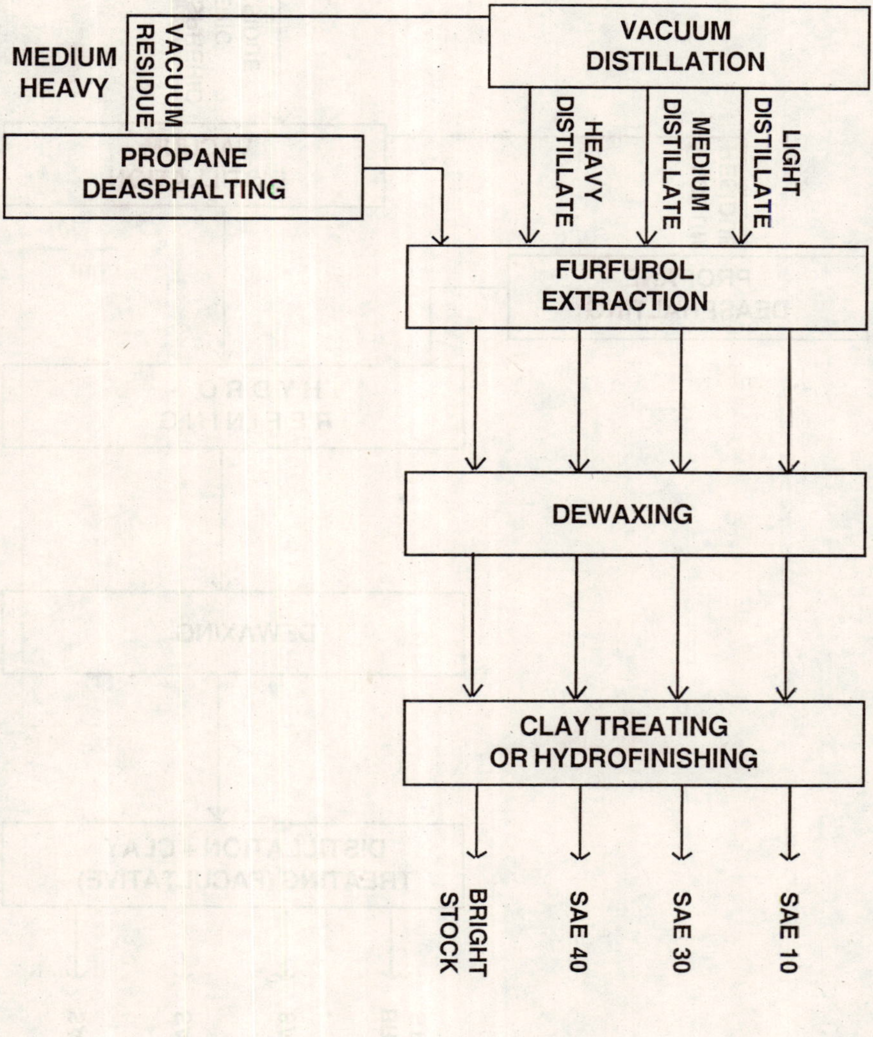

Figure 1 : Flow Diagram for a Process on Regeneration of Used Lubricating Oil.

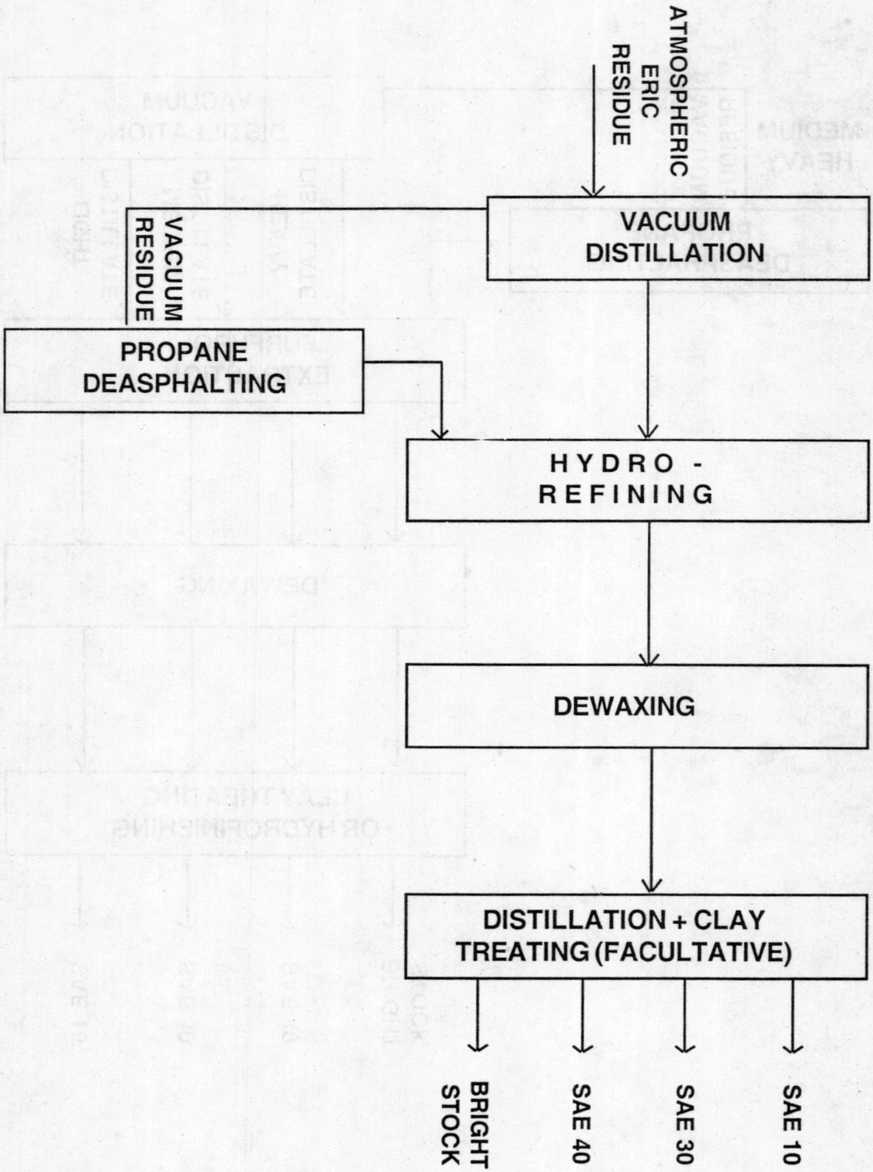

Figure 2 : Flow Diagram for a Process on Regeneration of Used Lubricating Oil.

of the oil. Distillation residue comprises most of the spent additive and is discarded.

4. Blending

Distilled lubricating oil (step 3) is blended with additives to improve viscosity index and other properties.

Novelty of the Process

Novelty of the process lies in the elimination of sulphuric acid treatment by a severe clay treatment step thereby avoiding acid sludge handling and disposal problem and in turn making the whole process more economical.

Lubricant Recycling

Considerable effort is underway to improve and expand recycling of lubricating oils. Although typical processes result in 80-90% yield, questions remain regarding the initial collection and the separation of the used oil from water and other contaminants. Subsequent treatment varies from simple cleaning to essentially the complete refining process used with virgin oil. The following are typical steps involved in reprocessing used petroleum lubricating oils are indicated schematically in Fig.3.

Reprocessing

It involves simple separation of contaminants by gravity settling of water and dirt, centrifuging, filtering and membrane techniques. Chemical emulsion breakers are first added and consist of sulphuric acid and then aluminium sulphate as a coagulant. Polymers sometimes are used to speed up the process. The separated oil is then decanted, skimmed or centrifuged and commonly is burned. 1-5% reprocessed waste oil generally may be added to fuel.

Reclamation

It involves flash distillation in an evaporator at about 100-200°C in partial vacuum to remove water and low boiling contaminants e.g. gasoline and solvents.

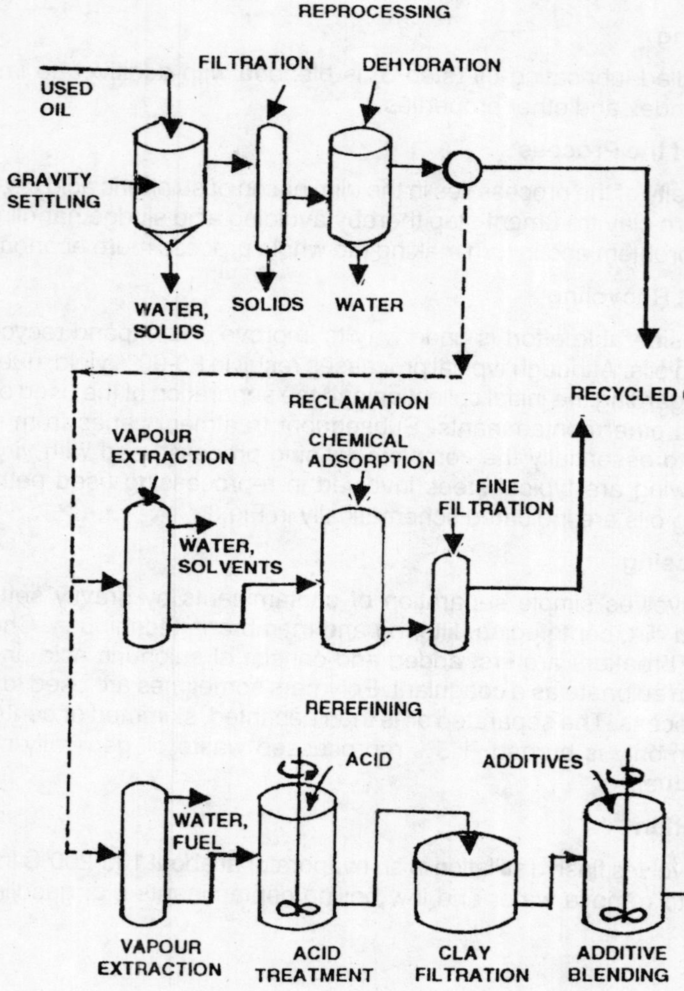

Figure 3 : Process Flow diagram in the Recycling of used Lubricating

Chapter 15

RE-REFINING OF USED LUBE OIL

Introduction

Re-refining of used lubricating oil has been a subject widely disussed during the last two decades. Regeneration/re-refining of used lube oil is based on the fact that the petroleum oils are almost indestructible. Lube oils are impared temporarily only because of the accumulation during use or handling of contaminants resulting from certain deteriorative chemical changes due to oxidation.

Re-refined lubricating oils are petroleum products obtained from rerefining of used lubricating oils (automotive and industrial) and blended with suitable additives i.e., detergents (to dissolve engine deposits), dispersants, oxidation inhibitors (to reduce susceptibility to oxidation at high temperatures) corrosion inhibitors, viscosity index improvers, pour - point depressants, antiwear additives antifoamants to provide desired properties.

Properties:

The properties of re-refined base stock and finished re-refined lubricating oils (obtained after adding additives to base oils) are listed in the following table.

Special Feature of Re-refining Process :

i) Petroleum being an exhaustible resources, the re-refining of used lubricating oils will help in oil conservation. This process also helps in solving the waste disposal problem.

ii) Re-refined lubricating oils have almost similar characteristics to that of new lube oils, are available at comparatively lower price.

iii) The re-refined lubricating oils can be used in all applications where new lube oils are being used.

Technical specification of refined Base stock & Re-refined lubricating oils

Sl. No.	Property	Value Required	
		Re-refined oil (finished)	Re-refined Base stock
1	2	3	4
1.	Appearance at 27°C	Oil should be clear bright and free from turbidity and Sediments.	
2.	Kinematic Viscosity at 100°C (Cst)	9.3 to 12.5	Same but a change upto 2cst between finished oil and base stock permitted.
3.	Viscosity index (Min.)	95	90
4.	Pour Point (°C) Max.	6	-
5.	Flash Point (°C)	215	215
6.	Carbon Resideu (% Mass) Max.	-	0.4
7.	Ash Sulphated (% Mass) Max	-	0.01
8.	Total Acid Number Mg. KOH/Gm. Max.	-	0.05
9.	Water Content (% vol.) Max.	-	0.03
10.	Saponification Value Mg KOH/Gm. (Max.)	-	1.00

Uses and Applications

Technically speaking re-refined lube oils can be used to replace some of the original base stocks. For some applications, in fact, they are better. But the usages depend heavily on the process used to manufacture the re-refined oil and so many other things like the chemical compatibility etc.

The major application area, for re-refined lubricating oils include lubrication of I.C. engines of cars. scooters, buses, trucks. It is also used in lubrication of army equipments/machines, etc. It is applied in lubrication of locomotives. Re-refined lube oil is utilised as base stocks by the manufacturers of lubricants, greases, finished lubricating oils, industrial oils and speciality oils etc. It is extensively used in lubricating the machine parts in industries.

Standard and Quality

In order to standardise the quality of re-refined lubricating oils in India,

Bureau of Indian standards, New Delhi have laid down some IS specifications to be followed by the manufacturers. In line with the international development, BIS issues guidelines as per specifications and performance parameters of API and CCMC etc.

Market Scenario

Since India is a major importer of lubricating oils. Much of the indigenous crude produced is non-lube bearing. As such, the substantial of the existing demand is fulfilled through import on the cost of outlay of valuable foreign exchange. Hence the re-refining of used lubricating oils will be one of the most efficient and cheap ways of meeting the increased demand of the country.

Major Users of Re-refined Lube Oils

i) Automobile Industry

ii) Indian Army

iii) Indian Navy

iv) Manufacturers of lubricants greases

v) Industries

Major Manufacturers of RE-refined Lube Oil in India (Private Sector)

i) M/s Castrol India Ltd., Mumbai

ii) M/s Gujrat Oiland Ltd., Ankleshwar

iii) M/s Rinki Industrial Oils Ltd., Baroda

iv) M/s Continental Petroleum Ltd., Alwar

v) M/s Unique Oils Ltd., Mumbai

vi) Small Scale Units (Combined)

Technology

The India's Technology developed by Indian Institute of petroleum, Dehradun is based on Acid-Clay Process. It is a batch process with low process yields 70% of re-refined oil (by vol. %) of used oil. The quality of the product is inferior. Indian re-refiners of used lubricating oils have been using this conventional technology. The imported technology based on solvent re-refining process for used lubricating oils is the most efficient one.

Industrial Licencing

The proposed article of manufacture does not fall underthe list of industries in respect of which Industrial Licencing is compulsory. Thus industrial undertaking shall have tofile a memorandum with secretariat of Indutrial approvals (SIA), Ministry of Industries, Govt. of India. The undertaking will have to procure licence from concerned Director of Industries of the state.

Process of Manufacture:

i) Re-refining of Used Lube Oil

First of all the used tube undergoes to mechanical separation. In this process, the oil is screened through fine mesh metal cloth for removal of insoluble matters like dirt, fibre, metal particle, suspended impurities and coarser impurities.The oil is stored in storage tank. Then the oil is subjected to vacuum de-hydration at about 150°C. The pressure is maintained at 600-700 mm Hg vacuum. The emulsified water is removed by operation and the whole mass after cooling to a temperature of 50°C is transferred to acid treatment reactor. In this process a predetermined quantity of sulphuric acid is added and then thoroughly agitated. The sludge formed is allowed to settle and finally removed. The decanted clear oil is then neutralised with activated fullers earth at elevated temperature under vacuum of 600 to 700 mm Hg. The clear oil slurry is then cooled and filtered to remove spent clay and other solids. Finally, the filtered oil is refiltered through a vacuum filter system.

The reclaimed oil is tested for quality, required doses additives are added and stored in the tank.

ii) Lubricating Greases

A known quantity of fatty acid like (tallow, hydrogenated castor oil, palm fatty acid, mahua oil, and acid oil) are charged into the cooking kettle, and then added the equivalent quantity of lubricating oil, heated to 80 to 90°C, mixed with alkali (sodium hydroxide, calcium hydroxide and lithium hydroxide etc. depending on the type of greases to be manufactured) and saponification is carried out upto 23°C. After the saponification is complete, the required quantity of lubricating oil is charged into the kettle with continuous stirring. After this, the whole mass is transferred to the cooling kettle and then milled through the milling machine. The product is deaerated and filled into the barrels.

iii) Specialities Oils

A number of oils are manufactured which are used for special purposes, generally not connected with lubrication. These oils are called speciality oils. These oils may be divided into following broad groups

(a) Insulating oil, (b) white oil, (c) Textile oils, (d) Refrigeration oils, (e) Metal oils, (f) Heat Treatment oils, (g) Petroleum Jelly, (h) Transformer oil.

For manufacture of speciality oils, the selected base stock of appropriate viscosity is firstly dehydrated. It is cooled and treated with sulphuric acid.The sludge formed is allowed to settle and removed. The decanted acidic oil is then neutralised with alkali and finally treated with activated clay. The oil clay mixture is finally filtered under vacuum and blended with additives according to the type of specialities to be manufactured.

iv) Industrial Fuel Oil (IFO)

IFO is manufactured by simply blending of lighter fraction oil (a by-product of re-refining of lube oil unit), superior kerosene oil (S.K.O) with heavy oil tank bottom sludges in the blending vessels at room temperature and finally filtered.

Raw Materials & Consumables

i) For Re-refined Lube Oil

The main raw material is used lube oil. The used lube oil is generated by all major consumers of lube oil products viz. Industries like chemical, En,gg., Fertilizer, Textile, Mining, State Road Transport undertakings, Defence, Shipping corporation, Steel plants. The other sources are from private automotive garriages.The other raw materials are sulphuric acid activated fullers earth, filter cloth. These are available in open market.

ii) For Lubricating Greases

The major raw materials for manufacturing greases is re-refined tube oil produced by the unit.The other raw materials are like calcium hydroxide, sodium hydroxide and lithium hydroxide. These are available in open market.

iii) For Specialities

The raw materials are ones used hydraulic oil, turbine oil, transformer oil, gear oil compressor oil etc. These are purchased from heavy industries like thermal power stations through a sealed tender or through agents. The other required chemicals are purchased from open market.

iv) For Industrial Fuel Oil

The main raw material is heavy oil tank bottom sludge which is obtained through agents. The other diluent i.e., lighter fraction oil which is the product of the re-refining of used lube oil unit. The third raw material is superior kerosene oil (S.K.O.) which is purchased from I.O.C.

Utilities: Service Facilities

i) Electric Power: Average Power reqd :110 H. P. (82 KW) 440 volt.

ii) Diesel oil: for D.G. set of 120 Kva.

iii) Industrial fuel oil : for oil fired furnace

iv) Water : Water will be required in the process as well as for general drinking and sanitation purposes. The same will be arranged through sinking tube-well in the factory premises.

v) Effluent : Solid Effluent : Acid sludge which is to be neutralised with lime and stored into sludge pit.

Liquid Effluent

The oily water effluent should be passed through oil catcher to entrap all the floating oil - films. The water free from oil is discharged to the drain. The skimmed oil with residual oil content is sent to settlerfor proper settling. The settled water is drained.

Gaseous Effluent

The height of the chimney should be sufficient to avoid the pollution from flue - gases.

vi) Fire Fighting : The factory should install the following fire extin guishers

a) Trolley mounted foam type

b) Portable dry chemical type

c) Portable CO_2 gas type

In addition to the above, the factory should be equipped with the fire hydrant on different locations.

vii) Safety Appliances

a) PVC apron

b) Asbestos apron

c) PVC gum boots

d) PVC hand gloves

e) Face shield

f) Dust mask

g) Leather hand gloves

h) First aid boxes containing emergency medicines.

i) On site emergency plan to meet the casualties.

Government Permissions

i) Concerned pollution control authority

ii) State factory inspector

iii) Storage licence for petroleum class 'B' & 'C' from controller of explosive, Nagpur.

Locational Consideration

For setting up a plant for re-refining of used lubricating oil and manufacture of various lubricants, the following aspects should be taken into account in selecting the site

i) Availability of raw materials

ii) Marketing facility

iii) Transport facility

iv) Availability of water and power

v) Availability of manpower

vi) Waste disposal facility

vii) Local objection

viii) Free from local population problem

ix) Local climate

x) Government permission

xi) Local township

xii) Other infrastructure facilities like school, college, hotel, recreation centres etc.

Project Implementation Schedule :

Barring inforeseen circumstances, the unit will go into commercial production in 18 months from its inception, which can be shown as follows:

Activity	*Month*	
	From	To
i) Preparation of TEFR, market survey, arrangement of land etc.	0	3
ii) Application to financial institution and sanction of term loan	4	6
iii) Construction of factory building	6	10
iv) Placement of order for supply of machinery and delivery at site	8	10
v) Installation of machinery	10	14
vi Arrangement of power and water	8	10
vii) Sanction of working capital loan	8	10
viii) Arrangement for raw materials	11	13
ix) Government permissions	13	14
x) Trial production	14	15
xi) Marketing strategy preparation	15	16
xii) Commercial production	17	18

PROJECT ECONOMY

1. Installed Capacity

The plant will produce 3000 MT/year of re-refined lubricating oil and 150 MT/year of lighter fraction oil as by product, of which 500 MT/year of re-refined tube oil will be sold as it is and rest 25.00 MT/year will be utilised to manufacture various lubricants/product. 150 MT/year of lighter fraction oil will be utilised to manufacture 600 MT/year of industrial fuel oil (IFO). The above capacity has been assumed on the basis of single shift operation and 300 working days in a year.

2. Product Mix

	Product	Qty/year
i)	Re-refined tube oil	500 MT
ii)	Automotive grease	200 MT
iii)	Antifriction bearing grease	200 MT
iv)	Sodium - calcium based grease	300 MT
v)	Lithium based grease	300 MT
vi)	Multipurpose grease	125 MT
vii)	Industrial fuel oil	600 MT
viii)	Motor oil	800 MT
ix)	Cutting oil	
	(a) Soluble	100 MT
	(b) Neat	80 MT
x)	Petroleum jelly	150 MT
xi)	Brake fluid	150 MT
xii)	Gear oil	150 MT
xiii)	Transformer. oil	150 MT
xiv)	2 - T oil	100 MT
xv)	Hydraulic oil	125 MT
xvi)	Synthetic cutting oil	80 MT
xvii)	Brake oil	75 MT
xviii)	Industrial oil	
	(a) Machine oil	50 MT
	(b) Quenching oil	60 MT
	(c) Refrigeration oil	70 MT
xix)	Coolant	60 MT

3. List of Plant & Machinery;

i) Storage tanks
ii) Dehydration kettle
iii) Clay treatment kettle
iv) Oil cooling kettle
v) Acid treatment tank
vi) Acid neutralizing & washing kettle
vii) Condenser
viii) Alkali Settling Tank
xi) Filter press
x) Fittered oil receiving tank
xi) Vacuum pump
xii) Vacuum filter
xiii) Heat exchanger
xiv) Air compressor
xv) Blending tank
xvi) Grease cooking kettle
xvii) Grease cooling kettle
xviii) Grease milling machine
xix) Oil furnace
xx) Container sealing machine
xxi) Ovens
xxii) Motor, pump, valves & pipe fittings
xxiii) D. G. set
xxiv) Pollution control equipments

4. Project Cost

		Rs in lakh
i)	Land and land development	20.00
ii)	Building and other civil works	45.00
iii)	Plant and machinery	100.00
iv)	Electrical installations	5.00
v)	Misc. fixed assets	40.00
vi)	Contingencies	21.00
vii)	Preliminary & pre-operative expenses	35.00
viii)	Margin for working capital	35.50
	Total :	301.50

5. Total Capital Investment

i) Fixed Capital	266.00
ii) Working Capital	128.10
Total :	394.10

6. Sources of Finance

i) Promoter's capital	75.38
ii) Long term loan	226.12
iii) Working capital loan	92.60
Total :	394.10

7. Working Capital Requirement

Sl.No.	Particulars	Period (month)	Value Rs. in lakh
i)	Raw materials and consumables in stock	1	50.00
ii)	Materials in process	1/8	7.20
iii)	Finished goods in stock	1/2	28.80
iv)	Sales on credit	1/2	37.50
v)	Working expenses	1	4.60
		Total :	128.10
	Bank finance		92.60
	Margin money		35.50

8. Cost of Production and Profitability/year :

		(Rs in lakh)
i)	Raw materials and consumables	600.00
ii)	Power fuel	15.00
iii)	Salary - wages	40.00
iv)	Repairs and maintenance	3.90
v)	Rent, taxes and insurance	2.50
vi)	Administrative expenses	1.20
vii)	Sales and publicity	30.00
	Total :	692.60

vii)	Annual Sales income	900.00
ix)	Profit before interest and depreciation	207.40
x)	Interest	
	on long term loan	40.70
	on w/c loan	18.52
xi)	Depreciation :	20.00
xii)	Profit before tax	128.18
xiii)	Provision for income tax	57.68
xiv)	Profit after tax	70.50

9. Break Even Point Analysis

Rs in lakh

A.Variable Cost

i)	Raw materials and consumables	600.00
ii)	Power - fuel	15.00
iii)	Salary and wages (25 %)	10.06
iv)	Interest on working capital loan	18.52
v)	Direct selling expenses	30.00
	Total :	673.52

B.Semi variable and Fixed Cost

i)	Salary - wages (75 %)	30.00
ii)	Repairs and maintanance	3.90
iii)	Rent, taxes and ensurance	2.50
iv)	Administrative expense	1.20
v)	Interest on term loan	40.70
vi)	Depreciation	20.00
	Total :	98.30

C. Surplus :

Rs. in Lakhs

i)	Income from sales	900.00
ii)	Less : Variable expense	673.52
		226.48

$$\text{Break even point} = \frac{98.30}{226.48} \times 100$$

$$= 43.40\%$$

Chapter 16

FORMULATIONS OF GREASES

Introduction

Greases are the important items for maintenance and smooth running of various machineries, automobiles, equipments, instruments and other mechanical items. The Greases and Lubricants are required in almost all Engineering Operations. Completed with the help of machineries. It adds the longitivity and durability of machineries by reducing the frictions between two parts. Several formulations applicable for different parts are mentioned here, with the use of indigenously available raw materials and plant and machineries. The quality products can be manufactured by the manufacturers in accordance with the norms of Bureau of Indian Standards specifications.

1. Sodium Based Grease

Ingredient	*Kg.*
Caustic soda	25
Fats or stearic acid	25
Water	25
Mineral oil	150

2. Sodium Based Soap

Tallow	600
Mineral oil	600
Caustic soda (40%)	90

The grease manufactured by using above formulations are used for lubricating wheels of car and truck.,

3. Cup Grease

Ingredient	*Kg.*
Mineral oil,white	20
Rosin oil	12
Caustic potash (10°Be)	1
Mineral oil, yellow	

4. Ball-Bearing Grease

Ingredient	*kgs.*
Stearic acid	20
Paraffin oil, white	180
Lime water	4

Take 20 kg. stearic acid and 20 kg. paraffin oil in a kettle. Heat these ingredients till complete melting takes place. Now add 4 kg. of lime water with continuous agitation. After complete saponification add rest of the paraffin oil with continuous agitation where the grease reaches the temperature of 40°C, pack it in desired packings.

5. High Speed Ball Bearing Grease

Ingredient	*kgs.*
Calcium soap	8,0
Sodium soap	33.0
Mineral oil (100 - 300 saybolt at 100°F)	160.0
Free Alkol	0.3

6. Carbon Black Grease

Ingredient	*kgs.*
Acetylene carbon black	24
Paraffin oil (pale yellow)	176

7. Silicon Based Grease

Ingredient	*kgs.*
Calcium soap	2.8 - 40
Fine silicon	0.2 - 15
Mineral oil	50 - 90

8. Aluminium Based Grease

Ingredient	*kgs.*
Aluminium stearate (6 to 8%)	40
Mineral oil	500

9. Mixed Base Grease

Ingredient	*kgs.*
Tallow	135.000
Lime water	0.525
Caustic soda	1.500
Water	0.200
Paraffinox oil, pale yellow	84.275

10. Mixed Base Grease

Ingredient	*Patts*
Stearic acid	15.0
Lime water	1.0
Sodium hydroxide	1.5
Aluminium sulphate	3.0
Magnesium chloride	2.0

11. Grease for High Speed Wheels

Ingredient	*Kgs.*
Soap	2
Rope oil	2
Water	10
Talc	4

12. Axle Grease

Ingredient	*Kgs.*
Palm oil	7.0
Anthracene oil	11.0
Rosin oil	5.0
Soap	0.5
Ingredient	*Kgs.*
Fats	114
Spindle oil	870
Slaked lime	14

13. Transparent Grease

Ingredient	*kgs.*
Spindle oil	50
Aluminium Stearate	3
Vegetable tallow	2

14. Roller Bearing Grease

Ingredient	*kgs.*
Sodium stearate	8,0
Sodium naphthenate	3.5
Mineral oil (medium heavy)	40.0
Caustic soda	0.15
Water	as per requirements

15. Grease for Driving Belts

Ingredient	*Kgs.*
Castor oil	90
Litharge	40
Water	40

16. Cup Grease Based on the Formulations

Ingredient	*Kgs.*
Mineral oil (white or yellow)	50
Rosin oil	24
Caustic potash (10° Be') or Hydrated lime	2
Mineral oil (Pale oil)	15

17. Formula for Mixed Soda-Lime Base Grease using Fire

Fire Heated Grease Mixer

Ingredient	%
Hydrated lime	0.5
Inedible tallow	13.5
Caustic soda (to be mixed with 1.5% water)	1.5
Water	0.2
Pale oil having saybolt viscosity of 400 at 100°F	84.3

18. Formula for Gear Grease

Ingredient	*Pounds*
Flaked caustic soda	15
Prime tallow	100
Water	22
Black oil (100 vis/210°F)	4500

19. Formula for Calcium Base Lubricating Grease

This is stable when repeatedly heated above 212°F consists of fatty acids, soaps and a special low viscosity index oil.

Ingredient	%
Soyabean fatty acid	6.7
Animal fatty acid	6.7
Cottonseed fatty acid	6.7
Hydrated lime	3.5
Lubricating oil having viscosity of 115.2 S.U.S. at 210°F.	76.4

20. Composition of Cold Set Calcium Base Grease

This is used for the lubrication of water pumps. It essentially consists of an emulsion as well as a soap thickened oil.

Ingredient	*kgs.*
Paraffiin wax	7
Unsaponified tallow	8
Calcium soap of animal fatty acids	36
(100 viscosity S.U.S. at 100°F) oil	40
Water	7

21. Water Resistant Grease

Ingredient	*Kgs.*
Calcium soap	7
Powdered graphite	15
Talc	5
Lanolin	14
Oil with viscosity of 135 S.U.S. at 210 F	59

22. For Lubrication of Submarine Propeller Shafts, Periscopes, and Gun Mounts

A calcium base lubricating grease is loaded with finely dispersed metallic lead in order to increase density of the lubricant and make it non-floating.

A frost removing grease is a non-corrosive, paste-like composition for preventing tenacious adhesion of frost to chilled surfaces. It contains 60 to 80 percent of white mineral oil, 15% of calcium chloride, the remainder being a calcium soap to provide a grease-like consistency.

23. Formulation For Lithium Soap Base Lubricating Grease

Ingredient	*Parts*
Lithium stearate	72
Naphtha (of 100°F flash point)	100
Phenyl silicone	22
Another composition is -	
Lithium stearate	3
Deodorized kerosene	35
(1 : 1 mixture) of dimethyl and diphenyl silicones	25

24. Mixed Soap Grease which are Reversible

Ingredient	*Parts by wt*
Soyabean oil fatty acids	5.5
Animal fatty acids	3.5
Cottonseed fatty acids	6.5
Hydrated barium oxide	10.0
Aluminium stearate	10.0
Lubricating oil of 50 SUS viscosity at 200°F	65.0

25. Formulation for high temperature lubricating grease

Ingredient	%
Lithium stearate	11.0
Aluminium stearate	2.2
Tributyl phosphite	0.5
Petrolatum	86.3
Total	100. 00

Composition for a wire rope lubricant which has improved internal friction and fatigue life with both anti-rust and low temperature qualities -

Ingredient	%
Lithium soap of hydrogenated fish oil fatty acids	13.0
Aluminium stearate	0.5
Zinc stearate	0.5
Sulfurized sperm oil	7.5
Naphthenic type Mineral oil	Rest

26. Formula for lubricating greases which are useful for lubricating heavy duty gear and chassis are prepared from a mixture of soda and lead soaps composition

Ingredient	%
Sodium soap of rapeseed oil	8 to 18
Mineral oil	20 to 50
Sodium sulphonate	0.1 to 1

The above ingredients are heated to a temperature of 500°F.

To this is added 30 to 60 percent of an oxidised asphalt having a viscosity at 210°F of 100 to 500 S.U.S. This mixture is cooled to 225°F, after which 8 to 12 percent of lead oleate is added.

27. A Soda Base Lubricating Grease containing

Methyl Cellulose is prepared as -

One part of oil soluble in methyl cellulose and insoluble in water (having one methoxy group per glucose unit) is dissolved in 30 parts of water. To this solution is added a mixture of 16 parts of mineral oil and 11 parts of hydrogenated fatty acids and the resulting emulsion is heated to 160°F. 3.5 parts of 45% sodium hydroxide solution is added to this emulsion and agitation is carried on for 3 hours while the mixture is heated to 280°F. The lubricating grease is finally dehydrated at 330°F. Polyvinyl alcohol or casein, or gelatin or natural gum may be used as thickeners.

28. Formula for a Wheel Bearing Lubricant

Two hundred sixty pounds of tallow fatty acids, 50 pounds of tallow and the 70 gallons of low viscosity oil are warmed to 120°F in an open kettle. 46.8 pounds of solid caustic soda (as 35 percent solution in water) is then added while the kettle contents are agitated. 70 gallons of 150 S.U.S. oil at 100°F is added and then further 100 gallons at 210°F is added. The mixture is agitated and then cooled.

29. Formula for a Mixed Base Lubricating Greases

Thirteen parts of stearic acid is melted and then 1 part calcium hydroxide is added. Next 1.5 parts sodium hydroxides is introduced, after which heating is continued until the acids are neutralized. Finally, 3 parts aluminium sulphate and 2 parts magnesium chloride are added in the solution.

Lead Base Lubricant Greases

Ingredient	*lbs.*
Petroleum oil	8.6
Litharge	22.8
Dry caustic soda	7.8
Sodium mahogany soap	14.2
Tallow	28.4

Procedure

Add tallow and the sodium mahogany soap in a mixer, together with about 5 lbs. of oil. Then, heat the mixture to a temperature of 160-180°F. Add caustic soda lye (48°βe). Maintain the temperature of this whole mixture at about 190°F until the mixture thickens. Now add litharge and slowly raise the temperature at about 500°F. Hold this batch until the temperature becomes down. Now add oil and agitate continuously until the temperature is at 300°F. At this stage fill it into containers.

Composition of Mixed Base Lubricating Greases

(1) As per U.S. Patent No. 1,477,611 following lubricant grease to be used on heavy bearing surfaces -

Ingredient	*Wt.*
Mineral oil	33
Water	9
Lead soap	10
Caustic soda	80
Fatty oil	40

(2) Lubricant grease for extreme temperatures, used in Engines, etc. U.S. Patent 2,349,358.

Ingredient	*%*
Sodium lead tallow soap	15 to 4.2

Sodium glyceroxide	1.8 to o-.5
Sodium mahogany soap	2.5 to 0.7
Carbon black	6.0 to 1.7
Litharge and free alkali	0.5 to 0.2
Petroleum oil	74.2 to 92.7

(3) Mixed soap lubricating grease : water insoluble, transparent, temperature stable and reversible:

Ingredient	%
Animal fatty acids	6.72
Cottonseed fatty acids	6.72
Soybean oil fatty acids	6.72
Hydrated barium oxide	12.00
Aluminium stearate	5.00
Lubricating oil	62.40

Procedure

The fatty acids and one-third of the oit are to be heated to 150°F and the barium hydroxide should be added. Stirring and heating to be continued until a temperature of 200°F is reached, then another third of the oil should be added. After this the aluminium stearate is to be dispersed in the remaining oil and is added to the bulk. Temperature should be remained between 300 and 350°F. It is to be filled into containers when the mass is thin and liquid.

Mixed Base Lubricating Greases

Ingredient	%
Hydrogenated fish oil fatty acids	13.00
Lithium hydroxide, 54% strength	2.05
Aluminium stearate	0.50
Zinc naphthenate	0.50
Low pour coastal lubricating oil	41.875
Low viscosity, low pour lubricating oil	41.875
Phenyl alpha naphthylamine	0.20

Procedure

In compounding the lubricating grease, the acid and about one-fourth of the oil is charged to a free-heated kettle and mixed and heated to about 150°F until the acids dissolves in the oil. The lithium hydroxide, dissolved in boiling water, is then added. Heating and agitation be continued and temperature should be raised to 200°F. Then aluminium stearate is added. In the whole process agitation should be continued, adding lubricating oil. After the mixture becomes liquid, at about 370°F, the phenyl alpha naphthylamine and zinc naphthenate, is to be dissolved in the remainder of the oil, is added. Heating is to be discontinued and the lubricating grease is stirred until the temperature drops below 100°F. The bulk is ready for packaging.

Journal Grease

(US Patent 1,989,186)

Ingredient	*lb.*
Heavy black petroleum oil	5.9
Heavy steam refined petroleum oil	34.4
Stearic acid	40.5
Caustic soda (48°Be)	13.1
Lard oil	6.1

Spring Leaf Lubricant

Ingredient	*lbs.*
White lead in linseed oil (92 lead, 8 oil)	83-84
Graphite powder	5.2
Petroleum grease	10.4-10.5
Glycerin	0.1-3

Corrosion Protecting Grease

Ingredient	(1)	*oz.*
Neutral petroleum grease		100
Zinc chromate powder		2 1/2
Pyridin bases (crude)		1

Rub together to form smooth grease.

Ingredient	(2)	*oz.*
Sodium peroxide		1/4
Methanol		2
Hydrogenated phenol		4
Lubricating oil		100

Rod Lubricant

Ingredient	(1)	*gallon*
Ceresin, yellow		25
Sperm oil		25
Tallow		50

Melt together.

Ingredient	(2)	*gallon*
Ceresin, yellow		1
Spindle oil, refined		3.8

Hard Grease

Ingredient	gallon
Train oil fatty acid	12
Lime, hydrated	2
Zinc oxide	2
Spindle oil	82
Water	2

Melting point 75°C

Lubricant Insoluble in Organic Solvents

Ingredient	*oz.*
Anhydrous glycerin	25
Dextrin	7
Pure d - mannitol	3.5

Heat carefully with constant stirring until the solid material is dissolved and the solution begins to boil, then cool to room temperature with stirring. To increase fluidity add more glycerin; to increase greasiness add more mannitol.

Colouring Lubricating Oils

Lubricating oils are improved in colour by adding a solution in mineral oil or other blending agent of the product obtained by heating together until fluorescence develops, an acridine, rhodamine, cosine, or eurhodine dye with stearic acid and a water insoluble soap. Soaps specified are aluminium stearate, magnesium stearate, oleate, or resinate, and zinc soaps. For example, 1 lb. of phosphine 5 g., 1 lb. of stearic acid, and 3 lb. of aluminium stearate are heated to 120°C until the fluorescence is a maximum; the mixture is cooled, pulverized, and dissolved to a 10% solution in a mineral oil, miscible with lubricating oil 0.25 - 0.5 gal. of the solution is added to 100 gal. of lubricating oil.

Refining of Lubricating Oil

Stock of about 68 viscosity index is subjected to the simultaneous action of 10% of aluminium chloride and 10% of fullers earth at a temperature of about 350°F for 1/2 hour.

Purification of Lubricating Oil

If lubricating oil is shaken with phenol, the lower layer consists of oil and impurities in phenol; the upper layer consists of phenol dissolved in pure oil. The phenol is removed and recovered by distillation or by washing with sulphuric acid.

Reclaiming, Used Lubricating Oil

(U.S. Patent 1,936,901)

Ingredient	*Qty.*
Used lubricating oil	100 gal.
Red oil	1 gal.
Calcium hypochloride	6-8 gal.
Sulphuric acid	6 lb.

Mix together and then add

Ingredient	*Quantity by wt.*
Sodium silicate	500 - 100 lb.
Water	10 - 20 gal.

Heat at 52 - 122°C for two hours.
Cool, add water, 3 gal. and separate clear oil.

Fat and Oil Bleaching

In refining fats and oils the colour is improved by adding 8 to 10% soap stock to the fat.

Industrial Cup Greases

	Ingredient	*Pts. by wt.*
(1)	Hydrated lime	1
	Mineral oil	52
	Oleic, stearic, or margaric acid	14

	Ingredient	*Pts. by wt.*
	Animal fat	5
	Mineral oil residue	75
	Slaked lime	15
	Manganese oxide	5

	Ingredient	*Pts. by wt.*
(3)	Lime	2
	Rendered suet	35
	Sulphur	14
	Graphite	19
	Heavy petroleum oil	30

	Ingredient	*Qty.*
(4)	Lard oil	150 gals.
	Inedible tallow	300 lbs.
	Hydrated lime	198 lbs.
	Western mineral lubricating oil	900 gals.

	Water	75 gals.
	Oil mirbane	6 lbs.
	Ingredient	*Wt.*
(5)	Hydrated lime	1.64
	Tallow	10.00
	Pale oil	60.64
	Asphalt	18.00
	Caustic soda	0.02
	Water	6.70

(Black cup grease)

Ingredient	Wt.
Hydrated lime	1.85
Tallow	11.74
Pale oil	64.62
Asphalt	14.17
Caustic soda	0.02
Water (Black sup grease)	7.30

Free Lubricant

Ingredient	Pts. by wt.
Palm oil	4 1/2
Cottonseed oil	10
Crude petroleum	25

Wire Cable Compound

Ingredient	Percent by wt.
100 to 120 penetration blown asphalt	23.00
Degras	23.00
Raw linseed oil	5.30
Fish oil	2.70
300 S.U.V. at 100° F naphthenic pale oil	23.00
Pine tar	23.00

The use of sulphur for manufacturing lubricants of high film strength is rapidly gaining popularity. The formula given here will produce a base which can be diluted with mineral oils to make cutting oil and other extreme pressure compounds.

Ingredient	*wt.*
Flower of sulphur	10 lb,
Lard oil	90 lb.

Mix well and slowly raise the temperature to 425°F. Maintain mild agitation throughout.

Calcium Base Cold Neck Grease

Ingredient	Kgs.
Tallow	75.00
Hydrated lime powder	10.00
Talc	12.50
Water	10.00
Flake graphite	30.00
Fine powdered graphite	10.00
Caustic potash	1.00
Cylinder stock	100.00

Calcium Base Gear Grease with Filler

Ingredient	Gallons
Oleic acid	2
Spindle oil	10
Lime water	6
Saw dust	45

Antirust Compound

Ingredient	Qty.
Paraffin wax	6 lb.
Asphaltic still residue (Above 1000 visc. at 210°F.)	94 lb.

Steering Gear Lubricant

Ingredient	Qty.
Oleic acid	300 lb.
Lime	43 lb.
Water	16 gal.
Western cylinder oil	475 gal.
Sulphur base	1000 lb.

Non-Bleeding Grease

One of the difficulties encountered in the use of pressure grease is the tendency of the light oil to separate and bleed away leaving the bearing choked with a hard soap. The present formula is for automobile chassis lubrication and similar application -

Ingredient	*Qty.*
Green petroleum	250 lb.
Paraffin pale oil (280Be')	92 gal.
Lime	9 lb.

Rust preventive oil

Ingredient	*Parts by wt.*
Triethanolamine	0.20
Sodium rosinate	1.00
Sodium petroleum sulphonate	10.00
Oleic acid	0.20
Tetrachlorophenol	0.25
Alcohol	0.40
Mineral oil	85.45
Water	1.45

Non-Greasy Lubricant

Ingredient	*(U.S.Patent 1,970,902)*
Sodium alginate	19 oz.
Water	100 oz.
Mix to a smooth paste while heating to 100° C add	
Glycerine	76 oz.

Boil off nearly all of the water

Chain Lubricant

Ingredient	*gal.*
Stearin	85
Bees wax	5
Carnauba wax	5
Japan wax	5
Total	100

Ingredient	*gal.*
Stearin	85
Bees wax	2.5
Carnauba wax	5
Japan wax	5

Pour at lowest possible temperature and allow to cool slowly and (undisturbed.

Penetrating Oil (Useful for loosening rusted metal parts)

Ingredient	*Qty.*
Engine oil	1 qt.
Naphtha or kerosene	3 qt.
Carbon disulphide	2 oz.
Oil of camphor	1-2 oz.
Graphite powder	1-4 oz.

Core Oil

Ingredient	*Qty.*
Linseed oil	300 oz.
American gas oil	600 oz.
Dark whale train oil	100 oz.
Ingredient	Qty.
Rosin	200 oz.
Train oil	200 oz.
Vulcan oil	600 oz.

Stuffing Grease

Ingredient		
(Melting point over 96°C)		gal.
(a)	Tallow	12
	Lard oil	3
(b)	Lime hydrate	2.5
(c)	Zinc oxide	2.5
(d)	Machine oil	79
	Refined 4-5°E. Viscosity 50°C.	
(e)	Yellow aniline dye, oil soluble	0.03
(f)	Water	1.00

Non-Corrosive Cutting Oil (US Patent 1,979,250)

Ingredient	*Qty.*
Mineral oil	71-74lb.
Castor oil	8¼-9½lb.
Rapeseed oil	8¼-9½lb.
Caustic potash	8¼-9½lb.
Soda ash	0.6-1¼lb.

Mix and dilute with water.

Most plants have the laboratory to make consistency determinations before batches are packed. The most reliable result will be obtained if the samples are cooled to 77°F before penetrations are taken, but some laboratories make such tests at higher temperatures. In such cases, charts are prepared showing the correction required for various temperatures so that the results will correspond with those obtained at 77°F.

Some Suggested Formulas

Ingredient	*Pts. by wt.*
1. Oleic acid	8.00
Hydrated acid	1.04
Coastal distillate	18.20
Coastal bright stock	72.76
Total	100.00

The oleic acid is to be dissolved in a portion of the oil and the hydrated lime mixed with another portion before combining.

2. A calcium based lubrication grease which is stable when repeatedly heated above 212'F consists of fatty acid soaps and a special low V.I. oil. AU.S. Patent 2,332,825 gives the following formula

Ingredient	
Animal fatty acids	6.76
Cottonseed fatty acids	6.72
Soyabean fatty acids	6.72
Dephenolized phenol extract	76.60
Hydrated lime	3.20
Total	100.00

The above oil has a viscosity of 115.2 SUS at 210'F and a V.I, of -45, The fatty acids are dissolved in 4/5 of the oil and heated to 180°F, after which the lime as a slurry with the remainder oil, is added to the mixing vessel. Agitation and heating to 180'F is then continued until the reaction is complete, which will be an hour or longer. If desired the mixture can be dehydrated at 250' - 300"F. In either case the finished product is cooled before packaging. Penetration 150 - 72'F.

3. Lubricant particularly useful for water-Pumps

Ingredient	%
Calcium soap of animal fatty acids	36
100 viscosity SUS at 100°F oil	40
Paraffin wax	7
Unsaponified tallow	8
Water	9
Total	100

The fatty acids, tallow, and paraffin were melted with half the oil at a temperature of about 140°F. The hydrated lime required to neutralize the fatty acids was mixed with the remainder of the oil and the water then added. The latter mixture was added to the first with very vigorous agitation and the product was filled into packages at once.

4. Automobile Lubricants

	Ingredient	*Qty.*
(i)	Fat	12.55
	Hydrated lime	1.93
	Oil with a viscosity of 1200 to 1500 SUS at 100°F	35.52
	Powdered graphite of 25% graphite carbon content	50.00

(ii)	Animal fatty acids	98 lbs.
	Hydrated lime	135 lbs.
	Oil with a viscosity of 2000 SUS at 100°F	195 gls.
	Flux oil, viscosity 3000 SUS at 210°F	105 gls.
	Black oil, viscosity 190 to 210 SUS at 210°F1115lbs.	
	Powdered graphite	

5. Water-resistant Grease

Ingredient	*Qty.*
Calcium soap	6 to 8
Powdered graphite	12 to 15
Talc	4 to 5
Tallow	5 to 6
Degras	12 to 15
Oil with viscosity 135 to 145 SUS at 210°F	51 to 61

6. Axle Greases

The production of axle grease depends upon the neutralization with lime of the acids in rosin oil. The reaction takes place readily at temperature of about 100°F in a period of less than one minute.

Two mixtures are cited. One is named "Compound"' the other is "Sett".

Compound

Rosin oil	300 pounds
Black oil	225 gallons

Sett

Black oil	105 gallons
Rosin oil	5 pounds
Hydrated lime	200 pounds

In mixing the Sett, stir the rosin oil with the black oil before the lime is added. The two mixtures are heated to approx. 100°F. If only one mixing kettle has provision for heat, the contents of this vessel can be slightly higher than 100°F, so that the final mix of the two will be close to the desired temperature. For the actual grease formulation a proportioning device is desirable so that 2 parts of the above compound can be mixed with 1 part of Sett.

Compound

Rosin oil	600 pounds
Black oil viscosity 60 to 80 SUS at 210°F	360 gallons

Sett

Hydrated lime	550 pounds
Black oil	300 gallons

All the above formulas are useful for making a dark axle grease, with an unmarked penetration of 140 to 170 and a worked penetration of 300 to 330.

Light Axle Grease

Light axle grease is similar in procedure except for the oil used, having a low viscosity, and light coloured.

Compound

Roisn oil	600 pounds
Oil, viscosity 100-120 SUS at 100°F	300 gallons

Sett

Hydrated lime	550 pounds
Water	18 gallons
Oil, viscosity 100-120 SUS at 100°F	280 gallons
Rosin oil	10 pounds

In making the Sett, the rosin oil is mixed with the mineral oil, after which the hydrated lime is added while agitation continues. After a thorough mixture is obtained, the water is added, and then mixing is continued until a good emulsion results. Equal amount of the Compound and of the Sett are then brought together to form a lubricant with an unworked penetration of 130 to 160. The water used with low viscosity oil product seams to reduce oil separation in the finished product.

Fillers in Axle Grease

1.5% flake mica may be used; so is the case for talc. Clays of various kinds are also added. These may be added from 10% to 30%. Graphite is the most widely used filler in axle greases. The proportion varies from a fraction of 1% to 10%, as desired. Fullers earth, and even water is also used as fillers.

Lubricant containing Carbohydrates

Ingredient	*Parts by Wt*
Wormwood salts	80
Ammonium hydrochlorate	10
Phenol	1
Water	50

Heat Stable Ball Bearing Grease

Ingredient	*Parts by Wt.*
Sardine oil	10.0
Stearic acid	2.0
Hydrated lime	2.0
Caustic soda	1.0

Aluminium base pressure gum grease	10.0
Lead oleate	5.0
Carnauba wax	5.0
Degrease	4.0
300 Western neutral	51.0

Procedure

The sardine oil and stearic acid may be saponified by heating with hydrated lime and water in an open vessel. The 300 western neutral oil is added to the lime soap. The aluminium base gurn grease, lead oleate, carnauba wax, and degras are then added. A fluid product results. It seems probable that the free fatty acids from the carnauba wax and degras are responsible for the fluid condition of the product. 45°Be' Caustic soda is therefore added to neutralize the fatty acids. The final product is heated to 250°F, and allowed to cool.

Water-proof Grease for Plug Valves

Ingredient	*Part by Wt.*
Powdered graphite	2
Petroleum residue (M.P. 85 - 100°F)	2
Anhydrous calcium soap	1

Pin Cup Greases

Ingredient	*Part by Wt.*
Free fat	1.7
Free fatty acids	1.04
Combined fat	7.96
Free Cao	0.22
Combined Cao	0.79
Water	1.25
Mineral oil	86.94

Ingredient	*Part by Wt.*
Hydrated lime	1.345
Caustic soda (dissolved in water to 40°Be')	0.048
Water	1.400
Mineral oil	2.500

Pneumatic Tool Grease

Ingredient	*Part by Wt.*
Soap	13.6
Ash	1.55
Iron and acid insoluble	3.20
Sodium carbonate	4.40

Calcium oxide	88.30

Winter Grade Curve Grease

Ingredient	*gals.*
Prepared oil	3.0
Asphalt base fuel oil, 16°Be'	3.5
Kidney rosin oil	1.0
Dark sett	5.5

Finished Grease

Ingredient	*Part by Wt.*
Fuel oil	78.17
Kidney rosin oil	7.80
Calcium oxide	5.61
Water	8.42
Total	100.00

Summer Grade Curve Grease

Base	gals.
Prepared oil	3.00
Asphalt base fuel oil, 16°Be'	3.50
Kidney rosin oil	1.00
Dark sett	5.00

Finished Grease

Ingredient	*Part by Wt.*
Fuel oil	78.13
Kidney rosin oil	8.30
Calcium oxide	5.43
Water	8.14

Axle Grease Medium

Ingredient	*Pts. by wt.*
Rosin oil	0.05
Water	2.80
Hydrated lime	3.36
Light vacuum distillate	29.05

Prepared Oil or Rosin Oil

Ingredient	*Pts. by wt*
Rosin oil	22.36
Fuel oil	42.38

Sett Greases

Ingredient	*Pts. by wt.*
Borax	5
Water	15
Tallow	45
Powdered sulfur	5
Lime	5
Graphite	10
White lead	4
Rosin	6
Mineral oil	5
	gals.
Black oil	6
Rosin	5
Lime water	5
Melted tallow	1
	lbs.
Talc	6
Spanish whiting	6
	quart
Spirits of niter	1

Fibre Grease

Ingredient	*lbs.*
Prime tallow	22.5
Caustic soda	150
Water	33
Paraffin oil 130 vis./100°F	600

PROCEDURE

The tallow and an equal weight of the paraffin oil are charged in a fire heated kettle and the temperature brought to 100°F.

The caustic soda dissolved in the water is then added to the mixture in the kettle and the temperature brought to 250° to 300°F, in from one to two hours.

The balance of the oil is run and the temperature brought to 400°F.

The fire is then drawn and the batch cooled to 200°F while stirring. It then may be filled into containers.

Lead Naphthenate base Hypoid Gear Lubricant

Ingredient		*Part by Wt.*
Lead naphthenate		18.0
Sulphur		1.5
1000 S.U.V. at 100° F black oil		80.0
80 Tar		0.5
	Total	100.0

Hot Bearing Grease (for heavy loaded hot bearings)

Ingredient	*Qty*
Tallow fatty acid	i 4.0
Refined montan wax	3.0
Engine oil (6.7°F at 50°C)	79.5
Lime hydrate	1.5
Caustic soda (40°Be')	3.0

Leather Stuffing Grease

Ingredient		kg.
1. Montan wax, crude		12
Ceresin		3
Woolfat, neutral		5
Car waste oil		50
Birch Tar		3
Train oil		27
	Total	100

Ingredient		*Qty.*
2. Woolfat, neutral		30
Train oil		50
Tallow		20
	Total	100

Ingredient	*lb.*
3. Sulphonated grease	1
Castor oil	1 /2
Mineral oil	1/2
4. Train oil, brown, clear	40
Woolfat, crude	25
Rubber solution (6%)	10
Crude montan wax	10

Ingredient	Qty.
Spindle oil	12
Birch tar	1
Total	100

Ingredient	Qty.
5. Yellow: Ozokerite-ceresin, yellow (58/60°C)	17
Spindle oil, distilled	83
Total	100

Ingredient	lb.
6. Yellow: Scale wax, yellow, 50/52°C	10
Montan wax, bleached	10
Rosin, pale	5
Spindle oil, distilled	75
Total	100

Ingredient	Qty.
7. Brown: Montan wax, crude	10
Rosin, dark	10
Scale wax	5
Spindle oil, distilled	75
Total	100

Ingredient	Qty
8. Black: Montan wax, crude	12
Rosin, dark	10
Scale wax	3
Spindle oil, distilled	73
Nigrosin, oil soluble	2
Total	100

Ingredient	kg.
9. Black: Montan wax, crude	15
Ozokerite ceresin, yellow	3
Woolfat,crude	5
Black leather dye, oil soluble	2
Spindle oil, distilled	75
Total	100

Liquid Belting Lubricant

Ingredient	*lb.*
(a) Rosin	7.5
Woolfat	7.5
(b) Train oil	30.0
Rosin oil or Mineral oil	55.0
Total	100.0

Melt (a) in a kettle. Dilute with (b) which is stirred slowly.
To get more viscous compositions, the liquid components may be reduced.

Belt Preserving Grease

Ingredient	*kgs.*
1. Woolfat, neutral	30
Tallow, free of acid	25
Degras	15
Train oil	30
Total	100

2. For protecting and softening the leather

Ingredient	*gals.*
Woolfat, neutral	30
Tallow	30
Train oil	25
Degras	14
Birch tar	1
Total	100

Ingredient	
3. Beef tallow	50
Paraffin wax (50/52°C)	10
Turpentine	10
Saturated steam cylinder oil, very fluid	50
Rosin, ground	10

Melt the first three ingredients on the steam bath, add the oil, stir until cooled, and stir in the rosin.

Ingredient	*lbs.*
4. Bees wax	4
Pitch	5

Resin	3
Neatsfood oil	13

The beeswax is melted first and the other ingredients are added in the order described above.

Lubricating Grease

[German Patent 613,362]

Neutral oil (Paraffin base viscosity 6.22 E, at 37.8°C) 1970 kgs.

Aluminium stearate 270 kg.

Heat up slowly to 127°C (in about 7 hours). Cool quickly.

Adherent Lubricating Grease

Ingredient	*[French Patent 797,054]*
Calcium soap	12
Rubber	0.5
Glycerol	1
Water	1
Red solar oil	85.5
Total	100.0

The rubber is heated to 188° and agitated to reduce the water content to 1 %.

Ball Bearing Grease

Ingredient	*kgs.*
(a) Stearic acid	10
Paraffin oil, white	30
(b) Lime hydrate water	2
(c) Paraffin oil, whits	56

1. White

Melt (a), saponifying hot with (b); add (c) in small portions. Keep stirring until cold, homogenize.

Ingredient	*kgs.*
(a) Train oil fatty acid	16
Mineral oil, pale	30
(b) Lime hydrate water	2
(c) Mineral oil, pale	40

2. Yellow

High Speed Ball Bearing Grease [Canadian Patent]

Ingredient	*OZ.*
Calcium soap	3.9
Sodium soap	16.0
Mineral oil (100-300 saybolt at 100°F)	78.7
Lime hydrate	1.5

Lubricant for Rubber Bearings [U.S.Patent 2,083,176]

Ingredient	*OZ.*
Glycerin	50.0
Water	50.0
Graphite, fine powdered	0.2

Lubricating Grease of low softening point for Rollar and Similar Bearings

Ingredient	
Oleic acid	8 oz.
Spindle oil, refined (visc, 2.5 - 4°E at 20°C)	86.7 kg.
Lime hydrate	1.3 kg.

Lubricating Grease for Hot Bearings

Ingredient	*kg.*
1. Tallow	300
Caustic soda, solid	42
Engine oil, refined (Viscosity 3.5°E at 50°C)	658

Kettle should be filled only to one-third. Heat the tallow to 50°C. start the mixer.

Dissolve the soda in 158 liters of water (yields 200 kg. lye) ; and add it to the melted tallow slowly. Heat until the tallow is completely saponified.

Add slowly 50 kg. oil, wait until smooth, add 250 kg. oil in small portions. Heat to 150°C., until all water is boiled away.

Add the remaining; pre-heated oil to the kettle, stir until cooled to 90°C., pour off.

A softer product can be held by adding the oil (50°C) to the finished soap, stirring thoroughly, and by only heating to 65 - 70°C.

Ingredient	*kg.*
2. Tallow	250
Caustic soda, solid	3
Engine oil, refined (viscosity 3.5° E at 50°C.)	715

Hot Bearing Grease

Ingredient	*kg.*
Tallow fatty acid	14.0
Montan wax, refined	3.0
Engine oil (6 - 7 E at 50°C.)	79.5
Lime hydrate	1.5
Caustic soda (40°Be')	3.0

Grease for Pressure Lubrication

Ingredient	*kg.*
Stearic acid	10
Oleic acid	8
Engine oil (6 - 7°E at 50°C.)	76
Lime hydrate	3

Cold-Roller Grease

Ingredient	*kgs.*
1. (Lubricant for rollers, pulleys, bearings)	
Crude woolfat	15
Woolfat stearin	5
Engine oil (viscosity 7 - 8°E at 50°C.)	78
Caustic soda (40° Be')	6
2. Train oil fatty acid	15
Tallow	3
Engine oil (Viscosity 7 - 8° E at 50°C.)	79
Caustic soda (40°Be')	8

Lubricant Briquets

Ingredient	*kg.*
1. Woolfat fatty acid	14
Rosin	8
Engine oil (7 - 8°E at 50°C.)	75
Caustic soda (40°Be')	9
2. Crude woolfat	10.0
Rosin	10.0
Engine oil (7-8E at 50°C.)	77.5
Caustic soda (40°Be')	8.0

Carriage Greases

(a) Woolfat fatty acid	15
Mineral oil	20
(b) Lime hydrate (in water)	2
(c) Mineral oil, pale	62

Light Brown

The melted (a) is saponified with (b) and thinned by (c).

Black

	Ingredient	*kgs.*
(a)	Woolfat fatty acid	17
	Paraffin oil. dark	25
(b)	caustic soda (24° Be')	10
(c)	paraffin ~ oil, dark	53
	Ceres black	0:5

Yellow: (Unfilled)

(a)	Rosin (stock) oil	27
	Mineral oil, pale	40
(b)	Lime hydrate	9
	Mineral oil, pale	24

Dissolve (a) with heat and stirring, and grind (b) separately until smooth. Add the thin paste (b) to the oil (a) with thorough agitation. A very heavy gel is formed.

Carriage, Greases Filled

	Ingredient	kgs.
(a)	Rosin oil	18
	Gas oil	31
(b)	Lime hydrate	6
	Gypsum	15
	Talc	5
	Paraffin oil, dark	25
	Total	100

Brown

Make up solution (a) and suspension (b) separately, mix to obtain gel.

(a)	Montan wax, crude	18
	Woolfat fatty acid	2
(b)	Paraffin oil, dark	22
(c)	Caustic soda (24° Be')	7
(d)	Gas oil	44
(e)	Barytes	10

Natural Colour:

Carriage Grease, Medium Quality

(a)	Rosin oil	21
	Mined oil, pale	30
(b)	Lime hydrate	7
	Gypsum	12
	Gas oil	30
	Total	100

Yellow:

(a)	Rosin oil	21
	Mineral oil, pale	30
(b)	Lime hydrate	7
	Gypsum	12
	Gas oil	30
	Total	100

Lubricating Greases for Driving Gears

Castor oil	30
Tallow	20
Colophony	20
Sodium hydroxide, solid	14
Cylinder oil (Viscosity 3.4°E at 100°C)	1916

Procedure

Kettle should be open, steam heated, to operate at 130 - 150°C, should be equipped with cooling system and its stirring gear should be able to make 35-40 revolutions per minute.

1. Put in the castor oil, tallow, colophony and 66 kg. of the cylinder oil.
2. Mix thoroughly at 90°C.
3. Make a 40°Be' aqueous solution of the sodium hydroxide.
4. Keep stirring all the time.
5. Add slowly the caustic soda.
6. Heat up slowly to 140°C, until after about 2 hours, the water will be boiled away.
7. Now add slowly the cylinder oil (about 400 kgs. should enter the kettle during 1 hour). Keep at 140°C.
8. Test, as soon as all is added, if enough water has boiled away.
9. If ready, cool as quickly as possible to secure a good consistency. Keep stirring until 35°C is reached.
10. Beware of too much air beaten into the mixtures.
11. Draw off at 35°C.

Chapter 17

LUBRICANTS AND THEIR MANUFACTURE

Introduction

Lubricants include substances having a wide range of physical properties. They are usually in the liquid state, although solids (graphite) and gases (air) may be used in certain applications. Liquid lubricants in turn vary widely in their physical properties. Mineral oils, ranging from extremely fluid liquids to highly viscous products are commonly used. The primary purposes of a lubricant is to reduce friction. However these may serve many purposes such as conducting the heat of friction away from the bearings, serving as a seal to exclude undesirable substances from the bearings, and acting as a carrier for rust preventives, antifrictipn agents, extreme pressure additives etc.

Composition of Mineral Oil

Lubricants other than mineral oils are sometimes used. These are synthetic compounds and other naturally occurring products obtained from a source other than petroleum. Since petroleum lubricants are relatively inexpensive, the non-petroleum products find a use only where petroleum is scarce.

Crude petroleum consists of very complex mixture of hydrocarbons plus minor amounts of other organic compounds, chiefly those containing oxygen, sulfur, or nitrogen.

Refining

The refining of lubricating oil involves various steps, to remove certain undesirable components. Some refining methods are chemical, while others are purely physical. The physical methods include distillation, solvent precipitation, solvent extraction, crystallization, and adsorption. In the chemical methods of refining, treatmentwith sulfuric acid is mostly adopted. Others include hydrogenation and treatment with aluminium chloride.

Blending

Blending in lubricating oils imparts required viscosity requirements and the incorporations of specific additives. Additives are added up to five percent.

Additives are added for the following reasons -

(a) To impart extreme pressure characteristics.
(b) To reduce pour point.
(c) To improve viscosity temperature relationship.
(d) To inhibit oxidation.
(e) To reduce bearing corrosion.
(f) To cause emulsification.
(g) To reduce or elimimate rusting.

Process of blending consists of mixing, since the final product is a homogeneous solution.

Non-Petroleum Lubricants

Various lubricants of this category vary from low grade subtitutes to high grade products for highly specialized applications. Some of the lubricants are -

Molasses and its dehydration residue for transmission.

Two percent dextrose solutions as soluble oils.

Polymerized anthracene and solutions of orthosilicates for various purposes.

Mixture of sea-mud and potassium soaps as axle grease.

Vegetable oils, including olive, castor, and cottonseed oil are used as crank case lubricants.

Synthetic Hydrocarbons

Lubricating oil made by the polymerization of olefins do not form insoluble oxidation products (sludge) when heated in the presence of air. Synthetic oils of the olefin polymer type may be made from coal by utilizing the Fischer-Tropsch process, in which carbon monoxide and hydrogen, which are produced from coal via the water gas reaction, are converted to a mixture of olefinic and paraffinic hydrocarbon. Lubricating oils maybe made by polymerizing these olefins. Aluminium chloride or other metal halide are usually employed as catalyst in this reaction. Other catalyst include sulfuric acid and clay. Synthetic oil may also be made by reacting an olefin with an aromatic. This may be accomplished by chlorinating the olefin, and allowing the chlorinated olefin to react with an aromatic, e.g. xylene, by the Friedel-crafts reaction. Coke oven tar and coke oven gas have been used as starting materials in the manufacture of lubricating oils of this type.

Synthetic Non-Hydrocarbons

Four different types of non-hydrocarbons lubricants are used in the industry. These are silicones, polyalkylene glycols, diesters, and fluorocarbons. All are more expensive than mineral oils.

Silicones

The silicones derive their name from the similarity between their empirical formula, R2Si0, to that of ketone.

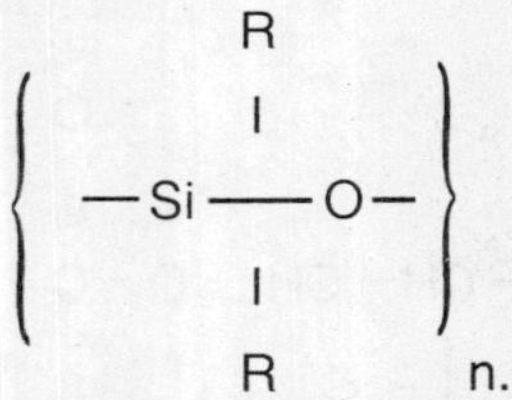

Silicones are made by the hydrolysis of dialkyl dichloro silanes, SiC12R2, which are in turn made either through the Grignard reaction, or by direct action of silicon on an alkyl halide.

$2RMgCl + SiCl_4 \rightarrow R_2SiCl_2 + 2MgCl_2$

or,

$Si0_2 + 2\ C \rightarrow Si + 2CO$

$Si + 2RCl \rightarrow R_2SiCl_2$

Properties of the polymer may be varied, by changing the 'R' group or by changing the chain length. The commercially available silicones have been classified into the following four groups according to their properties -

1. Varnishes and Resins
2. Rubbers
3. Greases
4. Fluids.

The silicones are chracterized by a high stability and low volatility. The fluids have low freezing points and very flat viscosity temperature curves.

They are virtually insoluble in mineral oil. They are used as hydraulic fluids and liquid dielectrics. Both the heavy fluids and the greases are used as lubricants for special application.

Polyalkylene Glycols

The polylkyalene glycols have several unique properties which recommend them as lubricating oil. They have viscosity temperature curve which, while considerably steeper than those of the silicones, are flatter than those of mineral oils. They are only partially miscible with most mineral oils at room temperatures, but become completely miscible at elevated temperature.

Diesters

Number of esters of diabasic acids, e.g. phthalic, adipic, and sebacic are used as light lubricating oil. Di -2 ethyl hexyl sebacate the most common of this category is

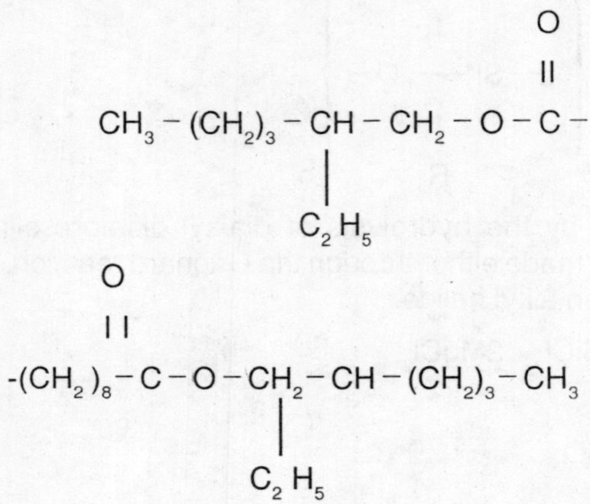

It has a very low freezing point and a low volatility. Its viscosity is that of a very light lubricating oil. This combination of properties makes this compound useful as an instrument oil e.g. for use in aircraft.

Esters of monobasic acids and polyhydric alcohols have also been used as lubricating oils.

Fluorocarbons

These are made by fluorinating bydrocarbons in the liquid phase with silver fluoride. Their outstanding characteristic is their extreme stability. They are therefore suitable for applications involving very high temperatures.

Chapter 18

VARIOUS FORMULATIONS OF LUBRICANTS AND GREASE

Textile Lubricants

		Ingredient	*Lb.*
1.		Monoamylamine/oleate	4
		Paraffin oil (28°Be')	96
		Mix the above and stir into water	100
			G.
2.	(a)	Rosin	6.4
		Mineral oil	20
	(b)	Olein, light	10.5
	(c)	Spindle oil	73.4
	(d)	Alcohol	5.4
	(e)	Caustic soda (40°Be')	2.2

Melt up (a) with agitation, until clear. Add (b), (c), cool down to 45°C, add (d) and, with vigorous mixing, (e) in small portions, until the cloudiness disappears.

Some olein may also be needed if it does not work clearly.

Lubrication for Wool

Ingredient	*G.*
Olive oil	87
Oleic acid	10
Trigamine	3
Water	100 cc.

The above emulsion Is suggested as a wool lubricant so that the wool fibers in the carding and combing operations pass over one another with the least possible amount of frictional resistance. The oil in emulsions made with trigamine is of an extremely fine particle size and comes into contact with the fibers very rapidly, thoroughly and uniformly. Furthermore, the oil emulsion is very easily removed during scouring.

Lubricant for Worsted Yarn

Ingredient	*kg.*
Oleic acid	40
Triethanolamine	2
Water	60

Stir together at about 35°C, and transfer immediately into a homogenizer, where the emulsion is homogenized under about 150 atmos- phere pressure.

Textile Lubricant for Spinning Jute, etc.

Ingredient	*kg.*
Train oil, dark	30 - 50
Spindle oil, distilled	30 - 50

Rope Lubricant (British Patent 455,652)

Ingredient	*oz.*
Mineral oil	72
Aluminium oleate	2 1/2
Hydroquinone	1/2

Warm together and stir until disolved.

Some Important Formula

Ingredient	*Parts*
Sea-fish oil soap (50%)	31.8
Menhaden oil	5.0
Sodium hydroxide	3.0
Residuum of a Furol viscosity at 210°F of 850 sec.	49.5
Low cold test oil of 80 - 85 SUS at 100°F	10.7

The procedure of manufacture is as above. The menhaden oil being added to the mixture before the sodium hydroxide is introduced. This lubricant is stirred as it cools to 300°F, at which point it is filled.

U.S.Patent 2,349,058

Ingredient	*Lb.*
Tallow	28.4
Sodium mahogany soap	14.2
Dry caustic soda	7.8
Litharge	22.8
Petroleum oil	8.6

The tallow and the sodium mahogany soap are added to a mixer, together with about 5 pounds of oil. After this mxture is heated to 160 to 180°F the caustic soda is added as a 48°Be'solution and the temperature of the batch maintained at 180 to 200°F until the mixture thickens. The litharge is then added and the temperature raised slowly to about 500°F. The batch is held at this temperature until it becomes smooth, after which the remainder of the oil is added and agitation continued until the temperature drops to about 300°F at which point the product is filled into containers or further processed.

Such lulbricating greases are formulated with a slight excess of litharge and alkali and will therefore have from 0.02 to 1.2% of such material in the final product. Lubricating greases prepared from these complex lead soaps are smooth, stringy, and tacky, but still fibrous enough to be pulled back to the face of the gear teeth after each revolution. These lubricating greases have good worked stability and are resistant to hot water.

Preparation of Complex Soap Lead Base Greases

Another U.S. Patent 2,292,672, gives a method for lead based complex soap greases : A very small amount of low viscosity oil is added to mixer, followed by the required amount of litharge. This mixture is stirred until a smooth paste results. The menhaden oil and an equal amount of low viscosity oil are then mixed with the paste and the entire mixture heated at 300 to 325°F for two to three hours, by which time the reaction should be complete. The remainder of the mineral oil and also blown asphalt are then added and mixed at a temperature of 200 to 250°F.

Formulas, as given in U.S. Patent 2,292,672:

	Light(%)	Medium(%)	Heavy(%)
Menhaden oil	4.49	4.49	4.49
Litharge	3.51	3.51	3:51
Blown asphalt .	30.00	40.00	51.00
80/85 at 100°F, Low cold test oil	26.00	30.00	41.00
175/185 at 210°F, Bright stock	36.00	22.00	X

Lead Base Lubricating Greases Containing Fillers

Lubricating greases containing complex lead soaps and also from 1.0 to 20.0% of carbon black are described in a US Patent 2,349,058. Its containing free litharge, is considered a filler. Another filler added is the carbon black. It increases the water resistance and improves the heat resistance of the lubricant and greases. Other fillers are asbestos, talc, and graphite.

Lead based Lubricating Greases Formula

	Heavy (%)	Medium (%)	Light (%)
(i) Lead-sodium soap	15.0	11.3	4.2
Sodium grlyceroxide	1.8	1.3	0.5
Sodium mahogany soap	2.5	1.9	0.7
Carbon black	6.0	4.5	1.7
Litharge and free alkali	0.5	0.5	0.2
Oil 5900 SUS at 100°F	74.2	80.5	92.7
			Parts
(ii) Litharge			5.95
Menhaden oil			11.80
Sodium hydroxide			2.55
Low cold test 80/85 SUS at 100°F oil			29.40
Residum 850 Sec. Furol at 210°F			35.30
Heavy black oil			15.00

Application of Lead Base Lubricating Greases

Except in the case of the lead soap of 12 hydroxy stearic acid, lead soaps are not employed as thickeners for lubricating oils, because,

(1) lubricating greases in which they are present resist the scrapping and sliding action of such mechanisms as worm gears, etc., (2) and to provide a carrier for lead which may later react with another ingredients, such as chlorine and sulfur for preventing seizure and scoring of metal surfaces under heavy loads.

Types of Greases Manufactured in India (According to information received from Standard Vacuum Oil Company Ltd., Bombay) :

Industrial Greases

Lime base cup greases for plain bearings.

Lime base greases for open gear lubrication.

Lime base semifluid greases for loose boss arbors, weight hooks, light duty guarded open gems, etc., in textile industry.

Lime base graphite greases for heavy duty plain bearings.

Lime base soft grease for mechanical grease lubrication systems.

Lime base grease for cold roll necks in steel mills.

Soda base grease for open type bearings in industrial machinery.

Aluminium base graphited grease.

Asphaltic base grease/Lubricants for open gears.

Automotive Greases

Lime, soda, and aluminium base greases for different parts of automobiles, and other vehicles.

Railroad Greases

Fraction gear greases.

Lime base rail and flange lubrication greases. Lime base low consistency grease for locomotive lubrication.

Soda base journal and road cup greases.

Soda base grease for general lubrication.

Specifications

Greases are graded on the basis of their worked penetration values. The 'dropping point' that is the temperature at which grease drops out of cup having an orifice at the bottom, is also employed for characterising greases. It gives an approximate idea of the maximum temperature at which the grease can be used in a bearing. Free alkalinity, and free acidity are generally specified, so also the ash content which provides a check on the soap content of the grease. The viscosity of the lubricating oil component is also spacified as this is useful to lubricating engineers in recommending greases for different purposes. The Indian Standards Institution has formulated various standards. Some of the main standards' content is given here:

Specification for Soda and Lime Greases

Nature of soap base	S.S. of loco Grease Soda	Grease 1 No.3 Lime
Ash (sulphate), % max.	5.50	5.00
Evaporation Loss, max	1.00	1.50
Consistency of worked material at 77°F, penetration in 0.1 mm.	200-250	230-280
Free acidity as oleic acid, % max.	0.40	1.00
Free alkalinity as ca$(OH)_2$, NaOH, % max	0.30	0.25
Drop. Pt. min	150°C	25°C
Water content, % max.	X	1.0
Viscosity of mineral oil Component, redwood No.	64-86 at 210°F	93-136 at 140°F

Strontium Based Lubricating Grease

Use: Strontium bases are particularly important because unlike other bases, they are soluble in water-cold as well as hot.

RAW MATERIALS

For forming strontium base grease the strontium compounds needed are (1) strontium hydroxide, and (2) strontium stearate. The former is primarily and mostly useful as they can be procured during manufacturing process, and comparatively economical as well. Strontium hydroxide may also contain some barium or calcium compounds.

As a soap base, tallow, lard oil, hog fat, stearic acid, oleic acid, the higher molecular weight acids resulting from the oxidation of petroleum fractions, rosin, higher molecular weight naphthenic acid, sulfonic acid, beeswax, sperm oil, and degras are needed for the manufacture of strontium base greases.

A variety of lubricant oils can be employed in strontium base lubricating greases. Oils varying from a viscosity of 55 SUS at 100°F to 200 SUS at 210°F and with a V.I. range of 20 to 105 is to be used.

Additives are the same as in other bases.

Preparation of Lubricating Grease from Normal Strontium Soap

A US Patent 2,417,430 describes the procedure as follows, two processes are cited :

In the first,18.5 grams of dry powdered normal strontium oleate having 5 ml. of water is to be added drop-wise and stirred into wet soap thoroughly. Approx. 200 grams of naphthenic type mineral oil of a viscosity of 207 SUS at 100°F is then added and the mixture is heated to 400°F. Subsequent cooling to 250°F resulted in a partial gelation.

In the second method a normal strontium soap lubricant is prepared as follows :

50 grams of tallow fatty acids, 25.3 grams of strontium hydrate, and 200 grams of SAE 40 solvent extracted 90 V.I. oil. The tallow fatty acids were first melted with 50 grams of oil. The strontium hydrate is then added and while being stirred the mixture is heated to 450°F. After foaming had almost ceased, the remainder of the oil was added, and after a heat of 450° was reached the product was set aside to cool to room temperature. The resulting, substantially anhydrous product, containing 22.0% of normal strontium soap and having a free acid content of 0.03% (calculated as acetic acid), had a melting point of 300°F. The mixture is now semifluid in consistency and too soft for a conventional ASTM penetration determination and analysis.

Preparation of Strontium Base Lubricating Greases with Complex Soap Thickeners

According to US Patent 2,417,430, this type of grease is prepared :

A mixture of 109 grams of cottonseed oil, 16 grams of sperm oil, 60 grams of SAE 60 lubricating oil and 46.4 grams strontium hydroxide is heated to 200 to 300°F until the vigour of the reaction subsided. Then an additional 250 grams of the same oil is added, and the mixture is heated for about 12 hours at 500°F at which time no substantial amount of free alkalinity remained. Finally 466 grams of oil was mixed in and the mass is cooled at room temperature.

The lubricant obtained about 17% of soap, and 0.01 % of the strontium hydroxide. This lubricating grease is smooth, unctious, dark in colour, and exhibits no syneresis. The worked penetration of the product remains 229, dropping point over 400°F.

Additional Formulas and Processes

Ingredient	grams
(1) Tallow fatty acids	50
Acetic acid	10.7
Strontium hydrate	48.0
SAE 40 grade solvent extracted 90 V.I. oil	200.0

The fatty acids are melted in a beaker and mixed with 50 grams of oil. When the temperature of this mixture reaches 180°F the acetic acid is to be added, followed by the strontium hydrate. While the material is being stirred its temperature is gradually increased, and after partial dehydration, the remaining oil is gradually added. The mixture is finally heated to 450°F before it is set aside for cooling.

Ingredient	kg.
(2) US Patent 2,595,556	
Prime tallow	7.0
Tallow fatty acids	21.0
Urea	1.5
Acetic acid (80% strength)	1.8
Strontium hydrate	24.3
SAE 40 grade naphthenic base oil	82.2

The tallow, tallow fatty acids, 14 kg of oil and the strontium hydrate is to be charged to a steam jacketed kettle of about 1 barrel capacity, equipped with a means of agitation. This mixture is heated to 235°F and while agitation is continued the urea and 14 kg of water is introduced. The acetic acid is next added, after which the temperature is raised to 250 to 275°F while agitation is continued for 1 hour. The remainder of the oil was mixed with the batch while cooling to 200°F, after which 0.5 kg of water is added to hydrate the lubricating grease. Dehydration is subsequently effected by raising the temperature to 285°F. The resulting strontium soap complex lubricating grease is slightly less fibrous than a corresponding barium base grease.

Mixed Base Strontium Soap Lubricating Greases

A US Patent 2,540,533 cites the composition of mixed base grease ; a description of the formation of this type of grease is as follows :

20 to 50% concentrate of the strontium salt of a 450 molecular weight petroleum sulfonic acid is dissolved in an acid treated coastal oil having a viscosity of 55 SUS at 210°F, 20% aqueous solution of calcium acetate in sufficient quantity to introduce the desired amount of calcium acetate is then added and the batch is partially dehydrated ; lead acetate is then added as a 30% solution ; finally the mixture is dehydrated at 240°F and then placed in an oven at 300°F for 2 to 3 hours.

Another Formula

	%
Strontium sulfonate	10.0
Calcum acetate	5.0
Ethane sulfonic acid	3.5
Hydrated lime	1.5
Coastal mineral oil, 55 SUS at 210°F	85.0

To manufacture this type of grease, the ethane sulfonic acid is to be dissolved in twice its weight of water and neutralized with the hydrated lime. When the reaction appeared to be complete, the solution is added to a blend of the strontium sulfonate and the mineral oil and the batch is stirred to 180 to 200°F until no solid particles are present. The calcium acetate is then added as a 20% aqueous solution and the mixture is dehydrated slowly, with stirring, until a temperature of 300°F is reached. The product is to be cooled at room temperature, without stirring.

Applications and Characteristics of Strontium Base Lubricants

(1) Resistance to the disintegrating effects of water, at ordinary or elevated temperatures; resistance to the leaching action of hydrocarbons.

(2) Reversible character over a wide temperature range, due to their anhydrous character and their freedom from gelation.

(3) Superior protective action against moisture or salt spray corrosion.

(4) Relative stability when used at high temperatures.

(5) Stability of grease structure when subjected to mechanical working.

Other Specific Applications Are

In rubber plants, bearings operating in ovens at approx. 325°F. and in an atmosphere where sulfur and solvent vapours are present, these can successively be lubricated.

Mixed Base Lubricating Greases

It is estimated that mixing two metals for a base in producing lubricating greases is more effective. It gives the structural stability in some mechanical devices. It also gives the variety, and thus effects on nature or texture of a grease. It actually softens the greases.

Only some of important greases are discussed below :

I. The addition of zinc soap together with phenyl alpha naphthylamine is found to stabilize acid reacting lubricating greases against oxidation. This is mixed with sodium, calcium, barium, aluminium, or lithium base greases.

A Suitable Working Formula is

Ingredient	%
Hydrogenated fish oil acids	13.00
54% lithium hydroxide	2.05
Aluminium stearate	0.50
Zinc naphthenate	0.50
Low pour coastal lubricating oil	41.875
Low viscosity, low pour point oil	41.875
Phenyl alpha naphthylamine	0.20

The fatty acids are dissolved in about one-quarter of the oil in fire heated kettle. The lithium hydroxide, dissolved in boiling water is added at a temperature of about 150°F, and heating and agitation are continued until the temperature reaches about 200°F. At this stage the aluminium stearate is added, after which heating and agitation are continued along with intermittent additions of lubricating oil until all but a small portion of the oil has been added. When a temperature of 370°F is reached and the mass is fluid, the phenyl alpha naphthylamine and the zinc naphthenate, dissolved in the remainder of the oil, are added. Heating is then discontinued and the mixture is stirred until the temperature has dropped to below 100°F when the lubricating grease is drawn into containers.

Graphite Lubricating Greases

Graphite lubricating greases for general application consists of a cup grease which contains upto 5 percent of powdered graphite as filler, Graphite is most commonly used filler in calcium base lubricating greases. Graphite lubricating greases are widely used in water pumps, ocean vessels of different types and in slides for elevators. Graphite used for lubricating greases must contain at least 95 percent of graphite carbon and must be free from gritty materials. These types of lubricating greases are particularly effective for use in rail and flange lubricants for rail roads. Such greases reduce the wear on both the rail and the flange of the car wheels, especially on high rails on curves. Colloidal graphite, commonly as a water dispersing agent, is employed as a lubricant for drawing tungsten wire through diamond dies at a temperature of 600°C. Another advantage of graphite solid lubricant is that it is effective at higher temperature and does not oxidise upto a temperature of 650°F.

Fine grade graphite powder as a filler in aluminium base lubricating grease is most widely used as sealant or pipe-thread lubricant. It is used to seal the irregularities in pipe threads better than most lubricants. Commonly used composition is 50 per cent of lubricating grease and 50 per cent of high clay content graphite powder. Graphite is also used in antiseize compounds for general use. One of the composition is -

Ingredient	%
White lead	60
Petrolatum	10
Graphite	10
Asphalt	10
Lubricating oil	10
Total	100

GENERAL PRECAUTION

Addition of graphite to calcium base lubricating greases has a softening effect. For this the addition of graphite is done when the product is partially or almost completely finished. This can be achieved by having a separate mixing kettle, as it is difficult to entirely free a vessel of the filter once it has been used in equipment. Secondly an appropriate oil must be used, so that slurry can be fed to the finishing kettle without dusting, as addition of powdered graphite is accompanied by dust which settles on the sides of the mixing vessel.

II. Mixed Base Lubricating Greases having Extreme Pressure Qualities

Ingredient	%
Fatty oil	40
Caustic soda	8
Lead soap	10
Mineral oil	33
Water	9
Total	100

Or

Ingredient	%
Sodium-lead tallow soap	15 to 4.2
Sodium glyceroxide	1.8 to 0.5
Sodium mahogany soap	2.5 to 0.7

Carbon black	6.0 to 1.7
Litharge and free alkali	0.5 to 0.2
Petroleum oil	74.2 to 92.7

A water-resistant, high temperature, extreme pressure lubricating grease is made from 78 to 81 % of sulfurized asphaltic base oil, of 50 to 100 SUS viscosity at 210°F, 9% of lithium soap, of hydrogenated fish oil acids, 9% of lead oleate, 0.5% of aluminium stearate, 0.5% of zinc naphthenate and 0% to 2% of chlorinated wax.

Ingredient	%
Magnesium soap of C_{10} to C_{12} alkenyl succinic acid	10
Lead soap of menhaden (fish oil) acids	10
Sulfurized sperm oil .	10
SAE 20 grade paraffin base lubricating oil	70
Total	100

III. Mixed Soap Lubricating Greases which are Reversible

The U.S. Patent 2,332,247 gives an excellent formula for a grease which is water-insoluble, transparent, temperature stable and reversible :

Ingredient	%
Animal fatty acids	6.72
Cottonseed fatty acids	6.72
Soyabean oil fatty acids	6.72
Hydrated barium oxide	12.00
Aluminium stearate	5.00
Lubricating oil, 50 SUS viscosity at 210°F	62.80

The fatty acids and one-third of the oil is heated to 150°F and the barium hydroxide added. Stirring and heating were continued until a temperature of 200°F is reached, when another third of the oil, is added. Following this, the aluminium stearate, dispersed in the remaining oil, is added and the temperature of the mixture raised to between 300 and 350°F. When the mass is fluid and clear it is poured into containers and permitted to cool. The cooled lubricating grease has a penetration of 200 and melting point of 265°F.

Thermally Reversible Lubricating Greases (US Patent 2,389,523)		
Composition	I %	II %
Stearic acid	17.85	16.50
Barium hydrate	7.52	6.95
Hydrated lime	0.47	0.44
Magnesia	0.20	0.18
Solvent refined oil 350 SUS viscosity at 100°F	73.96	X
Naphthenic oil 450 SUS at 100°F	X	75.93

Characteristics

Penetration 77°F, unworked
Penetration 77°F, worked
Melting point °F

Methods of Production of Mixed Base Lubricating Greases

Mixed base lubricating greases may be produced by one of the following methods or by a combination of these processes:

(1) By **saponification**, employing a mixture of bases, all of which may be added at once or they may be added in sequence.

(2) By formation of one soap from fatty material and alkali in a portion of the lubricating fluid; followed by addition of a preformed soap.

(3) By the addition and **dispersion** of two or more preformed two soaps to lubricating fluid.

(4) By **preparation** of lubricating greases of individual bases followed by cold mixing of the finished products.

Use of Alkalies and Salts in Mixed Base Grease Production

Formulas and methods of preparation of special valve or cock lubricants are suggested by Mass, W. (**Petroleum** Z, 28, No. 38 1-16) in which not only more than one base is used but also salts of metals, which will convert some of the soaps formed by the bases into soluble soaps. Such products are made from fatty acids in the presence of mineral oil or petrolatum.

After the fatty acids are melted in the hydrocarbon material, calcium hydroxide is added, if this is to be used. Next sodium or potassium hydroxide is introduced, after which heating is continued until the acids are neutralized. Finally, salts such as aluminium sulfate or magnesium chloride are added as solutions. If aluminium or magnesium soaps are thus formed, sodium or potassium sulfates or chlorides must remain in the mixture.

Ingredient	*Parts*
Stearic acid	13.0
Calcium oxide	1.0
Sodium hydroxide	1.5
Aluminium sulfate	3.0
Maganesium chloride	2.0

To this fillers of various kinds may be added.

Ingredient	*lbs.*
Stearic or any other fatty acid	100
Tallow or other glycerides	100
Petrolatum or oil of 150 SUS at 210°F	200
Caustic soda in aqueous solution of 35°Be'.	42
Aluminium sulfate, in 20 gallons of water	54

The method of manufacture consists of melting the acids and fat in the petrolatum or oil in a kettle provided with agitation. After these ingredients are thoroughly mixed, the caustic soda solution is introduced, while heating is continued. As soon as saponification has started, the aluminium sulfate solution is slowly added. As the aluminium sulfate is mixed in, the heat of the mass is raised to 375 to 425°F. Agitation and heat are continued until the product is dehydrated. After the batch is dehydrated, the lubricant is permitted to partially cool before it is drawn.

Formed Soaps with Preformed Soaps

In the production of mixed base lubricating greases the predominate soap is frequently formed in the lubricating oil by saponification of a fat or fatty acids, after which a preformed soap is added.

A barium-aluminium soap mixed grease is described here

Ingredient	*Parts*
Animal fatty acids	6.76
Cottonseed fatty acids	6.72
Soyabean oil fatty acids	6.72
Hydrated barium oxide	12.00
Aluminium stearate Lubricating oil of 50 SUS viscosity at 210°F	62.80

Procedure

The fatty acids are heated to 150°F in a third of the total oil. The barium hydroxide is then added and agitation and heating continues until the temperature reaches 200°F. Another third of the oil is then stirred into this mixture. The aluminium stearate is mixed with the remaining oil and then it is added to the barium soap mixture, after which the temperaure is raised to between 300 and 350°F. When the mixture becomes fluid and clear it is poured into containers to cool.

A **lithium base** lubricating grease containing both aluminium and zinc soap has the following proportions and ingredients

Ingredient	%
Hydrogenated fish oil fatty acids	13.000
Lithium hydroxide, 54% strength	2.050
Aluminium stearate	0.500
Zinc naphthenate	0.500
Low pour coastal lubricating oil	41.875
Low viscosity, low pour lubricating oil	41.875
Phenyl alpha naphthylamine	0.200

In compounding the above, the acid and about one-fourth of the oil are charged to a fire-heated kettle and, mixed and heated to about 150°F until the acids dissolved in the oil. The lithium hydroxide, dissolved in boiling water is then added. Heating and agitation are continued and the temperature is permitted to rise to 200°F. The aluminium stearate is then added and heating and stirring is being continued alongwith intermittent additions of lubricating oil until all but a small portion of the oil is added. After the mixture becomes fluid, at about 370°F, the phenyl alpha naphthylamine and zinc naphthenate, dissolved in the remainder of the oil, are added. Heating is then discontinued and lubricating grease to be stirred until the temperature drops below 100°F.

Fillers in Mixed Base Lubricating Greases

Generally, fillers are not mentioned by the industrial consultants. But a small-scale manufacturer may add, 20% of leaf lead mixed with the thickened petrolatum (temperature below 150°F).

Complex Soap Lubricating Greases

"Complex", is theoretically described as "A complex salt or absorption compound", but in manufacturing industry it is really meant "to refer to the soap modifications ; i.e. hydrated soaps, basic soaps, and soaps associated or combined with various other compounds, as complex soaps". Since many such soap combinations, and lubricating greases formed from them, has been accepted over a considerable period as normal products, they are important as well for a manufacturer like other grease products.

There are many kinds of complex soap lubricating greases, such as hydrated soaps, hydrated calcium soaps, hydrated aluminium soaps, barium soaps, lithium soaps, sodium soaps, strontium soaps, acid soaps etc. only some of the important of these complex soap lubricants will be discussed here.

Importance of Soap Salt Complexes, and their Characteristics

The particular characteristics which make soap-salt complexes valuable for the manufacture of lubricating greases are:

(1) Their solubility characeristics;

(2) Their freedom from change in aggregation state over a wide temperature range; and

(3) Their stability as regards dissociation of soap and salt.

Most soap thickeners for lubricating fluids should be soluble or dispersible in the fluid at elevated temperatures, and, as the temperature decreases, crystallize in fibrous crystallites which serve to immobilize the fluid. Still, all complex soaps formed from metal soaps and salts will not exhibit this characteristic. Some will not exhibit this characteristic. Some will be so soluble that they will fail to crystallize and consequently no plastic body will form. Other complexes may be too insoluble and either not disperse, ever, by a proper choice of the metal, of the higher fatty acids and the low molecular weight acids, suitable complex soaps can be found for the production of lubricating greases.

General claims for Soap-Salt Complexes for -Lubricating Greases

The most generalized claim for soap-salt complexes is to thicken the lubricating oils. It covers complexes at least two metals, one of which must be polyvalent. This polyvalent metal is preferably selected from the alkaline earth metals, such as : barium, calcium, magnesium, and strontium. But, aluminium, beryllium, zinc, cadmium, boron, tin. zirconium, cerium, vanadium, antimony, bismuth, arsenic, copper, molybdenum, germanium, columbium, chromium, selenium, tellurium, tungsten, manganese, iron, cobalt, nickel may be used as the polyvalent metal.

The second metal of the soap complexes must be different from the first and is preferably an alkali metal, namely: lithium, sodium, potassium, or cesium, or an alkaline earth metal, such as : barium, calcium, magnesium or strontium. The other metals listed above may also be taken as substitutes. These soap complexes are not limited to the use of two metals, as three or even more metals can by used provided at least one is polyvalent.

The saponifiable materials which contain high molecular weight fatty acids, either in a combined or a free state, include tallow, lard oil, hog fat, horse fat, stearic acid, oleic acid, higher molecular weight acids resulting from the oxidation of petroleum fractions, rosin and other related products, higher molecular weight naphthenic acids, sulfonic acids, and saponifiable waxes such as beeswax, sperm oil, degras, etc.

Suitable organic acids of low molecular weight whose salts may be employed for formation of complexes include monocarboxylic and polycarboxylic acids containing less than carbon atoms per molecule. Included in such groups are formic, acetic, propionic, valeric, oxalic, malonic, succinic, the low molecular weight alkyl and aryl sulfonic acids, and the low molecular weight carboxylic acids such as glyceric, glycollic, thioglycollic, etc., heterocyclic carboxylic acids, such as furoic, etc., and phenolic and thiophenolic compounds such as phenol, cresol, thiophenol,etc.

Some Methods for Forming Soap-Salt Complexes

There are numerous methods for manufacture of metal soap-metal salt complexes. Some of them are :

1. The one method for the formation of the complex soaps, and the resulting lubricating greases, consists of starting with a normal soap, which may be preformed or produced by reacting a saponifiabie material with a basically reacting compound. Such normal soap is dissolved in all or a portion of the mineral oil to be used, and subsequently a solution or a dispersion of the desired metal salt or salts in a polar solvent is added Agitation and heat are maintained on this mixture until all or a portion of the polar solvent is removed. Once the complex soap is formed, the production of the lubricating grease follows the usual pattern.

2. Another method for the manufacture of complex soaps and the resulting lubricating greases is to dissolve a normal metal soap in mineral oil, add to this solution a quantity of basically reacting compound, followed by sufficient low molecular weight carboxylic acid to neutralize a portion, only, of the base present. Finally,carbon dioxide is led into the mixture to neutralize the remaining base. A modification of this method is to mix mineral oil, normal metal soap, metal salt of a low molecular weight carboxylic acid, saponification reagent and water, and contact the mixture with carbon dioxide until the product is substantially neutral. The neutral product may then be dehydrated and finished in a normal manner.

3. Still another method is one in whcih a dry metal soap-metal salt complex is formed without any mineral oil being present. A suggested formula and procedure is given below

Ingredient	*lbs.*
Tallow fatty acids	50.0
Glycerol	5.0
Calcium oxide	9.5
Water	50.0

The materials are added to a steam jacketed kettle, mixed and heated to 240°F to effect saponification and partial dehydration. After cooling to room-temperature a brittle solid is obtained. This is removed from the kettle, powdered, and returned to the vessel. This powder is then heated in contact with air for 4 hours at a temperature of 300 to 350°F. Under these conditions the free calcium hydroxide content decreases to a value of 0.1% and the water content to 0.1%. Under these conditions the free calcium hydroxide content decreases to a value of 0.1% and the water content to 0.1%. Then this product is being dispersed in a mineral oil.

Complex Aluminium Soap Lubricating Greases

The complex greases are produced from a mixture of low molecular weight aromatic carboxylic acids and higher molecular weight acids, are again a combination of co-precipitating water solutions of soaps of alkali metals with an aluminium salt.

Examples of such soaps are aluminium benzoate stearate, aluminium toluate stearate, and aluminium didodecyl benzene sulfonate. These soaps are said to impart high melting points and resistance to emulsification with water to lubricating greases. For instance, 12 parts of aluminium benzoate stearate is dispersed in 108 parts of refined paraffin oil by heating to 450°F. The resulting product is a light brown, translucent lubricating grease with a dropping point of over 400°F.

An aluminium-barium complex lubricating grease can be formed thus:

Ingredient	*gms.*
Aluminium stearate	300
Urea	15
Acetic acid, 80%	19
Barium hydrate	160
SAE 30 naphthenic type oil, of 35 V.I.	600

The aluminium stearate is dissolved in about one-half of the oil, the barium hydrate, urea, and acetic acid are then added during constant agitation. The reaction mixture is heated to a temperature of 300 to 350°F for a period of two hours, after which the remainder of the lubricating oil is added while the batch cooled to about 200°F. Finally 0.05% of water is added to improve the body and smoothness of the lubricant. This product contains 3.9% of metal soap complex.

Complex Barium Soap Lubricating Greases

A US Patent 2,595,556 gives the following ingredients to form such a grease

Ingredient	*Kilos*
Prime tallow	7.00
Tallow fatty acids	21.00
Urea	1.50
Acetic acid (80% strength)	1.88
Barium hydrate	28.50
SAE 40 naphthenic type oil	82.20

The tallow, tallow fatty acids, 14 kg. of oil, and the barium hydrate are charged to a steam jacketed grease kettle and heated to about 235°F with agitation. The urea and an additional 14.0 kg. of oil are then added and the mixture is heated to 300°F while agitation continues. After 1¼ hours at this temperature, the batch is cooled to 200°F and 0.5 kg. of water is added. The acetic acid is then added to the kettle and the temperature increased to 250 to 275°F while mixing is continued for 1 hour. The remainder of the lubricating oil is then added while cooling the charge to 200°F, after which 0.5 kg. of water is added. Dehydration is then accomplished by heating to 285°F. The finished lubricating grease is slightly fibrous and had an unworked penetration of 272.

For barium-sodium complex greases the following formula is found suitable:

Ingredient	%
Stearic acid	14.0
Candelilla wax	4.0
Glacial acetic acid	4.0
Glycerol	6.5
Barium octahydrate	19.0
Lubricating oil	52.5
Total	100.0

Complex Calcium Soap Lubricant

Ingredient	%
Hydrogenated fatty acids	5.5
Cottonseed fatty acids	5.5
Refined or crude montan wax	4.0
Acetic acid	4.0
Lime flour	4.6
100 second paraffin oil	76.4
Total	100.0

The method of production is the usual compounding procedure followed by dehydration to the extent of giving the finished product increased temperature stability.

A calcium soap-calcium chloride complex formula is

Ingredient	%
Hydrogenated fish oil	20.0
Hydrated lime	2.9
$CaCl_2 . H_2O$	0.3
Ethylene glycol mono-butylether	2.0
Lubricating oil	74.8
Total	100.0

The hydrogenated fish oil, calcium hydroxide, calcium chloride and a trace of water are stirred and slowly heated to 450°F. With the calcium chloride present, it is said to be necessary to heat the mixture to 450°F in order to form a calcium soap. After all the water is removed at 450°F the m neral oil is mixed in at such a rate that the temperature is maintained at 400 to 450°F. Following the oil, the ethylene glycol monobutyl ether is added and the batch is permitted to cool, without any agitation, to room temperature after which it is stirred until smooth. The melting point of the product is 375°F.

There is a considerable choice of either mineral oils or soap stocks for the manufacture of these calcium soap-calcium chloride lubricating greases. The points which are emphasized about the manufacture of such lubricating greases are that the soap be prepared before mineral oil is added and the reaction carried out at 400 to 500°F.

A reversible high-temperature lubricating grease can be prepared by the following procedure :

A steam jacketed kettle is charged with 3000 grams of a 30% concentrate of calcium sulfonate of approx. 900 molecular weight, and 3000 grams of naphthenic oil of 65 viscosity SUS at 210°F. This mixture is agitated and heated to 180 to 200°F, after which 180 grams of calcium acetate as an 18.4% aqueous solution is added. Five drops of an organic silicon polymer are added to control foaming and the temperature of the charge is readily increased to 250°F. Cold water is then poured into the kettle jacket and agitation continues until the charge reaches a temperature of 100°F, at which point the lubricating grease is packaged. The finished product has a melting point above 400°F, and unworked penetration of 242 and a worked penetration of 278.

The recommended ingredients for producing a **calcium sulfonate complex for thickening lubricating oils** is as follows:

Ingredient	%
Calcium sulfonate as 40% concentrate in oil	41.0
Technical calcium acetate	18.0
Calcium stearate	1.5
Naphthenic type mineral oil	39.5
Total	100.0

The procedure for compounding is to dissolve the calcium sulfonate concentrate in half the lubricating oil to be used and add the calcium stearate while agitating. When a paste is obtained with the above mixture, the calcium acetate is added as a 15% aqueous solution. This addition is gradual and when the mixture acquires the appearance of a homogeneous, milky emulsion, heating is started. When the charge is substantially dehydrated, at about

280°F, heating is discontinued and the remainder of the oil is added. Agitation is continued until the temperature drops about 280°F, heating is discontinued and the remainder oil is added. Agitation is continued until the temperature drops to about 150°F when the lubricating grease can be drawn. The lubricating grease thus formed is a stable, having worked penetration of 285, and dropping point of 425 to 450°F.

Another Example is :

Ingredient	*grams*
Prime tallow	450.0
Urea	24.3
Acetic acid (80%)	34.0
Calcium oxide	51.5
Sodium hydroxide	42.0
SAE 30 naphthenic type oil, 35 V.I.	1200.0

The tallow is mixed with 225 g. of the oil and the slaked calcium oxide is added. The batch is heated and mixed to effect saponification, after which the mass is cooled and another 225 g. portion of oil is added. The sodium hydroxide (as a solution) and the urea are then added to the mixture, which is re-heated to 300 to 350°F for a period of 45 minutes. After cooling to 200°F the acetic acid is added to neutralize the remaining sodium hydroxide. A substantial neutral lubricating grease resulted with a melting point of 275°F.

Complex Lithium Soap-Salt Lubricating Greases

A preparation of lithium soap complex lubricating grease is described in an US Patent 2,417,428, in which 980 grams of stearic acid, 3940 grams of sperm oil, and 5000 grams of waxy gas oil are mixed in a steam jacketed kettle before a slurry of 1130 grams of lithium monohydrate in 1060 grams of gas oil is added. While the temperature is increased to 300°F the remaining gas oil, consisting of 10,000 grams, are added. The batch is then cooled to room temperature and worked through a 200 mesh screen.

The finished lubricating grease is smooth, buttery, and translucent. This product has an unusual character i.e. it bodied up when heated to 200 to 300°F and yet when it is cooled to room temperature the lubricant grease returns to a soft consistency.

A lubricating grease containing both the lithium soap of a fatty acid and lithium acetate has the following ingredients :

Ingredient	*grams*
Hydrogenated fish oil fatty acids (54 titer)	150
Palm oil	25
Naphthenic acid	25
Acetic acid	40
Coastal pale oil, 100 viscosity at 100°F	700
Lithium hydroxide (added as a water solution)	80
Coastal red oil, 2000 viscosity at 100°F	800

Complex Strontium Soap Lubricating Greases

One method of the preparation of lubricating grease from a strontium soap complex is as follows : 109 grams of cottonseed oil (approx. 0.38 equivalent), 16 grams of sperm oil (0.04 equivalent), 60 grams of a naphthenic type SAE 60 grade lubricating oil, and 102 grams of strontium hydrate (equal to 46.4 grams of strontium hydroxide or 0.76 equivalent), are heated at 200 to 300°F until the vigour of the reaction subsided. Then an addition 250 grams of the some oil added, the mixture is heated for about 12 hours at about 500°F at which time no substantial amount of free alkalinity remains. Finally 466 grams of the oil is stirred in, and the mass is cooled to room temperature.

An Extreme Pressure Lubricating Grease in which the preferred thickening agents for lubricating oil are strontium sulfonate, calcium acetate, and the calcium salt of ethane sulfonic acid

Ingredient	%
Strontium sulfonate	10.0
Calcium acetate, anhydrous	5.0
Ethane sulfonic acid	3.5
Hydrated lime	1.5
Acid extracted coastal oil of 55 SUS at 210°F	85.0

The ethane sulfonic acid is dissolved in twice its weight of water and neutralized with the hydrated lime. When the reaction appears to be complete, the neutralized solution is added to a blend of the strontium sulfonate and the oil. The batch is stirred at 180 to 200°F until no soild particles remained. Then the calcium acetate is added as a 20% aqueous solution and the mixture is dehydrated slowly, with stirring, until a temperature of 300°F is reached. The product is cooled to room temperature without stirring.

Chapter 19

ACETIC ACID FROM ETHANOL

MANUFACTURING PROCESS

The acetic acid is produced by the steps process.

1. Production of Acetaldehyde from Ethyl Alcohol.
2. Production of Acetic Acid from Acetaldehyde.

Chemical Reaction:-

Step - 1

$CH_3CH_2OH + 1/2\ O_2 \longrightarrow CH_3CHO + H_2O$ = 85-95% yield

Step - 2

$$CH_3CHO + 1/2\ O_2 \xrightarrow[\text{88-95\% yield}]{(CH_3COO)_2\ Mn} CH_3COOH$$

Step - 1 :

Alcohol vapors (50 to 95 percent) and preheated air are mixed in such proportions that the exothermic heat of oxidation will just exceed the absorbed heat of dehydrogenation, in which case the reaction will proceed without the external application of heat. The vapors pass through a reactor containing a silver gauze catalyst. Reactor temperature depends on the air-ethanol-steam ratio and the velocity of the gases over the catalyst and may vary from 375 to 550°C. Exit gases from the comvertor, containing alcohol and acetaldehyde, are led to a scrubbing column where cold dilute alcohol cools the gases and dissolve both the alcohol and acetaldehyde. The stripped gases leaving the top of the scrubber are scrubbed again with water and realeased to the atmosphere. The dilute alcohol acetaldehyde solution from the bottom of the scrubbing column is rectified in a refining column to produce 99 percent acetaldehyde as overhead. The dilute alcohol solution leaving the bottom of the column is concentrated in the conventional manner. Conversion per pass generally ranges from 25 to 35 per cent.

Step -2 :

A highly concentrated acetaldehyde solution (99 to 99.8 percent) is introduced into a stainless-steel reaction kettle in which air at 70 to 75 psi bubbles through the liquid (55 to 65°C) that contains 0.1 to 0.5 per cent manganous acetate used to decompose the explosive intermediate - per acetic acid. The gases leaving the reactor are scrubbed with water, releasing nitrogen to the atmosphere. The dilute acetaldehyde solution leaving the bottom of the scrubber is sent to a column for recovery. The crude acetic acid (94 to 96 per cent) is discharged from the reactor and continuously rectified to yield 99 per cent glacial acetic acid.

Basis :
Acetic Acid = 10 Tons/day = 250 Tons/Month
For 1 ton Acetic acid

Raw materials requirements :-
Acetaldehyde = 820 Kgs.
Manganous Acetate = 3 Kgs.
Air = 230 m^3.

For 1 ton Acetaldehyde
Ethanol (100% Basis) = 1150 Kgs.
Steam (7 atm) = 2600 Kgs.

SO_3 For 1 ton Acetic Acid
Ethanol (100% Basis) = 943 Kgs.
Manganous Acetate = 3 Kgs.

Air = 230 m^3.
Steam (7 atm) = 2150 Kgs.

PLANT ECONOMICS OF ACETIC ACID FROM ETHANOL

Rated Plant Capacity = 10.00 Tons/Day
LAND & BUILDING (Land 5 acres) = Rs. 1,19,50,000.00

PLANT & MACHINERY

1. Alcohol storage tank
2. Alcohol Vapouriser
3. Reactor for oxidation
4. Scrubber
5. Refining Column
6. Alcohol Concentration column
7. Air Compressor
8. Reactor
9. Scrubber
10. Distillation
11. Storage tank

12. Water storage tank
13. Pipes, fittings, structures, Pumps, Valves, tanks, etc.
14. Instrumentations & Process Control equipments.
15. Laboratory testing equipments
16. Boiler oil fired
17. Miscellaneous tools, jigs, fixtures etc.

FIXED CAPITAL

1.	LAND & BUILDING	Rs.	1,19,50,000.00
2.	PLANT & MACHINERY	Rs.	4,60,00,000.00
3.	OTHER FIXED ASSETS	Rs.	99,50,000.00
	TOTAL	Rs.	6,79,00,000.00

RAW MATERIALS

1. Ethanol
2. Manganous Acetate
3. Laboratory testing chemicals
4. Containers

TOTAL WORKING CAPITAL/MONTH

1.	RAW MATERIAL	Rs.	30,45,000.00
2.	SALARY & WAGES	Rs.	5,16,500.00
3.	UTILITIES & OVERHEADS	Rs.	7,30,000.00
	TOTAL	Rs.	42,91,500.00

TOTAL CAPITAL INVESTMENT

TOTAL FIXED CAPITAL	Rs.	6,79,00,000.00
TOTAL WORKING CAPITAL FOR 3 MONTHS	Rs.	1,28,74,500.00
TOTAL	Rs.	8,07,74,500.00

TURN OVER/ANNUM

By sale of 3000 MT of Acetic Acid	Rs.	9,00,00,000.00

PROFIT SALES RATIO = Profit / Sales x 100 = 18.24 %

RATE OF RETURN = Operating profit / T.C.I x 100 = 20.32 %

BREAK EVEN POINT (B.E.P) = 63.10 %

Chapter 20

COOLANT (ENGINE)

PROCESS OF MANUFACTURE

The process of manufacture for coolant consistes or two main heads. First of all we have to concentrate or :-

a) Section of raw materials and second
b) Blending/mixing of all the raw materials.

Ethylene glycol: (Ethylene alcohol; glycol; 1,2-ethandiol). CH_2OHCH_2OH. The simplest glycol.

Properties : Clear, colorless, syrup liquid; sweet taste; hydroscopic; lowers freezing point of water. Relatively non-volatile. Odourless. Soluble in water, alcohol, and ether, sp.gr. 1.1155 (20°C); b.p. 197.2°C, f.p. -13.5°C, wt/gal 9.31 lbs (15/15°C); refractive index 1.430 (25°C); flash point 240.8°F; combustible; auto-ignition temp. 775°F.

Derivation:- (a) By heating ethylene chlorohydrin with oxidation of ethylene with air, followed by hydration of the ethylene with air, followed by hydration of the ethylene oxide formed; (c) from formulation of the resulting glycolic acid.

Grade Technical
Container : Drums; tankers.

Hazard: Toxic by ingestion; lethal dose reported to be 100 cc.

The another component of the coolant is anti- carrosion elements or substances. All antifreezes conatin inhibitor designed to oliminate or at least minimize, corrosive attack. These may include organic, Inorganic and silicons compounds. The organic compounds include mineral and vegetable oils and their sulfonated products and amines, amides, bensoates mercaptans, and atrazold, The inorganics include borates, nitrates, mitrides, phosphates, molydates, silicate, and carbonates. Since no single compound gives complete corrosion protection to all metals under all conditions, most antifreze formulations contain various combinations of two or more inhibitors. The choice of individual components and their relative porportions affect the performance of the antifreeze. Some materials pass through a concentration of maximum effectiveness and may become more aggressive toward some of the metals at higher concentrations. Another problem in formulating the antifreese is dissoling enough inhibitors in the antifreeze concentrate to be effective after dilution for use.

Important factors are:- most inhibitor formulations are patented or kept a trade secret.

Ethylene glycol is to be taken in a steam jacketed cooking kettle or vessel or reaction vessel. It should be heated by boiler. In the uniform stirring. Make it a point that the stirring must not vigorous. Heating temperature will be between 70 to 80°C. Add inhibitors

Benzene sulfonic acid, Benzotriazole, Tohytriazole and other chemicals, Additives slowly are by one with uniform stirring, see that mixture must be homogeneous in nature. Caution is to be taken that there will be no separation of mixtures. If so, continuous stirring should be needed keeping thermostate upto a complete mixture.

The cool the whole mixture and filled it and despatch it filling in 1 litres plastic containers with all printing.

FORMULA OF COOLANT

Ethylene Glycol	70%
Propylene	20%
Sodium Benzoate	2.5-5%
Organic Pigments	0.5-1%
Silicats	1-2%
Sulfonated Card OIl	2-4%

PLANT ECONOMICS OF COOLANT (ENGINE)

Rated Plant Capacity = 500.00 LIT/Day

LAND & BUILDING (Land area 500 sq. mts.) = Rs. 4,10,000.00

PLANT & MACHINERY

1. Stainless steel Jacketed Vessel oil heated with Stirrer
2. Small Stainer to strain the coolant
3. Steel tank

4. Laboratory testing equipment.
5. Weighing balance, weights, and other miscellaneous.
6. Pipes fittings, motors pumps.

FIXED CAPITAL

1. LAND & BUILDING	Rs.	4,10,000.00
2. PLANT & MACHINERY	Rs.	3,65,000.00
3. OTHER FIXED ASSETS	Rs.	1,11,000.00
TOTAL	Rs.	8,86,000.00

RAW MATERIALS

1. Ethylene glycol
2. Propylene glycol
3. Sodium Benzoate
4. Sodium Silicate
5. Sulfonated Lard oil
6. Organic Dye
7. Packaging material Tin container

TOTAL WORKING CAPITAL/MONTH

1. RAW MATERIAL	Rs.	5,70,375.00
2. SALARY & WAGES	Rs.	16,875.00
3. UTILITIES & OVERHEADS	Rs.	48,300.00
TOTAL	Rs.	6,35,550.00

TOTAL CAPITAL INVESTMENT

TOTAL FIXED CAPITAL	Rs.	8,86,000.00
TOTAL WORKING CAPITAL FOR 3 MONTHS	Rs.	19,06,650.00
TOTAL	Rs.	27,92,650.00

TURN OVER/ANNUM

By selling of Coolant Engine 1,50,000 litre Coolant.	Rs.	90,00,000.00

PROFIT SALES RATIO = Profit / Sales x 100 = 8.05 %
RATE OF RETURN = Operating profit / T.C.I x 100 = 25.6 %
BREAK EVEN POINT (B.E.P) = 57.01 %

Chapter 21

CUTTING OIL

While there are numerous cutting fluids on todays market, almost all of them fall into one of three categories.

1. **Cutting oils**
2. **Emulsifiable oils**
3. **Chemical fluids (often referred to as synthetic)**

There are many possible breakdowns listed here are the three types with one exomplany break down.

1. Straight cutting oils (Not mixed with water)

A. Inactive oils

i) Straight mineral oils
ii) Fatty oils
iii) Fatty oil-mineral blends
iv) Sulfurized fatty mineral-oil blends.

B. Active Oils

i) Sulphrized mineral oils
ii) Sulfo-chlorinated minerals oils
iii) Sulfo-or sulfo chlorinated fatty oil blends.

(2) Emulsifiable oils (soluble oils)

A. Emulsifiable mineral oils
B. Super farry emulsifiable oils
C. Extrance pressure emulsifiable oils.

(3) Chemical (Synthetic) cutting fluids

A. True solution type
B. Wetting agent type
C. Wetting Agent type with extrence pressure lubricant.

PROCESS OF MANUFACTURE

Formula

(Base)	**% age by weight**
Lard oil No. 1	4.0
Flowers of sulfur (finished oil)	
Sulphur	0.8
Lard oil	15.2
Mineral oil, 100 to 200 Viscosity, (Pale Oil)	80.0

Procedure:-

i) Charge in a fire heated grease mixer 355 kg of lard oil and heat to a temperature of 380 - 420°F.

ii) At this temperature shift in gradually 63 kg of grounds sulfur. The lower the temperature and shorter the process, the lighter will be the colour of the finished base.

iii) After heating for about 15 min. A drop of the oil should be tested by placing on a cold bright surface for the presence of free sulfur heating should be continued until there is no precipitate of sulfur.

iv) The base should be left in the kettle to cool and after cooling 1254 kgs of lard oil having an acid value of 18.22% calculated of oleic should be run in.

v) About 1820 gallons of 100 viscosity at 100°F pale oil should be mixed with the ingredients in the kettle.

The product will be found to be satisfactory for general use.

PLANT ECONOMICS OF CUTTING OIL

Rated Plant Capacity = 1500.00 LIT/Day
LAND & BUILDING (Land area 800 sq.mt) = Rs. 15,60,000.00

PLANT & MACHINERY

1. Mixing Kettle
2. Storage Tanks
3. Hydraulic drum
4. Lab Testing Eqpt.
5. Scrubber
6. Filter
7. Other jigs, fixture & pumps etc.
8. Condenser
9. Blowers
10. Miscellaneous fittings pipes etc.

FIXED CAPITAL

1.	LAND & BUILDING	Rs.	15,60,000.00
2.	PLANT & MACHINERY	Rs.	22,85,000.00
3.	OTHER FIXED ASSETS	Rs.	7,00,000.00
	TOTAL	Rs.	45,45,000.00

RAW MATERIALS

1. Mineral oil
2. Sulfur powder
3. Lard oil
4. Miscellaneous chemicals
5. Packaging Materials

TOTAL WORKING CAPITAL/MONTH

1.	RAW MATERIAL	Rs.	8,11,290.00
2.	SALARY & WAGES	Rs.	40,875.00
3.	UTILITIES & OVERHEADS	Rs.	57,500.00
	TOTAL	Rs.	9,09,665.00

TOTAL CAPITAL INVESTMENT

TOTAL FIXED CAPITAL	Rs.	45,45,000.00
TOTAL WORKING CAPITAL FOR 3 MONTHS	Rs.	27,28,995.00
TOTAL	Rs.	72,73,995.00

TURN OVER/ANNUM

By sale of 1500x300 litres of cutting oil of different grades	Rs.	1,57,50,000.00

PROFIT SALES RATIO = Profit / Sales x 100 = 18.31 %

RATE OF RETURN = Operating profit / T.C.I x 100 = 39.65 %

BREAK EVEN POINT (B.E.P) = 45.65 %

Chapter 22

ETHANOL (BIOFUEL) FROM MOLASSES

MANUFACTURING PROCESS

Ethyl Alcohol is produced from sugar-containing materials such as molasses by fermentation utilising yeast enzymes to convert the sugar into alcohol. Blackstrap molasses is the most widely used raw material which is the waste syrup remaining after the extraction of crystallised sugar from evaporated sugar-cane juice obtained in sugar mill operations. It contains about 55% sugar by weight of which 35-40% is sucrose and 15-20% is invert sugar (glucose and fructose).

Molasses are charged into a mixing tank where it is diluted with sufficient warm water to give a sugar concentration of 10 to 15%. Sulphuric acid is added to reduce the ph from above 5.3 to between 4.0 and 5.0. The dilute acidified molasses, called mash, is run into large wooden or steel fermentation tanks where a selected strain of yeast is added. The yeast charge, previously grown in-oculating sterile mash under controlled conditions is added with the mash charge to the extent of about 5%. Alcoholic fermentation of molasses is carried out on industrial scale by cultivating the yeast culture of sacchromyces cerevisiae in yeast vessels and pre fermentors. Fermentation takes place at around 30°C. Usually ammonium sulphate is added to the mash in the proportion of 70-400 g/kl mash. Instead of ammonium sulphate an equivalent amount of urea can also be used. The addition of tripple super phosphate improves the fermentation efficiency. The PH of the mash is adjusted between 4.5-5.0 to keep down the growth of bacteria and wild yeast.

Due to the exothermic nature of the reaction, cooling coils or sprays are generally used. The temperature at the end of fermentation is around 38°C. The fermentation time is around 28 to 72 hours to produce 8 to 10% concentration of alcohol. The yeast supplies the enzyme, invertase which catalyses the hydrolysis of sucrose and produces the enzyme, zymase, which converts the monosaccharide to alcohol and carbon dioxide. The carbon di-oxide envolved is vented.

Distillation: The liquor in the fermentors after the fermentation is called cooled beer or wash. It is allowed to settle for a new hours and then distilled to obtain rectified spirit and fusel oil. For distillation most of the smaller distilleries employ pot stills, while the large distilleries make use of patent stills, such as coffey's still or Barnet's still.

Beer containing 8 to 10% alcohol is cooled and pumped to the top of a beer still. The alcohol and other volatiles such as aldehydes are distilled off. The residue known as slop or stillage is discharged as a waste from the bottom of a sill through a heat exchanger. The overheads from the beer column are condensed, and charged into an aldehyde a heads column where aldehydes and other low boiling impurities are separated as overhead. The potable alcohol is taken from this stage and stored in wooden barrels for ageing. The remaining alcohol is sent to the rectification column where 96% ethyl alcohol is separated from the top. Fusel oil is removed from the aldehyde column and reactification column and stored. The bottoms from aldehyde as well as rectification column are called low wines and can be sent to beer column for concentration.

The 95% ethyl alcohol from the rectification column is stored in silo. The ethyl alcohol water azeotrope boils at 78.2°C compared to 78.3°C for ethyl alcohol and 100°C for water and contains 95.6% by weight of ethyl alcohol and balance water. This was the highest concentration which could be reached by ordinary distillation. benzene water azeotrope boiling at 69.4°C containing 91.1% benezene and rest water Benzene did bring over water in azeotrope at the top of the column; it was a ternary azeotrope of benzene, ethyl alcohol, and water. It had a boiling point of 64.6°C and contained 74.1% benzene, 18.5% alcohol and balance water.

An additional column will be required to separate the ternery azeotrope. The 95% alcohol is dehydrated to 100% alcohol by azeotropic distillation of the alcohol with benzene.

PLANT ECONOMICS OF ETHANOL (BIOFUEL) FROM MOLASSES

Rated Plant Capacity = 17.77 KL/Day
LAND & BUILDING (Land area 20000 Sq.mtr)= Rs.1,50,10,000.00

PLANT & MACHINERY

1. Feed water tank
2. Cultivation tanks
3. Molasses bulk storage tank

4. Fermentation tanks
5. Pot stills fitted
6. Aldehyde column
7. Storage tank
8. Other miscellaneous equipments
9. Rectification column.
10. Distillation column alongwith heat
11. Boiler.
12. Cooling tower
13. Water softening plant
14. Heat exchangers.
15. Distillation column.
16. Reboilers.
17. Condensers.
18. Stripping column.
19. Pumps & compressors
20. Piping, fittings, valves.
21. Control and instrumentation.
22. Boiler.
23. DM Plant .
24. Effluent treatment plant.
25. Packing

FIXED CAPITAL

1.	LAND & BUILDING	Rs.	1,50,10,000.00
2.	PLANT & MACHINERY	Rs.	2,00,00,000.29
3.	OTHER FIXED ASSETS	Rs.	45,80,000.00
	TOTAL	Rs.	3,95,90,000.29

RAW MATERIALS

1. Ethyl Alcohol
2. Make up Benzene
3. Misc.consumables lot (Lump sum)

TOTAL WORKING CAPITAL/MONTH

1.	RAW MATERIAL	Rs.	16,02,200.00
2.	SALARY & WAGES	Rs.	3,73,125.00
3.	UTILITIES & OVERHEADS	Rs.	15,63,500.00
	TOTAL	Rs.	35,38,825.00

TOTAL CAPITAL INVESTMENT

TOTAL FIXED CAPITAL	Rs.	3,95,90,000.29
TOTAL WORKING CAPITAL FOR 1 MONTHS	Rs.	35,38,825.00
TOTAL	Rs.	4,31,28,825.29

TURN OVER/ANNUM

By sale of 5330 KL Ethanol	Rs.	6,71,58,000.00

PROFIT SALES RATIO = Profit / Sales x 100 = 20.57 %

RATE OF RETURN = Operating profit / T.C.I x 100 = 32.03 %

BREAK EVEN POINT (B.E.P) = 59.35 %

Chapter 23

FORMALDEHYDE

The applications of Formaldehyde can be summarized as below:-

1. It is used as an antiseptic and disinfectant for surgical.
2. It is used in the manufacture of phenol-formaldehyde and urea-formaldehyde resins in the plastic industry.
3. It is used in the preparation of hexamine or urotrophine , which is used as a remedy in out and as a urinary anticeptic.
4. Formalin is used for the preparation of anatomical and biological specimens as it renders protein hard and insoluble.
5. It is used in the preparation of synthetic plastics like Bakelite and Galalith- a hrn like substance obtained from formaldehyde and casein of milk.
6. Mixed with lactose it is used for the preparation of formalint-throuat lozenges.
7. Rongalite obtained by reducing formaldehyde sodium bisulphite derivative with zinc dust and ammonia is used as a reducing agent in vat dyeing.
8. It is used in the manufacture of synthetic dyestuff such as para-resoniline, indigo etc.
9. It is used in silvering Mirror.
10. Formaldehyde and its derivatives are finding its use as antiseptic to and disinfectant in food and agriculture industry.

PROCESS OF MANUFACTURE

1. From Methyl Alcohol:

In laboratory or on small scale formaldehyde can be prepared by catalytic oxidation of methyl alcohol. Vapours of methyl alcohol mixed with air are passed over heated (250-300°c) platintized asbestos. Instead of plstinized asbestos copper or silver may also be used. A catalyst consisting of molybdnum trioxide and ferric oxide converssts 95% of methyl alcolhol to formaldehyde.

100 C,C methyl alcohol is taken in the round bottom flask in the laboratory which is connected to one end of a hard glass tube packed with platinized asbestos. the other end of the tube is connected to suction pump through a receiveer containing water.

In the beginning, the platinized asbestos is heated to redness and the flask is heated on a water bath. Then with the help of suction pump air is sucked in through the apparatus. Vapours of methyl alcolhol and air come in contact with heated catalyst, when methyl alcohol geyts oxidized to formaldehyde, the latter being absorbed in water ins the receiver. The solution of formaldehyde so obtained is distilled to remove excess of methyl alcohol.

2. Formaldehyde production from methane:

Theory : Controlled oxidation of methane or natural gas under presure , in presnece of molybedenum oxides, yields formaldehyde.

$$\underset{\text{methane}}{CH_4} + \underset{\text{oxygen}}{O_2} \xrightarrow[\text{molybdenum oxide}]{\text{heated}} \underset{\text{formaldehyde + water}}{HCHO + \text{water}}$$

This process is much more economical where natural gas availabilty is more.

PLANT ECONOMICS OF FORMALDEHYDE

Rated Plant capacity	=		5.00 MT/Day
LAND & BUILDING (Land Area 1500 sq.mt.)	=	Rs.	25,90,000.00

PLANT & MACHINERY

1. Methanol storage tank
2. Air compressor
3. Vapourizing Chamber electrically
4. Preheating chamber
5. Fixed bed tubular reactor
6. Counter-current scrubbing chambers
7. Fractionating column
8. Various storage tanks
9. Boiler
10. Pumps
11. Insulation and other Misc.

FIXED CAPITAL

1.	LAND & BUILDING	Rs.	25,90,000.00
2.	PLANT & MACHINERY	Rs.	24,80,000.00
3.	OTHER FIXED ASSETS	Rs.	3,80,000.00
	TOTAL	Rs.	54,50,000.00

RAW MATERIALS

1. Methyl alcohol
2. Catalyst

TOTAL WORKING CAPITAL/MONTH

1.	RAW MATERIAL	Rs.	6,75,000.00
2.	SALARY & WAGES	Rs.	1,55,125.00
3.	UTILITIES & OVERHEADS	Rs.	4,02,500.00
	TOTAL	Rs.	12,32,625.00

TOTAL CAPITAL INVESTMENT

TOTAL FIXED CAPITAL	Rs.	54,50,000.00
TOTAL WORKING CAPITAL FOR 3 MONTHS	Rs.	36,97,875.00
TOTAL	Rs.	91,47,875.00

TURN OVER/ANNUM

By sale of 1500 MT FormaldehydeRs. 2,02,50,000.00

PROFIT SALES RATIO = Profit / Sales x 100 = 17.56 %

RATE OF RETURN = Operating profit / T.C.I x 100 = 38.87 %

BREAK EVEN POINT (B.E.P) = 56.29 %

Chapter 24

FOOD GRADE GREASE OR LUBRICANT

FORMULATIONS OF FOOD GRADE GREASE

FORMULATIONS:-1

QUANTITY	
Refined Petrolatums (IP/FCC grade) or Petroleum Jelly	35%
White Mineral oil (IP grade)	65%
Total	100

FORMULATIONS:-2

QUANTITY	
Refined Petrolatums (IP/FCC grade) or Petroleum Jelly	40%
White Mineral oil (IP/FCC grade)	60%
Total	100

MANUFACTURING PROCESS

To manufacture of food grade grease the following processing steps have to be followed.

1. Procure all the raw materials from the market of IP/FCC grades
2. Check the quality of all the raw materials.
3. Weigh the raw materials into desired quantities as specified in the formulations.
4. Now heat the IP/FCC grades petrolatum in a stainless steel jacketed reaction vessel fitted with S.S. stirrer, at 70°C. To this petrolatum, add the white mineral oil (IP/FCC grade) slowly and mix uniformly little by little, till all the white mineral oils are mixed with petrolatum by forming a semi solid viscous mass.
5. Now, cool the grease to room temperature.
6. Test the quality of finished product by checking the product as per FDA regulation or Toxic regulation to pass through these norms.
7. The finished food grade grease is now filled in the lacquer coated containers and seal the lid of the containers.
8. It is now stored and sent for marketing.

PLANT ECONOMICS FOOD GRADE GREASE OR LUBRICANT

Rated Plant Capacity =		5.00 TON/Day
LAND & BUILDING (Land Area 3000sq.mts.) =	Rs.	44,00,000.00

PLANT & MACHINERY

1. Reaction Vessel
2. Boiler
3. Condenser
4. S.S. Storage & filling tank
5. Laboratory & Testing Equipment
6. Drop point for grease appratus
7. Standard Pentrometer
8. Acidity Test
9. Cloud and Pour point
10. Specific gravity meter
11. Melting point apparatus
12. Thermometers
13. Other misc equipment & accessories including weight balance etc.

FIXED CAPITAL

1. LAND & BUILDING	Rs.	44,00,000.00
2. PLANT & MACHINERY	Rs.	20,60,050.00
3. OTHER FIXED ASSETS	Rs.	20,00,000.00
TOTAL	Rs.	84,60,050.00

RAW MATERIALS

1. White Petrolatum
2. White Mineral oil
3. Cartons, Lables, lacquer coated tin containers,

TOTAL WORKING CAPITAL/ANNUM

1. RAW MATERIAL	Rs.	6,75,00,000.00
2. SALARY & WAGES	Rs.	17,95,500.00
3. UTILITIES & OVERHEADS	Rs.	33,50,000.00
TOTAL	Rs.	7,26,45,500.00

TOTAL CAPITAL INVESTMENT

TOTAL FIXED CAPITAL	Rs.	84,60,050.00
TOTAL WORKING CAPITAL FOR 3 MONTHS	Rs.	1,81,61,375.00
TOTAL	Rs.	2,66,21,425.00

TURN OVER/ANNUM

By sale of Food Grade Grease 1500 Tons	Rs.	9,00,00,000.00

PROFIT SALES RATIO = Profit / Sales X 100 = 14.82 %

RATE OF RETURN = Operationg profit / T.C.I X 100 = 50.09 %

BREAK EVEN POINT (B.E.P) = 31.31 %

Chapter 25

GAS FILLING OF L.P.G. CYLINDER

LPG BOTTLING PROCESS

The following steps to consider during whole operation of LPG filling in cylinders.

1. LPG Gas procurement from the refineries or suppliers sources.
2. Storage of LPG in the tanks or hortons sphere.
3. Empty cylinder testing for leakage of body or valves.
4. Cylinder filling with the specified quantity as mentioned for the cylinder size, volume etc.
5. Filled LPG cylinder testing.
6. Storage in the cool & dry place.
7. Marketing & distribution.

PLANT ECONOMICS OF GAS FILLING OF L.P.G. CYLINDER

Rated Plant Capacity =	10000.00 Cylinders/Day	
LAND & BUILDING		
(Land area 10,000 sq.mts.) =	Rs.	40,80,000.00

PLANT & MACHINERY

1. Storage tanks
2. Cylinder filling systems complete with pumps
3. Fire fighting arrangements and equipments
4. Testing equipments
5. Gen. Set
6. Miscellaneous.

FIXED CAPITAL

1.	LAND & BUILDING	Rs.	40,80,000.00
2.	PLANT & MACHINERY	Rs.	57,60,000.01
3.	OTHER FIXED ASSETS	Rs.	3,03,50,000.00
	TOTAL	Rs.	4,01,90,000.01

RAW MATERIALS

1. L.P.G. Gas

TOTAL WORKING CAPITAL/MONTH

1. RAW MATERIAL	Rs.	99,40,000.00
2. SALARY & WAGES	Rs.	62,250.00
3. UTILITIES & OVERHEADS	Rs.	1,08,000.00
TOTAL	Rs.	1,01,10,250.00

TOTAL CAPITAL INVESTMENT

TOTAL FIXED CAPITAL	Rs.	4,01,90,000.01
TOTAL WORKING CAPITAL FOR 3 MONTHS	Rs.	3,03,30,750.00
TOTAL	Rs.	7,05,20,750.01

TURN OVER/ANNUM

By sale of 30,00,000 cylinders of 14.2 kgs.	Rs.	18,00,00,000.00

PROFIT SALES RATIO = Profit / Sales x 100 = 24.62 %

RATE OF RETURN = Operating profit / T.C.I x 100 = 62.85 %

BREAK EVEN POINT (B.E.P) = 25.50 %

Chapter 26

GREASES (LITHIUM BASED)

MANUFACTURING PROCESS OF LUBRICANT GREASES

Lubricating greases are manufactured by both batch and continuous processes. Due to the low capital Investment and case of processing, batch processes is best suited in small scale manufacture. The batch process is illustrated by the following formulation.

	% By Weight
Stearic acid or fat/oil	11
NacH(KOH/Ca(OH)$_2$ 76°Be	11
Water	11
Mineral Oil/Rosin Oil	67

The fat/oil and about 10 percent of the mineral oil charged in the fire-heated kettle, the fat melted and mixed thoroughly with oil. A mixture of alkalies and water as indicated is then added to the kettle them steam is passed and saponification is carried on until all the water has been evaporated from the reaction mixture. When the temperature reaches around 400°F oil is run in slowly and the temperature is maintained above 350°F until all or the oil is added. The batch is then cooled and drawn at 200°F and stored.

i. Batch Process.
ii. Continuous Process.

Following steps are used in Processing.

a. The required materials are properly weighed.
b. For saponification mixing and heating of ingredients is involved.
c. Dispersion of bodying agent in the lubricating fluid, dehydration by vaccum treatment of the finished or semi finished products.
d. Cooling of the soap.

The value of a lubricating grease and in service depends upon the following physcial characteristics.

1. Stability to working or shear.
2. Body or consistency.
3. Viscosity or flow.
4. Thermal stability.
5. Structure.

6. Synerisis.
7. Texture and appearance.

Most lubricates are produced by the batch, process, which is still popular particularly for a small scale manufacturer. In this process the amount of lubricants made in one lot may be from few hundred pounds to 60 or 100 barrels. Batch process may further to be divided into two parts;

i. Open kettle, and

ii. Closed kettle manufacture.

Simply, this process have the following successive steps in the production of lubricants.

i. OPEN KETTLE MANUFACTURE

a. Saponification and finishing carried out in one vessel.
b. Dispersion of preformed soap and finishing of product performed in the same kettle.
c. Saponification and dispersion of soap carried out in vessel, followed by cooling in auxiliary equipments.
d. Saponification concluded in one kettle and finishing carried out in a second vessel.
e. Fatty materials preferably fatty acids resin acids, mixed with a portion of the total oil in another vessel.

   The two mixtures are then brought together to the places where saponification takes place.

ii. CLOSED KETTLE MANUFACTURE

a. Saponification is carried out under pressure and finishing is done in a second vessel.
b. Saponification is carried out in a pressure vessel, soap dispersion in a second vessel and cooling in auxiliary equipment.

Greases Formulations (Lithium Based)

1.

Ingredients	Parts
Lithium stearate	72
Naphtha (of 100°F flash point)	100
Phenyl silicone	22

2.

Ingredients	Parts by wt.
Lithium stearate	3
Deodorized kerosene	35
(1:1 mixture) of dimethyl & diphenyl silicones	25

PLANT ECONOMICS OF GREASES (LITHIUM BASED)

Rated Plant Capacity =		2.00 MT/Day
LAND & BUILDING (Land 500 sq. mt.) =	Rs.	12,62,500.00

PLANT & MACHINERY

1. Mixing vessel
2. Storage tank
3. Cooling kettle
4. Drum
5. Oil fired furnace
6. Thermometer & other testing equipments
7. Other misc. equipments and accessories eg pipes, motors, starter switches etc.
8. Weighing balance digital

FIXED CAPITAL

1. LAND & BUILDING	Rs.	12,62,500.00
2. PLANT & MACHINERY	Rs.	15,93,000.00
3. OTHER FIXED ASSETS	Rs.	6,50,000.00
TOTAL	Rs.	35,05,500.00

RAW MATERIALS

1. Lithium stearate
2. Aluminium stearate
3. Tributyl phosphite
4. Petrolatum

TOTAL WORKING CAPITAL/MONTH

1. RAW MATERIAL	Rs.	20,37,250.00
2. SALARY & WAGES	Rs.	1,06,125.00
3. UTILITIES & OVERHEADS	Rs.	85,000.00
TOTAL	Rs.	22,28,375.00

TOTAL CAPITAL INVESTMENT

TOTAL FIXED CAPITAL	Rs.	35,05,500.00
TOTAL WORKING CAPITAL FOR 3 MONTHS	Rs.	66,85,125.00
TOTAL	Rs.	1,01,90,625.00

TURN OVER/ANNUM

By sale of 600 MT. lithium based Greases	Rs.	3,30,00,000.00

PROFIT SALES RATIO = Profit / Sales X 100 = 13.73 %

RATE OF RETURN = Operating profit / T.C.I x 100 = 44.47 %

BREAK EVEN POINT (B.E.P) = 36.85 %

Chapter 27

LUBE OIL FROM CNSL TO REDUCE FRICTION

The main basic raw material comes from petroleum distillation i.e. red oil cashew nutshell oil (C.N.S.L). Red oil has viscosity equivalent to light SAE. It is obtained from redistillation of petroleum in the still. It is distilled into three fractions. The residue in the still refined to meet quality requirements.

Cashewnut shell oil is obtained from the spongy layer between the inner and outer shell of cashew nut. The raw liquid contains about 90% ancardic acid, $C_{12}H_{32}O_3$ and a blistering compound containing sultur. Most of the liquid used incommerce has been heated or treated with chemicals to make it safe to handle. The liquid is non-drying, but can be made drying by proper treatment. It polymerize a heating and forms condensation products with aldehydes.

PROCESS OF MANUFACTURING

The manufacturing process of lube oil is quite simple. It involves blending of various ingredients in appropriate proportion in a particular manner. This blending is carried out in a kettle. The kettle draws its ingredients from out in a kettle. The kettle draws its ingredients from various storage tanks for raw materials and ingredients and additives.

Before feeding the ingredients, they are blended firstly in ball-mill. Then blended ingredients are fed to kettle, where it is further blended with CNSL. During the blending process, compressed air is sent in for a homogenous mass. Special care is to be taken when various additives are added according to the demand.

The required colour may be obtained by adding naphlhode. 2-naphthal may be added to get the yellowish tinge. The finished product is packed in tins of various volume and weights. The manufacturing process may be both batch and continuous process. Due to low capital investment and case of processing batch processes are best suited in small scale manufacture.

The fat oil in about 10 % by wt and mineral oil are charged in fire-heated kettle. The compressed air and steam is passed through the kettle for the homogenous mass and until all the water has been evaported from the reaction mixture when the temperature reaches around 400°f oil is run in slowly and up to 350°F all the oil is added up. The batch is then cooled and drawn at 200°F and stored.

Most lubricants are produced by the batch processes which is still particular for small scale manufacturer. Batch processes are classified as:-

1. Open kettle process.
2. Closed kettle process.

PLANT ECONOMICS OF LUBE OIL FROM CNSL

Rated Plant Capacity =		200.00 Lit/Day
LAND & BUILDING (Land area 300 sq.mt) =	Rs.	1,60,000.00

PLANT & MACHINERY

1. Mildsteel kettle steam jacketed
2. Ball mill
3. Storage tanks
4. Centrifugal pumps
5. Air compresser
6. Weighing Balance
7. Other Miscellaneous equipments and accessories eg. pipes, fitting etc.

FIXED CAPITAL

1. LAND & BUILDING	Rs.	1,60,000.00
2. PLANT & MACHINERY	Rs.	70,000.00
3. OTHER FIXED ASSETS	Rs.	52,500.00
TOTAL	Rs.	2,82,500.00

RAW MATERIALS

1. Cashewnut shell oil
2. Napthol
3. Butyl stearate
4. Tricrgysle phosphate
5. Barium sulphonate

TOTAL WORKING CAPITAL/MONTH

1. RAW MATERIAL	Rs.	1,00,630.00
2. SALARY & WAGES	Rs.	9,000.00
3. UTILITIES & OVERHEADS	Rs.	8,250.00
TOTAL	Rs.	1,17,880.00

TOTAL CAPITAL INVESTMENT

TOTAL FIXED CAPITAL	Rs.	2,82,500.00
TOTAL WORKING CAPITAL FOR 3 MONTHS	Rs.	3,53,640.00
TOTAL	Rs.	6,36,140.00

TURN OVER/ANNUM

Receipts by sale of 60,000 lit Lube Oil	Rs.	19,20,000.00

PROFIT SALES RATIO = Profit / Sales x 100 = 20.61 %

RATE OF RETURN = Operating profit / T.C.I x 100 = 62.21 %

BREAK EVEN POINT (B.E.P) = 32.72 %

Chapter 28

LUBE OIL AND GREASES

Lubricants and greases are one of the important products derived from crude petroleum. Though the percentage yield of the lubricating fractions from crude petroleum is relatively low, their value is for greater in terms of their essentiality to industry and other sectors of the economy lubricants are greases are essential for the proper functioning of nearly every machine, equipment & instrument.

Lube-oil is applied in various fields. The main are as follows:-

1) Plant & Machinery
2) Automobile engine
3) Textile industry

And in many others.

To improve the life of engines, machinery and other parts, lube oil is used. It is also used to reduce the friction between various parts & thereby increasing its life.

MANUFACTURING PROCESS

Lube Oil:

The manufacturing process of Lube oil is quite simple.

It is the blending of various ingredients in appropriate proportion in a particular manner. Usually, it is done in a kettle. The kettle draws the ingredients from various storage tanks for raw material & ingredients.

Before feeding the ingredients, these ingredients are blended First, in a Ball Mill, then the blended ingredients are fed to the kettle, where further blended with Red oil.

During this blending process, compressed air is sent in for a homogeneous mass. Special care is to be taken when additives are added.

The required colour may be obtained by adding naphlthode. 2 Naphthol may be added to get yelloiwsh linge.

The finished product is packed in tins of various volume and weights.

Greases:-

Lubricating grease are manufactured by both batch & continuous processes. Due to the low capital investment and case of processing, batch processes is best suited in small scale manufacture. the batch process is illustrated by the following formulation:-

Stearic acid or Fat/oil	11% by wt.
NaOH/KOH/$Ca(OH)_2$ 76° Be'	11
Water	11
Mineral oil/ resin oil	67

The Fat/oil and about 10% of the mineral oil are charged in the fire-heated kettle, the fat meeted and mixed throughly with oil. A mixture of alkalies and water as indicated is then added to the kettle. The steam is passed and saponification is carried on until all the water has been evaporated from the reaction mixture. When the temperature reaches around 400°F oil is run in slowly 350°F until all the oil is added. The batch is then cooled and drawn at 200°F and stored.

1) Batch Process
2) Continuous Process

Following steps are used in processing :-

a) The required materials are properly weighed.
b) For Saponification, mixing & heating of ingredients are involved.
c) Dispersion of binding agent in the lubricating fluid, dehydration by vacuum treatment of the finished or semi-finished products.
d) Cooling of the soap.

The value of lubricating grease & in service depends upon the following physical characteristics:

1) Stability to working or shear.
2) Body or consistency.
3) Viscosity or flow.
4) Thermal stability.
5) Syneresis.
6) Texture & apperance.

Most lubricants are produced by the batch process, which is still popular particular for a small scale manufacturer. In this process the amount of lubricants made in one lot may be from few hundred pounds to 60 or 100 barrels. Batch process may further to be divided into two parts:-

1) Open kettle &
2) Closed kettle manufacture.

Simply, this process have the following successive steps in the production of lubricants.

1) Open kettle Manufacturer

a) Saponification & Finishing carried out in one vessel.

b) Dispersion of product performed soap & finishing of product performed in the same kettle.

c) Saponification and dispersion of soap carried out in vessel, followed by cooling in auxillary equipment.

d) Dispersion of performed soap in one vessel, followed by cooling in auxiliary equipments.

e) Saponification concluded in one kettle & finishing carried out in a second vessel.

f) Fatty materials preferably fatty acids or resin acids mixed with a portion of the total oil in another vessel.

The two mixtures are then brought together to the places where saponification takes place.

2) Closed Kettle Manufacture:

a) Saponification is carried out under pressure and finishing is done in a second vessel.

b) Saponification is carried out in a pressure vessel, soap dispersion in a second vessel and cooling in auxiliary equipment.

PLANT ECONOMICS OF LUBE OIL AND GREASE

Rated Plant Capacity	=		400.00 KGS/Day
LAND & BUILDING (Land area 500 sq.mt)	=	Rs.	3,10,000.00

PLANT & MACHINERY

1. Mild steel kettle steam jacked
2. Ball mill
3. Mini boiler
4. Centrifugal pumps
5. Air compressor
6. Storage tanks
7. Weighing balance
8. Other miscellaneous equipments & accessories eg. pipes, fittings etc

FIXED CAPITAL

1.	LAND & BUILDING	Rs.	3,10,000.00
2.	PLANT & MACHINERY	Rs.	1,19,000.00
3.	OTHER FIXED ASSETS	Rs.	20,000.00
	TOTAL	Rs.	4,49,000.00

RAW MATERIALS

1. 2-Naphthol
2. Butyl stearate
3. Tricresyl phosphate
4. Barium sulphonate
5. Mineral oil
6. Resin oil
7. Hydrated lime

TOTAL WORKING CAPITAL/MONTH

1.	RAW MATERIAL	Rs.	26,255.00
2.	SALARY & WAGES	Rs.	12,000.00
3.	UTILITIES & OVERHEADS	Rs.	43,750.00
	TOTAL	Rs.	82,005.00

TOTAL CAPITAL INVESTMENT

TOTAL FIXED CAPITAL	Rs.	4,49,000.00
TOTAL WORKING CAPITAL FOR 3 MONTHS	Rs.	2,46,015.00
TOTAL	Rs.	6,95,015.00

TURN OVER/ANNUM

1. Receipts by sale of 60,000 Lit/p.a of Lube oil
2. 60,000 kgs/Annum of Grease

TOTAL	Rs.	14,10,000.00

PROFIT SALES RATIO = Profit / Sales x 100 = 20.48 %
RATE OF RETURN = Operating profit / T.C.I x 100 = 41.55 %
BREAK EVEN POINT (B.E.P) = 58.36 %

Chapter 29

MICROCRYSTALLINE WAX

MANUFACTURING PROCESS

Micro crystalline wax is produced either from the residual fraction of crude-oil distillation or from crude-oil tank bottoms. Here we are discribing the method followed for microcrystalline wax from crude oil tank bottoms called sludge obtained from petrochemical refineries. The high molecular weight fraction in crude oil precipitate from solution in large storage tanks. These crude-oil tank bottoms are essentially crude oil with very high wax contents and have to processed to obtain microcrystalline wax. The sludge accumulate from crude tanks bottoms are heated to separate dirt, diest and any foreign matter. The melted wax obtained is dehydrated and distilled to free the wax from its oil content as much as possible. The wax is recovered in Residual tank bottoms. From the residual tank bottoms the wax has to be freed from Asphalt by the desphalting process. The Desphalted wax is further subjected to deoiling process in the refinery. After being described it is treated in a separate tanks known as decolourising tank. After being decolorised the wax recovered from tank bottom is microcrystalline wax.

PLANT ECONOMICS OF MICROCRYSTALLINE WAX

Rated Plant Capacity = 1.00 TON/Day
LAND & BUILDING (Land Area 3000 sq.mt) = Rs. 93,50,000.00

PLANT & MACHINERY

1. Crude storage tanks
2. Dehydrator tank
3. Distilalation tank
4. Residual storage tank
5. Deasphalting systems
6. Solvent Storage tanks
7. Boiler
8. Laboratory equipments testing and analytical equipments
9. Misc. tank, pumps, valves, pipes, structures and other fittings

10. tools, Jigs, fixtures
11. Pollution control equipments and accessories

FIXED CAPITAL

1. LAND & BUILDING	Rs.	93,50,000.00
2. PLANT & MACHINERY	Rs.	1,49,50,000.00
3. OTHER FIXED ASSETS	Rs.	37,00,000.00
TOTAL	Rs.	2,80,00,000.00

RAW MATERIALS

1. Crude oil sludge
2. Solvent
3. Clay

TOTAL WORKING CAPITAL/MONTH

1. RAW MATERIAL	Rs.	36,00,000.00
2. SALARY & WAGES	Rs.	2,18,125.00
3. UTILITIES & OVERHEADS	Rs.	5,43,000.00
TOTAL	Rs.	43,61,125.00

TOTAL CAPITAL INVESTMENT

TOTAL FIXED CAPITAL	Rs.	2,80,00,000.00
TOTAL WORKING CAPITAL FOR 3 MONTHS	Rs.	1,30,83,375.00
TOTAL	Rs.	4,10,83,375.00

TURN OVER/ANNUM

Receipt of sale of 3000 tonnes Microcrystalline wax	Rs.	8,10,00,000.00

PROFIT SALES RATIO = Profit / Sales x 100 = 19.13 %
RATE OF RETURN = Operating profit / T.C.I x 100 = 37.72 %
BREAK EVEN POINT (B.E.P) = 52.05 %

Chapter 30

PETROLEUM JELLY

PROCESS OF MANUFACTURE

The natural petrolatum is produced by fractional distillation of still residues from the steam distillation of paraffin base petroleum or from steam reduced crude oils from which the light fraction have been removed.

Manufacturing Process of Synthetic Petrolatum

Petrolatm or petroleum jelly can also be made synthetically by blending mineral oil and microcrystalline wax. Paraffin wax is also incorporated. The mineral oil used should be highly refined medicinal white oil (liquid paraffin) if the petroleum jelly is to be used in pharmaceuticals and cosmetics. For less critical application technical white oil or even less retained mineral oils can be used. The waxes should of food grade if the petroleum jelly is to be used in pharmaceuticals. Stabilizers are also added to keep the wax-oil blend from separating or deteriorating other wise.

Manufacture of synthetic jelly consists of mainly blending the direct constituents proper mixing of the constituents is very important to ensure proper stability of the wax-oil system. If the mixing is not proper the oil mill separate from the wax and render the petroleum jelly grainy. For proper mixing the mixing vessel may be rotated or agitation may be done with the help of a turbing.

The blending is done in a kettle provided with electrical heating device, steam heating coils or steam jacket. Microcrystalline wax and paraffin wax is melted and a temperature of 120 to 130 C is maintained, oil is added and the vessel is agitated at a speed of 150-200 r.p.m. to get the whole mass thoroughly mixed. The mixing is continued for 1-2 hours, if the oil is not fully refined white oil and the waxes are of high quality the petrolatum is directly packed.

The formulation adopted here for the production of synthetic petrolatum is :

Petrolatum can be separated from reduced crude in several ways. The original method was cold settling. Reduced crude dissolved in a suitable amount of naphtha was allowed to stand over winter until the micro - waxes settled out. This method is still used but the reduced crude naphtha solution is held in refrigerated tanks until the petrolatum settles out. The supernatant naptha - oil layer is pumped to a still where the naphtha is removed leaning cylinder stock which can be further treated to produce bright stock. The petrolatum layer is also distilled to remove naptha. The resulting crude petrolatum may be clay treated or acid and clay treated to improve the colour.

Another method of separating petrolatum from reduced crude is centrifuge dewaxing. In this process, the reduced crude is dissolved in naphtha and chilled to 0^0F or lower . This cause the wax to separate gining the mixture the appearance of watery mud. The mixture is then fed to a battery of centrifuges where the wax is separated from the liquid.

A centrifuge consists of a vertical cylinder rotating at 15,000 revolutions per minute. The naptha - oil mixture with its suspension of wax crystals is fed into the bottom of the cylinder. As the mixture travels up the cylinder the centrifugal force causes the mixture to separate into a naptha oil layer and a petroleum layer. Mechanical means at the top of the cylinder direct each layer into separate exits. The naptha is then separated from the oil and petroleum by distillation.

Basis : 500 kg

White Oil/Pale oil	300 kg
Micro Crystalline Wax	100 kg
Paraffin Wax	50 kg
Clay	50 kg
Total	500 kg

PLANT ECONOMICS OF PETROLEUM JELLY

Rated Plant Capacity	=		500.00 Kg/Day
LAND & BUILDING (Land 300 Sq.mts.)	=	Rs.	4,50,000.00

PLANT & MACHINERY

1. Pale /white oil storage tank
2. Steam jacketed vessels
3. Finished prodict storage tank
4. Other misc. including electrificati on installtion office furniture and equipment technical

FIXED CAPITAL

1. LAND & BUILDING		Rs.	4,50,000.00
2. PLANT & MACHINERY		Rs.	1,90,000.00
3. OTHER FIXED ASSETS		Rs.	75,000.00
	TOTAL	Rs.	7,15,000.00

RAW MATERIALS

1. Wite oil/pale oil
2. Microcrystalline wax
3. Paraffin wax
4. Clay

TOTAL WORKING CAPITAL/MONTH

1. RAW MATERIAL		Rs.	2,73,500.00
2. SALARY & WAGES		Rs.	36,750.00
3. UTILITIES & OVERHEADS		Rs.	53,500.00
	TOTAL	Rs.	3,63,750.00

TOTAL CAPITAL INVESTMENT

TOTAL FIXED CAPITAL		Rs.	7,15,000.00
TOTAL WORKING CAPITAL FOR 3 MONTHS		Rs.	10,91,250.00
	TOTAL	Rs.	18,06,250.00

TURN OVER/ANNUM

Sales of 150 M.T of Jelly	Rs.	60,00,000.00

PROFIT SALES RATIO = Profit / Sales x 100 = 19.75 %

RATE OF RETURN = Operating profit / T.C.I x 100 = 66.03 %

BREAK EVEN POINT (B.E.P) = 43.18 %

Chapter 31

RECLAMATION OF USED ENGINE OIL

RECLAMATION OF USED ENGINE OIL

Re-refining of used oils is now accepted and recognised as a legitimate source of supplementing petroleum oils. Prior to the escalation of oil prices, petroleum lubricants and other industrial oils were very cheap and their conservation and saving was not economically attractive. Users did not care to recovery and preserve used oils, which were allowed to be lost or were disposed of by easiest possible means. Rise in Oil prices has compelled the users firstly to economise the use of oils and secondly to recover, grade and store the used oils. Attractive prices and ready acceptability have given a boost to this industry.

PROCESS OF MANUFACTURE

RE-REFINING PROCESSES

Different commercial processes and changes that occur in the re-refined oil as compared to the original oil are as follows:

1. ACID CLAY PROCESS

This involves the following major process steps.

(a) Treatment with 5 to 10 percent (wt) sulfuric acid (98 per cent) at 40 to 50°C, under mild agitation conditions. This removes asphaltic and carbonaceous material and also metal particles, water and aromatic hydrocarbons. Only active and degraded hydrocarbons are required to be removed; however substantial quantity of aromatic and other hydrocarbons are also lost.

(b) Acid Treated oil is meutralised by sodium hydroxide or sodium carbonate. It is further weather washed to remove the residual acid and water soluble salts.

(c) Neutral oil is dietlled up to 300°C to remove the volatile material.

(d) Neutralised oil is treated with an adsorbant to remove final traces of water, colouring materials, asphalt, and particulate matter.

Step (b) and (c) do not alter the volatility or GCC of the oil. In the acid treatment, asphaltic and the acid treatment, asphaltic and aromatic hydrocarbons are removed. Some other hydrocarbons are also lost, Fig.2 shows the volatility and GCC changes in the acid tyreated oil. The oil after acid treatment becomes more paraffinic, apparently showing a rise in pour point lowering of density and poorer thermal and hydrolytic stability IV of the acid re-refined oil will be obviously higher. Compatability with additives and additive response may undergo considerable change because of loss of aromaticity. This does not show off in the normal physico-chemical testing but may have serious problems in engine performance. Performance of detergency additives, E.P. additives, oxidation inhibitors and pour point depressants may be considerably affected. Volatility of the oil in acid clay re-refining remains practically unchanged.

2. TOTAL DISTILLATION PROCESS

In this process, the used oil after "Preparation" is subjected to fractionation under atmospheric pressure, to remove the volatile contaminants, followed by total distillation under vacuum 5 to 8% heavy residue is recovered after the vacuum distillation which is constituted of heavy hydrocarbons and aspheltic material. Thus re-refining results in loss of 5 to 8 per cent heavy cut and also a 3 to 5 per cent over all of the light fraction. This increases the volatility of the oil; average boiling temperature is lowered and viscosity is reduced elightly.

3. SOLVENT EXTRACTION PROCESS

Several solvents, like liquid propane, pentane, iso-propyl alcohol, phenol, furfural etc. have been used for the separation of degraded components from the used oils. In solvent extraction, while the degraded components are substantially extracted considerable quantity of desirable components are also lost in the extract. The re-fined oil is therefore more paráffinic that the original oil but less paraffinic than the acid treated oil.

After solvent stripping the raffinale is treated with an absorbent to improve the colour. Volatility of the oil remains more or less unchanged. An oil re-refined by this process may show poorer additive compatibility and response. This will have a higher pour point, better oxidation stability, higher VI and poorer thermal add hydrolytic stability.

4. HYDROGENATION

Hydrogenation is used as a total process of re-refining only is selected cases. Often, it is combined with total distillation or solvent extraction processes to eliminate residual unsaturation of the oil. Oils after hydrogenation become slightly poorer in aromatics, giving poorer additive response. However VI and oxidation stability is improved. Volatility of the oil remains practically unchanged.

PLANT ECONOMICS OF REFINING OF USED LUBRICANTS

Rated Plant Capacity	=		1.00 MT/Day
LAND & BUILDING (Land 2400 Sq.mts.)	=	Rs.	7,80,000.00

PLANT & MACHINERY

1. Storage tanks
2. Settling & decantation tank
3. Vacuum kettle
4. Reaction vessel
5. Vacuum kettle
6. Filter press
7. Reaction vessel
8. Refined lubricant storge tank
9. Boiler
10. Sulphuric acid storage tank
11. Instrumentation
12. Laboratory testing equipment
13. Pipe fitting Pumps (PP) valves

FIXED CAPITAL

1.	LAND & BUILDING	Rs.	7,80,000.00
2.	PLANT & MACHINERY	Rs.	3,75,000.00
3.	OTHER FIXED ASSETS	Rs.	23,000.00
	TOTAL	Rs.	11,78,000.00

RAW MATERIALS

1. Used lubricant
2. Sulphuric acid
3. Lime
4. Activated clay
5. Additives like antioxidants
6. Packing drum

TOTAL WORKING CAPITAL/MONTH

1.	RAW MATERIAL	Rs.	4,23,100.00
2.	SALARY & WAGES	Rs.	36,936.00
3.	UTILITIES & OVERHEADS	Rs.	46,600.00
	TOTAL	Rs.	5,06,636.00

TOTAL CAPITAL INVESTMENT

TOTAL FIXED CAPITAL	Rs.	11,78,000.00
TOTAL WORKING CAPITAL FOR 3 MONTHS	Rs.	15,19,908.00
TOTAL	Rs.	26,97,908.00

TURN OVER/ANNUM

By sale of 300 MT reconditioned (refined) lubricant (reclaimed engine oil)	Rs.	78,00,000.00

PROFIT SALES RATIO = Profit / Sales x 100 = 12.54 %
RATE OF RETURN = Operating profit / T.C.I x 100 = 36.62 %
BREAK EVEN POINT (B.E.P) = 53.13 %

Chapter 32

RUST PREVENTION LUBE OIL

Rust Prevention lubricating oils are used for prevention of rust on the mettallic parts of automobile with which it comes is contact, as basically into the base stock (Lube oil) are incarporated rust inhibitors, vi improvers, & other additives,etc.

Rust prevention lubricating oils are used as antioxidants/ stabilizers,etc.

These lubricating oil is used in the machinery for reducing the friction and due to the presence of rust preventives it acts as an anti-corrosion agent.

FORMULATION OF RUST PREVENTION LUBRICATING OIL
FORMULATION NO:1

1.	Base Stock (Lube Oil)	98.45%
2.	Corrosion Inhibitor viz Inida Zoline	1.00%
3.	Sarcosine	1.00%
4.	Antiwear ajent viz. Diamyl ammonium lauratc	0.50%
5.	VF Improver viz Polyisobutylene	0.05%
		100.00%

NO:2

1.	Base Stock (Lube Oil)	98.45%
2.	Corrosin Inhivitor viz Ininoester/Amidoxime	1.50%
3.	Alkanolamine/Alkylamine	0.50%
4.	Antiwear agent viz Phosphoric acid	0.50%
5.	V.I.Improrer - viz Polymethacrylate	0.05%
		100.00%

MANUFACTURING PROCESS OF RUST PREVENTATION LUBRICATING OIL

As Per Formulation NO:1....

The Base Stock (Lube Oil) in requisite quantity charged into a Reaction Kettle (S.S) (Jacketed) fitter with an agitator and heating is accomplished by thermic fluid heater.

Then into the reaction vend are added corrosion inhivitors viz. Imidazoline Sarcosine & Anti-wear Agents viz, Dianyl ammonium laureate in requisite quantites and the contents are well stirred for 1/2 Hour to 1 Hour and the temperature of 75-80°C is maintenance.

Thus is followed by addition of V.I.Improver viz Polyisobutylene.

The contents are well stirred for about 15 Minuts-1/2 Hour and the tempt of 75-80°C ic maintained. The product formed is then cooled.

It is checked for quality and then despatched in suitable centaines viz barrels (20 litres capacity) Sometimes, if need br(205 litrd hsrrels) may as well be employed.

PLANT ECONOMICS OF RUST PREVENTION LUBRICATING OIL

Rated Plant Capacity = 5.00 MT/Day
LAND & BUILDING (Land Area 1000 Sq.Mt.) = Rs. 21,82,500.00

PLANT & MACHINERY

1. Mixing Kettle
2. Storage Tanks
3. Thermic Fluid Heater
4. Packing Machine (Semi-Automatic)
5. Lab Equipments
6. Misc. equipment viz pipe, valves, motors, etc.

FIXED CAPITAL

1.	LAND & BUILDING	Rs.	21,82,500.00
2.	PLANT & MACHINERY	Rs.	28,30,000.00
3.	OTHER FIXED ASSETS	Rs.	4,60,000.00
	TOTAL	Rs.	54,72,500.00

RAW MATERIALS

1. Base Stock (Lube Oil)
2. Corrosion Inhibitor viz
3. Sarcosine
4. Antiwear agent viz Diamyl Ammonium Laurate
5. V.I. Improver viz Polyisobutylene
6. Packaging Materials

TOTAL WORKING CAPITAL/MONTH

1.	RAW MATERIAL	Rs.	46,37,250.01
2.	SALARY & WAGES	Rs.	1,06,400.00
3.	UTILITIES & OVERHEADS	Rs.	85,000.00
	TOTAL	Rs.	48,28,650.01

TOTAL CAPITAL INVESTMENT

TOTAL FIXED CAPITAL	Rs.	54,72,500.00
TOTAL WORKING CAPITAL FOR 3 MONTHS	Rs.	1,44,85,950.03
TOTAL	Rs.	1,99,58,450.03

TURN OVER/ANNUM

By sale of 1500 MT. of Rust Prevention Lubricating Oil	Rs.	6,45,00,000.00

PROFIT SALES RATIO = Profit / Sales x 100 = 5.08 %
RATE OF RETURN = Operating profit / T.C.I x 100 = 16.41 %
BREAK EVEN POINT (B.E.P) = 56.18 %

Chapter 33

SILICON GREASE

MANUFACTURING PROCESS OF SILICONE GREASE USING (IA) THICKENER

For the manufacture of silicone grease, first thickener is to be prepared which is mentioned below:-

PREPARATION OF CHROMIUM METHYL PHENYL PHOSPHINATE DIOCTYL PHOSPHINATE THICKENER

(1A)	Formulation	Qty.	%Age.
1.	Chromium Methyl Phenyl-phosphinate $Cr(H_2O)(OH)[Cop(me)(Ph)O]_2$(38 mmol) soln.)	15 gms.	8.52
2.	Dioctylphosphinate $(C_8H_{17})_2P(o)$ oH (38 m mol)	10.95 gm.	6.22
3.	Tetrahydrofuran (THF)	150ml(gm)	85.26
	Total	175.95gms	100.00

PLANT ECONOMICS OF SILICON GREASE

Rated Plant Capacity =		2.00 Ton/Day
LAND & BUILDING (Land Area 1250 sq.mt.) =	Rs.	35,25,000.00

PLANT & MACHINERY

1. Reaction Vessel
2. Boiler
3. Condenser
4. S.S. Storage
5. Laboratory & Testing Equipment
6. Drop point
7. Standard Pentrometer
8. Acidity Test apparatus Digital display complete
9. Cloud and Pour point Apparatus
10. Specific gravity meter

11. Melting point apparatus
12. Thermometers
13. Other misc equipment & accessories including weighing balance etc.

FIXED CAPITAL

1.	LAND & BUILDING	Rs.	35,25,000.00
2.	PLANT & MACHINERY	Rs.	25,60,050.00
3.	OTHER FIXED ASSETS	Rs.	20,00,000.00
	TOTAL	Rs.	80,85,050.00

RAW MATERIALS

1. Poly (methylphenyl-siloxane)
2. Thickener (Chromium methylphenyl
3. Cartons, Lables, lacquer coated tin containers
4. Laboratory chemicals, miscellaneous consumables and others

TOTAL WORKING CAPITAL/ANNUM

1.	RAW MATERIAL	Rs.	15,01,00,000.00
2.	SALARY & WAGES	Rs.	17,95,500.00
3.	UTILITIES & OVERHEADS	Rs.	28,40,000.00
	TOTAL	Rs.	15,47,35,500.00

TOTAL CAPITAL INVESTMENT

TOTAL FIXED CAPITAL	Rs.	80,85,050.00
TOTAL WORKING CAPITAL FOR 1 MONTHS	Rs.	1,28,94,625.00
TOTAL	Rs.	2,09,79,675.00

TURN OVER/ANNUM

By sale of Silicon Grease 600 Tons Rs. 18,00,00,000.00

PROFIT SALES RATIO = Profit / Sales x 100 = 11.82 %
RATE OF RETURN = Operating profit / T.C.I x 100 = 101.38 %
BREAK EVEN POINT (B.E.P) = 21.57 %

Chapter 34

WIRE DRAWING LUBRICANTS

WIRE DRAWING LUBRICANTS

Wire drawing lubrication is an extremely complicated, often poorly understood subject. Whatever the chemical complexity of wire and rod drawing lubrication, some rather definite physical behaviour can be cited. At one extreme, the absence of lubrication, local or general, can lead to adhesion of the die. In such cases the surface of the wire is stripped off and a torn, rough, heavily striated finish results. The value of the friction is theoretically about 0.5, but value of about 0.25 are more realistic averaged over the whole surface. When a minimal possibly monomolecular lubricant film exists, sticking no longer occurs and the wire assumers the contour of the die on a microscopic scale. This mode is called boundary, or thin film lubrication. If the die is smooth, surface asperities on the wire are ironed, out by the intimate die contact and a bright wire surface emerges. Rather thin lubricant films develop when solid soaps of relatively high shear strength are used. Dry lubricants may be applied by putting the wire through a box. A great amount of the wire or rod after the drawing pass.

TECHNOLOGY & PROCESS OF MANUFACTURE

Technology :

Although, there is a vast development in the field of lubricants. Sophisticated technology has been developed in the manufacturing of lubricants. A complete technical know-how is available indigenously for manufacture good quality wire drawing lubricants.

Process of Manufacture

The process of manufacture of powder wire drawing lubricants is simple. But there is some technicality involved in the formulation and process. At the same time, it is quite important to know how the particular wire drawing lubricant is used for particular quality of wire.

First of all, for manufacture of wire drawing lubricants (powder form), the materials are weighed in required proportions. These are fed to the ball mill or edge runner. The materials are ground properly as per required fineness. The ground material is screened. The oversize coarse material is recharged to the ball mill with next batch for grinding. The under size fine product is packed in different sizes of bags and sent for sale.

PLANT ECONOMICS OF WIRE DRAWING LUBRICANTS

Rated Plant Capacity =		600.00 Kg./Day
LAND & BUILDING (Land area 500 sq.mt.) =	Rs.	6,00,000.00

PLANT & MACHINERY

1. Ball mill
2. Vibrating set
3. High Speed Mixer/Blender
4. Testing & Material Handling Equipments
5. Miscellaneous tools & tackles, Process control instruments, stand by power generator.
6. Drying oven & dry grinder.

FIXED CAPITAL

1.	LAND & BUILDING	Rs.	6,00,000.00
2.	PLANT & MACHINERY	Rs.	11,00,000.00
3.	OTHER FIXED ASSETS	Rs.	2,85,000.00
	TOTAL	Rs.	19,85,000.00

RAW MATERIALS

1. FROM OF CALCIUM BASED LUB:
   (a) Calcium Stearate
2. (b) Zinc Sulphide
3. p-Dichloro, Diphenyl, Trichloroethane
4. FOR OF SODIUM-BASED LUB:
   (a) Sodium Stearate
5. (b) Titanium dioxide
6. (c) Alumina
7. (d) Borax
8. SYNTHETIC-BASED LUB:
   (a) polyethylone glucal
9. (b) p - Dichloro, Dipheneyl Trichloroethane
10. Talc Powder

TOTAL WORKING CAPITAL/MONTH

1.	RAW MATERIAL	Rs.	6,05,860.00
2.	SALARY & WAGES	Rs.	48,000.00
3.	UTILITIES & OVERHEADS	Rs.	46,840.00
	TOTAL	Rs.	7,00,700.00

TOTAL CAPITAL INVESTMENT

TOTAL FIXED CAPITAL	Rs.	19,85,000.00
TOTAL WORKING CAPITAL FOR 2 MONTHS	Rs.	14,01,400.00
TOTAL	Rs.	33,86,400.00

TURN OVER/ANNUM

By sale of 180 MT of wire drawing lubricants powder in suitable packs	Rs.	1,08,00,000.00

PROFIT SALES RATIO = Profit / Sales x 100 = 13.65 %

RATE OF RETURN = Operating profit / T.C.I x 100 = 43.54 %

BREAK EVEN POINT (B.E.P) = 48.21 %

Chapter 35

SUPPLIERS OF PLANT & MACHINERIES

BOILER

Fluidtech Boilers Pvt. Ltd.
2703, Phase-IV
GIDC, Vatva
Ahmedabad,
Gujarat-382445
India
TEL : +91 (0) 79 5840105
FAX : +91 (0) 79 5840041
E-mail: info@fluidltd.com

Shri Indtex Boiler Pvt. Ltd.
Plot No. 1601
GIDC Est., Phase-I
Naroda, Ahmedabad,
Gujarat-382330
India
TEL : +91 (0) 79 2823057
FAX : +91 (0) 79 2820047
E-mail:
shiyug@wilnetonline.net

MJ Patel (India) Ltd.
118, P D'Mello Rd.
Nr. Carnac Bridge
Mumbai, Maharashtra-400009
India
TEL : +91 (0) 22 3422114
FAX : +91 (0) 22 3427410
E-mail: mjpil@vsnl.net.in

Kemtech International Ltd.
A-125, Shivalik
Malviya Ngr. P.O.
New Delhi,
NCT of Delhi-110017
India
TEL : +91 (0) 11 6688343
FAX : +91 (0) 11 6680899
E-mail:
info@kemtechinternational.com

Bharat Heavy Plate & Vessels Ltd.
A Unit Of Bharat Yantra
Nigam Ltd.
PO BHPV, Visakhapatnam,
Andhra Pradesh-530012
India
TEL : +91 (0) 891 517381
FAX : +91 (0) 891 517626
E-mail:
bhpv.ec@rmj.sprintrpg.ems.vsnl.net.in

Precitech India
207, G K Towers, 29
G K Ngr., Dr. A S Rao Ngr.
Secunderabad,
Andhra Pradesh-500003
India
TEL : +91 (0) 40 7223824
E-mail:
sudhakar_valiv@yahoo.com

Nitasha Envirotech Pvt. Ltd.
1062-63, Phase-II
Indl. Area, Chandigarh,
Chandigarh (UT)-160002
India
TEL : +91 (0) 172 656700
FAX : +91 (0) 172 652998
E-mail: nitasha1@glide.net.in

National Furnaces
21/731, Bakshi House
Faiz Rd., Karol Bagh
New Delhi,
NCT of Delhi-110005
India
TEL : +91 (0) 11 3637605
FAX : +91 (0) 11 3510557
E-mail: natfur@rediffmail.com

Flare Combustion Systems
A-18, Hauz Khas
New Delhi,
NCT of Delhi-110016
India
TEL : +91 (0) 11 6867768
FAX : +91 (0) 11 6868382
E-mail:
flarecombustion@id.eth.net

Heatex Boilers (India) Pvt. Ltd.
2nd Flr., 1, Motia Khan
Rani Jhansi Rd.New Delhi,
NCT of Delhi-110055
India

TEL : +91 (0) 11 3530642
FAX : +91 (0) 11 3530645
E-mail:
heatexboilers@rediffmail.com

Balkrishna Boilers Inds.
Plot No. 14
Jay Khodiyar Indl. Est.
Nr. Subhash Est.
Ramol Rd.
Ahmedabad, Gujarat-380026
India
TEL : +91 (0) 79 5855883
E-mail: info@balkrishn.com

Isotex Corp.
3rd Flr., Laxmi Chmbrs.
Navjivan Rd.
Ahmedabad,
Gujarat-380014
India
TEL : +91 (0) 79 7544321
FAX : +91 (0) 79 7541224
E-mail: isotex@icenet.net

Vivek Chem-Fabs
Plot No. 71, Sect. 27A,
15/1 Mile Stone, Mathura Rd.
Faridabad, Haryana-121003
India
TEL : +91 (0) 129 5274848
FAX : +91 (0) 129 8843308

Hitze Equipments (India) Pvt. Ltd.
45-B, Indl. Area, Phase-II
Peenya, Bangalore,
Karnataka-560058
India
TEL : +91 (0) 80 3722281
FAX : +91 (0) 80 3327519
E-mail:
hitzindia@mantramail.com

Asian Boiler Engineers Pvt. Ltd.
130-A, Golanji Hill Rd.
Sewree, Mumbai,
Maharashtra-400015
India
TEL : +91 (0) 22 4131630
FAX : +91 (0) 22 4139624
E-mail:
abengg@bom3.vsnl.net.in

COOLANT FILTERS

Jaypee Industries Pvt. Ltd.
J-86, Sarita Vihar
New Delhi,
NCT of Delhi-110044
India
TEL : +91 (0) 11 6972106
FAX : +91 (0) 11 6972167

Electro Magnetic Industries
989/13, GIDC
Makarpura, Vadodara,
Gujarat-390010
India
TEL : +91 (0) 265 642017
FAX : +91 (0) 265 645430
E-mail:
sales@electromagneticindia.com

DI Filter Systems Pvt. Ltd.
C-94, 1st Flr., Shivalik
Gurgaon, Haryana-122001
India
TEL : +91 (0) 124 6219575
FAX : +91 (0) 124 6226920
E-mail: difsp@ndl.vsnl.net.in

Mag Tools
B-465, Indl. Est.
Gokul Rd., Hubli,
Karnataka-580030
India
TEL : +91 (0) 836 332297
FAX : +91 (0) 836 332297
E-mail:
magtools@bgl.vsnl.net.in

AR Engineering
L-77, Additional MIDC
Satara, Maharashtra-415004
India
TEL : +91 (0) 2162 44385
FAX : +91 (0) 2162 47569
E-mail:
arengineering@vsnl.com

CUTTING OIL FILTERS

Jaypee Industries Pvt. Ltd.
J-86, Sarita Vihar
New Delhi, NCT of Delhi-110044
India
TEL : +91 (0) 11 6972106
FAX : +91 (0) 11 6972167

Gopani Product Systems
104, Kashiparekh Cmplx.,
Swastik Cross Rd.
B/h Bhagwati Chmbr., C G Rd.
Navrangpura
Ahmedabad, Gujarat-380009
India
TEL : +91 (0) 79 6441972
FAX : +91 (0) 79 6441951
E-mail:
gopani@wilnetonline.net

Bhagyashree Accessories Pvt. Ltd.
S. No. 1/3B, Dhayari
Sinhgad Rd., Pune,
Maharashtra-411041
India
TEL : +91 (0) 20 4392276
FAX : +91 (0) 20 4392712
E-mail: chitale@vsnl.net

SAF Filter Pvt. Ltd.
34, C R Avenue
Kolkata,
West Bengal-700012
India
TEL : +91 (0) 33 2376168
FAX : +91 (0) 33 2373604
E-mail: safilterpltd@vsnl.com

AOF Filtration Systems Pvt.

Ltd.
Plot No. 282, Phase-II
Kamalapuri Cly.
Hyderabad,
Andhra Pradesh-500073
India
TEL : +91 (0) 40 3545993
FAX : +91 (0) 40 3547627
E-mail: aof@sify.com

GREASE MIXERS

Machinkraft Equipment
337, 3rd Rd.,
Sindh Hsg. Soc.
Aundh, Pune,
Maharashtra-411007
India
TEL : +91 (0) 20 5887464
FAX : +91 (0) 20 5880353
E-mail:
info@machinkraftequipment.com

Surya Industrial Equipments
D-109, Phase-I
IDA, Jeedimetla
Hyderabad,
Andhra Pradesh-500055
India
TEL : +91 (0) 40 3096355
FAX : +91 (0) 40 3098163

Cosywo Engg. Co.
15, Laxmi Co-op. Indl. Est.
Nr. Nagarvel Hanuman Mandir
Amraiwadi Rd., Ahmedabad,
Gujarat-380026
India
TEL : +91 (0) 79 2748168
FAX : +91 (0) 79 2748001
E-mail: cosywo@usa.net

Mixrite Engineering Pvt. Ltd.
Leela, 355, S V Rd.
Vile Parle (W)
Mumbai,
Maharashtra-400056
India
TEL : +91 (0) 22 6716143
FAX : +91 (0) 22 8365726
E-mail: mixrite@vsnl.com

Schurtek Engineers
18, Mistry Indl. Cmplx.
Cross Rd.-A, MIDC
Andheri (E), Mumbai,
Maharashtra-400093
India
TEL : +91 (0) 22 8325903
FAX : +91 (0) 22 8351358
E-mail:
schurtek@bom3.vsnl.net.in

Standard Engineers
3rd Flr., Sharda Sadan
Opp. Gunbow St.,
Fire Brigade, 11 S A Brelvi Rd.
Mumbai,
Maharashtra-400001
India
TEL : +91 (0) 22 2614419
FAX : +91 (0) 22 2626152
E-mail: agitator@vsnl.com

LUBRICANT MACHINERY

Aerotech India Pvt. Ltd.
202, Shivam House
Karampura Comml. Cmplx.
New Delhi,
NCT of Delhi-110015
India
TEL : +91 (0) 11 5433375
FAX : +91 (0) 11 5459768
E-mail:
headoffice@aerotech.wipro.net.in

Lubgraf Synoils Pvt. Ltd.
2011/A, Phase-IV
GIDC, Vatva
Ahmedabad,
Gujarat-382445
India
TEL : +91 (0) 79 5894912
FAX : +91 (0) 79 5894912

Sterling Lubricants Pvt. Ltd.
205-A, 2nd Flr.
Hare Krishna Cmplx.
B/h Dipali Cinema
Ashram Rd., Ahmedabad,
Gujarat-380009
India
TEL : +91 (0) 79 6581270
FAX : +91 (0) 79 6584296
E-mail:
autorol@satyam.net.in

Standard Oil Additives Pvt. Ltd.
938, 16th Main
2nd Stage, BTM Layout
Bangalore,
Karnataka-560076
India
TEL : +91 (0) 80 6684261
FAX : +91 (0) 80 6684257
E-mail: soapl@blr.vsnl.net.in

Pensol Industries Ltd.
307, Classic Centre, 575
M G Rd., Indore,
Madhya Pradesh-452001
India
TEL : +91 (0) 731 532609
FAX : +91 (0) 731 545984
E-mail: pensol@sancharnet.in

Mosil Lubricants Pvt. Ltd.
Plot No. 166/1, 'Kalanidhi'
P.O. Box No. 16791
Sion (W), Mumbai,
Maharashtra-400022
India
TEL : +91 (0) 22 4076680
FAX : +91 (0) 22 4075541
E-mail: sales@mosil.com

ELF Lubricants India Ltd.
1-2, Apple Heritage, 54-C
Sir Madhurdas Vasanji Rd.
Andheri (E), Mumbai,

Maharashtra-400093
India
TEL : +91 (0) 22 6871500
FAX : +91 (0) 22 6871520
E-mail: mktho@elf.co.in

Gulf Oil India Ltd.
In Centre, 49/50, MIDC
12 Rd., Marol
Andheri (E), Mumbai,
Maharashtra-400018
India
TEL : +91 (0) 22 8390789
FAX : +91 (0) 22 8376179

Sah Petroleums Ltd.
406/407, Embassy Centre
Nariman Point, Mumbai,
Maharashtra-400021
India
TEL : +91 (0) 22 2301911
FAX : +91 (0) 22 2875751
E-mail: ipol@vsnl.com

Subhash Chemical Industries
Shed W-2, S-Block,
MIDC, Bhosari
Pune,
Maharashtra-411026
India
TEL : +91 (0) 20 7120632
FAX : +91 (0) 20 7122554
E-mail:
subhaschem@vsnl.com

Crown Lubricants
34/35, Gandhi Rd.
Puzhal, Chennai,
Tamil Nadu-600066
India
TEL : +91 (0) 44 6590171
FAX : +91 (0) 44 6591271
E-mail: crownlub@eth.net

Mahatha Petrochemicals
Sree Meenakshi Gardens,
34, Mount Medavakkam Rd.
Keela Kattalai, Chennai,
Tamil Nadu-600117
India
TEL : +91 (0) 44 2471542
FAX : +91 (0) 44 2473800
E-mail:
mahatha@md5.vsnl.net.in

Atma Lubricants & Specialities Ltd.
54-5-41, 5th Rd.
Autonagar, Vijayawada,
Andhra Pradesh-520007
India
TEL : +91 (0) 866 544491
FAX : +91 (0) 866 542854
E-mail:
atma@md3.vsnl.net.in

Godavari Lubricants Pvt. Ltd.
D-33, Phase-I, IDA
Jeedimetla, Hyderabad,
Andhra Pradesh-500855
India
TEL : +91 (0) 40 3096154
FAX : +91 (0) 40 3098032
E-mail:
mohan58@hd2.dot.net.in

LUBRICATING TESTERS

SS Appliances Pvt. Ltd.
B-29, Sect. 7
Noida, Uttar Pradesh-201301
India
TEL : +91 (0) 120 4555332
E-mail:
ssengg@giasdl01.vsnl.net.in

Quantum Equipment Company Ltd.
5/28, Dhanalaxmi Chmbrs.
Gokhale Rd.
Thane, Maharashtra-400601
India
TEL : +91 (0) 22 5429561
FAX : +91 (0) 22 5418574
E-mail:
quantum@giasbm01.vsnl.net.in

LUBRICATING PUMPS : OIL & GREASE

Flowtech Pumps & Hydraulics
69, New Modella Indl. Est.
Padwal Ngr., Waghle Est.
Thane, Maharashtra-400604
India
TEL : +91 (0) 22 5836217
FAX : +91 (0) 22 5824761
E-mail: flowtech@bol.net.in

Cenlub Systems
184, Sect. 16
Faridabad, Haryana-121002
India
TEL : +91 (0) 129 5277746
FAX : +91 (0) 129 5277747
E-mail:
cenlub@ndb.vsnl.net.in

SMD Pump & Engineering India Pvt. Ltd.
Post Bag No. 1058, 96-A
TTK Rd., Alwarpet
Chennai,
Tamil Nadu-600018
India
TEL : +91 (0) 44 4997392
FAX : +91 (0) 44 4990966
E-mail: smdpump@vsnl.net

ITW Signode India Ltd.
3rd Flr., 5, Merchant Towers
Rd. No. 4, Banjara Hills
Hyderabad,
Andhra Pradesh-500034
India
TEL : +91 (0) 40 3353781
FAX : +91 (0) 40 3353791
E-mail: info@itwsignode.co.in

Industrial Engineering Works
J22/B, Ramesh Ngr.

P.O. Box No. 6280
Bander Wali Khui
New Delhi,
NCT of Delhi-110015
India
TEL : +91 (0) 11 5190862
FAX : +91 (0) 11 5437988

Flowchem Engineering Pvt. Ltd.
Plot No. 2001, Phase-IV
GIDC Est., Vatva
Ahmedabad,
Gujarat-382445
India
TEL : +91 (0) 79 5831361
FAX : +91 (0) 79 5831361
E-mail: flowchem@icenet.net

Hydro Power Corporation
258, GIDC Indl. Est.
Makarpura, Vadodara,
Gujarat-390010
India
TEL : +91 (0) 265 642741
FAX : +91 (0) 265 642741
E-mail:
hydro@hypopump.com

ARO Equipments Pvt. Ltd.
805, Phase-V
Udyog Vihar, Gurgaon,
Haryana-122015
India
TEL : +91 (0) 124 6450181
FAX : +91 (0) 124 6450185
E-mail:
aro@mantraonline.com

Dynamatic Technologies Ltd.
Dynamatic Park
Jalahalli Cross
Peenya Indl. Area
Bangalore,
Karnataka-560058
India
TEL : +91 (0) 80 8394933
FAX : +91 (0) 80 8394936
E-mail: bsh@dynamatics.net

LABORATORY EQUIPMENTS

Sunjay Technologies Pvt. Ltd.
A-32, Shri Ram Indl. Est., 13
G D Ambedkar Rd.
Wadala, Mumbai,
Maharashtra-400031
India
TEL : +91 (0) 22 4118800
FAX : +91 (0) 22 4111540
E-mail:
info@sunjaytechnologies.com

Technico Laboratory Products
21/34, Poomagal St.
Ekkattuthangal
Chennai,
Tamil Nadu-600097
India
TEL : +91 (0) 44 2344965
FAX : +91 (0) 44 2344965
E-mail:
technico@md3.vsnl.net.in

Thermolab Scientific Equipments Pvt. Ltd.
218, Sterling Chmbrs.,
1st Flr., 56
Mogra Village, Andheri (E)
Mumbai, Maharashtra-400069
India
TEL : +91 (0) 22 8353017
FAX : +91 (0) 22 8394562
E-mail:
madhav@bom3.vsnl.net.in

Bellstone Hi-Tech International
3755, Chawri Bazar
Delhi,
NCT of Delhi-110006
India
TEL : +91 (0) 11 3939951
FAX : +91 (0) 11 3939953
E-mail:
sales@bellstonehite.com

Erection & Instrumentaion Engineers
1001/1002
Span Trade Centre
Opp. Kochrab Ashram
Nr. Paldi Circle
Ahmedabad, Gujarat-380006
India
TEL : +91 (0) 79 6579074
FAX : +91 (0) 79 6584099
E-mail: vindish@icenet.net

Amarchand & Company Pvt. Ltd.
56, Indl. Est.
Ambala Cantt.,
Haryana-133006
India
TEL : +91 (0) 171 699499
FAX : +91 (0) 171 699806
E-mail: accolab@accolab.com

Murhopye Scientific Co.
B-11, Metagalli Indl. Est.
Mysore, Karnataka-570016
India
TEL : +91 (0) 821 582235
FAX : +91 (0) 821 581235
E-mail: murhopye@eth.net

Omega Electronics
36, Hathi Babu Ka Bagh
Jaipur, Rajasthan-302006
India
TEL : +91 (0) 141 2203694
FAX : +91 (0) 141 2204481
E-mail: omega@sancharnet.in

LUBRICATING RECYCLING SERVICES

Kamal Envirotech Pvt. Ltd.
834/1, Block-K
Mahipalpur New Delhi,

NCT of Delhi-110037
India
TEL : +91 (0) 11 6781200
FAX : +91 (0) 11 6783405
E-mail:
kamal_envir@vsnl.com

Product Mix
148-A,Sect.-A,
Indl. Area, Mandideep
Madhya Pradesh-462011
India
TEL : +91 (0) 7480 53102
FAX : +91 (0) 7480 756438

AR Engineering
L-77, Additional MIDC
Satara, Maharashtra-415004
India
TEL : +91 (0) 2162 44385
FAX : +91 (0) 2162 47569
E-mail:
arengineering@vsnl.com

Industrial Products
M-5, Laxminagar
WHC Rd., Nagpur,
Maharashtra-440022
India
TEL : +91 (0) 712 243682
FAX : +91 (0) 712 243682
E-mail:
hdiddee@nagpur.dot.net.in

Crown Lubricants
34/35, Gandhi Rd.
Puzhal, Chennai,
Tamil Nadu-600066
India
TEL : +91 (0) 44 6590171
FAX : +91 (0) 44 6591271
E-mail: crownlub@eth.net

Verma Electric Works
747, Phase-II
Indl. Area, Chandigarh,
Chandigarh (UT)-160002
India
TEL : +91 (0) 172 652988

PETRO CHEMICAL PLANTS

Ciria India Pvt. Ltd.
A-125, Neeti Bagh
New Delhi,
NCT of Delhi-110049
India
TEL : +91 (0) 11 6566581
FAX : +91 (0) 11 6528221
E-mail: ciria@vsnl.com

Engineers India Ltd.
Engineers India Bhavan, 1
Bhikaji Cama Place
New Delhi, NCT of Delhi-110066
India
TEL : +91 (0) 11 6104132
FAX : +91 (0) 11 6194760
E-mail: eil.mktg@eil.co.in

Lurgi India Co. Ltd.
B1/G-8
Mohan Co-op. Indl. Est.
Mathura Rd.
New Delhi,
NCT of Delhi-110044
India
TEL : +91 (0) 11 6945812
FAX : +91 (0) 11 6942811
E-mail:
li@lurgin.axcess.net.in

Punj Lloyd Ltd.
Punj Lloyd House, 17-18
Nehru Place
New Delhi,
NCT of Delhi-110019
India
TEL : +91 (0) 11 6436091
FAX : +91 (0) 11 6466106
E-mail: info@punjlloyd.com

Alpha Project Services Pvt. Ltd.
1-B, Patriot Cmplx.
Ellora Park
Race Course Circle
Vadodara, Gujarat-390007
India
TEL : +91 (0) 265 337316
FAX : +91 (0) 265 337307
E-mail:
alphaltd@giasbm01.vsnl.net.in

Gujarat State Petroleum Corporation Ltd.
A Govt. of Gujarat Undertaking.
Blk. 15, 2nd Flr.
Sect. 11
Udyog Bhavan
Gandhinagar, Gujarat-382011
India
TEL : +91 (0) 2712 36372
FAX : +91 (0) 2712 36375
E-mail:
ramana@guraratpetro.com

Fluor Danie India, Inc.
Block 4B
Corporate Park, Phase-III
DLF Qutub Enclave
Gurgaon, Haryana-122015
India
TEL : +91 (0) 124 6226917
FAX : +91 (0) 124 6226920
E-mail:
frank.robben@fluordaniel.com

John Brown Technologies (I) Pvt. Ltd.
No. 19, Primrose Rd.
Bangalore, Karnataka-560025
India
TEL : +91 (0) 80 5585210
FAX : +91 (0) 80 5585221

Rotary Mec Engg. (I) Pvt. Ltd.
9th Flr., Discoverer Bldg.
International Tech Park
Whitefield Rd.
Bangalore, Karnataka-560001
India

TEL : +91 (0) 80 8410025
FAX : +91 (0) 80 8410027
E-mail: rotban@blr.vsnl.net.in

PETRO CHEMICAL

Shree Heat-Tech Engineers Pvt. Ltd.
Plot No. W-361, Rabale MIDC
Navi Mumbai,
Maharashtra-400701
India
TEL : +91 (0) 22 7692614
FAX : +91 (0) 22 7690354
E-mail:
rashree@bom3.vsnl.net.in

Essar Projects Ltd.
Essar House
Keshavarav Khade Marg
Mahalakshmi
Mumbai, Maharashtra-400034
India
TEL : +91 (0) 22 4950606
FAX : +91 (0) 22 4954324

Richardson & Cruddas (1972) Ltd.
A Government Of India Undertaking
Sir J J Rd.
Byculla Iron Works
Mumbai, Maharashtra-400008
India
TEL : +91 (0) 22 3776832
FAX : +91 (0) 22 3731491

Technimont ICB Ltd.
168, Vidyanagari Marg
Kalina, Mumbai,
Maharashtra-400098
India
TEL : +91 (0) 22 6526595
FAX : +91 (0) 22 6528325
E-mail: icbbby@vsnl.com

Avant-Garde Engineers & Consultants Pvt. Ltd.
68A, Porur Kundrathur High Rd.
Porur, Chennai,
Tamil Nadu-600116
India
TEL : +91 (0) 44 4828717
FAX : +91 (0) 44 4828531
E-mail:
avantgarde@vsnl.com

Mabel Engineers Pvt. Ltd.
4th Flr., 185, Anna Salai
Chennai,
Tamil Nadu-600006
India
TEL : +91 (0) 44 8524538
FAX : +91 (0) 44 8521449
E-mail: mabel.mds@gnmds.globalnet.ems.vsnl.net.in

Bridge & Roof Company (India) Ltd.
A BYN Group Co.
17-18, Harrington Mansion
8, Ho-Chi-Minh Sarani
Kolkata,
West Bengal-700071
India
TEL : +91 (0) 33 2820351
FAX : +91 (0) 33 2822879
E-mail:
bridgeroof@gems.vsnl.net.in

Tata Construction & Projects Ltd.
6-A, Middleton St.
Kolkata,
West Bengal-700071
India
TEL : +91 (0) 33 2401441
FAX : +91 (0) 33 2402843
E-mail: tcpl@tata.com

Mecon Ltd.
A Govt. of India Enterprise
Vivekananda Path
P.O Doranda
Ranchi, Jharkhand-834002
India
TEL : +91 (0) 651 502197
FAX : +91 (0) 651 502189
E-mail: mecon-rnch@hub.nic.in

Satyadev Precision Engg. Works
B 15, Auto Ngr.
Visakhapatnam,
Andhra Pradesh-530012
India
TEL : +91 (0) 891 517654

Lloyds Steel Industries Ltd.
Engineering Divn.
Modern Mills Compound
101, Keshavrao Khade Marg
Mahalakshmi
Mumbai, Maharashtra-400025
India
TEL : +91 (0) 22 3080097
FAX : +91 (0) 22 3080069
E-mail:
nvbhat@lloydsgroup.com

SP Consultants
206, "Narmada"
Laxmi Cmplx.
Varkat Ngr., Thane (W)
Thane, Maharashtra-400606
India
TEL : +91 (0) 22 5375217
FAX : +91 (0) 22 5374369
E-mail:
response@spconsultantsweb.com

UHDE India Ltd.
A Krupp Uhde GmbH Company
UHDE House
L B S Marg, Vikhroli (W)
Mumbai, Maharashtra-400083
India
TEL : +91 (0) 22 5968000
FAX : +91 (0) 22 5784327
E-mail: uhdein@vsnl.com

Pioneer Erectors Pvt. Ltd.
10m Crescent Rd.
Shenoy Ngr.
Chennai, Tamil Nadu-

600030
India
TEL : +91 (0) 44 6262708
FAX : +91 (0) 44 6211798

Techno Electric & Engg. Co. Ltd.
P-46 A
Radha Bazar Lane
Kolkata, West Bengal-700001
India
TEL : +91 (0) 33 2254671
FAX : +91 (0) 33 2254478
E-mail: techno@cal.vsnl.net.

PETRO CHEMICALS FILTERS

Micro Filters
S-5, Jalaram Cmplx.
Opp. Bahucharaji Mandir
Karelibaug
Vadodara, Gujarat-390018
India
TEL : +91 (0) 265 464756
FAX : +91 (0) 265 465151

Dipesh Engineering Works
3, Sheroo Villa
87, J P Rd., Andheri (W)
Mumbai, Maharashtra-400053
India
TEL : +91 (0) 22 6336729
FAX : +91 (0) 22 6315507
E-mail:
kjpatel_71@hotmail.com

Pragati Engineering Works
Plot No. 114, New Chikhloli
MIDC, Ambernath,
Maharashtra-421505
India
TEL : +91 (0) 251 687407
FAX : +91 (0) 251 685054
E-mail:
shantaflaker@vsnl.com

Capitron Engineers
606, Shanti Ngr.
Shell Cly., Chembur
Mumbai, Maharashtra-400071
India
TEL : +91 (0) 22 5223449
FAX : +91 (0) 22 5223449
E-mail: priya005@usa.net

Ultrafilter international,
AG Branch Office
334, 14th Main Rd.
Rajmahal Vilas Extn.
Bangalore, Karnataka-560080
India
TEL : +91 (0) 80 3612304
FAX : +91 (0) 80 3614128
E-mail: ufiag@vsnl.net

Thermax Ltd.
Enviro Divn.
D-13, MIDC Indl. Area
Chinchwad
Pune, Maharashtra-411019
India
TEL : +91 (0) 20 7475941
FAX : +91 (0) 20 7440845
E-mail:
dbhanja@thermaxindia.com

PETROLEUM TESTING INSTRUMENTS

Kwality Traders
91, Bhagat Singh Mkt.
New Delhi,
NCT of Delhi-110001
India
TEL : +91 (0) 11 3347333
FAX : +91 (0) 11 3346939
E-mail: thermometer@yahoo.co.in

Khushboo Scientific Pvt. Ltd.
132, Princess St.
Mumbai, Maharashtra-400002
India
TEL : +91 (0) 22 2032174
FAX : +91 (0) 22 2081346
E-mail:
khushboo.sc@bol.net.in

Labindia Instruments Pvt. Ltd.
201, Nand Chmbrs.,
Nr. Vandana Cinema
LBS Marg
Thane, Maharashtra-400602
India
TEL : +91 (0) 22 5335389
FAX : +91 (0) 22 5335940
E-mail:
labindia@bom3.vsnl.net.in

Ratan Industries
30, New Khailand Mkt.
Ajmer, Rajasthan-305001
India
TEL : +91 (0) 145 421949
FAX : +91 (0) 145 420747

JR Mullick & Company Pvt. Ltd.
16/7/2B, Keyatala Rd.
Kolkata, West Bengal-700029
India
TEL : +91 (0) 33 4641621
FAX : +91 (0) 33 4643087
E-mail: jrmcal@vsnl.com

Orlab Instruments
A Divn. Of Orbit Technologies
Pvt. Ltd.
404, 4th Flr.,
Golden Edifice
Khairatabad,
Hyderabad,
Andhra Pradesh-500004
India
TEL : +91 (0) 40 3302526
FAX : +91 (0) 40 3325760
E-mail:
orlabindia@yahoo.com

STORAGE TANKS

Mellcon Engineers Pvt. Ltd.
B-297, Phase-I
Okhla Indl. Area
New Delhi, NCT of Delhi-110020
India
TEL : +91 (0) 11 6816530
FAX : +91 (0) 11 6816573
E-mail: mellcon@vsnl.net
www.mellcon.com

Devson Steels
C-15, Bulandshahr Rd.
Indl. Area, Ghaziabad,
Uttar Pradesh-201003
India
TEL : +91 (0) 120 4700804
FAX : +91 (0) 120 4700003
E-mail:
rakesh@devsonsteels.com

Steelite Engineering Ltd.
103/5, Blackie House
Opp. GPO, V T
Walchand Hirachand Marg
Mumbai, Maharashtra-400001
India
TEL : +91 (0) 22 2324093
FAX : +91 (0) 22 2610803
E-mail:
samir@steelitegroup.com

Dipesh Engineering Works
3, Sheroo Villa
87, J P Rd.
Andheri (W)
Mumbai, Maharashtra-400053
India
TEL : +91 (0) 22 6336729
FAX : +91 (0) 22 6315507
E-mail:
kjpatel_71@hotmail.com

Pragati Engineering Works
Plot No. 114, New Chikhloli
MIDC, Ambernath,
Maharashtra-421505
India
TEL : +91 (0) 251 687407
FAX : +91 (0) 251 685054
E-mail:
shantaflaker@vsnl.com

Richard Engineering (Bom.) Pvt. Ltd.
1st Flr., Brij Cmplx., K B Rd.
Railway Flyover Junction
Ambarnath (W)
Ambernath, Maharashtra-421501
India
TEL : +91 (0) 251 892421
FAX : +91 (0) 251 892418
E-mail: richsnow@vsnl.com

Machinkraft Equipment
337, 3rd Rd., Sindh Hsg. Soc.
Aundh, Pune,
Maharashtra-411007
India
TEL : +91 (0) 20 5887464
FAX : +91 (0) 20 5880353
E-mail:
info@machinkraftequipment.com

Aero Engineers
Plot No. 3419
GIDC, Phase-IV
Vatva
Ahmedabad, Gujarat-382445
India
TEL : +91 (0) 79 5840720
FAX : +91 (0) 79 5841041
E-mail:
aero@aeroengg.com

Dhopeshwar Engineering Pvt. Ltd.
A-16, CIE
Balanagar, Hyderabad,
Andhra Pradesh-500037
India
TEL : +91 (0) 40 3771579
FAX : +91 (0) 40 3772450
E-mail:
dhopesh@hd2.dot.net.in

Ampower Equipment
G-6/B, Ashoka Bhopal Chmbrs.
S P Rd.,
Secunderabad,
Andhra Pradesh-500003
India
TEL : +91 (0) 40 7892919
FAX : +91 (0) 40 7892919
E-mail: ampower@eth.net

Base Industries
Plot No. 138-B
IDA, Mallapur
Hyderabad,
Andhra Pradesh-501507
India
TEL : +91 (0) 40 7823073
FAX : +91 (0) 40 7823073
E-mail:
enfabs@hd1.vsnl.net.in

Essel Fabs
9B/1, Type III,
APIIC,
Kukatpally Indl. Est.
Hyderabad,
Andhra Pradesh-500072
India
TEL : +91 (0) 40 3075852

Buildworth Pvt. Ltd.
G S Rd., Dispur
Guwahati, Assam-781005
India
TEL : +91 (0) 361 340352
FAX : +91 (0) 361 341411
E-mail:
bwpl1@sancharnet.in

Mech Engineers
920-A, Phase-II,
Indl. Area
Ramdarbar
Chandigarh,

Chandigarh (UT)-160002
India
TEL : +91 (0) 172 652417
FAX : +91 (0) 172 652417

Indcon Boilers Ltd.
D-170, Phase-I
Okhla Indl. Area
New Delhi,
NCT of Delhi-110020
India
TEL : +91 (0) 11 6811440
FAX : +91 (0) 11 6812425
E-mail: indcon@vsnl.com

WEIGHING MACHINE

Transducers India
Kh. No. 38, Lane No. 1
Dabri, P.O. Palam
New Delhi,
NCT of Delhi-110045
India
TEL : +91 (0) 11 5395640
FAX : +91 (0) 11 5395637
E-mail: loadcell@vsnl.com

Kalsi Micro Measurements & Instrumentation Pvt. Ltd.
K-35
Site-III
Panki Indl. Area
Kanpur,
Uttar Pradesh-208022
India
TEL : +91 (0) 512 691971
FAX : +91 (0) 512 691628
E-mail:
kalsi_micro@sify.com

Hytech Micro Measurements Pvt. Ltd.
43, Avtar Enclave
Paschim Vihar
New Delhi,
NCT of Delhi-110063
India
TEL : +91 (0) 11 5260382
FAX : +91 (0) 11 5259315
E-mail: hytech@bol.net.in

Weitex India Ltd.
28/1/A, IDA
Nacharam
Hyderabad,
Andhra Pradesh-500078
India
TEL : +91 (0) 40 7152294
E-mail:
weitexindia@yahoo.com

Modern Systems Pvt. Ltd.
SCO 92, Sect. 35 C
Chandigarh,
Chandigarh (UT)-160022
India
TEL : +91 (0) 172 607529

Alexandra Scale Pvt. Ltd.
12/2, Amee Bazar,
Pattharkuva
B/h Jyoti Sangh
Ahmedabad,
Gujarat-380001
India
TEL : +91 (0) 79 5355777
FAX : +91 (0) 79 5321859
E-mail:
alexndra@ad1.vsnl.net.in

Aprotech Engineers Pvt. Ltd.
1573, Sect. 7E
Faridabad,
Haryana-121006
India
TEL : +91 (0) 129 5242140
FAX : +91 (0) 129 5243452
E-mail: aprotech@vsnl.com

Esge Load Cells & Weighing Systems
A-32, Manish Cmplx.,
#10, Convent Rd.,
Bangalore,
Karnataka-560001
India
TEL : +91 (0) 80 6711731
FAX : +91 (0) 80 6711731

IPA Pvt. Ltd.
472/B2, 12th Cross,
Phase-IV
Peenya Indl. Area
Bangalore,
Karnataka-560058
India
TEL : +91 (0) 80 8362851
FAX : +91 (0) 80 8360520
E-mail:
ipapvtld@giasbg01.vsnl.net.in

Chapter 36

SUPPLIERS OF RAW MATERIALS

LUBRICANT ADDITIVES

Electro Ferro Alloys Pvt. Ltd.
208, Aditya Bldg.
Nr. Khadayata Cly.
Mithakhali Six Roads
Ellisbridge
Ahmedabad, Gujarat-380006
India
TEL : +91 (0) 79 6400846
FAX : +91 (0) 79 6466663
E-mail: alloys@vsnl.com

Standard Oil Additives Pvt. Ltd.
938, 16th Main
2nd Stage, BTM Layout
Bangalore, Karnataka-560076
India
TEL : +91 (0) 80 6684261
FAX : +91 (0) 80 6684257
E-mail: soapl@blr.vsnl.net.in

Mosil Lubricants Pvt. Ltd.
Plot No. 166/1, 'Kalanidhi'
P.O. Box No. 16791
Sion (W)
Mumbai, Maharashtra-400022
India
TEL : +91 (0) 22 4076680
FAX : +91 (0) 22 4075541
E-mail: sales@mosil.com

Nitika Chemicals
FO-05, Amarjyoti Palace
Wardha Rd., Dhantoli
Nagpur, Maharashtra-440012
India
TEL : +91 (0) 712 542870
FAX : +91 (0) 712 534055
E-mail:
nitika@nagpur.dot.net.in

Endeavour Chemicals Pvt. Ltd.
R-393, MIDC,
TTC Indl. Area, Rabale
Navi Mumbai,
Maharashtra-400701
India
TEL : +91 (0) 22 7691469
E-mail:
ecpl@maharashtradirectory.com

Prachi Poly Products Ltd.
107, Chawala Warehouse
Sect. 18, MAFCO Area
Vashi, Navi Mumbai,
Maharashtra-400705
India
TEL : +91 (0) 22 7616104
FAX : +91 (0) 22 7616103
E-mail: prachiltd@vsnl.net

Indian Additives Ltd.
Manali Express Highway
Manali, Chennai,
Tamil Nadu-600068
India
TEL : +91 (0) 44 541267
FAX : +91 (0) 44 5941184
E-mail: venm@ialindia.com

Standard Industries Oils Pvt. Ltd.
41, Vaidyanatha St.
Tondiarpet, Chennai,
Tamil Nadu-600081
India
TEL : +91 (0) 44 5955912
FAX : +91 (0) 44 5958095

JD Jones & Company Pvt. Ltd.
C-3/1, Gillander House, 8
N S Rd., Kolkata,
West Bengal-700001
India
TEL : +91 (0) 33 2203314
FAX : +91 (0) 33 2206228
E-mail:
comments@jdjones.com

Shree Nathji Dyestuffs
R-60/1, Model Town-III
Delhi, NCT of Delhi-110009
India
TEL : +91 (0) 11 7133896
FAX : +91 (0) 11 7444651
E-mail: jatin@satyam.net.in

PETROCHEMICALS

Bongaigaon Refinery & Petrochemicals Ltd.
P.O.Dhaligaon
Bongaigaon, Assam-783385
India
TEL : +91 (0) 3664 41320
FAX : +91 (0) 3664 41203
E-mail: brpla2@gwl.dot.net.in

Gas Authority Of India Ltd.
16, Bhikaji Cama Place
Ring Rd., R K Puram
New Delhi,
NCT of Delhi-110066
India
TEL : +91 (0) 11 6172580
FAX : +91 (0) 11 6185941

Gujarat State Fertilizers & Chemicals Ltd.
P.O. Fertilizernagar
Vadodara, Gujarat-391347
India
TEL : +91 (0) 265 372451
FAX : +91 (0) 265 372966
E-mail: mail@gsfclimited.com

Indian Petrochemicals Corporation Ltd.
A Govt. Of India Undertaking
P.O. Petrochemicals
Vadodara, Gujarat-391346
India
TEL : +91 (0) 265 373144
FAX : +91 (0) 265 373163
E-mail: pac@wilnetonline.net

Narmada Chematur Petrochemicals Ltd.
National Highway No. 8
P.O. Narmadanagar
Bharuch, Gujarat-392015
India
TEL : +91 (0) 2642 47160
FAX : +91 (0) 2642 46497
E-mail: jidesai@narmada-chematur.com

Shravathy Petro Chemicals Pvt. Ltd.
9, Mile Old Madras Rd.
Virgonagar
Bangalore, Karnataka-560001
India
TEL : +91 (0) 80 8510646

Kochi Refineries Ltd.
P.O. Box No. 2
Ambalmugal
Ernakulam, Kerala-682302
India
TEL : +91 (0) 484 780261
FAX : +91 (0) 484 720855

Benazeer Chemicals Pvt. Ltd.
E-3/172, Arera Cly.
Bhopal,
Madhya Pradesh-462016
India
TEL : +91 (0) 755 566119
FAX : +91 (0) 755 566119
E-mail:
benazeer@bom6.vsnl.net.in

Ava Chemicals Pvt. Ltd.
1/20 B, Narayan Plaza
26-A, Chandivli Rd.
Mumbai, Maharashtra-400072
India
TEL : +91 (0) 22 8523955
FAX : +91 (0) 22 8525790
E-mail:
ava@bom2.vsnl.net.in

Bharat Petroleum Corporation Ltd.
Bharat Bhavan, 4 & 6
Currimbhoy Rd., Ballard Est.
Mumbai, Maharashtra-400001
India
TEL : +91 (0) 22 2618281
FAX : +91 (0) 22 2616793
E-mail:
okesy@bharatpetroleum.com

Deepak Fertilisers & Petrochemicals Corporation Ltd.
Opp. Golf Course
Shastri Ngr., Yerawada
Pune, Maharashtra-411006
India
TEL : +91 (0) 20 6684155
FAX : +91 (0) 20 6687499
E-mail:
deepak@deepakfertilisers.com

Ess Dee Exports Ltd.
124/A, Mittal Tower
Nariman Point
Mumbai, Maharashtra-400021
India
TEL : +91 (0) 22 2840519
FAX : +91 (0) 22 2874229

Herdillia Chemicals Ltd.
A Duncan Goenka Group Co.
Air India Bldg., 13th Flr.
Nariman Point
Mumbai, Maharashtra-400021
India
TEL : +91 (0) 22 2024224
FAX : +91 (0) 22 2042379
E-mail:
herdillia@herdillia.com

Himatlal & Co.
6th Flr., Doli Chmbrs.
Strand Rd., Colaba
Mumbai, Maharashtra-400005
India
TEL : +91 (0) 22 2833013
FAX : +91 (0) 22 2854815
E-mail:
himtlal@bom3.vsnl.net.in

Laffans Petrochemicals Ltd.
10, Luthra Indl. Est.
Safed Pool, Saki Naka
Andheri, Mumbai,
Maharashtra-400072

India
TEL : +91 (0) 22 8511919
FAX : +91 (0) 22 8513186
E-mail: lplho@vsnl.com

Mangalore Refinery & Petrochemicals
7th Flr., Arcadia
Nariman Point, Mumbai,
Maharashtra-400021
India
TEL : +91 (0) 22 2836380
FAX : +91 (0) 22 2029772
E-mail: mrplbom@vsnl.com

Rama Petrochemicals Ltd.
812, Raheja Chmbrs.
Nariman Point
Mumbai, Maharashtra-400021
India
TEL : +91 (0) 22 2834182
FAX : +91 (0) 22 2049946

Ramredis Pvt. Ltd.
68, STICE, Sinar Co-Op. Indl. Est.
Sinnar, Nasik,
Maharashtra-422001
India
TEL : +91 (0) 253 21248

Reliance Industries Ltd.
3rd Flr, Maker Chmbrs. IV, 222
Nariman Point
Mumbai, Maharashtra-400021
India
TEL : +91 (0) 22 2831633
FAX : +91 (0) 22 2042268

Shivdham Petrochemical Ltd.
63, Mittal Towers
Nariman Point
Mumbai, Maharashtra-400021
India
TEL : +91 (0) 22 2872460
FAX : +91 (0) 22 2872461

Topack Industries
4/5, Swastik Chmbrs.
Sion-Trombay Rd.
Chembur
Mumbai, Maharashtra-400071
India
TEL : +91 (0) 22 5227321
FAX : +91 (0) 22 5225773
E-mail: topack@naam.com

Oswal Agro Mills Ltd.
G T Rd.
Phagwara
Kapurthala, Punjab-144401
India
TEL : +91 (0) 1822 60301

Tamilnadu Petroproducts Ltd.
6, Nungambakkam High Rd.
Chennai, Tamil Nadu-600034
India
TEL : +91 (0) 44 8254545
FAX : +91 (0) 44 8255798
E-mail:
tpl@epages.webindia.com

Haldia Petrochemicals Ltd.
1, Auckland Place
Kolkata, West Bengal-700017
India
TEL : +91 (0) 33 2812611
FAX : +91 (0) 33 2471361

MCC PTA India Corporation Pvt. Ltd.
4th Flr., Siddha Point, 101
Park St., Kolkata,
West Bengal-700016
India
TEL : +91 (0) 33 2175493
FAX : +91 (0) 33 2174467

Precision Balance (I)
6, Wood St.
Kolkata, West Bengal-700016
India
TEL : +91 (0) 33 2403476
FAX : +91 (0) 33 2402427

Andhra Petrochemicals Ltd.
Opp. Naval Dockyard
P.O. Box 1401
Venkatarayapuram
Visakhapatnam,
Andhra Pradesh-530014
India
TEL : +91 (0) 891 578340
FAX : +91 (0) 891 577751

PETROLEUM TREATING CHEMICALS

Tagrose Chemicals (India) Ltd.
19, Marshall's Rd.
Egmore, Chennai,
Tamil Nadu-600008
India
TEL : +91 (0) 44 8587875
FAX : +91 (0) 44 8587873

Lalit Nitro-Chem Pvt. Ltd.
Plot No.14
F-II Block, MIDC
Pimpri Area
Pune, Maharashtra-411018
India
TEL : +91 (0) 20 7485272
FAX : +91 (0) 20 7477693
E-mail:
shubham@pn2.vsnl.net.in

Baker Oil Treating (I) Ltd.
Liberty Bldg., New Marine Line
Sir Vithaldas Thackersey Marg
Mumbai, Maharashtra-400020
India
TEL : +91 (0) 22 2017130
FAX : +91 (0) 22 2096976
E-mail: boti@vsnl.com

Chapter 37

LIST OF PRESENT MANUFACTURERS

COOLANTS

ITW Signode India Ltd.
3rd Flr., 5, Merchant Towers
Rd. No. 4, Banjara Hills
Hyderabad, Andhra Pradesh-500034
India
TEL : +91 (0) 40 3353781
FAX : +91 (0) 40 3353791
E-mail: info@itwsignode.co.in

Anand Group
1 Aurbindo Marg
New Delhi,
NCT of Delhi-110016
India
TEL : +91 (0) 11 6852161

Avertech Speciality Chemicals Pvt. Ltd.
17, Chetak Apt., Plot 27/2
Sect. 9, Rohini
New Delhi, NCT of Delhi-110085
India
TEL : +91 (0) 11 7561824
FAX : +91 (0) 11 7265685

Caltex Lubricants India Ltd.
2A & 2B, 2nd Flr.
Berjaya House, Comm. Centre
New Friends Cly.
New Delhi, NCT of Delhi-110065
India
TEL : +91 (0) 11 6332520
FAX : +91 (0) 11 6332522
E-mail: info@caltex.com

Plasticizers & Allied Chemicals
16, Rajasthani Udyog Ngr.
G T Rd., Azadpur
Delhi, NCT of Delhi-110033
India
TEL : +91 (0) 11 7463394
FAX : +91 (0) 11 7251790
E-mail: jain@del2.vsnl.net.in

Shineguard (I) Ltd.
X-32, Phase-II
Okhla Indl. Area
New Delhi, NCT of Delhi-110020
India
TEL : +91 (0) 11 6848148
FAX : +91 (0) 11 6829217
E-mail:
sarvo@del2.vsnl.net.in

Sunstar Lubricants Ltd.
Suite-2, 10 Hailey Rd.
New Delhi, NCT of Delhi-110001
India
TEL : +91 (0) 11 3329649
FAX : +91 (0) 11 3326709

Thakar Petrochemicals Ltd.
201, Shivlok House-II
Karampura Comml. Cmplx.
New Delhi, NCT of Delhi-110015
India
TEL : +91 (0) 11 5418878
FAX : +91 (0) 11 5434924

Autocola Lubricants & Autocare Pvt. Ltd.
42, Shrimall Soc.
Navrangpura, Ahmedabad,
Gujarat-380009
India
TEL : +91 (0) 79 6447318
FAX : +91 (0) 79 6431881
E-mail:
autocola@hotmail.com

Coolcent Coolants Pvt. Ltd.
9/A, Shreyansnath Soc.-1
Vasna, Ahmedabad,
Gujarat-380007
India
TEL : +91 (0) 79 6638970
FAX : +91 (0) 79 6575115

Gypsy Interlink Industries
310, Panorama Com.,
Opp. Bai Adalta
Gondal Rd., Rajkot,
Gujarat-360002
India

TEL : +91 (0) 281 220950
FAX : +91 (0) 281 220950
E-mail:
gypsysolex@yahoo.com

Navrang Enterprises
Mahalaxmi Audhyogik
Sahkari Vasahat, Nr. Swad
Restaurant
Phase-I, GIDC, Vatva
Ahmedabad, Gujarat-382445
India
TEL : +91 (0) 79 5896485
FAX : +91 (0) 79 5896485
E-mail:
mailtonavrang@yahoo.com

Parasmani Industries
301, Nr. Makarpura Bus
Depot
P.O. Box No. 730
Swastik Chmbrs.
Vadodara, Gujarat-390010
India
TEL : +91 (0) 265 643350
FAX : +91 (0) 265 641876
E-mail:
vardhman@wilnetonline.net

Prafful (I) Pvt. Ltd.
762, Phase-I
Modern Indl. Est.
Bahadurgarh, Haryana-124507
India
TEL : +91 (0) 1183 313906
FAX : +91 (0) 1183 317363

Cresent Industrial Lubricants
984, 9th Cross
HMT Main Rd., Divanarapalya
Bangalore, Karnataka-560054
India
TEL : +91 (0) 80 3372785
E-mail:
basheerak@satyamonline.com

Pensol Industries Ltd.
307, Classic Centre, 575
M G Rd., Indore,
Madhya Pradesh-452001
India
TEL : +91 (0) 731 532609
FAX : +91 (0) 731 545984
E-mail:
pensol@sancharnet.in

Castrol India Ltd.
P.O. Box 16172,
White House, 91 Walkeshwar
Rd.
Mumbai, Maharashtra-
400006
India
TEL : +91 (0) 22 3632511
FAX : +91 (0) 22 3635447
E-mail: sumitst@vsnl.com

Chem-Verse Consultants (I) Pvt. Ltd.
120/5, Jasood Bhavan
Rd. No. 24-A, Sion (W)
Mumbai, Maharashtra-
400022
India
TEL : +91 (0) 22 4095503
FAX : +91 (0) 22 4097858
E-mail:
sales@chemverse.com

Gandh Sugandh
Divn. of Vishudha
Rasayanee Pvt. Ltd.
1st Flr., Shrirang Shopping
Centre
Shrirang Soc.
Thane, Maharashtra-400604
India
TEL : +91 (0) 22 5343211
FAX : +91 (0) 22 5344292
E-mail:
phoenix@bom3.vsnl.net.in

Indian Oil Corporation Ltd.
Marketing Divn.
Indianoil Bhavan, G-9
Ali Yavur Jung Marg
Bandra (E)
Mumbai, Maharashtra-400051
India
TEL : +91 (0) 22 6400545
FAX : +91 (0) 22 6427384

Mirajkar Chemicals (Sangli) Pvt. Ltd.
N-17/2, MIDC
Kupwad Block
Sangli, Maharashtra-416436
India
TEL : +91 (0) 233 344251
FAX : +91 (0) 233 301151

Mytol Petroleums Pvt. Ltd.
E-10, Nand Dham Est.
Marol Maroshi Rd.
Andheri (E), Mumbai,
Maharashtra-400059
India
TEL : +91 (0) 22 8500705
FAX : +91 (0) 22 6938662
E-mail: mytol@vsnl.com

Oemeta Span (I) Pvt. Ltd.
63, Alankar Hsg. Soc.
Karve Ngr. Pune,
Maharashtra-411029
India
TEL : +91 (0) 20 340688

Sah Petroleums Ltd.
406/407, Embassy Centre
Nariman Point
Mumbai, Maharashtra-400021
India
TEL : +91 (0) 22 2301911
FAX : +91 (0) 22 2875751
E-mail: ipol@vsnl.com

The Lubz Corporation (I) Pvt. Ltd.
2, Vailankanni, Plot 637
8th Rd., Khar (W)
Mumbai, Maharashtra-400052
India
TEL : +91 (0) 22 6497949

Anabond Ltd.
3-A, 3rd Flr., Adyar Bridge

Rd.
Adyar, Chennai,
Tamil Nadu-600020
India
TEL : +91 (0) 44 4917529
FAX : +91 (0) 44 4919105
E-mail: anabond@vsnl.com

Chemical Specialities (I) Pvt. Ltd.
19, Karpagambal Ngr.
Mylapore, Chennai,
Tamil Nadu-600004
India
TEL : +91 (0) 44 4994127
FAX : +91 (0) 44 8251820

Priyadarishini Chemicals
D-6, Madani Cmplx., 2nd Flr.
100 Feet Rd., Gandhipuram
Coimbatore, Tamil Nadu-641005
India
TEL : +91 (0) 422 495985
E-mail:
pritrac_cool@yahoo.com

IBP Co. Ltd.
IBP House, 34-A
Nirmal Chandra St.
Kolkata, West Bengal-700013
India
TEL : +91 (0) 33 2369441
FAX : +91 (0) 33 2216934
E-mail: kcs_sinha@ibpoil.com

Sun Oil Company Pvt. Ltd.
10 B, British India St.
Kolkata, West Bengal-700069
India
TEL : +91 (0) 33 2201292
FAX : +91 (0) 33 2480850

LUBRICATING OILS

Unicity Petrochems & Co.
414, Rewa Chmbrs.
Sir V T Marg
Mumbai, Maharashtra-400020
India
TEL : +91 (0) 22 2066635
FAX : +91 (0) 22 2065605
E-mail: unicity@vsnl.com

Atma Lubricants & Specialities Ltd.
54-5-41, 5th Rd.
Autonagar, Vijayawada,
Andhra Pradesh-520007
India
TEL : +91 (0) 866 544491
FAX : +91 (0) 866 542854
E-mail:
atma@md3.vsnl.net.in

Crystal Polymers & Additives Ltd.
1-8-144/152, AVA Sangam Bldg.
P G Rd., Secunderabad,
Andhra Pradesh-500003
India
TEL : +91 (0) 40 7814887
FAX : +91 (0) 40 7845994

Godavari Lubricants Pvt. Ltd.
D-33, Phase-I, IDA
Jeedimetla, Hyderabad,
Andhra Pradesh-500855
India
TEL : +91 (0) 40 3096154
FAX : +91 (0) 40 3098032
E-mail:
mohan58@hd2.dot.net.in

Lucky Oil Co.
5-3-773, Shanker Bagh
Topkhana, Hyderabad,
Andhra Pradesh-500012
India
TEL : +91 (0) 40 4612960

Hindustan Grease Mfg. Company Pvt. Ltd.
K-31, Udyog Ngr.
Peeragarhi, New Delhi,
NCT of Delhi-110041
India
TEL : +91 (0) 11 5472041
E-mail:
tr_bhalla@hotmail.com

Siddharth Petro Products
301, Mohan Tower
Wazirpur Comml. Cmplx.
Delhi, NCT of Delhi-110052
India
TEL : +91 (0) 11 7125389
FAX : +91 (0) 11 7416140
E-mail:
sidpro@del2.vsnl.net.in

Sun Chem Pvt. Ltd.
F-2, DSIDC Cmplx.
Rohtak Rd., New Delhi,
NCT of Delhi-110041
India
TEL : +91 (0) 11 5472641
FAX : +91 (0) 11 5471502
E-mail:
sunchem@del6.vsnl.net.in

Electro Ferro Alloys Pvt. Ltd.
208, Aditya Bldg.
Nr. Khadayata Cly.
Mithakhali Six Roads
Ellisbridge
Ahmedabad, Gujarat-380006
India
TEL : +91 (0) 79 6400846
FAX : +91 (0) 79 6466663
E-mail: alloys@vsnl.com

Hiko Oils
15, Ajit Soc., Nr. Polo Club
Bagikhana Rd.
Vadodara, Gujarat-390001
India
TEL : +91 (0) 265 433691
FAX : +91 (0) 265 433635
E-mail:
vdesai@pi.zeverchand.co.in

Lubgraf Products
2610, GIDC, Phase-IV

Vatva, Ahmedabad,
Gujarat-382445
India
TEL : +91 (0) 79 5833726
FAX : +91 (0) 79 5894912
E-mail: lubgraf@vsnl.com

Lubgraf Synoils Pvt. Ltd.
2011/A, Phase-IV
GIDC, Vatva
Ahmedabad, Gujarat-382445
India
TEL : +91 (0) 79 5894912
FAX : +91 (0) 79 5894912

Self Lubricants
158, Opp. Chandola Talav
Nr. Ruby Marbles
Goodluck Mkt., Ahmedabad,
Gujarat-380028
India
TEL : +91 (0) 79 5329735
FAX : +91 (0) 79 5321937

Shanmukh Petrochem Pvt. Ltd.
Plot No.4715, GIDC Est.
Ankleshwar, Gujarat-393002
India
TEL : +91 (0) 2646 26010
E-mail:
shanmukh@narmada.netin

Shreeji Petro Lubricators
79-80, Phase-I
Gundlav, GIDC Est.
Valsad, Gujarat-396001
India
TEL : +91 (0) 2632 20335

Tashkent Oil Company Pvt. Ltd.
A-301, Alkapuri Arcade
P.O. Box 2558, R C Dutt Rd.
Vadodara, Gujarat-390007
India
TEL : +91 (0) 265 341514
FAX : +91 (0) 265 338083
E-mail: tashoil@usa.com

Cauvery Petrochemicals Pvt. Ltd.
No. 49, Kodavasamaja Bldg.,
2nd Flr., 1st Main
Vasantnagar, Bangalore,
Karnataka-560052
India
TEL : +91 (0) 80 2255158
FAX : +91 (0) 80 2256164
E-mail:
bnarang@hotmail.com

Cresent Industrial Lubricants
984, 9th Cross, HMT Main Rd.
Divanarapalya, Bangalore,
Karnataka-560054
India
TEL : +91 (0) 80 3372785
E-mail:
basheerak@satyamonline.com

Hyklass Lubricants (I) Pvt. Ltd.
#90/1, 3rd Main, Magadi Rd. Cross
Rajaji Ngr., Bangalore,
Karnataka-560044
India
TEL : +91 (0) 80 3400337

Kerala Lubricants & Chemicals
No. 82, Major Indl. Est.
Kalamassery Devp. Plot P.O.
Kalamassery, Kerala-683109
India
TEL : +91 (0) 48455 541284

Oilwell Industries
Daga Sadan,
Freeganj
Ujjain, Madhya Pradesh-456001
India
TEL : +91 (0) 734 553436

Pensol Industries Ltd.
307, Classic Centre,
575, M G Rd.,
Indore,
Madhya Pradesh-452001
India
TEL : +91 (0) 731 532609
FAX : +91 (0) 731 545984
E-mail:
pensol@sancharnet.in

Mosil Lubricants Pvt. Ltd.
Plot No. 166/1, 'Kalanidhi'
P.O. Box No. 16791
Sion (W), Mumbai,
Maharashtra-400022
India
TEL : +91 (0) 22 4076680
FAX : +91 (0) 22 4075541
E-mail: sales@mosil.com

Amol Oils
92, Ajanta Rd.
Chincholi, Jalgaon,
Maharashtra-425001
India
TEL : +91 (0) 257 237007
FAX : +91 (0) 257 237207
E-mail:
babhay@bom6.vsnl.net.in

Arihant Lubricants Pvt. Ltd.
Gat No. 622/1/1/B
Pune-Nasik Highway
Village Kuruli
Pune, Maharashtra-410501
India
TEL : +91 (0) 20 6122214
FAX : +91 (0) 20 622214
E-mail:
rmvasa@rediffmail.com

Bharat Petroleum Corporation Ltd.
Bharat Bhavan, 4 & 6
Currimbhoy Rd., Ballard Est.
Mumbai, Maharashtra-400001
India
TEL : +91 (0) 22 2618281

FAX : +91 (0) 22 2616793
E-mail:
okesy@bharatpetroleum.com

Castrol India Ltd.
P.O. Box 16172
White House, 91, Walkeshwar Rd.
Mumbai, Maharashtra-400006
India
TEL : +91 (0) 22 3632511
FAX : +91 (0) 22 3635447
E-mail: sumitst@vsnl.com

Essess Lube Products Pvt. Ltd.
W-9/1, MIDC, Nagpur,
Maharashtra-440028
India
TEL : +91 (0) 712 37989

Fuchs Lubricants (I) Ltd.
A Wholly Owned Subsidiary Of Fuchs Petrolub AG,
Karmayog Bldg.
Parsi Panchayat Rd.
Andheri (E)
Mumbai, Maharashtra-400069
India
TEL : +91 (0) 22 8313982
FAX : +91 (0) 22 8313989
E-mail:
fuchsindia.bom@vsnl.com

Gandhar Oil Refinery (I) Ltd.
T-10, Taloja
Main Rd., Panvel
Panvel, Maharashtra-410206
India
TEL : +91 (0) 21546 7412047
FAX : +91 (0) 21546 4132804

Hindustan Petroleum Corporation Ltd.
Hindustan Bhavan
P.O. Box No. 155
8, Shoorji Villabhdas Marg
Mumbai, Maharashtra-400001
India
TEL : +91 (0) 22 2618031
FAX : +91 (0) 22 2611822
E-mail: info@hindpetro.com

ICCON Oil Petroleums Pvt. Ltd.
E-11, Nand Dham Indl. Est.
Marol Maroshi Rd.
Andheri (E), Mumbai,
Maharashtra-400059
India
TEL : +91 (0) 22 8505801
FAX : +91 (0) 22 8501640

Ideal Industrial Lubricant (I) Pvt. Ltd.
407/1, Top Flr., Diamond Mansion
Ganpatrao Kadam Marg
Worli, Mumbai,
Maharashtra-400018
India
TEL : +91 (0) 22 4931122
FAX : +91 (0) 22 4373797

Indian Oil Blending Ltd.
254 C, Mahalaxmi Rly. Stn.
Opp. Income Tax Office,
Dr. A B Rd., Mahalaxmi
Mumbai, Maharashtra-400025
India
TEL : +91 (0) 22 4930904
FAX : +91 (0) 22 4930353

Indian Oil Corporation Ltd.
Marketing Divn.
Indianoil Bhavan, G-9
Ali Yavur Jung Marg
Bandra (E), Mumbai,
Maharashtra-400051
India
TEL : +91 (0) 22 6400545
FAX : +91 (0) 22 6427384

Integrated Network Products Pvt. Ltd.
S. No. 143/2/2/4
Tathawade, Pune,
Maharashtra-411033
India
TEL : +91 (0) 20 725877
FAX : +91 (0) 20 725877
E-mail: imp@pn2.vsnl.net.in

Macmil Corp.
18/135, Phule Ngr.,
Opp. New RTO
Alandi Rd., Pune,
Maharashtra-411006
India
TEL : +91 (0) 20 6696852
FAX : +91 (0) 20 6696852
E-mail: macmil@indiaco.com

Martol Petroproducts Pvt. Ltd.

7, Shreenath-II
Nav Mithagar Link Rd.
Mulund (E), Mumbai,
Maharashtra-400081
India
TEL : +91 (0) 22 5688332
FAX : +91 (0) 22 5650528
E-mail: martol@vsnl.com

Meet Petroproducts Pvt. Ltd.
J-39, MIDC, Taloja,
Maharashtra-410208
India
TEL : +91 (0) 215 7412767

Nandan Petrochem Ltd.
19, A Wing, Sita Est.,
Aziz Baug, Mahul Rd.
Chembur, Mumbai,
Maharashtra-400074
India
TEL : +91 (0) 22 7410527
FAX : +91 (0) 22 7411313

Panama Petrochem Ltd.
Mahavir Darshan, 416
Narshi Natha St.
Masjid Rd., Mumbai,
Maharashtra-400009

India
TEL : +91 (0) 22 3427700
FAX : +91 (0) 22 3428702
E-mail:
panama@bom4.vsnl.net.in

Reema Oil Co.
9, Anjaline Apts.
Old Police Stn. Rd.
Vile Parle (W), Mumbai,
Maharashtra-400056
India
TEL : +91 (0) 22 6102251

Rohit Trading Corp.
Manchando Compound No. 2
Gala No. 27/A
CST Rd., Kalina
Mumbai, Maharashtra-400098
India
TEL : +91 (0) 22 6112400
FAX : +91 (0) 22 6104741

Sah Petroleums Ltd.
406/407, Embassy Centre
Nariman Point
Mumbai,
Maharashtra-400021
India
TEL : +91 (0) 22 2301911
FAX : +91 (0) 22 2875751
E-mail: ipol@vsnl.com

Sarbi Petroleum & Chemicals Pvt. Ltd.
9, Moonstone Apts.
Link Rd., 65/E, Santacruz (W)
Mumbai, Maharashtra-400054
India
TEL : +91 (0) 22 6043722
FAX : +91 (0) 22 6056195

Savita Chemicals Ltd.
66/67, Nariman Bhavan
6th Flr., Nariman Point
Mumbai, Maharashtra-400021
India
TEL : +91 (0) 22 2883061
FAX : +91 (0) 22 2029364
E-mail:
savitacorp@vsnl.com

Stanlubes & Specialites (I) Pvt. Ltd.
C-463/464
TTC Indl.Area, MIDC
Pawne, Navi Mumbai,
Maharashtra-400613
India
TEL : +91 (0) 22 7680679
FAX : +91 (0) 22 7906572
E-mail:
stanlubes_sp@vsnl.com

Starol Petroleum Ltd.
3rd Flr., 11, Gold Mohur, 174
Princess St., Mumbai,
Maharashtra-400002
India
TEL : +91 (0) 22 2003042
FAX : +91 (0) 22 2003042
E-mail:
starol_petro@hotmail.com

Subhash Chemical Industries
Shed W-2
S-Block, MIDC
Bhosari, Pune,
Maharashtra-411026
India
TEL : +91 (0) 20 7120632
FAX : +91 (0) 20 7122554
E-mail:
subhaschem@vsnl.com

Sunitha Petrochemicals Pvt. Ltd.
G-2, Balrajeshwar Apts.
Balrajeshwar Rd.
Mulund (W), Mumbai,
Maharashtra-400080
India
TEL : +91 (0) 22 5694259
FAX : +91 (0) 22 5672203
E-mail:
trinitypetro@rediffmail.com

Synochem
A/404, Shreenath CHS,
Nr. New Kalwa High School
Kalwa, Thane,
Maharashtra-400605
India
TEL : +91 (0) 22 5401832
E-mail:
synochem@maharashtradirectory.com

Taxoil Lubricants Pvt. Ltd.
R-591, MIDC
Rabale, Navi Mumbai,
Maharashtra-400701
India
TEL : +91 (0) 22 7692536
FAX : +91 (0) 22 3739384

Universal Silicones & Lubricants Ltd.
Unit: 6, 7 & 8
Udyog Mandir No. 2, 7-C
Pitamber Lane
Mahim (W), Mumbai,
Maharashtra-400016
India
TEL : +91 (0) 22 4443820
FAX : +91 (0) 22 4457710

V-Chem
Ajay Sahawas A
Nariman Rd.
Vile Parle (E), Mumbai,
Maharashtra-400057
India
TEL : +91 (0) 22 6142237
FAX : +91 (0) 22 6115249

Viscolube Corp.
11, Ramesh Mahal
A B Nair Rd.
Juhu, Mumbai,
Maharashtra-400049
India
TEL : +91 (0) 22 6200789
FAX : +91 (0) 22 6208558
E-mail:
visco70@hotmail.com

Wecaba Chemicals
308-A, Niranjan Bldg.
Marine Lines (W)
Mumbai,
Maharashtra-400002
India
TEL : +91 (0) 22 2814760
FAX : +91 (0) 22 2088506
E-mail:
corochem@bom3.vsnl.net.in

White Petroleum Industries
306, Runwal Center
Nr. Lakme
Govandi Stn. Rd.
Govandi, Mumbai,
Maharashtra-400088
India
TEL : +91 (0) 22 5577626
FAX : +91 (0) 22 5566148
E-mail: wpind@vsnl.com

Jain Oil Stores
546-547
Indl. Area-B
Ludhiana, Punjab-141003
India
TEL : +91 (0) 161 530992
FAX : +91 (0) 161 531862
E-mail:
vipin35@satyam.net.in

Sun Oil Co.
546-547, Indl. Area-B
Ludhiana, Punjab-141003
India
TEL : +91 (0) 161 530992
FAX : +91 (0) 161 531862
E-mail:
vipin35@satyam.net.in

Continental Petroleums Ltd.
A-2, Opp. Udyog Bhawan
Tilak Marg, C-Scheme
Jaipur, Rajasthan-302005
India
TEL : +91 (0) 141 2411641
FAX : +91 (0) 141 2381561
E-mail:
conpetco@jp1.dot.net.in

Om Petrochemicals Pvt. Ltd.
E-221, Rd. No. 10
VKI Area
Jaipur, Rajasthan-302013
India
TEL : +91 (0) 141 2402327
FAX : +91 (0) 141 2261120

Chemoleums Ltd.
37, 1st Main Rd.
C.I.T Ngr., Chennai,
Tamil Nadu-600035
India
TEL : +91 (0) 44 4330574
FAX : +91 (0) 44 4342242
E-mail:
cml.city@rmy.sprintrpg.ems.vsnl.net.in

Crown Lubricants
34/35, Gandhi Rd.
Puzhal, Chennai,
Tamil Nadu-600066
India
TEL : +91 (0) 44 6590171
FAX : +91 (0) 44 6591271
E-mail: crownlub@eth.net

Indian Additives Ltd.
Manali Express Highway
Manali, Chennai,
Tamil Nadu-600068
India
TEL : +91 (0) 44 541267
FAX : +91 (0) 44 5941184
E-mail: venm@ialindia.com

Industrial Lube Products
355, 4th Link St.
Nehru Nagar, Kottivakkam
Chennai, Tamil Nadu-600096
India
TEL : +91 (0) 44 4926982
FAX : +91 (0) 44 4926982
E-mail:
radhoo@md4.vsnl.net.in

Mahatha Petrochemicals
Sree Meenakshi Gardens, 34
Mount Medavakkam Rd.
Keela Kattalai
Chennai,
Tamil Nadu-600117
India
TEL : +91 (0) 44 2471542
FAX : +91 (0) 44 2473800
E-mail:
mahatha@md5.vsnl.net.in

Mekuba Petroleum India Pvt. Ltd.
4D/3 Third Main Rd.
Ambatur
Chennai,
Tamil Nadu-600058
India
TEL : +91 (0) 44 6243917

Sri Chakra Lubes Pvt. Ltd.
No. 31, Sadhulla St.
T Nagar,
Chennai,
Tamil Nadu-600017
India
TEL : +91 (0) 44 4332885
FAX : +91 (0) 44 4333360

Sunshine Oil Co.
12, Periyar Salai
Chennai,
Tamil Nadu-600018
India
TEL : +91 (0) 44 4323288

SB Maheshwari & Co.
80/55
Coolie Bazar,
Kanpur,
Uttar Pradesh-208001
India
TEL : +91 (0) 512 361636
FAX : +91 (0) 512 311627
E-mail:
rm007@rediffmail.com

117. MANUFACTURE OF TIN CONTAINERS
118. MANUFACTURE OF STORAGE TANKS, PRESSURE VESSELS, HEAT EXCHANGERS
119. MARK II HAND PUMPS
120. MARUTI WORKSHOP CUM - SERVICE STATION
121. MECHANICAL JACKS
122. METAL CUTTING DIE DESIGN
123. METAL CUTTING OF AND GRINDING WHEELS (ABBRASIVE CUTTING WHEELS)
124. METAL HOOKS & CLIPS
125. METAL SEPARATION (COPP- ER , TIN, LEAD) FROM SPENT WASH ACID
126. METALLIC RING JOINTS
127. METALLIC GASKET (SPIRAL WOUND)
128. MICROVEE & ABSOLUTE FILTER
129. MICROWAVE OVEN
130. MILD STEEL INGOTS
131. MINI STEEL PLANT
132. MODERN VEHICLE WORKSHOP
133. MOPED
134. M.S.HINGES
135. M.S.INGOT AND HR. STEEL STRUCTURALS
136. M.S.INGOT BY INDUCTION FURNACES
137. M.S.PIPES
138. M.S. WELDING ELECTRODE
139. MUFFLERS & SILENCERS FOR THREE WHEELERS
140. NAIL CUTTER WITH FILER & MANICURE
141. NICHROME WIRE
142. NICKEL LINED SCREENS
143. NON-FERROUS ALLOY ROLLING
144. NON-FERROUS FORGING
145. NON-FERROUS FOUNDRY
146. NON PRESSURE
147. INCANDESCENT LAMP
148. NUMBER COMBINATION LOCKS FOR LUGGAGES
149. NUTS & BOLTS
150. PAPER COATED ALUMINIUM AND COPPER WIRE
151. PETROMAX CONTAINER
152. PHOTO ETCHING OF STAINLESS STEEL PLATES
153. PIPE GALVANIZING PLANT
154. PISTON RING-AUTOMOBILE
155. PLANT PROTECTION EQUIPMENTS
156. PLATINUM LABORATORY APPARATUS
157. PRESSURE COOKER & ALUMINIUM UTENSILS
158. PRESSURE COOKER (ALUMINIUM)
159. PRESSURE DIE CASTING
160. PRINTED ALUMINIUM COLLAPSIBLE TUBES
161. PRINTED TIN CONTAINERS
162. PRINTING PRESS (CYLINDER MACHINE)
163. PUMPS FOR CHEMICAL INDUSTRY (SPECIAL)
164. RAILWAY SLEEPERS (M.S.)
165. RAZOR TWIN BLADE
166. R.C.C SPUN PIPES
167. RECONDITIONING OF M.S. DRUMS/BARRELS
168. RE-ROLLING COPPER AND BRASS SHEET AND RODS
169. RE-ROLLING MILLS
170. RESIN COATED SAND
171. RESIN CORED SOFT SOLDER WIRES
172. ROLLING MILL (BY INDUCTION FURNACE) & MANUFACTURE OF BARS, ANGLES, SQUARES, TUBES AND OTHERS
173. ROLLER BEARING & FORGING
174. ROLLING OF STAINLESS STEEL PATTA
175. RUBBER INSULATED PLIERS (HAND TOOLS)
176. RUBBING COMPOUND FOR AUTOMOBILES
177. SCIENTIFIC LABORATORY EQUIPMENTS
178. SCOOTER ASSEMBLING
179. SECONDARY LEAD EXTRAC -TION BY SCRAP BATTERY PLATES,PIPES & SHEET
180. SEAMLESS M.S. TUBES & PIPES
181. SELF TAPPING STEEL SCREW
182. SEWING NEEDLES
183. S.G. IRON & ALLOY STEEL
184. SHEET METAL PRODUCTS, (FERROUS/NON-FERROUS)
185. SHIP/MARINE CONTAINER
186. SHOCK ABSORBERS
187. SHOE EYELETS
188. SHOT AND GRITS BY AUTOMIZATION PROCESS
189. SHOVELS
190. SILICO MANGANESE ALLOYS
191. SILENCERS (MUFFLERS) EXHAUST & TAIL PIPE FOR ALL TYPES OF VEHICLES
192. SINTERED BEARING
193. SINTERED BUSHES
194. SINTERED METAL PRODUCTS
195. SOFT AND HARD FERRITES
196. SPANNERS
197. SPARK PLUGS
198. STEEL PLANT (ELECTRIC ARC FURNACE BASED- EAF)
199. SPHERIODAL GRAPHITE CAST IRON
200. SPRAY DRYER
201. STAINLESS STEEL HINGES
202. STAINLESS STEEL SHEET ROLLING TO PRODUCE STAINLESS STEEL UTENSILS
203. STAINLESS STEEL UTENSILS
204. STAPLE PINS,PAPER PIN , GEM CLIPS ETC.
205. STEEL CASTINGS
206. STEEL CHAIN
207. STEEL FOUNDRY
208. STEEL FURNITURES AND ELECTRICAL APPLIANCES
209. STEEL PLANT (MINI)
210. STEEL RODS AND COILS FROM SCRAPS
211. STEEL ROLLING MILL
212. STEEL STRIPS (COLD ROLLED) SILICON WITH GRAIN RIENTED FOR ELECTRIC USE
213. STEEL TRANSMISSION LINE TOWERS & ROLLING MILL TO PRODUCE STEEL SECTION
214. STEEL FURNITURES AND ELECTRICAL APPLIANCES
215. STEEL WIRE DRAWING AND GALVANIZING
216. STEEL WOOL
217. SUBMERGED ARC WELDED PIPES
218. SUBMERSIBLE PUMP MANUFACTURING
219. SUPER ENAMELLED COPPER WIRE
220. THREE WHEELERS
221. TIE-ROD ENDS
222. TIN CONTAINERS
223. TOOLROOM AND SHEET METAL PRODUCTS
224. TRACTOR TRAILERS
225. TRANSMISSION POWER FITTING
226. TUBULAR POLES
227. SUPER ENAMELLED COPPER WIRES
228. TUBULAR POLES FOR ELECTRICAL TRANSMISSION (BY FABRICATION PROCESS)
229. TUBULAR POLES OF M.S. & HIGH TENSILE STEEL
230. VACUUM CLEANERS
231. VACUUM FLASK (STAINLESS STEEL)
232. VALVES FOR REFRIGERA TION AND AIR-CONDITION
233. VEHICLE WELDING & PAINTING
234. VENETION BLIND
235. WASHING MACHINES (AUTOMATIC & COMPUTERISED)
236. WATER CONTROLLER (AUTOMATIC)
237. WATCH STRAPS/CHAINS/ BRACELETS/BELT BRASS & STAINLESS STEEL
238. WATER COOLERS
239. WELDED WIRE MESH
240. WELDING ELECTRODES
241. WICK STOVES
242. WIND MILL WINDOW FRAME (FERROUS & NON-FERROUS)
243. WRIST WATCH

359. DI ETHYL OXALATE
360. DI METHYL ORTHOPHTHALATE
361. DI-METHYL PHTHALATE
362. DICLOFENAC GEL
363. DIOCTYL PHTHALATE (DOP)
364. DI PHENYL GLYCERINE
365. DI PHENYL OXIDE
366. DINITRO-CHLORO BENZENE
367. DISTILLED WATER
368. DODECYL BENZENE SULPHONATE
369. DUSTLESS CHALK
370. EDTA & ITS SALTS
371. ELECTROLESS NICKEL PLATING ON PLASTICS
372. ENDOSULFAN
373. EPOXY RESIN BASED COMPOUND
374. ETHYL ACETATE
375. EHTYL ETHER
376. ETHYL ALCOHOL (POTABLE LIQUOR)
377. ETHYL HEXANOL
378. EXTRACTION OF ESSENTIAL OILS BY SUGAR CRITICAL FLUID (CARBON DIOXIDE) METHOD FROM FLOWERS, HERBAL & SPICES
379. FERRIC ALUM
380. FERRO CHROME LIGNO SULPHONATE
381. FERRO MANGANESE
382. FERRO SILICONE
383. FERRO VANADIUM FROM VANADIUM SLUDGE
384. FERROUS SILICATE
385. FERROUS SULPHATE
386. FERTILIZER FROM ANIMAL BLOOD & LEATHER WASTE
387. FLUORESCENT TUBE LIGHT POWDER
388. FOAMED PVC COMPOUNDING & ITS PRODUCTS
389. FORMALDEHYDE
390. FRACTIONAL DISTILLATION OF D.M.O (DEMENTHOLIZED OIL)
391. FRACTIONAL DISTILLATION OF ESSENTIAL OIL & MEDICINAL PLANT EXTRACT
392. FRICTION DUST (LIQUID & POWDER) FROM CNSL
393. FRUIT FLAVOURS
394. FURFURAL FROM RICE HUSK
395. GARLIC ACID
396. GASKET SHELLAC COMPOUND
397. GEAR OIL
398. GIBBERELLIC ACID
399. GLASS PUTTY
400. GLYCERINE
401. GOSSYPOL (POLY PHENOL) FROM COTTON SEED OIL
402. GUAR GUM POWDER
403. HAIR FIXER (HAIR GEL TYPE)
404. H - ACID
405. HENNA PASTE MAKING
406. HEPTAL DEHYDE
407. HIGH CARBON FERRO CHROME
408. HYDRATED CALCIUM SILICATE BRICK
409. HYDRATED LIME FROM SEA SHELL
410. HYDROCHLORIC ACID
411. HYDRO FLUORIC ACID
412. HYDROGEN PEROXIDE (BY AUTO-OXIDATION PROCESS)
413. ICE PACKS (SOLUTIONS TYPE, WHITE GEL TYPE, VIOLET SEMI SOLID POLYMER TYPE)
414. IMPROVING DROP POINT PARAFFIN WAX FROM 45-50^{0}C TO 75-80^{0}C
415. INDUSTRIAL ALCOHOL
416. INTEGERATED COMPLEX OF EASTER & ALLIED PRODUCTS (D.O.P, D.B.P, ETHYL ACETATE WIRE ENAMEL & CABLE JELLY)
417. IMFL (WHISKY) & COUNTRY LIQUOR
418. IRON OXIDE FOR MAKING FERITTE
419. IRON SULPHIDE
420. JUTE BATCHING OIL
421. KESH KALA TEL (HAIR DYE LOTION) (VASMOL 33, BLACK NITE TYPE)
422. L-LYSINE MONOHYDROCHLORIDE
423. LACTIC ACID FROM WHITE SUGAR BY FERMENTATION PROCESS
424. LDPE GRANULES FROM VIRGIN (LDPE RESIN)
425. LEAD EXTRACTION FROM BATTERY SCRAP
426. LEAD OXIDE (A) LEAD MONOXIDE (B) LEAD TETRA OXIDE (C) GREYLEAD OXIDE
427. LIQUID GLUCOSE & ITS BY PRODUCTS
428. LIQUID OXYGEN BOTTLING PLANT
429. LIQUID SHOE POLISH
430. LIQUID FLOOR POLISH
431. LUBE OIL VISCOSITY IMPROVED FOR P.P.G/P.E.G.
432. LUBRICANTS ASHLESS 100% COMBUSTION
433. MAGNESIUM CARBONATE AND MAGNESIUM BICARMONATE
434. MAGNESIUM HYDROXIDE POWDER
435. MAGNESIUM SILICATE
436. MAGNESIUM SULPHATE
437. MALACHITE GREEN
438. MALEIC ANHYDRIDE
439. MANGANESE SULPHATE
440. MANUFACTURING OF CARBON MONO-OXIDE WATER GAS
441. MENTHOL BOLD CRYSTALS FROM FLAKES
442. MENTHOL CRYSTAL & MENTHA OIL
443. MERCURIC OXIDE
444. METAL PRE-TREATMENT CHEMICALS
445. METHANE GAS BY SODIUM ACETATE & SODA LIME
446. METHYL ACETYL RICINOLATE
447. METOL
448. METOL FROM HYDROQUINONE & METHYLAMINE
449. MICANITE
450. MICRO NUTRIENT MIXTURE
451. MINERAL WATER
452. MINERAL WATER AND PET BOTTILNG PLANT
453. MINERAL WATER IN BOTTLES, GLASS AND POUCHES
454. MINI CEMENT PLANT (BY ROTARY KILN PROCESS)
455. MIXED FERTILIZER
456. MOSQUITO & FLIES REPELLENT AGARBATTI (INCENSE STICKS)
457. MONO CHLORO ACETIC ACID
458. MONOCROTOPHOS (TECHNICAL)
459. MOSQUITO COIL
460. MOSQUITO COIL & MAT
461. MOSQUITO MAT
462. MOTHER TINCTURE & BIO CHEMIC MEDICINES
463. NAPHTHALENE & PHENYL (INTEGRATED UNIT)
464. NATURAL MINERAL WATER BY REVERSE OSMOSIS PROCESS
465. NICKEL PLATING BRIGHTNER (PRIMARY OR CARRIER BRIGHTNER & SECONDARY BRIGHTNER)
466. NICKEL SULPHATE
467. NICOTINE FROM TOBACCO WASTE
468. NICOTINE SULPHATE FROM TOBACCO WASTE
469. NITRO BENZENE
470. NITRO CELLULOSE SANDING SEALER/LACQUER
471. NITRO MUSK
472. NITROGEN & OXYGEN GAS PLANT
473. NON-IONIC SURFACTANT (WETTING AGENT)
474. NO-CARB PASTE
475. OCTANOL
476. ORTHO NITRO PHENOL
477. OXALIC ACID FROM MOLASSES
478. OXALIC ACID FROMRICE HUSK
479. OXALIC ACID FROM TREE BARK
470. OXALIC ACID FROM WASTE VEGETABLES
471. OXYGEN GAS PLANT
472. OXYGEN GAS PLANT (AIR SEPERATION METHOD)
473. PARA-AMINO BENZOIC ACID
474. PARA-AMINO PHENOL
475. PARA TOLUENE SULPHONIC ACID
476. PECTIN FROM RAW PAPAYA
477. PERFUME (LEMON & OTHERS)

CRUDE NAPHTHA
570. TRIMETHYL AMMONIUM CHLORIDE
571. TRIPHENYL PHOSPHITE (T.P.P)
572. ULTRAMARINE BLUE (LIQUID)
573. UREA FORMALDEHYDE & MELAMINE FORMALDEHYDE POWDER
574. UNDECYLINIC ACID
575. VINYL ACETATE MONOMER
576. VITAMIN C
577. VITAMIN E
578. WASTE WATER TREATMENT PLANT FOR INDUSTRIAL SECTOR IN INDIA (ONLY MARKER SURVEY)
579. WIRE DRAWING LUBRICANT
580. WIRE ENAMEL
581. XANTHATES
582. YELLOW DEXTRIN
583. ZINC CHLORIDE
584. ZINC OXIDE
585. ZINC PHOSPHATING BY COLD PROCESS
586. ZINC SILICATE
587. ZINC STEARATE
588. ZINC SULPHATE
589. ZINC SULPHATE MONOHYDRATE
590. ACID BLACK
591. AURAMINE'O'
592. AZO DYES STUFF
593. DYE & DYE INTERMEDIATE
594. DYE INTERMEDIATES
595. MALACHITE GREEN
596. METHYLENE BLUE
597. PHTHALOCYANINE BLUE
598. PHTHALOCYANINE BLUE & GREEN
599. REACTIVE DYES
600. SULPHUR BLACK DYE
601. VAT DYES
602. WATER CHILLING PLANT
603. WADDING OIL (100%) FOR WADDING OF COTTON HOSIERY CLOTH IN THE DYEING PROCESS
604. WHITE OIL
605. WAX FLOOR POLISH

ELECTRICAL, ELECTONICS, COMPUTERS AND INFOTECH/IT PROJECTS

606. AIR CONDITIONING
607. ALUMINIUM ALLOY CONDUCTOR
608. ALUMINIUM CABLE
609. ALUMINIUM ELECTROYTIC CAPACITORS
610. AUDIO CASSETTE ASSEMBLING & RECORDING
611. AUDIO CASSETTES DUPLICATING RECORDING
612. AUDIO CASSETTES & AUDIO STUDIO
613. AUDIO CASSETTES PLANE & RECORDED
614. AUDIO MAGNETIC HEADS
615. AUDIO MAGNETIC TAPE
616. AUDIO/VIDEO CASSETTES
617. AUTO BULB/LAMPS
618. AUTOMATIC VOLTAGE STABILIZER
619. BATTERY PLATES
620. BACK OFFICE (Rs. 5000/-)
621. B/W TV & COMPUTER MONITOR PICTURE TUBE
622. BREAD BOARDS
623. CALL CENTRE
624. CAMERA (35 MM)
625. CAPACITORS
626. CARBON ELECTRODE USED FOR BATTERY CELL
627. CARBON POTETIOMETERS
628. CEILING FAN
629. CERAMIC INSULATOR
630. CHILDREN INFOTECH TRAINING INSTITUTE (Rs. 5000/-)
631. CHOKE AND PATTI
632. CHOKE AND STARTER
633. CHOKE USED FOR FLUORESCENT LAMPS
634. COLOUR TELEVISION
635. COLOUR AND BLACK & WHITE TELEVISION
636. COMPACT DISC
637. COMPACT DISC PLAYER (AUDIO/VIDEO)
638. COMPUTER EDUCATION INSTITUTE
639. COMPUTER ASSEMBLY
640. COMPUTER HARDWARE
641. COMPUTER KEYBOARD
642. COMPUTER PERIPHERALS
643. COMPUTER PRINTERS
644. COMPUTER RIBBON
645. COMPUTER RIBBON REINKING OR REFILLING
646. COMPUTER STATIONERY
647. COMPUTER STATIONERY &

IMPORTED HARDWARE PARTS
648. COMPUTER TERMINALS
649. COMPUTERISED WASHING MACHINE (AUTOMATIC)
650. COMPUTER SOFTWARE
651. CONDENSER FOR MOTOR USING MPP FILM
652. CONTENT DEVELOPMENT CENTRE (EOU) (Rs. 5000/-)
653. CONTROL PANEL BOARD
654. COOLING COIL FOR AIR CONDITIONERS
655. COPPER STRIP COIL FROM SCRAP
656. CORDLESS TELEPHONES
657. CYBER CAFE
658. CYBERKIOSK (Rs. 5000/-)
659. DATA PROCESSING CENTRE (Rs. 5000/-)
660. D.C. MICRO MOTORS
661. D.G.SETS
662. DISH ANTENNA AND CABLE T.V. NETWORK EQUIPMENT
663. DISTRIBUTION TRANSFORMERS & REPAIRS
664. DOMESTIC ELECTRICAL APPLIANCES- ROOM COOLER, WASHING MACHINE, WATER HEATER, ELECTRIC ROOM HEATER
665. E-SCHOOL
666. E-COMMERCE/BUSINESS
667. ELECTRIC ENERGY METER
668. ELECTRIC FANS
669. ELECTRIC HORN FOR AUTOMOBILE
670. ELECTRIC LAMP/GLS (INCANDESCENT LAMP)
671. ELECTRIC MIXER
672. ELECTRIC MOTORS UP TO 10 HP. REWINDING OF ALL TYPES OF MOTORS WATER PUMPS
673. ELECTRIC MOTOR WINDING (FOR FAN, MIXIES, ETC.)
674. ELECTRIC STEAM IRON
675. ELECTRICAL APPLIANCES
676. ELECTRICAL FIXTURES
677. ELECTRICAL STAMPING
678. ELECTROLYTIC CAPACITORS
679. ELECTROMAGNETIC RELAY
680. ELECTRONIC BALAST/CHOK
681. ELECTRICAL CHOKE
682. ELECTRONIC DIGITAL WATCHES
683. ELECTRONIC DIGITAL WEIGHING MACHINE
684. ELECTRONIC FIRE ALARM
685. ELECTRONIC GAS STOVE LIGHTERS
686. ELECTRONIC PRESSURE INDICATORS, ELECTRICALS, ELECTRONIC LIQUID LEVEL INDICATORS, ELECTRONIC TEMPERATURE INDICATOR, DIGITAL TACHOMETER
687. ELECTRONIC TELEPHONE INSTRUMENTS
688. ELECTRONIC TOYS
689. ELECTRONIC WATCHES & CLOCKS
690. FAX MACHINES
691. F.H.P MOTORS
692. FLOPPY DISKETTES
693. FLUORESCENT LAMP STARTER
694. FLUORESCENT TUBULAR

Above all the Detailed Project Reports are available at *"ENGINEERS INDIA RESEARCH INSTITUTE"*. 4449, Nai Sarak (D), Main Road Delhi - 110 006
●Ph : 91-11-23918117, 2391 6431, 23840361, 31082370 ●Fax : 91-11-2391 6431
●E-Mail : eirisidi@bol.net.in

LAMPS WITH INTRODUCTION TO MERCURY VAPOUR LAMP
695. FRANCHISEE COMPUTER EDUCATION CENTRE (Rs. 5000)
696. GAS DETECTOR (L.P.G)
697. GENERATOR SET & PUMP SETS
698. GENERATOR (BATTERY OPERATED)
699. GIS SERVICE CENTRE (GEOGRAPHICAL INFORMATION SYSTEMS)
700. HARDWARE FITTING FOR TRANSMISSION LINE (OVERHEAD LINE MATERIAL
701. HEADERS FOR TRANSISTOR ICS SEMI CONDUCTOR
702. H.T & L.T INSULATORS
703. H.T & M.V INDUSTRIAL CUBICAL SWITCH BOARD
704. INFORMATION MOVING DISPLAY (L.E.D TYPE)
705. INSURANCE CLAIM PROCESSING CENTRE (EOU) (Rs. 5000/-)
706. INTEGRATED CIRCUITS
707. INTERNET BASED STOCK TRADING (Rs. 5000/-)
708. INTERNET SERVICE PROVIDER (I.S.P.)
709. JELLY FILLED TELEPHONE CABLES
710. LAP TOP COMPUTERS
711. LEAD ACID BATTERIES
712. LEAD ACID BATTERY PLATES AND ASSEMBLING OF BATTERY
713. LEGAL TRANSCRIPTION & SECRETARIAL SERVICES CENTER (EOU)(Rs. 5000/-)
714. LIGHT EMITTING DIODES (L.E.D)
715. LINEAR ICS TRAINER KIT
716. LOUD SPEAKER
717. L.T TRANSFORMER REPAIRING
718. MEDICAL TRANSCRIPTION CENTRE
719. METAL FILM RESISTORS
720. METALLISED POLYPROPYLENE, POLYESTER FILM CAPACITOR
721. MICA BASE ELECTRONIC COMPONENTS
722. MICA PAPER WASTE PAPER FROM MICA WASTE
723. MICRO PROCESSORS TRAINER KITS BASED ON MICRO PROCESSORS
724. MINI COMPUTER (PERSONAL COMPUTER)
725. MINIATURE CIRCUIT BREAKER (M.C.B)
726. MINIATURE WATCH BATTERIES (BUTTON CELL)
727. MIXER/GRINDER (MIXI)
728. MONO CHROME COMPUTER MONITOR
729. MOTOR START ELECTROLYTIC CAPACITOR
730. MULTI LAYER P.C.B
731. MULTIPLE RELAY FOR LOW VOLTAGE
732. NEON INDICATOR
733. NEON SIGN MANUFACTURE
734. OPTICAL FIBRE CABLES
735. ON LINE SHOPPING MALL (Rs. 5000/-)
736. OPTO MECHANICAL & ELECTRICAL EQUIPMENTS
737. PHOTO COLOUR LAB
738. PICTURE TUBE (B/W)
739. PLAIN PAPER COPIER
740. PLASTIC FILM CAPACITORS
741. POLYESTER CAPACITORS
742. PORTABLE GENERATOR SET
743. PORTAL
744. PORTABLE TELEVISION(TV)
745. POWER CAPACITORS
746. POWER INVERTERS
747. POWER PLANT
748. POWER TRANSFORMERS UP TO 600 KVA
749. PRINTED CIRCUIT BOARD
750. PVC WIRES & CABLES
751. RE-CONDITIONING OF PICTURE TUBE
752. RESIN CAST CT & PT (1 KV)
753. SEMI CONDUCTOR DEVICE
754. SEMI CONDUCTORS FOR TRANSISTORS & DIODES
755. SETTING UP OF A VIDEO STUDIO
756. SMOKE DETECTORS
757. SOLAR CELLS
758. SOLAR MODULES
759. SOLAR PHOTO VOLTAIC SYSTEM
760. SOLDER FLUXES
761. SOLAR WATER HEATING PANELS
762. STEEL FURNITURE & ELECTRICAL APPLIANCES
763. STEREO AMPLIFIERS
764. STEREO CASSETTE RECORDERS/PLAYERS
765. STREET LIGHT FITTINGS SURGE SUPPRESSOR
766. TANTALUM CAPACITORS
767. TEFLON COATED ELECTRIC CABLE
768. TELEMEDICINE (DISTANCE HEALTH CARE) (Rs. 5000/-)
769. TELEPHONE CORD/CABLE
770. TELEPHONE (PUSH BUTTON TYPE)
771. TELEPHONE (PUSH BUTTON & CORDLESS)
772. TELEVISION (CTV & B/W)
773. TELEVISION (3-D)
774. TELEVISION DEFLECTION COMPONENTS
775. TELEVISION SIGNAL BOOSTERS
776. TELEVISION TUNERS
777. TRACTION BATTERIES
778. TRAINING INSTITUTE OF MEDICAL TRANSCRIPTION
779. TRANSFORMER FOR B/W TV
780. TRANSFORMER FOR VOLTAGE STABILIZER & E.H.T
781. TRANSMISSION POWER LINE FITTING
782. TRANSMISSION TOWER FITTING
783. TV AUDIO EQUIPMENT CABINETS & THEIR ASSEMBLING UNIT
784. UN-INTERRUPTED POWER SUPPLY (U.P.S)
785. VARIABLE FREQUENCY
786. VARIABLE VOLTAGE A.C. DRIVE
787. VIDEO CASSETTES (COMPLETE MANUFACTURING & ASSEMBLING)
788. VIDEO CASSETTES RECORDER (V.C.R)
789. VIDEO FILM STUDIO
790. VOLTAGE REGULATOR FOR AUTOMOBILES
791. VOLTAGE STABILIZERS
792. VOLTAGE STABLIZER & T.V. GAIN BOOSTER
793. WAX AND CHEMICAL COATED, BRAIDED TINSEL WIRE
794. WEBSITE DESIGN & E-MAIL REGISTERING
795. WELDING ELECTRODES
796. WIND ENERGY POWER PROJECT (10 MW)
796A WIRES (METAL)

FOOD, AGRO FOOD, PROCESSED FOOD, AGRO PLANTATION, CULTIVATION, FARMING, DAIRY/MILK, TOBACCO/PAN MASALA, BREWERY & DISTILLERY, EDIBLE OILS, EOU FOOD PRODUCTS AND ALLIED PRODUCTS

797. ALCOHOLIC BEVERAGES & VENEGAR FROM COCONUT WATER
798. ALCOHOL DRINKS FROM ETHYL ALCOHOL BY MIXING OF VARIOUS FLAVOURS
799. ANTI SCALE COMPOUND FOR ADDING INTO SUGAR JUICE BOILING
800. APPLE JUICE CONCENTRATED & DEHYDRATED FRUIT & VEGETABLES
801. ARTIFICIAL FISH MEAL FOR POULTRY FEED
802. AUTOMATIC BISCUIT PLANT
803. BABY CEREAL FOOD AND MILK POWDER
804. BACTERIA FOR CANE JUICE
805. BAKER'S YEAST
806. BAKERY INDUSTRY
807. BANANA PUREE
808. BEER & WINE
809. BEER PLANT (BREWERY)
810. BIDI
811. BIDI & CIGARETTE
812. BISCUIT PLANT

813. BREAD (AUTOMATIC PLANT)
814. BLACK PEPPER (SPICES)
815. BREAD AND BISCUITS
816. BREEDING FARM
817. BROILER CHICKEN
819. BUTTON MUSHROOM CULTIVATION & PROCESSING
820. CANNING OF RASAGULLAS IN METAL CANS
821. CAFFEIN FROM TEA WASTE
822. CANNING OF FRUITS & VEGETABLES
823. CASEIN AND BY-PRODUCTS
824. CASHEW FRUIT JUICE FROM CASHEW FRUIT APPLE
825. CASHEWNUT KERNEL EXTRACTION FROM CASHEWNUT FRUIT
826. CASHEWNUT SHELL LIQUID & KERNEL PROCESSING
827. CASHEW FENI
828. CATECHEU (BY CHEMICAL PROCESS)
829. CATTLE FEED FROM TAPIOCA
830. CHEWING & BUBBLE GUM
831. CHICKEN/SHEEP MEAT PROCESSING
832. CHOCOLATE (MILK)
833. CIGARETTE AND BEEDIES
834. COCOA BUTTER FROM COCOA MASS
835. COCONUT PRODUCTS & BY PRODUCTS PROCESS COMPLEX
836. COLD/SOFT DRINKS
837. COLLECTION OF MILK AND MILK MAKING POWDER
838. COLLECTION OF MILK AND PACKING IN POLYTHENE POUCH (1/2 KG.1 KG. & 2 KG.)
839. CONDENSED MILK (SWEETNED)
840. CONFECTIONERY INDUSTRY (TOFFEE & CANDY, SEMI-AUTOMATIC PLANT)
841. COUNTRY LIQUOR FROM MOLASSES
842. CIGARETTE
843. DAIRY FARM AND DAIRY (MILK) PRODUCTS (PASTEURISED MILK, BUTTER, GHEE, PANEER)
844. DAIRY FARM TO PRODUCE MILK & PACKING IN POUCHES (50%) & CAN(50%)
845. DAIRY FOR MILK PROCESSING
846. DAIRY FARM (BUFALO)
847. DAL (PULSE) MILL UNIT
848. DEHYDRATION OF CARROT & GARLIC
849. DEHYDRATION & CANNING OF FRUITS & VEGETABLES
850. DEHYDRATION OF FIGS
851. DEHYDRATION OF FRUITS AND VEGETABLES
852. DEHYDRATED ONIONS AND ONION POWDER
853. DRY ICE BY BREAKING OF AIR
854. DRYING OF RED CHILLIES, HALDI, DHANIA, AND GREEN PEAS
855. EGG POWDER (40,000 EGGS PROCESSING PER DAY)
856. EXPORT OF PROCESSED FOODS AND MARINE PRODUCTS
857. FISH CANNING & POUCHING
859. FISH FARMING (PRAWN & OTHER MARINE PRODUCTS)
860. FISH MEAL
861. FLOUR MILL AND MUSTARD OIL
862. FOOD COLOUR & ORASTED GROUNDNUT GRAM PEAS, ETC IN POUCHES
863. FROG LEGS PROCESSING
864. FROZEN MEATS PROCESSING
865. FOOD FLAVOURS (WHISKY) VODKA, GRAPE, BUTTER SCOTCH)
866. FOOD PRODUCTS COMPLEX (DEHYDRATED ONIONS, GARLIC POWDER & FLAKES, CATTLE FEED, TOMATO POWDER, TOMATO PRODUCTS, CANNED FRUITS & VEGETABLES, TOMATO PURE, GROUN NUT OIL, REFIND OIL, DEHYDRATED GRAPES, BANANA POWDER & WAFFERS)
867. FRUIT JUICE, JAM, JELLIES & ALLIED PRODUCTS
868. FRUIT JUICE, PICKLES PROCESSING AND CANNING
869. FRUIT JUICE MAKING & PACKING IN PLASTIC CONTAINER/POUCHES
870. FRUIT PROCESSING (JAM & JELLIES)
871. FRUIT PULP & JUICE CONCENTRATES
872. FRUIT & VEGETABLE DRYING (FREEZE DRYING METHOD)
873. GOAT & SHEEP FARMING
874. GRAM DALL/PULSE MILL
875. GRAPE DEHYDRATION
876. HARD BOILED CANDY (TOFFEE & CANDY)
877. HERBAL CIGARETTES
878. HONEY PROCESSING & PACKAGING
879. ICE CREAM OF DIFFERENT FLAVOURS
880. ICE CREAM STABILIZER
881. ICE MAKING PLANT
882. INDIAN MADE FOREIGN LIQUOR (I.M.F.L)
883. INSTANT FOOD (IDLI MIX, DOSA MIX, GULAB JAMUN MIX)
884. INSTANT FOOD (INSTANT FOOD & FAST FOOD PARLOUR)
885. INSTANT NOODLES
886. INSTANT TEA
887. INSTANT TEA FROM BLACK TEA
888. INTEGERATED STARCH BAKING POWDER/YEAST INDUSTRY
889. IODIZED SALT
890. IODIZED SALT (ORDINARY MOISTURE-LESS/FREE FLOWING IN PLASTIC BAGS AND CONTAINERS)
891. JAM, JELLIES, FRUIT JUICE & ALLIED PRODUCTS
892. KATHA AND CUTCH
893. KHANDSARI SUGAR
894. KHANDSARI SUGAR & IMFL
895. LACTIC ACID FROM WHITE SUGAR BY FERMENTATION PROCESS
896. LACTOSE & BY PRODUCTS PROCESSING FROM MILK
897. LIQUID GLUCOSE AND ITS BYE PRODUCTS
898. MACRONI AND VERMICILLI
899. MALT EXTRACTION FROM BARLEY
900. MANGO PROCESSING (MANGO PULP, JUICE & SLICES)
901. MAYUR BRAND TYPE CHEWING TOBACCO
902. MINERAL WATER
903. MILK PRESERVATION & MARKETING TO WHOLE SELLERS (INPOUCH PACKING BY UHT TECHNOLOGY)
904. MILK PROCESSING AND PACKAGING OF MILK PRODUCTS
905. MILK PRODUCTS (CASEIN, LACTOSE, GHEE & WHEY POWDER)
906. MILK TOFFEE
907. MINI FLOUR MILL
908. MINI SUGAR PLANT
909. MISRI (PEARL SUGAR CANDIES)
910. MODERN RICE MILL
911. MURABBA
912. MUSTARD OIL EXTRACTION & REFINING
913. MUTTON TALLOW
914. NAMKEEN INDUSTRY (BHUJIA, CHANA CHUR ETC.)
915. NAMKEEN & SWEETS
916. NON-BASMATI RICE FROM PADDY
917. OLEORESIN, ESSENTIAL OIL, DYES & POWDER OF SPICES
918. OLEORESIN EXTRACTION FROM DIPTERO-CARPUT TURMINATUS AND PINUS KHASYANA
919. OLEORESIN EXTRACTION FROM CHILLI
920. PAN MASALA AND POUCH

1059. BUFFALO HORN TIP, HOOF
1060. BANQUET HALL
1061. BUTTON
1062. CALCINED PETROLEUM (C.P) COKE
1063. CANVAS SHOES
1064. CANVAS SHOES, JUNGLE BOOTS
1065. CARBON BRUSH, BRUSH HOLDER & SLIP RING
1066. CEMENT SHEETS WITH COIR FIBRE & OTHER SEGMENTS
1067. CERAMIC TILES (GLAZED) BY DOUBLE FIRING/HEATING
1068. CHILDREN RECREATION CENTRE
1069. COAL BRIQUETTES
1070. COLD STORAGE & ICE
1071. COLD STORAGE FOR FRUITS AND VEGETABLES
1072. COMPRESSOR (HERMETIC) FOR AIR CONDITIONER
1073. COSTUME JEWELLERY/ IMITATION JEWELLERY
1074. DECORATIVE LAMINATED SHEET (SUNMICA)
1075. DIAMOND CUTTING & EXPORTS
1076. DRINKING STRAW FROM PROPYLENE
1077. ENGINEERING COLLEGE
1078. ENTERTAINMENT CLUB
1079. FASHION TECHNOLOGY INSTITUTE
1080. FAST FOOD PARLOUR
1081. FAST FOOD (INSTANT FOOD & FAST FOOD PARLOUR)
1082. FIRE EXTINGUISHERS (SODA ACID TYPE)
1083. FISH NET
1084. FLORICULTURE (CUT FLOWER ROSE) WITH GREEN HOUSE
1085. FLOOR COVERING SHEET
1086. FILM STUDIO (VIDEO)
1087. FLUSH DOOR, CHIP BOARD, WOOD WOOL & OTHER INSULATING BOARDS
1088. GAS DETECTORS OF L.P.G
1089. GEMS MANUFACTURING
1090. GLASS BOTTLE BY SCRAP
1092. GOAT & SHEEP FARMING
1093. GOLD ELECTROPLATING
1094. GOLD JEWELLERY (E.O.U)
1095. GOLD PLATED SILVER JEWELLERY & CUTLERY
1096. GRANITE SLAB AND TILES
1097. GREEN HOUSE
1098. HARD CHROMIUM PLATING
1099. HEALTH CLUB AND BEAUTY PARLOUR CUM HAIR SALOON WITH SONA BATH
1100. HEALTH CLUB CUM BEAUTY PARLOUR TRAININGINSTITUTE
1101. HORN TIP,HOOVE BUTTON
1102. HOSPITAL
1103. HOSPITAL (100 BEDS)
1104. HOSPITAL (200 BEDS)
1105. ICE MAKING PLANT
1106. IMITATION AND COSTUME
1107. JEWELLERY (NECKLACE, EARRINGS EAR TOP ETC.)
1108. INITMATE SCENT ETCHEMICALS FROM ALL TYPES OF FLAVOUR
1109. INVESTMENT CASTING
1110. JUTE, COIR, GLASS ROPE/ SUTLI
1111. JUTE TWINE
1112. L.P.G BOTTLING PLANT
1113. L.P.G REGULATOR (DOMESTIC PURPOSE)
1114. LAMINATED PARTICLE BOARD & HARD BOARD
1115. LAMINATED SAFETY AND TOUGHENED GLASS
1116. LEASING & HIRE PURCHASE
1117. LICHEN (CHARILA)
1118. MANILA ROPES
1119. MEDICAL COLLEGE
1120. MATCH UNIT FROM WAXED PAPER
1121. MEDIUM DENSITY FIBRE BOARD
1122. MELAMINE CROCKERY
1123. MINERAL WATER
1124. MINI CEMENT PLANT
1125. MIRROR SILVER, GOLDEN, PINK, BLACK & SMOKES
1126. MODERN ADVERTISING AGENCY WITH DTP & FILM STUDIO
1127. MOTEL/SMALL HOTEL
1128. MULTI COLOUR PRINTING
1129. MULTI STOREY COMMERCIAL COMPLEX ALONGWITH RESIDENTIAL AND DELUX FLATS FOR FOREIGN TOURISTS & REVOLVING RESTAURENT AT THE TOP
1130. MULTIPLE LAMINATION INDUSTRY
1131. MUSHROOM GROWING AND PROCESSING (BY DEEP FREEZING METHOD)
1132. NEWS PAPER PRINTING
1133. NICKEL LINED INDUSTRIAL SCREEN
1134. OFFSET COLOUR PRINTING PRESS (SIX COLOUR)
1135. OFFSET PRINTING PRESS
1136. P.C.C ELECTRIC POLES
1137. PHOTOGRAPHIC DEVELOPER & FIXER
1138. PVC EXTRUSION PROFILE (DOOR & WINDOWS)
1139. POP-CORN
1140. PHOTO ETCHING OF S.S.
1141. PRE STRESSED CEMENT CONCRETE PIPES
1142. PILFER PROOF CAPS
1143. PILFER PROOF CAPS AND CROWN CAP
1144. POUCH MAKING & GRAVURE PRINTING (ROTO PRINTING)
1145. POULTRY & FISH FARMING (INTEGERATED UNIT)
1146. PRINTING OF TIN SHEETS
1147. READYMADE GARMENTS
1148. RESTAURANT
1149. ROSE PLANTATION AND ROSE OIL EXTRACTION
1150. ROTOGRAVURE PRINTING
1151. SAFETY BELTS
1152. SAFETY MATCHES
1153. SHOE LACES
1154. SILK COCOON CULTIVATION (GROWING OF SILK COCOON WARM)
1155. SILK SCREEN PRINTING FORMULATIONS FOR PLASTIC, PAPER & CLOTH
1156. SPIKENARD (JATAMANSI)
1157. STENCIL COATING SOLUTION
1158. SUGAR CANDY (MISRI)
1159. SUGAR CANE PLANTATION
1160. SUGAR CANE JUICE PRESERVATION
1161. SURAT ZARI
1162. SYNTHETIC SHOES & SOLES
1163. TEA PACKAGING INDUSTRY
1164. TENNIS BALLS
1165. THREE STAR HOTEL
1166. TRAVELLING AGENCY
1167. TRAYS, TROLLEYS FOR HOSPITAL WITH SCRATCHLESS COATING
1168. WAX EXTRACTS (TANNING POWDER)
1169. WIRE ROPE SLINGS
1170. WOOD WOOL SLAB
1171. WOODEN CANE FURNITURE WITH EXPORT POTENTIAL
1172. WOODEN FURNITURE
1173. WOODEN PANEL INCLUDING KILN SEASONING
1174. WOODEN FURNITURE
1175. WATCH CASE BUFFING
1176. WATCH DIAL
1177. WRIST WATCHES
1178. WATCHES (ELECTRONIC)
1179. ZEDOARY (KACHUR)

EDIBLE OILS, ESSENTIAL OILS LURICATIING OILS, GREASES, VEGETABLE OILS, WAXES. CAMPHOR, PERFUMES & PERFUMERY COMPOUNDS AND REFINED OILS ETC.

1180. AROMATIC PERFUMERY COMPOUND
1181. AEROSOL
1182. AGARBATTI PERFUMERY COMPOUND
1183. BEES WAX MANUFACTURE
1184. CAMPHOR
1185. CARDANOL FROM CASHEW NUT SHELL LIQUID
1186. CASTOR OIL
1187. CASTOR OIL DERIVATIVE OLEORESINS
1188. CHILLI OIL
1189. CITRONELLA OILS
1190. CLOVE OIL
1191. CONCENTRATE OF ROSE JASMINE & LILY ETC.
1192. COLOURED FLAME CANDLE

1193. CANDLES (SEMI-AUTOMATIC)
1194. CORN OIL (MAIZE OIL)
1195. DEHYDRATED CASTOR OIL
1196. EUGENOL FROM CINNAMON LEAF OIL
1197. EXTRACTION OF ESSENTIAL OIL (CARDAMON, JEERA, AJOWAN, GINGER OILS ETC. & PACKAGING OF GROUND SPICES)
1198. EXTRACTION OF JASMINE ESSENCE
1199. EXTRACTION OF ESSENTIAL OILS BY SUPER CRITICAL FLUID METHOD FROM FLOWERS, HERBS & SPICES
1200. EUCALYPTUS OIL
1201. EXTRACTION OF OIL FROM OIL SEED EXPANDEREXTRUSION TECHNOLOGY)
1202. FAT LIQUOR SULPHATED OIL
1203. FLAVOURS FOR FOOD
1204. GARLIC OIL & POWDER
1205. GINGER OIL, SANDALWOOD OIL AND NAGARMOTHA OIL
1206. GINGER OIL
1207. GINGER OIL & GINGER DUST
1208. INTEGERATED WAX COMPLEX
1209. IONONE FROM LEMON GRASS OIL
1210. JASMINE & LILLY FLOWER OIL
1211. LEMON GRASS OIL
1212. LIQUID PARAFFIN
1213. LUBE OIL & GREASE
1214. LUBRICATING OIL
1215. MENTHOL CRYSTALS
1216. MENTHOL OIL & CRYSTAL
1217. MICRO CRYSTALLINE WAX
1218. MUSTARD OIL (EDIBLE OIL)
1219. OIL FROM ARTEMISIA HERBS
1220. PALM OIL CRUSHING UNIT
1221. PAN MASALA
1222. PARAFFIN WAX
1223. PARAFFIN WAX FROM SLACK WAX
1224. REFINED OIL-SUN FLOWER OIL, GROUNDNUT OIL, STAFF FLOWER OIL & COTTON SEED OIL
1225. REFINED VEGETABLE OIL
1226. RECLAMATION OF USED ENGINE OIL
1227. RICE BRAN OIL (R.B.O)
1228. ROSE OIL EXTRACTION
1229. SMOKE LESS CANDLE
1230. SPICE OIL & OLEORESINS
1231. SOLVENT EXTRACTION PLANT (OIL CAKE BASED)
1232. SYNTHETIC ALMOND OIL
1233. SYNTHETIC TALLOW
1234. SYNTHETIC GHEE
1235. VEGETABLE OIL EXTRACTION & REFINING
1236. WADDING OIL (100%) FOR WADDING OF COTTON HOSIERY CLOTH IN DYEING PROCESS
1237. WAX EMULSION FOR TEXTILE
1238. WAX FLOOR POLISH

PAINT, ENAMEL, SOLVENTS, THINNERS, INKS & VARNISH

1239. ACRYLIC EMULSION PAINTS
1240. ALUMINIUM PAINT
1241. AUTOMOBILE PAINTS
1242. BALL POINT PEN REFILL INK
1243. BITUMINIOUS ROAD EMULSION
1244. BITUMEN
1245. BITUMINIOUS FELTS FOR WATER & DAMP PROOFING
1246. BITUMINIOUS ROAD EMULSION RAPID MEDIUM & SLOW SETTING
1247. BUFFING & POLISHING
1248. CEMENT PAINT FOR WHITE & GREY CEMENT

1249. DISPERSANT
1250. DRY DISTEMPER
1251. DRY DISTEMPER & CEMENT PAINT
1252. DUPLICATING INK BLACK FOR GESTNER DUPLICATOR
1255. EMULSION PAINTS (WATER BASED)
1256. HAMMERTONE PAINT
1257. INSULATING VARNISH & WIRE ENAMEL
1258. IRON OXIDE PIGMENTS
1259. INSULATING VARNISH (POLY VINYL BUTYRAL BASED, FFC GRADE)
1260. LIME COLOUR (CEMENT COLOUR)
1261. SYNTHETIC RED OXIDE FOR FLOORINGS
1262. SOLVENT & THINNERS
1263. MARKING INKS (WATER PROOF)
1264. METAL NAPHTHANATE (AS DRIER FOR PAINTS)
1265. N.C.PUTTY
1266. OFFSET PRINTING INK
1267. OIL BOUND DISTEMPER PAINT
1268. PAINT BRUSHES
1269. PAINT REMOVERS
1270. PAINT INDUSTRY
1271. PAINT & VARNISH
1272. PICTURE VARNISH
1273. POWDER COATING PAINT
1274. PRINTING INKS (OFFSET, FLEXO & ROTO GRAVURE)
1275. PRIMER PAINT & ENAMEL PAINT
1276. PUTTY & WATER PROOFING PAINT
1277. PRINTING INKS (FLEXO-GRAPHIC INK)
1278. PUTTY (METAL CASEMENT)
1279. RED OXIDE PRIMER (ANTI CORROSIVE)
1280. REFRECTORY PAINT (GRAPHITE BASED)
1281. SCREEN PRINTING INKS
1282. SILK SCREEN PRINTING INK FORMULATION FOR PLASTIC, PAPER, CLOTH
1283. STAMP & PAD INK
1284. STOVING PAINT
1285. SPIRIT SOLUBLE MALEIC RESIN
1286. TEXTURE PAINT
1287. THINNERS AND ITS ALLIED PRODUCTS
1288. TONER INK
1289. VARNISH THINNER (SOLVENT)
1290. VACUUM METALLIZING LACQUERS
1291. WOOD PRIMER

PHARMACEUTICAL, DRUGS, AYURVEDIC/HERBAL COSMETICS & MEDICINES, HOMOEOPATHIC MEDICINES, DISPOSABLE SYRINGE, DENTAL COLLEGE & FINE CHEMICALS ETC.

1292. AROMATIC PILLS
1293. ASPIRIN
1294. AYURVEDIC PAIN BALM OINTMENTS
1295. AYURVEDIC CHURAN AND TABLETS
1296. AYURVEDIC TABLETS (HAJMOLA TYPE)
1297. AYURVEDIC/HERBAL PHARMACY
1298. AYURVEDIC SHERBATS
1299. AYURVEDIC PRODUCTS
1300. BULK DRUGS (E.O.U)
1301. BLOOD BAGS
1302. CALCIUM GLUCONATE
1303. CAPSULE, TABLET & INJECTION WITH MODERN INSTRUMENTS
1304. CASHEW FENI
1305. CHLOROQUINONE PHOSPHATE (BULK DRUGS)
1306. CLINICAL THERMOMETER
1307. DENTAL CLINIC

Above all the Detailed Project Reports are available at *"ENGINEERS INDIA RESEARCH INSTITUTE"*. 4449, Nai Sarak (D), Main Road Delhi - 110 006

● Ph : 91-11- 23918117, 2391 6431, 23840361, 31082370 ●Fax : 91-11- 2391 6431
●E-Mail : eirisidi@bol.net.in

1308. DENTAL COLLEGE
1309. DENTAL GRADE EUGENOL
1310. DEXTROSE MONOHYDRATE, LIQUID GLUCOSE
1311. DEHYDRATED ONION & ONION POWDER
1312. DEXTROSE POWDER (ANHYDROUS FROM STARCH)
1314. DEXTROSE SALINE SOLUTION
1315. DISTILLERY (I.M.F.L)
1316. DISPOSABLE NEEDLES FOR SYRINGES
1317. DISPRIN
1318. DISTILLED WATER
1319. EMPTY HARD GELATINE CAPSULES
1320. FILLING & PACKING OF CAPSULES
1321. GLUCOSE - D - POWDER
1322. GLYCERINE
1323. HERBAL COSMETICS
1324. HERBAL SHAMPOO
1325. HERBAL HAIR OILS (AYURVEDIC)
1326. HOMOE & BIO-MEDICINES WITH MOTHER TINCTURE
1327. HOMOEPATHIC MEDICINES
1328. HYPODERMIC NEEDLES
1329. I.V. FLUIDS
1330. IBUPROFEN
1331. INFUSION & TRANSFUSION SETS (I.V. SET)
1332. INJECTABLE FOR PHARMACEUTICALS
1333. INJECTION AMPOULES PACKAGING BOX
1334. INTEGERATED SURGICAL COTTON
1335. ICE MAKING PLANT
1336. ICE & COLD STORAGE
1337. LACTOSE & BY PRODUCTS PROCESSING FROM MILK
1338. LICHEN (JATAMANSI CHARILA)
1339. LIQUID GLUCOSE AND ITS BY-PRODUCTS
1340. L-LYSINE MONOHYDRO CHLORIDE
1341. LIQUID GLUCOSE FROM POTATOES
1342. MEDICAL COLLEGE
1343. NICOTINE FROM TOBACCO WASTE
1344. OINTMENT-AYURVEDIC (YELLOW & WHITE)
1345. PHARMACEUTICAL AND FOOD GRADE GELATINE
1346. PHARMACEUTICAL INDUSTRY (TABLETS, CAPSULES, LIQUID, GEL, OINTMENT POWDER INJECTABLE)
1347. PHARMACEUTICAL UNIT (EOU) WITH FORMULA TIONS, INJECTABLES, ETC. PYRIDINE & DERIVATIVES
1348. SALT (IODIZED SALT)
1349. SALINE & INJECTION WATER
1350. SALINE WATER & DEXTROSE SOLUTION (I.V.FLUID IN PLASTIC BOTTLES)
1351. SORBITOL
1352. STARCH (MAIZE)
1353. SURGICAL ADHESIVE PLASTER
1354. SURGICAL BANDAGES
1355. SURGICAL GLOVES
1357 SURGICAL COTTON
1358. SURGICAL COTTON AND BANDAGE
1359. SYNTHETIC CAMPHOR POWDER
1360. TABLETS & CAPSULES
1361. TISSUE CULTURE
1362. TINCTURE FROM RECTIFIED SPIRIT
1363. TRIMETHOPIME
1364. VETERENARY MEDICINES (ONLY FORMULATIONS)
1365. VITAMIN 'C', SORBITOL' ANHYDROUS DEXTROSE, STARCH

PULP, PAPER, STRAW/GREY BOARD, KRAFT PAPER, PACKAGING, PAPER CARRY BAGE, PAPER FROM AGRO WASTE & STATIONERY ETC.

1366. AMMONIA PAPER
1367. AUTOMATIC BOOK BINDING
1368. ADHESIVE (FEVICOL TYPE)
1369. ALL PIN & GEM CLIPS
1370. CARBON PAPER
1371. CARD BOARD
1372. CARBON LESS PAPER
1373. CELLPHANE PAPER
1374. COMPUTER FORMS & SECURITY PRINTING PRESS
1375. CORRUGATED BOARD & BOX (PRINTED & LAMINATED)
1376. CORRUGATED BOARD AND BOXES FROM FROM CARD EOARDS
1377. CORRUGATED CARTONS FROM PLAIN PAPERS
1378. CORRUGATRED PACKING & MATERIAL (BULB & TUBES PACKING)
1379. DESK TOP PUBLISHING
1380. DEFOAMING AGENT FOR PAPER PLANT
1381. DRINKING STRAW PAPER
1382. D.T.P CUM OFFSET PRESS
1383. EGG TRAYS
1384. EXERCISE NOTE BOOK, REGISTER AND PAD
1385. FLEXOGRAPHIC INK
1386. GREETING CARD BY OFFSET PRESS
1387. HAND MADE PAPER FILTER PAPER
1388. HARD BOARD
1389. INJECTION AMPOULES PACKAGING BOXES
1390. INSULATIING PAPER
1391. KRAFT PAPER
1392. KRAFT PAPER FROM BAGASSE
1393. LAMINATED PACKAGING PAPER WITH PRINTING
1394. LAMINATION & COATING ON PAPER
1395. M.G. PAPER FROM WASTE PAPER
1396. MILL PAPER FROM WASTE PAPER
1397. MILL BOARD FROM RICE & WHEAT STRAWS
1398. MILL BOARD FROM WASTE PAPER
1399. MINI PAPER PLANT FROM SISAL
1400. MINI PAPER PLANT
1401. MULTI WALL PAPER SACKS
1402. NEWS PAPER FOR CHILDREN
1403. NEWS PRINT PAPER FROM RICE STRAW BAGASSE
1404. NEWS PAPER CHILDRENS
1405. NEWS PRINT PAPER
1406. OFFSET AND TREADLE TYPE PRINTING PRESS
1407. MILL BOARD BASED ON RICE STRAW
1408. PAPER AND BOARD FROM STRAW
1409. PAPER & PAPER PRODUCTS
1410. PAPER ENVELOPES
1411. PAPER CARRY BAGS
1412. PAPER BOARD CARTON
1413. PAPER CONES FOR LOUD SPEAKERS
1414. PAPER FROM AKRA
1415. PAPER FROM BAGASSE WITH CORRUGATED BOARD & BOXES
1416. PAPER FROM BAMBOO
1417. PAPER GLASSES FOR BEVERAGES
1418. PAPER FROM RICE HUSK & WHEAT HUSK
1419. PAPER FROM TREE BARK, EUCALYPRUS WOOD
1420. PAPER PRODUCTS
1421. PAPER PLANT (WHITE WRITING & NEWS PAPER FOR PULP & WASTE PAPER)
1422. PAPER PLATES, PAPER GLASS
1423. PAPER CONES & TUBES
1425. PAPER PLANT WITH DTP & PRINTING & PUBLISHING UNIT
1426. PAPER BASED PHENOLIC SHEET
1427. PAPER CUP FOR ICE CREAM
1428. PAPER TUBES SPIRAL WINDING COMPOSIT CONTAINER
1429. PAPER LABLE FOR BEER BOTTLES
1430. PARTICLE BOARD & BLACK BOARD WITH SANDING & LAMINATION OF PARTICLE BOARD
1431. PARTICLE BOARD FROM RICE HUSK
1432. POUCH FILLING & MAKING FOR TOMATO SAUCE
1433. POUCH MAKING &

GRAVURE PRINTING
1434. PROCESSING OF PAPER FOR FEEDING IN COMPUTER
1435. PULP FROM BAMBOO & WOOD
1436. PAPER FILES
1437. PLAYING CARDS
1438. ROSIN SIZING AGENT (FOR PAPER PLANT)
1439. SAND PAPER
1440. SANITRY NAPKINS
1441. SILICON COATED PAPER
1442. STENCIL PAPER
1443. STRAW BOARD AND GREY BOARD
1444. STRAW BOARD & MILL BOARD
1445. STRAW BOARD AND PAPER BOARD
1446. TISSUE PAPER FACIAL
1447. TISSUE MOIST TOILETERY CLEANSING TISSUE AND RELATED PRODUCTS
1448. TISSUE PAPER ROLLS
1449. TETRA PACK FOR MILK PACKAGING, GHEE & OTHER LIQUIDS
1450. TOILET PAPER ROLLS
1451. TOILET PAPER & NAPKINS
1452. WAX COATED PRINTED PAPER
1453. WET FACE FRESHNER TISSUE
1454. WHITE WRITING & PRINTING PAPER
1455. WRITING & PRINTING PAPER (PAPER MILLS)

PLASTIC, B.O.P.P, ACRYLIC, DISPOSABLE PLASTIC PRODUCTS, PET PRODUCTS, P.V.C, H.D.P.E, P.P, L.D.P.E., P.U, A.B.S, THERMOFOARMING, MASTER BATCHES, & POLYMER AND RUBBER PRODUCTS, TYRE, TUBE, ADHESIVE, SHEET, COIR & MANY OTHERS

1456. ABS GRANULES FROM ABS SCRAPS FROM OLD T.V. CABINETS, WHITE GOODS ETC.
1457. ACRYLIC BEADS
1458. ACRYLIC COPOLYMER EMULSION
1459. ACRYLIC LATEX
1460. ACRYLIC SHEET
1461. ACRYLIC SHEET & MOULDED PRODUCTS
1462. ACRYLIC TEETH
1463. AUTO TUBES
1464. AUTO FLAPS FOR TRUCKS & BUSES
1465. AUTO TYRES & TUBES
1466. BABY BOTTLES (PLASTIC) WITH WHITESILICON RUBBER NIPPLES
1467. B.O.P.P. FILM
1468. B.O.P.P. PRESSURE SENSITIVE SELF ADHESIVE TAPE
1469. BABY NIPPLE (SILICON)
1470. BABY NIPPLE (BIG SIZE)
1471. BALLOON PLASTIC ADVERTISING
1472. BLISTER FILM PVC
1473. BLISTER PACKAGING & POUCH PAKAGING
1474. BLOW MOULDING PLASTIC CONTAINER
1475. COATING ON METALIZED POLYESTER FILM/METALISED PAPER/ ALIMINIUM FOIL
1476. COATING ON PLASTIC (ELECTROLYSIS) & GLASS
1477. COIR FOAM (RUBBERISED)
1478. COLOUR COATING ON PLASTICS
1479. COLOUR MASTER BATCHES FOR VARIOUS PLASTICS
1480. CYCLE TYRES AND TUBES
1481. DISPOSABLE PLASTIC CUPS GLASSES, ETC.
1482. DISPOSABLE PLASTIC SYRINGES & NEEDLES
1483. DISPOSABLE PLASTIC SYRINGES
1484. DOUGH MOULDING COMPOUND (D.M.C)
1485. EPOXY RESIN
1486. EXPANDED POLYESTRENE MOULDING (THERMOCOLE)
1487. F.R.P AUTO,SCOOTER ROOFS & CEILINGS
1488. F.R.P PRODUCTS (HELMET, WASHBASIN SHEETS, ROOFING SHEETS)
1489. FIBRE REINFORCED PLASTIC (HIGH PRESSURE MOULDING WITH SMC BMC AND DMC)
1490. FIELD RUBBER CONVERTED TO THE 60% LATEX RUBBER
1491. FLEXIBLE P.U. FOAM
1492. FORMALDEHYDE CROCKERY & OTHER ITEMS
1493. FORMALDEHYDE RESIN (UREA, PHENOL,MELEMINE)
1494. GASKET SHEET
1495. GUM BOTTLE (PVC)
1496. GLASS BEADS
1497. HDPE COATED PAPER SACK
1498. H.D.P.E. BAGS
1499. H.D.P.E. CONTAINERS (BLOW MOULDING)
1500. H.D.P.E. CONTAINER, POLY JARS BY INJECTION MOULDING (FOOD GRADE)
1501. H.D.P.E. JERRY CANS
1502. HDPE MANUFACTURING FROM ETHYLALCOHOL
1503. H.D.P.E PIPE AND FITTINGS
1504. H.D.P.E. PIPES
1505. H.D.P.E PRINTED BAGS
1506. H.D.P.E TWINES AND ROPES
1507. H.D.P.E. & L.D.P.E PIPES AND FITTINGS
1508. H.D.P.E/PP BOX STRAPPING
1509. H.D.P.E/PP WOVEN SACKS USING PLAIN LOOMS
1510. HOLOGRAM STICKERS-3D
1511. H.M BAG PLANT WITH PRINTING UNIT
1512. HAWAI CHAPPALS (RUBBER)
1513. I.V PLASTIC BOTTLE
1514. ICE CREAM CUP (PLASTIC)
1515. INJECTION MOULDED AUTO COMPONENTS
1516. INJECTION & BLOW MOULDED PLASTIC PRODUCTS
1517. INJECTION MOULDED PLASTIC PRODUCTS
1518. INTEGERATED COMPLEX ESTER'S & ALLIED PRODUCTS (D.O.P,D.B.P, & ETHYL ACETATE, BUYTL ACETATE, WIRE ENAMELS, JELLY CABLE COMPOUND)
1519. L.D.P.E. (LOW DENSITY POLY ETHYLENE) GRANULES FROM VIRGIN (L.D.P.E. RESIN)
1520. INTEGERATED SURGICAL RUBBER GOODS INDUSTRY
1521. INJECTION MOULDED PLASTIC BALLS
1522. L.D.P.E FROM ETHYL ALCOHOL
1523. LDPE MOULDED PRODUCTS
1524. LAMINATION OF COEXTRUSION MULTILAYER FILM IN ROLL FORM
1525. LATEX RUBBER
1526. LATEX RUBBER CONDOM
1527. MASTER BATCHES (COLOURED, P.V.C, L.D.P.E, H.D.P.E, ETC.)
1528. MELAMINE FORMALHYDE RESIN
1529. MOULDED LUGGAGE
1530. MULTI-LAYER (3 LAYER BAGS)
1531. MULTI-LAYER (3 LAYER) FILM WITH LAMINATION & PRINTING
1532. OIL SEAL
1533. PET BOTTLE/CONTAINERS
1534. PET BOTTLES FROM PRE FORM
1535. PET BOTTLE & MINERAL WATER
1536. PET PRE-FORM FROM PET RESIN
1537. PET PRE-FORM CUM PET BOTTLES
1538. PET PRE-FORM PET BOTTLES CUM MINERAL WATERS
1539. POLY CARBONATE RESIN
1540. PTFE COMPONENTS
1541. PU/PVC SOLE FOR SPORT SHOE BY IMPORTED M/C.
1542. PVC BATTERY SEPARATOR
1543. P.V.C COMPOUNDS (FRESH)
1544. P.V.C COMPOUNDS (SCRAP)
1545. P.V.C ELECTRICAL INSULATING TAPE
1546. P.V.C. EXTRUSION PROFILES
1547. P.V.C FITTINGS
1548. P.V.C FLEXIBLE FUSIBLE POWDER HEAT FUSIBLE POWDER
1549. P.V.C GRANULES (FOR

INSULATION & SHEETS GRADES)
1550. P.V.C GRANULES FROM PVC SCRAPS (WITH POLLUTION CONTROL)
1551. P.V.C HOSES
1552. P.V.C LEATHER CLOTH
1553. P.V.C FLEXIBLE PIPES
1554. P.V.C PIPES AND FITTINGS
1555. POLYTHENE BAGS (PRINTED)
1556. PVC PLASTICS FILM SHEET SOFT/RIGID
1557. PVC RESIN AND COMPOUND
1558. PVC RULAR
1559. PVC STABLIZERS (SINGLE PACK SYSTEM)
1560. PVC WIRE AND CABLES
1561. PAPER BASED PHENOLIC SHEET FOR ELECTRICAL
1562. PHENOL FORMALDEHYDE RESIN
1563. PHENOLIC RESIN
1564. PLASTIC BEADS FROM PLASTIC SCRAPS
1565. PLASTIC BUTTONS
1566. PLASTIC CANS
1567. PLASTIC COLLAPSIBLE TUBE
1568. PLASTIC CORRUGATED SHEET & BOXES
1569. PLASTIC FILM AND SHEETS WITH PRINTING FLEXO & ROTO/LDPE/HDPE/PP/HM/PVC
1570. PLASTIC FILTER MASTER BATCH & OTHER MASTER BATCHES FOR VARIOUS PLASTICS
1571. PLASTIC JERRY CANS
1572. PLASTIC GRANULES OR POWDER FROM PLASTIC SCRAP
1573. PLASTIC INJECTION MOULDED T.V. CABINETS
1574. PLASTIC ITEMS MANUFAC TURE FROM POWDER MELAMINE
1575. PLASTIC GOODS
1576. PLASTIC PIPES & TARPAULINES
1577. PLASTIC SHEET FROM SCRAP
1578. PLASTIC PLANT (BLOW MOULDING & INJECTION MOULDING)
1579. PLASTIC PRODUCTS (GOLD, SILVER, NICKEL)
1580. PLASTIC TOYS
1581. POLYESTER BEADING
1582. POLYESTER FILM
1583. POLYTHENE BAGS & AUTOMATIC PRINTING
1584. POLYTHENE PRINTED BAGS
1585. POLYURETHANE FOAM AND ITS PRODUCTS
1586. PROPYLENE FILM (PRINTED) & BAG MANUFACTURING
1587. PLASTIC MATS
1588. RAINBOW COLOUR ON PVC FILM & SHEET
1589. RED MUD PVC PIPES AND FITTINGS
1590. RE-RUBBERISED OF SOLID TYPE
1591. RESIN COATED SAND REXINE
1592. REXINE CLOTH & ALLIED PRODUCTS
1593. RUBBER ADHESIVE
1594. RUBBER AUTO PARTS
1595. RUBBER BELTING
1596. RUBBER MOULDING UNIT INCLUDING LINING RUBBER SHEETING
1597. RUBBER RECLAIMING
1598. RUBBER ROLLERS FOR TEXTILE MILLS & PAPER INDUSTRIES
1599. RUBBER & PLASTIC SHEETS, MATS & FLAPS
1600. RUBBER SHEET AND ALLIED HOSPITAL RUBBER GOODS
1601. RUBBERIZED PVC GASKET
1602. RUBBERISED COIR
1603. RUBBER COMPOUND FOR AUTOMOBILES
1604. SAFETY BELTS
1605. SILVER AND GOLD PLATING ON PVC AND NYLON-6
1606. SILICONE RUBBER NIPPLES/ TEATS
1607. SPECTACLE FRAMES (PLASTIC)
1608. SPUNGE RUBBER
1609. SURGICAL EXAMINATION GLOVES
1610. SYNTHETIC PEARL COATING ON POLYSTYRENE BEADS
1611. SYNTHETIC RUBBER ADHESIVE
1612. TEFLON MANUFACTURING
1613. TEFLON TAPE
1614. TEFLON TAPES & CABLES
1615. THERMOCOLE SHEET AND MOULDED PRODUCTS EXPANDED POLYESTERENE EXTRUSION PROFILES
1616. THERMOFORMED PACKAGING (BLISTER PACKAGING & POUCH PACKAGING)
1617. THERMOPLASTIC POLYURETHANE
1618. THERMOFORMED CUPS, PLATES & GLASS WITH HIPS SHEET
1619. THERMOCOLE
1620. THERMOCOLE BASED DISPOSABLE GLASS, CUPS & PLATES
1621. TOOTH BRUSHES
1622. TOY BALLOON, DECORA TIVE & INDUSTRIAL BALLOONS
1623. TREAD RUBBER
1624. TYRE RETREADING (HOT)
1625. TYRE RETREADING BY COLD PROCESS
1626. TYRE TUBES & FLAPS
1627. TYRE & TUBES
1628. UNSATURATED POLYESTER FOR REXINE
1629. V-BELT AND FAN BELT
1630. VINYL ASBESTOS AND PVC WALL PAPER
1631. VITON (FLUORO ELASTOMER)

SOAP, COSMETICS & PERFUMS

1632. ACID SLURRY, SYNTHETIC DETERGENT POWDER
1632. ACID SLURRY
1633. AGARBATTI SYNTHETIC, PERFUMERY COMPOUND
1634. AFTER SHAVE LOTION
1635. ANTISEPTIC CREAM
1636. BETA IONONE
1637. BLEACHING POWDER
1638. BLUE DETERGENT POWDER
1639. CLEANING POWDER (VIMTYPE)
1640. COLD CREAM
1641. COLOURED FLAME & PERFUMED CANDLES (RED, BLUE, GREEN FLAME)
1642. COSMETIC INDUSTRY (MODERN)
1643. COSMETIC INDUSTRY (SHAMPOO, SPRAY PERFUME, TALCUM POWDER
1644. DETERGENT POWDER (ARIEL TYPE)
1645. DETERGENT POWDER (NIRMA TYPE) FULLY AUTOMATIC PLANT
1646. DETERGENT WASHING POWDER
1647. FISH OIL SOAP
1648. GLYCERINE TRANSPARENT SOAP
1649. HAIR REMOVING CREAM
1650. HERBAL COSMETICS
1651. HERBAL SHAMPO & CREAM
1652. HERBAL/AYURVEDIC COSMETICS
1653. INCENSE POWDER, INCENSE STICKS & INCENSE CAKE
1654. OPTICAL WHITENERS
1655. ROSE OIL EXTRACTION
1656. SHAMPOOS (COCONUT OIL BASED COLD PROCESS)
1657. SHAVING CREAM
1658. SINDUR (KUMKUM)
1659. SOAP COATED PAPER
1660. SPRAY DRIED DETERGENT POWDER
1661. STAIN REMOVER
1662. TALCUM POWDER (FACE & TOILET POWDER)
1663. TOILET AND HERBAL SOAP
1664. TOOTH PASTE & POWDER
1665. WASHING DETERGENT POWDER AND WASHING SOAP
1666. WASHING POWDER LIQUID DETERGENTS, LOTION & SHAMPOO

TEXTILE INDUSTRIES, READYMADE GARMENTS, COTTON, DYEING, BLEACHING, CLOTH, HOSIERY, POWER LOOM, HAND LOOM, WOOLLEN, SILK, SOCKS, SURGICAL COTTON & MANY OTHERS

1667. ANGORA RABBIT WOOL
1668. BUCKRAM
1669. CANVAS SHOES, JUNGLE BOOT, BOOT RUBBER KNEES & BOOT COMBAT
1670. CARPET FROM COTTON WASTE
1671. CERAMIC THREAD GUIDE
1672. COTTON BUDS/SWABS
1673. COTTON FROM WASTE YARN
1674. COTTON ROLLS
1675. COTTON SPIDERS FOR LOUD SPEAKERS
1676. DENIM CLOTH
1677. DENIM CLOTH (INTEGERATED UNIT WITH BLEACHING, DYEING AND PRINTING)
1678. DISPERSENT FOR TEXTILE
1679. DYEING & BLEACHING
1680. DYEING OF HANK YARN
1681. EMULSIFIER FOR WOOL BATCHING OIL
1682. EMBROIDERY ON FABRICS
1683. GARMENT DYEING, WASHING & STITCHING (JEANS, JACKETS, SKIRTS & SHIRTS)
1684. GOVES KNITTING
1685. GUNNY BAGS
1687. HDPE WOVEN SACKS
1688. HDPE TARPAULINS USING PLAIN LOOM WITH LAMINATION
1689. HDPE/PP WOVEN SACKS USING CIRCULAR LOOMS
1690. HOSIERY CLOTH (COTTON) PROCESSING (BLEACHING, DYEING, FINISHING OF CLOTH)
1691. HOSIERY INDUSTRY
1692. HOSIERY MERCERISING
1693. HOSIERY PRODUCTS LIKE VEST, BRIEF, T-SHIRTS & SOCKS
1694. JACQUARD FABRICS
1695. JUTE COIR, GRASS ROPE/ SUTLI MAKING
1696. JUTE FELT
1697. JUTE TWINES
1698. KNITTED FABRICS
1699. LAMINATED JUTE BAGS
1700. LAMINATION OF HDPE WOVEN CLOTH (JUTE,COTTON, PAPER)
1701. NYLON YARN CRIMPING, DOUBLING AND BLEACHING
1702. PIGMENT BINDER FOR TEXTILE PRINTING
1704. POLYESTER RESIN FOR WIRE ENAMEL
1705. POLYESTER RESIN
1706. POLYESTER YARN FROM WASTE POLYESTER ZIP FASTENERS
1707. POWER LOOM
1708. READYMADE GARMENTS & HOSIERY
1709. READYMADE GARMENTS MERCHANDISE
1710. READYMADE GARMENTS & COVERS
1711. READYMADE GARMENTS & EMBROIDERY OF GOWNS, SHIRTS, BLOUSES, T-SHIRTS ETC. (ONLY LADIES)
1712. READYMADE SALWAR SUIT
1713. RECOVERY OF NYLON FROM NYLON WASTE
1714. ROTARY PRINTING AND DYEING ON COTTON, SYNTHETIC TEXTILE
1715. SANITARY NAPKINS
1716. SCREEN PRINTING ON COTTON CLOTH
1717. SEWING THREAD REELS & BALLS MAKING INDUSTRIES
1718. SCREEN PRINTING ON COTTON, POLYESTER & ACRYLIC
1719. SHAWLS (WOOLLEN)
1720. SHOE LACES
1721. SILK FABRICS ON HANDLOOM
1722. SOCKS KNITTING
1723. SPINNING, DOUBLING DYEING MERCERISING & BLEACHING OF COTTON YARN
1724. SPINNING & CARDING OF WOOL INTO YARNS
1725. STARCH BOOK BINDING CLOTH
1726. SURAT JARI
1727. SURGICAL COTTON & BANDAGE
1728. SYNTHETIC TEXTILE INDUSTRY(SUITING, SHIRTING, SAREES) TERRY CLOTH
1729. T-SHIRTS
1730. TOWELS, BED SHEET COVERS
1731. TERRY TOWEL
1732. TERRY FABRICS WEAVING UNIT
1733. TEXTILE AUXILLIARIES & CHEMICALS
1734. TEXTILE BLEACHING, DYEING & FINISHING & PRINTING OF COTTON FABRICS
1735. TEXTILE (HOSIERY)
1736. TEXTILE MILL
1737. TEXTILE DYEING & PRINTING
1738. TEXTILE PRINTING (JOB WORK)
1739. TEXTILE PIGMENT PRINTING BINDER
1740. TOWEL (TERRY)
1741. VELVET CLOTH BY FLOCKING PROCESS
1742. VISCOSE STAPLE FIBRE
1743. WADDING OIL (100%) FOR WADDING OF COTTON HOSIERY CLOTH IN THE DYEING PROCESS
1744. WEAVING OF DASUTI CLOTH WITH PRINTING, DYEING, EMBROIDERY & FINISHING
1745. WASHING OF JEANS & OTHER GARMENTS
1746. WORSTED WOOLLEN YARN CLOTH
1747. ZARI GLITTER SALMA SITARA OF PLASTIC FILM

INFOTECH/IT, HOSPITALITY, HOSPITAL, COLLEGE, SCHOOL, MEDICAL, ENTERTAINMENT CLUB, WARE HOUSING & REAL ESTATE, PROJECTS

1748. AMUSEMENT PARK
1749. AMUSEMENT PARK CUM WATER PARK
1750. BANQUET HALL
1751. CALL CENTER (DOMESTIC)
1752. CALL CENTER (INTERNATIONAL)
1753. CHILDREN RECREATION CENTRE
1754. COLD STORAGE
1755. COMMUNITY HALL
1756. COMPUTER EDUCATION INSTITUTE
1757. COMPUTER SOFTWARE
1758. COLLEGE
1759. CYBER CAFE
1760. DENTAL CLINIC
1761. DENTAL COLLEGE
1762. DIAGONOSTIC CENTRE
1763. E-COMMERCE/BUSINESS
1764. E-SCHOOL (Rs. 5000/-)
1765. ENGINEERING COLLEGE
1766. ENTERTAINMENT CLUB
1767. ENTERTAINMENT CLUB, HOLIDAY RESORT, 4 STAR HOTEL, AMUSEMENT PARK CUM WATER PARK, MUSHROOM & ITS PRODUCTS, FISH FARMING, LAKE FOR BOATING, DEER PARK
1768. FASHION TECHNOLOGY INSTITUTE
1769. FAST FOOD PARLOUR
1770. FIVE STAR HOTEL
1771. FOOD PARLOUR
1772. FRANCHISE TRAINING PROGRAMME FOR IIT & ENGINEERING ENTRANCE EXAMS.
1773. GOLF COURSE
1774. HEALTH CLUB, BEAUTY PARLOUR
1775. HEALTH CLUB AND FITNESS CENTER
1776. HEALTH RESORTS
1777. HOLIDAY RESORTS
1778. HOLIDAY RESORT CUM

ENTERTAINMENT CLUB WITH 4 STAR HOTEL
1779. HOSPITALS
1780. ICE CREAM PARLOUR
1781. INTERNET SERVICE PROVIDER (I.S.P.)
1782. MEDICAL COLLEGE
1783. MEDICAL COLLEGE, HOSPITAL & RESEARCH INSTITUTE
1784. MEDICAL TRANSCRIPTION CENTRE
1785. MENTAL RETARDATION HOSPITAL & CEREBRAL PALSY
1786. MOTEL/SMALL HOTEL
1787. MULTISTOREY COMMERCIAL COMPLEX
1788. MULTISTOREY RESIDENTIAL COMPLEX
1789. NURSERY SCHOOL
1790. NATURE CARE CENTRE
1791. NURSING HOME
1792. ONLINE SHOPPING MALL (RS. 5000/- REPORT)
1793. PORTAL
1794. REHABILITATION CENTRE FOR AGED & NEEDY PERSONS
1795. RESIDENTIAL CUM COMMERCIAL COMPLEX
1796. RESTAURANT
1797. RESTAURANT WITH PUB
1798. SCHOOL (PRIMARY)
1799. SCHOOL (HIGHER SECONDARY)
1800. THREE STAR HOTEL
1801. TOURIST CLUB
1802. TRAINING INSTITUTE FOR MEDICAL TRANSCRIPTION
1803. VIDEO FILM STUDIO
1804. WARE HOUSE
1805. WEBSITE DESIGN & E-MAIL REGISTERING

AGRO BASED INDUSTRIES

1806. COAL BRIQUETTES FROM AGROWASTE
1807. FURFURALFROM RICEHULL
1808. MUSHROOM CULTIVATION & PROCESSING (BUTTON)
1809. MUSHROOM GROWING & PROCESSING WITH AIR CONDITIONING
1810. MUSHROOM CULTIVATION & PROCESSING UNIT DEHYDRATION & PACKAGING OF OYSTER & PADDY STRAW MUSHROOMS
1811. ORGANIC MANURE
1812. PAPAYA CULTIVATION
1813. PAPAYA & TOMATO CULTIVATION
1814. PROCESSING & UTILISATION OF COCONUT
1815. PROCESSING OF SHEEP HAIR TO PRODUCE WOOL

BAKERY, CONFECTIONERY & FOOD PRODUCTS

1816. AGROLACTOR SOYA MILK
1817. APPLE FRUIT JUICE WITH CANNING BOTTLING
1818. AYURVEDIC SHARBAT
1819. BAKERY UNIT (PASTRIES, BREAD, BUNS, CAKE, TOFFEE ETC.)
1820. BAKING POWDER
1821. BANANA & ITS BY PRODUCTS
1822. BANANA POWDER
1823. BANANA WAFERS
1824. BANANA CULTIVATION
1825. BEER INDUSTRY
1826. DEHULLING OF JAUN FOR BEER
1827. BEER & WINE
1828. BEER, ALCOHOL, IMFL
1829. BESEN PLANT
1830. BISCUIT PLANT
1831. BREAD & BISCUIT PLANT
1832. BOTTLING PLANT COUNTRY LIQUOR FROM RECTIFIED SPIRIT
1833. BRANDY
1834. BREAD RUSKS
1835. CANNED FRUITS & VEGETABLES
1836. CANNING & PRESERVATION OF MEAT
1837. CANNING & PRESERVATION OF VEGETABLES
1838. CANNING OF MANGO PULP & MANGO SLICES
1839. CARBONATED BEVERAGS
1840. CASHEW FENI
1841. CASHEW NUT (DRIED & FRIED)
1842. CATTLE BREEDING
1843. CATTLE BREEDING & DAIRY FARM TO PRODUCE MILK
1844. CATTLE FEED FROM TAPIOCA
1845. CHEWING GINGER & AMLOKI
1846. CHEWING GUM
1847. CHILLI SAUCE
1848. CHILLI POWDER
1849. CHOCOLATE
1850. CIDER PLANT
1851. COCOA POWDER
1852. COCOA BUTTER & COCOA POWDER
1853. COCONUT SHELL POWDER
1854. COCONUT WATER
1855. COCONUT SWEET (WATERY)
1856. COCONUT MILK POWDER (DEHYDRATED)
1857. COCONUT PRODUCTS & BY PRODUCTS (INTEGRATED PLANT)
1858. COLD DRINK
1859. CURRY POWDER
1860. DAIRY FOR MILK PROCESSING (GHEE, BUTTER & PANEER)
1861. DAIRY PRODUCTS
1862. DAIRY PRODUCTS MILK PACKAGING IN POUCH (GHEE, BUTTER, ETC.
1863. DAIRY FARM TO PRDUCE MILK WITH PACKAGING (COW)
1864. DAIRY FARM TO PRDUCE MILK WITH PACKAGING (BUFALLOE)
1865. DAIRY FARM & MILK PRODUCTS
1866. DAL MOTH, CHANACHUR & BHUJIYA
1867. DEHYDRATION OF FRUITS & VEGETABLE
1868. DESICCATED COCONUT POWDER FROM COCONUTS
1869. DEHYDRATION & CANNING OF FRUITS & VEGETABLES
1870. DRY FRUIT ROASTING & PACKAGING
1871. DRYING OF RED CHILLIES, HALDI, DHANIYA, PEAS & GROUND NUT
1872. EGG POWDER
1873. FISH CANNING IN TIN & POUCHES
1874. FISH DEHYRATION (DRYING OF FISH)
1875. FISH MEAL
1876. FISH PROCESSING (BEAST FREEZING PROCESSES)
1877. FLAVOURS FOR FOOD INDUSTRIES
1878. FLOUR MILL (ROLLER)
1879. FROZEN MEAT
1880. FOOD DEHYDRATION (FRUITS & VEGETABLES)
1881. FRIED & ROASTED GROUND NUT, GRAMS, PEAR ETC.
1882. FRUIT JUICE MAKING & PACKAGING IN PLASTIC CONTAINER
1883. FRUIT JUICE IN TETRA PACK (DRINKS)
1884. FRUIT JUICE, SQUASHES, SAUCE & KETCHUP, JAM, JELLY, VINEGAR ETC.
1885. GARLIC FLAKES
1886. GARLIC POWDER
1887. GHEE & BUTTER
1888. GINGER (PULVERISED)
1889. GINGER GLAZING & PRESERVATION
1890. GINGER STORAGE
1891. GINGER PROCESSING
1892. GINGER OIL & GINGER DUST
1893. GINGER POWDER (DRY) & OLEORESIN
1894. GRAPE DEHYDRATION
1895. GRAPE CULTIVATION
1896. GRAPE JUICE
1897. HONEY PROCESSING & PACKAGING
1898. ICE CREAM & ICE CANDY
1899. ICE CUBE
1900. INVERT SUGAR
1901. IDLI MIX, DOSA MIX SAMBHAR MIX, VADA MIX, GULAB JAMUN MIX
1902. INSTANT COFFEE & INSTANT TEA